The Poor under Globalization in Asia, Latin America, and Africa

UNU World Institute for Development Economics Research (UNU-WIDER) was established by the United Nations University as its first research and training centre and started work in Helsinki, Finland, in 1985. The purpose of the institute is to undertake applied research and policy analysis on structural changes affecting developing and transitional economies, to provide a forum for the advocacy of policies leading to robust, equitable, and environmentally sustainable growth, and to promote capacity strengthening and training in the field of economic and social policymaking. Its work is carried out by staff researchers and visiting scholars in Helsinki and via networks of collaborating scholars and institutions around the world.

United Nations University World Institute for Development Economics Research (UNU-WIDER)
Katajanokanlaituri 6 B, FIN-00160 Helsinki, Finland
www.wider.unu.edu

The Poor under Globalization in Asia, Latin America, and Africa

Edited by
Machiko Nissanke and Erik Thorbecke

A study prepared for the World Institute for Development Economics Research of the United Nations University (UNU-WIDER)

OXFORD
UNIVERSITY PRESS

OXFORD
UNIVERSITY PRESS

Great Clarendon Street, Oxford OX2 6DP

Oxford University Press is a department of the University of Oxford.
It furthers the University's objective of excellence in research, scholarship,
and education by publishing worldwide in

Oxford New York

Auckland Cape Town Dar es Salaam Hong Kong Karachi
Kuala Lumpur Madrid Melbourne Mexico City Nairobi
New Delhi Shanghai Taipei Toronto

With offices in

Argentina Austria Brazil Chile Czech Republic France Greece
Guatemala Hungary Italy Japan Poland Portugal Singapore
South Korea Switzerland Thailand Turkey Ukraine Vietnam

Oxford is a registered trade mark of Oxford University Press
in the UK and in certain other countries

Published in the United States
by Oxford University Press Inc., New York

First published 2010

British Library Cataloguing in Publication Data
Data available

Library of Congress Cataloging in Publication Data
Data available

Typeset by SPI Publisher Services, Pondicherry, India
Printed in Great Britain
on acid-free paper by
CPI Antony Rowe, Chippenham, Wiltshire

ISBN 978–0–19–958475–8

3 5 7 9 10 8 6 4 2

Foreword

As the globalization process has intensified since the 1990s, serious concerns have been raised over its impact on the world's poor. Today, these concerns have become even more pronounced because of the way globalization has been affected by the current global financial and economic crisis. The absence of a viable international financial system and adequate governance over the globalization process has inflicted great collateral damage on the developing world as a whole. In particular, the weak regulations and supervision of financial institutions and markets in advanced countries, as well as the generally unchecked global capital flows, have been major triggers for the present global recession.

Clearly, the downside of globalization is most vividly illuminated during times of global financial and economic crises. In fact, the costs of financial crises fuelled by the globalization process in the past have been borne often disproportionately, so it is the poor in the developing world who tend to be the most vulnerable group.

Today globalization is certainly at a crossroad. Globalization has a considerable potential to contribute to growth and to reducing poverty through the spread and transfer of technology as well as the transmission of knowledge and skills. This potential is large if globalization produces 'job-creating' economic growth for the poor. In fact, much of Asia benefited enormously from the forces of globalization over the last decades except for the earlier Asian Financial Crisis of 1997 and the present one. Thus, rather than opposing globalization and further integration, it is critical for the global community to find a way to improve its functioning so that globalization yields a better outcome in terms of poverty alleviation worldwide. Many countries in the developing world, particularly in Sub-Saharan Africa and Latin America, have so far benefited little from globalization, while poverty remains quite high in South Asia generally despite considerable progress. Globalization should be made to work for the poor and to reduce global inequality, rather than letting market forces alone determine a socially less desirable outcome. This is the message emanating most strongly from this volume, the last of the series of publications from the UNU-WIDER multi-year project on the Impact of Globalization on the World's Poor, which examines, from a comparative perspective, the relationships among growth, inequality, and poverty under globalization in three developing regions: Asia, Latin America, and Sub-Saharan Africa.

Though globalization and poverty could have been analysed within an interdisciplinary context taking into account a variety of dimensions (such as cultural, social, and political), the UNU-WIDER project concentrates predominantly, but not exclusively, on the economic manifestations of globalization and their effects on poverty. Hence, the chapters in this book examine and address the issue at hand from the viewpoint of development economics.

The research reported here by leading development scholars and specialists should be of great interest to academics, policymakers, and students who are dealing with the challenge of making the process of globalization more responsive to the reduction of poverty worldwide.

This volume represents the crowning achievement of a successful large-scale project directed by Machiko Nissanke and Erik Thorbecke that has illuminated the links between globalization, growth, inequality, and poverty in different parts of the developing world.

Augustin K. Fosu
Deputy Director and Officer-in-Charge, UNU-WIDER
July 2009

Acknowledgements

The UNU-WIDER project on 'The Impact of Globalization on the World's Poor' held three regional conferences, in Tokyo, Johannesburg, and Rio de Janeiro, respectively, between 2005 and 2007, following an initial conceptual conference held in Helsinki in October 2004. This volume presents thirteen papers selected from these three regional conferences to illustrate the differential effects of globalization on growth, inequality, and poverty in Asia, Latin America, and Africa in a comparative perspective. The papers presented at these conferences were partially commissioned or selected from over 450 applications received in response to our 'call for papers' posted separately for each of the regional conferences, on the strength of extended abstracts, the need for balance, and our aim at covering topics and aspects in the globalization–poverty nexus as comprehensively as possible. We are grateful to all the conference participants who contributed significantly as paper presenters, chairs, and discussants. We would like to express our sincere appreciation of the assistance we received from the co-hosting institutions in organizing these conferences in each of the three locations: UNU Centre and the Japanese International Cooperation Agency in Tokyo, the Trade and Industrial Policy Strategies in Johannesburg, and the Pontifícia Universidade Católica in Rio de Janeiro.

We are most grateful to the staff at UNU-WIDER who provided efficient logistic support to us in the management of this large research project. We would like to express our special thanks to Lisa Winkler for her editorial support of this volume, to Barbara Fagerman for exceptional administrative support, and to Tony Shorrocks for his intellectual leadership. Special thanks are also due to Adam Swallow who provided excellent and timely help and advice at all stages of the publication process.

UNU-WIDER is especially thankful to the Finnish Ministry for Foreign Affair for its support to this project, and also gratefully acknowledges the financial contributions to the research programme by the governments of Denmark (Royal Ministry of Foreign Affairs), Finland (Ministry for Foreign Affairs), Norway (Ministry of Foreign Affairs), Sweden (Swedish International Development Cooperation Agency–Sida), and the United Kingdom (Department for International Development).

M.N.
London

E.T.
Ithaca, New York
July 2009

Contents

III. Latin America

IV. Africa

List of Figures

List of Tables

List of Abbreviations

ADB	Asian Development Bank
AMPS	all media and products survey
APCE	average per capita consumption expenditure
ASEAN	Association of Southeast Asian Nations
ATPDEA	Andean Trade Preference and Drug Eradication Act
BMI	body mass index
BRIC	Brazil, Russia, India, and China
CCPP	centros poblados [populated centres] [of Peru]
CDFs	cumulative density functions
CGE	computable general equilibrium
CPI	consumer price index
CSGR	[University of Warwick] Centre for the Study of Globalization and Regionalization
CV	coefficient of variation
DER	Duclos–Esteban–Ray
DHS	demographic and health survey
ECLAC	Economic Commission for Latin America and the Caribbean
EGI	economic globalization index
ERD	economics and research department
ERHS	Ethiopian rural household survey
ERP	effective rates of protection
FDI	foreign direct investment
FFE	foreign-funded enterprise
FG	Flying Geese [model]
FOB	Free on Board/Freight on Board
GATT	General Agreement on Tariffs and Trade
GDP	gross domestic product
GDPPC	per capita gross domestic product
GEAR	growth, employment, and redistribution

GIC	growth incidence curve
GPS	global positioning system
GSDP	gross state domestic product
HAZ	height-for-age z-score
HOS	Heckscher–Ohlin–Samuelson
HPAE	high-performing Asian economy
HPCI	household per capita income
ICRIER	Indian Council for Research on International Economic Relations
IDB	Inter-American Development Bank
IES	income and expenditure surveys
IETS	Instituto de Estudos do Trabalho e Sociedade
IFPRI	International Food Policy Research Institute
IIA	independence of irrelevant alternatives [hypothesis]
ILO	International Labour Organization
IMF	International Monetary Fund
INPC	Indice Nacional de Preços ao Consumidor [consumer price index]
IPP	Instituto Pereira Passos
IRRI	International Rice Research Institute
IT	information technology
IV	instrumental variable
JMP	Juhn–Murphy–Pierce
LAC	Latin America and the Caribbean
LDC	least-developed countriy
LFS	labour-force survey
LSMS	living standards measurement survey
MDG	Millennium Development Goal
MV	modern [rice] variety
MV1	first-generation modern [rice] variety (susceptible to damage by brown plant hoppers)
MV2	second-generation modern [rice] variety (resistant to plant hoppers)
MV3	third-generation modern [rice] variety (better grain quality)
MVA	manufacturing [sector gross] value added
NAFTA	North American Free Trade Agreement
NBS	National Bureau of Statistics
NGO	non-governmental organization
NIE	newly industrialized economy
NSCB	National Statistical Coordination Board
ODI	Overseas Development Institute

OECD	Organization for Economic Co-operation and Development
OEM	original equipment manufacturing
OHS	October household survey
OLS	ordinary least squares
PDF	probability density function
PETT	programa especial de titulación de la tierra [special land-titling and registration]
PG	poverty gap
PGI	political globalization index
PME	Pesquisa Mensal de Emprego
PNAD	Pesquisa Nacional por Amostra de Domicílios
PPP	purchasing power parity
PRC	People's Republic of China
R&D	research and development
RER	real exchange rates
RHG	representative household groups
SADC	Southern African Development Community
SBTC	skill-biased technical change
SES	socio-economic status
SGI	social globalization index
SSA	Sub-Saharan Africa
SUNAT	Superintendencia Nacional de Administración Tributaria [National Superintendency of Tax Administration]
TNC	transnational corporation
TOT	terms of trade
TWFPR	total workforce participation rate
UN Comtrade	United Nations commodity trade [statistics database]
UNCTAD	United Nations Conference on Trade and Development
UNDP	United Nations Development Programme
UNECA	United Nations Economic Commission for Africa
UNESCO	United Nations Educational, Scientific, and Cultural Organization
WDI	world development indicator
WENAO	Western Europe, North America, Oceania
WGIC	wage-growth incidence curve
WHO	World Health Organization
WIID	World Income Inequality Database
WPI	wholesale price index
WTO	World Trade Organization

List of Contributors

N. R. Bhanumurthy is Associate Professor at the Institute of Economic Growth, Delhi. His research areas are development economics, macro-monetary economics, international money and finance, and macroeconomic modelling. He has worked at UNESCAP, Bangkok and also at UNDP Regional Centre in Colombo, Sri Lanka as Macroeconomist. He is Secretary of the Indian Econometric Society.

Alok Bhargava received his PhD in Econometrics from the London School of Economics in 1982. He is a Professor of Economics at the University of Houston, Adjunct Professor at the University of Texas School of Public Health, and a Visiting Professor at University of Paris 1. His research has concentrated on issues of nutrition, population health, child development, demography, and epidemiology.

Ronelle Burger is a researcher at the Department of Economics at the University of Stellenbosch. She is interested in poverty alleviation and development policy in African countries.

Stefan Dercon is Professor of Development Economics at the University of Oxford. Previously he worked at UNU-WIDER, University of Leuven, and the University of Addis Ababa. He works mainly on issues related to risk and poverty and rural institutions. Much of his work is on long-term patterns of wealth and poverty and he is closely involved in longitudinal surveys in Ethiopia, Tanzania, India, Peru, and Vietnam.

Francisco H. G. Ferreira is a Lead Economist with the World Bank's Research Department, from where he co-directed the World Development Report 2006 on Equity and Development. He holds a PhD from the London School of Economics and, prior to joining the Bank's Research Group, he was a Professor of Economics at the Catholic University of Rio de Janeiro.

Alfred J. Field is Professor of Economics at the University of North Carolina, Chapel Hill. His research lies in the area of international trade and economic development, and focuses on issues related to trade policy, structural adjustment, and development policy. Field has worked in Latin America and China, as well as several US and international agencies, and is co-author of *International Economics*, now in its sixth edition.

Erica Field is Assistant Professor in the Economics Department at Harvard University and a member of the National Bureau of Economic Research and Abdul Latif Jameel Poverty Action Lab (J-PAL). Her research focuses on the microeconomics of economic development. Her areas of interest include: property rights, microfinance, health and development, marriage markets in developing countries, and gender and development.

Yujiro Hayami is chairman of the Graduate Faculty at the Foundation for Advanced Studies on International Development and Professor at the National Graduate Institute of Policy Studies, Tokyo. He was professor of International Economics, School of International Politics, Economics, and Business, Aoyama-Gakuin University, 1986–2000, professor of economics at Tokyo Metropolitan University from 1966 to 1986, and Lee Teng Hui Professor of World Affairs at Cornell University from 1995 to 1996. Professor Hayami holds honorary lifetime membership of the International Association of Agricultural Economists and received a Purple Medal (Shiju Hōsho) from the Government of Japan for his work.

Phillippe G. Leite is an Economist with the World Bank's Social Protection Department. He holds a Masters degree in Statistics from the Brazilian Statistic School (ENCE) and a Masters degree in Economics from the École des hautes études en sciences sociales (new École d'économie de Paris), where he is currently finishing a PhD in Economics.

Megan Louw was a researcher in the Department of Economics at the University of Stellenbosch when this research was undertaken. She is interested in poverty, inequality, and economics of education.

David Mayer-Foulkes studied mathematics at the University of Oxford and University of California, Berkeley. He has undertaken research in economics at Centro de Investigación y Docencia Económicas (CIDE) in Mexico since 1991 and directs the journal *Economía Mexicana*. He has worked for Pan American Health Organization (PAHO), the World Bank, Inter-American Development Bank (IADB), United Nations Development Programme (UNDP), and UNU-WIDER, focusing on development and poverty traps. His recent research understands development and underdevelopment as different steady states in long-term endogenous technological change models.

Arup Mitra is Professor of Economics at the Institute of Economic Growth, Delhi. His specialization includes labour and welfare, urban development, industrial and service sector growth and productivity, and gender inequality. He did his post-doctoral study from Northwestern University as a Ford Foundation fellow. He has worked with the International Labour Organization (ILO), Geneva and many other international organizations. He also received the Mahalanobis gold medal from the Indian Econometric Society for his contribution to quantitative research.

Machiko Nissanke is Professor of Economics at School of Oriental and African Studies (SOAS), University of London. She previously worked at the University of Oxford, Birkbeck College, London and University College London. She was Research Fellow of Nuffield College, Oxford and the Overseas Development Institute, UK. She has published numerous books and journal articles on financial economics and international economics, and has served many international organizations as adviser and coordinator of research programmes.

Terutomo Ozawa is Emeritus Professor of Economics, Colorado State University, and Research Associate at the Centre on Japanese Economy and Business, Columbia Business School. He received a PhD from Columbia University, and has served as a consultant for the Organization for Economic Co-operation and Development (OECD), the United Nations Conference on Trade and Development (UNCTAD), the World Bank, and others. His latest publication is *The Rise of Asia: The 'Flying Geese' Theory of Tandem Growth and Regional Agglomeration* (Cheltenham: Edward Elgar, 2009).

Janice E. Perlman recently completed her new book, *Favela: Four Decades of Living on the Edge in Rio de Janeiro* (New York: Oxford University Press, 2010). She has won a Guggenheim, a Fulbright, and C. Wright Mills Awards. Dr Perlman is the Founder and President of The Mega-Cities Project, a global non-profit organization based in New York City, and has been a Professor at University of California, Berkeley, New York University, and Columbia University.

Jeffery I. Round is an Emeritus Reader in Economics at the University of Warwick, UK. He has been a Visiting Associate Professor at the Woodrow Wilson School, Princeton, a Harkness fellow at Harvard, and a consultant for the World Bank, the Department for International Development (DFID), United Nations Development Programme (UNDP), and other international organizations. His main research interests include the design and use of social accounting matrices for development policy analysis, and regional modelling.

David E. Sahn is a Professor of Economics at Cornell University. He received his PhD from MIT and an MPH from the University of Michigan. Prior to Cornell, he was an Economist at the World Bank and served as a Visiting Distinguished Scholar at the International Monetary Fund (IMF). Dr Sahn has published widely on issues of poverty, inequality, and health and serves as an advisor to several international organizations, such as the African Economic Research Consortium, World Bank, IMF, OECD, and various UN agencies, as well as working directly as an advisor to various government policymakers.

Erik Thorbecke is the H. E. Babcock Professor of Economics Emeritus, Graduate School Professor and former Director of the Program on Comparative Economic Development at Cornell University. He has published extensively in the areas of economic and agricultural development, the measurement and analysis of poverty and malnutrition, the social accounting matrix and general equilibrium modelling, and international economics. The Foster–Greer–Thorbecke poverty measure has been adopted almost universally by international organizations and researchers doing empirical work on poverty.

Servaas van der Berg is Professor of Economics at the University of Stellenbosch, and holds the National Research Foundation Research Chair in the Economics of Social Policy. His research interests are poverty, inequality, economic development issues, and economics of education.

Matthew Wai-Poi is an Economist at the Jakarta Office of the World Bank and currently completing his PhD at Columbia University. He has previously worked as a management consultant and holds degrees in law and business from the University of Auckland.

Guanghua Wan is a Senior Economist of the Asian Development Bank. Previously he was Senior Research Fellow and Project Director at UNU-WIDER. Guanghua Wan is Honorary Professor at several leading universities in China and a prolific researcher, having published over fifty analytical papers in refereed journals and more than ten academic books. He is a pioneer in developing regression-based decomposition techniques for inequality and poverty accounting.

Stephen D. Younger is Associate Director of the Cornell Food and Nutrition Policy Program and Scholar in Residence at the Department of Economics, Ithaca College, New York. Dr Younger received a PhD in Economics from Stanford University. His research and teaching interests include the impact of public policy on poverty and inequality and poverty measurement in multiple, non-income, dimensions of well-being.

Yin Zhang is a Lecturer in Economics at the School of Social Sciences, University of Dundee. Her research interests include economic development, applied macroeconomics, and applied econometrics.

Part I

Overview

1

Comparative Analysis of the Globalization–Poverty Nexus in Asia, Latin America, and Africa

Machiko Nissanke and Erik Thorbecke

1.1. Introduction

Globalization and poverty, alongside the issue of climate change, epitomize two of the most pressing contemporary international development issues. Despite the enormous potential of globalization in accelerating economic growth and development through greater integration into the world economy, the spread and transfer of technology, and the transmission of knowledge, its impact on poverty reduction has been uneven and even marginal in some regions such as in much of Sub-Saharan Africa (SSA). Both the prevalence and depth of poverty in many parts of the developing world remain unacceptably high.

A question often raised is whether the actual distribution of gains from globalization is fair and, in particular, whether the poor benefit proportionately less from globalization and could actually be hurt by it under some circumstances. The risks and costs brought about by globalization can be significant for fragile developing economies and the world's poor. The downside of globalization is most vividly illuminated at times of periodical global financial and economic crises. The costs of repeated financial crises fuelled by the globalization process, at least until the present major recession, have been borne overwhelmingly by the developing world and often disproportionately so by the poor who are the most vulnerable. On the other hand, the benefits from globalization during boom times are often not equally shared within the global community.

The fear that the poor have been bypassed, or actually hurt, by globalization was highlighted by the findings from a number of recent studies, which point towards a continuing prevalence of high inequality in world income distribution, and limited income convergence among participating national economies and across regions.[1] The regional trends in income inequality measured by the Gini coefficient show that within-country inequality has increased markedly since the early 1980s in almost all regions.[2]

The progress on poverty reduction has also been uneven. The share of the population of developing countries living below US$1 a day declined from 42 per cent to 16 per cent between 1981 and 2005, but this was mainly achieved by the substantial reduction of the poor in Asia, in particular in China.[3] Furthermore, over the period 1981–2005, the total number of people living under US$2 a day has actually increased worldwide by about 56 million to 2.6 billion in 2005, while the share of the world's population receiving less than US$2 a day fell from 69 per cent in 1981 to 48 per cent in 2005 (Chen and Ravallion 2008). There is a clear disparity in the regional trends in poverty reduction. While East Asia and the Pacific experienced the sharpest reduction in the number of poor living below US$1 a day, poverty has increased significantly in Africa in terms of poverty incidence as well as the depth of poverty.

Though any observed trend in poverty and income inequality cannot be exclusively or even mainly attributed to the 'globalization' effect as such, these various estimates cannot dismiss the concerns raised that the globalization process may have had adverse effects on income distribution and on poverty among some segments of the population.[4] Indeed, while most objective observers would argue that globalization is likely to have contributed to poverty alleviation on a net basis, it is also known to have created winners and losers at numerous levels throughout modern history.[5] These concerns have generated a passionate debate worldwide as well as a powerful anti-globalization movement.

The extent of controversy surrounding this debate reflects the fact that globalization is not a process, proceeding neutrally in a policy vacuum; it rather is a policy-induced condition.[6] Globalization is not purely driven by new technological innovations and progress or by 'neutral' market forces and

[1] See Nissanke and Thorbecke (2006b) for a review of literature and more detailed discussion on the concepts used for analysing the trends in world inequality and empirical evidence. Milanović (2005a; 2006) provides a detailed empirical analysis of 'global' income inequality. For the historical trends towards income divergence, see Pritchett (1997). Quah (1996) also discusses the twin peaks in world distribution dynamics, which are characterized by the tendency for stratification and polarization.

[2] Milanović (2005a); Milanović (2005b); and Birdsall (2006).

[3] Chen and Ravallion (2008). Chen and Ravallion show that 'when China is excluded, the number of people living on less than US$1 a day is fairly static with no clear trend' (Chen and Ravallion 2007: 2).

[4] The losers could include some of those who have actively participated in the process of globalization (see Aggarwal 2008 for such an example).

[5] See Williamson (2002), among others, for winners and losers from globalization in modern history.

[6] See Kozul-Wright and Rayment (2004) for an extensive discussion.

other inescapable sociopolitical forces, as often depicted in popular writings.[7] In particular, the current phase of globalization is, to a certain extent, an outcome emerging from the global acceptance and diffusion of the economic policy paradigm, emphasizing benefits and positive features of the liberalized policy regime.

As the process of economic integration has intensified since the 1990s, the question of how globalization affects the world's poor has become one of the central issues in international political economy and international relations. However, the precise nature of the various mechanisms through which globalization has altered the pattern of income distribution and the conditions facing the world's poor are yet to be carefully analysed. This is because the globalization–poverty relationship is complex, non-linear, and heterogeneous, involving multifaceted channels. Besides the 'growth' effects of globalization on poverty (that is, the effects of globalization on poverty filtered through economic growth), the integration process is known to create winners and losers directly through other channels, affecting both vertical and horizontal inequalities (Ravallion 2004). Because these multifaceted channels interact dynamically over space and time, the net effects of globalization on the poor can only be judged on the basis of context-specific empirical studies. Cross-country studies requiring precise measurements and definition of the two key concepts—globalization and poverty—tend to fail to give robust insights into this critical nexus. Both concepts are multidimensional, and not easily captured in a composite index that may be used in a meaningful manner in cross-country comparative studies or regressions.

Building on earlier research projects, UNU-WIDER initiated a project on 'The Impact of Globalization on the World's Poor' in 2004, to deepen our understanding into how conditions facing the world's poor have been evolving under the forces of globalization.[8] In the project framework paper (Nissanke and Thorbecke 2006a; 2006b) various channels and transmission mechanisms are identified and explored through which the process of globalization affects different aspects and dimensions of poverty in the developing world. The fourteen papers presented at the conceptual and methodological conferences in Helsinki (Nissanke and Thorbecke 2006d; 2006e) analysed several of these

[7] Helleiner (2001) emphasizes the need to distinguish two different phenomena associated with the term 'globalization'. Whilst the first is a consequence of technological revolutions in transport, communications, and information processing, the second usage points to policy choices. As he notes, despite this clear distinction, the recent association of external liberalization *policies* with the technology-driven *fact* of globalization has contributed to the confusion. For discussion on the effects of technological progress on the shrinkage in space and time, see Cairncross (1997).

[8] The aim of the project is to focus on the predominantly economic manifestations of globalization; hence, it does not attempt to provide a fully comprehensive and multidisciplinary treatment of the impact of globalization on poverty, covering other dimensions of globalization such as cultural, social, and political dimensions.

distinct channels through general, conceptual discussions, or through detailed empirical studies.

The present volume presents thirteen papers selected from the three regional conferences to illustrate the differential effects of globalization on growth, inequality, and poverty in Asia, Latin America, and Africa.[9] Significant differences in initial conditions as well as distinct internal dynamic processes of institutional and sociopolitical change triggered by the forces of economic integration have influenced the poor in Asia, Latin America, and Africa in quite dissimilar ways.[10] At an aggregate level, there are distinctive characteristics, specific to each of the three developing regions, of the ways in which globalization has affected the poor. This merits a comparative analysis of each region's experiences with globalization and integration.

Naturally, any attempt at estimating rigorously the impact of the globalization process on socio-economic performance (and more specifically on poverty) faces the almost insurmountable obstacle of the lack of a plausible counterfactual scenario. In order to derive robust inferences, one would have to compare the performance under the present forces of globalization to an alternative scenario of no or limited globalization. Within limits this could be done very approximately and roughly within a computable general equilibrium model for a given country or region of a country but this task is clearly infeasible for continents as large and diverse as Asia, Latin America, and Africa.

Instead, we first attempt to describe some major recent socio-economic trends in each of these continents that one can legitimately claim were influenced by the globalization process even if they were, in fact, the net consequences of a whole series of factors with some of them independent of the forces of globalization. Further, while there are clear intercontinental differences in the effects of globalization on the poor it is also true that significant differences can prevail *within* each regional block as well. Hence, the general picture we paint with a broad brush can usefully serve as a backdrop to the specific case studies included in this volume. Focusing on distinct manifestations of globalization and channels through which the latter affects poverty, these case studies cover the spectrum from broad macroeconomic regional and country analyses to micro-oriented village studies in each of the three continents. The case studies that have adopted diverse methodological approaches

[9] Three separate publications (containing a collection of the papers presented at each of the three regional conferences in Tokyo, Rio de Janeiro, and Johannesburg during 2005–6) cover region-specific case studies other than those included in this volume (Nissanke and Thorbecke 2008a; 2008b; and 2010). Nissanke and Thorbecke (2006c) and Nissanke (2007) present a preliminary policy framework for encouraging globalization to be more pro-poor.

[10] In their cross-country regression analyses on the globalization–inequality–poverty nexus both Heshmati (2006) and Kalwij and Verschoor (2006) underscore the significance of regional variations.

to examine the globalisation–poverty relationships illustrate clearly that the impact of globalization on poverty is extremely context-specific.[11]

The remainder of this overview chapter is structured as follows. Section 1.2 presents a brief summary of our analysis of channels and transmission mechanisms through which the process of globalization affects different aspects of poverty in the developing world. Section 1.3 provides a comparative analysis of the main characteristics of the ways by which the poor in three different regions are affected by globalization. Section 1.4 consists of a synopsis of the thirteen case studies (chapters) from Asia, Latin America, and Africa appearing in this volume. Section 1.5 offers concluding remarks, suggesting a policy framework that could make globalization more pro-poor.

1.2. Channels Linking Globalization to Poverty

What are the transmission mechanisms through which the process of globalization affects poverty directly and indirectly? In a general sense, the channel linking globalization (openness) to poverty can be visualized as a large river fed by a variety of economic tributaries. Figure 1.1 is our attempt to illustrate schematically the various critical links of the causal chain running from globalization (openness) to poverty, focusing on most critical tributaries and abstracting from several feed-back effects that exist among the constituting elements.

As listed in Figure 1.1, globalization, as defined in this volume, means greater economic integration manifested through increased openness via numerous transmission mechanisms, such as trade and investment liberalization, movements of capital, labour migration across borders and within countries, the nature of technological change and diffusion of knowledge and technology, the worldwide information flows, and institutional environments. These mechanisms affect poverty through two different paths: first, through their contributions to the growth channel (in the upper part of the diagram in Figure 1.1) and, second, through their impact on income distribution (in the lower part of the diagram).

The specific links shown in Figure 1.1 are from openness to growth, from openness to income distribution (inequality), from growth to income distribution and vice versa, from growth to poverty, and from income distribution to poverty, respectively. In turn, the two main channels of globalization—the 'growth' and 'distribution' channels—further interact dynamically over time to produce a growth–inequality–poverty triangular relationship, which is captured by the right-hand-side triangle of Figure 1.1, describing the arithmetic–

[11] See also Winters, McCulloch, and McKay (2004) for a detailed discussion on context-specific effects of trade liberalization on poverty in developing countries.

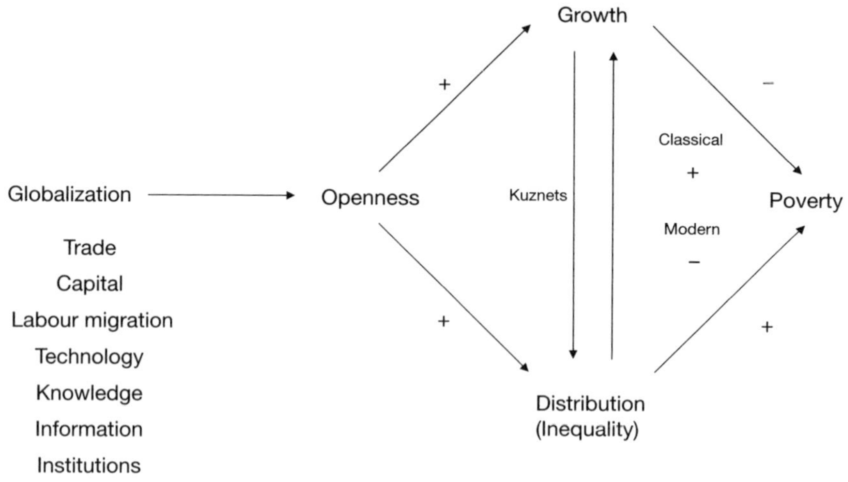

Fig. 1.1. The globalization–openness–growth–inequality–poverty link

statistical relationship among growth, inequality, and poverty investigated and popularized by Bourguignon (2003).

As discussed in Nissanke and Thorbecke (2006a) and Nissanke and Thorbecke (2006b), each subset of links embedded in the *globalization (openness)–growth–income distribution–poverty nexus*, schematically illustrated in Figure 1.1, can be contentious and controversial. For example, the direction of causality in the openness–growth link is still being debated (the consensus view is that trade contributes to growth rather than vice versa) as well as how trade and capital flows could be interlinked into a virtuous circle. In this context it can be argued that the positive openness–growth link is neither automatically guaranteed nor universally observable, as the growth-enhancing effects of trade openness depend critically on the way and extent to which a country is integrated into the global economy. Indeed, a greater integration/openness does not necessarily ensure uninterrupted growth spells. Rather, it also entails accepting great downside risks of contagion effects of crises, as plentifully demonstrated by the globally synchronized slowdown that has engulfed all the economies in the developing world since September 2008.

Further, relating the causal chain from income and wealth inequality to growth (the 'inequality–growth' link), there are two conflicting theoretical strands: the traditional (classical) approach and the 'new' political economy of development theories (modern). Whilst the former emphasizes the growth-enhancing effects of income inequality and wealth inequality through the saving-enhancing effects as well as the existence of investment indivisibilities and incentive effects,[12] the latter links greater inequality to reduced growth through various conditions such as the diffusion of political and social instability leading to greater uncertainty and lower investment, unproductive rent-seeking activities, high transaction costs, and increased insecurity of property rights.[13]

The Kuznets hypothesis of the inverted U-shaped relationship between growth and inequality that examines the opposite causal flow (i.e., the 'growth–inequality' link) is also challenged by a number of recent studies. Thus, the new political economy of development approach suggests that with two causal chains combined, growth patterns yielding more inequality would, in turn, engender lower future growth paths resulting in less of a growth-induced poverty reduction, as Figure 1.1 illustrates. Thus, we argued that while globalization-induced growth may benefit the poor, the ultimate poverty-reduction effects depend on how the growth pattern affects income distribution, as inequality acts as the *filter* between growth and poverty reduction. Poverty reduction would require some combination of higher growth and a more pro-poor distribution of the gains from growth.

In addition, several specific features associated with the current phase of globalization have contributed to possible adverse effects on the poor. These include: (a) the nature of technical changes biased in favour of capital and against unskilled labour, the asymmetrical access to new technology and knowledge, and the uneven process of technology diffusion; (b) the perverse pattern of international migration which yields a greater migration of skilled labour from developing countries to developed countries, while unskilled labour migration tends to be strictly controlled; (c) the perverse movements of capital, such as in the form of capital flight from developing or emerging market economies or *diversification* finance characterizing portfolio capital flows conducted through asset swapping for risk hedging and shedding, which results in global macro-imbalances and periodical financial crises; and (d) uneven, skewed foreign direct investment (FDI) flows, which have not necessarily guaranteed host developing countries access to potential benefits of management and knowledge transfer. These features have affected, in a number of instances, the functional income distribution between labour and capital against the former.

Concerns are particularly strong about the increased vulnerability of the poor to globalization forces that generate greater fluctuations in income and expenditure caused by global shocks, such as the various financial crises that have hit Latin America and Asia in the last two decades or the ongoing global financial crisis and earlier food crisis hurting disproportionately the poor. Thus, while globalization can be a major engine for growth in aggregate, it is critical to put

[12] See Kaldor (1956) and Aghion, Caroli, and Garcia-Peñalosa (1999) for discussion on the savings effects and the investment effects, respectively.

[13] See Thorbecke and Charumilind (2002).

in place strong institutions that mediate the various channels and mechanisms through which the globalization process influences poverty. Indeed, institutions act as a filter intensifying or hindering the positive and negative pass-through between globalization and poverty and can help explain the diversity, heterogeneity, and non-linearity of outcomes.[14]

1.3. Regional Characteristics Influencing the Globalization–Poverty Nexus

1.3.1. Income Divergence in the South under Globalization

Emerging empirical evidence on the recent increase in world income disparity between the rich and the poor can at least be partially attributed to the forces shaping the current process of globalization. In particular, the observed 'big time' divergence in inter-country income levels (when each country is weighted equally) brings into question the validity of the openness-induced income-convergence thesis, advanced by Sachs and Warner (1995) and others.

The reality is that the mere adoption of open trade and investment regimes does not guarantee, or necessarily promote, developing countries' entry into the 'income convergence club'.[15] Based on a 'human-development-trap model', Mayer-Foulkes (Chapter 2 in this volume) shows that in the presence of multi-equilibria, development and underdevelopment can coexist as steady states under globalization. His analysis leads him to conclude that globalization is a necessary, but not a sufficient condition for convergence to development. Indeed, many poor countries that have opened their economies since the 1980s have fallen behind, not having succeeded in reaching the take-off point necessary for benefiting from positive forces of globalization.[16] In addition, many countries that have seen a substantial increase in their trade/GDP ratios have undergone a worsening of their income distribution.[17] Empirical studies of countries and regions generally point to the existence of *threshold* effects in the globalization–inequality–poverty nexus, as postulated in section 1.1.

It can be argued, therefore that the conundrum of the persistent 'non-convergence' of world per capita income should be explicitly addressed in terms of structural features of the global economic relationships as they evolved over time and institutional and sociopolitical conditions found in participating countries. The income convergence trend among nation states, to the extent

[14] See Sindzingre (2006).

[15] This point was emphasized in Dowrick and DeLong (2001).

[16] See four studies on SSA included in Part IV of this volume, as well as six additional case studies focusing on SSA settings in Nissanke and Thorbecke (2008b), for empirical evidence.

[17] Sanchez (2003).

that it has been observed historically, is likely to be explained more effectively by the specific nature of the integration and specialization process followed by subgroups of countries, rather than by the degree of openness of the trade and investment regimes per se, as often claimed.

Above all, countries need to have reached the take-off point, as the effects of international trade on growth are critically dependent on the pattern of specialization and integration. Contrary to the conventional Heckscher–Ohlin trade model, with a symmetrical treatment of the two sectors, the pattern of specialization does matter, in reality, for welfare implications of a trade induced growth path, as two sectors need not be symmetrical on at least two accounts. First, because of the possibility of the 'immiserizing' effect of changes in the terms of trade (TOT) à la Bhagwati,[18] and second because of the possible differential impact of dynamic-scale economies through technological spillovers and the accumulation of knowledge capital. A country specializing in an industry endowed with a larger positive externality would experience a faster growth rate compared with the trading partner that specializes in an industry with a weaker externality. Thus, the growth rates of the two trading countries could differ considerably, depending on the pattern of specialization. A country with an initial comparative advantage in 'non-dynamic' sectors may end up in a low equilibrium trap through the evolving patterns of production and trade. Similarly, the effects of FDI on host economies diverge enormously, depending on the sectors into which transnational corporations (TNCs) are attracted to move in and invest. Low-income developing countries tend to attract natural-resource-based FDI in extracting mineral resources or FDI geared towards the lower end of TNCs' vertical integrated global operations (their global value chain) such as simple assembly-line operations. These sectors and activities are characterized by limited dynamic externalities and knowledge and skill spillovers.

In general, the globalization experiences in the South tend to be very heterogeneous. In this context, we argue that developing countries have to undergo substantial changes in trade and production structure, so as to be able to reap more benefits from the dynamic forces unleashed by globalization and experience income convergence. Indeed, sharp divergences have emerged in the development paths followed by different countries in the South over the recent decades. These divergences can be explained by the distinct internal patterns of economic growth and the forms of integration adopted. As a consequence, some countries in the South were able to benefit from *virtuous* cycles of

[18] Birdsall (2002) suggests that, measured by the trade : GDP ratio or tariff rates, most commodity-dependent countries have not been more reticent than less-commodity-dependent countries about participating in international trade, but the former group has failed to grow, especially after 1980, as they have remained dependent on exports of primary commodities. See also Maizels (1992).

globalization-induced growth, while others were left behind in *vicious* cycles of globalization-induced decline. Not only did the growth rates diverge widely but there emerged a marked difference in the ways the benefits of economic growth trickled down to the poor as these developing economies were integrating into the global economy. The sharp differential impact of the forces of globalization on the poor in the developing world can be analysed by focusing on the integration experiences of three broad regions (continents): Asia, Latin America, and Africa, respectively.

1.3.2. Comparative Globalization Experiences

INTEGRATION EXPERIENCES IN ASIA

Asia is the region widely regarded as having benefited most from the dynamic *growth* effect of the recent wave of globalization, which has also resulted in a very substantial reduction of abject poverty in many economies. Furthermore, the growth pattern achieved through increased trade and FDI in *East* Asia in the 1960s and 1970s was especially seen as highly inclusive, and often viewed as a model of 'shared growth' (World Bank 1993; Campos and Root 1996; Ahuja et al. 1997). Yet, there is growing evidence that in the last three decades inequality has been rising as part and parcel of the integration process in many parts of Asia. Hence, it is critically important to examine the mechanisms at work in the globalization–poverty nexus in Asia.

First, there is very little disagreement over the powerful growth-enhancing effects of openness through trade and FDI in the case of most Asian countries. In particular, following aggressively an 'outward-oriented development strategy', most *East* Asian economies had not only managed the process of integration into the world economy much earlier than other developing countries but also improved their form of linkages to the global economy in the years of their rapid economic growth. In addition, prior to the financial crisis of 1997–8, many of the East Asian economies registered spectacular growth performances accompanied by a substantial reduction in poverty—through dynamically evolving changes in their socio-economic structures. A number of earlier studies (World Bank 1993; Campos and Root 1996; Ahuja et al. 1997) attributed this successful growth performance to an appropriate set of economic policies and institutions well suited to the conditions prevailing in East Asia during that period. The relatively quick turnaround of many emerging economies in East Asia in the years following the severe crisis of 1997–8 is often attributed to their strong export performance and renewed adaptability and flexibility in responding swiftly to new opportunities offered by globalization.

Second, the structural transformation of most economies in East Asia has been facilitated considerably by the integration/globalization process. As discussed in Chapter 4 by Ozawa, the catch-up process and associated growth dynamism in Asia, as a whole, can be examined in terms of the 'Flying Geese Paradigm', wherein a sequence of staggered catch-up growth episodes has successively taken place in the region since the end of the Second World War. More specifically, as Ozawa observes, poverty alleviation has been occurring, in flying geese style (i.e., in tandem with growth) among these rapidly catching up Asian economies. The incidence of extreme poverty is estimated to have dramatically declined from 33 per cent in 1990 to 7 per cent in 2005 in East Asia including China, from 24 per cent to 7 per cent in Southeast Asia, and from 42 per cent to 32 per cent in South Asia, respectively.[19]

Thus, the growth performance—accompanied by a substantial reduction of abject poverty—in East Asia can be explained in terms of the region-wide *comparative advantage recycling* in the production and export of labour-intensive goods. The process involves a strong demand for unskilled and semi-skilled labour, driven by exporting labour-intensive goods and attracting pro-trade FDI, bringing about effective technology, knowledge, and skill transfer. Most of the East and Southeast Asian economies have successfully gone through the structural transformation of their production and trade structures with continuous upgrading of their human skill endowments and technology/knowledge base. By relying on their fast-evolving dynamic comparative advantages these countries were able to maximize the benefits from dynamic externalities. Their increasing specialization in sectors with large spillovers and dynamic externalities was conducive to engendering a pattern of equalizing growth.

Third, in most of East Asia, the pro-poor pattern of public expenditure in favour of the rural poor at early stages of development produced and sustained the 'shared' growth process at least until the 1970s. There were concerted efforts on the part of governments to facilitate building primary assets of the poor through such measures as an equitable distribution of land (through appropriate land reforms), extensive public provision of free and universal primary education, promotion of small-scale enterprises, and development of rural infrastructure—roads, irrigation, schools, agricultural support outposts, health stations, and irrigation systems. In this context, Ozawa argues in Chapter 4 that the observed pro-poorness of growth in East Asia is not purely a manifestation of market-driven growth effects.

Fourth, notwithstanding the ongoing urbanization process, the great majority of the poor in Asia continues to reside in the rural areas—63 per cent at last count (Cook 2006). The accelerating rural to urban migration in response to the rapid expansion of job opportunities has contributed both to economic growth

[19] Poverty based on the headcount ratio of US$1 a day in China fell from 74 per cent in 1981 to 8 per cent in 2005 (Chen and Ravallion 2008) and in Indonesia from 38 per cent to 7 per cent between 1984 and 2004. Similar progress occurred in Thailand (where the headcount ratio dropped from 18 per cent in 1988 to 1 per cent in 2003) and in India (where it declined from 46 per cent in 1987 to 31 per cent in 2003) (ADB 2004; 2005). In Vietnam, poverty is estimated to have declined from 51 per cent in 1990 to 7 per cent in 2005 (Ali and Zhuang 2007; ADB 2007).

in urban areas and to the alleviation of poverty in rural areas by (i) reducing surplus labour in agriculture, and (ii) through the remittances from migrant workers that presently account for a significant share of rural household income.[20] Further, as emphasized in Chapter 6 by Hayami, the employment-creating impact of globalization benefited landless labourers in both urban and rural areas as an important conduit for reducing rural poverty.

Yet, globalization and market-driven economic growth tend to increase inequality, as 'global markets are inherently disequalizing' (Birdsall 2006: 18).[21] With the current wave of globalization, 'within country' income inequality has been steadily rising (Milanović 2005a).[22] Asia is no exception to this trend. The earlier period of shared growth was followed by one of rising inequality in 1East Asia, which was further exacerbated by the financial crisis of 1997–8. Although both China and India have accelerated the catching-up process, resulting in very fast growth in their mean national incomes, income inequality among provinces and states, as well as inter-personal inequality, have been rising in both countries in recent decades particularly after a decisive step was taken towards opening the respective economies (detailed in Nissanke and Thorbecke 2008a and in Chapters 5 and 7 in this volume).[23] The rising inequality could put a brake on economic growth as it tends to tear apart social cohesion required for economic development in the region. The poor in Asia, as elsewhere, have been particularly subject to increased vulnerability from globalized market forces.[24]

Hence, while growth in Asia produced adverse distributional effects, it was so vigorous that it more than compensated for the latter in its capacity to reduce poverty (ADB 2004). A number of empirical studies have been carried out to examine the dynamic trajectory of the inter-relationships among poverty, growth, and inequality in Asia by decomposing the changes in poverty into two components: the growth component and the distribution component. The

[20] See Sawada and Estudillo (2008) for the effect of migrants' remittance on poverty in the Philippines.

[21] Milanović (2005b) notes that while the disequalizing force inherent to economic growth is noted by many classical development writers, an interesting question is whether there are countervailing forces to render growth spatially equalizing in the long run. Krugman and Venables (1995) argue that centripetal and centrifugal forces in a spatial economy will produce an inverted U-shaped trend in global inequality as market-driven globalization proceeds in the long run.

[22] The trends in world income inequality depend on which concept is used for measurement (Nissanke and Thorbecke 2006b; Milanović 2005a). Among different estimates, the 'between country' inequality weighted by population (but ignoring 'within country' inequality) shows a declining trend largely driven by the China factor, while all other estimates show clearly that the world inequality has been increasing.

[23] Among twenty-one developing countries in Asia, fifteen countries registered a rise in the Gini coefficient. A sharp increase of 5 to 10 percentage points in the Gini coefficient is observed in five countries, including Nepal and China (ADB 2007). Growing inequality is observed in terms of both income inequality and non-income inequality (such as in health and education).

[24] See Aggarwal (2008).

results of the earlier decomposition study for five countries in East Asia (Malaysia, Thailand, Indonesia, rural China, and the Philippines) confirm that growth was sufficiently buoyant to more than compensate for greater income inequality and keep poverty reduction on track (Ahuja et al. 1997).[25]

Overall, the process of integration of many Asian economies into the global economy has generated such a strong growth impact that the poor were not left out from its beneficiary effects.[26] This is particularly so when economic growth was accompanied by increasing employment opportunities for the poor. At the same time, the Asian experience underscores the importance of policy and institutional measures to build up productive assets of the poor through substantial investment in education, health, extension services, and infrastructure as well as through the redistribution of assets in favour of the poor—for example, through land tenure reforms. The pattern of growth in Asia has been pro-poor according to the weak definition (the poor benefit proportionately less than the non-poor) but not according to the strong definition of pro-poor growth (that is the poor benefit proportionately more than the non-poor).

Indeed, despite the sharp reduction in the incidence of extreme poverty (less than US$1 a day), poverty remains high in many developing countries in Asia, if it is measured on the basis of the US$2 a day poverty line. It is estimated that the latter declined from 87 per cent in 1981 to 74 per cent in 2005 in South Asia, and from 93 per cent to 40 per cent in East Asia (dominated by China) over the same period (Chen and Ravallion 2008). The reduction in this measure is appreciable in particular in East Asia, but poverty is still widespread in Asia as a whole, and the challenge facing policymakers in the region in attacking poverty of this magnitude is still daunting. The 'inequality increasing' effect of globalization should be attenuated by public policy measures to ensure that benefits from globalization-induced growth are shared more equally and equitably. In this context, it is worth remembering that the pattern of *shared* growth from wealth-sharing policy measures provided legitimacy for governments to pursue pro-growth and pro-business economic policy in the early drive for rapid industrialization in East Asia (Campos and Root 1996). Sustaining the shared growth process is hence critical for ensuring economic growth to continue under this era of globalization. Alternatively, growing inequalities can weaken social cohesion and risk reducing the momentum for economic growth and integration in the region.

INTEGRATION EXPERIENCES IN LATIN AMERICA

Latin America occupies an intermediate position in its integration experience compared to the other two regions. Like countries in SSA, many economies in

[25] See Chap. 5 of this volume for a decomposition analysis of the Indian economy.

[26] See Nissanke and Thorbecke (2008a) for detailed case studies that examine the effects of different aspects of globalization on inequality and poverty in Asia.

Latin America have been historically natural-resource based in their linkage to the global economy through primary commodity exports. Though the economies in the region are much more diversified in their production and trade structures than those in SSA, they have been largely susceptible to the 'global development cycle', dominated by external shocks (Ocampo and Parra 2006).[27] Many countries in the region were exposed to the deterioration in their TOT caused by the sharp drop in the prices of a number of primary commodities in the 1980s. In addition, as main recipients of commercial loans based on abundant petrodollars in the 1970s, middle-income countries in the region suffered from the sudden hike in real interest rates at the end of the 1970s. Resulting from the ensued severe debt crisis, the region had to endure the 'lost decade' of economic growth in the 1980s characterized by negative external resource transfer and negative growth rates in per capita income. The annual average growth of GDP in the 1980s for the Latin American region was barely above 2 per cent, resulting in stagnant per capita income.

After the belated market-based debt restructuring under the Brady Plan and the sweeping policy reforms of liberalization and deregulation, middle-income economies in the region reintegrated into the global economy as emerging market economies in the early 1990s. Yet, the region's economic integration, spurred by the liberalization and privatization drive and based on the premise of large 'growth' dividends from globalization, has not delivered the promised benefits of sustained economic growth to these economies. The average annual growth of GDP in Latin America during the 1990s was only around 3 per cent. Sanchez summarizes the prevailing view on the region's performances over the last two decades by noting that 'Latin America has wholeheartedly embraced the faith in open trade and freer capital markets and yet, subsequent growth is well short of expectation' (Sanchez 2003: 1977). On the whole, the globalization-induced economic growth in the region has been much more precarious and fragile than that recorded in Asia throughout the last three decades.

Under the impetus of highly volatile portfolio capital flows, economic growth has been interrupted by the periodic crises in capital accounts of balance of payments since the mid-1990s. Much of the eagerly anticipated increase in FDI took the form of asset acquisition of newly privatized public utilities rather than that of 'greenfield' investment in productive capital. Operating within the global production network, TNCs in the manufacturing sector in the region have adopted new production technologies with little new employment created. TNCs in Mexico and the Caribbean tend to specialize in low-technology manufactures, operating largely assembly plants with little

[27] Ocampo and Parra (2006) attribute the cycles of growth spurts and collapses of many developing economies since the 1950s to their susceptibility to external shocks originating from the global economy, and accordingly identify a 'global development cycle' that circumscribes the growth possibilities of these economies on a sustainable basis.

potential of technology and skill transfers (ECLAC 2004; Sáinz 2006). Thus, during the recent spell of globalization, Ocampo and Parra remark that 'South America has experienced premature deindustrialization, while Mexico and Central America avoided this trend by specializing in high import intensive manufacturing exports, but with limited benefits in terms of growth' (Ocampo and Parra 2006: 14). The growth spurt starting in 2004 (yielding an annual growth rate of GDP of around 5 per cent a year until 2008), largely fuelled by temporarily rising commodity prices, is not sustainable. Clearly the growth transmission channel has, at least until very recently, been much too weak to play a significant role in reducing poverty in the region.

In contrast to Asia, the Latin American region has experienced a very low rate of formal job creation in the tradable sector under globalization. In some cases, economic growth was 'jobless', with a negative rate of creation of formal jobs. Sáinz (2006) observes the sharp disparities in performance between large (often operated by TNCs) and small enterprises in the region: large-scale enterprises recorded high rates of productivity growth with a shrinking labour force, while the number of small and informal low-productivity enterprises continues to grow. Thus, labour markets in the region are characterized by a high degree of segmentation in parallel with an increasing casualization of the workforce.

As firms operating in the formal sector are subject to increased international competition as liberalization proceeds, the informal sector has expanded by absorbing negative income shocks as workers in the formal sectors are laid off. This process has given rise to the fear of 'social exclusion' of the self-employed, operating almost entirely in the informal sector. Popli (2008) notes that the self-employed now account for one-third of the labour force in the Mexican economy and are one of the most vulnerable groups. This process of casualization and informalization of the workforce can help explain the reduction in open unemployment in Mexico and other Central American countries during the 1990s, while open unemployment was rising steadily in Argentina, Brazil, and Columbia, and other Latin American countries. The share of the informal sector in urban employment rose significantly in most countries of the region (ECLAC 2004).

While the distribution of income and assets in this region is known to have been historically the most unequal in the developing world, many empirical studies confirm that income and asset inequality has continued to rise significantly during the integration process after 1980. In the second half of the 1990s, all Latin America and the Caribbean (LAC) countries were grouped at the very top end of the world inequality ranking according to the World Bank's World Development Indicators (WDIs) data set—with a median Gini of 56.7 per cent and mean of 54.7 per cent (Palma 2006). Further, according to the ECLAC study, in the 1990s, the share of total national income accruing to the top 10 per cent of households continued to rise: between the mid-1990s and mid-2000s, inequality rose in nine LAC countries, while it fell in only two countries and remained essentially the same in four countries. The lethal combination of low growth and increased income inequality resulted in little overall poverty reduction. The headcount ratio (based on the US$1 a day poverty line) fell from 7.4 per cent in 1981 to 5 per cent in 2005. Yet it is important to note that the aggregate statistics hide the good performance of some individual countries. The best performer in terms of growth and poverty alleviation was Chile, where the US$1 a day poverty has been practically eradicated, and Brazil and Mexico who succeeded in reducing both inequality and poverty substantially since the mid-1990s despite unspectacular growth (Nissanke and Thorbecke, 2010).

The increased income inequality is often explained by the widening income gaps between skilled and unskilled workers as well as between the formal and informal sectors, reflecting the differences in human capital endowments.[28] Brazil's experience since the late 1980s provides a revealing counterevidence marked by a falling wage inequality and income inequality (after 2000) as Ferreira, Leite, and Wai-Poi (Chapter 8 in this volume) make clear in their case study—illustrating thereby the risk of blanket generalizations.

However, Palma (2006) challenges the power of these explanations for the pattern of income distribution, exclusive of other factors, arguing that the effects of globalization on income distribution in the region are most pronounced at the extreme ends of the income distribution. In other words, Latin America is characterized by a greater income *polarization*. Palma explains this polarization by the way the LAC economies have integrated into the global economy, citing the Mexican case where the share of wages fell from 40 per cent of GDP in 1976 to just 19 per cent in 2000. Wages in low-technology manufacturing sectors, in which Mexican 'maquila' enterprises specialize, stagnated, while large productivity gains were appropriated in a sharp rise in profit margins. In short, globalization, at least partially, through its technology transmission channel appears to have shifted the functional income distribution against labour in the region and the rising income inequality dampened further the poverty alleviation effect of a modest growth performance.

Paradoxically, while the evidence is persuasive that income inequality is high and rising and contributing to perpetuate poverty in the region, much of the development literature ignores the fact that income inequality and income-based poverty are not necessarily the only or even best measures of economic and social well-being. Poverty and inequality are multidimensional concepts that can only be imperfectly reflected by money-metric measures. In this context, and further to muddle the development performance picture, Sahn and Younger (2006) found that during the 1980s and 1990s, inequality measured in the health and education dimension fell in Latin America and that this decline contributed to a substantial improvement in health and education indicators.

[28] See Harrison and Hanson (1999); Goldberg and Pavcnik (2004); and Chap. 8 in this volume for a literature review and empirical evidence relating to Mexico, Colombia, and Brazil, respectively.

They pointed out that this progress is important evidence of socio-economic development in Latin America—evidence that a narrow focus on money-metric measures alone would miss.

The poverty incidence is much higher in rural areas than in cities, although there is an ongoing increasing urbanization of poverty trends due to the rural–urban migration. While some major efforts have been in place in recent years to redress income inequality through such schemes as the Brazilian *Bolsas* and the Mexican *Progresa*, inequality in non-income measures such as education, nutrition, health, and access to utilities remains persistent. The poor are particularly disadvantaged in accessing these public goods. While a claim has been made that increasing international remittances could become a massive resource transfer mechanism to reduce poverty levels by increasing income of poorer households, de la Fuente (2008) shows that remittances are not going to the poorest members in rural communities in Mexico.

During the 1990s, there were some noticeable surges in social expenditures per capita through public transfers and human capital formation in many countries (ECLAC 2004). Through a rigorous empirical analysis of the relationship between growth patterns, poverty, and inequality in Brazil, Kakwani, Neri, and Son (2008) provide an important insight into the crucial role of incomes derived from social security and other government transfers in cushioning the effects of macroshocks, triggered by the forces of globalization, specifically among the poorest segments of Brazilian society for the period, 1995–2004. Skoufias, Lindert, and Shapiro (2009) also examine the performance of various schemes of public transfers in eight countries in the region. They found that, on the whole, public transfers in the region have not yet managed to redistribute income to the poor significantly. Mitigating the negative effects of globalization on inequality and the poor is of particular importance in the LAC region, where there is today widespread dissatisfaction with the social injustice associated with high poverty and inequality.

A strong case can be made that the high vulnerability to external shocks—the direct consequence of the way the LAC economies have integrated into the global economic system—has considerably impaired the institution-building process towards a more equitable society. Governments have faced serious constraints both in the fiscal front and monetary policy choices for sustaining public transfer programmes or other social policies in order to address growing inequality and the unacceptable prevalence of poverty. At the same time, the inconsistent (stop-and-go) and populist economic and monetary policies followed by many LAC regimes have contributed in no small measure to the mixed socio-economic performance described above. There appears little doubt that with sounder policies and governance the net and overall impact of globalization would have been more favourable to most segments of the population.

INTEGRATION EXPERIENCES IN SUB-SAHARAN AFRICA

Following largely an inward-oriented development strategy in the early decades of the post-independence period, the majority of SSA countries failed to take advantage of the potential provided by the dynamic growth spurt that characterized the global economy starting in the 1970s. The region was largely marginalized and experienced slow growth and stagnation. With growing recognition of their disadvantageous position, most economies in SSA significantly liberalized their trade and investment policy regimes as part of Structural Adjustment Programmes since the mid-1980s. Today, SSA is not behind other developing regions in TOT openness, as conventionally measured through a trade intensity index (imports and exports relative to GDP).[29] In spite of the increase in trade intensity, however, Africa's share of total world trade has fallen over the last two decades. Many countries in SSA have also intensified their efforts to attract FDI with the help of various fiscal and other incentive measures. However, FDI flows to the region have so far been largely limited to extraction of oil and other natural resources.

Thus, SSA presents a clear example in support of the argument that the shift to an open policy regime alone is not sufficient to bring about economic growth and consequent poverty reduction. After two decades of reforms dominated by liberalization, privatization, and deregulation, the economies of SSA have not yet been able to escape from the 'growth tragedy' syndrome—the term popularly used in characterizing the region's dismal economic performance in the comparative growth literature.[30] The recent upturn in economic growth recorded in many natural-resource-rich economies in SSA was closely associated with the temporary price hike of oil and mineral commodities in world markets. The sustainability of these high growth rates appears most questionable in the light of the free fall of commodity prices throughout 2008. Highly competent macroeconomic management over the commodity price cycle is required to avoid the 'Dutch disease' often associated with commodity booms. Otherwise, the foundation for long-term economic development of these natural resource-rich economies would remain fragile.

Indeed, the high primary commodity dependence remains one of the most conspicuous characteristics of the trade linkage of countries in SSA with the rest of the world. As UNCTAD (2002) suggests, any low-income countries dependent on primary commodity exports and natural-resource-based structure could be locked in an *international poverty trap* through integration. It is not a mere historical accident that the beginning of the debt crisis in many countries in SSA in the late 1970s coincided exactly with that of the 'commodity crisis' (Maizels 1992).

[29] See Chap. 11 by Round in this volume for key aggregate statistics on trends in openness, growth, inequality, and poverty.

[30] See O'Connell and Ndulu (2000) for a review of literature on Africa's 'growth tragedy' and further explanations for the poor growth performance in SSA.

The demand management of commodity-dependent economies governed by external shocks should be *countercyclical* to the commodity price movements. Yet, at times of an externally induced balance of payment crisis accompanied by a sharp drop in domestic demand, in the absence of alternative financial facilities, these countries have been forced to adopt stabilization policy measures that aim at a further contraction in aggregate domestic demand.[31] Effective and flexible facilities of *contingency financing* to deal with external shocks on an *ex ante* basis have been largely absent in debt-relief mechanisms such as the Heavily Indebted Poor Countries and Multilateral Debt Relief Initiative programmes.[32]

The failure of SSA economies to diversify and undergo structural transformation, and hence to benefit from the technology-driven, highly dynamic aspects of the ongoing globalization process, has led to major drawbacks in terms of low economic growth and persistent poverty. The incidence and depth of poverty have deepened in the region. According to the recent estimates (Chen and Ravallion 2008), the number of poor below the US$1.25 a day international poverty line almost doubled in SSA from about 212 million in 1981 to 388 million in 2005. The poverty incidence (the headcount ratio) in SSA fell marginally during this same period from about 53 per cent to 51 per cent—by far the highest incidence among the major regions in the world. Ali and Thorbecke (2000) argue that poverty in SSA is both most prevalent and severe in rural areas.

Furthermore, as Milanović (2003) notes, countries in SSA display a relatively high intra-country inequality. This can be seen as a puzzle as Africa should be a low inequality continent according to the Kuznets hypothesis because 'African countries are poor and agriculture-based, and also because the main productive asset—agricultural land—is relatively evenly distributed in most of SSA (except the region of Southern Africa) in part thanks to the tradition of communal land holding' (Milanović 2003: 2). The degree of income inequality in Africa has increased sharply between the 1980s and the 1990s, as shown in Chapter 11.

While it has become almost universally accepted that sustained poverty reduction requires economic growth, the *pattern* of growth, as discussed in section 1.2, does significantly affect the rate of poverty reduction. In this context, it can be argued that Africa's growth has been distinctly against the poor not only in terms of its ability to deliver the required (high) growth rate to ensure that the poor could benefit from economic growth, but also in terms of its pattern. Economic growth in SSA, where it has occurred, has not been translated into significant poverty reduction. Critically, the nature and pattern of integration of the SSA economies into the global economy, the slow rate of

[31] See Nissanke (1993 and 2010a) for a critical review of macroeconomic adjustment policies over the commodity price cycles in mineral-based developing countries.

[32] See Nissanke (2010b) for discussion on examples of a state-contingent debt-relief mechanism based on the proposal made in Krugman (1988).

structural transformation, and the neglect of the agricultural sector all combined have not been conducive to generating *virtuous* cycles of globalization-induced growth and poverty reduction.

Governments in SSA have systematically ignored (if not exploited) their agricultural sectors—failing to undertake pro-poor public investment in rural areas; rather, tending to extract a surplus from agriculture at an early stage of development. It has also been argued that divisive fiscal instruments such as subsidies or preferential credits were more extensively used by politicians in SSA than other regions as the favoured mechanisms to buy political support or to appease various interest groups.[33] Furthermore, with the advent of the debt crisis in the 1980s, fiscal retrenchment (hence reduced spending on rural infrastructure) has been consistently pursued as part of the stabilization-cum-adjustment policies. Governments were typically left with little capacity and resources to undertake public investment on a sustained basis. Under such conditions, it is difficult to expect structural transformation to take place. The majority in rural areas were de facto disenfranchised from the developing process. Private agents and rural farmers were likely to have refrained from making forward-looking productive investments.[34] Today, many parts of SSA remain isolated from global markets and the global community as the region's access to information and technology is limited.

On the whole, while globalization has made some contribution to economic growth in SSA, it has not yet facilitated the process of structural transformation required for countries to reach the take-off stage and accelerate the process of economic development and poverty reduction: instead, the forces of globalization have increased intra-country inequality and done very little to reduce poverty. Whilst the impact of globalization on poverty is extremely context-specific, the limited scope of globalization in SSA appears to be generally the result of a combination of poor initial conditions, such as fundamental disadvantages of location (disease-prone tropical countries with a harsh environment), inadequate political institutions, poor governance, extremely underdeveloped physical infrastructure, and a related high-risk investment climate.[35]

[33] This line of characterization of African states is found in Bates (1981 and 1983). See also Teranishi (1996).

[34] See Nissanke and Aryeetey (2003) for detailed discussion on the relationships between private agents and governments in SSA in a comparative perspective with that found in East Asia.

[35] See Chap. 12 in this volume for a more thorough discussion of these issues. See also Nissanke and Thorbecke (2008b) for six case studies that examine the effects of different aspects of globalization on poverty in SSA.

1.4. Overview of the Book

The book is divided into four parts: Part I consists, in addition to this introduction, of two chapters that examine cross-country divergence in inequality and poverty dynamics as well as in other indicators of economic development across the regions of the developing world under globalization—one from a theoretical perspective and the other in the form of cross-country regressions. Chapter 2, by David Mayer-Foulkes, develops a theoretical model to examine how a human development trap can persist throughout the process of globalization. The model can explain persistent income inequality between and within countries, and compare the consequences of different policy regimes such as import substitution and export promotion. By allowing for multiple equilibria, the model shows that development and underdevelopment can coexist as steady states in the context of globalization. An initial uneven distribution of assets can give rise to a human development trap that divides the population into classes where the lower class (the poor) is caught in a poverty trap from which they can not escape under the prevailing global and national policy regimes.

The model relies on two types of market imperfections: (i) incomplete markets in human capital investment (poor households cannot borrow to educate their children), and (ii) innovation provides market power (technological leaders have an inherent advantage). As a result of those reasonable assumptions—negating competitive markets—resources under the impact of globalization will not flow so as to lead to convergence. Mayer-Foulkes applies his model to explain cross-country convergence–divergences in income and life-expectancy since the 1980s across the world, including developing countries in different regions.

Chapter 3, by Alok Bhargava, examines the effect of globalization on GDP growth rates, inequality, and poverty by analysing the statistical relationships among relevant variables with aggregate panel data of fifty-four developing countries at five-yearly intervals for the period 1990–2000. Using the trade-intensity indices as representative of globalization measures, he investigates the non-linear effects of literacy levels and measures of openness. His empirical results underscore the importance of high literacy rates and life expectancy for developing countries in order to reap the benefits of globalization. Further, while his results reveal that the levels and growth rates of GDP are important for reducing poverty, globalization measured in export : GDP ratio and import : GDP ratio separately were not a significant predictor of poverty incidence. This is interpreted as little evidence that globalization has been affecting poverty—either positively or negatively on the aggregate. His results also indicate that the imports : GDP ratio and the proportion of the labour force with high skill levels may exacerbate inequality. This leads him to suggest that since the diffusion of technical knowledge to developing countries and the availability of an educated labour force are critical ingredients for economic growth, short-run increases in inequality may be inevitable. Overall, he concludes that developing countries need to invest additional resources in education and health to create a skilled labour force capable of enjoying greater benefits from globalization.

Part II of the book contains four papers examining the globalization–inequality–poverty relationships in Asia. In Chapter 4, Terutomo Ozawa explains the staggered catch-up process and associated growth dynamism in Asia and the very substantial reduction of abject poverty that has occurred in tandem in terms of the 'Flying Geese Paradigm' of *comparative advantage recycling*. He argues that the economies in this region have effectively initiated a succession of growth spurts based on a strong demand for unskilled labour, driven by exporting labour-intensive goods and pro-trade FDI through effective technology, knowledge, and skill transfer. In flying geese style, growth clustering develops, in which a hegemon economy (the lead economy) propagates growth stimuli to its closely aligned cohort of countries that are at various earlier stages of development and structural transformation. The stimuli include dissemination of technology, knowledge, information, skills, and provision of development finance, and, above all, transplantation of growth-inducing institutional arrangements. Ozawa suggests that the region's synergistic interactions result in agglomeration economies, enabling the *entire* hierarchy of countries mutually to gain, grow, and prosper.

Ozawa further emphasizes that the substantial poverty reduction in East Asia as a whole is not purely a manifestation of market-driven growth effects. In addition, proactive policy interventions and institutional arrangements were in place to lessen the adverse distributional effect and produce shared, pro-poor growth. Ozawa argues that because poverty reduction is a public good, pro-poor policy interventions and institutional set-ups can always be justified and required to spawn growth-led poverty reduction. For example, the pro-poor pattern of public expenditures in favour of rural poor, such as extensive public provision of education, physical, and social infrastructure was a decisive contributing factor in sustaining the shared growth process in many countries in East Asia.

Chapter 5, by N. R. Bhanumurthy and Arup Mitra, examines the dynamic trajectory of the inter-relationships among poverty, growth, and inequality across Indian states through a decomposition analysis. They show that the growth effect dominates the inequality (distribution) effects in poverty reduction in the two periods: (i) 1983 to 1993–4 and (ii) 1993–4 to 1999–2000 (the two periods are taken to represent broadly the pre-reform and post-reform periods, respectively) as India's economic growth increased from the 'Hindu rate of growth' of 4 per cent to the 'Bharat rate of growth' of 6 per cent after the deliberate policy shift towards pro-growth and pro-globalization in the early 1990s. This growth acceleration succeeded in reducing overall poverty, despite the rise in inequality in the second period. As growth accelerated, there was a marked shift in the composition of GDP with a sharp decline in the share of agriculture and a corresponding increase in the share of services. However, since no such shift was observed in the employment structure, with the agricultural sector still absorbing a majority of the labour force, the debate continues whether the increase in output growth is a 'jobless growth' or not.

In this context, Bhanumurphy and Mitra also examine the net effect of population mobility on poverty. The decline in the incidence of poverty (rural–urban combined) depends on whether urban employment opportunities are large enough to absorb the increasing supply of labour migrating from the rural areas. According to their decomposition analysis, there is a small 'population-shift effect' in poverty reduction in the rural areas due to the rural–urban migration in the first period, but that effect was marginal compared to the growth effect. They conclude that, despite some variations across states, overall, the economic growth realized through pro-globalization reforms has produced a large decline in the poverty incidence in India by raising labour productivity and employment opportunities with the shift in value-added mix towards industry and tertiary activities such as information technology, business process outsourcing services, financial institutions, and infrastructure services.

In Chapter 6, Yujiro Hayami emphasizes the employment-creating impact of globalization benefiting landless labourers as an important conduit for reducing rural poverty. Using the survey data collected over three decades (1966–97) in a rice-cultivating village in East Laguna in the Philippines, he examines the transformation of the village community under the forces of globalization manifested through: (i) population growth due to the importation of advanced medical and public health technology; (ii) the Green Revolution bringing along the transfer of advanced agricultural technology and the introduction of irrigated double cropping; (iii) land-reform programmes, shifting the land-tenure status from share-cropping tenancy towards leasehold tenancy and owner-farming; and (iv) the expansion of non-farm employment opportunities as well as the greater use of hired labourers who had been negatively affected by the land reforms. Whilst the Green Revolution reduced real rice prices received by farmers, it also kept the cost of wage goods, and thus the wage rates in labour-intensive manufactures, from rising. This process allowed this rural community, as elsewhere in East Asia, to gain a competitive edge in producing industrial goods at the lower end of skill requirements, as part of the region's recycling of comparative advantages.

Hayami further reckons that the creation of non-farm employment opportunities associated with rural-based industrialization is a most significant and direct factor for creating an opportunity for rural communities to reduce poverty and inequality in East Asia. In this context, he emphasizes the importance of public investment in transportation and communication infrastructure, industrial extension activities, and school education as well as building market-supporting institutions to protect property rights and enforce contracts.

Despite the impressive achievement in poverty reduction, the growing inequality under globalization has become a particularly pressing concern in China. Zhang and Wan explain in Chapter 7 that since the late 1980s the engine of China's economic take-off shifted from agricultural growth spurred by the de-collectivization of the rural areas to manufacturing exports fuelled by large FDI inflows. At the same time, progress in poverty reduction has stalled in urban China since the late 1980s. In a study of *urban* poverty in China it has been found that: (i) the income of the poor has not grown as fast as average income and the income shares of the poor have fallen accordingly; (ii) the income growth of the poor has been particularly slow since the mid-1990s and in several provinces real income growth of the poor has stagnated; and (iii) the further one moves away from the coast, the less favourable income distribution tends to become for the poor.

Further, they present the results of a number of regression analyses, based on provincial-level data, of the impact of globalization measured in openness to foreign trade and foreign investment on *urban* poverty. Their findings indicate that when globalization is separately accounted for, in addition to the income growth, globalization in general and trade openness in particular increase the income shares of the poor. However, their results also indicate that growth in China has not been pro-poor or distribution-neutral and confirm that the inequality-reducing effect of trade was significantly weakened after 1992. Further, they find that the benefit from globalization accrues to the urban poor in the inland provinces just as much as it does to their counterparts in the coastal region, suggesting globalization cannot be simply characterized as a process of pro-rich or pro-coastal provinces in China as popularly feared.

Part III of the book contains three studies examining the globalization–inequality–poverty relationships in Latin America and the Caribbean. In Chapter 8, Francisco H. G. Ferreira, Phillippe G. Leite, and Matthew Wai-Poi explore the impact of trade liberalization on wage inequality in Brazil. Using a nationally representative sample of workers in all sectors of the economy, the chapter seeks to quantify the effects of the 1988–95 trade liberalization episode on Brazilian wage distribution. The main finding is that trade reforms did contribute to the observed reduction in income inequality in the last decade through: (i) trade-induced changes in employment levels across sectors, industries, and formality categories and (ii) changes in the economy-wide skill premium which fell together with the returns to education.

The Brazilian experience is in conflict with most of the literature on trade liberalization in Latin America, which suggests that it has contributed to an increase in inequality—or at least to the gap between skilled and unskilled wages. The authors explain that Brazil was an exception to the Latin American pattern in that effective protection prior to trade liberalization was higher in skill-intensive industries. The lesson for policymakers would seem to be that in countries where protection was stronger for industries intensive in skilled workers there need not exist any mandatory trade-off between gains in efficiency and productivity, on the one hand, and increases in inequality or poverty, on the other, following trade liberalization.

On the basis of a longitudinal study of the *favelas* (shantytowns) of Rio de Janeiro spanning over three decades (1969–2004) and four generations, in Chapter 9 Janice E. Perlman derives some fascinating insights on the determinants of geographical and social mobility, how people's lives changed over time and generations over thirty-five years. A first observation is that at the community (*favela*) level the improvements in infrastructure and standard of living have been enormous. A comparison of socio-economic status indices at the end and at the beginning of the sample period reveals clear indication of movement away from poverty. Yet, there are some disappointing trends. Due to the perversity of prejudice, educational gains for *favelados* are not fully reflected by their income; for every additional year of schooling (after the first four), the gap in expected income between the *favelados* and non-*favelados* grows wider. Barriers to upward mobility may have become stronger in the era of globalization and include community-level obstacles (increased violence related to drug and arms traffic and decreased social capital) and economic obstacles (such as the stigma of *favela* residence, labour market conditions in Rio, and extreme inequality).

Looking at indicators of individual or collective consumption or educational levels one would conclude that there have been striking improvements in well-being. In contrast, looking at unemployment or violence (triggered by the drug trade) one would conclude that life is much worse now. Presumably, in the minds of most *favela* households these two opposite trends tend to compensate each other. The majority of the respondents across all three generations stated that globalization had not made any difference in their overall welfare. Perlman interprets the survey results as pointing that even as progress is being made at the material and educational levels, the goal of breaking out of poverty is a moving target. It is quite likely that the increasing flow of information about the living standards of others, both within and beyond country borders, triggered by globalization can result in changing reference norms and increased frustration with relative income differences, even among respondents whose own income is rising. Somehow, economic achievements are not capturing the sense of lingering marginalization, disrespect, and exclusion that the poor feel, despite indicators that objectively show that they are now less poor.

In Chapter 10, Alfred J. Field and Erica Field explore the impact of trade liberalization and other reforms reducing market distortions on the shift away from traditional agricultural crops and towards export crops in rural Peru. The opening up of the economy after 1994 brought about changes in relative prices between these two types of crops, favouring the export crops. The econometric results confirmed that changes in these relative prices increased the likelihood that households would shift production towards new export products. These tendencies appear to be strengthened if the farm household obtained title to their property. Hence, they suggest that weak property and titling institutions may inhibit the degree to which households can reap the benefits of the forces of globalization.

The authors also found that those households that began producing an export-oriented crop were much less likely to be poor at the end of their sample period (2004) while those who were unable to alter production due to reasons such as location, access to credit, or lack of title to property continued to produce traditional crops and were caught in a poverty trap. Hence, a passive approach to globalization is not enough to insure that poverty will be reduced; the liberalization of markets must be accompanied by appropriate social programmes and institutional reforms directed to the specific nature of the problems and constraints faced by those socio-economic groups suffering from poverty.

Part IV of the book contains four papers examining the globalization–inequality–poverty relationships in SSA. In examining the aggregate economic 'openness' indicators and their trends over time, Jeffrey I. Round in Chapter 11 observes that: (i) SSA is not behind other developing regions in terms of a trade-intensity index (imports and exports relative to GDP) and the average trade intensity has increased in SSA in line with the overall global increase; (ii) in spite of the increase in trade intensity and inflow of FDI, however, Africa's shares of total world trade and FDI has fallen over these two decade.

Further, the incidence and depth of poverty have risen in the region. In terms of the headcount ratio, the poverty incidence in SSA is the highest in the world. He also notes that the degree of income inequality in Africa has also risen sharply between the 1980s and the 1990s and within-country inequality in SSA is now higher than in the rest of the world. Thus, he argues that, despite considerable variations across countries in the region, empirical evidence and existing studies tend to suggest that globalization may be associated with increasing inequality and poverty in SSA.

However, a key issue in any attempt to estimate the impact of globalization on the poor is the lack of an appropriate counterfactual. While recognizing this methodological difficulty, Stefan Dercon in Chapter 12 proceeds to bring forth persuasive evidence on the likely impact of trade liberalization on households. Noting little effect on sustained growth from trade liberalization, he argues that, even with liberalization, growth was stifled by poor infrastructure, low education, and corruption. In particular, many African countries suffer from the fundamental disadvantages of location; landlocked, disease-prone tropical countries with harsh natural environments face a fundamental cost disadvantage. There is much evidence that marketing, transport costs, and transaction costs are very significantly higher in Africa than in Asia. Thus, he suggests that the limited scope of globalization in Africa and its slight impact on growth and poverty reduction is the result of a combination of poor initial characteristics, such as inadequate political institutions, greatly underdeveloped physical infrastructure, and a related high risk investment climate.

Taking Ethiopia as an example of an insulated, landlocked country, Dercon proceeds to analyse the impact of trade liberalization on living standards and poverty during the period 1989–95. He concludes that the trade reforms contributed to growth and poverty reduction in the surveyed villages but that the inadequately endowed poor, in terms of land and location, benefited least. Further liberalization and engagement with the world economy may offer new opportunities for those areas enjoying good infrastructure and communications, whilst poorly endowed areas within Ethiopia are at risk of becoming even more marginalized during the era of globalization. Also, rural households are becoming more vulnerable to market-related risks triggered by trade-induced shocks such as sudden changes in demand or in prices and need new instruments to cope with these emerging risks.

In Chapter 13, David E. Sahn and Stephen D. Younger explore how globalization affected non-income measures of well-being—health and education—in Africa over the past fifteen to twenty years. It is important to note that both anthropometry and educational attainment are far less subject to measurement errors than income and expenditures measures, and both are directly attributable to individuals, so that the difficult issue of intra-household allocation is avoided. The data used in the analysis came from fifty-four Demographic and Health Surveys conducted in twenty African countries that have at least two surveys. Overall, Sahn and Younger could rely on thirty-two spells of change in health and education poverty—usually five years long.

Their results indicate that in the area of health little progress is being made in terms of reducing pre-school age-stunting, a clear and robust manifestation of poor overall health. For children's height there were thirteen cases where the headcount ratio worsened, ten in which it improved, and nine where it remained the same. Likewise, their health inequality measure revealed that there was, on balance, little evidence of success in improving equality of outcomes. With regard to inequality of children's heights the authors found more cases of worsening than improvements. Similar results obtained in their examination of underweight women as an indicator of general current health of adults. The story is somewhat more positive with regard to education. Reflecting the complexity and context-specific nature of the dynamic process, their empirical analysis of the effect of globalization does not suggest that globalization is correlated (positively or negatively) with health and education outcomes. However, the overall picture emerging gives little cause for optimism that Africa has reaped, or will soon reap, the benefits of the process of globalization.

In Chapter 14, Servaas van der Berg, Ronelle Burger, and Megan Louw analyse the impact of globalization in the post-apartheid era on growth, employment, income distribution, and poverty in South Africa. The picture they paint is that trade and financial liberalization appear to have positively, but modestly, influenced economic growth. On the other hand, employment was only marginally affected—with the jobs created being largely located towards the upper hand of the skill spectrum. Consequently, South Africans in the upper range of the income distribution seem to have reaped most of the gains from globalization.

The evidence regarding the poverty trend is somewhat ambiguous. However, the authors claim that, on the basis of a different data set than the usual Income and Expenditure Surveys, the headcount ratio fell between 2000 and 2004, from 51 per cent to 47 per cent. Rather than crediting the process of globalization for this reduction in poverty, the authors make a strong case that government action through social grants has been the most important contributor to poverty alleviation. Amongst groups, blacks continue to experience high and increasing intra-group income inequality, yet one polarization measure appears to indicate that improvements in living conditions associated with expanding grants and the emergence of a black middle class have dampened to some degree the social tensions associated with material inequality.

1.5. Concluding Remarks

The empirical case studies from the three regions support our contention laid out at the outset that the effects of globalization on poverty are diverse and, in many ways, context-specific.[36] Indeed, our studies confirm the view that 'the forces of globalization as such are not *inherently* beneficial or deleterious for development prospects' (Sanchez 2003: 1978).

Yet, our comparative analysis of the globalization experiences across the three developing continents also suggests that globalization works best for the poor through the 'growth' channel when globalization-induced economic growth generates secure employment opportunities continuously at a steady rate for a growing population and labour force. On the whole, the employment-creating effect of growth is pronounced in East Asia, where globalization has brought about a substantial poverty reduction due to vigorous growth, despite increasing inequality. The process of poverty reduction in the Asia and Pacific region has closely followed the waves of employment creations for unskilled labour and the poor in tandem with the evolution and shifts of comparative advantages within the region in the ever-accelerating integration process. In contrast, such a poverty-reduction process through globalization could not be achieved in SSA and ECLAC regions, where liberalization of trade and investment regimes failed to produce either strong or significant employment-creating growth. Instead, trade liberalization has tended to result in 'jobless' growth, casualization of employment, and informalization of their economies. This observation leads us to argue that the employment-creation effect achieved

[36] See Ravallion (2006) and Bardhan (2006) for the detailed discussion on the tenuous but complex nature of the openness–poverty relationships. Winters, McCulloch, and McKay (2004) also presents a careful examination of multiple mechanisms found in the link between trade liberalization and poverty.

through globalization-induced economic growth is a most direct and powerful channel through which globalization can make a noticeable dent on poverty.

Thus, the potential of sustained poverty reduction is realized only when globalization-induced growth is characterized by a relatively high 'employment elasticity'. However, such growth outcome cannot be guaranteed whenever globalization/integration is embraced, on its own, as a development strategy. Instead, the dynamic integration experiences in Asia point to the need for policies of *strategic integration*, not of *passive integration or delinking* from the global economy. Such a strategic position should, first of all, aim at facilitating the transformation of production and trade structures from the narrowly based commodity dependence that is bound to expose economies to external shocks. In terms of sustained economic growth, developing countries that have successfully diversified their exports structures into manufactured goods—in particular, increasingly into medium- and high-technology sectors—have systematically outperformed those dependent on primary commodities and natural-resource-based processing goods.[37] Thus, whether global market forces establish a virtuous circle or vicious circle depends not only on the initial conditions at the time of exposure but also importantly on the effective design and implementation of national policies to manage the integration process. As Kaplinsky notes, 'the issue [confronting policymakers] is thus not *whether* to participate in the global economy but *how* to do so in a manner which provides for sustainable and equitable income growth' (Kaplinsky 2000: 117).

Clearly, a strategic position towards globalization cannot be equated with a mere adoption of liberal trade and investment regimes, or a simple fine-tuning of the pace and sequence of liberalization measures. At the same time, there is no place for an old-style, poorly designed and implemented protection policy, which is mired in unproductive rent-seeking activities, patron-client relationships between governments and private agents, or consolidation of 'vested' interests of the protected sectors. Import-substitution strategy can work only when protection is granted to firms with a clearly specified 'graduation' clause in a performance-based system. That is, protection should always be seen as temporary and 'time-bound' by agents in return for better performances.

In particular, national integration strategies should be designed in light of the skewed nature of the ongoing process of globalization. First, dynamic externalities and rent-rich activities are increasingly concentrated in high-skill, knowledge-intensive sectors—in short, the skill- and technology-related divide has become wider over recent decades. This trend is clearly reflected in the continuously declining TOT of less-skill-intensive manufactured goods relative to high-skill- and technology-intensive goods over recent decades. The markets for many labour-intensive products have come to resemble those for primary

[37] Ocampo and Perra (2006: tables 2 and 3 and fig. 9).

products (Maizels 1998). The entry of China and India into global markets for these products has depressed and will continue to depress real wages and returns in these low-technology and low-skill sectors. On the other hand, a number of primary commodities experienced a sharply upward phase in their commodity price-cycles in recent years, in the face of the surge in demand for raw materials and other commodities from fast-growing economies in Asia such as India and China. Consequently, many natural-resource-based economies in SSA and Latin America did enjoy a period of 'growth spurts' associated with the 'commodity' boom. However, the subsequent sharp fall in commodity prices, as the world economy entered into a severe downturn phase, has illustrated the high vulnerability of these economies to commodity price shocks. This demonstrates once again the difficulties in sustaining a structure of economic growth that is capable of creating job opportunities for a rising labour force, exclusively on the basis of the primary commodity boom. A broadly based development pattern for these economies would require a strategy of using resource rents and windfalls for economic diversification.

Second, intra-firm trade in parts, components, and other intermediate goods and intra-industry trade with highly differentiated products make up a predominant share of contemporary global trade. In particular, international trade is less and less conducted in arm's-length relationships among firms. Rather, a growing share of world trade is accounted for by intra-firm trade undertaken within TNCs. There has been a tremendous growth in offshore outsourcing and global division of labour, dictated by TNCs' globally integrated production and marketing strategies. TNCs' activities are strategically organized and integrated either horizontally or vertically. In particular, with a sharp decline in transport and communication costs over the recent decades, TNCs have been aggressively organizing their operations vertically by slicing up the production process finely into numerous separate operations and locating them in different parts of the world according to cost advantages of each location.[38]

Furthermore, considerable asymmetries in market power and access to information, technology, and other intangible knowledge assets between TNCs, on the one hand, and local entrepreneurs, farmers, and traders in developing countries, on the other, have resulted in a hugely skewed distribution of gains from trade. This is reflected in the TNCs' dominance in commodity and value chains of traded goods, as well as in frequently observed conditions such as the sharp decline in real wages in export-processing zones (Kaplinsky 2000). Under this condition, the benefits of productivity improvements, instead of going to the fragmented producers and farmers, are largely appropriated by the TNCs and global supermarket chains. This uneven distribution of market power points to the need to improve the negotiating positions of developing country

[38] Krugman (1995) and Kaplinsky (2000).

governments vis-à-vis TNCs, aiming at a strategic, targeted approach to FDI, so that FDI could facilitate skill and technology transfer and generate strong positive productivity spillovers benefiting domestic firms.

Generally, given the observed trends towards inequality both globally and within many nations, developing countries have to take strategic steps to position themselves more favourably in the globalization process in order to derive greater benefits from globalization's dynamic forces. They need a long-term vision for upgrading their comparative advantages towards high value-added activities by climbing the technology ladder step-by-step through learning and adaptation. To succeed, developing country governments should consciously engage in building institutional capacities for integration, including a capable nation state that is ready to take on the enormous challenges posed by globalization. The positive benefits from globalization are neither automatic nor guaranteed, whilst passive liberalization would risk perpetual marginalization.

Furthermore, since openness could potentially benefit the poor in countries which have already reached the take-off stage, low-income countries should embark on the path towards *structural transformation* of their agrarian economies, as a necessary condition for successful integration. The importance of this critical step is underscored by the existence of critical *thresholds* in the globalization–poverty nexus that need to be reached before the positive effects of globalization on poverty reduction can be realized.[39] By demonstrating the possible coexistence of development and underdevelopment under globalization through the human-development-trap model (Chapter 2 in this volume), David Mayer-Foulkes also underscores the critical importance of national policies to enhance human capital endowments and develop technological capabilities. Thus, sizable public investment in skill upgrading, as a specific pro-poor measure, is the key for ensuring positive benefits from globalization for the poor. In conjunction with building assets of the poor in their human capital base, there is a complementary need to invest in rural physical and social infrastructures and create market-supporting institutions, so that the poor can be connected and networked beyond isolated communities and villages. In terms of inter-sectoral flows, a continuing *gross* flow of resources should be provided to agriculture—irrigation, inputs, research, and credit—to increase this sector's productivity and potential capacity of contributing an even larger return flow to the rest of the economy and hence provide a *net* agricultural surplus to finance the subsequent development of the rest of the economy.

Finally, our project case studies unequivocally point to the need for instituting safety nets and appropriate regulations to protect the poor from large downside risks associated with globalization. Clearly, globalization has significantly

[39] Agénor (2002).

increased the vulnerability of the poor in all three developing regions through channels such as: (i) the increased scale and frequency of macroeconomic shocks; (ii) larger exposure to changes in the ecosystem or new unknown technology with often uncertain pay-offs; and (iii) their deteriorating working conditions and weakening bargaining powers in global value chains.[40] Thus, governments should take a proactive and pro-poor stance in instituting various schemes of public transfers and safety nets to shelter the poor from these adverse conditions.[41] In this context, Bardhan (2006) argues that the distributional issue raised in the debate is not an argument against globalization (open trade and investment regimes) per se but for proactive public programmes to protect the poor.

All in all, our comparative analysis of the three regions suggests that governments of developing countries need to pursue both strategic integration and a proactive domestic development agenda to ensure that the poor benefit from globalization, while they are adequately protected from negative impacts. Bardhan (2006) notes that globalization should not be allowed to be used, either by its critics or by its proponents, as an excuse for inaction on the domestic as well as the international fronts. What is *at minimum* called for is liberalization to be accompanied by a comprehensive policy package for enhancing the capability of the poor and instituting a safety net for people who lose from the globalization process. In order to achieve this goal, the capacity of the nation states should be strengthened rather than weakened.

References

Agénor, P.-R. (2002) 'Does Globalization Hurt the Poor?'. Policy and Research Working Paper 2922. Washington, DC: World Bank.

Aggarwal, R. (2008) 'Resource-poor Farmers in South India: On the Margins or Frontiers of Globalization?'. In M. Nissanke and E. Thorbecke (eds), *Globalization and the Poor in Asia: Can Shared Growth Be Sustained?* Basingstoke: Palgrave Macmillan for UNU-WIDER.

Aghion, P., E. Caroli, and C. Garcia-Peñalosa (1999) 'Inequality and Economic Growth: The Perspective of the New Growth Theories', *Journal of Economic Literature*, 37: 1615–60.

Ahuja, V., B. Bidani, F. H. G. Ferreira, and M. Walton (1997) *Everyone's Miracle? Revisiting Poverty and Inequality in East Asia*. Washington, DC: World Bank.

Ali, A. A. G., and E. Thorbecke (2000) 'The State and Path of Poverty in Sub-Saharan Africa: Some Preliminary Results', *Journal of African Economies*, 9 (Suppl.): 9–40.

[40] See various case studies included in Nissanke and Thorbecke (2006d; 2006e; 2008b; and 2008d).

[41] See Kakwani and Son (2008) and Kakwani, Neri, and Son (2008), among other project case studies.

Ali, I., and J. Zhuang (2007) 'Inclusive Growth Toward a Prosperous Asia: Policy Implications'. ERD Working Paper 97. Manila: ADB.
Asian Development Bank (ADB) (2004) *Key Indicators of Developing Asian and Pacific Countries*. Manila: ADB.
—— (2005) *An Initial Assessment of the Impact of the Earthquake and Tsunami of December 26, 2004 on South and Southeast Asia*. Manila: ADB.
—— (2007) *Key Indicators 2007: Inequality in Asia*. Manila: ADB.
Bardhan, P. (2006) 'Globalisation and Rural Poverty', *World Development*, 34: 1393–404. Also in M. Nissanke and E. Thorbecke (eds), *The Impact of Globalization on the World's Poor: Transmission Mechanisms*. Basingstoke: Palgrave Macmillan for UNU-WIDER.
Bates, R. H. (1981) *Markets and States in Tropical Africa: The Political Basis of Agricultural Policies*. Berkeley, Calif.: University of California Press.
—— (1983) *Essays on the Political Economy of Rural Africa*. Cambridge and Berkeley, Calif.: Cambridge University Press/University of California Press.
Birdsall, N. (2002) 'A Stormy Day on an Open Field: Asymmetry and Convergence in the Global Economy'. Paper presented at the conference, 'Globalization, Living Standards, and Inequality', 27–8 May 2002, Sydney.
—— (2006) 'The World is Not Flat: Inequality and Injustice in our Global Economy'. WIDER Annual Lecture 2005. Helsinki: UNU-WIDER.
Bourguignon, F. (2003) 'The Poverty–Growth–Inequality Triangle'. Washington, DC: World Bank. mimeo.
Cairncross, F. (1997) *The Death of Distance*. London: Orion.
Campos, E., and H. L. Root (1996) *The Key to the East Asian Miracle*. Washington, DC: Brookings Institution.
Chen, S., and M. Ravallion (2007) 'The Changing Profile of Poverty in the World'. 2020 Focus Brief on the World's Poor and Hungry People. Washington, DC: IFPRI.
—— —— (2008) 'The Developing World is Poorer than We Thought, But No Less Successful in the Fight against Poverty'. Policy Research Working Paper 4703. Washington, DC: World Bank.
Cook, S. (2006) 'Asian Paths to Poverty Reduction and Inclusive Development'. Asia 2015 Conference Paper. Brighton and London: IDS/ODI.
de la Fuente, A. (2008) 'Remittances and Vulnerability to Poverty in Rural Mexico'. Research Paper 2008/17. Helsinki: UNU-WIDER. Rev. and repr. *World Development, UNU-WIDER Special Issue: Globalization, Poverty, and Inequality in Latin America* (forthcoming).
Dowrick, S., and J. B. DeLong (2001) 'Globalization and Convergence'. Paper presented at the NBER conference, 'Globalization in Historical Perspective', 4–5 May 2001, Davis, Calif.
Economic Commission for Latin America and the Caribbean (ECLAC) (2004) *A Decade of Social Development in Latin America, 1990–1999*. Santiago: ECLAC.
Goldberg, P., and N. Pavcnik (2004) 'Trade, Inequality and Poverty: What Do We Know? Evidence from Recent Trade Liberalization Episodes in Developing Countries'. National Bureau for Economic Research Working Paper 10593. Cambridge, Mass.: NBER.
Harrison, A., and G. Hanson (1999) 'Who Gains from Trade Reform? Some Remaining Puzzles', *Journal of Development Economics*, 59: 125–54.

Helleiner, G. K. (2001) 'Markets, Politics and Globalisation: Can the Global Economy be Civilized?', *Journal of Human Development*, 2: 27–46.

Heshmati, A. (2006) 'The Relationship between Income Inequality, Poverty, and Globalization'. In M. Nissanke and E. Thorbecke (eds), *The Impact of Globalization on the World's Poor: Transmission Mechanisms*. Basingstoke: Palgrave Macmillan for UNU-WIDER.

Kakwani, N., M. C. Neri, and H. H. Son (2008) 'Linkages between Pro-poor Growth, Social Programmes and Labour Market: The Recent Brazilian Experience'. Research Paper 2009/26. Helsinki: UNU-WIDER. Rev. and repr. *World Development, UNU-WIDER Special Issue: Globalization, Poverty, and Inequality in Latin America* (forthcoming).

Kaldor, N. (1956) 'Alternative Theories of Distribution', *Review of Economic Studies*, 23: 83–100.

Kalwij, A., and A. Verschoor (2006) 'A Decomposition of Poverty Trends across Regions: The Role of Variation in the Income and Inequality Elasticities of Poverty'. In M. Nissanke and E. Thorbecke (eds), *Globalization and the Poor in Asia: Can Shared Growth Be Sustained?* Basingstoke: Palgrave Macmillan for UNU-WIDER.

Kaplinsky, R. (2000) 'Globalisation and Unequalisation: What Can Be Learned from Value Chain Analysis?', *Journal of Development Studies*, 37: 117–46.

Kozul-Wright, R., and P. Rayment (2004) 'Globalisation Reloaded: An UNCTAD Perspective'. Discussion Paper 167. Geneva: UNCTAD.

Krugman, P. (1988) 'Financing vs Forgiving a Debt Overhang', *Journal of Development Economics*, 29(3): 253–68.

—— (1995) 'Growing World Trade: Causes and Consequences', *Brooking Papers on Economic Activity*, 1995: 327–77.

—— and A. J. Venables (1995) 'Globalization and the Inequality of Nations', *Quarterly Journal of Economics*, 110: 857–80.

Maizels, A. (1992) *Commodities in Crisis*. Oxford: Clarendon Press.

—— (1998) 'The Prebish–Singer Hypothesis Revisited'. In D. Sapsford and J. Chen (eds), *Development Economics and Policy*. London: Macmillan Press.

Milanović, B. (2003) 'Is Inequality in Africa Really Different?'. Policy Research Working Paper 3169. Washington, DC: World Bank.

—— (2005a) *World Apart: Measuring International and Global Inequality*. Princeton, NJ: Princeton University Press.

—— (2005b) 'Half a World: Regional Inequality in Five Great Federations'. Policy Research Working Paper 3699. Washington, DC: World Bank.

Nissanke, M. (1993) 'Stabilization-cum-Adjustment over the Commodity Price Cycle'. In M. Nissanke and A. Hewitt (eds), *Economic Crisis in Developing Countries: New Perspectives on Commodities, Trade and Finance*. London: Pinter Publishers.

—— (2007) 'Pro-poor Globalisation: An Elusive Concept or a Realistic Perspective'. Inaugural Lecture Series. London: SOAS, University of London.

—— (2010a) 'Commodity Market Structures, Evolving Governance and Policy Issues'. In M. Nissanke and G. Mavrotas (eds), *Commodities, Governance and Economic Development under Globalization*. Basingstoke: Palgrave.

—— (2010b) 'Reconstructing the Aid Effectiveness Debate'. In G. Mavrotas (ed.), *Foreign Aid for Development: Issues, Challenges, and the New Agenda*. Oxford: Oxford University Press for UNU-WIDER.

—— and E. Aryeetey (2003) *Comparative Development Experiences of Sub-Saharan Africa and East Asia: An Institutional Approach*. Aldershot: Ashgate.

——and E. Thorbecke (2006a) 'Overview'. In M. Nissanke and E. Thorbecke (eds), *The Impact of Globalization on the World's Poor: Transmission Mechanisms*. Basingstoke: Palgrave Macmillan for UNU-WIDER.

———— (2006b) 'Channels and Policy Debate in the Globalization–Inequality–Poverty Nexus'. In M. Nissanke and E. Thorbecke (eds), *The Impact of Globalization on the World's Poor: Transmission Mechanisms*. Basingstoke: Palgrave Macmillan for UNU-WIDER. Repr. *World Development*, 34 (2006): 1338–60.

———— (2006c) 'A Quest for Pro-poor Globalization'. Research Paper 2006/46. Helsinki: UNU-WIDER. Repr. G. Mavrotas and A. Shorrocks (eds), *Advancing Development: Core Themes in Global Development*. Basingstoke: Palgrave Macmillan for UNU-WIDER, 2007.

———— (eds) (2006d) 'The Impact of Globalization on the World's Poor', *World Development*, UNU-WIDER Special Issue, 34.

———— (2006e) *The Impact of Globalization on the World's Poor: Transmission Mechanisms*. Basingstoke: Palgrave Macmillan for UNU-WIDER.

———— (2008a) *Globalization and the Poor in Asia: Can Shared Growth be Sustained?* Basingstoke: Palgrave Macmillan for UNU-WIDER.

———— (eds) (2008b) 'The Impact of Globalization on the Poor in Sub-Saharan Africa', *African Development Review*, UNU-WIDER Special Issue, 20.

———— (eds) (2010) 'Globalization, Poverty and Inequality in Latin America', *World Development*, UNU-WIDER Special Issue.

O'Connell, S., and B. Ndulu (2000) 'Africa's Growth Performance: A Focus on Sources of Growth'. Nairobi: African Economic Research Consortium.

Ocampo, J. A., and M. A. Parra (2006) 'The Dual Divergence: Growth Successes and Collapses in the Developing World since 1980'. Working Paper 24. New York: UN-DESA.

Palma, G. J. (2006) 'Globalizing Inequality: "Centrifugal" and "Centripetal" Forces at Work'. Working Paper 35. New York: UN-DESA.

Popli, G. K. (2008) 'Trade Liberalization and the Self-employed in Mexico'. Research Paper 2008/05. Helsinki: UNU-WIDER. Rev. and repr. *World Development, UNU-WIDER Special Issue: Globalization, Poverty, and Inequality in Latin America* (forthcoming).

Pritchett, L. (1997) 'Divergence, Big Time', *Journal of Economic Perspectives*, 11: 3–17.

Quah, D. T. (1996) 'Twin Peaks: Growth and Convergence in Models of Distribution Dynamics', *Economic Journal*, 106: 1045–55.

Ravallion, M. (2004) 'Pro-poor Growth: A Primer'. Policy Research Working Paper 3242. Washington, DC: World Bank.

——(2006) 'Looking Beyond Averages in the Trade and Poverty Debate', *World Development*, 34: 1374–92. Repr. M. Nissanke and E. Thorbecke (eds), *The Impact of Globalization on the World's Poor: Transmission Mechanisms*. Basingstoke: Palgrave Macmillan for UNU-WIDER.

Sachs, J. D., and A. Warner (1995) 'Economic Reform and the Process of Global Integration'. Brookings Papers on Economic Activity 1. Washington, DC: Brookings Institution.

Sahn, D. E., and S. D. Younger (2006) 'Changes in Inequality and Poverty in Latin America: Looking Beyond Income', *Journal of Applied Economics*, 9: 215–34.

Sáinz, P. (2006) 'Equity in Latin America since the 1990s'. Working Paper 22. New York: UN-DESA.

Sanchez, O. (2003) 'Globalization as a Development Strategy in Latin America?', *World Development*, 31: 1977–95.

Sawada, Y., and J. P. Estudillo (2008) 'Trade, Migration and Poverty Reduction in the Globalizing Economy: The Case of the Philippines'. In M. Nissanke and E. Thorbecke (eds), *Globalization and the Poor in Asia: Can Shared Growth Be Sustained?* Basingstoke: Palgrave Macmillan for UNU-WIDER.

Sindzingre, A. (2006) 'Explaining Threshold Effects on Globalization on Poverty: An Institutional Perspective'. In M. Nissanke and E. Thorbecke (eds), *The Impact of Globalization on the World's Poor: Transmission Mechanisms*. Basingstoke: Palgrave Macmillan for UNU-WIDER.

Skoufias, E., K. Lindert, and J. Shapiro (2009) 'Globalization and the Role of Public Transfers in Redistributing Income in LAC'. Research Paper 2009/26. Helsinki: UNU-WIDER. Rev. and repr. *World Development, UNU-WIDER Special Issue: Globalization, Poverty, and Inequality in Latin America* (forthcoming).

Teranishi, J. (1996) 'Sectoral Resource Transfer, Conflict and Macro-stability in Economic Development: A Comparative Analysis'. In M. Aoki and M. Okuno-Fujiwara (eds), *Role of Government in East Asia: A Comparative Institutional Analysis*. Oxford: Oxford University Press.

Thorbecke, E., and C. Charumilind (2002) 'Economic Inequality and its Socioeconomic Impact'. *World Development*, 30: 1477–95.

UNCTAD (United Nations Conference on Trade and Development) (2002) *The Least Developed Countries Report 2002*. Geneva: UNCTAD.

Williamson, J. G. (2002) 'Winners and Losers over Two Centuries of Globalization'. WIDER Annual Lecture 2002. Helsinki: UNU-WIDER.

Winters, L. A., N. McCulloch, and A. McKay (2004) 'Trade Liberalization and Poverty: The Evidence So Far', *Journal of Economic Literature*, 42: 72–115.

World Bank (1993) *The East Asian Miracle: Economic Growth and Public Policy*. New York: Oxford University Press.

2

Globalization and the Human Development Trap

David Mayer-Foulkes

2.1. Introduction

Even before the 2008 economic crisis, for many of the poor in Latin America, Africa, and Asia, globalization has failed to be a source of hope. The pro-market liberalization policies that have been followed for two decades have been only mildly successful in Latin America and Africa, and many parts of Asia. These policies have essentially followed the Washington Consensus, consisting mainly of opening to trade and foreign direct investment (FDI), maintaining macroeconomic stability, and entrusting economic development to market functioning. Faced with the stagflation crisis of the 1970s and the first oil crisis, Ronald Reagan and Margaret Thatcher restarted economic growth by freeing trade and investment. Many underdeveloped countries faced similar crises at the time, especially those following import-substitution models, and fell into debt through rising interest rates and oil prices. Thus, essentially the same macroeconomic and growth policies were applied in developed and underdeveloped countries. Because East Asian economies had experienced a transition to development by following export promotion, the expectation was that liberalization would put many underdeveloped economies on the same path. However, dissatisfaction with the results has shifted economic policies towards government intervention for direct poverty alleviation in a series of countries.

An economic explanation is needed that can answer to this reality. Why was export promotion better than import substitution? Yet, why have the results of liberalization been meagre? What role has the high level of inequality had, for example, in the case of Latin America? Why do millions not believe in market-guided policies? Why is globalization perceived as unfair? Where to go from here to address the problems of poverty and development? The objective of this chapter is to provide just such an explanation, fully grounded in economic theory. To do so, I combine several important strands of research on economic growth, human development, and the role of early child development.[1]

2.1.1. *Trade, Technological Change, and Economic Growth*

The first strand of research I draw from is on economic growth. Two decades of research have reached the consensus that differences in income per capita between countries are mainly due to differences in technology.[2] Thus, economic growth is mainly and above all the process through which technological levels of production rise.[3] Hence, to understand the impact of globalization on economic growth, it is necessary to understand how technological change takes place under trade and FDI.

I address here the question, how does the international allocation of *production* under trade and FDI, which has been studied extensively, affect the international allocation of *innovation*?[4] This question is examined by Mayer-Foulkes (2006a), who finds that standard trade theory implies the following natural, real, macroeconomic *principle*[5] governing the international allocation of innovation under trade. The principle is that under trade, the volume of innovative sectors that a country can dominate (and, consequently, under certain conditions, its rate of technological change) is proportional, *ceteris paribus*, to its productive capacity. Suppose that the economy consists of a continuum of sectors, whose production involves distinct technologies and comparative advantages between countries. Lagging economies with low levels of productivity will only be able to cover world demand for a small number of sectors. Hence, in lagging economies, technological change will be limited to a small set of sectors, implying low returns to investment in technological change, even after taking technology transfer into account. Hence free trade introduces innovation imbalances between countries.

The result is extended to include FDI, a salient feature of globalization in both the nineteenth and twentieth centuries, in Mayer-Foulkes (2006c). When foreign investors produce abroad to benefit from cheap labour and cheap resources, as their profits rise so do their incentives to innovate. Moreover, innovation in the

[1] The implications of this viewpoint for global governance and the role of globalization in generating the 2008 crisis are discussed in Mayer-Foulkes (2009 and 2010).

[2] See Howitt and Mayer-Foulkes (2005: 1–2) for references to studies attributing cross-country differences in per capita GDP to differences in productivity.

[3] Schumpeterian analysis of endogenous technological change first concentrated on R&D in developed countries as the source of economic growth (Aghion and Howitt 1988; 1992) and convergence (Howitt 2000). It can also explain convergence clubs, underdevelopment, and divergence (Howitt and Mayer-Foulkes 2005; Aghion, Howitt, and Mayer-Foulkes 2005).

[4] *Innovation* is broadly understood to include R&D as well as imitation and technology adoption.

[5] By economic *principle* I mean a result that can be proved from microeconomic assumptions in a series of contexts, such as the existence of general equilibrium and the welfare theorems.

sectors they occupy in host countries is crowded out by their unassailable competition. Thus, FDI generates asymmetric incentives to innovation that both favour leading countries and retard lagging countries, compounding the innovation imbalances introduced by trade. Technology transfer from FDI, which can play a very significant role favouring economic growth in the host country, tends to occur with high-enough intensity only under appropriate regulation or negotiation. It follows that development and underdevelopment persist as different steady states under globalization. Both this result and the previous one on trade are strong theoretical results, relying only on the assumptions commonly used in models of trade and of endogenous technological change, and not on assumed asymmetries between countries, which underlie most explanations of underdevelopment.

These theoretical results can explain the simultaneous historical emergence from stagnation to modern economic growth, and the appearance of underdevelopment, or the Great Divergence (Mayer-Foulkes 2006a). Development and underdevelopment appeared and were stable, and the Great Divergence (Pritchett 1997) proceeded, not only under free trade but also under FDI through the First Great Age of Globalization (approximately from the 1820 to 1914), and up to the present. The results apply equally well to the present era of globalization, which accelerated with the liberalization policies of Ronald Reagan and Margaret Thatcher in the 1980s, combined with the introduction of market mechanisms in China in December 1978 and the fall of the Berlin Wall in 1989, all of which contributed to the formation of a global market economy open to trade and FDI.[6]

Since technological leaders trade, their innovators enjoy global incentives for innovation. Thus, steady states for closed economies will be lower. Openness is therefore a necessary condition for development, for all except possibly the largest countries. As a consequence, an import substitution strategy is likely to exhaust itself when technology reaches levels requiring world market incentives for innovation. An export promotion strategy will not hit these limits. But, openness is not a sufficient condition for development. *ceteris paribus*, under market forces only economies not lagging too far behind converge to the developed steady state. For smaller and more backward countries market forces must be augmented with export promotion and technology adoption to provide enough push for a change of steady state.

[6] Other articles by the author focus on a historical model and discussion (Mayer-Foulkes 2006a); a model of globalization (Mayer-Foulkes 2006c); a discussion of the challenges for global governance in making globalization equal rather than polarized (Mayer-Foulkes 2008a); an alternative model of human development under globalization emphasizing the role of economic geography, with empirical applications to early child development and cognitive ability (Mayer-Foulkes 2008a; 2008b); and an explanation of the 2008 financial crisis in relation to globalization, also calling for the reform of globalization to ensure the provision of the full spectrum of public goods (Mayer-Foulkes 2009).

2.1.2. Human Development and Economic Growth

The second strand of research I draw from is historical research on the strong, long-term, mutual impact between human development and economic growth. This research attributes about a third of long-term economic growth to improvements in health—that is, to human development. As economic development took place, very remarkable changes in human health occurred. Life expectancy and average adult height and weight rose tremendously.[7] The synergism between technological and physiological improvements has produced a dynamic, long-term, culturally transmitted form of human evolution that is biological but not genetic, called by Fogel (2002) 'techno-physio evolution'. The term *human development* includes here this long-term dimension of change.

A third strand of research underlines the intergenerational nature of human development. Microeconomic studies have found that early child development (ECD) is a crucial link in the intergenerational transmission of socio-economic status and in the adult correlation between health and income. Using the 1958 National Child Development Study, which follows all children born in Great Britain in the week of 3 March 1958, Case, Fertig, and Paxson (2003) found that, controlling for parental income, education, and social status, children who experience poor health have significantly lower educational attainment and significantly lower average adult health and earnings. More specifically, Heckman and Carneiro (2003) identified ECD as a crucial stage of investment in human capital formation, with especially high returns.

Now, it is a commonly accepted fact that investment in human development in general and ECD in particular are characterized by market failures, in so far as the level of these investments depends heavily on parental wealth, rather than on the returns to human capital investment. Thus, from the economic point of view, the investment process sustaining human development is *characterized by market failures*. Human development can be understood as an intergenerational process of human capital accumulation, slowed by the presence of market failures limiting the necessary investment, in which early child development plays a critical role.[8]

[7] Average stature rose from 164 cm to 181 cm in Holland between 1860 and 2002 and from 161 cm to 173 cm in France and Norway between 1705 and 1975. Average weight rose from 46 kg to 73 kg in Norway and France between 1705 and 1975. Life expectancy rose from 41 years to 78 years in England between 1841 and 1998; and from 29 years to 60 years in India between 1930 and 1990 (Fogel 2002; Cervellati and Sunde 2005).

[8] For an extensive discussion and references on human development and economic growth and the role of child development, see Mayer-Foulkes (2008d).

2.1.3. Globalization and Development

To analyse the interaction of human development and economic growth under globalization, I construct a human-development-trap model representing an intergenerational poverty trap in human capital investment, and set it in the context of trade and endogenous technological change.

I first describe the human-development-trap model in some detail. It is an overlapping generations model in which altruistic parents make their children a bequest. A high enough bequest provides them with the opportunity for an indivisible investment in human capital. In the present context this investment acquires both skills and the current human development potential. If the bequest is too low, the absence of credit markets makes the investment impossible. The construction closely follows Galor and Zeira's (1993) well-known, simple, poverty-trap model, building upon it in two ways.

First, the usual assumption of increasing returns to human capital is removed. Instead, investment indivisibilities and the absence of credit markets lead to an undersupply of human capital. Under the assumption that skilled and unskilled labour are complementary, undersupply implies that human skills command *extraordinary* returns, defined as higher returns than the interest rate.

Second, a *dynamic* trap is defined, which subsists under economic growth. Poverty-trap models are usually static and therefore unrealistic in the long term. Here the trap defines two population classes. One is skilled, attains the current human development potential, and is able to bequeath its children with the next generation's human-development potential. The other is unskilled, lives beneath the human development potential, and is unable to bequeath it. Yet, both experience income growth as technology rises through time.[9] At lower levels of development, human capital may be thought to be more intensive in nutrition and health, while at higher levels successively higher levels of education become a more important component. This combination of inequality and growth is consistent with the extraordinary persistence of within country inequality, at widely different income levels and growth rates.[10]

I assume that, because of the non-marketable benefits of human development, including lifelong health, knowledge for living, and life expectancy, the whole population will opt for human capital investment if given the opportunity. The trap exists if the proportion of unskilled workers is high enough that human capital is undersupplied. If instead the trap disappears and skills become oversupplied, some skilled workers will work at unskilled jobs and the whole population will attain the current human development potential.

[9] Income growth does not make class differences trivial or irrelevant. At a 2 per cent growth rate, a proportional class income gap of 4 represents a seventy-year lag.

[10] As Kanbur states: 'There is no statistical correlation between changes in per capita income and changes in inequality, taking countries as the unit of observation' (Kanbur 2005).

Mayer-Foulkes (2008c) presents strong evidence for the existence of such a human development trap in contemporary Mexico, including extraordinary returns to education, high returns to ECD, and a multiple-peaked distribution of human capital across households. In fact, extraordinary returns to education, defined as returns significantly higher than OECD levels, exist, on average, throughout the underdeveloped world.[11] This constitutes evidence for the existence of a human-development poverty trap or prolonged transition (when the poor need several generations to attain the local human-development potential) in non-OECD Asia, Latin America, and Africa.

The human-development-trap model is placed in the context of trade and endogenous technological change by means of a reduced-form expression including the following components. (1) Human capital raises production levels and contributes to technological change by increasing the resources for innovation. (2) Under trade, each sector produces for the global market and has higher resources for innovation. (3) The operation of comparative advantage also increases resources for innovation. (4) The transfer of ideas, which may rise under trade, also contributes to convergence. (5) Specialization under trade implies that the number of productive sectors in each country, where innovation occurs, is proportional to each economy's GDP, once comparative advantage and innovation are taken into account. (6) The productivity of innovation investment in each country is higher when more sectors are involved in innovation.[12]

The result is an analysis of the interaction of multiple steady states across countries in the context of globalization, with the human development trap occurring within countries.[13]

2.1.4. Development and Underdevelopment: Distinct Steady States

To see how the full model deepens the discussion on human development and economic growth, let us first discuss the comparison of East Asia and Latin America. Comparing the performance of the two regions, Birdsall, Ross, and Sabot (1997) stress the two-way causality between human capital and inequality, on the one hand, and economic growth, on the other. The success of the export-oriented development strategy was more labour and skill demanding. As

[11] See Psacharopoulos and Patrinos (2004: tables 1 and 2). For a full discussion, see Mayer-Foulkes (2008*c*).

[12] This assumption is implicit in many models of endogenous technological change. For example, this occurs when research in a continuum of sectors contributes through an externality to raise the leading technological frontier, in turn raising the productivity of innovation investment for all sectors (Aghion and Hewitt 1988 and 1992).

[13] Mayer-Foulkes gives an alternative model of stratified and divergent economic growth, integrating economic geography, human development, and endogenous technological change (Mayer-Foulkes 2008a and 2008b).

higher growth was achieved, a higher GDP led to higher investments per pupil, higher educational quality, lower income inequality, and lower absolute levels of poverty. On the other hand, the unequal distribution of the quantity and quality of education in Latin America led to forgone opportunities in labour productivity and economic growth.

The two examples of interaction between economic growth and human development can be explained in two ways by the model. A first explanation, not resorting to multiple steady states, is simply that policies such as promoting exports and technology adoption matter for the success of the productive sector under globalization. When higher rates of technological change are achieved, improvements in production raise the returns to education and the resources available for human capital investment.

A second, deeper explanation is the following. Latin America remained in a lower steady state, with lower returns to human capital, because of its higher levels of initial inequality, and because it followed a strategy of import substitution that not only did not promote trade but also depended on unregulated FDI that crowded out innovation. In contrast, East Asia converged to development. Enjoying lower levels of initial inequality, it followed a careful globalization strategy featuring export promotion and technology adoption, and experienced miracle growth as it changed steady state to become a successful global partner in trade and development, with high returns to human capital. It is worth noting that the larger East Asian countries, Japan, Korea, and Taiwan, jealously nurtured their technological independence and avoided dependence on FDI.[14] A change of steady state perspective for East Asia is supported extensively and explicitly in Wan's (2004) comparative country case studies.

An additional result that emerges from jointly analysing human development and economic growth is a tension between the policy preferences of the skilled and unskilled. Assume that both human capital investment and innovation require government support. Skilled workers will favour innovation. Increases in productivity will raise the returns to human capital, while extraordinary returns to skills will fall with human capital investment on the unskilled. In contrast, unskilled workers favour human capital investment. This unlocks productive capabilities without the need for technological change. Under the skilled workers' preferred policies, the human development trap will persist.

[14] To the contrary, Singapore, a small country, promoted FDI by consistently underpricing its human capital. Hong Kong's development is based on geographical advantages for trade: an excellent natural harbour ideally situated to serve Pacific and China-West trade. An example of innovation crowding out is provided by the automotive industry. Europe and America, original inventors of the motor car, produce, import, and export cars. Japan and Korea, which did not allow foreign production of cars, only produce and export their own brands. In contrast, Latin America, an FDI host in cars, did not develop its own cars (Mayer-Foulkes, 2006c: table 1; data from ILO 2000). At the present time, China has installed its own automobile industry.

Under the unskilled workers' preferences, human capital investment will be carried out at the cost of worsening the country's relative technological lag. By entrenching the economy in a lower steady state, this could make emerging from underdevelopment impossible. In addition, once the human capital trap is overcome, government support will have to change its focus to technological change. This may require quite a strong institutional and policy shift, as occurred in the ex-socialist countries. The tension between policies to help the poor (here modelled as human capital investment) and policies for economic growth (here modelled as investment in technological change) is a significant problem in Latin America, as in much of the underdeveloped world. According to the model, both extremes generate inferior policies. However, in practice, the two objectives can intersect: generating human capital to support technological change for export promotion is an example of an optimal combination.

Our model gives quite a general explanation for the qualitative diversity of development experiences across Africa, Asia, and Latin America. It does so by describing dynamics in both human capital accumulation and technological innovation that can give rise to the existence of low steady states. As will be shown below, two types of low steady states arise due to technological dynamics. In the first, *divergence in growth rates*, countries experience low income growth rates, as compared to leading economies. In the second, *divergence in levels*, countries grow at similar rates to leading economies, but do not catch up, remaining instead at an equilibrium lag in income levels. Human development dynamics introduce further qualitative differentiation between countries, according to their degree of inequality and average human capital level.

In an econometric study, Mayer-Foulkes (2006b) gives evidence for the presence of a steady state structure in the cross-country context for the period 1960–97. To illustrate the relevance of the qualitative diversity generated by the model, I first describe these results and then discuss them in the light of the model.

Mayer-Foulkes (2006b) clusters countries into five groups according to a simple criterion embracing both income and human development. The criterion is to maximize the proximity of countries' income and life expectancy trajectories within groups, placing weights on both levels and growth rates. Because the purpose is to analyse market-driven growth, only countries with market economies during the period 1960–97 are included in the sample. Mainly petroleum-exporting countries are excluded from the sample because their economic performance depends mainly on the behaviour of the oil market. The clustering assigns countries into five groups that provide a succinct descriptive analysis of the diversity of development experiences. The five groups of countries are illustrated geographically in Figure 2.1. The geographical distribution of these groups by continents is shown in Table 2.1. Income and life-expectancy levels for the five groups of countries are shown in Table 2.2. This table shows that group 1 corresponded to high-income countries with an

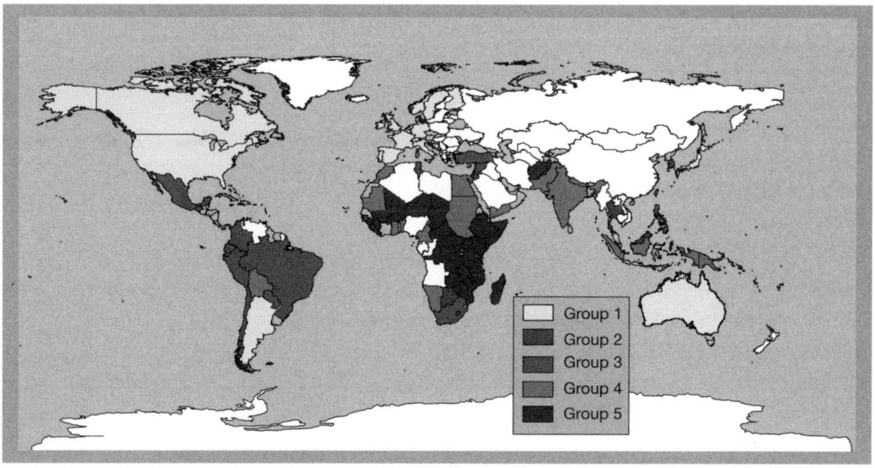

Fig. 2.1. Clustering of non-mainly petroleum-exporting countries with market economies during the period 1960–1997

average income growth rate of 2.5 per cent. Group 3 corresponded to middle-income countries with a somewhat lower income-growth rate of 1.9 per cent. Group 2 instead represents a transition group of countries with very high average growth rates averaging 5.0 per cent over thirty years, beginning at incomes lower than group 3 and ending with much higher incomes than this group that approached group 1. Group 4 had lower incomes and lower average growth than group 3. Group 5 had really low incomes which actually decreased on average over the period. A look at life expectancy gives a different picture. Life expectancy for the five groups is ordered monotonically, decreasing from group 1 to group 5 both in 1962 and 1997. Improvements in life expectancy *increase* from group 1 to group 4, therefore exhibiting absolute convergence. However, group 5 improves much less than group 4, remaining at a very low life expectancy.

Table 2.1. The five groups of countries by continents

Group	West Europe and North America	East Asia Pacific	Latin America and Caribbean	Middle East, North Africa, and Turkey	South Asia	Sub-Saharan Africa	Total
1	19	3	7	1	0	0	30
2	3	7	2	0	0	2	14
3	0	3	15	5	1	3	27
4	0	2	4	3	5	13	27
5	0	0	1	0	1	26	28
Total	22	15	29	9	7	44	126

Table 2.2. Average income and life expectancy levels for the five groups of countries—initial and final levels and growth rates (1985 US$)

		Income			Life expectancy		
		Levels		Growth Rate	Levels		Growth Rate
Group	Interpretative Description	1960	1995	1960–95	1962	1997	1962–97
1	Developed	5,631	13,064	2.5%	70	77	0.27%
2	Transition	1,409	8,891	5.0%	62	73	0.49%
3	Middle income	1,739	3,483	1.9%	57	71	0.62%
4	Transition	926	1,500	1.4%	43	60	0.94%
5	Semi-stagnant	693	610	−0.3%	39	47	0.49%

Summarizing, group 1 corresponds to developed countries with high incomes and life expectancies;[15] group 2 to countries enjoying relatively high life expectancies and experiencing pronounced income growth; group 3 to countries with middle incomes and life expectancies; group 4 to lower incomes and life expectancies but a notable transition in life expectancy; and group 5 to countries stagnating in incomes and with life expectancies improving relatively slowly from low levels.

The clustering throws light on the issues of cross-country convergence and divergence. In effect, the clustering is a decomposition of divergence and convergence, divergence occurring *between* groups and convergence *within* them (Mayer-Foulkes 2006b). Now we come to the important point. The five groups of countries correspond to the possibilities that our theoretical model predicts. Groups 1, 3, and 5 correspond quite closely to the steady states predicted by technological dynamics. Group 1 is the high steady state development. Group 3 is a middle state diverging in levels, but having similar income growth rates with leading countries. Group 5 diverges in growth rates. Finally, groups 2 and 4 represent transitions between these steady states. The transition experienced by group 2 is in incomes, rather than life expectancies. Our comparison above on East Asia and Latin America outlines the role that a low-education trap can play in selecting the countries accessing the transition. By contrast, the transition experienced by group 4 is in life expectancies. Here what is crucial is overcoming a basic health trap indicated by very low life expectancies. Figures 2.1, 2.2(a), and 2.2(b) show three standard deviation corridors for the income and life-expectancy trajectories of the five groups of countries.

[15] Although Argentina may be considered a notable exception, its relatively high income and relatively low growth make the relatively coarse clustering algorithm allocate it to Group 1.

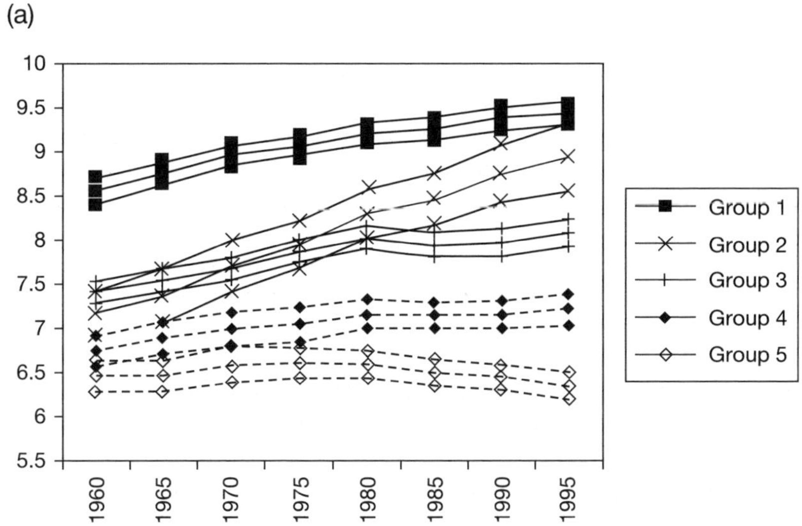

Fig. 2.2(a). Income per capita

Notes: Three standard deviation corridors by groups of countries (constructed on the logarithmics of the variables).

Source: Mayer-Foulkes (2006c).

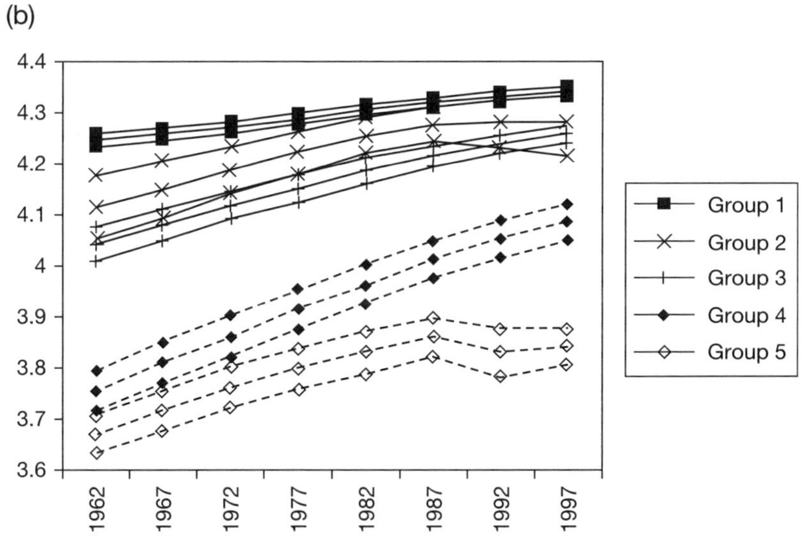

Fig. 2.2(b). Life expectancy

Although the period of globalization we are concerned with here started in the 1980s, it is useful for the discussion following below to compare initial conditions for underdeveloped countries in 1960. Groups 2 and 3 had per capita incomes of US$1,409 and US$1,739, respectively, on the one hand (1985 dollars), and life expectancies of 62 years and 57 years, reflecting higher inequality in group 3 than group 2 countries. By contrast, groups 4 and 5 had much lower incomes, of US$926 and US$693, and life expectancies of 43 years and 39 years. These very low income and life-expectancy levels are close to those experienced in antiquity, according to Pritchett (1997). They reflect societies that by and large have not experienced modernization in production, as represented, for example by the rural to urban transition, and that do not count with the most basic sanitary arrangements. At such a stage, labour markets for engaging in manufacturing have hardly developed. Even so, countries in group 4 were able to achieve a health transition taking them to a life expectancy of 60 years in 1997, while group 5 remained at 47 years.

Let us now discuss the role of globalization. Essentially, the model of endogenous technological change under trade and FDI predicts that open countries with low aggregate production will dominate production in and innovate for only a small number of sectors, while closed economies will have low incentives for innovation. In both cases, if they have agricultural or mineral resources, low-income countries' trade will specialize in these sectors. By contrast, middle- and high-income countries will produce in these sectors as well as in other, additional sectors. FDI will follow a similar pattern, concentrating in resources when not much other production or wealth exists, making production for export or for supplying local demand possible. This is consistent with the points made in Chapter 11 (by Round) about the impact of globalization in Africa, most of which corresponds to groups 4 and 5: 'resource intensive countries have grown faster, are significantly more open to trade, and attract a higher proportion of FDI relative to GDP,' with most other impacts on inequality, poverty, and growth dependent on local conditions.

It is also consistent with the points made in Chapter 4 (by Ozawa), about economic development in Asia. Here the idea is that local labour markets engage in the manufacturing sector for exports, climbing the skill ladder, so that countries follow a 'sequence of staggered or lagged catch-up events across the region,' 'flying geese style'. These countries are comparable to group 2 countries and also, more recently, to some group 4 countries, which by 1997 had reached income and life-expectancy levels comparable with those of group 2 countries in 1960. For example, in the case of India, income and life expectancy were US$1,624 dollars and 63 years in 1997.

Two basic preconditions apply for the labour-based flying-geese-style pattern of economic growth to take place. First, there must be a sufficient supply of labour for manufacturing, which depends on a sufficiently large and healthy urban population. Second, the population must be ready to acquire skills. Both of these demand a sufficient level of health, represented by a life expectancy of, say, 60 years.

These preconditions do not apply to groups 5 and, until recently, to group 4, explaining why Africa has been following a different pattern of growth. What about group 3 countries—for example, Latin America? The contrast between group 2 and group 3 is precisely the contrast between Latin America and East Asia discussed above. The presence of a human development trap made the level of inequality, and perhaps also conflicts between alternative growth and development, too high for a sufficiently large pool of skilled labour to be developed.

What does the model conclude? First, no asymmetric assumptions between countries (for example, in geography or institutions) are necessary to show the existence of multiple steady states under globalization–development and underdevelopment. The usual assumptions used in models of trade and endogenous technological change suffice, since they can explain the allocation of production and therefore innovation across countries by trade and FDI. Second, the assumption of increasing returns in human capital is not a necessary condition for a human-capital poverty trap to exist. It is enough if a large enough portion of families cannot endow their children with human capital–due to incomplete or malfunctioning markets. The ensuing undersupply will lead to extraordinary returns to skills and the population will divide into two classes, whose different living standards will evolve in parallel according to each country's technological level.

When these phenomena—human development, trade, and innovation—are analysed together, multiple steady states in human and technological development emerge that coexist under globalization. At the highest steady states the human development trap has disappeared and high levels of technology are enjoyed. At lower steady states the human development trap may persist and low levels of technology cannot be escaped. A diversity of growth experiences, including the existence, especially in highly unequal underdeveloped countries of pro-rich and pro-poor policy regimes, that is consistent with the true life physiognomy of development and underdevelopment, results.

2.1.5. Does Globalization Yield Development?

We now let the model answer the questions that motivated this chapter. Why was export promotion better than import substitution? Because high-level technologies are based on innovations that require world market incentives. Domestic markets of all but the largest countries cannot hope to support the innovative capacity of leading economies involved in world trade. The purposeful, strategic policies promoting exports and technology adoption that East Asian economies followed supplied large markets and fed their economic growth.

Why have the results of liberalization been meagre? Because globalization—that is, openness to trade and foreign investment—will not automatically lead to development. Success depends on economy size, human resource levels, and on implementing policies promoting exports and technology adoption. Other determinants of aggregate production, such as institutional and financial development, also affect steady state membership.

What role does a high level of inequality, for example in Latin America, play? Inequality, representing the presence of a human development trap and low human-resource levels, is a determinant of steady state membership. In its presence, and in the absence of policies truly promoting competitive technologies for the global market, development is impossible.

Why do millions not believe in market-guided policies? Because millions of people are subject to an intergenerational poverty trap that exists precisely because it is impervious to market forces. (This and the following statement are consistent with rational expectations.)

Why is globalization perceived as unfair? Because it provokes innovation imbalances and innovation crowding out favouring advanced countries.

Where to go from here? Globalization is a necessary condition for development, in so far as it promotes economic efficiency and high incentives for innovation. But it is not sufficient. What is required is to govern globalization through policies compensating the long-term imbalances it creates, favouring successful integration of weaker economies, promoting technology transfer, encouraging exports from lagging countries, bolstering universal knowledge integration. China has been successful at regulating trade and FDI, to ensure its own growth in the process of integration. To extend such arrangements for mutual benefit to the many smaller countries, global governance and regulation are required. Macroeconomic measures for achieving control and coordination with the same objectives may exist as well, to be implemented as a part of global governance.

Furthermore, the trade and innovation model discussed here shows that development is not a zero sum game. Leading countries' welfare depends essentially on the world growth rate, and this is maximized when the world is fully developed. This can only occur when human development is achieved everywhere and every country enjoys its full share of innovation. Concerted nutrition, health, skills, know-how, research, and infrastructure transfers to the underdeveloped world are therefore in the interest of leading countries, and constitute an instrument for global prosperity and peace.

The rest of the chapter is organized as follows. Section 2.2 presents a concise, simple economic model defining a dynamic human development trap which is then interacted with economic growth. The results are summarized verbally. Then, the world growth rate, and the effects of opening to globalization, particularly on the poor, are discussed. Section 2.3 concludes.

2.2. The Model

Our discussion in the section on human development leads to the following stylized facts about long-term human development. First, technological improvements lead to techno-physio evolution: improvements in stature, health, and longevity. Second, higher human development provides inputs for raising technological levels. Third, the presence of market failures inhibits the human capital investment that each new generation must make to achieve current levels of human development; only the wealthier part of the population may reach the human development potential that is currently available, while the poorer part may remain trapped away from achieving its full potential. Here we formalize these ideas in a concise economic model of a human development trap and its interaction with economic growth.

A classical example of a static human capital trap is provided by Galor and Zeira (1993). This trap is based on the need for an indivisible investment for acquiring skills, and on the presence of a credit constraint not allowing the poor to make the investment. I take this model, as presented in Basu (2003: sect. 3.4), as point of reference to construct a dynamic human-development-trap model.

2.2.1. The Human-Development-Trap Model

This section of the model appears in Mayer-Foulkes (2008c). Thus, here only the necessary elements to understand it are included. Consider an economy with S_t skilled workers, each with human capital A_t, so that the aggregate human capital stock is $H_t = A_t S_t$, and with L_t unskilled workers. A single good is produced according to the production function $Y_t = \Phi(A_t L_t)^{\beta} H_t^{1-\beta} = \Phi A_t L_t^{\beta} S_t^{1-\beta}$, with technology level also A_t. Φ is a fixed productivity effect. Wage rates for labour and human capital are therefore given by $w_t{}^L = \beta\Phi A_t(S_t/L_t)^{1-\beta}$ and $w_t{}^s = (1-\beta)\Phi A_t(S_t/L_t)^{\beta}$, and are proportional to A_t. Note that increasing returns to human capital are *not assumed* in the model. Instead, complementarity between skills and labour implies that the undersupply of human capital (following from barriers to its acquisition) will result in an endogenous wage gap between skilled and unskilled labour.

In period t, each young person receives a bequest x_t, and decides whether to invest hA_t units in acquiring an indivisible package of A_{t+1} units of human capital consisting of ECD, health, and education ('becoming skilled').[16] The alternative is to work earning $\eta w^L{}_t$, where $0 < \eta \leq 1$ represents the ratio of child to adult wages. Any remaining bequest is saved and earns an interest rate r. For

[16] I assume technological change transforms both production and human capital. Thus, A_t units of human capital acquired in youth become A_{t+1} units of adult human capital. Alternatively, let the package of A_{t+1} units of human capital available to the young cost $h\,A_{t+1}$, and substitute h with hg_{t+1} in the results.

simplicity, a credit market is assumed to be missing: it is impossible to borrow to acquire nutrition, health, and education. In the second period of life, each adult earns y_{t+1}, the sum of her skilled or unskilled wage ($w^S{}_{t+1}$ or $w^L{}_{t+1}$) and accrued savings. Each adult consumes c_{t+1} and decides on a bequest b_{t+1} to her one child. Young people maximize:

$$\max U_t = c_{t+1}^{\alpha} b_{t+1}^{1-\alpha} + \delta_t u^H A_t, 0<\alpha<1$$

subject to the budget constraint $c_{t+1} + b_{t+1} = y_{t+1}$. The utility function contains two terms. The first represents preferences over consumption and bequests. The second term represents the non-labour benefits of acquiring health and education. δ_t takes the value 1 if skills and health capital were acquired, and 0 otherwise, while $u^H A_t$ (with u^H constant) measures the non-labour benefits of human capital. For simplicity, so as not to include consumption in both periods to define a discount rate, the interest rate is assumed to be exogenous.

Assume that the model parameters are such that (1) independently of the ratio S_t / L_t of skilled to unskilled workers, anybody receiving a bequest $x_t \geq A_t h$ will decide to acquire human capital; (2) given a technological level A_t, skilled workers' children can acquire skills and human development; (3) the maximum feasible level of human development is bounded.

For now, suppose that the rate of technological change $A_{t+1}/ A_t = 1 + g_t$ is constant and exogenous, and define the deflated variable $\tilde{x}_t = x_t/A_t$.

Proposition 1. Under these assumptions, a higher steady state $\tilde{x}^{High}$ in which skills are acquired exists. A lower steady state $\tilde{x}^{Low}$ in which skills are not acquired also exists (see Figure 2.3) if the skilled to unskilled workers ratio lies below the critical level:

$$\frac{S_t}{L_t} < \eta_{\text{Crit}} \equiv \left(\frac{(1 + g_t - (1 - \alpha)(1 + r))h}{\beta(1 - \alpha)\Phi(\eta(1 + r) + 1 + g_t)} \right)^{\frac{1}{1-\beta}} \quad (1)$$

In this case S_t and L_t remain constant. For higher growth rates g_t, higher skilled to unskilled ratios are necessary to escape the trap, and returns to education are higher.

For the proof see Mayer-Foulkes (2008a: appendix). At both steady states, wages rise with the technological level A_t, implying growing levels of nutrition and health even for the unskilled. However, the unskilled population is trapped away from reaching the full current human development potential, which is only accessible at the higher steady state. In this sense, the model defines a *dynamic poverty trap*. The rising indivisible human capital investment models successive investments at different stages of development, such as adequate nutrition, literacy, primary school, secondary school, higher education, and so on, as mentioned above.

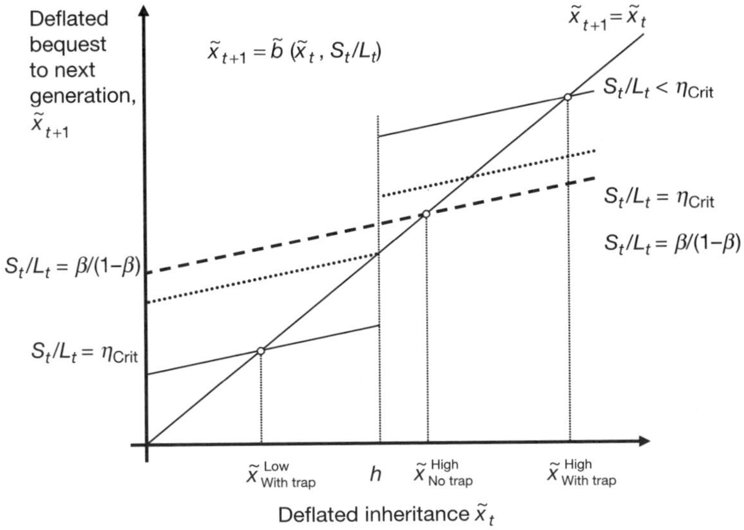

Fig. 2.3. Dynamic human development trap

Notes: Children who inherit more than hA_t (deflated to h) chose to be skilled. They earn higher wages and bequest more to their children. Wages for skilled and unskilled workers are endogenous and depend on the aggregate ratio of skilled to unskilled workers S_t/L_t. If this ratio lies below the critical level η_{Crit}, there is a trap, which otherwise disappears. Near the critical level η_{Crit}, workers receiving bequests below hA_t will go through a prolonged transition towards the higher steady state. Human development is 'viable and bounded' when steady state $\bar{x}_{\text{NoTrap}}^{\text{High}}$ exists.

As long as the trap exists, children would like to borrow to acquire human capital. Thus, investing in human capital offers higher returns than the interest rate, that is, *extraordinary returns* to investment.

Define the human resources level:

$$HR_t = L_t^{\beta} S_t^{1-\beta} \tag{2}$$

In the absence of a trap, all workers are skilled and wages for skilled and unskilled labour will equalize ($w_t^L = w_t^S$). Skilled and unskilled jobs will be allocated in the ratio $S_t/L_t = (1-\beta)/\beta$. If the population numbers $N_t = S_t + L_t$, then $HR_t = L_t^{\beta} S_t^{1-\beta} = \beta^{\beta}(1-\beta)^{1-\beta} N_t$. This is the optimal level for HR_t and its higher bound. Instead, when a human development trap holds, HR_t will be lower and production less efficient.

If the dynamic trap condition (1) does not hold, a prolonged transition may nevertheless take place in which several generations must pass before the offspring of a poor dynasty achieve the full human development potential. Under a prolonged transition, incomplete markets slow the transition to a steady state through prolonged, systematic underinvestment in human capital. A transition under perfect markets would be faster.

2.2.2. Endogenous Technological Change

A simple equation for endogenous technological change is now stated.[17] For an open economy, set an endogenous rate of technological change:

$$1 + g_t = \frac{A_{t+1}}{A_t} = \left(\frac{\phi Y_t^{\text{World}}}{A_t}\right)^{\gamma} \left(\frac{\theta Y_t}{\bar{\theta}_{\text{World}} Y_t^{\text{World}}}\right)^{\kappa} exp\left(\chi^{\text{FT}} - \frac{A_t}{\bar{A}_t}\right) \tag{3}$$

The first entry expresses that firms innovate more the higher their level of production. It is assumed here that firms serve a demand proportional to the world product, and that they innovate with certainty. Division by A_t accounts for the fishing-out effect: innovation at higher technological levels is proportionally harder. ϕ is a constant including the propensity with which income is invested in innovation, depending, for example, on institutional arrangements. Decreasing returns to innovation investment in each given sector is assumed, so $0 < \gamma < 1$.[18]

The second entry expresses the impact of innovation allocation across countries. Countries innovate on the sectors they produce for, whose measure is proportional to their productive capacity. We let proportionality depend on a fixed country effect θ for country factors that may affect innovation races, and the corresponding average world parameter θ^{World}. Also, there are innovation externalities between sectors. The more sectors a country innovates in, the higher the returns for innovation in each sector. This means that specialization in a small number of sectors involves a disadvantage. This assumption is especially credible in the case of a long-term model. The degree of cross-sectoral externalities in innovation is given by κ. Externalities are absent if $\kappa = 0$; in this case knowledge for production can be completely specialized and a country needs no knowledge about sectors it does not produce for. In the case $\kappa = 1$, aggregate technological change equals average technological change in all sectors. This would be the case if knowledge worked through a local leading technological edge resulting from externalities from local innovation. It is assumed that κ lies somewhere in between. In fact, it is assumed that $\gamma < \kappa < 1$, that is, decreasing returns to specialization hold, even in the presence of convergence forces. The negative effects for backward economies

[17] Extended versions of this model are available in Mayer-Foulkes 2006a and 2006b.

[18] Note that under this simple specification the returns to innovation are unbounded. It will follow that the scale of resources applied to innovation has an unbounded effect on growth. However, under a more complex, bounded specification, the scale effect would be bounded as well.

of investing their innovation in a small segment of sectors will be stronger than the advantage of backwardness due to convergence.

In the third entry, $\bar{A}_t$ is the leading technological edge, assumed here to be generated in some other country or countries. Thus the economy we are concerned with is a small, lagging country. Technology is assumed to rise faster for lower relative technological levels $a_t = A_t/\bar{A}_t$, due to technology transfer from leading countries, an advantage of backwardness effect generating convergence (Gerschenkron 1952). The functional form chosen here assumes the convergence effect is bounded by $\exp(\chi^{FT})$ as a_t becomes small. This makes divergence in growth rates possible under autarchy.

Under autarchy, the same equation is assumed to hold, with Yt^{World} replaced by Y_t and θ^{World} by θ. Hence:

$$1 + g_t = \frac{A_{t+1}}{A_t} = \left(\frac{\phi Y_t}{A_t}\right)^{\gamma} exp\left(\chi^A - \frac{A_t}{\bar{A}_t}\right) \tag{4}$$

It is reasonable to assume $\chi^A < \chi^{FT}$—that is, that technology transfer works less strongly under autarchy than under free trade, when not only ideas but also goods travel between countries. Also, in the presence of comparative advantage (Mayer-Foulkes 2006a), it can be assumed that the fixed-country productivity effects are higher under free trade than under autarchy, so $\Phi_A < \Phi_{FT}$.[19] Let $\lambda = Y_t^{World}/\bar{A}_t$ and define $1 + \bar{g} = \bar{A}_{t+1}/\bar{A}_t$.

Summarizing, technological change is governed by:

$$\frac{a_{t+1}}{a_t} = \begin{cases} H_{FT}(a_t) \equiv \dfrac{1}{1+\bar{g}} \left(\dfrac{\theta \Phi_{FT} HR_t a_t}{\bar{\theta}_{World}\lambda}\right)^{\kappa} \left(\dfrac{\phi\lambda}{a_t}\right)^{\gamma} exp(\chi_{FT} - a_t) \\ H_A(a_t) \equiv \dfrac{1}{1+\bar{g}} (\phi \Phi_A HR_t)^{\gamma} exp(\chi_A - a_t) \end{cases} \tag{5}$$

where the human resource level HR_t defined by (2) is used. This variable defines a scale effect in the equations governing technological change, depending on effective labour force. A more complete model might also include a higher demand for human capital for innovation than for production.

The steady state found in Proposition 1 extends to a free trade or autarchic steady state in relative technological levels if the relative technological level a_t is also at a steady state. There are two types of steady states a^*. Let H_X represent either H_{FT} or H_{FT}. The first type of steady state is $a^* = 0$. This exists if and only if $H_X(0) < 1$, because then $\lim_{t\to\infty} a_t = 0$. When a lagging country approaches this

[19] It is assumed throughout that a full human development potential is feasible both under autarchy and free trade. However, under extreme conditions of comparative advantage, the full human development potential may only be feasible under free trade, when $\Phi_A < \frac{h}{(1-\alpha)\epsilon(\beta)} < \Phi_{FT}$. See condition (2) in Mayer-Foulkes (2008a: appendix A).

type of steady state, its growth rate becomes lower than the leading technological edge growth rate:

$$\lim_{t\to\infty} \frac{A_{t+1}}{A_t} = \lim_{t\to\infty} \frac{a_{t+1}}{a_t}\frac{\bar{A}_{t+1}}{\bar{A}_t} = H_X(0)(1+\bar{g})<1+\bar{g}$$

The second type of steady state occurs for $0 < a^* \leq$. It exists when $H_X\,(a^*) = 1$. The growth rate is then $1 + g^{\bar{}}$, and the economy tends to a fixed^{-} technological lag a^*.

For ease of language, we say that at these two types of steady states technology 'diverges in growth rates' or 'diverges in levels' (equivalently 'converges in growth rates').

In the autarchic case, $H_A\,(a_t)$ is a decreasing function. At most a single steady state exists. In the case of free trade, the following properties hold.

1) $H_{FT}\,(a_t)$ is a quasiconcave function.

2) $H_{FT}\,(0) = 0$.

3) $H_{FT}\,(a_t)$ has a single maximum at $a_t = \kappa - \gamma \in (0, 1)$.

4) H_{FT} is increasing in ϕ, $\theta/\theta^{\text{-World}}$, Φ_{FT}, HR_t, χ_{FT}, and decreasing in λ a_t and $\bar{g}$.

For the proof of these properties, on which Proposition 2 and its Figures 2.4 and 2.5 are based, see the Appendix to this chapter.

Proposition 2. Under autarchy (Figure 2.4), a lagging country has the following steady states, which depend only on its parameters.

A.1 If $H_A\,(0) \leq 1$, there is divergence in growth rates. The absolute rate of growth tends from below to $(\phi\Phi_A HR_t)^{\gamma} exp(\chi_A)<1+\bar{g}$.

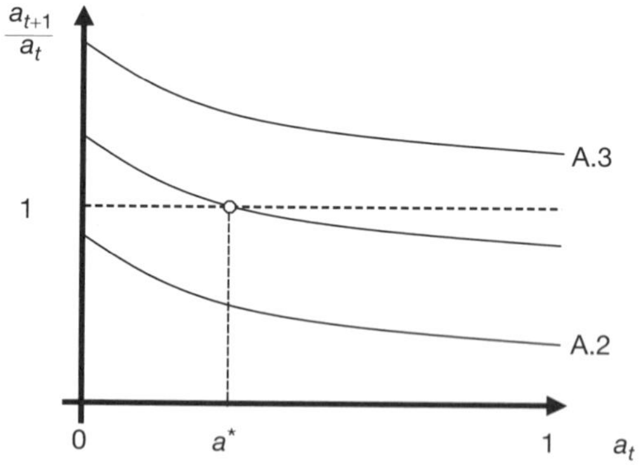

Fig. 2.4. Dynamics of technological change under autarchy

Notes: The diagram shows the three cases that arise for the case of autarchy in Proposition 2: A.1, A.2, and A.3.

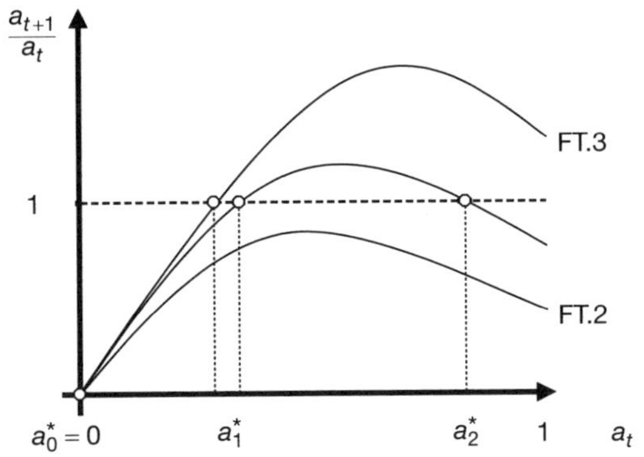

Fig. 2.5. Dynamics of technological change under free trade

Notes: The diagram shows the three cases that arise for the case of free trade in Proposition 2: FT.1, FT.2, and FT.3.

A.2 If $H_A(0) > 1$ and $H_A(1) < 1$ there is a steady state $0 < a^* < 1$ at which the economy diverges in levels, with growth rate $1 + \bar{g}$.

A.3 If $H_A(1) > 1$, the lagging country will overtake the leaders.

In case A.1, steady state growth rates, and in case A.2, steady state levels, are increasing in the propensity to innovate ϕ, fixed productivity effects Φ_A, human resources HR_t, and technology transfer rates as measured by χ_A.

Under free trade (Figure 2.5), the following dynamic configurations for a lagging country exist. The steady states may depend on initial conditions as well as parameters.

FT.1 If $H_{FT}(\kappa-\gamma) \leq 1$, the only stable steady state is $a^* = 0$. The lagging country's relative growth rate decreases towards 0. In the special case $H_{FT}(\kappa-\gamma) = 1$ there is an unstable steady state $a^* = \kappa-\gamma$, from which the economy converges to $a^* = 0$ under any negative perturbation.

If $H_{FT}(\kappa-\gamma) > 1$, a stable and an unstable steady states a_0^*, a_1^*, exist, satisfying $0 = a_0^* < a_1^* < \kappa-\gamma$ and $H_{FT}(a_0^*) = 0$, $H_{FT}(a_1^*) = 1$, $H'_{FT}(a_1^*) > 0$. Two possibilities arise:

FT.2 $H_{FT}(1) \leq 1$. A further stable steady state $a_2^* \in (\kappa-\gamma, 1]$ exists with $H'_{FT}(a_2^*) < 0$.

FT.3 $H_{FT}(1) > 1$. In this case $H_{FT}(a_t) > 1$ on $(a_1^*, 1]$.

For initial values $a_{t_0} < a_1^*$, the lagging country tends to $a_0^* = 0$, where its growth rate descends to 0. For initial values $a_{t_0} > a_1^*$, in case FT.2 the lagging country tends to a_2^*, where it diverges in levels, with growth rate $1 + \bar{g}$. In case FT.3 it overtakes the leading economy. If the lagging country becomes a leader, a higher world growth rate and leading technological edge will emerge.

It follows from property (4) of H_{FT} that: (a) the higher the lagging country's propensity for innovation; (b) the more sectors it dominates; (c) the higher its fixed productivity effects; (d) the higher the level of human development the more efficient its allocation between skilled and unskilled labour; and (e) the higher the rate of technology transfer, the higher will its rate of technological change be. The larger the world economy or its rate of growth, though, the lower its relative steady state. At steady states divergent in growth rates or levels, these comparative statics translates into growth or level effects.

Note that backward countries may diverge in growth rates under free trade even when they might converge to the leading growth rate under autarchy. At any given level a_t, the relative growth rate under free trade is higher than under autarchy, $H_{\mathrm{FT}}(a_t)/H_{\mathrm{A}}(a_t) > 1$, only if

$$\frac{Y_t}{Y_t^{\mathrm{World}}} = \frac{HR_t a_t}{\lambda} > \left(\frac{\bar{\theta}^{\kappa}_{\mathrm{World}} \Phi^{\mathrm{A}\gamma} exp(\chi_{\mathrm{A}})}{\theta^{\kappa} \Phi^{\kappa}_{\mathrm{FT}} exp(\chi_{\mathrm{FT}})}\right)^{\frac{1}{\kappa-\gamma}} \tag{6}$$

that is, if the relative size of the aggregate product is high enough. In addition, if the lagging country is good at capturing innovation sectors (θ high), enjoys high benefits from comparative advantage ($\Phi_{\kappa\mathrm{FT}}$ sufficiently larger than $\Phi_{\gamma\mathrm{A}}$), and if technological transfer under trade is sufficiently high (χ_{FT} sufficiently larger than χ_{A}), growth will tend to be higher under trade. Policies for human development will raise H_t R_t and contribute to the viability of growth under free trade.

Promoting exports and technological change, as well as concentrating on comparative advantage (that is raising θ, χ_{FT} and $\Phi^{\kappa}{}_{\mathrm{FT}}$), also contribute to growth under free trade. Steady state membership also depends on institutional and financial development, which can raise aggregate production.

One defining characteristic of the economic unit whose size is referred to by the model, is that it shares knowledge for production and for skill formation. One policy for breaking the size constraint is therefore knowledge integration. Integration through trade and investment must be complemented by integration in education and technology.

Under autarchy, the behaviour of the lagging country only depends on its parameters. Instead, under free trade, its initial conditions matter. If they are low too, a lagging country will diverge in growth rates.

The following corollary restates the results to bring out the role of human development in economic growth and globalization (proof in the Appendix to this chapter).

Corollary 1. The following conclusions about globalization and human development hold.

HD.1 If human resources HR_t in the lagging country are too low, it will necessarily diverge in growth rates. A minimum-level HR_t for converging in growth rates under free trade is given by the condition $H_{\mathrm{FT}}(\kappa-\gamma) > 1$, that is,

$$\left(\frac{\theta \Phi_{FT} HR_t}{\bar{\theta}_{World}}\right)^{\kappa} > \frac{(1+\bar{g})\lambda^{\kappa-\gamma}}{\phi^{\gamma}(\kappa-\gamma)^{\kappa-\gamma} exp(\chi_{FT}-\kappa+\gamma)}$$

HD.2 Growth will only be faster under free trade than under autarchy if human resources HR_t are sufficiently high, as in (6); otherwise, too many innovation sectors will be lost to trading partners.

HD.3 Economic growth performance is better for higher levels of human resources HR_t. At steady states divergent in growth rates or levels, higher human resources HR_t translate into growth or level effects. For higher human resource levels HR_t, the lagging country is more likely to converge rather than diverge in growth rates, since the threshold level a^*_1 is lower.

HD.4 If a government carries out policies for human capital investment for the children of the unskilled, a steady state can only occur once human resources reach their maximal level $HR_t = \beta^{\beta}\,(1-\beta)^{1-\beta}\,N_t$ and the human development trap has disappeared. Under autarchy, the economy will eventually converge to a steady state diverging in levels only. Under free trade, the feasibility for convergence in growth rates will occur only if from some time on $a_t > a^*_1$, with $HR_t = \beta^{\beta}\,(1-\beta)^{1-\beta}\,N_t$.

HD.5 An economy converging to a^*_2 will be able to achieve human development. However, human capital equality does not guarantee development.

2.2.3. Summary of Results

The propositions concentrate on lagging countries. In the autarchic case, a single stable steady state exists, independently of initial conditions. Country parameters and the level of human development determine whether the lagging country diverges in growth rates, diverges in levels, or overtakes the leading economy. It is assumed that convergence forces are bounded, making divergence possible under autarchy as well.

In the case of free trade, small economies can only innovate in a handful of sectors, with a consequently low rate of technological change. Thus, for low country parameters and/or low levels of human development, divergence in growth rates is the only steady state. For higher parameters or levels of human development, lagging economies with sufficiently high initial conditions will either converge in levels or overtake the leading economy.

There is a scale effect inherent in the technological change model. However, this effect is unbounded only for mathematical tractability. If innovation rates are bounded, so will the scale effect. Because of the scale effect, the relevant measure translating human development into growth is human resources, meaning aggregate units of combined skilled and unskilled labour. Under a human development trap, human capital undersupply will reduce aggregate human resources. Human resources affect economic growth under free trade as follows. First, productive efficiency will be higher for higher levels of human resources, increasing resources for innovation. Second, there is a minimum level of human resources needed for convergence in growth rates. If these are too low, the lagging country will necessarily diverge in growth rates. Third, there is also a minimum human resource requirement for growth to be faster under free trade than under autarchy; otherwise too many innovation sectors will be lost to trading partners. Hence, at steady states diverging in growth rates or levels, higher human resources translate to higher growth rates or levels. Fourth, lagging countries are more likely to converge rather than diverge in growth rates for higher levels of human resources. Fifth, a successful development path will be able to achieve human development. On the other hand, since the level of human development depends on the level of technology, equality does not of its own guarantee development.

The presence or absence of government human capital investment raising the skilled to unskilled ratio S_t / L_t is a condition of the steady state. A human development trap can only exist at steady state if there is no human capital investment for the poor. Conversely, if there is human capital investment, S_t / L_t will rise until the human development trap disappears before a steady state can be reached. Beginning from low levels of development, even if it is feasible to reach a developed, higher-technology steady state, too much or too little investment in human capital may make this impossible. Even if human capital equality is achieved, underdevelopment may persist, with technological levels diverging in levels or growth rates from leading countries. A careful balance is needed between supporting human capital investment—an essential component of growth—and a favourable insertion in globalization to reach high technological levels.

2.2.4. Optimal World Growth Rate

It has been assumed above that only research in leading countries advances the leading technological edge. This is a reasonable assumption for countries lagging sufficiently far behind. However, when countries converge to the leading countries, eventually their research will also push the leading technological edge. In this case, under trade, the world growth rate will rise. Since the leading countries' welfare increases with the world growth rate, convergence of the underdeveloped countries is in their long-term interest. This result is proved formally in Mayer-Foulkes (2006a and 2009).

2.2.5. The Impact of Opening to Globalization

Liberalization policies take the form of a transition from an autarchic to an open steady state. This is costly in itself. I discuss here some implications of this process, particularly on poverty.

First, the model predicts dramatic structural economic change, as does any trade model. Many productive sectors will disappear as the economy specializes in its most productive tradable sectors, which must be competitive in world markets. The expected magnitude of this process of specialization is large for most underdeveloped countries. The reason is that the share of world competitive sectors can at most be proportional to productive capacity and is therefore small. If in practice commercial integration is regional rather than global, fewer sectors will be lost, but those remaining will have less market power and therefore fewer incentives for innovation.

The reform process has usually been very fast. Economies have been subjected to large, multifaceted shocks, structured as follows. In non-world-competitive sectors, physical and human capital lose value and unskilled labour demand falls. In sectors receiving FDI by higher-technology foreign firms, competing domestic firms are displaced. Skilled and unskilled labour demand will depend on the specific FDI sectors involved. In world-competitive domestic sectors, or in sectors supplying FDI, volume, innovation incentives, and labour demand will tend to increase, with possible bottlenecks in specialized human capital. Summing up, a negative initial shock to unskilled wages is likely, with some skilled wages rising. To this must be added a series of transition costs and risks, whose impact can be very high for the poor. It is no surprise that this process of sudden change has given rise to volatility and financial crises.

This is where the predictions of trade models based on competitive production end. The expected benefits are short- and medium-term gains in comparative advantage, with sketchy links to further economic growth. The present model points out that the longer-term success of opening to trade and FDI depends on the success of innovation in surviving domestic sectors. However, the reforms have not planned for this. Instead, the results have been left 'to the market'. To be successful, sectors with comparative advantage that have been supplying only the domestic market should now not only preserve this advantage in the face of foreign technological improvement but grow to become innovative, world suppliers!—with little or no investment in public physical, human, or research infrastructure, and scant negotiation for spillovers from FDI. Although the future wealth of the population depends on these sectors, these disadvantages and neglect translate into even lower initial conditions.

The panorama of the impact of globalization coincides with the model predictions. Positive and negative impacts are distributed with great variance across sectors, regions, and countries. Inequality tends to rise, with increased insecurity and a very real risk of falling into poverty for those employed in unlucky sectors or regions, or those who need to bear the costs of transition or retraining. The poor require safety nets and appropriate social protection schemes. Resulting inequality may lead to conflict and difficulties for growth.

Firms in successful sectors may be too small to face the challenge of multinational marketing chains, and obstacles may occur to firm size, an important determinant of world competitiveness. As successful sectors suddenly require new technologies to increase production, the tendency to use ready-made technologies from abroad suited to higher levels of skills will result in skill-biased technological change and inefficiencies.

2.3. Final Remarks

The model presented here explains persistent income inequality between and within countries, compares import substitution and export promotion, and accounts for episodes of miracle growth. It shows that development and underdevelopment can coexist as steady states in the context of globalization.

The results rely on just two types of market imperfections, both of which are commonly accepted facts. Increasing returns to education or in production are not assumed. The first type of imperfection are incomplete markets in human capital investment. Children are not endowed by the market with their human capital investment, in spite of its notable returns. Instead, initial conditions in wealth determine the incidence of investment. This problem can result in a human development trap that subdivides the population into classes and can persist under economic growth. Strong evidence for the presence of such a trap in Mexico is provided by Mayer-Foulkes (2008c). Surely this is not an isolated phenomenon.

The second type of imperfection is market power derived from innovation. To remove any doubt on the relevance of market power, note that aggregate world exports in 1998 amounted to US$7 trillion, while aggregate sales from foreign affiliates of transnational corporations amounted to US$11 trillion (UNCTAD 1999). The combined sales of the top 200 corporations were higher in 2000 than the combined economies of all countries minus the biggest nine; that is, they surpassed the combined economies of 182 countries (Anderson and Cavanagh 2000). Property rights over innovation, and the resulting market power, are considered a condition for its existence. As has been explained, under free trade the corresponding assumptions in the theory of endogenous technological change, including innovation externalities between sectors, imply the existence of multiple steady states (Mayer-Foulkes 2006a; 2006c).

The fact that human development and technological change, the main processes of economic growth, are subject to market imperfections, results in the existence of a diverse set of steady states: widely varying incomes and growth rates, episodes of miracle growth (understood as transitions between steady states), economic growth without inequality reduction, positive and negative impacts of trade on growth, convergence to parallel growth paths of a lucky group of countries, long-term divergence and stagnation for many others, and pro-rich and pro-poor policy regimes. Thus, the theoretical model explains the broad physiognomy of economic growth.

The idea that under globalization resources will flow so that economies equalize is based on the predominance of competitive markets. If this were the reality, the Great Divergence would not have occurred, and development would have spread equally around the world since its origins. For, what forces could keep competitive markets so out of balance?

Sound global economic policies must recognize the powerful impact of these market imperfections in human development and innovation. Globalization—free trade and FDI—generates innovation imbalances that must be compensated for lagging countries to develop. It is a matter of experience that countries that have implemented complementary measures promoting their exports and regulating FDI so as to develop their technological capabilities have been able to achieve sustained economic growth for long periods—that is, miracle growth. When this has occurred, as in the case of the Asian tigers and China, both the countries involved and their commercial partners have benefited. Such policies can be implemented by individual countries or regions. However, it would be optimal if they were carried out as an integral part of global governance. The very institutions that regulate trade and investment—WTO, IMF, and the World Bank—must commit to balance the incentives for innovation and technological change, to ensure that globalization brings economic development for all.

The model shows that in the presence of a human development trap there is a natural policy conflict between emphasizing human development or technological change. Both extremes have their problems. If only technological change is pursued, the human development trap can persist. From this point of view, the UN Millennium Development Goals are an essential component of economic growth. Instead, if only human capital investment is pursued, the technological lag may become too large for development to be feasible. Eventually a policy change will become inevitable as the ex-socialist countries have experienced.

Development is not a zero sum game. It is in the economic interest of leading countries to foster productive and innovative capabilities around the world. The world growth rate is maximal when all countries are developed. Successful technology transfer and adoption will raise economic growth in both lagging and leading countries. In turn, economic growth will increment the incentives and the resources to dismantle the human development trap, liberating vast economic and human potential. Making globalization successful for all will provide a foundation for global peace and prosperity.

APPENDIX

Properties of $H_{\mathrm{FT}}(a_t)$. Observe that the function $f(a_t) = a_t^{\kappa-\gamma}\,exp\,(1 - a_t)$ satisfies $f(0) = 0$, $f'(1) = \kappa-1-\gamma < 0$, since $0 < \gamma < \kappa < 1$. Also, $f(a_t)$ is quasiconcave, since

$$\frac{d}{da_t}\ln\left(a_t^{\kappa-\gamma}\,exp\,(1-a_t)\right) = \frac{d}{da_t}((\kappa-\gamma)\ln a_t + 1 - a_t) = \frac{\kappa-\gamma}{a_t} - 1$$

is positive for $a_t < \kappa-\gamma$ and negative for $a_t > \kappa-\gamma$, with its unique maximum at $\kappa-\gamma$.

Proof of Corollary 1. Parts 1 and 2 are proved in their statements. Part 3 follows directly from (5) and the properties of $H_{\mathrm{FT}}(a_t)$, $H_{\mathrm{A}}(a_t)$. Part 4 is evident as follows. So long as there is human capital investment the ratio S_t / L_t will change. Hence a steady state cannot be reached until the human development trap ceases to exist. Convergence in growth rates (or divergence in levels) means reaching a steady state a_2^*. Since $a_2^* > a_1^*$, converging trajectory must from some time on satisfy this inequality. The first statement in Part 5 follows from noting that at any point in such a trajectory at some finite proportion of income can be invested in human capital without compromising $a_t > a_1^*$. Under this condition, achieving human development takes finite time. On the other hand, human capital equality, or equivalently human development, is also possible at a lower, divergent, steady state.

References

Aghion, P., and P. Howitt (1988) 'Growth and Cycles through Creative Destruction'. Cambridge, Mass.: MIT. mimeo.

———(1992) 'A Model of Growth through Creative Destruction', *Econometrica*, 60: 323–51.

———and D. Mayer-Foulkes (2005) 'The Effect of Financial Development on Convergence: Theory and Evidence', *Quarterly Journal of Economics*, 120: 173–222.

Anderson, S., and J. Cavanagh (2000) 'Top 200: The Rise of Global Corporate Power'. Corporate Watch. <http://www.globalpolicy.org/socecon/tncs/top200.htm>.

Basu, K. (2003) *Analytical Development Economics: The Less Developed Economy Revisited.* Cambridge, Mass.: MIT Press.

Birdsall, N., D. Ross, and R. Sabot (1997) 'Education, Growth and Inequality'. In N. Birdsall and F. Jaspersen (eds.), *Pathways to Growth: Comparing East Asia and Latin America*. Washington, DC: IDB.

Case, A., A. Fertig, and C. Paxson (2003) 'From Cradle to Grave? The Lasting Impact of Childhood Health and Circumstance'. National Bureau for Economic Research Working Paper 9788. Cambridge, Mass.: NBER.

Cervellati, M., and U. Sunde (2005) 'Human Capital Formation, Life-expectancy and the Process of Economic Development', *American Economic Review*, 95: 1653–72.

Fogel, R. W. (2002) 'Nutrition, Physiological Capital, and Economic Growth'. Pan American Health Organization and Inter-American Development Bank. <http://www.paho.org/English/HDP/HDD/fogel.pdf>.

Galor, O., and J. Zeira (1993) 'Income Distribution and Macroeconomics', *Review of Economic Studies*, 60, 35–52.

Gerschenkron, A. (1952) 'Economic Backwardness in Historical Perspective'. In B. F. Hoselitz (ed.), *The Progress of Underdeveloped Areas*. Chicago: University of Chicago Press.

Heckman, J., and P. Carneiro (2003) 'Human Capital Policy'. National Bureau for Economic Research Working Paper 9495: Cambridge, Mass.: NBER.

Howitt, P. (2000) 'Endogenous Growth and Cross-country Income Differences', *American Economic Review*, 90: 829–46.

——and D. Mayer-Foulkes (2005) 'R&D, Implementation and Stagnation: A Schumpeterian Theory of Convergence Clubs', *Journal of Money, Credit and Banking*, 37: 147–77.

International Labour Organization (ILO) (2000) 'The Social and Labour Impact of Globalization in the Manufacture of Transport Equipment'. Report for discussion at the Tripartite Meeting on the Social and Labour Impact of Globalization in the Manufacture of Transport Equipment, Geneva, 8–12 May 2000. Geneva: ILO.

Kanbur, R. (2005) 'Growth Inequality and Poverty: Some Hard Questions', *Journal of International Affairs*, 58: 223–32.

Mayer-Foulkes, D. (2006a) 'Development and Underdevelopment: 1500–2000'. Unpub. mimeo.

——(2006b) 'The Impact of Free Trade and FDI: Banana Republic or Miracle Growth?'. mimeo.

——(2006c) 'Global Divergence'. In Gleb P. Severov, *International Finance and Monetary Policy*. Hauppauge, NY: Nova Science Publishers.

——(2008a) 'The Cognitive Transition in Mexico: Economic Geography and Local Governance Impacts'. <http://ssrn.com/abstract¼1303867>.

——(2008b) 'Economic Geography of Human Development: Stratified Growth in Bolivia, Brazil, Guatemala and Peru'. <http://ssrn.com/abstract/1287962>.

——(2008c) 'The Human Development Trap in Mexico', *World Development*, 36: 775–96.

——(2009) 'Long-term Fundamentals of the 2008 Economic Crisis'. *Global Economy Journal*, 9: 4.

——(2010) 'Economic Challenges for Global Governance'. In A. Kumar and D. Messner (eds), *Power Shifts and Global Governance: Challenges from South and North*. London: Anthem Press.

Pritchett, L. (1997) 'Divergence, Big Time', *Journal of Economic Perspectives*, 11: 3–17.

Psacharopoulos, G., and H. A. Patrinos (2004) 'Returns to Investment in Education: A Further Update', *Education Economics*, 12: 111–34.

UNCTAD (United Nations Conference on Trade and Development) (1999) *World Investment Report 1999*. New York: United Nations.

Wan Jr., H. Y. (2004) *Economic Development in a Globalized Environment: East Asian Evidences*. Dordrecht: Kluwer Academic Publishers.

3

Globalization, Literacy Levels, and Economic Development

Alok Bhargava

3.1. Introduction

The recent trends in globalization reflected in the increased production of goods and services across the globe have important implications for policy-makers in developing and developed countries. While the conventional economic analysis such as the Heckscher–Ohlin model implies benefits of cheap labour in developing countries, production of goods and services demanded by developed countries entails the availability of at least a semi-skilled labour force and industrial infrastructure that are often inadequate in developing countries, especially in Africa. While unskilled labour can produce agricultural commodities, such exports are hampered due to subsidies and protection programmes for agriculture in developed countries. Because countries such as Japan and China have succeeded in producing goods requiring advanced technology, it is of interest to investigate the effects of variables such as education, population health, exports, imports, and foreign investment on economic growth in developing countries. Moreover, since poverty has not declined in many developing countries despite greater economic integration, it is important to analyse the effects of variables reflecting globalization on measures of poverty and inequality (e.g., Dollar and Kraay 2004; Harrison 2005).

Further, analyses of time-series data on a small group of countries such as those in East Asia (Kim and Lau 1994) and China (Ravallion 2004) can provide insights into the effects of factors such as foreign investment and trade on economic development. However, many developing countries have poor educational and healthcare infrastructures and there are lags between investments in education and health and the availability of a skilled labour force (Bhargava 2001a). Moreover, increased life expectancy enables countries to reap the benefits of such investments over long time spans (Bhargava et al. 2001) Thus, high literacy levels can enhance the benefits of globalization, though the time profiles of imports and exports may have differential effects on economic development (e.g., Santos-Paulino and Thirlwall 2004). For example, it may be necessary for developing countries to import technology and to have a relatively skilled labour force that can compete in producing goods demanded in developed countries. Thus, panel data on developing countries with differing levels of education, population health, and economic environments can provide insights for formulating trade and development policies.

A shortcoming in analysing aggregate panel data on countries is that observations on many important variables are often missing, especially for developing countries. Moreover, while databases have recently begun compiling variables on alternative indicators of globalization, corruption, and political freedom (e.g., Rodriguez and Rodrik 2001; Winters 2004), it is essential to incorporate the gradual effects of education and health on economic growth rates. These problems are compounded by the fact that health and demographic variables are often compiled via surveys by agencies such as the World Bank (2005a; 2005b) only at a few time points: the observations in remaining periods are projections from statistical models. Similar issues arise for measures of poverty and inequality where the numbers of observations are further reduced. Finally, there are complexities in creating comparable data series for even the basic variables such as GDP levels; it is desirable to use GDP series based on exchange rates and on PPP that is assessed via the costs of purchasing a similar basket of goods in other countries. The stochastic properties of GDP series can differ partly due to exchange-rate fluctuations, though GDP growth rates separated by five-year intervals can circumvent some of the econometric problems (Bhargava 2001b).

The structure of this chapter is as follows. The data are briefly described in section 3.2. The analytical framework is developed in section 3.3 and some econometric issues are addressed in section 3.3.2. The empirical results for growth rates in fifty-four developing countries in 1990, 1995, and 2000 are presented in section 3.4.1 using exchange rate and PPP-based GDP series. The results from models for poverty and inequality using data in 1990 and 2000 are presented in sections 3.4.2 and 3.4.3, respectively. The conclusions are summarized in section 3.5.

3.2. The Data

The data used in the analysis were taken for the years 1985, 1990, 1995, and 2000 primarily from the World Development Indicators (2005) (henceforth WDI (2005)) (World Bank 2005a). The *per capita* GDP series in constant US$2,000 and that using an index of PPP were available in WDI (2005), the data on exports and imports expressed as percentages of the GDP were also from WDI (2005).

Other measures of globalization such as FDI and capital flows were available in WDI (2005), though these variables were mainly insignificant predictors of growth rates, and poverty and inequality measures, and hence are not discussed further in the chapter.

The adult literacy rates available in WDI (2005) were compiled by UNESCO and were available for more countries than, for example, education variables such as the percentages of labour force with primary, secondary, and tertiary education literacy rates. Similarly, life-expectancy data were taken from the WDI (2005). The use of five-yearly data minimized some of the problems such as the projection of these variables from statistical models. The education series constructed by Barro and Lee (2000) and the census data from various countries were used to create the series for the proportions of labour force with 'low', 'medium', and 'high' skill levels (Docquier and Marfouk 2006). Overall, for estimating the model for GDP growth rates, complete observations were available for fifty-four developing countries (excluding those in the Middle East with oil reserves) in four time periods.

The data on poverty measures in WDI (2005) were often missing for developing countries in the three time periods (1990, 1995, and 2000) Thus, poverty measures based on consumption surveys in developing countries, percentages of people below the poverty line ('headcount ratio'), and the mean distance below poverty line expressed as a proportion of poverty line ('poverty gap') were taken from a World Bank website (World Bank 2005b). To minimize the numbers of missing observations, the data for 1990 and 2000 available for thirty-six countries were analysed. Last, the data on Gini coefficients reflecting inequality were taken from UNU-WIDER (2005) for the years 1990 and 2000. These years were again selected to minimize missing observations as the data were available for thirty-five developing countries.

3.3. The Analytical Framework

3.3.1. Analysing the Effects of Globalization on Growth Rates, Poverty, and Inequality Measures

With globalization, developing countries are likely to see an increase in their exports and imports and greater opportunities to produce finished goods that enhance economic productivity. While microeconomic data are useful for analysing the effects of greater trade on economic well-being of population groups, it is difficult to monitor large numbers of households employed in different sectors of the economy for long time periods. Moreover, the effects of globalization may be more visible in the data at regional levels especially in large countries such as China where economic activity has been concentrated in certain geographical regions. However, aggregate data on GDP growth rates reflect the overall economic activity and can provide broad insights into the effects of globalization.

While countries such as Japan and South Korea have benefited from globalization, the initial literacy levels attained by the population were high. Apart from natural resources such as oil and minerals, an increase in production of goods demanded in developed countries entails a mix of production technology with skill levels of the labour force. Moreover, domestic agriculture may not benefit directly from globalization since technology transfer such as improved variety of seeds are achieved via agricultural institutes supported by international agencies. In addition, the exports of agricultural commodities to developed countries are restricted. By contrast, the quality of products such as textiles and clothing in developing countries has improved in part by importing machinery and the employment of skilled labour. Similarly, the availability of high-skilled labour in countries such as India has raised productivity levels in the information and technology sectors and has had spin-offs in the production of goods and services.

At a general level, one is likely to see beneficial effects of globalization in countries with a skilled labour force, though the time profile of the development processes are likely to differ. Some developing countries, for example, might initially become exporters of low-priced garments, though with the import of technology they can compete with producers in developed countries. While disaggregated data on exports and imports are seldom available, empirical analyses can model the potential synergisms between literacy levels and the imports and exports of developing countries. Such interactions have not been explored in the previous literature in part because there has been less emphasis on the value added by skilled labour. Instead, the exploitation of cheap unskilled labour was emphasized. In fact, unskilled labour such as that engaged in food production on small farms may require protection if food prices fall due to better technologies for food storage and distribution. One might see some of these effects in analyses of poverty and inequality measures at the country level. The preceding discussion is reflected in the empirical models outlined below.

THE MODELS

The empirical model for GDP growth rates using exchange-rate- (or PPP-) based series is given by:

$$\text{(GDP growth rate)}_{it} = a_0 + a_1\text{(East Asia)}_i + a_2\text{(Latin America)}_i + a_3\text{(South Asia)}_i + a_4 \ln\text{(Literacy rate)}_{it\text{-}5} + a_5[\ln\text{(Literacy rate)}_{it\text{-}5}]^2 + a_6 \ln\text{(Export/GDP)}_{it\text{-}5} + a_7[\ln\text{(Export/GDP)}_{it\text{-}5}]^2 + a_8 \ln\text{(Import/GDP)}_{it\text{-}5} + a_9[\ln\text{(Import/GDP)}_{it\text{-}5}]^2 + a_{10} \ln\text{(Medium-skill/Total labour)}_{it\text{-}10} + a_{11} \ln\text{(Life-expectancy)}_{it\text{-}5} + a_{12} \ln\text{(GDP)}_{it\text{-}5} + u_{1it}$$

$$(i = 1, \ldots, Nt = 1,2,3) \qquad (1)$$

The model in equation (1) included three indicator variables for the geographical regions—that is, the means of the variables were assumed to be different in East Asia, Latin America, and South Asia, with the coefficients interpreted with reference to countries in Africa. The model in equation (1) was the general formulation containing export : GDP and import : GDP ratios and enabled testing of the null hypothesis that these variables can be combined as the trade : GDP ratio (see below) While the non-linearities with respect to literacy rates were taken into account in the models, interaction terms such as those between literacy rates and export : GDP and import : GDP ratios were invariably insignificant and were dropped from the models to reduce multicollinearity. Note that the models were in the spirit of the earlier work by Barro and Sala-i-Martin (1995) in that the lagged values of the explanatory variables were included. Moreover, life expectancy and GDP levels were treated as endogenous variables due to previous findings (Preston 1976; Bhargava et al. 2001).

A simple random-effects formulation for the errors affecting the models is given by:

$$u_{1it} = \delta_i + v_{it} \tag{2}$$

where δ_i were country-specific random effects that were distributed with zero mean and finite variance and v_{it} were independently distributed random variables with zero mean and finite variance. However, equation (2) was a special case of the general assumption invoked in the analysis that the variance covariance matrix of u_{1it} was positive definite (Bhargava 1991). The methods for testing parameter restrictions and exogeneity null hypotheses are briefly explained in Section 3.2.

The model for the poverty headcount or poverty gap is given by: $(\text{Poverty measure})_{it} = b_0 + b_1(\text{East Asia})_i + b_2(\text{Latin America})_i + b_3(\text{South Asia})_i + b_4 \ln(\text{literacy rate})_{it-10} + b_5 \ln(\text{export : GDP})_{it-10} + b_6 \ln(\text{import : GDP})_{it-10} + b_7 \ln(\text{low-skill : total labour})_{it-10} + b_8 \ln(\text{GDP})_{it-10} + b_9 \ln(\text{GDP growth rate})_{it-10} + u_{2it}$

$$(i = 1, \ldots, Nt = 1,2) \tag{3}$$

The non-linearities with respect to literacy rates and export : GDP and import : GDP ratios were not evident in these models perhaps due to the reduction in numbers of countries and time observations. The role of GDP growth rates for reducing poverty has been emphasized in the literature and it was useful to employ the GDP series based on exchange rates and PPP. While exogeneity null hypotheses were tested for the lagged GDP levels and growth rates, dynamic models were also estimated for poverty measures dropping the lagged GDP variable. The errors (u_{2it}) were assumed to be randomly distributed with a bivariate distribution, though without restricting the variance covariance matrix.

Last, the model for Gini coefficient is given by:

(Gini coefficient)$_{it}$ = $c_0 + c_1$(East Asia)$_i$ + c_2(Latin America)$_i$ + c_3(South Asia)$_i$ + c_4 ln(Literacy rate)$_{it-10}$ + c_5 ln(Export/GDP)$_{it-10}$ + c_6 ln(Import/GDP)$_{it-10}$ + c_7 ln (Medium skill/Total labour)$_{it-10}$ + c_8 ln(High-skill/Total labour)$_{it-10}$ + c_9 ln (GDP)$_{it-10}$ + c_{10} ln(GDP growth rate)$_{it-10}$ + u_{3it}

$$(i = 1, \ldots, Nt = 1,2) \tag{4}$$

The inclusion of the proportions of labour force with medium and high skill levels was likely to capture the effects of different income shares on inequality. As in the model for poverty measures, the variables reflecting non-linearities with respect to literacy rates and export : GDP and import : GDP ratios were not significant predictors of the Gini coefficients.

3.3.2. The Econometric Framework

The methodology used for estimation of static random-effects models for GDP growth rates in situations where some of the explanatory variables are endogenous was developed in Bhargava (1991). Let the model be given by:

$$y_{it} = \sum_{j=1}^{m} z_{ij}\gamma_j + \sum_{j=1}^{n_1} x_{1ij}\beta_j + \sum_{j=n_1+1}^{n} x_{2ijt}\beta_j + u_{it} \tag{5}$$

where zs are time-invariant variables, x_1 and x_2 are, respectively, exogenous and endogenous time-varying variables. In the models estimated for GDP growth rates, the indicator variables for East Asia, Latin America, and South Asia were time-invariant explanatory variables. Time-varying regressors consisted of (lagged) literacy rate, export : GDP and import : GDP ratios with their respective squared terms, ratio of medium skill to total labour, life expectancy, and GDP levels.

Further, one can distinguish between two sets of assumptions for endogeneity of the time-varying variables x_2 such as GDP levels and life expectancy. First, x_2 may be correlated with the errors u_{it} in a general way—that is, x_2 are fully endogenous variables, x_{2jt} must be treated as different variables in each time period. Let X_1 and X_2 be, respectively, the $n_1 \times 1$ and $n_2 \times 1$ vectors containing the exogenous and endogenous time-varying variables ($n_1 + n_2 = n$), and let Z be the $m \times 1$ vector of time-invariant variables. We can write a reduced form equation for the fully endogenous variables X_2 as:

$$X_{2it} = \sum_{j=1}^{T} F_{tj} X_{1ij} + F_t^* Z_i + U_{2it} \tag{6}$$

where F_{tj} ($t = 1, \ldots, T$; $j = 1, \ldots, T$) and F_t^*($t = 1, \ldots, T$) are, respectively, $n_2 \times n_1$ and $n_2 \times m$ matrices of reduced form coefficients; U_{2it} is the $n_2 \times 1$ vector of errors.

The reduced form equation (6) is a general formulation for correlation between the time-varying endogenous variables and errors u_{lit}-affecting model (5). For example, lagged GDP levels have often been included as an explanatory variable in models for growth rates and were treated as a fully endogenous variable (Bhargava et al. 2001). However, owing to the small number of time observations, it may be difficult to achieve identification of the model parameters under the general correlation pattern.

An alternative assumption for endogeneity of variables such as GDP and life-expectancy is to assume that these are correlated only with the country-specific random effects δ_i, i.e.:

$$x_{2ijt} = \lambda_j \delta_i + x^*_{2ijt} \tag{7}$$

where x^*_{2ijt} are uncorrelated with δ_i, and δ_i are randomly distributed variables with zero mean and finite variance. This correlation pattern was invoked by Bhargava and Sargan (1983) in the spirit of the commonly used random-effects models. Endogenous variables of the type in equation (7) have sometimes been referred to as 'special' endogenous variables. Moreover, instrumental variables estimators based on differencing the variables also invoke similar assumptions (e.g., Anderson and Hsiao 1981).

The advantage in assuming the correlation pattern (7) is that deviations of the x_{2ijt}'s from their time mean:

$$x^+_{2ijt} = x_{2ijt} - \bar{x}_{2ij}(t = 2, \ldots, T; j = n_1 + 1, \ldots, n, i = 1, \ldots, N) \tag{8}$$

where

$$\bar{x}_{2ij} = \sum_{t=1}^{T} x_{2ijt}/T(j = n_1 + 1, \ldots, n; i = 1, \ldots, N) \tag{9}$$

can be used as $[(T-1)n_2]$ additional instrumental variables to facilitate identification and estimation (Bhargava and Sargan 1983). Efficient Three Stage Least Squares type instrumental variables estimators were used to estimate the models in equations (1), (3), and (4) assuming the correlation patterns for x_{2jt} in equations (6) and (7) and without restricting the variance covariance matrices of the errors.

While in ordinary time series models a misspecification test can be applied to test the over-identifying restrictions (Sargan 1958), it is possible to test various exogeneity assumptions for explanatory variables in the panel data framework. As shown in Bhargava (1991), one can sequentially test exogeneity assumptions using statistics based on instrumental variables estimates because the correlation pattern for special endogenous variables in (7) is a special case of the general formulation (6). The sequential Chi-square test for exogeneity would first test the validity of the special correlation pattern (6). If n_2 time-varying variables are postulated to be endogenous, then under the null hypothesis, the first-test statistic is asymptotically distributed (for large N and fixed T) as a Chi-square variable $[(T(T-1)n_2]$ degrees of freedom. If the null hypothesis cannot be rejected, then we can further test if the time means of x_2 given in equation (9) are uncorrelated with the random effects δ_i. The test statistic for the second set of hypotheses is asymptotically distributed as a Chi-square variable with Tn_2 degrees of freedom.

SOME TESTS OF PARAMETER RESTRICTIONS IN NON-LINEAR MODELS

The model in equation (1) is a general quadratic formulation that enabled testing of the null hypotheses that export : GDP and import : GDP ratios may be combined as the trade : GDP ratio. First, a translogarithmic formulation would allow for interaction terms between literacy rates, export : GDP, and import : GDP ratios (Sargan 1971; Christensen, Jorgenson, and Lau 1973). However, since the coefficients of the interaction terms were invariably insignificant in the models for GDP growth rates, one can simplify the testing procedures for combining the export : GDP and import : GDP ratios by splitting the test procedures into two stages. In the first stage, one can test the null hypothesis that the interaction term between export : GDP and import : GDP ratios is zero. A Chi-square test statistic can be developed using the sample criteria for the exogeneity test statistics mentioned above that are asymptotically equivalent to likelihood ratio tests. Since three time observations were available for the estimation, these statistics were distributed as Chi-square variables with three degrees of freedom. In practice, however, it was not necessary to compute these statistics since the null hypotheses that the coefficients of interaction terms were zero were accepted using t-tests.

In the second stage of the tests for the model in equation (1), one can test the null hypotheses that:

$$H_0 : a_6 = a_8 \text{ and } a_7 = a_9 \tag{10}$$

against the alternative hypothesis that:

$$H_1 : a_6 \neq a_8 \text{ and } a_7 \neq a_9 \tag{11}$$

Because three time observations were available, the statistic for testing the null against the alternative was asymptotically distributed as a Chi-square variable with six degrees of freedom. While one can control the overall size of sequential tests (Anderson 1971; Sargan 1980), the above procedure was better suited for investigating the effects of imposing equality restrictions on the coefficients of export : GDP and import : GDP variables as commonly done in the trade literature.

Table 3.1. Efficient instrumental variable estimates from random-effects models for five-yearly GDP growth rates for developing countries (1990–2000)

	Five-yearly GDP growth rates (constant 2000 US$)				Five-yearly GDP growth rates (purchasing power parity 2000)			
	Specification 1		Specification 2		Specification 1		Specification 2	
	Coefficient	SE	Coefficient	SE	Coefficient	SE	Coefficient	SE
Constant	−0.125	0.231	0.268	0.277	−0.168	0.219	0.179	0.266
East Asia indicator variable	0.009	0.012	0.011	0.014	0.016	0.011	0.018	0.013
Latin America indicator variable	0.001	0.011	0.023	0.014	−0.014	0.009	−0.003	0.011
South Asia indicator variable	−0.013	0.012	−0.019	0.015	−0.010	0.011	−0.010	0.013
ln (literacy)$_{-5}$, %	−0.143*	0.071	−0.260*	0.088	−0.118*	0.062	−0.210*	0.077
[(ln literacy)$_{-5}$]^2	0.021*	0.010	0.039*	0.012	0.017*	0.009	0.032*	0.011
ln (Export/GDP)$_{-5}$, %	−0.054*	0.024	–		−0.046*	0.023	–	
[(ln Export/GDP)$_{-5}$]^2	0.010*	0.004	–		0.006	0.004	–	
ln (Import/GDP)$_{-5}$, %	−0.065*	0.033	–		−0.046	0.030	–	
[(ln Import/GDP)$_{-5}$]^2	0.009*	0.005	–		0.007*	0.005	–	
ln (Trade/GDP)$_{-5}$, %	–		−0.148*	0.047	–		−0.118*	0.043
[(ln Trade/GDP)$_{-5}$]^2	–		0.019*	0.006	–		0.014*	0.006
ln (Medium-skill/total labour)$_{-5}$	0.001	0.004	0.008	0.005	0.007	0.004	0.004	0.005
ln (Life expectancy)$_{-5}$	0.196*	0.044	0.200*	0.049	0.207*	0.043	0.219*	0.049
ln (GDP)$_{-5}$	−0.036*	0.007	−0.056*	0.008	−0.040*	0.007	−0.063*	0.009
Chi-square test for exogeneity (12 d.f.)	50.38*		50.29*		54.82*		48.11*	
Chi-square test for exogeneity (6 d.f.)	12.12*		30.45*		8.53*		25.97*	
Chi-square test for specification 1 against 2 (6 d.f.)	22.73*				21.38*			
Literacy rate at which partial derivative = 0, %	30.4		28.5		29.1		27.3	
Export/GDP ratio at which partial derivative = 0, %	14.6		–		46.2		–	
Import/GDP ratio at which partial derivative = 0, %	36.6		–		21.9		–	
Trade/GDP ratio at which partial derivative = 0, %	–		49.8				62.8	

Notes: There were fifty-four developing countries with three time observations (1990, 1995, 2000) used in the estimation.
Slope coefficients and standard errors are reported.
* $P<0.05$.

One can compute the levels of literacy, and export : GDP and import : GDP ratios (or trade : GDP ratio) for which the derivatives of GDP growth rates with respect to these variables are zero. While these threshold levels are informative and are reported in Table 3.1, there are difficulties in computing their confidence intervals—that is, the levels beyond which the overall impacts are statistically significant. Although one can develop a one-sided analogue of Wald (1943) statistics for the overall effects, the problems are compounded by the modest number of the countries in the sample leading to wide confidence intervals. Thus, we mainly report the points of inflexions in Table 3.1 and these provide insights into the non-linearities in the relationships between GDP growth rates, literacy rates, and export : GDP and import : GDP ratios. We also present the results for specifications that included the trade : GDP ratio and report the points of inflexion with respect to literacy rates in these models to assess the robustness of the results.

3.4. The Results from Panel Data on Developing Countries in the Period 1990–2000

3.4.1. Empirical Results for GDP Growth Rates

The results for GDP growth rates based on the GDP series using constant US$2000 and PPP are presented in Table 3.1. In specification 1, the export : GDP and import : GDP variables were introduced as separate explanatory variables together with their respective squared terms. These two variables were combined as the trade : GDP ratio and its square in specification 2. Specifications 1 and 2 were non-linear in literacy rates; the points of inflexion with respect to literacy rates and export : GDP and import : GDP ratios (or trade : GDP ratio) are reported in Table 3.1. The Chi-square tests for exogeneity and for testing parameter restrictions in equation (10) are also reported.

First, focusing on the results from the exchange-rate-based GDP series for specifications 1 and 2, the null hypothesis that the export : GDP and import : GDP ratios can be combined as the trade : GDP ratio was firmly rejected at the 5 per cent significance level. The Chi-square statistic assumed the value 22.73 that was above the critical level of 12.6. Moreover, it was evident from the coefficients of export : GDP and import : GDP variables and their respective squared terms that these differed from the corresponding coefficients of trade : GDP ratio and its square. It would have been useful further to analyse the differential lag patterns with respect to export and import variables, though this was not feasible in view of the fact that only three time observations were available for the estimation.

Second, the threshold values for the export : GDP ratio beyond which it had a positive impact on GDP growth rates in specification 1 was 14.6 per cent; the corresponding figure for the import : GDP ratio was 36.6 per cent. By contrast, using the results from specification 2, the point of inflexion with respect to the trade : GDP ratio was 49.8 per cent. As noted above, the patterns of imports, especially those involving the transfer of advanced technology for production, were likely to be important for developing countries for enhancing productivity and economic growth. Third, there were significant non-linearities in specifications 1 and 2 with respect to the literacy rates. However, the threshold levels beyond which the effects of literacy rates on economic growth were positive were 30.4 per cent and 28.5 per cent from specifications 1 and 2, respectively. These levels were quite nominal especially since only two countries in the sample had lower literacy rates. However, it is important to reiterate that the cut-off points at which the overall effect was *statistically* significant were difficult to compute and could be quite high.

Fourth, the coefficients of the dummy variables for geographical regions were generally insignificant in specifications 1 and 2. This was perhaps not surprising since GDP growth rates exhibit considerable variation over time, though the use of five-yearly growth rates alleviates many problems. The coefficients of the variable for proportion of the labour force with medium-skill levels were not significant in specifications 1 and 2 for GDP growth rates. By contrast, coefficients of the lagged life expectancy and GDP variables were highly significant. These results showed the importance of population health indicators such as life expectancy (or adult survival rates) for economic growth previously underscored by Bhargava et al. (2001). However, possible non-linearities with respect to the life expectancy variable were not evident in this sample presumably because developed countries were excluded. The coefficients of (lagged) GDP were invariably negative and significant, implying conditional convergence in the growth rates, though with the qualification that the equilibrium GDP levels were affected by the unobserved country-specific random effects (Bhargava 2001b).

Last, the sequential tests for exogeneity hypotheses rejected the random-effects correlation patterns in equation (7) for the life expectancy and GDP variables. These variables were treated as fully endogenous, though the results for the two formulations for endogeneity in equations (6) and (7) were close. Owing to the small number of time observations available, it was better to rely on the random-effects decomposition for the correlation pattern, the results for specifications 1 and 2 assumed the special endogeneity patterns for life expectancy and GDP variables.

The second set of results in Table 3.1 for specifications 1 and 2 employed the PPP-based GDP series that were likely to exhibit less variation due to interpolations used to compute the PPP indices. The results were broadly similar to those obtained for the exchange-rate-based GDP series, though there were certain differences. For example, while the points of inflexion with respect to literacy rates were similar for the two GDP series using specification 1, the corresponding inflexion points with respect to export : GDP ratios were 14.6 per cent for the exchange-rates-based GDP series and 46.2 per cent for the PPP GDP series. The corresponding results for import : GDP ratios were 36.6 per cent and 21.9 per cent, respectively. The results from specification 2 for the trade : GDP ratio for the exchange rate and PPP-based GDP series were 49.8 per cent and 62.8 per cent, respectively. The points of inflexion with respect to literacy rates using specification 2 were 28.5 per cent and 27.3 per cent, respectively, for the exchange rate and PPP-based GDP series that were close. Overall, the results in Table 3.1 cast doubt of the usefulness of combining the exports and imports ratios as the trade : GDP ratio. Last, other indicators of globalization such as FDI and capital flows were not significant predictors of GDP growth rates partly because the numbers of countries in the sample were lower due to missing observations.

3.4.2. Empirical Results for the Two Measures of Poverty

The results for the percentages of people below the poverty line (headcount ratio) and the mean distance below the poverty line as the proportion of poverty line (poverty gap) in 1990 and 2000 for thirty-six developing countries are presented in Table 3.2. Similar results were obtained for the measure of poverty based on consumption surveys and hence were omitted to economize on space. The non-linearities with respect to literacy rates and export : GDP and import : GDP ratios were not apparent in these models. In fact, the coefficients of these three variables were statistically not different from zero in the specifications using the exchange rates and PPP-based GDP series. By contrast, the lagged GDP levels were statistically significant predictors of the headcount ratio and poverty gap using the two GDP series. The GDP growth rates were significant predictors of the headcount ratio and the poverty gap, though in the model for the poverty gap the coefficient of the exchange-rate-based GDP growth rate series was not significant.

The Chi-square tests for exogeneity of the lagged GDP and growth-rates series were within the confidence intervals for accepting the null hypotheses that these variables may be treated as exogenous in the models. This was in contrast with the results for GDP growth rates where the exogeneity null hypotheses for lagged GDP levels and the life-expectancy variable were rejected. A possible interpretation of these findings was that while poverty was likely to be reduced by lagged GDP levels and growth rates, the factors underlying the evolution of poverty profiles were complex and entailed differential benefits of economic growth for various income groups. Such factors, in turn, need not be systematically related to the error terms affecting the lagged GDP levels and growth rates.

Table 3.2. Efficient estimates from random-effects models for two poverty measures at ten-year intervals in developing countries (1990–2000)

	Using GDP levels (constant 2000 US$)				Using GDP levels (purchasing power parity 2000)			
	Poverty headcount ratio		Poverty gap		Poverty headcount ratio		Poverty gap	
	Coefficient	SE	Coefficient	SE	Coefficient	SE	Coefficient	SE
Constant	9.184*	1.493	9.818*	1.810	12.095*	1.982	14.138*	2.336
East Asia indicator variable	−0.606	0.454	−1.167*	0.548	−0.492	0.463	−0.980	0.543
Latin America indicator variable	−0.023	0.376	0.270	0.458	−0.357	0.358	−0.097	0.421
South Asia indicator variable	−0.647	0.467	−1.249*	0.572	−0.678	0.481	−1.282*	0.571
ln (literacy)$_{-10}$, %	0.296	0.374	0.341	0.451	0.267	0.389	0.367	0.456
ln (Export/GDP)$_{-10}$, %	−0.044	0.325	−0.070	0.401	−0.399	0.321	−0.495	0.386
ln (Import/GDP)$_{-10}$, %	−0.275	0.260	−0.303	0.317	−0.113	0.266	−0.146	0.317
ln (Low-skill/total labour)$_{-10}$	0.826	0.972	0.817	1.206	0.645	1.019	0.531	1.232
ln (GDP)$_{-10}$	−0.927*	0.202	−1.204*	0.246	−1.069*	0.262	−1.489*	0.309
ln (GDP growth rate)$_{-10}$	−7.097*	3.894	−8.301	4.800	−7.496*	3.766	−9.117*	4.580
Chi-square test for exogeneity (4 d.f.)	9.09		9.54		8.55		9.16	
Chi-square test for exogeneity (4 d.f.)	3.54		4.78		0.95		1.26	

Notes: There were thirty-six developing countries with two time observations (1990, 2000) used in the estimation.
Slope coefficients and standard errors are reported.
* $P<0.05$.

Table 3.3. Efficient estimates from random-effects models for Gini coefficients at ten-year intervals in developing countries (1990–2000)

	Gini coefficients			
	Using GDP levels (constant 2000 US$)		Using GDP levels (purchasing power parity 2000)	
	Coefficient	SE	Coefficient	SE
Constant	3.502*	0.442	3.337*	0.461
East Asia indicator variable	−0.341*	0.066	−0.347*	0.065
Latin America indicator variable	−0.185*	0.064	−0.170*	0.062
South Asia indicator variable	−0.341*	0.074	−0.343*	0.073
ln (literacy)$_{-10}$, %	0.027	0.108	0.025	0.110
ln (Export/GDP)$_{-10}$, %	−0.013	0.042	0.0003	0.041
ln (Import/GDP)$_{-10}$, %	0.076*	0.036	0.071*	0.035
ln (Medium-skill/total labour)$_{-10}$	− 0.079*	0.034	−0.081*	0.034
ln (High-skill/total labour)$_{-10}$	0.067*	0.024	0.064*	0.024
ln (GDP)$_{-10}$	0.042	0.031	0.053	0.040
ln (GDP growth rate)$_{-10}$	0.170	0.462	0.207	0.433
Chi-square test for exogeneity (4 d.f.)	7.17		6.46	
Chi-square test for exogeneity (4 d.f.)	0.68		0.73	

Notes: There were thirty-five developing countries with two time observations (1990, 2000) used in the estimation. Slope coefficients and standard errors are reported.
* P<0.05.

In fact, further Chi-square tests indicated that the errors affecting GDP growth rates were less likely to be correlated with the errors affecting the two poverty measures modelled in the analysis.

3.4.3. Empirical Results for the Gini Coefficients

The results for Gini coefficients for thirty-five developing countries in 1990 and 2000 are presented in Table 3.3 using the two GDP series. In contrast with the poverty measures, the indicator variables for East Asia, Latin America, and South Asia were estimated with negative and significant coefficients. Thus, there appeared to be a decline in inequality in these regions in comparison with African countries. Second, while the coefficient of the export : GDP ratio was not statistically different from zero, this was not the case for the coefficient of the import : GDP ratio that was estimated with a positive sign. These results indicated that imports were associated with higher inequality in developing countries and there may be many reasons for this finding. For example, importing goods and services needed for domestic production may initially be beneficial for the well-off and educated population subgroups.

Third, while the ratio of medium-skill to total labour was estimated with a negative and significant coefficient in the models using the two GDP series, the ratio of high-skill to total labour was estimated with positive and significant coefficients. Moreover, the coefficient of the ratio of low-skill to total labour was not a significant predictor, coefficients of GDP levels and growth rates were also not significantly different from zero. These results suggested the importance of differences in the education levels of the labour force in countries for inequality measures. Because the exports and imports of the countries and literacy rates were controlled for in the analysis, globalization may exacerbate inequality owing to skill differentials of the populations. Moreover, in view of the results in Table 3.1, developing countries need to invest in creating an educated labour force, educated population groups are likely to have higher life expectancy that in turn would enhance the benefits of globalization for economic growth. Last, the Chi-square test statistics for exogeneity of the GDP levels and growth rates were not significant in the models for the Gini coefficients. This was perhaps not surprising since coefficients of these variables were insignificant predictors in the models.

3.5. Conclusion

This chapter presented analyses of GDP growth rates, poverty measures, and inequality using aggregate panel data on developing countries in the period 1990–2000, during which trade levels have increased. While additional measures of globalization are being compiled for more recent years (e.g., Heshmati 2006), analyses using the data on exports and imports of the countries provided useful insights. It was seen that while the effects of export : GDP and import : GDP ratios on GDP growth rates were different, studies analysing the effects of exports and imports on economic growth, poverty, and inequality do not restrict these coefficients from being the same. As data on additional globalization-related variables become available, researchers will be able to model the differential lag patterns in exports and imports affecting economic growth in developing countries.

Second, the importance of protecting the poor in the face of increased globalization has been emphasized in the literature. The results in this chapter underscored the importance of high literacy rates and life expectancy for developing countries for reaping the benefits of globalization. With the demand in developed countries for inexpensive high-quality goods rising and the import of agricultural commodities hampered by agricultural subsidies, it is evident that developing countries with an educated labour force are likely to benefit from opening their markets and competing with producers in developed countries. From this viewpoint, countries in Sub-Saharan Africa especially need to devise careful policies for reaping the benefits of globalization. In particular, the AIDS pandemic is reducing life expectancy and the school participation of orphaned children (Bhargava 2005), thereby hindering the benefits of globalization.

Third, the analysis of the poverty measures showed the importance of GDP levels and growth rates for reducing poverty. However, variables such as export : GDP and import : GDP ratios were not significant predictors of poverty measures suggesting that, at least at an aggregate level, these broad indicators of globalization were not exacerbating poverty. Finally, the models estimated for inequality indicated that import : GDP ratios and the proportion of the labour force with high skill levels may exacerbate inequality. Since the diffusion of technical knowledge to developing countries and availability of an educated labour force are critical ingredients for economic growth, short-run increases in inequality due to globalization may be inevitable. Overall, developing countries need to invest additional resources in education and health so as to create a skilled labour force to enjoy greater benefits of globalization.

References

Anderson, T. W. (1971) *Statistical Analysis of Time Series*. New York: John Wiley.

—— and C. Hsiao (1981) 'Estimation of Some Dynamic Models with Error Components', *Journal of American Statistical Association*, 76: 598–606.

Barro, R. J., and J. W. Lee (2000) 'International Data on Education Attainment: Updates and Implications'. Working Paper 42. Cambridge, Mass.: Harvard University Center for International Development.

—— and X. Sala-i-Martin (1995) *Economic Growth*. New York: McGraw Hill.

Bhargava, A. (1991) 'Identification and Panel Data Models with Endogenous Regressors', *Review of Economic Studies*, 58: 129–40.

—— (2001a) 'Nutrition, Health and Economic Development: Some Policies Priorities', *Food and Nutrition Bulletin*, 22: 173–7.

—— (2001b) 'Stochastic Specification and the International GDP Series', *Econometrics Journal*, 4: 274–87.

—— (2005) 'AIDS Epidemic and the Psychological Well-being and School Participation of Ethiopian Orphans', *Psychology, Health and Medicine*, 10: 263–75.

—— and J. D. Sargan (1983) 'Estimating Dynamic Random Effects Models from Panel Data Covering Short time Periods', *Econometrica*, 51: 1635–60.

—— D. Jamison, L. Lau, and C. Murray (2001) 'Modeling the Effects of Health on Economic Growth', *Journal of Health Economics*, 20: 423–40.

Christensen, L. R., D. W. Jorgenson, and L. J. Lau (1973) 'Transcendental Logarithmic Production Frontier', *Review of Economics and Statistics*, 55: 28–45.

Docquier, F., and A. Marfouk (2006) 'Measuring International Migration by Educational Attainment in 1990–2000: Release 1.1'. In C. Ozden and M. Schiff (eds), *International Migration, Remittances, and the Brain Drain*. Washington, DC: World Bank.

Dollar, D., and A. Kraay (2004) 'Trade, Growth and Poverty', *Economic Journal*, 114: F22–F49.

Harrison, A. (ed) (2005) *Globalization and Poverty*. Chicago: University of Chicago Press.

Heshmati, A. (2006) 'The Relationship between Income Inequality, Poverty and Globalization'. In M. Nissanke and E. Thorbecke (eds), *The Impact of Globalization on the World's Poor: Transmission Mechanisms*. Basingstoke: Palgrave Macmillan for UNU-WIDER.

Kim, J. I., and L. J. Lau (1994) 'The Sources of Economic Growth in the East Asian Newly Industrialized Countries', *Journal of Japanese and International Economies*, 8: 235–71.

Preston, S. (1976) *Mortality Patterns in National Populations*. New York: Academic Press.

Ravallion, M. (2004) 'Looking beyond Averages in the Trade and Poverty Debate'. Working Paper 3461. Washington, DC: World Bank.

Rodriguez, F., and D. Rodrik (2001) 'Trade Policy and Economic Growth: A Skeptic's Guide to the Cross-national Evidence'. In B. Bernanke and K. S. Rogoff (eds), *NBER Macroeconomics Annual 2000*. Cambridge, Mass.: MIT Press for NBER.

Santos-Paulino, A., and A. Thirlwall (2004) 'The Impact of Trade Liberalization on Exports, Imports and the Balance of Payments of Developing Countries', *Economic Journal*, 114: F50–F72.

Sargan, J. D. (1958) 'The Estimation of Economic Relationships Using Instrumental Variables', *Econometrica*, 26: 393–415.

—— (1971) 'Production Functions, Part 5'. In P. R. G. Layard, J. D. Sargan, M. E. Ager, and D. J. Jones (eds), *Qualified Manpower and Economic Performance*. London: Allen Lane.

—— (1980) 'Some Tests of Dynamic Specification for Single Equations', *Econometrica*, 48: 879–98.

UNU-WIDER (2005) World Economic Inequality Database V. 2.0a. Helsinki: UNU-WIDER. <http://www.wider.unu.edu/research/Database/en_GB/database/>.

Wald, A. (1943) 'Tests of Statistical Hypotheses Concerning Several Parameters When the Number of Observations is Large', *Transactions of the American Mathematical Society*, 54: 426–82.

Winters, L. A. (2004) 'Trade Liberalisation and Economic Performance: An Overview', *Economic Journal*, 114: F4–F21.

World Bank (2005a) *World Development Indicators*. Washington, DC: World Bank.

—— (2005b) *Povcalnet*. Washington, DC: World Bank. <http://iresearch.worldbank.org/PovcalNet/jsp/index.jsp>.

Part II

Asia

4

Asia's Labour-driven Growth, Flying Geese Style: Types of Trade, FDI, and Institutions Matter for the Poor

Terutomo Ozawa[1]

4.1. Introduction

Despite the financial crises of 1997–8, Asia as a whole has experienced rapid growth since the end of the Second World War. During the post-war 'golden age of capitalism' (1950–71) Japan's per capita income multiplied sixfold, enabling the country to join the ranks of the advanced world. Shortly thereafter, the newly industrialized economies (NIEs) Hong Kong, Singapore, Taiwan, and South Korea achieved equally remarkable catch-up growth. In fact, Hong Kong and Singapore's per capita incomes soon surpassed that of Britain, their former mother country. Korea's economic growth was so successful that in 1996 it was able quickly to join the OECD, 'the rich men's club'. ASEAN-4 (Association of Southeast Asian Nations: Thailand, Malaysia, Indonesia, and the Philippines), too, began to emulate the NIEs' achievements. More recently, China and India also have begun quickly to scale the ladder of economic development, emerging as members of the so-called BRIC (Brazil, Russia, India, and China). Likewise, Vietnam is following suit. Thus, Asia's growth as a whole is characterized as a sequence of *staggered* or *lagged* catch-up events across the region, a pattern of what I term 'tandem growth', which is well envisioned in the so-called 'flying geese' (FG) model of economic development.

Asia's recent economic development, especially in its early phases, has been simultaneously accompanied by an impressive poverty reduction as a consequence of the sharp rise in demand—hence, incomes—for unskilled labour.

[1] The author is grateful to Professor Yasuyuki Sawada of Tokyo University and Dr Charles Oman of OECD's Development Centre for their valuable comments.

In fact, this 'unique' feature (a double play of growth and poverty alleviation) was already identified as 'shared growth' by the World Bank in its 1993 study of the development experiences of the high-performing Asian economies (HPAEs), the phenomenon of 'unusually low and declining levels of inequality, contrary to historical experience and contemporary evidence in other regions' (World Bank 1993: 29).[2]

Indeed, the incidence of extreme poverty practically first disappeared in Japan after the Second World War and then in the NIEs. There has also been a considerable reduction of abject poverty in ASEAN-4 and more recently—and most dramatically—in China. It is estimated by the Asian Development Bank (2004) that in China, for example, the headcount ratio of the population living on US$1 a day decreased from 53.1 per cent in 1984 to 26.5 per cent in 2001, from 37.8 per cent in 1984 to 7.5 per cent in 2002 in Indonesia, and from 17.8 per cent in 1988 to 1.9 per cent in 2000 in Thailand. These are, indeed, remarkable accomplishments. India, too, has been experiencing noticeable alleviation in poverty, especially in urban areas; as a consequence of its recent stepped-up pace of economic development, the headcount ratio declined from 46.3 per cent in 1987 to 36.0 per cent in 2000—though, admittedly, the absolute number of the poor is still large.[3] Interestingly enough, poverty reductions have been occurring, again FG style (i.e., in tandem), among these rapidly catching-up Asian economies. Given such a track record of poverty alleviation, most Asian countries are expected to meet without much difficulty the goal of the UN Millennium Project of halving the proportion of the population in extreme poverty (US$1 a day line) by 2015.[4]

Then, the major question we must ask is: why has Asia as a whole—but especially East Asia, relative to other developing regions—been so successful in managing its economic growth so as to lessen poverty? Why has the same phenomenon not occurred evenly across the world? Is there any particular reason specifically endemic to East Asia? So far, the usual answer is that the East Asian countries have adopted both pro-growth and pro-poor policies, and

[2] The World Bank's original study did not include China as an HPAE, but would certainly have treated it as such if the study had been made more recently: 'recently China, particularly southern China, has recorded remarkably high growth rates using policies that in some ways resemble those of the HPAEs. This very significant development is beyond the scope of our study' (World Bank 1993: 1).

[3] Despite the recent sharp decline in abject poverty, it should, however, be noted that East, Southeast, and South Asia still had almost 690 million poor people in 2002 in terms of the US$1 a day poverty line, and as many as 1.9 billion people on the basis of the US$2 a day poverty line (ADB 2004). Furthermore, a preliminary estimate indicates that the Indian Ocean tsunami may add nearly two more million people to poverty (ADB 2005).

[4] 'On the assumptions that (i) current rates of economic growth continue in most developing member countries of ADB, but decline to more sustainable levels in the PRC and the Central Asian republics, and (ii) that distributions are no more unequal than those experienced in recent years, many DMCs are poised both to meet the MDG target of halving the 1990 proportion of extremely poor by 2015 and to reduce the number of people living in extreme poverty' (ADB 2004: 45).

established the appropriate institutional set-ups to achieve equality, as epitomized in the practice of 'shared growth'. The region has also benefited from its egalitarian tradition based on communitarianism stemming from many centuries of rice paddy cultivation, as well as from the influence of Confucianism (or a 'strong culture'[5] adaptable to the forces of globalization).

This chapter, however, argues that although such practice and tradition are no doubt instrumental and necessary for the desirable outcome, what matters most is a distinct way in which East Asia has initiated, and continues, its catch-up growth: first by capitalizing on its most abundant asset, unskilled labour, for labour-intensive manufacturing for export at the start of their interactive development. In this connection, what may be called the 'FG paradigm of comparative advantage recycling in labour-intensive goods' can provide a useful framework within which Asia's effective poverty alleviation is explainable in a comprehensive fashion. The paradigm includes all the pro-poor attributes of economic activities (such as trade and investment) that have so far been identified, but rather separately in a fragmented manner and without any broad unifying frame of reference. Indeed, there is strong ground to argue that those Asian countries that have actively participated in the FG formation of labour-driven tandem growth are the ones that experienced significant poverty reductions.

4.2. Globalization, Growth, and Poverty Reduction

To explore the impact of globalization on poverty, three key events and two causal linkages between them are generally recognized: globalization affects growth, and such globalization-driven growth then impacts on poverty (that is, in two logical steps), as illustrated in Figure 4.1. These two linkages are considered the key macroeconomic channels of causality and constitute a general frame of analysis. For example, Nissanke and Thorbecke (2005) lay out this conceptual framework for the UNU-WIDER study on globalization and poverty, but they also bring in other variables such as capital and labour mobility, technology, information diffusion, and institutions as growth enhancing intermediaries (Nissanke and Thorbecke 2008; also see Chapter 1) In contrast, Chapter 11 (by Round) stresses and surveys empirical findings (as opposed to theories) on the channels, while cautioning us about some intrinsic deficiencies of econometric analysis and simulation approach (usually involving computable general equilibrium modelling). Given the fact that a host of institutional factors (including culture, traditions, customs, and ethos) play a vital role in growth and income distribution, empirical analysis is constrained by the inadequacy of variables that can appropriately measure intangible determinants.

[5] The distinction between a strong culture and a weak culture is attributed to Huntington (Berger and Huntington 2002).

What makes this chapter's approach distinct is that when we talk about the growth of economies they are not treated as equals, in the sense that developing economies are necessarily at different stages of development. That is, a hierarchy of economies matters, especially in the context of the Asian experience, as it engenders dynamic externalities (i.e., 'concatenation economies'). In addition, institutional factors within individual countries and political relations (and geopolitics) between them—and a 'demonstration effect'—are far more decisively important than normally treated and revealed in econometric studies (which use crude proxies at best). And so are the natures of exports (whether they are manufactures or primary goods, and, if manufactures, whether they are labour intensive or capital intensive) and investment (whether it is pro-trade or anti-trade). As seen below, these are the powerful factors that underlie the globalization–growth–poverty alleviation nexus in Asia.

In general, one can take a reduced form of analysis and/or a structural form of analysis, and two opposing views, positive and negative, prevail about the impact of globalization on poverty via growth. The positive view argues (i) that globalization favourably affects (fosters) developing countries' growth and incomes for workers, thereby contributing to poverty alleviation, whereas the negative view holds (ii) that globalization aggravates poverty—whether or not it stimulates or stunts developing countries' growth because globalization (via international businesses) entails inequality in favour of the rich and against the poor.

The negative view emphasizes the belief that the market-driven (capitalistic) process of economic development causes an adverse income distribution against the poor. On the other hand, the positive view argues that even with such an adverse income distribution effect, the growth effect of globalization

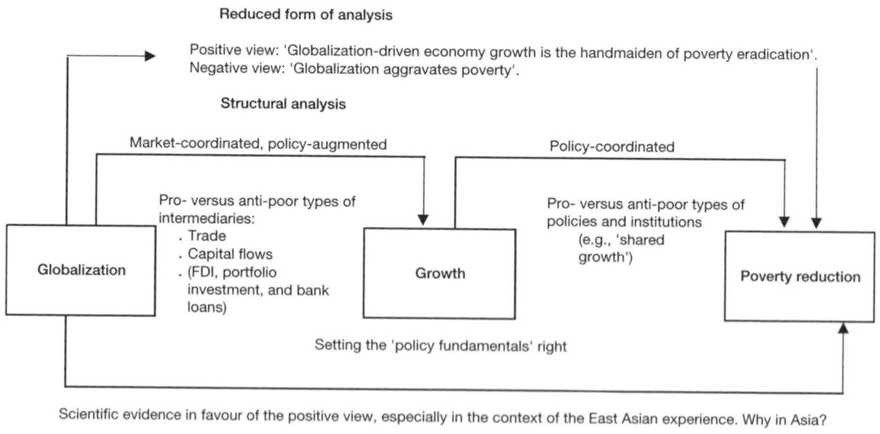

Fig. 4.1. Globalization, economic growth, and poverty reduction

Source: Compiled by the author.

(via freer trade and inward FDI) can more than compensate for any income inequality—so long as developing countries implement appropriate policy and set up necessary institutional arrangements. And this has been the case, especially with East Asia.

Each side has legitimate grounds to support their position. For reasons to be discussed later, however, the general consensus among economists is that both 'shrewd [on-the-field] observation and scientific evidence' are in strong support of the positive view and as summed up by Bhagwati that 'the scientific analysis of the effect of trade on poverty is even more compelling' (Bhagwati 2004: 52–3).

4.2.1. Scientific Evidence for Growth-led Poverty Reduction

Indeed, scientific evidence is strong. As shown in Figure 4.2, Dollar and Kraay (2001; 2002) found a close correlation between growth and poverty reduction

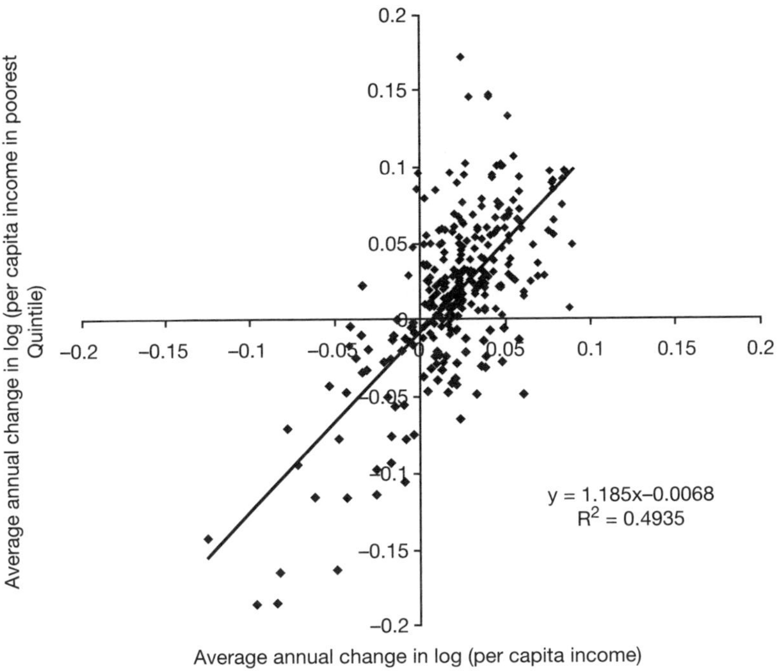

Fig. 4.2. Growth is good for the poor

Notes: Figure shows average annual growth rates of indicated variables over non-overlapping periods of at least five years, in a sample of 285 observations covering ninety-two developed and developing countries. Per capita income growth refers to real per capita GDP growth. Per capita income growth in the poorest quintile is equal to per capita income growth plus growth in the income share of the poorest quintile.

Source: Dollar and Kraay (2001).

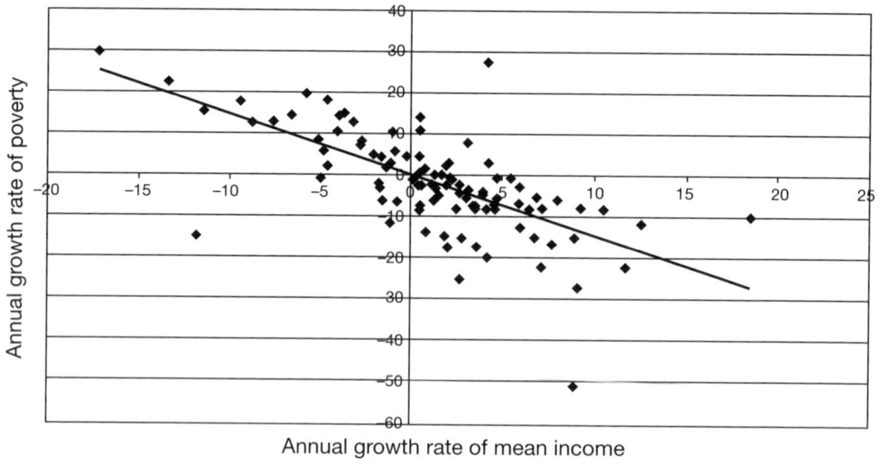

Fig. 4.3. Growth and poverty reduction in the developing world (percentage)

Source: ADB (2004).

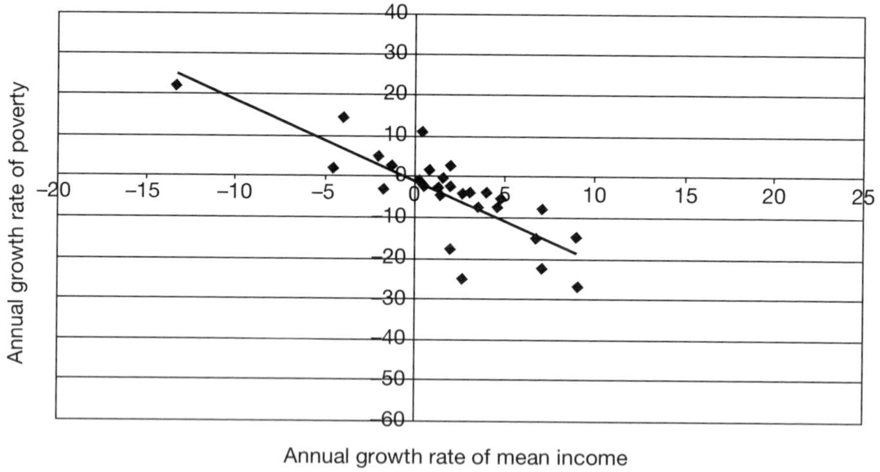

Fig. 4.4. Growth and poverty reduction in selected developing member countries (percentage)

Source: ADB (2004).

by observing ninety-two developed and developing countries. A similar study was made and a similar result obtained by the Asian Development Bank (ADB 2004: fig. 6) that focuses on developing countries alone (Figure 4.3). 'In particular, growth of 1 per cent is associated with a 1.5 per cent decline in the incidence of US$1 a day poverty on average' (ADB 2004: 32). In the case of

Asia (twenty-seven countries in East Asia, Southeast Asia, and South Asia), however, there is a much *stronger* relationship between growth and poverty alleviation (as shown in Figure 4.4). 'Each 1 per cent of growth is associated with an almost 2 per cent decline in poverty incidence on average (ADB 2004: 33). In other words, the efficacy of growth in lessening poverty is as much as one-third higher for Asia. No doubt, if East Asia and Southeast Asia alone are studied by excluding South Asia where the magnitude of poverty is very high, growth would be even more pro-poor—that is, more effective in poverty eradication.

Growth tends to cause an unfavourable distribution (in relative terms) against the poor. But if an economy grows vigorously enough (which is the case with capitalism, since it is the most powerful engine of development), there is a positive spillover effect from growth that more than compensates for the adverse distribution effect. And, indeed, this is what has happened in Asia:

> *[T]he driver of rapid poverty reduction in Asia has been growth and not distribution change.* Indeed, the largest reductions in poverty in Asia have all taken place in the context of distribution changes that went *against* the poor. There were nine spells in which poverty declined on average by 1.5 percentage points or more a year. In each of these nine spells, distribution changes were such that poverty would have increased in the absence of growth. In the case of *rural* PRC, for example... distribution changes alone (i.e. in the absence of any growth), would have increased poverty by 1.2 percentage points a year on average during the 1993–6 spell. Nevertheless, poverty reduction was rapid over this period (4.8 percentage points a year on average) *because the positive growth effect more than matched the adverse effects of purely distribution change on the poor.* [These] episodes... have been experienced widely across the region, encompassing countries not only from East Asia and Southeast Asia but even two South Asian economies (namely, Bangladesh and Pakistan in the late 1980s and early 1990s). (ADB 2004: 35; emphasis added)

It should be noted, however, that the governments did intervene proactively to lessen the adverse distribution effect on the poor rather than focusing only on the pro-growth strategy. It cannot be overemphasized, therefore, that both policy and institutional arrangements need to be specifically crafted to enhance the positive growth effect and concurrently abate the negative distribution one. Asia's practice of shared growth epitomizes such policy-cum-institutional matrices.

As early as the start of the 1990s, the World Bank (1993) took notice of the fact that the HPAEs achieved *both* high growth and income equality simultaneously, and reduced poverty to a much greater extent than any other economies in other regions:

> For the eight HPAEs, rapid growth and declining inequality have been shared virtues, as comparisons over time of equality and growth using Gini coefficients illustrate... The developing HPAEs clearly outperform other middle income economies in that they have *both* lower levels of inequality and higher levels of growth. Moreover... improvements in income distribution generally coincided with periods of rapid growth... Given rapid growth and declining inequality, these economies have of course been *unusually successful*

in reducing poverty... Increases in life-expectancy have also been larger than in any other region. (World Bank 1993: 31–2; emphasis added)

One legitimate question, then, is: 'why has growth served the poor in East Asia better than the rest of the developing world on average (World Bank 1993: 33)? Why has the region been so 'unusually successful in reducing poverty' (World Bank 1993: 32)?

So far, one explanation is the one given by the World Bank: East Asia has been able to get the policy fundamentals right by way of (i) carefully limited and market-friendly (pro-business) government activities; (ii) strong export orientation; (iii) high levels of domestic savings; (iv) accumulation of human capital (via emphasis on universal education and vocational training, inside and outside firms); (v) good macroeconomic management; (vi) effective acquisition of foreign technology and advanced knowledge through openness to licensing, inward FDI, and foreign training; (vii) flexible labour markets; (viii) land reform and productive agricultural sectors; and (ix) a conscious adoption of the principle of shared growth (low-income inequality with rapid growth).[6]

These Asian approaches are in sharp contrast, however, to the neoclassical stance to place full trust in the market mechanism, an approach best exemplified by the Washington consensus. In the East Asian experience, rapid growth is consciously governed in such a way to moderate the adverse distribution change. As Bhagwati puts it, 'it's policy, stupid' (Bhagwati 2004: 52). In reference to India's experience:

growth was not a passive, trickle-down strategy for helping the poor. It was an active, pull-up strategy instead. It required a government [of India] that would energetically take steps to accelerate growth, through a variety of policies, including building infrastructure such as roads and ports and attracting foreign funds. (Bhagwati 2004: 54)

Here, Bhagwati's growth model jibes with Stiglitz's formulation of what he calls 'a new paradigm of development' (Stiglitz 2003: 92), a paradigm that is an amended version of the Washington consensus.

The rapid growth of most of the East Asian economies showed that development was possible, and that successful development could be accompanied by a reduction of poverty, widespread improvements in living standards, and even a process of democratization... these countries did not follow the standard prescriptions. In most cases, national governments played a large role. (Bhagwati 2004: 81)

[6] All these features are often mutually augmenting and cumulatively causational. For example, a rapid rise in income with declining income inequality led to higher primary and secondary school enrolments (human capital formation), which in turn fostered further catch-up growth and a further drop in poverty. And these desirable characteristics/attributes are clearly advanced by appropriate government policies. Indeed, policy and institutional set-ups matter in creating market-compatible yet pro-poor growth.

Stiglitz's new paradigm (i.e., post-Washington consensus) constitutes a 'more holistic approach to development', whose features 'were, in fact, incorporated in the development strategies of the fastest [Asian] developers'. In other words, the new paradigm is built on, and modelled after, the successful experiences of East Asia's shared growth. Stiglitz's model, though not explicitly so stated, boils down to the notion of 'social capacity' to learn from and catch up with the advanced world, a term that was coined by Ohkawa and Rosovsky (1972) and popularized by Abramovitz (1986). Such capacity depends on government policies and institutional set-ups to create a market-compatible if not totally market-dictated economy. The social capability requires more than mere (unconditional) acceptance of the so-called Washington consensus (a set of 'neo-liberal' economic policy prescriptions).[7]

In this connection we may argue that growth under globalization (i.e., the globalization–growth link) can be best coordinated by market forces—that is, should be left fundamentally to the market by adopting market-enhancing policy if growth is to be most effectively maximized. On the other hand, however, growth-led poverty reduction (i.e., the growth–poverty link) ought to be coordinated proactively by policy and relevant institutional set-ups. In other words, we can have the best of both worlds: growth (an increase in the size of the pie) should be market-driven whereas poverty eradication (an equitable division of the pie) is the task assigned largely to both the state and the public (inclusive of enterprises) through appropriate policies. This is because poverty eradication is basically a public good (a social desideratum) which the market itself is poorly qualified to resolve (and, in fact, incapable of resolving). As Dunning observes, the market is 'less well designed for the production and exchange of public or social goods and services than private goods and services' (Dunning 2003: 32). It is, indeed, often said that 'like fire, the market is a good servant, but a poor master' (Eatwell 1982).[8] Put differently, the market is basically neither goal setting nor goal pursuing; it is goal neutral at best and sometimes even goal hindering. In essence, the market is merely a resource-allocative mechanism, not a goal-oriented and fulfilling entity (Ozawa 1996). Poverty amelioration is certainly a social goal of our human endeavour.

In short, the growth–poverty-reduction nexus has been both conceptually explored and empirically verified throughout Asia where trade and investment have been liberalized and pro-poor policies and institutional arrangements are

[7] India has recently decided to keep outward-oriented development and economic changes on track when its government announced its budget and spending plans for the fiscal year 2005. Even at the cost of not trimming its fiscal deficit, New Delhi will focus on three objectives: job creation, infrastructure improvements, and social programmes for the rural poor. All three will moderate the adverse distributive effect of rapid growth (which India pursues by further opening up its economy for inward investment), having hence a favourable impact on poverty reduction.

[8] Some say that this famous statement was originally made by Joan Robinson.

actively organized. Yet, as seen below, by contrast, the nexus between globalization and growth seems still lacking in a comprehensive framework that can capture the more fundamental/underlying forces of global capitalism.

4.2.2. Globalization and Growth

This section briefly reviews and summarizes the causality of globalization and growth as conceptualized so far by economists. In economics, trade and capital flows (notably FDI by multinational corporations) are naturally considered the major conduits of globalization impacting on the growth of the developing world.

The nexus between trade liberalization and growth has already been well established as positive in terms of trade theory (i.e., trade is a national income-raising activity) and empirically so verified in most cases (for a survey on this topic, see Winters 2004). Furthermore, the impact of trade on growth is examined with respect to two opposing trade policies; outward-focused export-led policy versus inward-oriented import-substituting policy. The former has proven growth conducive, whereas the latter is not as much growth conducive—or is even growth stunting. East Asia, in particular, has succeeded in outward-focused export-driven growth. And it is often compared with Latin America, which once experimented with, but suffered from, their inward-oriented import-substituting strategies and had to switch to the East Asian model. Strong export promotion is thus now regarded as more preferable as the desideratum for successful catch-up growth than import substitution. Yet, the kinds of goods a country specializes in, and exports, influence how trade impacts demand for labour, hence poverty.

In this respect, the promotion of exports of primary goods has long been recognized as a less desirable strategy of economic development for many reasons, but particularly if technological progress, structural upgrading, job creation, and income distribution in favour of labour are aimed at as objectives. The so-called Prebisch–Singer thesis (Prebisch 1950; Singer 1950) was introduced in the 1950s to argue against primary-goods export expansion, since such exports are subject to the secular deterioration of the commodity terms of trade and as a consequence the primary exporting countries may experience a loss of growth and income. Similarly, the immiserizing growth theory (Bhagwati 1958) stressed the danger of expanding—and relying only on—primary production for export because of the same (though short-run) terms of trade deterioration that causes negative growth.[9] Furthermore, a sudden

[9] It should be noted in passing that as early as the 1920s the so-called Australian case for protection argued against specialization and free trade in the primary goods which would lead to the problems of (i) diminishing returns in agriculture; (ii) income distribution in favour of landowners but against workers; and (iii) a deterioration of the terms of trade (Irwin 1996). In

boom in resources exports (as often seen in oil exports) may cause the so-called Dutch disease, with a sharply appreciated home currency undermining manufacturing and traditional exports.

On a financial level, moreover, resource extraction and revenues from primary exports in developing countries are, as a norm, heavily regulated and controlled by the governments and lead to corruption and inept management of fiscal budgets and programmes. Some governments often experience financial crises due to the cumulative effect of the feast and fast cycle of public spending in which windfall revenues from resource exports in the time of each commodity boom create more government-funded programmes that are not cut, however, during the subsequent market bust. The end result is an inevitable fiscal crisis.[10]

On the other hand, a promotion of manufactured exports, especially labour-intensive goods in accordance with the Heckscher–Ohlin trade theory, is regarded as favourable for developing countries for two major reasons: (i) the demand for developing countries' abundance factor—namely, labour, rises (more than proportionately than for their scarce factor, capital); and (ii) the factor price (wage) magnification effect (the wage increases more than proportionately than the price of exports labour produces). In addition, other modern trade theories stress some dynamic benefits of trade such as increasing returns in manufacturing, and greater learning opportunities through contact with sophisticated customers in the advanced countries. (In fact, Indonesia's success in poverty reduction is attributable to its development strategy of promoting labour-intensive manufactured exports, along with primary exports.)

As to the impact of inward FDI by multinational corporations on the growth of host countries, there are both boon and bane stories. Graham (2000) distinguishes inward FDI in internationally competitive activities (competitive FDI) from one in internationally non-competitive activities (non-competitive FDI). He relates the former to a situation in which the host country pursues export-oriented development policy, and the latter to the host country's import-substituting protection policy. This distinction actually clearly coincides with the differentiation made much earlier by Kojima (1973) between pro-trade (export creating) and anti-trade (import substituting) FDI.

No doubt, FDI can thus be 'designed' to become a positive link between globalization and growth. It should be noted that another form of capital flows, portfolio investment ('hot money'), is by comparison less desirable—

other words, Australia, which was eager to expand its population and its national economy, needed the development of the manufacturing sector to attract and absorb immigration, and clearly understood that an expansion of the manufacturing industry, not agriculture and mining, was the only viable long-term avenue to build a strong economy.

[10] The 'feast-and-fast' theory of a fiscal crisis was introduced by Arthur B. Laffer in his explanation of the dire financial quagmire of the state of California. This theory, however, is equally applicable to the resource-exporting developing countries' fiscal problems.

and often disruptive for developing countries where the financial markets are underdeveloped, because of its speculative and short-term nature. International bank loans, which are mostly inter-bank loans, are considered not as desirable as FDI because of their relatively short-term commitments and volatility in loan renewals (though less volatility than hot money).

In sum, two forms of globalization linkage: trade, and capital flows, have been well studied—but only separately without any unifying framework. That is to say, the existing studies cannot really explain why trade and FDI in East Asia have been so strongly and so distinctly pro-growth and pro-poor simultaneously in the outcome. There are actually more fundamental forces at work in producing rapid growth—hence a more substantial poverty reduction—throughout East Asia than individual country-specific pro-growth and pro-poor policies and institutions themselves can explain. (This is the crux of the present chapter.)

As will be seen, the FG model of comparative advantage recycling in labour-driven goods, which most cogently fits the East Asian experience, can provide a holistic/comprehensive/integrative explanation by linking the process of globalization more directly with the successful decline in poverty in terms of a structural form of analysis.

4.3. Comparative Advantage Recycling in Labour-intensive Goods, Flying Geese Style, in the Context of the Hierarchies of Countries and Industries

As introduced elsewhere (Ozawa 1993), the model of comparative advantage (or market) recycling in labour-intensive goods is a comprehensive framework within which we can explain how Asian economies—first, Japan, and then the NIEs, the ASEAN-4, China, and Vietnam in tandem—have successfully initiated a succession of export-driven growth (by developing and exporting labour-intensive goods mostly to the relatively open markets of the USA), the event that has proved to be most effective in poverty reduction. It is a restatement of the so-called FG theory of economic development, originally introduced by Akamatsu (inter alia, 1935; 1961)[11] and further elaborated, inter alia, by Kojima (2003; 2004), Kojima and Ozawa (1985), and Ozawa (2003; 2005).

[11] Akamatsu conceived three different patterns of FG formation: (i) an intra-industry sequential pattern of import-substitution-cum-export-promotion (import→domestic production→export or M-P-E); (ii) a sequential pattern, both intra-industry and inter-industry, of qualitative/structural improvements in manufacturing activities and industrial structure from low-end to high-end products ('from crude/simple to complex/refined articles', in Akamatsu's own words); and (iii) an international (cross-border) sequential pattern of catch-up growth among a closely interacting group of countries aligned along, and moving up, the different stages of economic development. Akamatsu regarded the first pattern as the primary/basic one (which he found in

This reformulated model (Ozawa 1993; 2003; and 2005) explains:

- the stages of industrial upgrading pioneered and trail-blazed by two hegemons of global capitalism (first under the Pax Britannica and later under the Pax Americana) which can serve as the ladder of economic development for the followers to scale;
- the catch-up growth of each Asian economy initiating from the bottom rung of the development ladder—that is, labour-intensive manufacturing and exports (notably textiles and garments);
- the role of the US markets as the major demand provider;
- the sequential recycling/relaying of the US markets for labour-intensive goods from one Asian country to another;
- the role of Japan—and more recently, the NIEs—as the crucial capacity (comparative advantage) augmenter for the lower-ranking follower goose countries by way of FDI and technology transfer; and
- the resultant opportunity given to each follower goose to create demand for unskilled labour (so long as the labour market is kept flexible and appropriate government policies are adopted), thereby contributing to poverty reduction.

In short, the reformulated model serves as a comprehensive framework to capture not only the static gains (allocative efficiency) of trade and FDI but also, and more importantly, the dynamic gains (adaptive efficiency) and poverty alleviation of economic integration.

4.3.1. Two Hegemon-led Growth Clustering

First, let us take a quick look at how the modern industrial structure has been introduced, and has evolved in the world. The world economy has so far been led by two hegemonic powers (first the UK and then the USA). Indeed, the UK and USA have been the very first lead geese for two periods; the former during the Pax Britannica of 1846–1914, and the latter during the Pax Americana of 1950 onward, respectively. And, modern industrialization has been all moulded as 'derived' economic development under the forces of hegemon-led growth clustering (Ozawa 2005). In fact, Akamatsu (1935) found a basic pattern of such

his empirical studies of industrial development in pre-war Japan), and the other two as the derived patterns. It should be kept in mind that Akamatsu's findings were centred mostly on statistical studies and left the theoretical/causal dimension of his findings largely unexplored. My restatement of his model concerns his second pattern. For some reason, however, the third pattern—that is, a line-up of countries by stages of countries alone—has come to be widely accepted as the FG formation both in the media and in academia (though the academia, especially mainstream economics, has been much slower in accepting and expanding on the model). Moreover, Japan is erroneously interpreted by some advocates of the FG model and its critics alike as the lead goose that sparked the East Asian miracle.

a formation in the Japanese experience of industrial development under Pax Britannica-led growth clustering when in the 1930s he first studied Japan's pre-war industrial development.

Growth clustering is a phenomenon in which a hegemon economy (the lead goose) propagates growth stimuli to its closely aligned cohort of countries that are at various stages of development and structural transformation. The stimuli include dissemination of technology, knowledge, information, skills, and demand (via access to the hegemon's home market)—and, above all, transplantation of growth-inducing institutional arrangements of open market capitalism. This all contributes to the higher levels of industrial productivity, efficiency, and per capita income (i.e., economic growth). The lower-echelon countries (follower geese) can free ride and thrive on these growth stimuli, so long as they are willing to follow in the ideological steps of the hegemon. In other words, there is what may be called 'economies of hierarchical concatenation' (Ozawa 2005) that the follower countries can reap from the forces of hegemon-led growth clustering.

At the same time, furthermore, the hegemon itself and other high-echelon countries (second- and third-ranking follower geese) also benefit from rapid economic integration with lower-echelon countries (say, fourth-ranking follower geese), as the latter's vigorous economic development creates demand from the upper-echelon countries for goods (especially capital goods) and services (business-related). In sum, the group's synergistic interactions result in agglomeration economies, enabling the entire hierarchy of countries to mutually gain, grow, and prosper.

In fact, this mutual dependence has recently deepened around the world, but especially in the Pacific Rim between the USA (the first lead goose) and Asia's catching-up economies (follower geese) in the form of what may be called the 'Pacific Rim co-growth cluster' (Ozawa 2004). The USA has become ever more dependent on capital inflows, while the rest of the world, especially East Asia, depends on their exports of labour-intensive manufactures to the USA to kick-start and promote their economic growth. Consequently, the USA runs a rising trade deficit, while absorbing capital inflows to finance the deficit. This development is also called 'a global co-dependency' (Mann 2004). There is good reason, however, why such co-dependency has intensified on the Pacific Rim, as will be explored later.

4.3.2. Five Progressive Tiers of Industry: The Ladder of Development

Under the two hegemonic regimes, furthermore, a hierarchy of industries or the ladder of development has come into existence. And, as will be seen, this industrial hierarchy interacts, in the most cogent growth-conducive fashion, with the hierarchy of countries that exists in the present hegemonic world, especially in East Asia.

What is the hierarchy of industries or, a more popularly used phrase, the ladder of development? But it has not been clearly examined and defined, not to speak of its rungs. What is exactly the ladder of development and its rungs?

The world economy has so far witnessed five successive tiers of leading growth industry emerge in wave-like progression ever since the industrial revolution in England: the five tiers that are illustrated in Figure 4.5. The historical process of industrial development entailed the sequence of (i) 'Heckscher–Ohlin' labour-driven light industries (e.g., textiles and apparel)[12] → (ii) 'non-differentiated Smithian' scale-driven, resource-intensive, heavy and chemical industries (e.g., steel, machinery, and chemicals) → (iii) 'differentiated Smithian' assembly-based industries (e.g., cars) → (iv) 'Schumpeterian' R&D-driven industries (e.g., microchips and computers) → (v) 'McLuhan' Internet-based industries (e.g., information processing and transmission) (Ozawa 2005) These five tiers currently constitute the existing hierarchy of industries or the ladder of development.

What the Pax Britannica introduced were initially the labour-intensive light industries (the Heckscher–Ohlin stage/rung) and then the resource-intensive, scale-driven, heavy and chemical industries (the non-differentiated Smithian stage/rung). In contrast, the Pax Americana created the highly component intensive, assembly-based, genuinely consumer-oriented, and R&D-intensive industries (the differentiated Smithian and the Schumpeterian stages/rungs), and, most recently, the Internet-enabled information-intensive industries (the McLuhan phase as an offshoot/extension of the Schumpeterian stage/rung). The IT-driven industries are built on intellectual and entrepreneurial capital and strongly geared to the needs of final consumers. The New Economy is the latest creation of US-led consumer capitalism.[13]

The driver of this structural transformation is technological progress and knowledge accumulation in the hegemon economy, and advances in sciences and technology have been basically capital using and labour saving—and not the other way around (Rosenberg 1982). This characteristic is consistent with

[12] The Heckscher–Ohlin industries include the primary sector, such as agriculture and resource extraction. But primary production is not as conducive to long-term structural transformation as labour-driven manufacturing, for a variety of reasons, discussed earlier.

[13] Trade under the Pax Britannica was largely motivated by the search for resources and persistent differences in technology (i.e., differences on the supply side), for which the doctrine of comparative advantage (both the Ricardian and the Heckscher–Ohlin theories, which explain inter-industry trade) was pertinent. In contrast, trade under the Pax Americana has become increasingly knowledge-driven, scale-based, demand-sided, and intra-industry oriented; hence new theories such as Vernon's product-cycle theory, Linder's income-similarity theory, and the monopolistic competition theory of trade have gained in explanatory power, especially for trade in manufactures. In other words, a history of theoretical development in international economics can also be told and examined in terms of the above stages model of industrial upgrading.

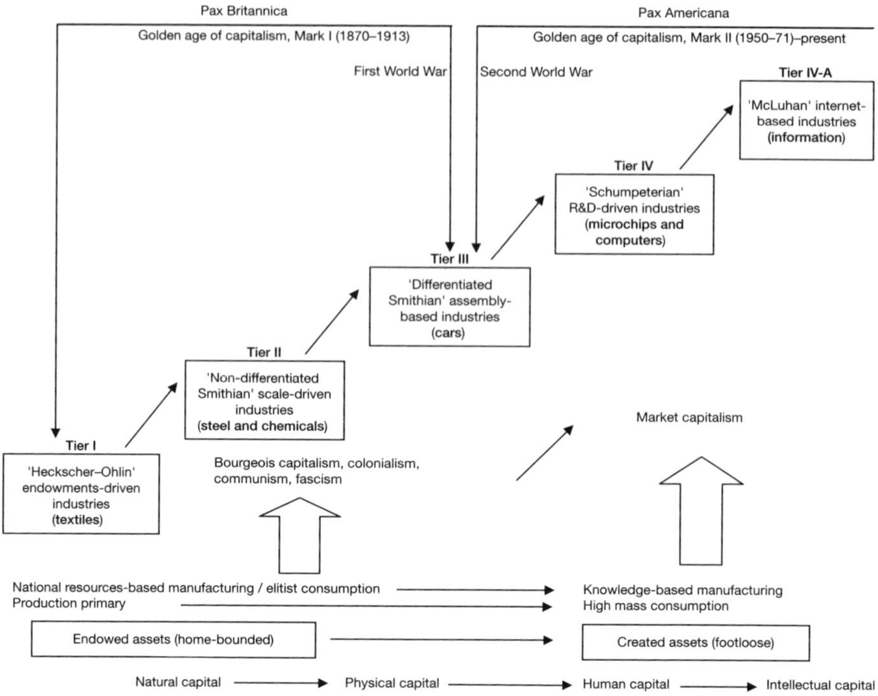

Fig. 4.5. Structural upgrading under Pax Britannica-led and Pax Americana-led macro-clustering

Source: Ozawa 2003; 2005.

the rising-factor endowment ratio of capital to labour *pari passu* with economic growth.

Obviously, the advanced countries no longer have competitiveness in lower-tier industries, especially labour-intensive, light manufacturing industries (e.g., textiles and apparel) and resource-based 'smoke stack' low-tech heavy industries (e.g., steel). Ironically, their own technological progress—hence their successful structural transformation—has made it impractical for them to retain competitiveness in lower-tier industries. This is necessarily the inevitable outcome of 'creative destruction' as emphasized by Schumpeter (1942). Labour-driven light industries (notably textiles) are the ideal 'entry' industries for developing countries to start out with in their effort to climb the ladder of economic development. These industries, indeed, can serve as jump-starters of development by mobilizing the developing countries' most abundant factor, relatively unskilled labour, to active employment—hence, the most effective market-coordinated way of reducing poverty. Being cognizant of this fact, many developing countries, particularly those still in the early stages of development,

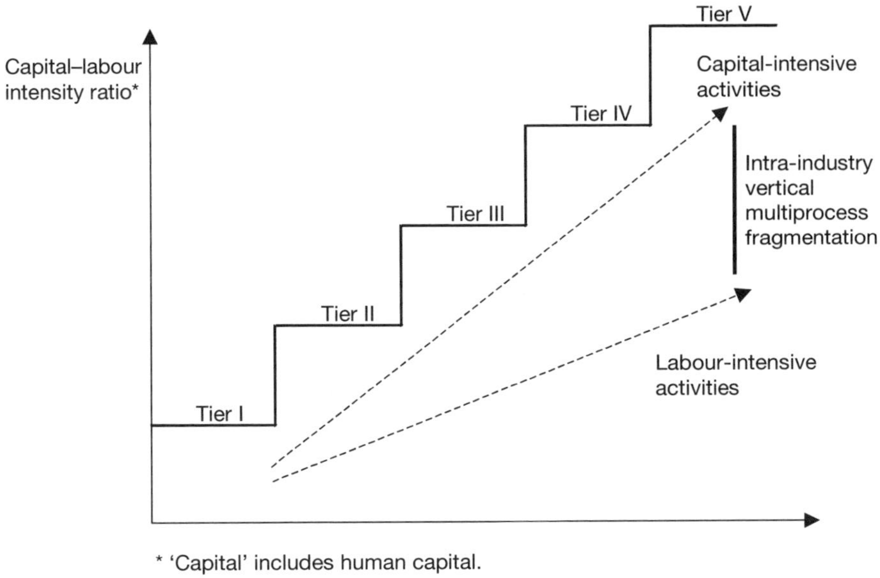

Fig. 4.6. Fragmentation of production along the capital–labour intensity ratios

Source: Ozawa 2003; 2005.

are eagerly producing and exporting textiles and apparel and standardized electronics goods as their major manufactured goods. Interestingly enough, this development strategy usually places female workers, especially from the poor rural areas, in great demand, since low-end manufacturing normally creates more jobs for female workers than for male workers, for whatever reasons.[14] Given their heavy reliance on this industry as a major earner of foreign exchange, these Asian textiles- and apparel-exporting countries are jealously guarding such industrial activity, as seen in the recent furore over the suspension of multi-fibre agreements that is likely to shift textiles production to China away from other poor developing countries.[15]

Furthermore, each advanced stage of structural transformation has produced a widening range of vertically concatenated multistage industries (or segments), the upper end of which is highly capital-intensive and technologically sophisticated, while the lower end is labour-intensive and technologically

[14] It is an important—often politically/emotionally charged—issue whether they are made better off, or exploited, as many feminists contend. But it is beyond the scope of this chapter, since it requires careful analysis. For a balanced analysis, however, see Bhagwati (2004, esp. Chap. 7).

[15] For example, Cambodia, whose garment industry currently 'employs over 200,000 people, and accounts for 80 per cent of the country's exports', is in dire danger of losing this only flourishing industry (*Economist* 2005: 42).

standardized—hence, the latter being more readily transferable to low-wage developing countries (see Figure 4.6) As a result, even higher-tier industries, especially cars, electronics, and telecommunications equipment, are transplanting or outsourcing their low-end production (mostly of standardized parts/components, as well as the low-value-added, low-profit lines of finished goods) to low-cost locations in the developing world. The same thing can be said about services such as back-office jobs, as seen in the growth of call centres in the developing countries, notably India.[16]

In the course of industrial progress, the manufacturing activities have become therefore vertically deep in production sequences, multiprocess/stage differentiable, and inter-process fragmented and divisible. In this connection, a division of labour between high-skilled and low-skilled jobs has deepened. And, in the context of globalization, the developing countries are increasingly given the opportunities to specialize in, and export, labour-intensive goods—not only final consumer goods (ranging from textiles, apparel, and toys to TV sets, computer monitors, and low-end cars) but also standardized intermediate capital goods such as parts and components in electronics, telecommunications, and cars.

Moreover, it should be emphasized that, thanks to the IT revolution and advances in transportation, the capacity of individual firms themselves in advanced countries—that is, at the firm level in addition to the economy and industry levels—to fragment their own vertical intra-firm chains of value-added activities and outsource low-end (non-core) businesses to the developing countries has sharply increased.

In short, both industrial upgrading (of the *inter*-industry/stage type) and refined vertical concatenation (of the *intra*-industry/stage type) have created godsend opportunities for the firms in the advanced and developing countries to pursue a new division of labour in productive activities across borders.

4.3.3. The USA as the First Lead Goose: The Originator of Concatenation Economies

What has happened in East Asia is owing to the convergence of three earlier structural dynamisms: (i) the USA pioneered in the development of new R&D-driven industries such as computers and microchips; (ii) Japan moved up the ladder of development from the lower tiers by first modernizing the war-torn light industries and heavy and chemical industries (that had already been established before the Second World War) and then, by entering into higher

[16] It should be noted, however, that outsourced back-office jobs create demand not for unskilled labour but for skilled labour (usually university graduates), hence causing a widening income gap. Yet the resultant rise in income—and economic growth—is likely to have a beneficial trickle-down effect on the poor.

value-added industries, as its wages rose and its capital accumulation proceeded; and (iii) other Asian countries at lower stages of economic development also soon initiated their catch-up growth by developing labour-intensive manufacturing for export, one group of economies at a time in a staggered sequence (first the NIEs, then ASEAN-4, and more recently China and Vietnam).

In the post-Second World War period, the USA, the hegemon of post-war capitalism, adopted a liberal trade policy toward Asia, especially during the cold war. It has been providing the major market for Asia's exports of labour-intensive goods. And the US import market for such goods, the market once captured but soon discarded by Japan, was quickly handed over to the NIEs, which in turn soon relayed it to ASEAN-4—and more recently to China and Vietnam. The successful growth of export-oriented labour-intensive manufacturing in Asia has been facilitated by FDI by multinational corporations not only from the USA and Europe but also—and more significantly—from Japan, the NIEs, and even ASEAN-4—that is, from within East Asia itself. Multinationals' FDI and outsourcing normally transplant onto the developing host countries'

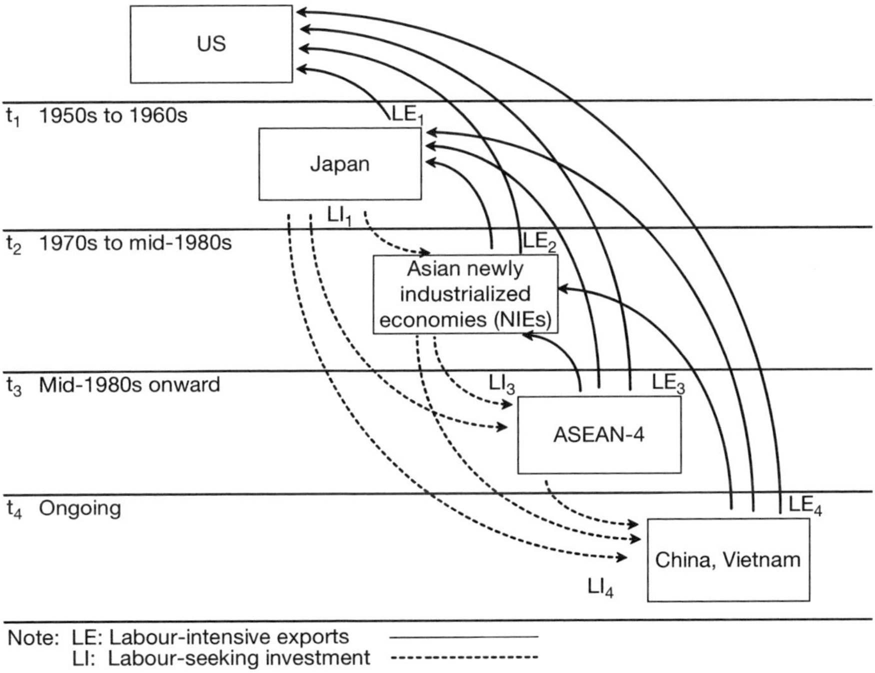

Fig. 4.7. Comparative advantage recycling in labour-intensive manufacturing via FDI and outsourcing

Source: Ozawa 1993.

modern management, technology, and access to export markets so as to activate or reinforce the developing countries' comparative advantage in labour-intensive goods and services (i.e., comparative advantage augmentation). These developments have combined to produce the phenomenon of intra-regional recycling of comparative advantage in low-end manufacturing via FDI, as illustrated schematically in Figure 4.7.

4.3.4. The Role of the Second Goose: Japan—and then the NIEs

In this connection, Japan has been playing a critical role as the second goose. It first captured the US market for labour-intensive exports and then handed it over to other Asian countries by way of transplanting Japan's comparatively disadvantaged industrial activities through Japanese multinational firms' operations. Simultaneously, Japan has been successful in scaling the ladder of development. As a consequence, Japan's rapid industrial upgrading has contributed to the spread of its low-end production of both the inter-industry and the intra-industry types to the rest of Asia. These structurally induced waves of overseas investment are depicted in Figure 4.8.

The evolutionary sequence of industrial upgrading—(i) labour-driven → (ii) scale-driven → (iii) assembly-driven → (iv) R&D-driven → (v) IT-driven—have been accompanied by its corresponding sequence of outward FDI and other business operations: (i′) the elementary stage of offshore production (or low-wage-seeking investment centred on labour-intensive light industries, such as toys and apparel); (ii′) resource-seeking and house-cleaning types of investment by heavy and chemical industries; (iii′) assembly-transplanting type of investment (inclusive of the low-cost labour-seeking type in parts, components, accessories, and low-end lines of products) by manufacturers of electronics and cars; and (iv′) alliance-seeking (strategically networking) type of business operations in production, marketing, and R&D (often and increasingly via mergers and acquisitions).

The faster the pace of Japan's catch-up growth by climbing up the ladder of industrial upgrading, the greater the pressure on—and the easier for—Japanese producers to transplant disadvantaged (low-value-added) industrial activities to low-cost locations in Japan's nearby countries so that they would be able to maintain and, in fact, enhance competitiveness in the world market (Ozawa 2005). Structural upgrading is no doubt one of the major sources of productivity growth, since it involves both technological progress and a reallocation of resources from low-value-added to higher-value-added activities. And the subsequent rises in productivity lead to higher wages overall, but especially to higher wages for skilled workers (thereby giving incentives for workers to upgrade their skills). Japan's high societal propensity to seek higher education and for firms to give on-the-job training under job security, prepared for, and facilitated, labour's adaptability to higher productivity activities. The supply of

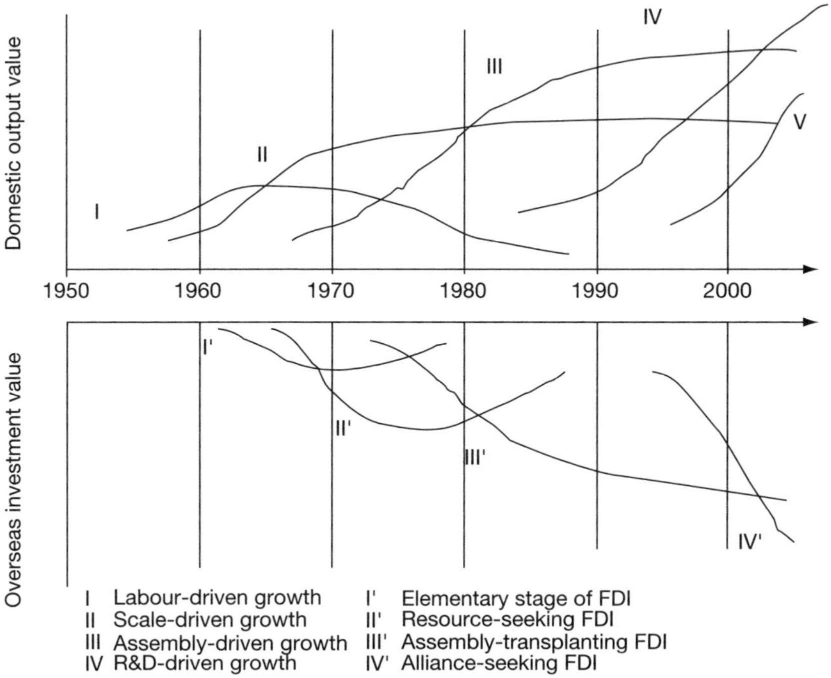

Fig. 4.8. Japan's stages of industrial upgrading and outward FDI

Source: Ozawa (1993).

low-skilled labour quickly declined, and such type of labour became a scarce factor. Japan's small archipelago and its nationwide network of compulsory universal education and public health did not allow the existence of any rural hinterland where an oversupply of uneducated and unskilled labour might have existed.[17]

The Japanese experience was soon to be replicated by the NIEs that followed Japan's footsteps. The NIEs in turn have quickly graduated from the labour-driven phase of catch-up growth and transferred (recycled) their labour-intensive manufacturing (hence their shares of the US markets) first to ASEAN-4 and more recently to China and Vietnam. This 'orderly' recycling/relaying of labour-intensive manufacturing is rather endemic to East Asia, a phenomenon that no other region has so far been able to replicate; and herein lies the key clue

[17] How Japan used policies and institutional arrangements during its high growth period is explored in Ozawa 2005. The post-Second World War land reform carried out during the occupation enabled about 4 million peasant households to acquire their own farmland and led to the eradication of rural poverty.

to East Asia's rapid growth and impressive rise in the overall standard of living (hence poverty alleviation).

4.3.5. Empirical Evidence

The above patterns of comparative advantage recycling as mirrored in the US import markets for labour-intensive goods are clearly revealed in Figure 4.9. The vertical axis measures the shares of the US market for labour-intensive manufactures captured by Japan, the NIEs, ASEAN-4, and China over the period of 1963–97. It can be seen that, on average, Japan lost its lead to the NIEs at the start of the 1970s. The NIEs, in turn, were able to attain a rising market share until the early 1980s and then began to experience a rapidly declining share; in 1992 they were finally taken over by China. By 1997, the shares of both the NIEs and Japan had dwindled and fallen behind both China and ASEAN-4, whose exports of labour-intensive goods to the USA had started soaring from the mid-1980s onward. It is also interesting to note that the US market shares of ASEAN-4 and China reversed in 1981, and that since then China's share has risen much faster than that of ASEAN-4, more than doubling in the late 1990s. China's soaring exports to the USA have been made possible by foreign multinationals' export-oriented investments and outsourcing operations attracted to, and induced by, China's low wages after the adoption of its open-door policy in 1987. In 1995, for example, FDI inflows in China registered US$35.8 billion, while those in ASEAN-4 were US$12.0 billion, the former nearly three times more than the latter (UNCTAD 1997).

The above patterns have also been econometrically tested in terms of co-integration analysis (Cutler, Berri, and Ozawa 2003 for labour-intensive exports; Cutler and Ozawa 2007 for TV set exports). These studies affirm the pattern of comparative-advantage recycling. The former in particular points out one interesting adjustment phenomenon: the first round of recycling from Japan to the NIEs was slower than the second round of recycling from the NIEs to ASEAN-4 (and from the NIEs to China). Why was this the case? There were several developments that were responsible for the phenomenon. First of all, Japan began to shift away from labour-intensive exports to more capital-intensive ones (such as steel, ships, and machinery) as early as the 1950s. In other words, Japan's graduation from the labour-intensive stage was so swift that the NIEs at that time were not yet fully prepared to take over Japan's US market share. The speed with which Japan moved up the ladder of development away from the labour-intensive tier is reflected in Figure 4.10, which shows that the ratio of labour-intensive exports to total manufactured exports from Japan declined precipitously from 40 per cent in 1960 to as low as 6 per cent in 1974. At that time, indeed, the NIEs (except Hong Kong) were still pursuing inward-looking, import-substituting strategies and were not in a position immediately to take possession of Japan's rapidly declining US market share.

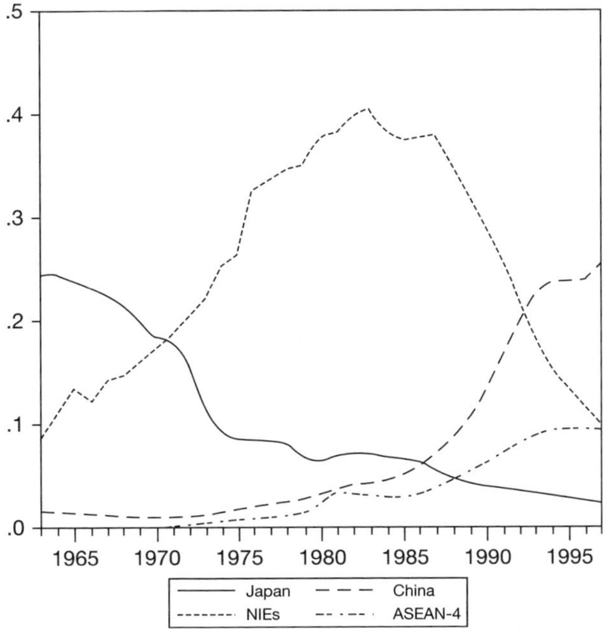

Fig. 4.9. US import market share for labour-intensive goods

Source: Cutler, Berri, and Ozawa (2003).

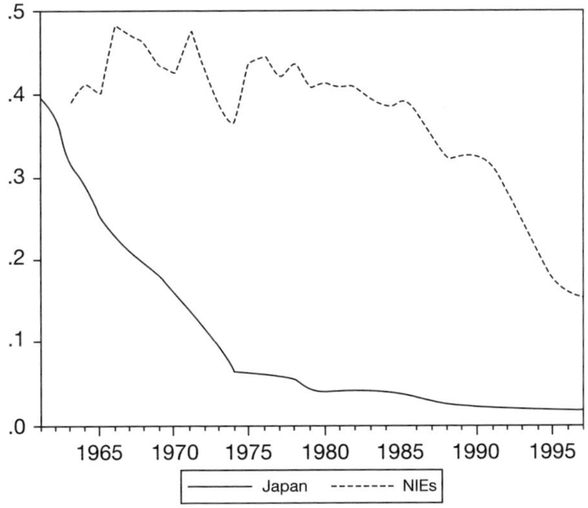

Fig. 4.10. The ratio of labour-intensive exports to total manufactured exports, Japan and NIEs

Source: Cutler, Berri, and Ozawa (2003).

It was not until 1965, for example, that Taiwan opened its first export-processing zone in Kaohsiung, and not until 1970 that South Korea set up an export-processing zone in Masan, the first landmark of their adoption of export-oriented policy. These zones soon hosted Japanese enterprises as major foreign investors and joint-venture partners. In short, there was thus a lag between Japan's retreat from, and the NIEs' full entry into, the labour-intensive export market.

In contrast, market recycling from the NIEs to ASEAN-4 and China was better coordinated in timing. As the NIEs began to lose competitiveness in labour-intensive goods as a result of rapid growth in the 1970s, ASEAN-4, almost simultaneously, and then China in the 1980s, opened up for inward investment in these goods. In fact, the miraculous growth of the NIEs triggered China's decision to switch to an export-oriented development strategy. Moreover, both ASEAN-4 and China came to be assisted by export-oriented investments not only from the NIEs but also from Japan and the USA, enabling them quickly to build up labour-intensive exports. In addition, so far as FDI in China is concerned, the largest group of investors is neither from Japan nor from the USA, but mainly from the ethnic Chinese NIEs (Hong Kong, Taiwan, and Singapore) and the overseas Chinese diasporas in ASEAN-4. Consequently, there were much faster transplantations of labour-intensive manufacturing through the networks of ethnic Chinese businessmen from one place to another.[18] (These geographical features are again endemic to East Asia alone, and not observable in any other regions.)

Reflective of the recycling of labour-intensive manufacturing for export, it is expected that FDI in East Asia's labour-intensive manufacturing is mostly from within East Asia itself—rather than from the advanced west.[19] The multinational corporations from the latter are, on the whole, more likely to set up production in capital-intensive, high-tech manufacturing, though some (especially mass merchandisers such as Walmart) are also active in outsourcing and procuring labour-intensive manufactures from the Asian suppliers. In contrast, Asian multinationals, especially from the NIEs and the Chinese diasporas, are more labour intensive in manufacturing activities—hence more wage sensitive and more capable of managing local workers in the Asian host countries.

This sequential process of comparative-advantage recycling can continue down the hierarchy of economies by repeating the same experience each time. Obviously, a multiplication of derived incomes is not as exact as depicted above; the size of the labour-intensive, low-end markets 'captured' from the leader economy by followers certainly varies each time, and the second-rank followers—and the third-rank followers—themselves in turn add to the markets

[18] For an earlier empirical work, see also Berri and Ozawa (1997).

[19] For example, more than half of FDI in ASEAN-4 is from Japan, the NIEs, and ASEAN-4 themselves, and the major investors in China are from the NIEs.

to be handed down to still lower-rank followers. These added details, however, do not negate the main point. There is a significant effect of the tandem development multiplier on the growth of outward-oriented, labour-driven economies in Asia, as low-end markets and industries are passed around and re-exploited among themselves.

Indeed, tandem development can alleviate one problem (the 'fallacy of composition') of outward-looking, export-focused industrialization: if the developing countries adopt such an export-dependent strategy all at once, will there still be enough markets for every country? Balassa answers in the affirmative:

> The stages approach to comparative advantage... permits one to dispel certain misapprehensions as regards the foreign demand constraint for manufactured exports under which developing countries are said to operate. With countries progressing on the comparative advantage scale, their exports can supplant the exports of countries that graduate to a higher level. (Balassa 1989: 28)

This ideal process of supplanting 'the exports of countries that graduate to a higher level' has indeed so far occurred from Japan and the NIEs to ASEAN-4 and to China. For a successful recycling of comparative advantages to occur, it is imperative for upper-echelon countries to climb up the chain value quickly, and willingly relay their increasingly comparatively disadvantaged production onto lower-echelon countries. In other words, their capacities to metamorphose themselves structurally are one key enabling factor in comparative-advantage recycling. In this regard, Japan and the NIEs, not to speak of the USA, have clearly demonstrated such capacity in part because of their institutional flexibilities, particularly in the labour markets.

It should be noted, however, that the emergence of China as the world's major labour-driven manufacturer is no doubt creating a problem to other developing countries that are in the same early phase of labour-driven development and are still unable to 'graduate to a higher level', as is largely the case with ASEAN-4 (and, for that matter, many Latin American countries). Because of the pure size of China, with its enormous labour supply, what is true for China (i.e., labour-driven development pays off for China) may no longer be true for the rest of the developing world as a whole—that is, a fallacy of composition.

4.4. Summing Up

In what way does this reformulated FG model, the model of comparative-advantage recycling in labour-intensive goods, provide a useful framework of analysis to shed light on the unusually strong nexus of globalization–growth–poverty alleviation in Asia, especially in East Asia? In the first place, as posited in the paradigm, the present hierarchy of industries that exists in the global economy provides the five-stage ladder of structural transformation any aspiring catching-up country could climb up, starting with the most labour-intensive segment of industrial activity. (Comparative-advantage recycling is most workable in this segment.) For example, it is clearly quixotic for any developing country (where the abundance of unskilled labour is the potential basis for its comparative advantage) to try, in its early developmental phase, to take up the task of building capital-intensive, high-tech manufacturing (such as cars and aircraft) or R&D-driven Schumpeterian industries. Such a country obviously needs to start out with the lowest tiers of industry (i.e., low-tech Heckscher–Ohlin industries) which are commensurate with its labour abundance and level of technological sophistication—hence the most practical, most appropriate, and easiest ones to develop in terms of its natural potential for comparative advantage. At the same time, however, the higher tiers of industry, especially assembly-based manufacturing and Internet -enabled services also have created godsend opportunities for developing countries to participate in the low-end and labour-intensive segments of advanced industries.

Indeed, all the successful Asian economies have been following such a natural sequence of orderly progression up the ladder of development, starting from labour-intensive production—natural in the sense of compatibility with their factor endowments and skill levels. The main asset of the poor countries for long-term growth, whether they are endowed with natural resources or not, is no doubt their abundant labour, which needs to be mobilized and activated for gainful employment as the first requisite of industrialization. After all, employment of unskilled labour is the *sine qua non* of any poor country's development and poverty eradication. Labour-intensive manufacturing is the mandate of early-stage development.

Fortunately, the USA, as the hegemon of post-Second World War global capitalism, has been willingly offering the developing countries, notably in East Asia, its domestic markets for labour-intensive goods and services throughout the post-war period—during the cold war for geopolitical reasons and more recently because of its high propensity to outsource production across borders to the lowest-cost-possible locations anywhere in the world and control inflation at home. Indeed, this segment of the US market has also come to be used as a tool of US foreign aid, as seen in the African Growth and Stabilization Act, US bilateral free trade agreements with some developing countries such as Chile and Jordan, and the Central American Free Trade Agreement. It is up to developing countries to capitalize on the US market.

It is against the backdrop of America's relatively liberal trade policy that as one developing Asian country (first, Japan) has graduated from the labour-driven stage of development, those US import markets for labour-intensive goods are being passed on/relayed to another country (the NIEs, then ASEAN-4, and, most recently, China and Vietnam) in a staggered fashion, FG style. And, in this process, the paradox of 'labour abundance as a labour shortage' has been observed repeatedly. The first lead goose, the USA, has unarguably been the foremost *market (demand) provider.*[20] In the meantime, Japan and the NIEs, as the second geese, have so far been mostly the *capacity augmenters*, transferring and supplying all the necessary managerial, technical, and marketing skills, as well as intermediate goods—in the capacity of direct investors in, and procurers from, the lower-ranking follower geese, ASEAN-4, China, and Vietnam. As a consequence, demand for low-skilled labour has been expanding, thereby contributing to the reduction of poverty.

This favourable outcome can thus best be understood in terms of the FG paradigm of comparative-advantage recycling in labour-intensive goods, the paradigm that includes all the pro-poor attributes of trade, investment, and growth that have fortuitously been created under the Asian Pacific co-growth cluster led by the USA. In short, the evolving hierarchies of countries and industries have most cogently meshed and interacted with each other—at both market (unconscious) and policy (conscious) levels—in Asia to produce the most dynamic pattern of mutual economic growth the world has seen. In particular, pro-trade type of FDI, that can magnify the comparative costs, led to an expansion of exports in labour-intensive sectors, providing employment opportunities for the unskilled. And this pro-growth system has so far provided an unprecedented opportunity for poverty reduction.

However, how long this regime of comparative-advantage recycling lasts all depends on the capacity of the USA to absorb Asia's labour-intensive goods and services. And fears are expressed that the rest of the world might no longer be willing to finance the ever-rising US current account deficit and budgetary deficit resulting from bailouts and huge stimulus packages, thereby leading to a crash of the US$. America's financial crisis that began to unfold in the autumn of 2008 quickly spread to the rest of the world, especially Europe. Even Asia that managed largely to escape from the initial subprime debacle is likewise plagued by investors' loss of confidence. The current global recession has already started to reduce employment across Asia. Even in still vibrant China migrant (poor) workers are forced en masse to return to their villages.

[20] It is said that China surpassed the USA in 2004 as Japan's top trading partner. True, China replaced the USA as the largest exporter to Japan (US$57.6 billion from the USA versus US$61.7 billion from China). This reflects Japan's own procurement-aimed FDI and original equipment manufacturing (OEM) in China, as well as transmigration of export-oriented manufacturers from the NIEs to China, especially in IT-related electronics industries. Yet, the USA is still Japan's largest market (US$118.6 billion to the USA versus US$39.9 billion to China in 2002), though China is closing the gap at double-digit rates (e.g., a 28.2 per cent jump in 2002 (JETRO 2003)).

References

Abramovitz, M. (1986) 'Catching Up, Forging Ahead, and Falling Behind', *Journal of Economic History*, 46: 385–406.

Akamatsu, K. (1935) 'Wagakuni Yomo Kogyohin no Susei' [Trend of Japan's Woollen Product Industry], *Shogyo Keizai Ronso*, 13: 129–212.

—— (1961) 'A Theory of Unbalanced Growth in the World Economy', *Weltwirtschaftliches Archiv*, 86: 196–215.

Asian Development Bank (ADB) (2004) *Key Indicators of Developing Asian and Pacific Countries*. Manila: ADB.

—— (2005) *An Initial Assessment of the Impact of the Earthquake and Tsunami of December 26, 2004 on South and Southeast Asia* (Jan.) Manila: ADB.

Balassa, B. (1989) *Comparative Advantage, Trade Policy and Economic Development*. New York: New York University Press.

Berger, P. L., and S. P. Huntington (eds) (2002) *Many Globalizations: Cultural Diversity in the Contemporary World*. New York: Oxford University Press.

Berri, D., and T. Ozawa (1997) 'Pax Americana and Asian Exports: Revealed Trends of Comparative Advantage Recycling', *International Trade Journal*, 11: 39–67.

Bhagwati, J. (1958) 'Immiserizing Growth: A Geometrical Note', *Review of Economic Studies*, 25: 201–5.

—— (2004) *In Defense of Globalization*. New York: Oxford University Press.

Cutler, H., D. J. Berri, and T. Ozawa (2003) 'Market Recycling in Labour-intensive Goods, Flying Geese Style: An Empirical Analysis of East Asian Exports to the US', *Journal of Asian Economics*, 14: 35–50.

—— and T. Ozawa (2007) 'The Dynamics of the "Mature" Product Cycle and Market Recycling, Flying Geese Style: An Empirical Examination and Policy Implications', *Contemporary Economic Policy*, 25: 67–78.

Dollar, D., and A. Kraay (2001) 'Trade, Growth, and Poverty'. Working Paper 2615. Washington, DC: World Bank, Development Research Group.

—— —— (2002) 'Growth is Good for the Poor', *Journal of Economic Growth*, 7: 195–225.

Dunning, J. H. (2003) *Making Globalisation Good: The Moral Challenges of Global Capitalism*. Oxford: Oxford University Press.

Eatwell, J. (1982) *Whatever Happened to Britain? The Economics of Decline*. London: BBC.

Graham, E. M. (2000) 'Fighting the Wrong Enemy: Antiglobal Activists and Multinational Enterprises'. Washington, DC: Institute for International Economics.

Irwin, D. A. (1996) *Against the Tide: An Intellectual History of Free Trade*. Princeton, NJ: Princeton University Press.

Japan External Trade Organization (JETRO) (2003) *JETRO Boeki Toshi Hakusho* (JETRO White Paper on Trade and Investment). Tokyo: JETRO.

Kojima, K. (1973) 'A Macroeconomic Approach to Foreign Direct Investment', *Hitotsubashi Journal of Economics*, 12: 1–21.

—— (2003) *Gankokei Keizai Hattenron* [The Flying Geese Theory of Economic Development], i. Tokyo: Bunshindo.

—— (2004) *Gankokei Keizai Hattenron* [The Flying Geese Theory of Economic Development], ii. Tokyo: Bunshindo.

——and T. Ozawa (1985) 'Toward a Theory of Industrial Restructuring and Dynamic Comparative Advantage', *Hitotsubashi Journal of Economics*, 26: 135–45.

Mann, C. L. (2004) 'Managing Exchange Rates: Achievement of Global Re-balancing or Evidence of Global Co-dependency?', *Business Economics*, July: 20–9.

Nissanke, M., and E. Thorbecke (2005) 'Channels and Policy Debate in the Globalization–Inequality–Poverty Nexus'. Discussion Paper 2005/08. Helsinki: UNU-WIDER.

————(2008) 'Introduction: Globalization–Poverty Channels and Case Studies from Sub-Saharan Africa', *African Development Review*, 20: 1–19.

Ohkawa, K., and H. Rosovsky (1972) *Japanese Economic Growth*. Palo Alto, Calif.: Stanford University Press.

Ozawa, T. (1993) 'Foreign Direct Investment and Structural Transformation: Japan as a Recycler of Market and Industry', *Business and the Contemporary World*, 5: 129–49.

——(1996) 'Japan'. In J. Dunning (ed.), *Governments, Globalization, and International Business*. Oxford: Oxford University Press.

——(2003) 'Pax Americana-led Macro-clustering and Flying Geese-style Catch-up in East Asia: Mechanisms of Regionalized Endogenous Growth', *Journal of Asian Economics*, 13: 699–713.

——(2004) 'The Chinese Miracle and the "Flying Geese" Paradigm of Catch-up Growth'. Paper presented at the Ninth International Conference of the East Asian Economic Association, 13–14 Nov. 2004, Hong Kong.

——(2005) *Institutions, Industrial Upgrading, and Economic Performance in Japan: The 'Flying Geese' Paradigm of Catch-up Growth*. Cheltenham: Edward Elgar.

Prebisch, R. (1950) *The Economic Development of Latin America and its Principal Problems*. New York: United Nations.

Rosenberg, N. (1982) *Inside the Black Box: Technology and Economics*. Cambridge: Cambridge University Press.

Schumpeter, J. A. (1942) *Capitalism, Socialism and Democracy*. New York: Harper & Row.

Singer, H. W. (1950) 'The Distribution of Gains between Borrowing and Investing Countries', *American Economic Review*, 40: 473–85.

Stiglitz, J. (2003) 'Towards a New Paradigm of Development'. In J. Dunning (ed.), *Making Globalization Good: The Moral Challenges of Global Capitalism*. Oxford: Oxford University Press: 76–107.

United Nations Conference on Trade and Development (UNCTAD) (1997) *World Investment Report*. Geneva: UNCTAD.

Winters, A. L. (2004) 'Trade Liberalisation and Economic Performance: An Overview', *Economic Journal*, 114: F4–F21.

World Bank (1993) *The East Asian Miracle: Economic Growth and Public Policy*. New York: Oxford University Press.

5

Globalization, Growth, and Poverty in India

N. R. Bhanumurthy and Arup Mitra[1]

5.1. Introduction

Globalization embodies increased import penetration, export sales, competition in services FDI, and exchange-rate fluctuations prompted by international capital movements. As Rama (2003) defines, globalization is the combination of these changes in the way the developing countries interact with the rest of the world. In other words, it is the process through which the domestic factors of production such as labour and capital will be integrated with the world economy. The process of globalization in India was initiated in 1991 in order to give an impetus to the output growth rate and to help the economy recover from the foreign exchange crisis and fiscal imbalances. But the benefits of these reforms in terms of rise in incomes are obviously not expected to reach different sections of the population equally. One view is that the poor may benefit from economic growth only indirectly and, hence, the proportional benefits of growth going to the poor will always be less than those accruing to the non-poor. In other words, in the process of economic growth in the initial stages, the positive effects of growth on the poor tend to get offset by the adverse effects of inequality rising, as suggested by Kuznets (1955). However, if economic growth is accompanied by a decline in inequality, the poor benefit more than the non-poor—the situation is described in the literature as *pro-poor growth* (see Kakwani, Prakash, and Son 2000; Kakwani and Pernia 2000). Even when inequality rises, observed poverty may still decline if the growth effect dominates the inequality

[1] The authors would like to thank Professors Machiko Nissanke and Erik Thorbecke as well as Professor Nanak Kakwani and other conference participants for their comments and suggestions. The authors are also grateful to Professor Jean Drèze for his insightful comments on the earlier version of the chapter.

effect—that is, the extent of fall in poverty due to growth is larger than the rise in poverty due to a rise in inequality.

Given the wide regional variations in India in terms of socio-economic development and initial conditions, economic reforms have been initiated at different levels and at different points in time across the states. Most of the reforms have been pursued in the industrial sector, the spread and growth of which show considerable regional variations. Availability of infrastructure, which is a strong determinant of industrial productivity, mobility, and income earnings, also varies significantly across the states (Mitra 1997) Hence, it is expected that economic growth would have wide regional variations and further that the changing income distribution in the process of growth would also be different across states.

Among several outcomes, population mobility across space is one, which is directly influenced by economic growth. The spatial composition of growth, reflected in terms of rural–urban development disparity, motivates people to shift to areas with better employment prospects. As total poverty is a weighted average of rural and urban specific poverty ratios, the net effect of population mobility on poverty depends on the changes in its rural and urban components. Since economic reforms are more urban-based, the spatial composition of growth is expected to change, resulting in a migration of population from rural to urban areas. The decline in the incidence of poverty (rural–urban combined) depends on whether urban employment opportunities are large enough to absorb the increasing supplies of labour from the rural areas. A large number of empirical studies exist to suggest that rural migrants have been able to escape poverty, though they could not graduate to the urban formal sector (Banerjee 1986; Mitra 1994; 2003; Papola 1981). Even when the incidence of urban poverty rises due to rural–urban migration, the decline in the combined poverty ratio may be evident with a fall in the rural poverty incidence occurring in response to out-migration. This is precisely because the weight of urban poverty is much less in the poverty for all areas combined poverty to the rural poverty.

It is not only the overall growth but also the composition of growth, which is important for poverty reduction. If the poor are mostly concentrated in the agricultural sector, it is natural that agriculture-led growth would reduce poverty. However, as Kuznets (1966) points out, in the process of economic development, both the value-added mix and workforce structure shift away from agriculture. Hence, recommending an agriculture-led growth may be counter-intuitive. One may, therefore, suggest that the growth of the industrial sector or that of the overall commodity-producing sector plays an important role in reducing poverty. However, several tertiary activities also play a key role in generating economic growth. It has been observed that the entire tertiary sector is not parasitic in nature (Bhattacharya and Mitra 1997); a large segment, particularly in the context of liberalization, is strongly associated with the commodity-producing sector. Activities, which were earlier conducted within the manufacturing sector, for example, are being undertaken separately because of greater specialization, and, hence, these may form a part of the tertiary sector. This would, therefore, call for a careful interpretation of the tertiary sector rather than treating it purely as redundant. In other words, tertiarization of value added may also play a role in poverty reduction as it can generate employment and simultaneously enhance real income. In other words, in the context of poverty reduction, the changing composition of growth does not imply a rise only in the share of industry, but rather in industry and tertiary sectors that both accompany the declining share of agriculture (see Ravallion and Datt 1996).

According to the 'over-urbanization thesis', if the industry can absorb on a large scale the semi-skilled and unskilled labour released from the agriculture sector, poverty would decline. Hence, it is not merely industrialization in terms of value added, but rather it is the poor vis-à-vis the employment generated in the manufacturing, that is crucial for reducing poverty. Similarly, a rise in industrial productivity translating into a rise in the income of the workers would have implications in terms of a decline in poverty (Mitra 1992). On the whole, both the industrialization of value added and the workforce, resulting in a rise in productivity, would help reduce poverty.

In order to examine some of these hypotheses in the context of globalization, we have conducted two decomposition exercises. The first exercise, following Kakwani (2000) and Mazumdar and Son (2002), decomposes the change in incidence of poverty over two time points in terms of pure growth effect (holding inequality constant), inequality effect (holding growth constant), and population-shift effect. Such an analysis enables a critical analysis of the policy issues and offers a profound understanding of the reform process. However, it may be noted that in doing such an exercise, only the expenditure inequality has been considered which is a gross underestimate of income/asset inequality. Similarly, the growth effect is envisaged in terms of mean effect—the mean of consumption expenditure per capita—which is again a gross underestimate of per capita income. As data on income and its distribution are not available, these crude proxies are followed and are based on the national sample survey data on expenditure per capita and its size distribution.[2]

In assessing the population-shift effect, the percentages of population residing in urban and rural areas are considered, which in addition to rural–urban migration also include the differentials in rural–urban natural growth of population, and the rise (fall) in the level of urbanization (percentage of rural population) due to reclassification of areas. Hence, it may not be justified to

[2] There are alternative measures of poverty figures estimated by independent researchers. But, since these are different from each other, we have considered the poverty figures based on Planning Commission's Modified Expert Group Methodology.

perceive the population-shift effect purely in terms of rural–urban migration, which can again comprise interstate as well as intra-state streams, not deciphered in the study. Therefore while interpreting the results, these limitations need to be kept in view. The second exercise expresses poverty in terms of per capita income, share of industry in GDP, manufacturing labour productivity, and the ratio of poor to manufacturing employment. The details about these exercises are discussed in section 5.4. Section 5.5 discusses the database used in this study. The empirical results are interpreted in section 5.6, while section 5.7 summarizes the major findings of the study. But, before discussing the technical framework, in the next section we discuss the impact of globalization on growth and in section 5.3 we discuss changes in some of the variables such as incidence of poverty, per capita income, and urbanization over time. The analysis has been carried out in the subsequent sections with a view to highlighting the changes that occurred in the pre-reform and reform periods.

5.2. Globalization and Growth

As part of globalization and liberalization in India, the government has undertaken initiatives in certain areas that possibly were hindering the growth of the economy. The production sectors were opened up for the private sector, both domestic and foreign. This has resulted in the inflow of foreign investment and at the same time the shrinking of the public sector. Hence, the focus has shifted from equity to growth. Further, the government has tried to remove the state-imposed market distortions to improve efficiency and productivity. The government has also significantly brought down the trade barriers. All these measures are expected to improve the growth performance of the economy.

The policy measures that were initiated in the early 1990s appear to have increased the output growth in the country. This is evident in Figure 5.1, wherein both actual and forecasts of GDP growth are plotted. The forecasts are based on an appropriate econometric model using the information from 1960–1 to 1990–1. In this exercise we try to see what could have been the GDP growth if the reforms had not been initiated in the early 1990s, or if there had been no regime shift. It is quite clear that if there was no reform, the GDP growth might have been well below the actual. This is also clear from Figure 5.2, wherein the figures on differences between the actual and forecasted GDP levels are presented. As appears from both charts, there has been a structural shift upwards since 1993–4. Furthermore, the average output growth in the reform period has been above 6 per cent, indicating that the Indian economy has shifted above from its 'Hindu rate of growth' of 4 per cent to 'Bharat rate of growth' at 6 per cent. This is a very significant shift and has come within a short period. Virmani (2005) argues that the reforms have indeed helped increase the total factor productivity growth and have resulted in higher economic growth.

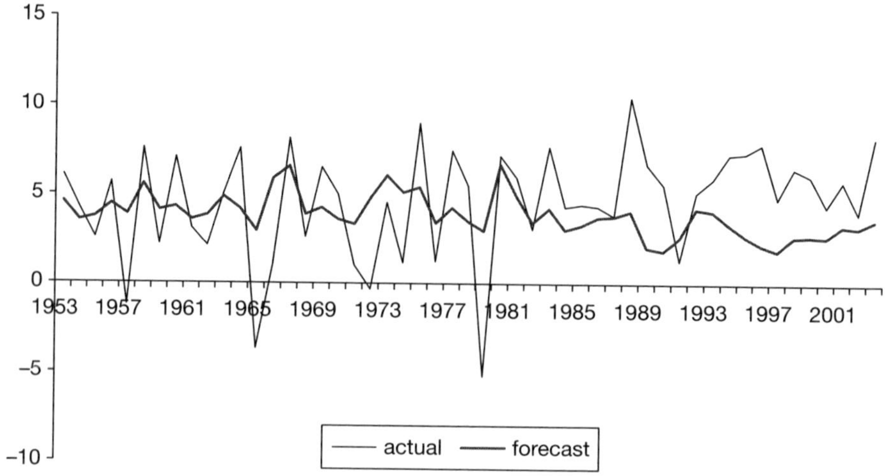

Fig. 5.1. Actual and projected GDP growth in India

Source: Actual growth figures taken from Reserve Bank of India 2003–4; projected growth computed by the authors.

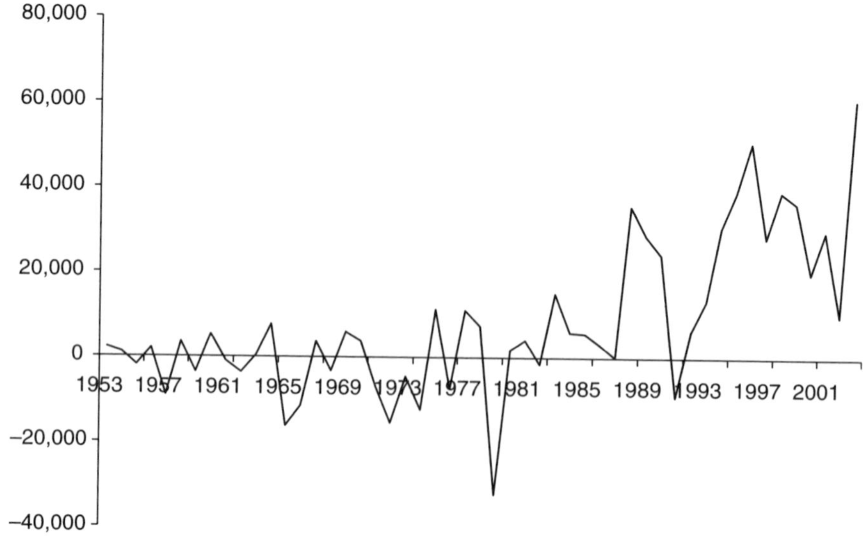

Fig. 5.2. GDP growth differentials in India

Source: Computed by the authors based on Figure 5.1.

Further, this rise in growth has contributed to reduction in poverty incidence more than expected.

This shift in the growth curve is basically due to the change in the composition of GDP. The share of the agricultural sector in GDP, which was nearly 50 per cent, has come down drastically to 22 per cent, while the share of the tertiary sector has gone up to 50 per cent, keeping the share of the industrial sector almost at its historical figures. But this shift in the value-added composition has not been reflected in the employment structure. Still, a large majority of the labour force depends on the agricultural sector for livelihood, whereas the industry and service sectors are unable to absorb the additional labour force. This has led to the criticism that the current rise in the output growth is basically a 'jobless growth'. One needs to examine whether these are some shortfalls occurring in the initial stages of the globalization process, after which positive gains would follow. Although the international experience is not clear in this regard, this issue needs to be addressed urgently as this would have severe adverse impact on the poor in the economy reducing the possibility of achieving the MDGs of the United Nations.

Increasing globalization also means that the domestic economy needs to share both global 'good' and 'bad'. What it means is that globalization provides both opportunities as well as risks. The spread of the recent global financial crisis, which emanated from the developed markets to the developing countries and least developed countries (LDCs), is a clear example of the risks that are associated with globalization. But the adverse effects of this global risk are expected to be much larger on the developing countries and LDCs than that on the developed nations.

The Asia Pacific region, which, together with Africa, is the largest home for people below the poverty line, is expected to see large adverse impact of the present global crisis on both growth and also on income distribution/poverty as well. The first-round effects of this crisis have already shown in terms of a sharp rise in the domestic inflation levels through increase in the world food and fuel prices. And the second round impact is expected to materialize through a fall in the growth of output that will hamper the income distribution. The World Bank (2008) study showed that rise in inflation alone would push nearly 100 million people below the poverty line across the globe. The recent study by UNDP (2008) showed that in the Asia Pacific region alone it would push nearly 57 million people below the poverty line by 2009. This means that the UN efforts to achieve the MDGs will be pushed back by nearly seven years. The same study shows that GDP growth in the Asia Pacific region is expected to decline by about 2 per cent in 2008 compared to 2007. Based on forecasts provided by the international agencies, it appears that the growth in 2009 could be much less than in 2008.

In India, as well, the impact of the global crisis has resulted in a sharp rise in inflation rates. But the peak rate of 12.44 per cent is much less compared to any other country in the South Asia region. In terms of output growth, it is predicted that India's growth would decline to 7 per cent in 2008–9, compared to nearly 9 per cent in 2007–8. Based on the theoretical framework that is presented in section 5.4, it is expected that globalization and growth are positively and negatively related with the poverty incidence. Hence, this global crisis is expected to reduce the output growth and, hence, increase the poverty incidence in India as well.

One important view in the context of growth and globalization suggests that economic growth is a positive function of globalization, as the latter facilitates free mobilization of resources. Hence, by specializing in labour-intensive exportable goods, low-income and labour-surplus countries can accelerate growth, generate employment, and reduce poverty. However, technological innovation can bring in a shift in the demand for skilled labour and, hence, can reduce the wages of the less skilled, implying a rise in wage inequality (Feenstra and Hanson 1996). Though this concern has been primarily expressed in the context of the developed countries, the same logic can be extended to the developing countries as well if they import technology from the former. Research for various Latin American countries is indicative of widening the impact of trade on wage inequality, and, more importantly this is spearheaded by the notion of skill-biased technological change induced through trade.

On the whole, though freer trade or trade openness is believed to enhance economic growth, the anti-globalization strand views it as socially malign on several dimensions including poverty (Bhagwati and Srnivasan 2002). However, highlighting the findings of Dollar (2001), Bhagwati and Srnivasan (2002) point out that countries which registered significant declines in poverty are also the ones which integrated faster into the world economy in terms of trade and direct investment, and, hence, it would not be correct to suggest that trade openness bypasses poverty. Rivera-Baitz and Xie (1992) also argued that knowledge diffusion and trade in ideas through a GATT-type patent system are needed for the whole world to grow faster, and thus argued for multilateral liberalization that comprises trade in goods and ideas both.

5.3. Some Broad Indicators

The incidence of poverty in rural India declined from 45.61 per cent in 1983 to 37.27 per cent in 1993–4 (see Table 5.1). Between 1993–4 and 1999–2000, it declined by 10.18 percentage points, the extent of fall being larger than in the previous period. This trend is similar even in urban India. The decline in poverty has been accompanied by an increase in the average per capita consumption expenditure, which rose by 18.3 and 11.3 per cent (in constant prices) over the period from 1983 up to and including 1993–4 and from 1993–4 up to and including 1999–2000, respectively. Per capita GDP also

Table 5.1. Trend in poverty and other variables in India, 1983–2000

	1983			1993–4			1999–2000		
Variables	Rural	Urban	Total	Rural	Urban	Total	Rural	Urban	Total
Poverty (%)	45.61	42.15	44.48	37.27	33.66	35.97	27.09	23.62	26.1
APCE (Rs.)	240.0	381.0	273.5	281.4	458.0	328.3	309.0	515.4	367.6
TWFPR	44.5	34.0	42.0	44.4	34.7	41.8	41.7	33.7	39.4
GDPPC (Rs)		6619.0			8740.0			11438.0	
Urbanization		23.79			26.57			28.4	

Notes: TWFPR Total workforce participation rate (principal and subsidiary status).
GDPPC Per capita gross domestic product (factor cost, 1993–4 prices).
Urbanization Urban population : total population.
APCE Average per capita consumption expenditure (1993–4 prices).

Source: Government of India (2001).

increased by 27.8 and 26.9 per cent over the same periods. This has been accompanied by an increase in the level of urbanization (defined as the ratio of urban population to total population). The workforce participation rate, which is defined as the principal plus subsidiary status worker as a percentage of the total population, remained more or less the same in the rural areas in the first subperiod, whereas it declined by almost 2.7 percentage points in the second subperiod. On the other hand, in the urban areas, it increased marginally by 0.7 percentage point in first subperiod and fell subsequently by almost one percentage point in the second period.

It appears that the decline in the incidence of poverty, particularly in the 1990s, has been accompanied by a fall in the workforce participation rate and a rise in per capita income and the per capita consumption expenditure. Can all this be viewed as the contribution of economic reforms, which led to higher growth in the 1990s; or to the change in the composition of growth and/or change in inequality in the process of growth? It would, therefore, be interesting to examine the contribution of different factors in reducing poverty over the 1980s and 1990s.

5.4. Technical Framework

Several studies in the Indian context have been pursued to assess the impact of economic growth on poverty. Ahluwalia (1978) cites evidence in favour of agricultural growth trickling down to benefit the poor in rural India. Jain and Tendulkar (1990) examine the relative strengths of growth and redistribution in changing the headcount ratio of poverty over the period 1970–1 to 1983. Mitra (1992) shows that the impact of industrial growth on urban poverty was only nominal, which is reconfirmed by Ravallion and Datt (1996) in the case of rural as well as urban areas. The recent report by ILO (2006) shows that in countries such as India and China growth has been very impressive and most of it had the potential to reduce poverty. The report also adds that because of this reason the overall poverty incidence in these countries has declined sharply compared to other countries in Asia. Overall, the debate around growth and poverty seems to have arrived at a consensus that growth is necessary, but not sufficient, for poverty reduction. Growth is said to be pro-poor 'when it is labour absorbing and accompanied by policies and programmes that mitigate inequalities and facilitate income and employment generation for the poor, particularly women and other traditionally excluded groups' (ADB 1999: 6 n. 6). It is defined as what enables the poor actively and directly to participate in and significantly benefit from economic activity (Kakwani and Pernia 2000). Chen and Ravallion (2000), for instance, argue that persistent poverty in many countries is the result of persistent inequalities—both economic and non-economic—that have prevented the poor from participating in the growth that did occur. Hence, a strategy that is biased in favour of the poor to enable them to benefit proportionally more than the rich needs to be the basis of pro-poor growth (Kakwani and Pernia 2000).

Decomposing the change in the poverty index into a growth and distribution effect was initiated by Kakwani and Subbarao (1990) and Jain and Tendulkar (1990), while quite a few alternative decomposition methods have been developed subsequently—for example, by Datt and Ravallion (1992), Kakwani (2000), and Mazumdar and Son (2002); a synthesis of these methods are given in the Appendix to this chapter. Based on this, the present study estimates below an equation to decompose the change in the incidence of poverty in terms of mean effect, inequality effect, and the effect due to population shift from rural to urban areas, in fifteen major Indian states individually, and at the all-India level for the two subperiods 1983 to 1993–4 and 1993–4 to 1999–2000.

$$\frac{\Delta P}{P} = \sum_i \frac{\bar{f}_i P_i}{P} \frac{M_i}{P_i} + \sum_i \frac{\bar{f}_i P_i}{P} \frac{I_i}{P_i} + \sum_i \frac{\bar{P}_i f_i}{P} \frac{\Delta f_i}{f_i}$$

where f_k and P_k are the population share and poverty index of the kth group, respectively, and M and I are mean and inequality effect.[3]

Equality, as defined by Tendulkar and Jain (1995), is an unambiguous reduction in poverty as well as an increase in social welfare. However, to judge distributional outcomes entirely on the basis of relative inequality—that is, in

[3] Besley, Burgess, and Esteve-Volart (2004) also examine these issues with the help of the decomposition exercise following Datt and Ravallion (1992). But, as it may be noted in the Appendix to this chapter, the problems in Datt and Ravallion (1992) were addressed in the methodology developed in Kakwani (2000) and Mazumdar and Son (2002) and, hence, the present study follows the exact decomposition methodology developed by the later.

terms of a reduction in the Gini coefficient, could be faulty. This is because the same value of Gini coefficient can be associated with different Lorenz curves reflecting very different kinds of relative inequalities. Similarly, a simple headcount measure of poverty or the poverty gap index is actually the special case of the class of Foster–Greer–Thorbecke (1984) poverty index, capturing the severity of poverty. Hence, limitations of our analysis arising due to the fact that we simply use the headcount measure of poverty and that the inequality index implicit in our analysis refers to the Gini coefficient, need to be kept in view while interpreting the results. Further, as the methodology adopted here is an exact decomposition, we safely derive the inequality effect as a residual after estimating the growth effect and the population-shift effect from the change in the incidence of poverty.

Further, to understand the linkage between poverty, per capita income, and sectoral value added, we have also estimated a multiplicative decomposition[4] of poverty ratio in a particular period:

$$\mathrm{P} = \left(\frac{\mathrm{GDP}}{\mathrm{Population}}\right)\left(\frac{\mathrm{Agriculture} + \mathrm{Industry}}{\mathrm{GDP}} * 100\right)\left(\frac{\mathrm{Poor}}{\mathrm{Agriculture} + \mathrm{Industry}}\right)$$

Here *P* is the poverty ratio. In this decomposition the headcount measure of poverty is expressed in terms of per capita income, the share of commodity sector (agriculture and secondary—that is, manufacturing, construction, electricity, gas, and water, etc.) in total GDP, and the poor-dependency ratio relative to the total commodity-sector value added. In the other two variants that are presented in the footnote, poverty is expressed as per capita income, industrialization as a share of organized manufacturing value added and the ratio of the poor to organized manufacturing value added, indicating the poor that the organized industry has to support. In the third variant, poverty is decomposed into per capita income, with industrialization defined as the percentage share of organized manufacturing value added, the ratio of the poor relative to employment in the organized manufacturing, and the inverse of labour productivity in the organized manufacturing.

Taking the logarithm transformation of both sides, each variant can be reduced to an additive form. Hence, the inter-temporal difference in each of these expressions gives the rate of growth of change in the headcount measure of poverty being expressed in terms of the rate of growth of each component listed on the right-hand side. The data that we have for this study are explained in the next section.

[4] The other two variants are $P = \left(\frac{GDP}{Population}\right)\left(\frac{Mfg.valueadded}{GDP} * 100\right)\left(\frac{Poor}{Mfg.valueadded}\right)$

$$P = \left(\frac{GDP}{Population}\right)\left(\frac{Mfg.valueadded}{GDP} * 100\right)\left(\frac{Poor}{Mfg.employment}\right)\left(\frac{Mfg.employment}{Mfg.valueadded}\right)$$

5.5. The Database

In this study we try to decompose the changes in poverty between two periods—1983 to 1993–4 and 1993–4 to 1999–2000—and between two regions—rural and urban—by using two methods that are specified in the previous section. But only the methodology developed by Kakwani (2000) and Mazumdar and Son (2002) is used in the case of fifteen major Indian states. For the purpose of comparison, we take the distribution of consumer expenditure data from the thirty-eighth, fiftieth, and fifty-fifth rounds of consumer expenditure surveys conducted by the National Sample Survey Organization for the years 1983, 1993–4, and 1999–2000, respectively.[5] Also, we have adjusted the base year expenditures with the prices of the terminal year. The price indices used are state-specific price deflators for rural and urban areas separately, which were used in the modified expert-group methodology to update the poverty line of Rs 49 and Rs 56.6 in 1973–4 prices for rural and urban areas, respectively (Government of India 2002). It is found that the distribution of expenditure–class intervals in each round is different. We have reclassified the base-year expenditure–class intervals in terms of terminal-year class intervals. In doing so, we assume that the number of persons and the per capita expenditure within the class interval are proportionately related. We have interpolated the population for 1983, 1993–4, and 1999–2000 based on the population census data for the years 1981, 1991, and 2001. For the second method, we have taken GDP (at factor cost, in 1993–4 prices), agricultural, and secondary-sector value-added data from the Government of India's Economic Survey 2002–3. The data on value added and workers employed in the organized manufacturing sector are taken from the Annual Survey of Industries for the requisite years and the value-added figures have been converted into 1993–4 prices. For employment in the manufacturing sector, we take the total number of workers instead of the total persons engaged, as the latter includes highly skilled jobs, which may not be available to the unskilled and semi-skilled job seekers. Hence, in assessing the relative burden of the poor in terms of the number of poor vis-à-vis employment in the high-productivity organized manufacturing sector, only the number of workers is considered to be appropriate.

[5] Strictly speaking, the results from the 55th round data on consumption expenditure are not comparable with the earlier rounds because of the possible intermingling of responses due to adoption of dual recall periods (7 days and 30 days) in the 55th round. For details, see Deaton and Drèze (2002) and Sundaram (2001).

Table 5.2. Change in the incidence of poverty in India in the 1980s and the 1990s

	Change in rural poverty between		Change in urban poverty between		Change in all areas poverty between	
States	1983 and 1993–4	1993–4 and 1999–2000	1983 and 1993–4	1993–4 and 1999–2000	1983 and 1993–4	1993–4 and 1999–2000
Andhra Pradesh	−10.61	−4.87	2.03	−11.7	−6.72	−6.42
Assam	2.41	−4.97	−14.0	−0.26	0.39	−4.77
Bihar	−6.16	−13.91	−12.83	−1.59	−7.26	−12.36
Gujarat	−7.62	−9.01	−11.25	−12.3	−8.58	−10.14
Haryana	7.46	−19.75	−7.77	−6.39	3.68	−16.31
Karnataka	−6.45	−12.5	−2.68	−14.89	−5.08	−13.12
Kerala	−13.27	−16.38	−21.13	−4.28	−14.99	−12.71
Madhya Pradesh	−8.26	−3.58	−4.68	−9.94	−7.26	−5.09
Maharashtra	−7.3	−14.21	−5.11	−8.34	−6.58	−11.84
Orissa	−17.81	−1.71	−7.51	1.19	−16.73	−1.41
Punjab	−1.25	−5.6	−12.44	−5.6	−4.41	−5.61
Rajasthan	−7.04	−12.72	−7.45	−10.64	−7.05	−12.13
Tamil Nadu	−21.51	−11.93	−7.19	−17.66	−16.63	−13.91
Uttar Pradesh	−4.17	−11.06	−14.43	−4.5	−6.22	−9.7
West Bengal	−22.25	−8.95	−9.91	−7.55	−19.19	−8.64
All India	−8.38	−10.18	−8.43	−8.74	−8.51	−9.87

Notes: The change is indicated in terms of the terminal year figure minus the base year figure.
Source: Computed by the authors.

5.6. Empirical Analysis

Looking at the observed change in the incidence of poverty, we note that at the all-India level the fall in the 1990s (1993–4 up to and including 1999–2000) ('reform period', hereafter) seems to be higher than during 1983 to 1993–4 ('pre-reform period', hereafter). The rural–urban differences are noteworthy: rural poverty dropped by a little more than 10 percentage points in the reform period, whereas it was around 8.3 percentage points in the pre-reform period; urban poverty fell by 8.38 and 8.74 percentage points in the pre-reform and reform periods, respectively (see Table 5.2).

Following the methodology of Mazumdar and Son (2002), the change in poverty has been decomposed into the growth effect, inequality effect, and the effect due to population shift from rural to urban areas. This exercise has been carried out for both pre- and reform periods, broadly classified as 1983 to

1993–4 and 1993–4 to 1999–2000. The decomposition has been done for rural and urban areas separately, for fifteen states, and also for the whole of India.

From Table 5.3 it may be noted that between 1983 and 1993–4 the growth effect was −14.28 and −5.66 per cent for rural and urban areas, respectively. It seems that in the process of growth, inequality had been accentuated, as the inequality effect was positive (0.19 and 0.89 per cent for rural and urban areas, respectively), implying that inequality raised poverty. However, the growth effect has been much larger than the inequality effect in terms of absolute magnitude and, hence, this helped the poverty decline during this period. As regards the population-shift effect, rural to urban migration obviously reduced the poverty in the rural areas (−2.59 per cent). Although in the urban areas it led to an increase in the incidence of poverty (by 2.28 per cent), the net effect judged in terms of the change in overall poverty (rural–urban combined) is seen to be beneficial as it dropped by 0.3 per cent. In other words, rural to urban migration helped reduce poverty by enabling the rural migrant poor to participate in urban-based activities, which could generate comparatively higher incomes than those in the rural areas. At the all-India level (rural and urban combined), the growth effect (−19.54 per cent) dominated over the inequality effect (1.07 per cent), though the latter is seen to have a tendency of increasing poverty. In other words, the adverse effects of a rise in inequality have been less than the beneficial effects of growth, which resulted in a decline in poverty by 19.17 per cent.

It is quite evident from Table 5.4 that in the reform period—that is, 1993–4 to 1999–2000, the growth effect continued to be beneficial as far as poverty reduction in the rural areas is concerned, and the magnitude increased to a considerably higher level (−22.12 per cent). However, the inequality effect rose from 0.19 per cent in the first period to 1.59 per cent. Though growth accentuated inequality in the 1990s, the inequality effect has been dominated by the growth effect and, hence, poverty declined to a larger extent than the corresponding fall in the previous period. Interestingly, in the urban areas, the inequality effect became almost zero (0.04) per cent in the second period which was nearly one (0.89) per cent in the first period. Growth possibly reduced inequality by helping the poor access the benefits of growth in the reform era. The growth effect on poverty also went up in magnitude from −5.66 to −6.72 per cent over the same period and thus reduced the incidence of urban poverty. The phenomenon of no adverse inequality effect in urban India in the post-reform period is noteworthy. However, urban economy being only one-fourth of the total, the inequality effect for the whole of India still turned out to be adverse (1.63 per cent) in the 1990s, indicating an increasing effect on poverty. But, since the growth effect (−28.83 per cent) dominated over the inequality effect, it could more than offset the adverse effects of inequality and, thus, reduce poverty (−27.42 per cent). As regards to the population-shift effect, rural to urban migration seems to have reduced poverty in the

Table 5.3. Decomposition of change in poverty in India between 1983 and 1993–4

	Growth			Inequality			Population			Total		
States	Rural	Urban	All areas	Rural	Urban	All areas	Rural	Urban	All areas	Rural	Urban	All areas
Andhra Pradesh	−28.69	1.3	−27.39	1.73	0.69	2.42	−2.17	3.81	1.64	−29.13	5.8	−23.33
Assam	4.96	−3.77	1.19	0.35	0.04	0.39	−1.48	0.5	−0.98	3.83	−3.23	0.6
Bihar	−8.72	−2.72	−11.44	0.1	0.06	0.16	−0.59	0.39	−0.2	−9.21	−2.27	−11.48
Gujarat	−12.54	−12.34	−24.88	−2.92	0.86	−2.06	−2.72	3.5	0.79	−18.18	−7.98	−26.16
Haryana	26.54	−7.79	18.75	1.25	−1.51	−0.26	−7.21	6.01	−1.19	20.59	−3.29	17.3
Karnataka	−11.75	−1.97	−13.72	0.03	−0.17	−0.14	−2.06	2.58	0.52	−13.78	0.44	−13.34
Kerala	−25.57	−12.06	−37.63	0.35	−0.06	0.29	−4.97	5.38	0.42	−30.18	−6.74	−36.92
Madhya Pradesh	−14.23	−2.58	−16.8	1.32	0.49	1.81	−2.5	2.83	0.33	−15.41	0.74	−14.66
Maharashtra	−11.92	−5.15	−17.07	1.44	0.72	2.16	−3.69	3.35	−0.34	−14.17	−1.08	−15.25
Orissa	−22.75	−1.53	−24.28	−1.0	0.04	−0.96	−1.49	1.16	−0.34	−25.25	−0.33	−25.58
Punjab	−7.82	−21.71	−29.53	2.36	−0.83	1.53	−1.99	2.78	0.79	−7.45	−19.76	−27.21
Rajasthan	−15.77	−4.64	−20.41	−0.12	−0.15	−0.28	−1.4	1.6	0.2	−17.29	−3.2	−20.5
Tamil Nadu	−27.42	−5.2	−32.62	0.28	0.36	0.63	−2.74	2.75	0.01	−29.88	−2.1	−31.98
Uttar Pradesh	−6.78	−6.23	−13.01	−0.38	0.34	−0.04	−1.71	1.65	−0.07	−8.87	−4.25	−13.12
West Bengal	−29.61	−4.98	−34.59	0.05	0.08	0.13	−0.9	0.47	−0.43	−30.46	−4.43	−34.89
All India	−14.28	−5.66	−19.94	0.19	0.89	1.07	−2.59	2.28	−0.3	−16.68	−2.49	−19.17
CV	−113.64	−92.87	−77.26	392.03	951.82	309.56	−67.79	65.50	940.77	−93.72	−161.96	−76.42

Notes: CV is coefficient of variation across the states (excluding All India).
Source: Computed by the authors.

Table 5.4. Decomposition of change in poverty in India between 1993–4 and 1999–2000

	Growth			Inequality			Population			Total		
States	Rural	Urban	All areas	Rural	Urban	All areas	Rural	Urban	All areas	Rural	Urban	All areas
Andhra Pradesh	−16.93	−14.43	−31.35	1.5	0.79	2.3	−0.06	0.16	0.09	−16.09	−14.08	−28.96
Assam	−11.72	−0.32	−12.04	1.01	0.11	1.12	−1	0.18	−0.82	−11.71	−0.03	−11.74
Bihar	−21.67	−0.43	−22.1	−0.28	0.04	−0.24	−0.12	0.08	−0.04	−22.07	−0.31	−22.38
Gujarat	−24.35	−18.31	−42.66	0.54	0.01	0.55	−1.23	1.51	0.28	−25.04	−16.79	−41.83
Haryana	−55.08	−8.55	−63.63	−1.82	0.39	−1.43	−0.16	0.11	−0.04	−57.06	−8.05	−65.11
Karnataka	−25.48	−14.14	−39.63	0.06	−0.48	−0.42	−1.29	1.78	0.49	−26.71	−12.84	−39.55
Kerala	−46.33	−3.56	−49.89	−0.23	0.16	−0.07	0.18	−0.22	−0.05	−46.39	−3.63	−50.01
Madhya Pradesh	−5.93	−5.62	−11.55	−0.45	−0.02	−0.48	−0.96	1.07	0.11	−7.35	−4.57	−11.92
Maharashtra	−21.73	−9.52	−31.24	−1.14	0.31	−0.83	−1.83	1.84	0.01	−24.7	−7.36	−32.06
Orissa	−3.45	0.34	−3.11	0.43	0.01	0.44	−0.95	0.82	−0.13	−3.97	1.17	−2.8
Punjab	−34.23	−15.67	−49.9	1.82	0.5	2.32	−2.01	1.88	−0.13	−34.42	−13.29	−47.71
Rajasthan	−35.5	−9.64	−45.14	−0.17	0.65	0.49	−0.22	0.27	0.06	−35.88	−8.71	−44.59
Tamil Nadu	−20.28	−20.36	−40.63	−0.38	0.52	0.14	−4.37	5.1	0.73	−25.03	−14.74	−39.76
Uttar Pradesh	−21.48	−2.16	−23.65	−0.05	−0.09	−0.14	−0.61	0.55	−0.06	−22.15	−1.7	−23.85
West Bengal	−17.62	−6.25	−23.87	−0.51	0.37	−0.14	−0.33	0.17	−0.16	−18.46	−5.71	−24.17
All India	−22.12	−6.72	−28.83	1.59	0.04	1.63	−1.65	1.43	−0.21	−22.17	−5.25	−27.42
CV	−57.84	−79.41	−51.35	4284.22	151.03	430.90	−114.24	131.32	1495.49	−55.91	−80.35	−51.73

Notes: CV is coefficient of variation across the states (excluding All India).
Source: Computed by the authors.

Table 5.5. Decomposition of change in poverty in India between 1983 and 1993–4

Variables	Model 1	Model 2	Model 3
ΔPOV%	−0.22	−0.22	−0.22
ΔGDPPC	0.28	0.28	0.28
ΔIND%	0.19		0.19
ΔCOMM%		−0.097	
Δ(POOR/COM)		−0.398	
Δ(POOR/MEM)			−0.06
Δ(MEM/MVA)			−0.626
Δ(POOR/MVA)	−0.694		

Notes: POV% Poverty ratio.
GDPPC Per capita GDP.
IND% Share of manufacturing output in total GDP (percentage).
COMM% Agricultural and allied activities value added and secondary sector value added (percentage).
POOR Total number of people below poverty line.
MEM Total number of workers in manufacturing sector.
MVA Gross value added by the manufacturing sector; Δ represents change between two periods.

rural areas (by 1.64 per cent) but raised the incidence of urban poverty (by 1.43 per cent). However, the net effect of the population shift on poverty has been beneficial (−0.21 per cent) suggesting that rural–urban migration helped the overall poverty to decline. But it may be noted that the population-shift effect on poverty declined in magnitude in the second period (−0.21) compared with the first (−0.3), which is suggestive of a possible decline in the net population shift from rural to urban areas in the 1990s compared with the 1980s.

Results from the second decomposition exercise, for which three variants are taken, are presented in Tables 5.5 and 5.6, for the 1980s and 1990s, respectively. From the results it is evident that the ratio of poor to organized manufacturing value added fell sharply by 69.4 per cent between 1983 and 1993–4. The other two components—namely, per capita income and industrialization index,

Table 5.6. Decomposition of change in poverty in India between 1993–4 and 1999–2000

Variables	Model 1	Model 2	Model 3
ΔPOV%	−0.32	−0.32	−0.32
ΔGDPPC	0.264	0.265	0.265
ΔIND%	−0.172		−0.172
ΔCOMM%		−0.65	
Δ(POOR/COMM)		0.06	
Δ(POOR/MEM)			−0.15
Δ(MEM/MVA)			−0.26
Δ(POOR/MVA)	−0.413		

Notes: See Table 5.5.

increased by 28 and 19 per cent, respectively. The net effect of all these changes is seen to have reduced poverty. Hence, it is the expansion of the organized manufacturing in terms of value added that has resulted in an overall decline in poverty in the first period. In the second period, too, the manufacturing value added per poor continues to reduce poverty, suggesting the importance of expansion of this sector in the context of poverty reduction. However, it may be clarified here that even when the growth rate of manufacturing value added is positive, its share in total GDP may still decline if other components within the tertiary sector in particular are growing rapidly. Since some of these components in the tertiary sector are actually expanding fast in the recent years and they hold possibilities of creating employment opportunities for the poor through direct or indirect linkages among sectors, the declining share of industry in total GDP also appears to be contributing to the reduction in poverty. This finding need not conflict with the statement made above that the expansion of the industry contributes to poverty reduction: both growth in manufacturing value added per poor and a very fast growth of the tertiary sector, which tends to reduce the overall share of industry in total GDP, possibly occur simultaneously. Hence, the findings relating to the role of industrialization in reducing poverty and, at the same time, the growth of tertiary sector activities holding opportunities for the poor both seem to have important policy implications.

In the second variant, this particular phenomenon is made more distinct. While in the first period, both the share of commodity-sector value added and the ratio of poor to commodity-sector value added resulted in a decline in the incidence of poverty, in the second period it is primarily the decline in the percentage share of commodity-sector value added that contributed to reduction in poverty, thus indicating the tertiary sector growth being pro-poor.

In the third variant, where the rate of growth of poverty is expressed in terms of the growth rate of per capita GDP, growth rate of industrialization, the rate of growth of inverse of manufacturing labour productivity, and the rate of growth of the ratio of poor to manufacturing employment, the last two factors primarily caused the decline in poverty in the first period. However, the fall in the ratio of the poor to manufacturing employment was only 6 per cent in the 1980s. On the other hand, in the second period, the contribution of this factor to the reduction in poverty went up to 15 per cent. Since the denominator—that is, employment in the organized manufacturing, actually fell in absolute terms in the second period, it is the decline in the absolute number of the poor which resulted in the fall in the ratio of the poor to manufacturing employment. If manufacturing employment would also have increased during 1993–4 and 1999–2000, the ratio of the poor to manufacturing workers could have caused a much larger decline in the incidence of poverty. The rise in manufacturing labour productivity seems to have contributed to a fall in poverty to a larger extent in the second period as compared with the first period. In addition, the expansion of the tertiary sector in the second period also seems to have brought down the incidence of poverty. On the whole, as the composition of growth has changed, labour productivity and employment growth in the organized industry are crucial to poverty reduction.

At the state level, from Tables 5.3 and 5.4, all the other states except for Assam and Haryana registered a fall in the incidence of rural poverty in the 1980s, and in the 1990s each of the major states recorded a decline. In the case of urban areas, with the exception of Andhra Pradesh and Orissa in the 1980s and 1990s, respectively, all the other states show a decline in the incidence of poverty. However, the extent of decline varies considerably across states, though in the rural areas it seems to have fallen in the 1990s compared with the previous decade. On the one hand, the coefficient of variation of the change in rural poverty dropped from 98.75 in the first period to 51.03 in the second period. On the other hand, the coefficient of variation increased from 61.58 to 70.21 in the urban areas of the states during the same period, indicating a rise in the interstate variations of change in the incidence of urban poverty in the reform period.

It may be interesting to spell out our hypothesis at this stage. As economic reforms are likely to bring in higher growth, the growth or mean effect is expected to go up in the reform period. Though the extent of fall in the incidence of urban poverty in the 1990s has been only marginally higher than in the 1980s, as noted above, the hypothesis of a higher growth or mean effect in the second period may still be valid. In addition to this, the inequality effect might have fallen in the second period compared with the first, if economic reforms aim at generating pro-poor growth—that is, employment generation occurring in the process of economic growth (Kakwani and Pernia 2000). Further, as the coefficient of variation of the change in the incidence of urban poverty rose in the 1990s over the 1980s we can hypothesize that the economic reforms executed at different levels across the states have generated different mean and/or inequality effects.

In the light of these hypotheses, we may examine the empirical results. From Table 5.3 it may be noted that the growth/mean effect dominated over the inequality effect as well as the population-shift effect in most of the states during 1983 to 1993–4, which brought in a decline in the observed poverty ratio. Even in rural Assam and Haryana, where the observed poverty ratio actually increased between 1983 and 1993–4, the growth effect mainly accounted for this rise. However, in urban Andhra Pradesh, the rise in observed poverty has been caused by all the three components. In fact the population-shift effect turns out to be slightly higher than the growth effect. In all the other states, a decline in the observed poverty incidence in the rural and urban areas is mainly attributed to the growth effect.

Although the inequality effect was positive in sign suggesting that in the process of growth inequality rose and accentuated poverty, it could not neutralize the beneficial effects of growth on poverty (see Table 5.3). In the rural areas of Gujarat, Orissa, Rajasthan, and Uttar Pradesh, and in the urban areas of

Haryana, Karnataka, Kerala, Punjab, and Rajasthan, the inequality effect turned out to be negative in sign, suggesting that inequality fell in the process of growth and thus contributed along with the mean effect to a reduction in poverty. This is an interesting feature and needs further analysis, as to why the inequality effect turned out to be beneficial in these states and not elsewhere, but this is outside the scope of our chapter.

Although urban poverty increased, owing to rising levels of urbanization (percentage of population residing in the urban areas) the decline in the percentage of rural population ushered in more than a proportionate fall in rural poverty in several states such as Assam, Bihar, Haryana, Maharashtra, Orissa, Uttar Pradesh, and West Bengal. Thus, in these states, the population-shift effect helped the all-area combined poverty to decline during the period 1983 to 1993–4 (see Table 5.3).

In the reform period, the growth effect continued to dominate over the other two effects, and it also accounted for much of the decline in the incidence of poverty in most of the states (see Table 5.4). The only exception in this respect is urban Orissa, where the observed poverty rose by 1.19 percentage points, caused by both adverse growth and inequality effects. In urban India, though, the growth effect continued to be dominant in the reform period, and it is interesting to note that the adverse effect of inequality fell in this period compared with the 1980s and became almost negligible. Second, despite a rise in the adverse effects of inequality in rural India in the second period relative to the first, in a large number of states (e.g., rural areas of Bihar, Haryana, Kerala, Madhya Pradesh, Maharashtra, Rajasthan, Tamil Nadu, Uttar Pradesh, and West Bengal) the inequality effect turned out to be beneficial in the sense that, like the growth effect, it also helped poverty to fall. This is possibly because growth became pro-poor in these states by generating employment opportunities. As regards the population-shift effect, it continued to be beneficial at the all-India level. In other words, the fall in the incidence of rural poverty due to a decline in the percentage of rural population continued to be more than the rise in the incidence of urban poverty caused by the rise in the level of urbanization between 1993–4 and 1999–2000. However, in terms of magnitude the population-shift effect for all areas fell marginally from −0.3 in the first period to −0.21 in the second period.

On the whole, the beneficial effect of growth on poverty increased in magnitude in the reform period relative to the pre-reform period in several states both in the rural and urban areas. Except for Andhra Pradesh, Madhya Pradesh, Orissa, Tamil Nadu, and West Bengal, the rural areas of all other states recorded an improvement in the growth effect. Similarly, except for Assam, Bihar, Kerala, Orissa, Punjab, and Uttar Pradesh, the urban areas of all other states registered an increase in the growth effect. The adverse effect of inequality corresponding to all areas (rural–urban combined) fell in several states like Andhra Pradesh, Bihar, Haryana, Karnataka, Kerala, Madhya Pradesh, Maharashtra, Tamil Nadu,

Uttar Pradesh, and West Bengal, although at the all-India level it went up from 1.07 per cent to 1.63 per cent.

Based on Tables 5.3 and 5.4, different size classes have been formed to represent the growth effects in both the periods, and the states have been distributed across these size classes. If the growth effect is greater than zero (> 0), it is considered to be adverse as it raises the incidence of poverty instead of reducing it. The higher the magnitude with a negative sign, the higher the beneficial growth effect. Table 5.7, which corresponds to the rural areas of the states, offers a mixed picture. While states like Madhya Pradesh, Orissa, Andhra Pradesh, West Bengal, and Tamil Nadu moved from relatively higher size classes in the pre-reform period to relatively lower size classes in reform period, several other states moved to higher size classes of growth effect from the lower size classes over the same period. On the other hand, in the urban areas, relatively few states like Orissa, Kerala, and Punjab moved down from higher size classes in the pre-reform period to lower size classes in the reform period, and states like Andhra Pradesh and Tamil Nadu experienced a perceptible rise in terms of growth effect (see Table 5.8). However, a large number of states remained in the same size class of growth effect in both the periods. But, notwithstanding this stagnancy, the growth effect in the urban areas does not seem to have deteriorated in a large number of states.

It would be interesting to examine whether states with a higher growth effect particularly in the urban areas in the 1990s over the previous decade also experienced lower magnitudes of an adverse population-shift effect in the urban areas. The answer is in the affirmative, because several states like Andhra Pradesh, Gujarat, Haryana, Karnataka, Madhya Pradesh, Maharashtra, Rajasthan, Uttar Pradesh, and West Bengal which recorded a higher growth effect in the urban areas in the 1990s relative to the 1980s also experienced a lower population-shift effect in the urban areas. The only exception is Tamil Nadu.[6] In other words, these are the states where higher growth effects in the reform period reduced the extent of rise in the incidence of urban poverty occurring in the process of expanding urbanization. From this it may be inferred that as reforms enhanced the growth effects in the urban areas of several states, they also reduced the deleterious effects of population rise on poverty in the urban areas of the same states.

[6] Tamil Nadu recorded a massive increase in urban population between the 1991 and 2001 census years possibly due to reclassification of areas as urban in 2001 which were rural in 1991. As a result, there has been a decline of the rural population in 2001 compared to 1991, even in absolute terms. Decline in fertility alone could not have caused this, because fertility could not have fallen only in rural areas but in both rural and urban areas. It is also unlikely that a fertility decline would bring in a fall in population in absolute terms. Rural to urban migration also could not have reduced the rural population in absolute terms. Rapid increase in so-called urban population caused urban poverty to rise.

Table 5.7. Cross-tabulation of states in India in terms of growth effect on poverty changes in two periods in the rural areas (in percentage points)

		1993–4 and 1999–2000					
	Growth effect	> 0	0 to −10	−10 to −15	−15 to −20	−20 to −25	< −25
1983 and 1993–4	> 0			Assam			Haryana
	0 to −10					Bihar, Uttar Pradesh	Punjab
	−10 to −15		Madhya Pradesh			Gujarat, Maharashtra, All India	Karnataka
	−15 to −20						Rajasthan
	−20 to −25		Orissa				
	< −25				Andhra Pradesh, West Bengal	Tamil Nadu	Kerala

Source: Computed by the authors.

Table 5.8. Cross-tabulation of states in India in terms of growth effect on poverty changes in two periods in the urban areas (in percentage points)

Growth effect		1993–4 and 1999–2000					
		> 0	0 to −10	−10 to −15	−15 to −20	−20 to −25	< −25
1983 and 1993–4	> 0			Andhra Pradesh			
	0 to −10	Orissa	Assam, Bihar, Haryana, Madhya Pradesh, Maharashtra, Rajasthan, Uttar Pradesh, West Bengal, All India	Karnataka		Tamil Nadu	
	−10 to −15		Kerala		Gujarat		
	−15 to −20						
	−20 to −25				Punjab		
	< −25						

Source: Computed by the authors.

It has been widely noted that economic growth varies considerably across space; even within India, states have recorded different growth rates, which do not seem to have any tendency towards convergence in the long run (Sachs, Bajpai, and Ramiah 2002). Such divergence across states is noted not only in terms of growth in state domestic product but also in terms of growth in average per capita consumption expenditure (Deaton and Drèze 2002). Among several factors that explain the divergence in the economic growth across the states, it is the extent of economic reforms initiated in these states that is important for discussion. For this purpose, some of the reform indicators were looked at. The reform indicators are looked at in terms of level of FDI, change in fiscal deficit (as a percentage of gross state domestic product (GSDP), and the change in the public-private employment ratio (in the organized sector). The data on FDI show considerable variations across states, which have again undergone changes over the years. In fact, only six states (namely, Delhi, Karnataka, Andhra Pradesh, Tamil Nadu, Gujarat, and Maharashtra) have attracted the bulk of FDI with a negligible share in other states. By the end of the last decade, the distribution of FDI among these top states was as follows: Delhi (9 per cent), Karnataka (19 per cent), Andhra Pradesh (11 per cent), Tamil Nadu (20 per cent), Gujarat (9 per cent), and Maharashtra (32 per cent) (Economic Survey of Karnataka 2001–2). From Table 5.9 it may be further noted that states such as

Table 5.9. Some indicators for the extent of economic reforms in India at state level

States	Ratio of public to private employment ratio in 1991 vis-à-vis 2000[1]	Change in fiscal deficit/gross state domestic product between 1994–5 to 1999–2000[2]
Andhra Pradesh	1.40	−0.8
Assam	0.94	–
Bihar	1.02	−5.6
Gujarat	1.15	−3.1
Haryana	1.06	−2.9
Karnataka	1.60	0.1
Kerala	1.08	−1.3
Madhya Pradesh	0.96	−1.5
Maharashtra	1.07	−2.7
Orissa	0.73	−2.8
Punjab	1.12	−1.6
Rajasthan	1.05	−3.2
Tamil Nadu	1.29	−1.5
Uttar Pradesh	1.03	−2.4
West Bengal	0.93	−5.4

Source: [1] Calculated by the authors from data in Government of India (2002);
[2] Government of India (n.d.).

Andhra Pradesh, Gujarat, Karnataka, Kerala, Maharashtra, Punjab, and Tamil Nadu experienced a sharp decline in the public–private employment ratio between 1991 and 2000. The figures in Table 5.9 give the proportion of base year (1991) public-private employment ratio to the terminal year (2000) public-private employment ratio; hence, the larger the ratio, the higher the shift away from the public sector, which is taken as an outcome of shrinking public sector following from the structural adjustment programme.

In terms of fiscal deficit as a percentage of GSDP, it may also be noted that fiscal reforms seems to have taken place in Andhra Pradesh, Karnataka, Kerala, Madhya Pradesh, Punjab, and Tamil Nadu. Taking FDI as a major indicator, and any one of the other two, the following states may be identified as the most reforming ones: Andhra Pradesh, Karnataka, Gujarat, Maharashtra, and Tamil Nadu. Interestingly these are the states which also experienced a perceptible increase in the growth/mean effect in the urban areas in the post-reform period over the pre-reform period (see Table 5.7). Even in the rural areas of Gujarat, Karnataka, and Maharashtra the growth effect on poverty increased during the same period (see Table 5.8). Though the growth effect in rural Andhra Pradesh and Tamil Nadu declined in the second period, it has still been much higher than that of many other states.

Inequality seems to have increased in Andhra Pradesh and Tamil Nadu in the process of growth in the urban areas in the second period, which raised the deleterious effect of inequality on poverty. However, in the other three states the inequality effect fell in the second period compared with the first period. Though urban poverty increased owing to a rise in urbanization, except in Tamil Nadu, in all other four states its adverse effect came down sharply.[7] On the whole, reforms seem to have had a positive effect on poverty in these states. And, conversely, the remaining nine states, where reforms have not been initiated on a large scale, do not seem to have experienced any major increase in growth/mean effect on poverty in the urban areas in the second period compared with the first. Hence, with wider implementation of reforms across states, poverty can be reduced sharply in the coming years.

Notwithstanding the divergences in reforms and growth, the convergence in the growth/mean effect on poverty in the reform period is quite evident from Tables 5.2 and 5.3. From the decomposition analysis, as we examine the coefficient of variation of the growth/mean effect across states, a perceptible decline seems to have taken place in the reform period compared with the pre-reform period. In the rural areas, it dropped from 113.64 in the pre-reform period to 57.84 in the reform period, and in the urban areas the fall was from 92.87 to 79.41 during the same period. This tends to support our argument that despite

[7] In Tamil Nadu, reclassification of areas, as mentioned above, led to a massive increase in urban population, which otherwise would have remained as rural areas.

the divergence arising from economic reforms pursued at different levels across states, the beneficial effects with regard to poverty reduction has a converging tendency.

5.7. Conclusion

The effect of globalization on the poor is a matter of serious concern and has raised both academic and political debates in various countries. In this chapter an attempt has been made to assess the impact of economic reforms on the headcount measure of poverty. This is done in terms of a decomposition analysis splitting the percentage change in the incidence of poverty between two time points in terms of growth/mean effect, inequality effect, and the population-shift effect. The decomposition has been pursued for two time periods: one from 1983 to 1993–4 and another from 1993–4 to 1999–2000, described as pre-reform and reform periods, respectively, although strictly speaking reforms were initiated from July 1991 onwards. While the growth/mean effect has been dominant, and has resulted in a decline in the incidence of poverty in both the periods and in most of the states, inequality, which in general rose in the process of growth, raised the poverty ratio at the all-India level. However, in the rural areas of a large number of states the inequality effect turned out to be beneficial in the reform period. Even in the urban areas of several states and at the all-India level, too, the adverse inequality effect fell considerably in the reform period compared with the pre-reform period. The population-shift effect, which measures the net effect of a rise (and fall) in the percentage of population residing in urban (and rural) areas on the incidence of poverty, appeared to be beneficial in at least seven of the fifteen major states and at the all-India level too, in both the periods. In other words, the overall incidence of poverty in these states fell, though rural–urban migration might have raised the incidence of urban poverty.

Economic reforms have been pursued at different levels across states, and this seems to have enhanced the interstate variations in economic growth. These reforms have also led to a change in the composition of growth—that is, the shift in value-added mix towards industry and tertiary activities, and it seems to have caused a larger decline in the incidence of poverty in the 1990s compared with the 1980s, which is evident from the second exercise in our study. Also, the labour productivity growth and employment growth in the organized industry are crucial to poverty reduction through their direct and indirect effects on the rest of the economy. Other than the role of agriculture in a few states like West Bengal, the rapid growth of new components of the tertiary sector, such as IT, business process outsourcing services, financial institutions, and infrastructure services must have impacted upon the economic growth at varied level across states. But, interestingly, the beneficial growth/mean effect on poverty increased in magnitude in most of the states in the reform period relative to the pre-reform period and, more importantly, its variation across states dropped considerably. This is possibly because of good governance in the rapidly growing and reforming states, and the demonstration effect of this in the slowly growing states. The deleterious effect of inequality on poverty also shows a declining tendency in several states in the reform phase compared with its previous period, possibly because growth became pro-poor. The population-shift effect, which showed a tendency of raising urban poverty, also fell across states in magnitude in the second period compared with the first. And states with greater (and beneficial) growth effects in the reform period relative to the pre-reform period also show lower (and adverse) population-shift effects in the urban areas—that is, a relatively smaller rise in the incidence of urban poverty caused by rural–urban migration. Reforms seem to have a close association with a rise in growth effects, indicating that both economic growth and its ability to reduce poverty are conceded in the reforming process. A strategy of growth with employment generation would help the poor benefit from economic reforms directly and rapidly, and this would not only enhance the growth effect but would also make inequality and population-shift effects more beneficial to poverty reduction.

The extent of globalization in India indeed enhanced the growth path of output from its traditional low levels. But the impact of this high growth on poverty seems to have been substantial, at least in terms of our empirical results, as it led to a fall in the incidence of poverty in both rural and urban areas and across the states depending upon the level of globalization. Further, our results show that the growth effect on poverty is much higher than the inequality effect, implying that there might have been an increase in the inequality but it was neutralized by the beneficial effect of growth. However, the fact that the inequality effect was unfavourable to the poor in at least some of the regions suggests that the direct benefits of globalization have been much higher among the rich compared with the poor. We are hesitant to say that the rise in output growth in India in the reform period is pro-poor. Further, this also indicates that if there were any shortfall in the output from the expected levels it would only hit the poor more adversely than the rich. Many emerging countries in Asia have also experienced this pattern of adversity, which affected different sections of the population unequally. It may be noted that at the time of the Asian financial crisis it was the poorer section that was affected badly through loss of employment and decline in the social support schemes. Hence, these results from India and other emerging market economies show that globalization has the potential to help the poor if and only if it is managed prudently.

APPENDIX

Synthesis of decomposition methods

Let the change in poverty between two periods j and k be ΔP_{jk} and the incidence of poverty be:

$$P = P(Z, \mu, L(t)) \tag{1}$$

where P is the poverty ratio, Z is the poverty line, μ mean income (or expenditure), and $L(t)$ the Lorenz ratio.
And the change in poverty can be defined as:

$$\Delta P_{jk} = Q(M_{jk}, I_{jk}) \tag{2}$$

where M_{jk} and I_{jk} are change in poverty due to mean and inequality effect, respectively. Kakwani and Subbarao (1990) estimate M_{jk} by taking the change in mean and keeping the Lorenz curve of the jth period constant. I_{jk} has been estimated by taking the change in the Lorenz curve and keeping the mean of the jth period constant. But this decomposition was not an exact one and contains the residual term. Datt and Ravallion (1992) have defined this residual term as:

$$\varepsilon_{jk} = -M_{kj} - M_{jk} \tag{3}$$

But this decomposition is not symmetric as it is sensitive to the reference period.
Another method suggested by Jain and Tendulkar (1990) defines that the change in poverty can be decomposed as:

$$\Delta P_{jk} = M_{jk} + I^*_{jk} \text{ and } \Delta P_{jk} = M^*_{jk} + I_{jk}$$

where

$$M^*_{jk} = P(Z, \mu_k, L_k(t)) - P(Z, \mu_j, L_k(t)) \text{ and}$$
$$I^*_{jk} = P(Z, \mu_k, L_k(t)) - P(Z, \mu_k, L_j(t)).$$

Though this procedure is an exact one, this was criticized on the ground that the mean effect and the inequality effect have been estimated by using different reference period. Kakwani (2000) tries to propose a method that takes care of the weaknesses that are found in the previous ones. It defines the mean and inequality effect as:

$$M^*_{jk} = \frac{1}{2}[P(Z, \mu_k, L_j(t)) - P(Z, \mu_j, L_j(t)) + P(Z, \mu_k, L_k(t)) - P(Z, \mu_j L_k(t))] \tag{4}$$

and

$$I_{jk}^{*} = \frac{1}{2}[P(Z, \mu_j, L_k(t)) - P(Z, \mu_j, L_j(t)) + P(Z, \mu_k, L_k(t)) - P(Z, \mu_k L_j(t))] \quad (5)$$

Hence the decomposition would be written as:

$$\varDelta P_{jk} = M_{jk}^{*} + I_{jk}^{*} \quad (6)$$

In addition to the growth and inequality effect, Mazumdar and Son (2002) include the population-shift effect in the decomposition exercise.

Assuming that there are two demographic groups as i = 1 and 2, the change in poverty can be expressed as:

$$\frac{\varDelta P}{P} = \sum_i \frac{\bar{f}_i P_i}{P} \frac{M_i}{P_i} + \sum_i \frac{\bar{f}_i P_i}{P} \frac{I_i}{P_i} + \sum_i \frac{\bar{P}_i f_i}{P} \frac{\varDelta f_i}{f_i} \quad (7)$$

where f_k and P_k are population share and poverty index of the *k*th group, respectively.

$$\text{And } \bar{f}_i = \frac{f_{ij} + f_{ik}}{2}, \text{—} P_i = \frac{P_{ij} + P_{ik}}{2}$$

It may be noted that *M* and *I* are mean and inequality effect, respectively, similar to that of *M** and *I** of Kakwani (2000), and this is an exact decomposition of the change in percentage of poverty. Here f_i and P_i are population share and poverty index of the *i*th group, respectively. $\bar{f}_i$ and P_i are the *i*th group averages of the respective values at two time points. *P* is the headcount ratio of poverty for all areas (rural and urban combined). $\varDelta P$ is the change in poverty between two time points. The third term on the right-hand side represents the change in poverty due to population shift. $\varDelta f_i$ is the change in population share between two time points of the *i*th group. In our present analysis, *i* stands for rural and urban areas.

References

Ahluwalia, M. S. (1978) ‘Rural Poverty and Agricultural Performance in India’, *Journal of Development Studies*, 14: 298–323.

Asian Development Bank (ADB) (1999) *Fighting Poverty in Asia and the Pacific: The Poverty Reduction Strategy*. Manila: ADB.

Banerjee, B. (1986) *Rural to Urban Migration and the Urban Labour Market*. New Delhi: Himalaya Publishing House.

Besley, T., R. Burgess, and B. Esteve-Volart (2004) ‘Operationalizing Pro-poor Growth: India Case Study’. London: London School of Economics. <http://siteresources.worldbank.org/INTPGI/Resources/342674-1115051237044/oppgindia.pdf>.

Bhagwati, J., and T. N. Srinivasan (2002) ‘Trade and Poverty in the Poor Countries’, *American Economic Review*, 92: 180–3.

Bhattacharya, B. B., and A. Mitra (1991) ‘Excess Growth of the Tertiary Sector: Issues and Implications’, *Economic and Political Weekly*, 1–6 June.

Bhattacharya, B. B., and A. Mitra (1997) 'Changing Composition of Employment in Tertiary Sector: A Cross-country Analysis', *Economic and Political Weekly*, 15 Mar.

Chen, S., and M. Ravallion (2000) 'How Did the World's Poorest Fare in the 1990s?'. Policy Research Working Paper 2409. Washington, DC: World Bank.

Datt, G., and M. Ravallion (1992) 'Growth and Redistribution Components of Changes in Poverty Measure: A Decomposition with Application to Brazil and India in the 1980s', *Journal of Development Economics*, 38: 275–95.

Deaton, A., and J. Drèze (2002) 'Poverty and Inequality in India: A Re-examination', *Economic and Political Weekly*, 7 Sept.

Dollar, D. (2001) 'Globalization, Inequality and Poverty since 1980'. Background Paper. Washington, DC: World Bank. <http://www.worldbank.org/research/global>.

Feenstra, R. C., and G. H. Hanson (1996) 'Globalisation, Outsourcing and Wage Inequality', *American Economic Review*, 86: 240–5.

Foster, J., J. Greer, and E. Thorbecke (1984) 'A Class of Decomposable Poverty Measures', *Econometrica*, 52: 761–6.

Government of India (GoI) (var. years) *Economic Survey of Karnataka*. <http://des.kar.nic.in/indexie.html>.

—— (2002) 'National Human Development Report, 2001'. New Delhi: Planning Commission for the Government of India.

International Labour Organization (ILO) (2006) *Labour and Social Trends in Asia and the Pacific 2006: Progress Towards Decent Work*. Geneva: ILO.

Jain, L. R., and S. D. Tendulkar (1990) 'Role of Growth and Distribution in the Observed Change in Headcount Ratio Measure of Poverty: A Decomposition Exercise for India', *Indian Economic Review*, 35: 165–205.

Kakwani, N. (2000) 'On Measuring Growth and Inequality Components of Poverty with Application to Thailand', *Journal of Quantitative Economics*, 16: 67–79.

—— and E. M. Pernia (2000) 'What is Pro-poor Growth?', *Asian Development Review*, 18: 1–16.

—— B. Prakash, and H. H. Son (2000) 'Growth, Inequality, and Poverty: An Introduction', *Asian Development Review*, 18: 1–21.

—— and K. Subbarao (1990) 'Rural Poverty and its Alleviation in India', *Economic and Political Weekly*, 25: A2–A16.

Kuznets, S. (1955) 'Economic Growth and Income Inequality', *American Economic Review*, 45: 1–28.

—— (1966) *Modern Economic Growth: Rate, Structure and Spread*. New Haven, Conn.: Yale University Press.

Mazumdar, D., and H. H. Son (2002) 'Vulnerable Groups and the Labour Market in Thailand: Impact of the Asian Financial Crisis in the Light of Thailand's Growth Process'. Paper presented at the NCAER workshop, 'The Impact of Globalization on the Labour Markets', New Delhi.

Mitra, A. (1992) 'Growth and Poverty: The Urban Legend', *Economic and Political Weekly*, 28 Mar.

—— (1994) *Urbanization, Slums, Informal Sector Employment and Poverty: An Exploratory Study*. New Delhi: D. K. Publishers.

—— (1997) 'Infrastructure and Human Development', *Productivity*, 38: 200–6.

—— (2003) *Occupational Choices, Networks and Transfers: An Exegesis Based on Micro Data from Delhi Slums*. New Delhi: Manohar Publications.

Papola, T. S. (1981) *Urban Informal Sector in a Developing Economy.* New Delhi: Vikas Publishing House.

Rama, M. (2003) 'Globalization and Workers in Developing Countries'. In R. Hasan and D. Mitra (eds), *The Impact of Trade on Labour: Issues, Perspectives and Experiences from Developing Asia.* Amsterdam: North-Holland Elsevier.

Ravallion, M., and G. Datt (1996) 'How Important to India's Poor is the Sectoral Composition of Economic Growth?', *World Bank Economic Review,* 10: 1–25S.

Reserve Bank of India (RBI) (2003–4) *Handbook of Statistics on Indian Economy.* <http://www.rbi.org.in/scripts/AnnualPublications.aspx?head=Handbook%20of%20Statistics%20on%20Indian%20Economy>.

Rivera-Baitz, L. A., and D. Xie (1992) 'GATT, Trade and Growth', *American Economic Review,* 82: 422–7.

Sachs, J. D., N. Bajpai, and A. Ramiah (2002) 'Understanding Regional Economic Growth in India'. Working Paper 88. Cambridge, Mass.: Harvard University, Center for International Development.

Sundaram, K. (2001) 'Employment and Poverty in 1990s: Further Results from NSS 55th Round Employment-Unemployment Survey, 1999–2000'. *Economic and Political Weekly,* 11 Aug.

Tendulkar, S. D., and L. R. Jain (1995) 'Economic Growth, Relative Inequality, and Equity: The Case of India', *Asian Development Review,* 13: 138–68.

United Nations Development Programme (UNDP) (2008) *Rising Food and Fuel Prices in Asia and the Pacific: Causes, Impacts and Policy Responses.* Draft Technical Report. Colombo: UNDP Regional Centre.

Virmani, A. (2005) 'Policy Regimes, Growth and Poverty in India: Lessons of Government Failure and Entrepreneurial Success!'. Working Paper 170. New Delhi: ICRIER.

World Bank (2008) 'Rising Food Prices: Policy Options and World Bank Response'. Background Note for the Development Committee. Washington, DC: World Bank.

6

Globalization and Rural Poverty: Perspectives from a Social Observatory in the Philippines

Yujiro Hayami

6.1. Introduction

Waves of modernizing forces under globalization, such as commercialization and new technology, have been pressing major changes upon rural communities in the third world. Fears have often been expressed that these forces are destroying the traditional community institutions based on the principles of mutual help and income sharing, thereby creating greater inequality and higher incidence of poverty in the rural sector (Griffin 1974; Scott 1976; Lipton with Longhurst 1989). This chapter aims to give a microscopic perspective on this concern by means of an intensive case study of one village (*barangay* or *barrio*) in the Philippines, which has been used as a social observatory over the past three decades by social scientists at the International Rice Research Institute (IRRI), including myself.

This village is located in the Province of Laguna lying along the coast of Laguna de Bay (the largest lake in the Philippines), south of Manila. At IRRI we called it East Laguna Village, because it faces the east coast of Laguna de Bay. A survey on this village was first conducted in 1966 by Hiromitsu Umehara (1967). Subsequently, the Social Sciences Division of IRRI conducted eight surveys covering all the households in the village in 1974, 1976, 1980, 1983, 1987, 1992, 1995, and 1997; an additional two surveys covering farmers' households were only carried out in 1996 and 1997.

Based on data collected from these surveys, as compiled in Hayami and Kikuchi 2000, this chapter aims to assess the possible impacts of modernization forces under globalization on rural communities in developing economies. The four major forces focused in this study are: (i) rapid population growth continuing to press on limited farmland available to villagers; (ii) diffusion of modern high-yielding varieties of rice associated with increased application of fertilizers, which is popularly called 'the green revolution'; (iii) land-reform programmes aimed at transferring land-cultivation rights from landlords to tenant farmers; and (iv) expansion of non-farm economic activities resulting from the increased integration of this village with wide urban and foreign markets.

How those forces are related to globalization may need explaining, with the exception of the fourth factor. First, it is important to recognize that major acceleration in population growth in this study site as well as in developing countries in general starting from around the 1920s–30s is considered a product of globalization because it resulted mainly from sharp declines in death rates due to the importation of advanced medical and public health technology from developed countries and also from the expansion of markets to developing economies with the result of preventing local crop failures from turning into famines (Hayami and Godo 2005: 64–73). Second, it is well known that the green revolution was essentially a transfer of advanced agricultural technology from temperate to tropical areas through adaptive research (Hayami and Ruttan 1985). Third, redistributive land reform may be considered a cure to the inequity that was brought about by earlier globalization. Particularly important in the Philippine context is that land reform was geared to correct the extremely inequitable land distribution that was a consequence of Spanish colonialism.

Since these four factors have commonly been operating in developing economies, though their strength differs each across countries, the intensive observations on the transformation of this village are expected to shed lights on the mechanism of how the forces of globalization may interact in influencing poverty and inequality in the rural sector.

All the figures presented hereafter are drawn by the author based on the data collected for Hayami and Kikuchi (2000).

6.2. Population Pressure on Land

East Laguna Village began to be settled in the 1880s. In a marshy lowland area adjacent to Laguna de Bay, initial settlers opened land and practised rain-fed rice monoculture under sharecropping contracts with landlords mainly living in local towns. Because of specialization in rice with no alternative crop suitable to the marshy lowland, together with the nature of the colonial Philippine economy based on the export of primary commodities, villagers were involved in market transactions from the beginning, though their income was predominantly produced from rice cultivation with virtually no cottage manufacturing activity as well as few non-farm employment opportunities available. Villagers were poor as they had to submit a half of their rice harvest to landlords but they were largely homogeneous, with no significant class differentiation within the village.

The most fundamental and sustained force to press on change in such a community structure was population growth. In this village the frontier of opening new land for cultivation had been closed by the late 1950s, but the population continued to increase at rates higher than 3 per cent per year, tripling the number of villagers from about 400 in 1966 to about 1,200 in 1995, associated almost parallel increases in the man : land ratio (Figure 6.1). The effect of importation of advanced medical and public health technologies on population growth was especially strong in this area. Not only natural growth was accelerated through reductions in the death rate but also immigration was encouraged because this marshy lowland area became less susceptible to contagious diseases, thereby encouraging immigration from surrounding hills and mountains where people had settled earlier for their better hygienic environments.

As the availability of rice field per capita decreased, it became progressively more difficult for children of farmers in this village and more so for migrants

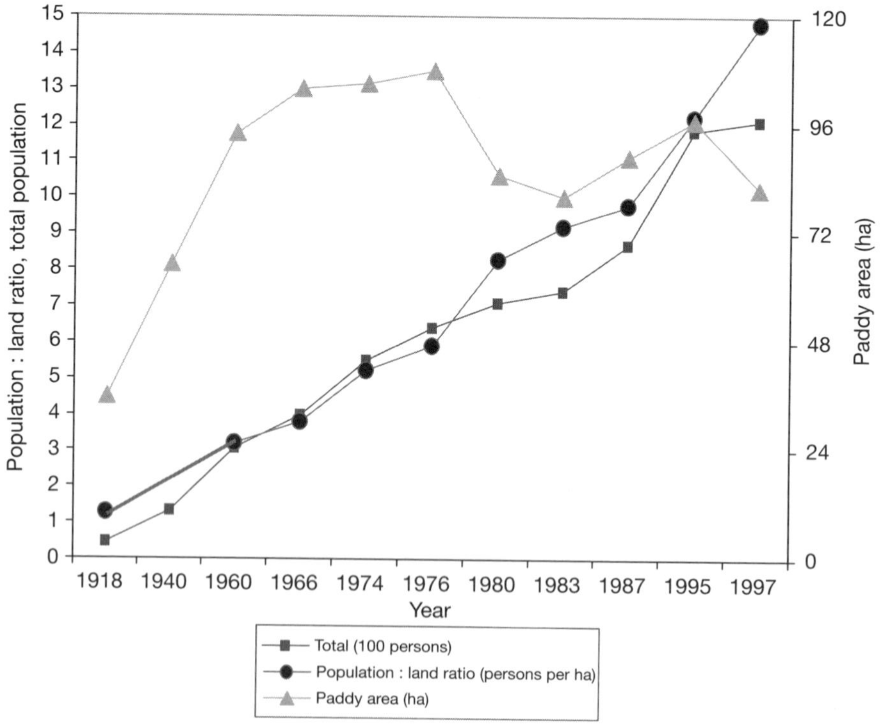

Fig. 6.1. Growth of population and riceland, East Laguna Village, 1918–97

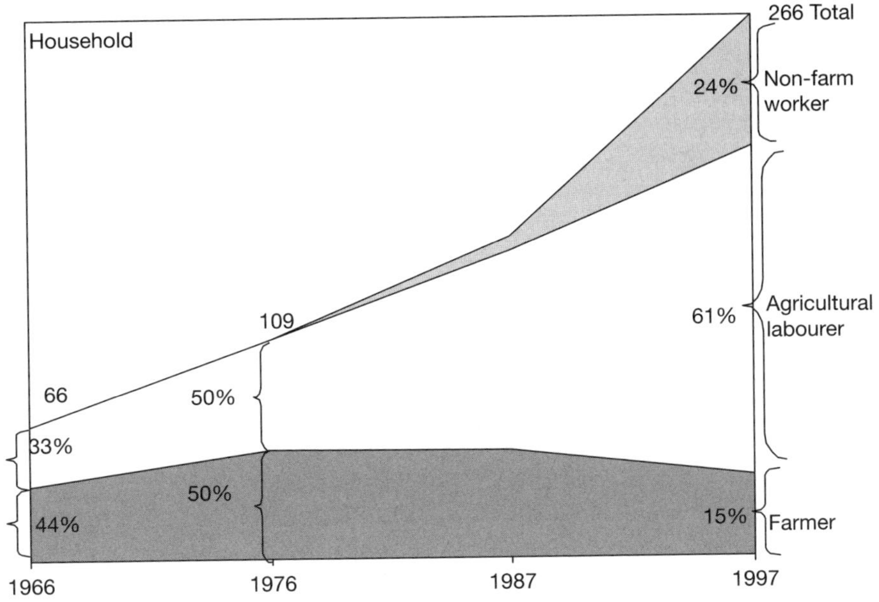

Fig. 6.2. Distribution of households by type, East Laguna Village, 1966–7

from other villages to acquire lands for establishing themselves as farmers. Thus, class segmentation between farm operators and agricultural labourers began to emerge in the hitherto homogeneous peasant community consisting mostly of sharecroppers. The share of agricultural labourers who held no land to cultivate but earned subsistence from hired farm work increased sharply relative to farmers (Figure 6.2). As the village became closely integrated with the urban economy, a new class of 'non-farm workers' was created in East Laguna Village. Typically, they commute from their residence within the village to permanent salaried jobs in nearby towns.

6.3. Impacts of the Green Revolution

The impoverishing effect of increased land scarcity was counteracted to some extent by the extension of a national irrigation system to this village in 1958 that converted rice production from rain-fed single cropping to irrigated double cropping. On this infrastructure, the dramatic diffusion of modern high-yielding varieties began from the late 1960s. Because of its close location to IRRI (within about 30 km), farmers in this area were the earliest to adopt modern rice varieties (MVs), not only in the Philippines but also among tropical rice-producing areas of the world. They were also quick to shift from the first-generation modern varieties susceptible to damage by brown plant hoppers (MV1) to MV2s resistant to the plant hoppers, and further to MV3s having better grain qualities (Figure 6.3., Panel I). Correspondingly, rice yields per hectare per cropping season in this village more than doubled, from the level of about two tons to five tons in less than thirty years (Figure 6.3., Panel II). Such quick turnovers of rice varieties to some extent reflected the advantage of this village being located close to IRRI. However, this pattern was common among irrigated rice villages in the Philippines as well as in other Southeast Asian economies such as Indonesia and Malaysia, even though some time lags were involved.

Despite the sharp increases in rice yields, it is doubtful how much farmers gained from this innovation. The successful green revolution not only in the Philippines but also in major rice-growing areas in Asia significantly increased global rice supply, resulting in large declines in rice prices in the world rice market. This global effect was transmitted to this village also, resulting in a reduction in the real price of rice received by farmers from about 20 pesos to about 7 pesos per kg of paddy, at the pace slightly faster than the pace of rice yield increase (Figure 6.3, Panel III). This means that the gains from new rice technology were mostly transferred to consumers, leaving little benefit to farmers. This adverse price effect should have been especially serious to large farmers and landlords whose marketable surplus ratios were high, while marginal farmers and agricultural labourers could have been better off to the extent that they were net buyers of rice (Hayami and Herdt 1977).

It is important to recognize that the adverse price effect of the green revolution on farmers was neither specific to this village nor to the Philippines, but was global, as is evident from the close correlation in rice price movements between the domestic price in the Philippines and the Bangkok fob price of Thai rice that is considered to represent the world rice market situation. It should also be recognized that it had the effect of reducing public supports to the rice sector, especially on irrigation systems. In this village the maintenance of a national irrigation system deteriorated as the result of the reduction in foreign aid to the National Irrigation Administration of the Philippines, forcing farmers to supplement water by installing private pumps (Kikuchi, Fujita, and Hayami 2001). The new biological technology in the green revolution itself was considered to be neutral with respect to scale since no statistically significant yield difference was observed between large and small farmers throughout the 1970s and 1980s. But large farmers' yields became significantly higher in the 1990s when it became necessary to use private pumps (Hayami and Kikuchi 2000: 101). In this way, foreign aid agencies' response to rice price declines as the very result of the successful green revolution should have worked as a force to increase inequality in this village.

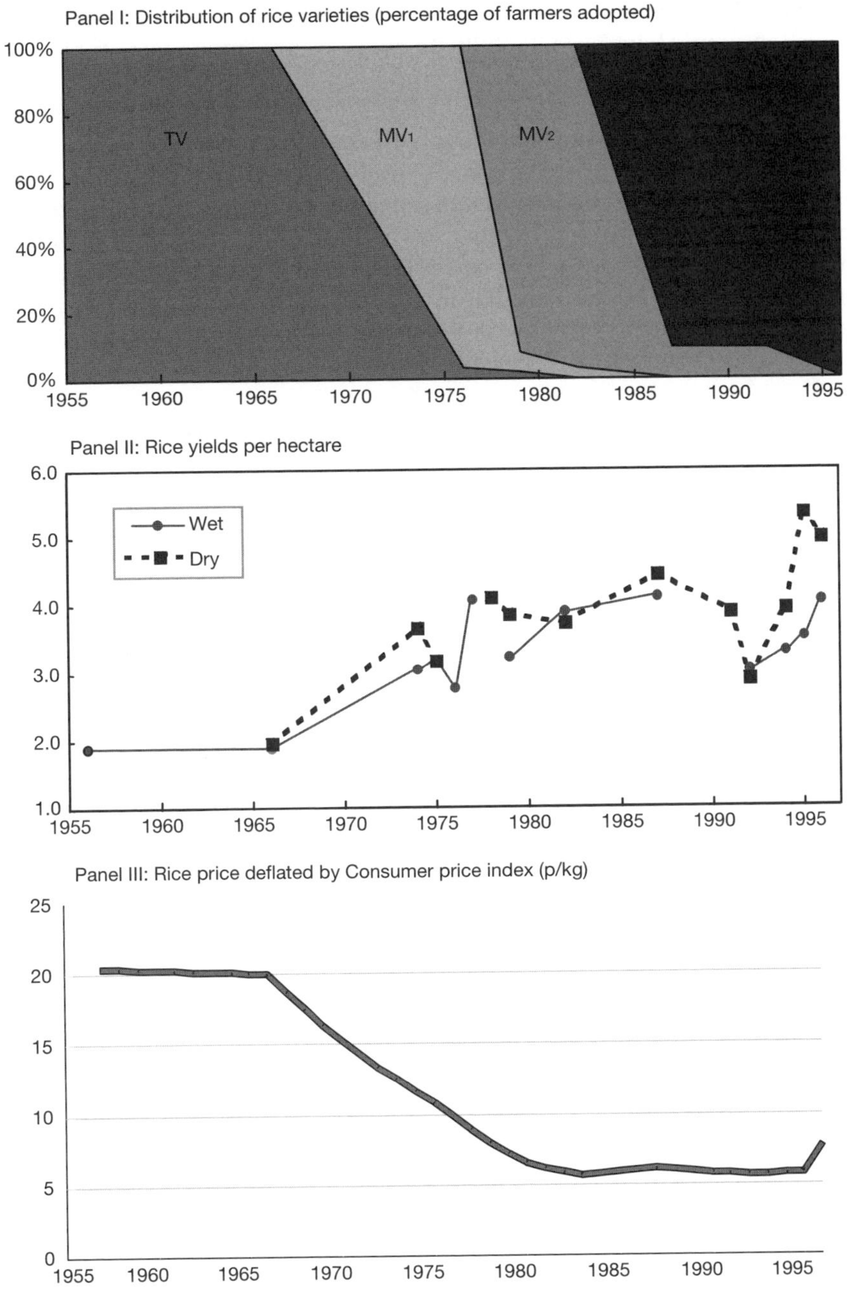

Fig. 6.3. Distribution of rice varieties adopted by farmers, average yield per hectare, and rice prices received by farmers, East Laguna Village, 1965–95

A major factor determining the impact of the new rice technology on poverty reduction should have been its ability to increase farm employment for agricultural labourers who belonged to the lowest income strata. As observed in Figure 6.4, in the initial stage of MV diffusion the average amount of labour used for rice production per hectare, including both family and hired labour, increased by around 20 per cent from the pre-MV level of 89 person days in 1966 to 105 days in 1976. The increase occurred mainly in weeding and harvesting/threshing activities, reflecting high yielding and fertilizer using characteristics of MVs. From 1976 to 1995, however, the labour use decreased by as much as around 40 per cent, to a level lower than that in 1966 owing to the diffusion of labour-saving practices such as the use of herbicides and portable threshers. Despite this sharp decline in total labour use, hired labour employment in 1995 was

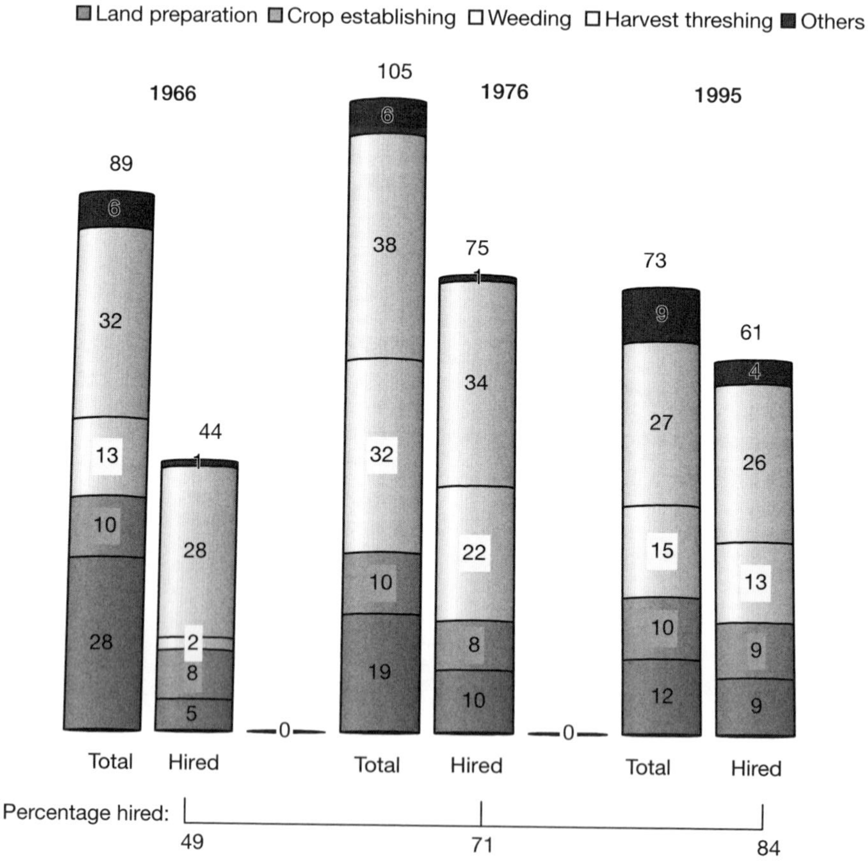

Fig. 6.4. Labour utilization in rice production per hectare (wet season), East Laguna Village, 1966–95

61 days or nearly 40 per cent higher than the pre-MV level of 44 days, implying that the share of hired labour in total labour use increased from about 50 per cent to about 80 per cent. This bias towards the greater use of hired labour is considered to be one of the results from changes in income distribution owing to interactions between the green revolution and land-reform programmes to be discussed in the next section.

6.4. Income Redistribution under the Land-reform Programmes

Compared with the independent effects of the MV technology alone on income distribution, as examined in the previous section, much greater impacts were produced when this technological progress interacted with land-reform programmes.

Land-reform programmes aimed to correct extreme inequality in land-ownership distribution, as the legacy of Spanish colonialism had been implemented strongly in this village and its surroundings under President Ferdinand Marcos' martial law regime during the period 1972–81. The programmes began with 'operation leasehold', converting traditional sharecropping tenancy to leasehold tenancy with land rent fixed at lower than market rates, to be followed by 'operation land transfer', transferring to tenants the ownership of lands under tenancy above landlords' retention limits (Hayami, Quisumbing, and Adriano 1990). Their outcomes in East Laguna Village are clearly observable in Figure 6.5. In 1966, before the start of land reform, about two-thirds of the paddy fields in the village were under shared tenancy and one-third under leasehold tenancy, whereas land owned by villagers was only 1 per cent of their farming area. With the progress of 'operation leasehold', leasehold tenancy became dominant, with its share rising to about two-thirds in 1970, while the share of sharecropping land decreased to less than one-third. But the share of owner-farming area was still only 2 per cent in 1976. Further progress in 'operation leasehold', together with the beginning of 'operation land transfer', increased the owner-farming area to 29 per cent of village land by 1995, while the sharecropping area decreased to only 15 per cent.

Initially, 'operation leasehold' resulted in an income transfer from landlords in towns to tenant farmers in this village of about 15 per cent of rice output, because land rent under the traditional 50 : 50 output and input-sharing contract was about 40 per cent of output, while the leasehold rent stipulated by the reform was fixed at 25 of normal rice yield at the time of programme implementation. The same applied to the beneficiaries of 'operation land transfer', because their amortization payments to land purchase were usually set about equal to leasehold rents. Later, however, their benefits rose sharply with the progress of the green revolution. Since the rent or amortization payments were fixed in kind, all the increases in rice yields went to tenants. Corresponding to

Fig. 6.5. Distribution of riceland by tenure status, East Laguna Village, 1966–95

more than twice the increases in rice yields during two decades from the early 1970s, the landlords' share went down from initially stipulated 25 to only about 10 per cent, resulting in major income gains to former sharecroppers.

Such a large income transfer resulting from the concurrent progress of the green revolution and land reform, no doubt, contributed greatly to the reduction of disparity between tenants and landlords, which had been the major woe in rural Philippines. Ironically, however, it became the source of major disparity within the village community, because this benefit of land reform was captured by tenant farmers alone, while no direct benefit accrued to landless agricultural labourers. Moreover, land-reform regulations resulted in an inactive land-rental market and closed opportunities for agricultural labourers to ascend to farm operators because, if new leaseholders or amortizing owners were to sub-rent their holdings to agricultural labourers, their rights to continue cultivating the lands would be forfeited and transferred to subtenants as 'the actual tillers of the soil'. Thus, subtenancy was practised only within the narrow circle of relatives and close friends. This, together with rapid inflows of labourers from surrounding hills and mountains, resulted in sharp increases in the number of agricultural labourers' households relative to farmers, as earlier observed in Figure 6.2.

How the problem of traditional disparity between tenant farmers and landlords was replaced by that of the newly emerged disparity between farmers and

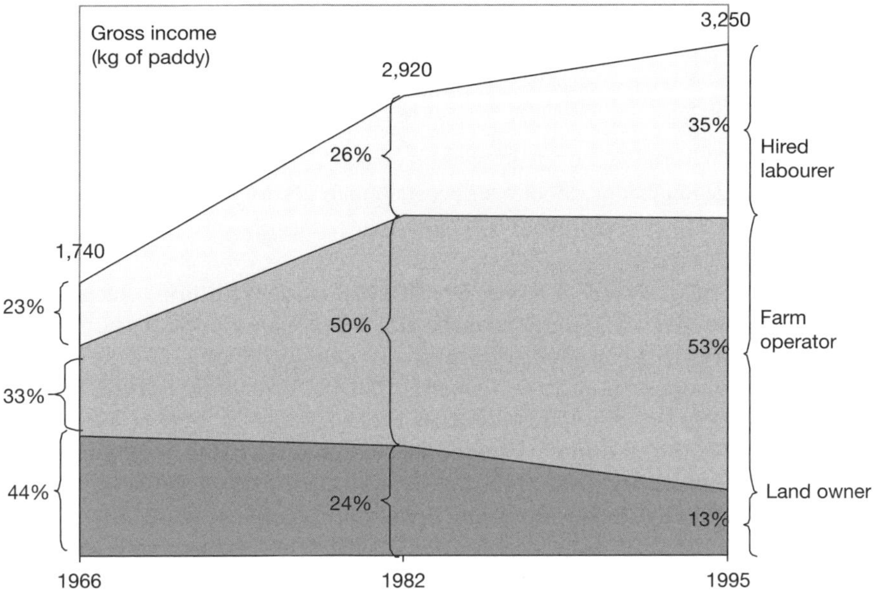

Fig. 6.6. Shares of income from rice production per hectare (wet season), East Laguna Village, 1966–95

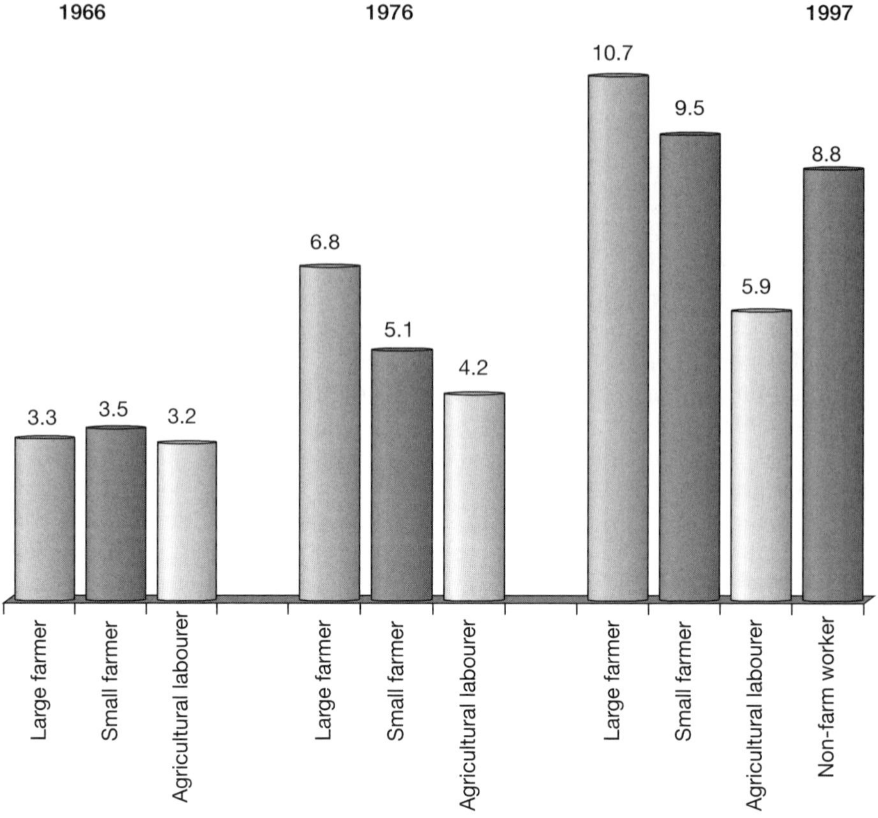

Fig. 6.7. Average number of school years per adult male (21–64 years old), East Laguna Village, 1966–97

labourers can be observed in Figure 6.6. In 1966, under traditional technology and land tenure systems, landlords received land rent amounting to as much as 44 per cent of income produced from rice production, while 23 per cent was paid to hired labourers, and the remaining 33 per cent only accrued to farm operators. By 1982, farmers' income share rose to 50 per cent at the expense of landlords, while the labourers' share increased only marginally. In 1995, farmers continued to receive a high share at the same level as in 1982, while the further decrease in landlords' share went to labourers, reflecting the increased use of hired labour relative to family labour as observed in Figure 6.4. In terms of the distribution of income from rice farming, it is obvious that the disparity in per capita income widened between farmers and labourers, since the population of the latter increased much faster than the former. Among farmers, income gains were larger for those holding larger lands covered by land-reform programmes.

The increasing inequality within the village community was reflected in widening differentials in the level of education across social classes. Figure 6.7 shows that in 1966 no significant difference was observed in the average number of school years per adult across the households of agricultural labourers—small and large farmers who operate farms above and below 2 hectares, respectively. However, significant differences emerged in 1976 and widened further in 1997, with the education levels of large and small farmers' family members becoming higher than that of labourers by 80 and 60 per cent, respectively.

Correspondingly, inter-class differentials also emerged in family size. Before land-reform programmes removed the 'agricultural ladder' allowing labourers to ascend to the status of farm operators, agricultural labourers mainly consisted of newly married couples with one or two babies, if any. Typically, as they accumulated farming experiences and small savings, they became sharecroppers on a small plot of land. Later, as their children increased in number and grew to be able to help farm work, they rented more lands. In fact, differences in family size observed for 1976 in Figure 6.8 seem to reflect the lifecycle of villagers associated

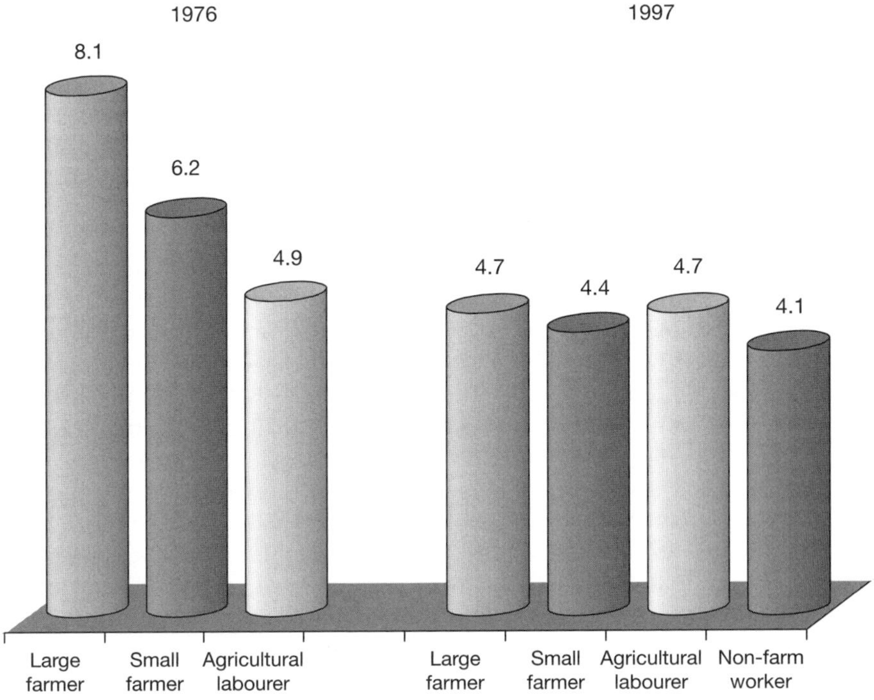

Fig. 6.8. Average family size, East Laguna Village, 1976–97

with the rising of agricultural labourers to small farmers, and further to large farmers. However, such differences in family size disappeared from the 1997 observations. The family sizes of farmers decreased because many of the farmers' children, who received higher education, moved out to urban areas for non-farm occupations. This reduction in farmers' family sizes tended to increase their per capita income relative to labourers. Furthermore, the farmers' income was further augmented by remittances from children working in urban areas as well as abroad. In short, the income disparity that was created in this village community through the combined effects of population pressure, new rice technology, and land reform continued to widen further over time through differential changes in education and family size.

6.5. Expansion of Non-farm Economic Activities

Despite the sharply increased population of agricultural labourers under apparently unfavourable conditions, they were able to subsist because of expansions in wage employment opportunities. As already observed, employment creation for them by the green revolution was modest at best, even when counting the effects of substitution of hired labour for family labour by farmers who benefited from land reform. It was the expansion of non-farm employment that helped landless labourers to maintain or even improve their subsistence.

Non-farm employment opportunities for villagers began to expand rapidly, especially after the late 1970s when major improvements in highway systems were accomplished, through which the major pulses of globalization were transmitted to rural areas. The west coast of Laguna de Bay, adjacent to Metro Manila, quickly became an industrial zone, with many modern factories built on the basis of FDI, to which villagers could commute daily or where they could stay working during the weekdays and return home at weekends. Even though permanent employment in the modern formal sector was limited mainly to farmers' children, who received higher than primary education, landless labourers were able to access casual employment in such activities as construction, informal transportation, petty trades, and small manufactures, which spilled out either directly or indirectly from the formal sector activities.

From the late 1980s, a new surge began in the expansion of non-farm employment opportunities through the spread of small manufactures in local towns and even inside villages. They engaged in the production of labour-intensive commodities, such as garments, shoes, toys, and Christmas ornaments for export, under various subcontracting arrangements. Typically, a trader in Manila who received a large bulk order from a foreign buyer representing a supermarket chain in the USA would send orders in small lots to these informal manufacturers under various subcontracting arrangements, because of advantages such as access to cheap labour and evasion from labour codes.

Inside East Laguna Village, traditionally characterized by the virtual absence of manufacturing activities, seven workshops were opened during 1991–5 for Christmas ornaments made from tin plates and wires, with the result that the share of village income from manufacturing jumped from only around 1 per cent before the mid-1980s to as much as 12 per cent in 1995–6 (Hayami and Kikuchi 2000). Much income from such local manufacturing went to the households of agricultural labourers and marginal farmers, as their family members were employed in these workshops or received payments for doing certain tasks at home under putting out contacts with the workshop operators.

This kind of rural-based industrialization was one of the bases of export-oriented industrialization in Japan to be followed by Asian newly industrialized economies (NIEs). As NIEs advanced to a higher stage of development, with their wage rate sharply rising in the 1980s, demand from high-income economies for labour-intensive, low-technology products shifted to ASEAN and other low-wage Asian economies (Hayami 1998). An important condition for Asian countries to be able to capture such opportunities in a 'flying geese' pattern should have been wide diffusion of elementary education and development in communication and transportation infrastructure, as clearly illustrated with the case of East Laguna Village.

6.6. Patterns of Income Growth

What would have been the net result of complex interactions of the four modernization forces under globalization on economic growth in East Laguna Village? The household income data prepared from our recurrent surveys may shed light on this question.

6.6.1. Database

Although full enumeration surveys were conducted nine times in East Laguna Village, we were able to collect sufficiently comprehensive data for estimating the incomes of all the village households for six years only (1974; 1976; 1980; 1983; 1987; and 1995). For those six years, we estimated the incomes of all the individual households by adding (i) incomes from self-employed activities such as rice farming; (ii) earnings from hired employment, capital. and land rentals (including rent from subtenancy contract); and (iii) transfer incomes such as remittances from family members living outside the village (minus transfers to the outside). The income from self-employed activities is obtained by subtracting from output values all the paid out costs. The values of self-employed products used for home consumption are imputed by market prices and included in income, whereas those used for production purposes such as seeds, feeds, and payments in kind to inputs are deducted as costs. The data are not available to apply the same estimation procedure before 1974. We tried, however, to estimate the total village income in 1965–6 (1965–6 dry season and 1966 wet season) through extrapolations mainly based on the available data of rice production, though it is not possible to estimate incomes for different classes of households separately.

Although we have relatively reliable data for the six survey years, a major problem in ascertaining the trend of real income growth from the surveys in such a small number of years are the influences of weather and other ecological variations on rice yields that resulted in major fluctuations in rice incomes. In order to mitigate the effects of random shocks such as weather and market fluctuations, our comparison over time is based on the averages of 1974 and 1976 data and of 1980 and 1983 data. For 1995, the average rice income for 1995 and 1996 is added to the non-rice income in 1995, because the 1996 survey covered farmers' households only.

6.6.2. Growth of Average per Capita Income

The first question is if East Laguna Village was able to achieve positive economic growth under strong population pressure on limited land. The answer depends, to a large extent, on what deflator to use for the conversion of nominal to real incomes. As a measure of economic welfare enjoyed by villagers, the consumer price index (CPI) outside Manila, prepared by the National Statistics Office (formerly National Census and Statistics Office), may be relevant. As a measure of product or value added by village factors, however, the farm-gate price of rough rice might be a more appropriate deflator, considering the dominant weight of rice production in the economy of East Laguna Village, particularly in earlier years. The problem is that the movements in CPI and the price of rice were very different, as already observed in Figure 6.3.

As is evident from Figure 6.9, the real income growth patterns are very different between the cases of using the price of rice and CPI as deflators. For the whole period from 1965–6 to 1995–6, CPI deflated per capita income remained largely stagnant, while that based on rice-price deflation recorded a high growth rate of 4.2 per cent per year. While it is certain that the rice-price deflation overestimates welfare gains to villagers as it eliminates the adverse price effect of the green revolution, the CPI deflation may result in underestimation because a significant share of rice output was consumed within village without being sold to the market and, also, because the weight of rice in villagers' consumption expenditure is higher than the average of households outside Manila, including not only rural villages but also urban towns. In any case, one certain conclusion we can draw is that East Laguna Village was somehow able to prevent per capita real income from decreasing during the past three decades under strong population pressure on limited land resources as well as the backwash of deterioration in the terms of trade for rice.

6.6.3. *Per Capita Income Growth by Type of Household and by Type of Economic Activity*

How did relative income positions change across different classes of households? Figures 6.9 and 6.10 compare average per capita incomes deflated by CPI across different categories of households. The per capita income growth of agricultural labourers was slower than that of farmers, resulting in declines in their relative incomes to large and small farmers from 35 per cent and 67 per cent, respectively, in 1974–6 to 23 and 44 per cent, respectively. Nevertheless, agricultural labourers were able to achieve net growth in per capita real income by 13 per cent during these two decades. This may not be an insignificant achievement, considering the sharply increased population of agricultural labourers competing for employment in a limited farmland area. It was only possible with major increases in incomes from non-farm sources as well as earnings from hired employment.

Indeed, as shown in Figure 6.11, the income of farm origin (aggregate of self-employed farm incomes and earnings from hired farm employment) decreased rapidly over time, whereas the income of non-farm origin increased. As a result, the share of the latter increased in the average household income from 13 per cent in 1974–6 to 64 per cent in 1995–6. The initial increase in the share of non-farm income from 1974–6 to 1980–3 resulted mainly from increased hired employment in both permanent employment in modern factories in the west coast of Laguna de Bay and casual employment in construction and

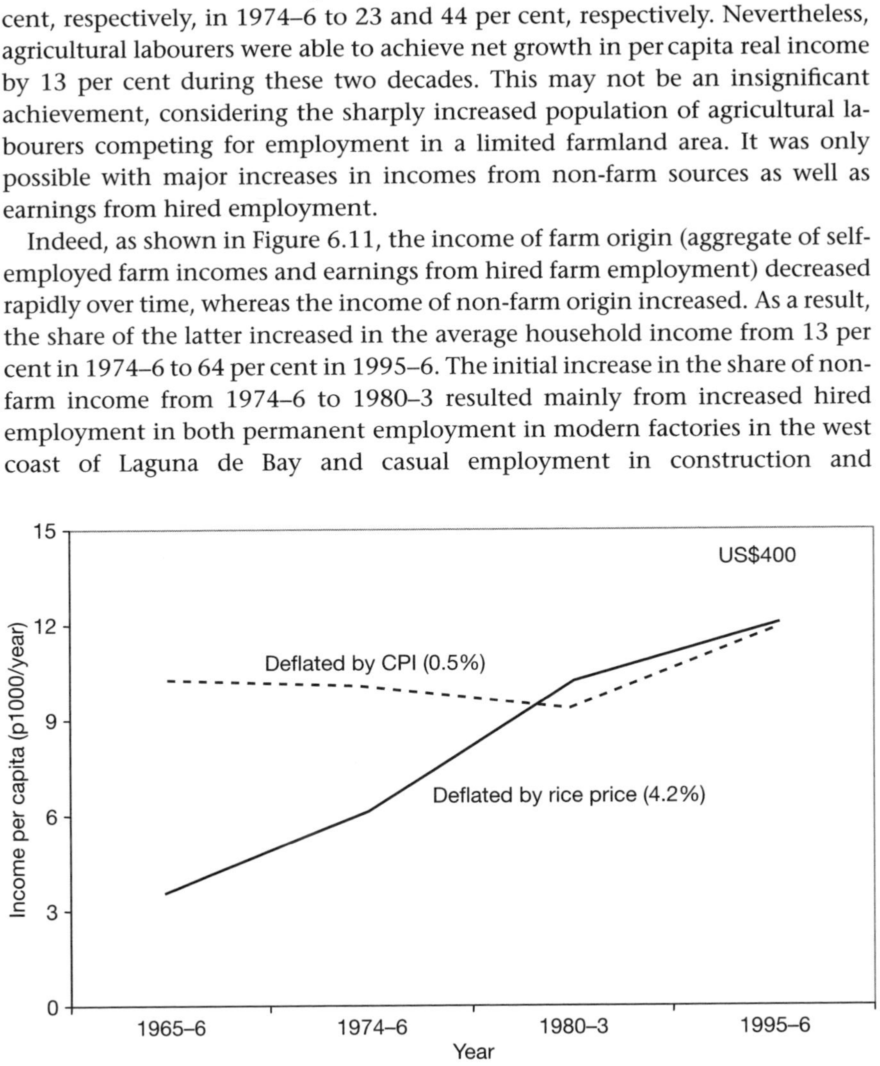

Fig. 6.9. Income growth per capita, East Laguna Village, 1965–96

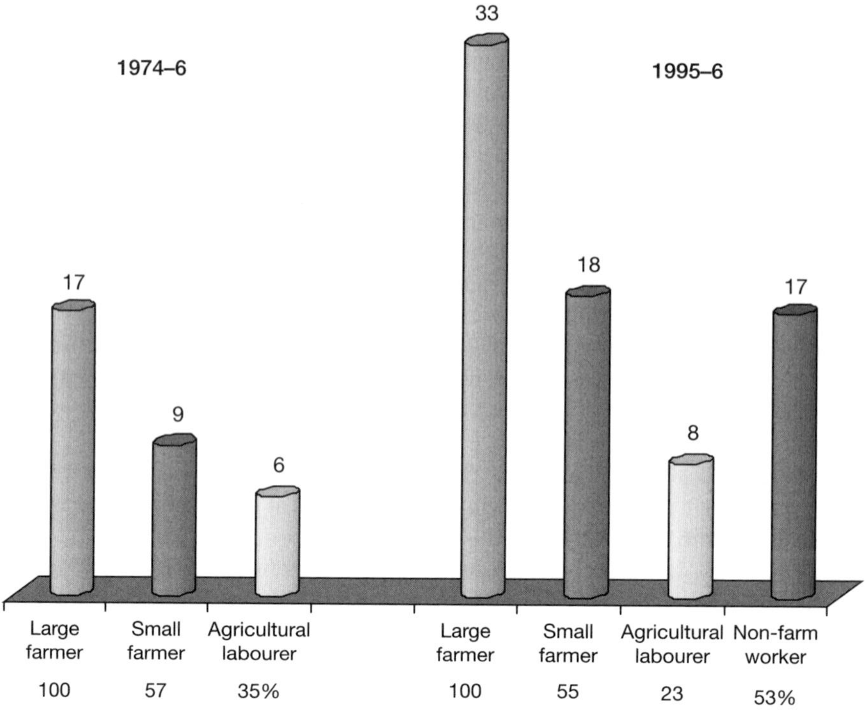

Fig. 6.10. Average per capita income (CPI deflation) by type of household, East Laguna Village, 1974–6 to 1995–6

transportation activities. The former opportunities were mainly captured by the educated youth in the farmer households, whereas a large share of the latter was captured by marginal farmers and agricultural labourers. On the other hand, from 1980–3 to 1995–6, the share of the income from non-farm self-employment increased faster than that of hired employment because of increases in cottage industries under subcontract arrangements as explained in the previous section.

The increased integration of East Laguna Village with urban labour markets was especially evident starting from the 1980s in the emergence of non-farm workers as a new social class. Their average household income, earned mainly from permanent salaried jobs in local towns, was about the same as that of small farmers and was more than double than that of agricultural labourers whose earnings were based mainly on casual daily wage employment. These non-farm workers and small farmers together composed the village middle class, comprising about a third of the population and earning nearly a half of the total village income in 1995–6.

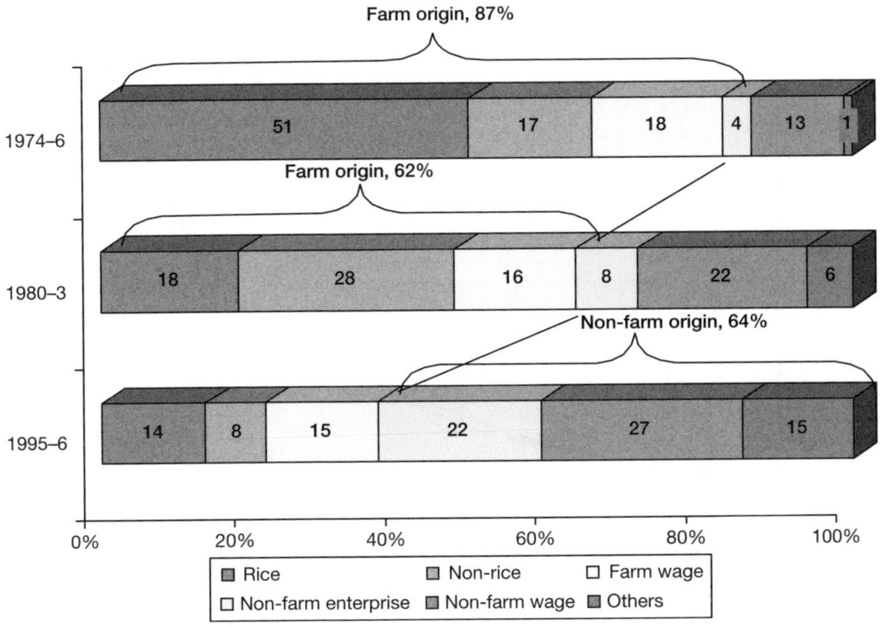

Fig. 6.11. Percentage composition of average household income, East Laguna Village, 1974–95

6.7. Changes in Income Distribution and Poverty Incidence

How did the distribution of income and the incidence of poverty change in East Laguna Village? Figures 6.12(a) and 6.12(b) compares changes in the Gini coefficients measuring inequality in the distribution of both income and operational landholdings together with changes in the percentage of people below the poverty line (the so-called headcount index) measuring the incidence of poverty in this community.

It is important to observe that the income Gini coefficient did not rise significantly in the past two decades. Indeed, changes in the Lorenz curve drawn from the household income data are almost not discernible over the years of 1974, 1983, and 1995 (Figure 6.12(a)). During this period large farmers achieved significantly faster per capita income growth than small farmers and agricultural labourers, as observed in Figure 6.10. Yet, large farmers' share of the village income did not rise but decline from about 45 per cent in 1974–6 to only about 20 per cent, owing to a sharp decline in their household members' share of the village population (dropping from 26 per cent in 1976 to mere 8 per cent

(a)

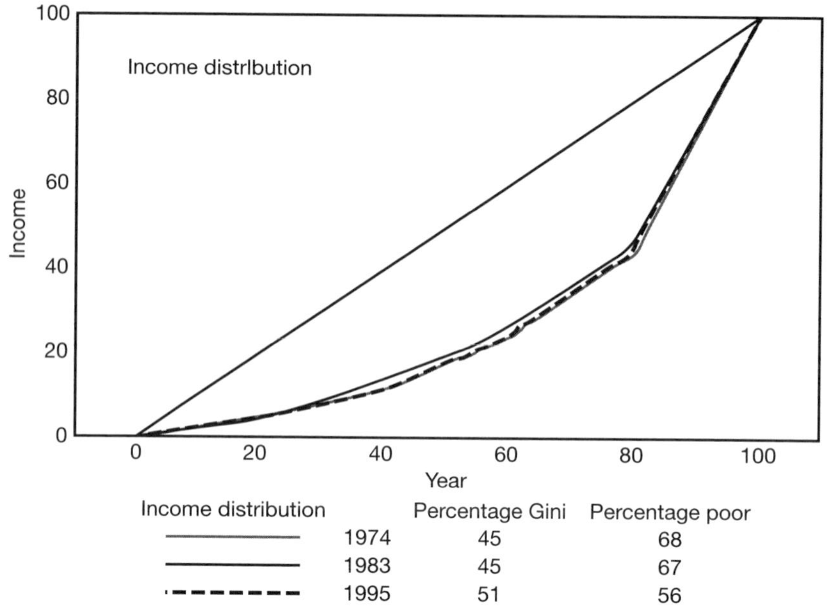

Fig. 6.12(a). Changes in income distribution, East Laguna Village, 1966–95

in 1975). Meanwhile, the income share of the village middle class, consisting of small farmers and non-farm workers, rose from about 30 per cent to 40 per cent.

Such movements in the income distribution represent a sharp contrast to those in the distribution of landholdings. The land Gini coefficient increased rapidly over time (Figure 6.12(b)), progressively diverging from the income Gini. In contrast to the changes in income share, large farmers' share of operational landholdings was maintained at about the same level of nearly 70 per cent, despite the sharply reduced shares in the number of households as well as population. As long as East Laguna Village was a purely agrarian community, relying mainly on rice production (as was the case before the 1970s), the major determinant of income distribution across households should have been the distribution of operational landholdings. However, as non-farm income earning opportunities increased, the power of land distribution to bind income distribution was progressively weakened; this should have been the main reason why the Gini coefficient of income inequality was prevented from rising significantly, despite the sharp increase in the Gini coefficient of land concentration from 0.54 in 1966 to as high as 0.89 in 1995.

Similar to other rural villages in the Philippines as well as other developing economies, East Laguna Village was characterized by the high incidence of

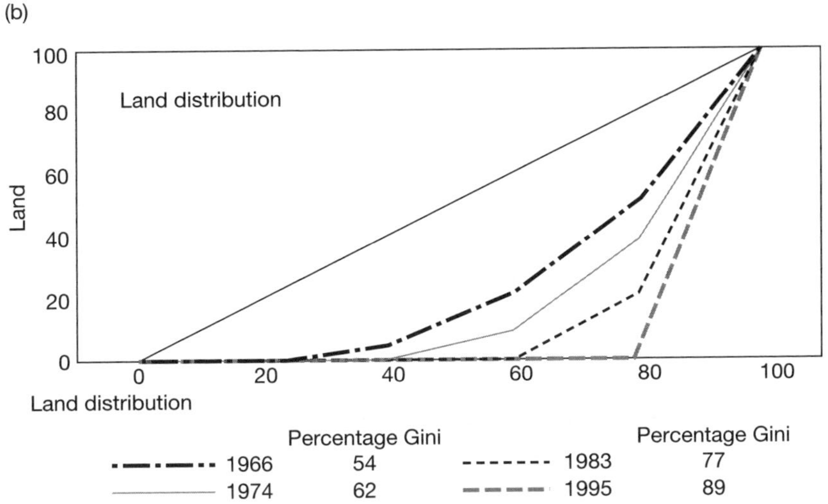

Fig. 6.12(b). Changes in land distribution, East Laguna Village, 1966–95

Notes: Percentage Gini: Gini coefficient calculated across individuals under the assumption that household income is distributed equally among the members of each household. Percentage poor: Percentage of population with incomes below the poverty line. The poverty line is defined as the annual per capital income required to satisfy basic nutritional requirements (2,000 calories) and other basic needs. The poverty line for respective years are estimated by deflating the 1994 poverty line by CPI estimated by the NSCB (1996) for the rural sector of the Philippines.

poverty. If we use the National Statistical Coordination Board's (1996) poverty line, the percentage of villagers being poor was 56 per cent in East Laguna Village in 1995, whereas it was 53 per cent in the rural sector of the Philippines in 1994 (28 per cent in the urban sector). The incidence of poverty, however, has not increased, but rather decreased in the last two decades. The share of population below the poverty line in East Laguna Village was as high as 68 per cent in 1974, remained about the same in 1987, and then dropped to 56 per cent in 1995, reflecting the increased non-farm employment opportunities in the 1990s.

It must be recalled that even though the basic factor underlying the increased inequality in the distribution of landholdings in East Laguna Village was strong population pressure on the limited land available for cultivation, a more immediate cause was the land-reform regulations that made the land-rental market inactive. This closed the opportunity for landless agricultural labourers to rent land for their own cultivation. Ironically, the land-reform programmes that aimed to achieve greater equity in the rural sector contributed to greater inequality within the village community, although the programmes were able to achieve the intended goal of transferring income from rich landlords living in towns to poor tenants in villages. The direct contribution of the green revolution to the well-being of the landless poor through added employment in rice production was minor at best. It was the increased employment in non-farm economic activities that prevented the incidence of poverty from increasing sharply among marginal farmers and agricultural workers. These non-farm activities were made accessible to villagers through closer integration of the village economy with wide markets available under the wave of globalization.

From Thomas More's *Utopia* to Russian Narodniks and US Populists in the nineteenth century, and further to the recent 'moral economy school' (Scott 1976), a popular perception has repeatedly been asserted that the encroachment of market into traditional agrarian communities tends to result in greater inequality and misery for the rural poor. Such a view does not seem to find support in the history of East Laguna Village. Instead, the experience of East Laguna Village in the past three decades, as observed in Figures 6.12(a) and 6.12(b), strongly suggests that the misery of the poor would have been magnified further by the rapid population growth under closed land frontiers if the village had continued to rely on traditional agriculture while being isolated from urban market activities.

6.8. Globalization in a Historical Perspective: A Concluding Remark

Finally, I will try to give a historical perspective to the nature of current globalization and its impact in East Asia with reference to the case of East Laguna Village.

Baldwin and Martin (1999) characterize the current wave of globalization beginning in the twentieth century in comparison with the earlier wave in the nineteenth century. According to these authors, the 'first globalization wave' in the nineteenth century was generated by the rise of industrial power in western countries, which resulted in the de-industrialization of the third world under the dictate of comparative advantage. In contrast, the 'second wave' currently in progress has been generated by the shift of comparative advantage in advanced economies from the industrial production of standardized commodities to the production of knowledge and information, having the effect of promoting manufacturing activities in developing economies.

While the above characterization of the two waves seems valid, it would be useful to specify the earlier wave that surged from the western to the tropical world from the fifteenth to seventeenth centuries. This wave was provoked by 'merchant capitalism' (Kuznets 1966) or mercantilism under the support of absolutism in western Europe, first led by Spain and Portugal and followed by England, France, and the Netherlands. Unlike in the wave of the nineteenth century in which western traders collected tropical cash crops and minerals in exchange for manufactured commodities under the free trade system, merchant adventurers in the mercantilist regime relied more heavily on plundering of the natives through tax and tribute as well as forced labour for monopoly export to their home countries under the charters of absolute monarchies.

Thus, it seems appropriate to consider that tropical economies have been integrated with the western world over the three globalization waves induced, first, by merchant capitalism in the fifteenth to eighteenth centuries, second, by 'industrial capitalism' à la Marx in the nineteenth to early twentieth centuries, and third by what may be called 'knowledge capitalism' currently in progress. The impacts of these three waves are clearly observable with respect to East Laguna Village. The two traditional characteristics of this village were pervasive landlordism and rice monoculture, which were commonly shared by rural communities in the Philippines. The former was clearly the legacy of Spanish colonialism established through plundering the rights of natives under the system of merchant capitalism backed by absolutism in a process similar to that of Latin America (Phelan 1959; McLennan 1969; Larkin 1972). On the other hand, rice monoculture with virtual non-existence of manufacturing activities until the 1970s would have been the reflection of the second wave that caused de-industrialization in the third world, especially in Southeast Asia (Resnick 1970; Bairoch 1975).

The third globalization wave has surged to this village in several ways. Explosive population growth through a reduction in the death rate due to the importation of modern medical and public health technologies, application of land-reform programmes, and the green revolution may be considered the outcomes of international knowledge transfer, which is the major characteristic of knowledge capitalism. However, the more obvious and stronger impact of the third wave on the life of villagers was its effect in promoting industrialization in developing economies, as manifested in the rapid expansion of non-farm employment opportunities. The impact of this effect in reducing poverty and inequality, as observed with East Laguna Village, should have been shared among high-performing economies in the East Asian Miracle (World Bank 1993).

The question is: how have these East Asian economies been able to achieve faster industrial growth by taking advantage of the third globalization wave than other developing regions? Our village study has shown that East Laguna Village and its surroundings were able to capture a fair share of the global demand for labour-intensive manufactures, partly because of public investment in transportation and communication infrastructure as well as industrial extension activities. Another major factor would be the increased school education among villagers. The same would have been the case among all the high-performing economies in East Asia.

Indeed, the current globalization wave has created a great opportunity for rural communities in developing economies to reduce poverty and inequality. However, whether this opportunity can be captured by the rural poor depends on how wise public investments are allocated in their support for infrastructure including education and extension services. The needed support should include improvements in the efficiency of markets by building institutions to protect property rights and enforce contracts, while the government should refrain as much as possible from direct intervention into markets.

A major hypothesis suggested but not confirmed by this village study is that technological progress in agriculture as represented by the green revolution might have provided a basis for the remarkable success of labour-intensive manufacturing in East Asia. As observed from the village data, major increases in rice yields resulting from the diffusion of modern varieties were associated with equally large reductions in real rice prices received by farmers. While this adverse market effect deprived the farmers in Asian villages of much of the direct gains from new rice technology, it would have worked to reduce industrial workers' cost of living and wage rates, thereby making Asia the attractive location for labour-intensive manufacturing. Considering this indirect effect, the success of the green revolution could have been a decisive factor underlying the East Asian miracle as compared with the economic growth and poverty reduction performance in other developing regions, especially Africa. This hypothesis—as well as many others—needs to be confirmed by studies larger than the microvillage study as reported in this study.

References

Bairoch, P. (1975) *The Economic Development of the Third World since 1900*. London: Methuen.

Baldwin, R., and P. Martin (1999) 'Two Waves of Globalization: Superficial Similarities and Fundamental Differences'. In H. Siebert (ed.), *Globalization and Labor*. Tübingen: Mohr Siebeck.

Griffin, K. (1974) *The Political Economy of Agrarian Change: An Essay on the Green Revolution*. Cambridge, Mass.: Harvard University Press.

Hayami, Y. (ed) (1998) *Toward the Rural-based Development of Commerce and Industry: Selected Experiences from East Asia*. Washington, DC: World Bank.

—— and Y. Godo (2005) *Development Economics: From the Poverty to the Wealth of Nations*, 3rd edn. Oxford: Oxford University Press.

—— and R. W. Herdt (1977) 'Market Price Effects of Technological Change on Income Distribution in Semisubsistence Agriculture', *American Journal of Agricultural Economics*, 59 (May): 245–56.

—— and M. Kikuchi (2000) *A Rice Village Saga: The Three Decades of Green Revolution in the Philippines*. London, Lanham, Md., and Makati: Macmillan/Barnes and Nobles/IRRI.

—— M. A. R. Quisumbing, and L. S. Adriano (1990) *Toward An Alternative Land Reform Paradigm: A Philippine Perspective*. Quezon City: Ateneo de Manila University Press.

—— and V. W. Ruttan (1985) *Agricultural Development: An International Perspective*. 2nd edn. Baltimore, Md.: Johns Hopkins University Press.

Kikuchi, M., M. Fujita, and Y. Hayami (2001) 'State, Community and Market in the Deterioration of a National Irrigation System in the Philippines'. In M. Aoki and

Y. Hayami (eds), *Communities and Markets in Economic Development*. Oxford: Oxford University Press.

Kuznets, S. (1966) *Modern Economic Growth: Rate, Structure and Spread*. New Haven, Conn.: Yale University Press.

Larkin, J. A. (1972) *The Pampangans: Colonial Society in a Philippine Province*. Berkeley, Calif.: University California Press.

Lipton, M., with R. Longhurst (1989) *New Seeds and Poor People*. London: Unwin and Hyman.

McLennan, M. S. (1969) 'Land and Tenancy in the Central Luzon Plain', *Philippine Studies*, 17: 651–82.

National Statistical Coordination Board (NSCB) (1996) *Philippine Poverty Statistics*. Makati: NSCB.

Phelan, J. L. (1959) *The Hispanization of the Philippines: Spanish and Filipino Responses, 1956–1700*. Madison, Wis.: University of Wisconsin Press.

Resnick, S. (1970) 'The Decline in Rural Industries under Export Expansion: A Comparison among Burma, Philippines and Thailand', *Journal of Economic History*, 30: 51–73.

Scott, J. C. (1976) *The Moral Economy of the Peasant*. New Haven, Conn. and London: Yale University Press.

World Bank (1993) *The East Asian Miracle: Economic Growth and Public Policy*. Oxford: Oxford University Press.

7

Globalization and the Urban Poor in China

Yin Zhang and Guanghua Wan

7.1. Introduction

Recent research has revealed the disturbing fact that since the late 1980s progress in poverty reduction has stalled in urban China (Ravallion and Chen 2007) or has even been reversed (Hussain 2003; Khan, Griffin, and Riskin 1999). The same period also witnessed the engine of China's economic take-off changed from agricultural growth spurred by decollectivization in the rural areas to manufacturing exports fuelled by large FDI inflows. Arguably, the latter is more directly related to the urban areas where most manufacturing industries congregate. In view of the ongoing debate on the marginalizing impact of globalization on the poor, the concurrence in China of increasing urban poverty and growing integration with the global economy deserves a careful examination.

Although a rich literature exists on inequality and poverty in China, relatively few studies have dealt with the effect of globalization on poverty in urban China. Two recent studies, Ravallion and Chen (2007) and Ravallion (2004), find little correlation between the expansion of trade and overall poverty reduction. This finding is based on national aggregate measures of poverty and trade openness. However, both the level of openness and the severity of poverty vary considerably across the Chinese provinces.[1] Also, because urban residents are generally more exposed to the vicissitudes of the global economy than are rural residents, the effects of globalization on urban and rural poverty may also differ. Hence, even if globalization does impact on poverty, either positively or negatively, the relationship may not show up in national average measures. Moreover, globalization can affect poverty via two channels: the growth effect

[1] For evidence on regional differences in openness, see Wei and Wu (2002) and Wan, Lu, and Chen (2004); for evidence on regional variations in poverty, see Khan (1998) and Hussain (2003).

and the distributional effect. Since there is a general consensus on the positive impact of trade (and FDI inflows) on growth, the finding of disassociation between absolute poverty and trade implies a negative distributional effect of trade. This is inconsistent with Dollar and Kraay (2002) who, in a widely cited cross-country study, conclude that the poor benefit from globalization just as much as the rest of the population. Is China an exception to this general pattern?

This chapter departs from earlier studies in three aspects. First, by placing the focus on the distributional effect of globalization on China's *urban* poor, it complements previous studies on the total impact of globalization and those on China's rural poverty. Second, it examines the impact of both openness to foreign trade and openness to foreign investment. Although these two aspects of globalization are closely related, their effects on poverty might differ. As shown below, urban China turns out to be a case in point. Finally, the chapter makes use of intra-province distributional data to assemble a provincial panel, whereby province-specific heterogeneity can be more readily accommodated. By accounting for regional diversity, we consider this one step towards the direction of 'looking beyond average', as Ravallion urges (2004).

The remaining part of the chapter is organized as follows. The next section explains our method of estimating three measures of the income shares of the poor from grouped household survey data. This is necessary because we are unable to access household records or congruent data for the poor. Preliminary analysis of the trend and regional pattern of the three measures is also presented. In section 7.3, the effects of globalization on the three income shares are explored and the robustness of the findings tested. Section 7.4 concludes.

7.2. Estimating the Income Shares of the Poor

As far as income poverty is concerned, globalization can help or hinder poverty reduction through two channels: the first one is through affecting average income growth, and the second one is by changing income distribution. On the first channel, Stiglitz observes that 'globalization may bring enhanced growth, but need not...' (Stiglitz 2003: 507). Openness to international trade and foreign capital makes it possible for a country to benefit from greater economies of scale and scope, more efficient allocation of resources, and faster acquirement of advanced technology and management know-how, thereby embarking on a trajectory of higher growth. The growth-promoting effects of globalization, however, cannot occur in the absence of the right initial conditions, institutions, and government policies (Nissanke and Thorbecke 2005). Moreover, globalization brings not only potential benefits but also risks. The opening up of capital markets, in particular, subjects an economy to the risks of pro-cyclical short-term capital inflows and large-scale capital flights. As evidenced by the financial crises in the 1990s, when not properly managed, such risks can cause significant growth setbacks (Stiglitz 2003). Therefore, economic theory provides no clear-cut prediction about whether the growth effects of globalization would be positive, negative, or negligible.

Empirically, despite lingering doubts about the robustness of the results from cross-country studies,[2] the balance of the evidence based on case studies as well as cross-country regressions indicates a positive relationship between growth and trade openness. In the growth and globalization literature, China's experience is often cited as a success story. The accumulated evidence—from studies fitting various econometric models, applying different estimation methods, and using data from disparate sources and of different sample periods and aggregation levels—points unambiguously to a positive contribution to China's impressive growth record by its expansion in trade and FDI inflows.[3]

The distributional effects of globalization on poverty can occur through a number of mechanisms, some of which may work in opposite directions. For example, the Stolper–Samuelson theorem predicts that trade will increase the relative wage of unskilled labour in developing countries and hence tend to improve the position of the poor in the division of national income. However, trade and FDI may also bring about skill-biased technological changes, which would increase the relative demand for skilled labour, resulting in lower relative wage for unskilled labour. Similar to the growth effects, therefore, there is no clear indication a priori as to what the confluence of such conflicting trends will be.[4]

Unlike in the case of growth effects, empirical evidence concerning China on this front is far from conclusive. Although the estimates of the values of inequality indices vary, overall income inequality undoubtedly increased markedly in the 1980s and 1990s.[5] And there exists some evidence that rising inequality is associated with growing integration with the world economy in the same period. For instance, Kanbur and Zhang (2005) show that the income gap between the coastal and inland regions and that between urban and rural areas are both positively correlated with openness to trade. However, two uncertainties prevent us from inferring from such evidence that the poor have been disadvantaged in the globalization process. The first uncertainty is when the unit of analysis moves from the national level to the local level the relationship between openness and inequality might change. Thus, employing

[2] For example, Rodriguez and Rodrik (2001) conclude, after examining several influential cross-country studies which find a negative relationship between growth and trade distortions that trade distortions are not well measured in those studies and the results therein are sensitive to the inclusion of other policy distortion variables.

[3] See, among others, Buckley, Clegg, and Wang (2002); Démurger and Berthélemy (2000); and Wei (1995).

[4] For discussion of the various mechanisms of the distributional effects of globalization, see Nissanke and Thorbecke (2005) and references cited therein.

[5] See, for example, UNU-WIDER (2008).

city-level data, Wei and Wu (2002) find that greater openness to trade narrows, rather than widens, the urban–rural income gap. The second uncertainty is that an increase in the value of such aggregate inequality measure as the Gini coefficient does not correspond to a reduction of the income shares of the poor in national income, and vice versa. If the high-income group gains a larger share of total income entirely at the expense of the middle class, overall income inequality rises with no adverse consequences for the poor. In light of the foregoing discussion, this chapter will focus on the distributional effects of globalization by examining its impact on the income shares of the poor.

To obtain the urban income distributions in different provinces over time, we draw on the annual urban household surveys administered by the National Bureau of Statistics (NBS).[6] The survey data are published in provincial statistical yearbooks in grouped format where households are classified into consecutive income classes and the percentage/number of households in each class is tabulated along with the group mean income and average household size. We were able to collect such data for a total of 375 distributions, covering twenty-nine out of the thirty-one provinces and province-level cities in mainland China (i.e., China excluding Taiwan, Macau, and Hong Kong) for most of the years between 1988 and 2001.

A problematic feature of the data is that the grouping format gives rise to irregular quantiles. To compound the problem, the categorization of income classes is not congruent across provinces and frequently changes over time. To enable spatial and temporal comparison, it is thus necessary to estimate the probability density functions (PDFs) of the distributions from the published data. In the income distribution literature, a number of parametric models have been proposed for such purpose. None of these models enjoys established superiority over the others. Considering that the 375 distributions are likely to be rather diverse both spatially and temporally and that the number of data points available for estimating each distribution also differs, we feel it unpromising to search for a parametric form that would approximate all the distributions reasonably well. By contrast, the non-parametric method of kernel density estimation offers an appealing alternative in that it does not require a priori specification of any particular functional form.[7]

[6] Most published studies about China's income distribution rely on the NBS data. Some studies use data from household surveys conducted by the Chinese Academy of Social Sciences in collaboration with a team of economists based outside China. The latter surveys cover around a third of the thirty-one provinces and are available for 1988 and 1995 only.

[7] At the exploring stage, we tried fitting parametric models to the data. We experimented with the log-normal distribution and the beta and general quadratic Lorenz curves, complete with the quantile-by-quantile mean-fitting method proposed in Shorrocks and Wan (2004). This procedure did not always yield meaningful Lorenz curves. Where it did, we found that the differences between the resulted distribution and that produced by kernel density estimation lie primarily with the upper tail.

The kernel density estimation was recently applied by Sala-i-Martin (2002a; 2002b) to estimate income inequality among world citizens.[8] Further explanation of the method can be found in the Sala-i-Martin papers. Suffice it to note here that we use the Rosenblatt–Parzen density estimator with the standard normal density function as the kernel.[9] The bandwidth of the kernel is set individually for each province at $0.9 \times \sigma \times n^{-1/5}$, where σ is the average of the standard deviations of the logarithmic income of the province and n is the number of available data points.

The estimated PDFs for each province for three selected years can be found in Appendix B in Zhang and Wan (2006). We summarize the main results there as follows. First, for nearly all provinces the entire income distribution has moved to the right. Unless there has been widespread switching of fortunes between the members of high and low income groups, this implies that an overwhelming majority of urban residents saw their real income grow in this period. Second, the distributions have become more dispersed in all cases except Gansu. This is a clear indication of increased income inequality within provinces. Furthermore, it appears that, for the three province-level cities, a second local mode is gradually taking shape on the high-income end, indicating a tendency towards polarization.[10] Third, the bottom tails of the distributions have grown longer over the period in all provinces. Thus, the income of the poor has not been growing as fast as the average income and, accordingly, the income shares of the poor must have fallen. The income growth of the poor seems to have been particularly slow since the mid-1990s. In a number of provinces (e.g., Shanxi, Anhui, Hunan, Guizhou, and Guangxi), real income growth of the poor may have stagnated.

We define the poor, variously, as the bottom 5 per cent, 10 per cent, and 20 per cent of the population with the lowest income. Given an estimated PDF $p(x)$ of log income, a person is considered poor if his or her annual real income Y satisfies $\int_{-\infty}^{lnY} p(x)dx < s$, where $s = 0.05$, 0.1, or 0.2 depending on which of the three definitions is used. The income shares of the poorest 5 per cent, 10 per cent, and 20 per cent of the provincial residents are calculated as:[11]

[8] Milanović's (2002) objection to the use of kernel density estimation in Sala-i-Martin (2002a; 2002b) is that, with quintile data, there is too little information (Sala-i-Martin uses quintile data) to infer the shape of entire distributions, especially that of the upper tails. This is essentially a criticism of the data rather than of the estimation method. Any estimation method, parametric or non-parametric, can only produce as good an approximation to the true distribution as the data allow. In our dataset, we have on average eight data points for a distribution and typically greater concentration of data for the lower part of the distribution which is the focus of this chapter.

[9] Using the Epanechinikov kernel yields similar results.

[10] This is of course subject to the caveat that data for the high-income groups are likely to contain more errors.

[11] $\int_{-\infty}^{\ln Y^*} e^x p(x)dx = \bar{Y}^P$ is the mean income of the poor, s is the population share of the poor, $\int_{-\infty}^{+\infty} e^x p(x)dx = \bar{Y}$ is the average income of all residents, the income share of the poor is thus given by $\bar{Y}^P \times s/\bar{Y}$.

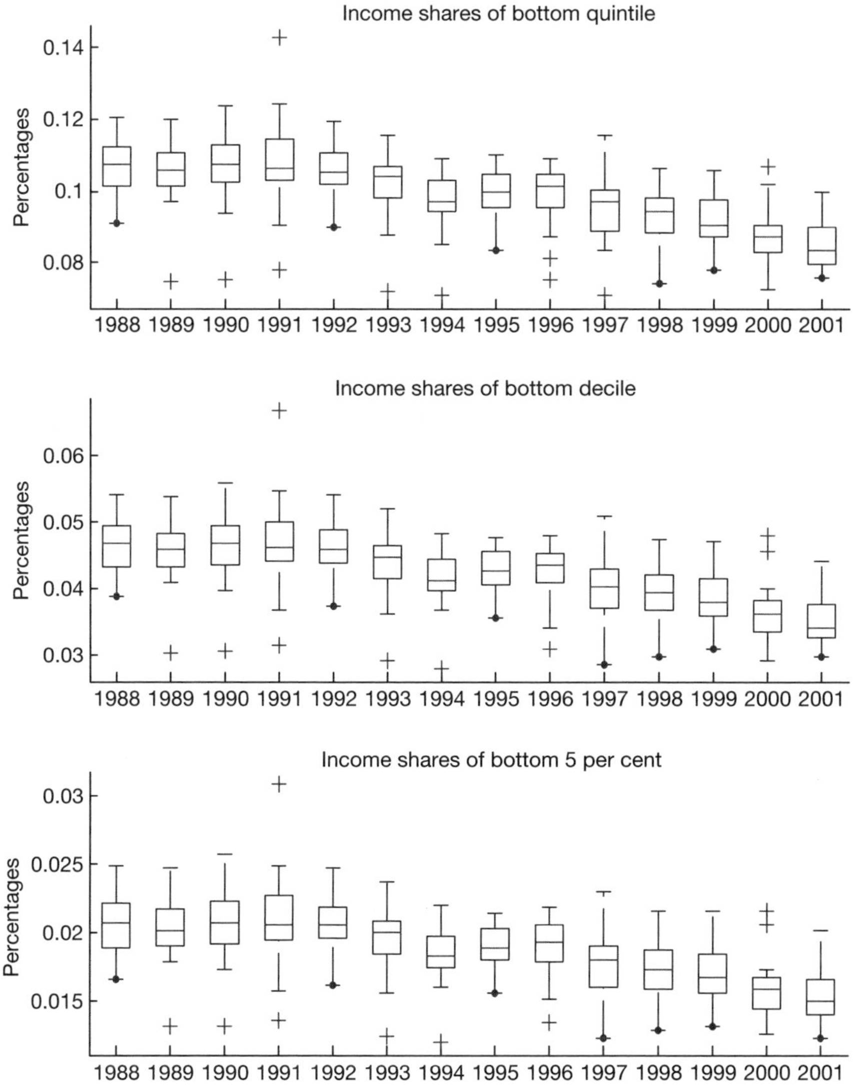

Fig. 7.1. Boxplots of the income shares of the poor in China

$$\frac{s\int_{-\infty}^{\ln Y^*} e^x p(x)dx}{\int_{-\infty}^{+\infty} e^x p(x)dx} \tag{1}$$

where $\int_{-\infty}^{\ln Y^*} p(x)dx = s$, and $s = 0.05$, 0.1, and 0.2, respectively.

Shown in Figure 7.1 are the cross-section boxplots over 1988–2001 for each of the three sets of income shares. The cross-section dispersions of the three measures do not appear to have changed much, yet a trend decline is visible in all of them. To assess the magnitude of the decline and to detect if any regional differences are present, four regressions were run using the pooled data on a time trend and dummy variables for three different groupings of the provinces.[12] As the results reported in Table 7.1 show, income distributions tend to become less favourable to the poor the further one moves away from the coast. In the two-region ('coastal' and 'inland') and three-region groupings ('coastal', 'central', and 'western' areas), the income shares of the poor in the coastal provinces are clearly higher than those in the other provinces (referring to the coefficients on the coastal dummies in regressions 2–3). Between the central and the western provinces, the poor in the former region obtain a larger share of total provincial income. When a finer classification of the provinces is adopted, the income distributions in the three province-level cities are the most favourable to the poor, followed by those in the three north-eastern provinces, and the other provinces along the coast. The sparsely populated yet resource-rich north-western provinces have the least favourable income distribution for the poor. However, there appear to be ample variations within the groups that the average income shares of the coastal, central, and north-eastern groups are not statistically different from that of the south-western group, the base group in regression 4. For all these regional differences in the levels of the income shares, an across-the-board decline is confirmed for all three of the income share measures. The magnitudes of the coefficient estimates on the time trend are stable across different specifications. At the estimated rates of decline, the three measures could have fallen by 20 per cent to 30 per cent over the period on average. We also tried introducing interaction terms between the time trend and the regional dummies into regressions 3 and 4. However, due to multi-collinearity caused by high correlations between the regional dummies and their interaction terms, the interaction terms are never precisely estimated and hence dropped from the regression.

What part might globalization have played in bringing about the above outcomes? In trying to answer this question, looking at the bivariate correlations between globalization and the income shares of the poor alone does not get one very far, as the temporal and spatial correlations between the two present a paradox. Two of the well-known facts about China's globalization process are: (i) China, as a whole, has markedly increased its integration with the world economy since the mid-1980s; and (ii) the scale, intensity, and speed of the opening-up process are much greater in the eastern seaboard than in the inland provinces. Thus, timewise, the presence of a trend decline in the income shares of the poor implies that globalization cannot be pro-poor in the sense that it benefits the rich more than proportionately; spacewise, however, the

[12] The members of the regional groups are listed in the notes to Table 7.1.

Table 7.1. Trend and regional differences in the income shares of the poor in China

	Regression 1			Regression 2			Regression 3			Regression 4		
	20%	10%	5%	20%	10%	5%	20%	10%	5%	20%	10%	5%
Intercept	11.241	4.926	2.206	10.999	4.786	2.132	10.762	4.660	2.072	11.252	4.920	2.201
	0.000	*0.000*	*0.000*	*0.000*	*0.000*	*0.000*	*0.000*	*0.000*	*0.000*	*0.000*	*0.000*	*0.000*
Time trend	−0.179	−0.092	−0.044	−0.180	−0.092	−0.045	−0.179	−0.092	−0.044	−0.181	−0.093	−0.045
	0.000	*0.000*	*0.000*	*0.000*	*0.000*	*0.000*	*0.000*	*0.000*	*0.000*	*0.000*	*0.000*	*0.000*
Coastal[a]				0.640	0.371	0.195	0.874	0.495	0.254	0.213	0.140	0.073
				0.000	*0.000*	*0.000*	*0.000*	*0.000*	*0.000*	*0.124*	*0.046*	*0.035*
Central[b]							0.449	0.238	0.115	0.098	0.051	0.022
							0.000	*0.000*	*0.000*	*0.411*	*0.400*	*0.470*
Three cities[c]										0.744	0.447	0.244
										0.000	*0.000*	*0.000*
North-east[d]										0.181	0.113	0.060
										0.176	*0.095*	*0.080*
North-west[e]										−0.816	−0.438	−0.221
										0.000	*0.000*	*0.000*

Notes: The figures in italics are the marginal significance values of the *t*-statistics of the coefficient estimates. In Regression 4, the base group consists of the south-western provinces: Guangxi, Guizhou, Sichuan, and Yunnan. The other groups are defined as follows:

[a] In Regressions 2–3, coastal provinces include Beijing, Fujian, Guangdong, Hainan, Hebei, Jiangsu, Liaoning, Shanghai, Shandong, Tianjin, and Zhejiang. In Regression 4, Beijing, Shanghai, Tianjin, and Liaoning are assigned to other groups.

[b] In Regressions 2–3, central provinces include Anhui, Heilongjiang, Henan, Hubei, Hunan, Inner Mongolia, Jiangxi, Jilin, and Shanxi. In Regression 4, Heilongjiang, Jilin, and Inner Mongolia are assigned to other groups.

[c] The three province level cities are Beijing, Shanghai, and Tianjin.

[d] The north-eastern provinces include Liaoning, Heilongjiang, and Jilin.

[e] The north-western provinces are Gansu, Inner Mongolia, Ningxia, Shanxi, Qinghai, and Xinjiang.

proposition that globalization is anti-poor would be in conflict with the finding that the poor in the provinces closer to the coast enjoy higher income shares. An easy compromise would be to conclude that globalization is a distribution-neutral force. But is that the true and full story? We now turn to a formal analysis of the relationship between globalization and the income shares of the poor.

7.3. Globalization and the Poor

We adopt the following econometric framework used in Dollar and Kraay (2002):

$$\bar{y}^P_{kt} = \alpha_0 + \alpha_1 \bar{y}_{kt} + \boldsymbol{\beta}' \mathbf{x}_{kt} + \boldsymbol{\mu}' \mathrm{k} + \varepsilon_{kt} \tag{2}$$

The equation states that the (logarithmic) mean income of the poor $\bar{y}^P_{kt}$ in location (province) k and period (year) t is, first of all, determined by the (logarithmic) per capita income, $\bar{y}_{kt}$, in province k. Over and above the effects of $\bar{y}_{kt}, \bar{y}^P_{kt}$ is influenced by a vector of other variables $\mathbf{x}_{kt}$ and a vector of time invariant yet province-specific factors $\boldsymbol{\mu}_k$. Upon subtracting $\bar{y}_{kt}$ from both sides of equation (2), we obtain:

$$l_{kt} = \alpha^*_0 + \alpha^*_1 \bar{y}_{kt} + \beta 1 g_{kt} + \boldsymbol{\beta}^{*\prime} \mathbf{x}^*_{kt} + \boldsymbol{\mu}_k{}' + \varepsilon_{kt} \tag{3}$$

where $l_{kt} = \bar{y}^P_{kt} - \bar{y}_{kt} + \log s,$[13] $s = 0.05$, 0.1 or 0.2, is the logarithms of the income shares of the poor, $\alpha^*_0 = \alpha_0 + \log \mathrm{s}$, $\alpha^*_1 = \alpha_1 - 1$ and g_{kt} is (the logarithms of) an indicator measuring the extent of globalization of the local economy. Our main concern in this chapter is of course whether g_{kt} enters equation (3) significantly and, if it does, what sign the coefficient β_1 takes on. On account of the results from the preceding section, it is also anticipated that α^*_1 will be negative, implying that the income shares of the poor fall as the average income grows.

It might be argued that a globalization indicator should reflect the 'openness' of local institutions, that is, it should be indicative of how conducive or restrictive local legal and bureaucratic procedures and regulations are to cross-border flows of goods, services, and capital. Data on such information are hard to come by, especially at the provincial level. Following the common practice, the ratio of imports and exports to GDP is used to indicate openness to foreign trade and the ratio of FDI stock to GDP to indicate openness to foreign investment. While these two ratios measure two different aspects of globalization, they are also highly correlated in our dataset, with a correlation coefficient of 0.79. To avoid multicollinearity and, in the meantime, ensure both aspects of globalization are

[13] See above, fn. 11.

represented in the regression analysis below, we use the first principle component constructed from the two ratios as the third globalization indicator.[14]

Several concerns might be raised about the estimation of equation (3). The province-specific effect term $\boldsymbol{\mu}_k$ can be dealt with in two ways. The first is known as the within or fixed-effect estimator, which amounts to transforming each variable into deviations from the means of the respective cross-section units. The alternative is to sweep out $\boldsymbol{\mu}_k$ by taking the first difference of the regression equation. Both methods have their problems. Estimating the equation in first differences results in information loss, which in our case is accentuated by the fact that our panel is punctured by missing observations at various years for different provinces.[15] The within estimator, on the other hand, requires for consistency the more stringent assumption that the right-hand-side variables are strictly exogenous. This assumption is likely to be untenable in the present context, particularly because per capita income $\bar{y}_k$ may be affected by income distribution l_k, though the causality may not be contemporaneous. For both methods, inconsistent estimates can arise from measurement errors. The omission of other potential determinants of l_k, albeit necessary to maintain a parsimonious model, may lead to a similar problem if the omitted variables are correlated with the explanatory variables included in the model.

To address the above concerns, variant specifications of equation (3) are considered and their modelling results are discussed in sections 7.3.1 and 7.3.2 below. In these regressions, potential simultaneity is addressed by introducing instruments for the problematic variables $\bar{y}_k$ and g_{kt}. Following Ravallion (2001), we use (the log of) real GDP per capita as the instrument for $\bar{y}_k$. Despite the recent divergence between these two income measures observed in the national data from a wide range of developing countries including China,[16] the two series in our dataset are highly correlated.[17] As for the instrument of the globalization indicators, we experimented with its lagged values, two-year averages, and using both. The regressions were conducted first by employing the within estimator, and then on the first differenced form. These different combinations of alternative instruments and data transformations produced broadly similar results. The signs and significance of the coefficients on $\bar{y}_k$ and g_{kt}, in particular, are always in agreement. For the sake of brevity, we present below the within estimates with g_{kt-1} as the instrument for g_{kt}.

[14] The first principal component explains just below 90 per cent of the total variance of the two ratios. Details about the compilation of these indicators, as well as definitions of the other variables used in this study, can be found in the Appendix to this chapter. Agénor (2003) also uses principal component analysis to derive a 'globalization index'.

[15] On taking first differences, the number of observations in our panel is reduced by 38, or about one-tenth of our sample size.

[16] Ravallion (2003a) examines discrepancies between income data from household surveys and those from national accounts.

[17] The logarithms of the two series have a correlation coefficient of 0.86.

7.3.1. The Differing Effects of Trade and FDI

In Tables 7.2–7.4, results are given for three sets of regressions where the dependent variable is the log income shares of, respectively, the bottom quintile, decile, and 5 per cent of the urban residents. Each table consists of three panels summarizing the results of using alternative globalization indicators in ten regressions. Column 1 gives the results of ordinary least squares (OLS) regression on pooled data (i.e., $\boldsymbol{\mu}_k = \boldsymbol{\mu}$ for $k = 1, \ldots, 29$) and column 2 OLS with fixed effects. As discussed above, the OLS estimates may be inconsistent and biased towards zero. They are reported here for purposes of comparison. The estimates in the remaining eight columns are all produced using instrumental variable (IV) estimation.

In a study of ninety-two countries over four decades, Dollar and Kraay (2002) conclude that 'the general relationship between growth of income of the poor and growth of mean income is one to one'. Translated into the notation in equation (3), that proposition is equivalent to the coefficient on real income per capita α_1^* being statistically insignificant. As can be seen from Tables 7.2–7.4, our results show that α_1^* is not only significant but also negative. This result holds consistently for all three income shares across different globalization indicators, model specifications, and estimation methods. Moreover, it seems that the further left down along the Lorenz curve the income share (the dependent variable), the greater is the magnitude of α_1^* in its equation. For China's urban poor, therefore, the rising tide has not lifted their boats by as much and/or as quickly as it has elsewhere. Considering that income inequality in China was low before the mid-1980s, it is perhaps not much of a surprise that China's experience should prove exception to the Dollar–Kraay proposition.[18] None the less, it reminds one that caution should be exercised when generalizing findings from cross-country studies to individual economies.

The result of a more surprising nature is that with the coefficient on the globalization indicator β_1. Across the first panels of Tables 7.2–7.4, β_1 is found to be positive and significant at conventional levels for every regression with the exception of the OLS with fixed effects in column 2. The latter estimates are probably biased anyway. Here, again, our results sit at odds with those in Dollar and Kraay (2002) and, for that matter, with those from several other cross-country studies on trade openness and income inequality.[19] In contrast to the findings in the other studies that trade openness has either no impact on the income share of the poor or is inequality-increasing, our results suggest that trade helps the poor gain a larger share from aggregate income growth or, equivalently, reduces the 'losses' they would otherwise suffer. However, the

[18] Ravallion (2003b) presents evidence that within country inequality in developing countries converges towards medium levels.

[19] See, for example, Barro (1999) and Spilimbergo, Londono, and Szekely (1999).

Table 7.2. Globalization and the income shares of the poor in China: bottom quintile

Independent variable	(1)	(2)	(3)	(4)	(5)	(6)	(7)	(8)	(9)	(10)
	Globalization indicator: Trade: GDP ratio									
Globalization g	0.029	0.011	0.030	0.032	0.028	0.029	0.030	0.025	0.040	0.045
	0.001	*0.301*	*0.021*	*0.052*	*0.035*	*0.028*	*0.028*	*0.057*	*0.007*	*0.003*
Per capita income y	−0.145	−0.300	−0.319	−0.319	−0.338	−0.354	−0.338	−0.309	−0.372	−0.381
	0.000	*0.000*	*0.000*	*0.000*	*0.000*	*0.000*	*0.000*	*0.000*	*0.000*	*0.000*
Coast × g				−0.004						
				0.843						
p1992 × g					−0.008	−0.010	−0.006	−0.008	−0.011	−0.012
					0.054	*0.026*	*0.155*	*0.058*	*0.009*	*0.008*
Liberalization						0.046				0.063
						0.113				*0.038*
Economic structure							0.056			0.096
							0.122			*0.015*
Education								−0.012		−0.011
								0.460		*0.510*
Inflation									−0.100	−0.134
									0.016	*0.002*
Adjusted R^2	0.096	0.691	0.815	0.812	0.807	0.808	0.808	0.808	0.807	0.798
	Globalization indicator: FDI stock/GDP ratio									
Globalization g	0.003	0.006	0.009	0.009	0.001	0.005	0.001	0.001	0.000	0.005
	0.647	*0.319*	*0.187*	*0.164*	*0.925*	*0.567*	*0.946*	*0.905*	*0.973*	*0.571*
Per capita income y	−0.115	−0.309	−0.329	−0.320	−0.325	−0.351	−0.325	−0.295	−0.346	−0.355
	0.000	*0.000*	*0.000*	*0.000*	*0.000*	*0.000*	*0.000*	*0.000*	*0.000*	*0.000*
Coast × g				−0.008						
				0.249						
p1992 × g					−0.009	−0.010	−0.009	−0.009	−0.012	−0.012
					0.004	*0.003*	*0.008*	*0.006*	*0.000*	*0.000*
Liberalization						0.051				0.060
						0.106				*0.081*
Economic structure							0.034			0.060

(*continued*)

Table 7.2. Continued

Independent variable	(1)	(2)	(3)	(4)	(5)	(6)	(7)	(8)	(9)	(10)
							0.332			*0.099*
Education								−0.013		−0.012
								0.443		*0.497*
Inflation									−0.081	−0.104
									0.039	*0.009*
Adjusted R^2	0.094	0.689	0.809	0.808	0.805	0.803	0.804	0.804	0.804	0.797
	Globalization indicator: 1st principal component of trade/GDP and FDI/GDP									
Globalization g	0.011	0.008	0.013	0.039	0.032	0.029	0.033	0.032	0.039	0.048
	0.035	*0.073*	*0.024*	*0.053*	*0.001*	*0.025*	*0.001*	*0.004*	*0.000*	*0.004*
Per capita income y	−0.133	−0.306	−0.323	−0.334	−0.346	−0.349	−0.350	−0.350	−0.373	−0.451
	0.000	*0.000*	*0.000*	*0.000*	*0.000*	*0.000*	*0.000*	*0.000*	*0.000*	*0.000*
Coast × g				−0.025						
				0.187						
p1992× g					−0.012	−0.011	−0.011	−0.012	−0.014	−0.015
					0.023	*0.051*	*0.032*	*0.025*	*0.007*	*0.013*
Liberalization						−0.026				−0.037
						0.572				*0.426*
Economic structure							0.155			0.258
							0.089			*0.021*
Education								0.002		0.012
								0.931		*0.487*
Inflation									−0.092	−0.124
									0.025	*0.005*
Adjusted R^2	0.097	0.690	0.815	0.814	0.806	0.805	0.804	0.804	0.805	0.798

Notes: See Appendix for the definition of the variables. Figures in italics are the marginal significance levels of the *t*-statistics of the corresponding estimates. Estimation methods used for each regression are as follows:

(1) OLS regression on pooled data. The standard errors of the coefficient estimates are adjusted for heteroscedasticity and first order autocorrelation using the Newey–West procedure.

(2) OLS estimation with fixed effects.

(3)–(10) IV estimation with fixed effects.

Table 7.3. Globalization and the income shares of the poor in China: bottom decile

Independent variable	(1)	(2)	(3)	(4)	(5)	(6)	(7)	(8)	(9)	(10)
	Globalization indicator: trade/GDP ratio									
Globalization g	0.040	0.015	0.040	0.039	0.037	0.039	0.038	0.033	0.047	0.052
	0.000	*0.229*	*0.014*	*0.059*	*0.024*	*0.018*	*0.021*	*0.045*	*0.008*	*0.006*
Per capita income y	−0.170	−0.360	−0.385	−0.385	−0.408	−0.431	−0.408	−0.363	−0.439	−0.436
	0.000	*0.000*	*0.000*	*0.000*	*0.000*	*0.000*	*0.000*	*0.000*	*0.000*	*0.000*
Coast × g				0.003						
				0.901						
p1992× g					−0.010	−0.013	−0.008	−0.010	−0.013	−0.015
					0.046	*0.018*	*0.112*	*0.049*	*0.013*	*0.009*
Liberalization						0.064				0.078
						0.070				*0.037*
Economic structure							0.052			0.089
							0.248			*0.064*
Education								−0.018		−0.018
								0.344		*0.366*
Inflation									−0.090	−0.126
									0.076	*0.018*
Adjusted R^2	0.082	0.681	0.809	0.810	0.804	0.802	0.803	0.804	0.803	0.795
	Globalization indicator: FDI stock/GDP ratio									
Globalization g	0.007	0.006	0.010	0.010	−0.001	0.004	−0.002	−0.001	−0.002	0.004
	0.452	*0.370*	*0.244*	*0.228*	*0.882*	*0.693*	*0.871*	*0.906*	*0.850*	*0.712*
Per capita income y	−0.135	−0.368	−0.391	−0.384	−0.386	−0.419	−0.386	−0.335	−0.403	−0.396
	0.001	*0.000*	*0.000*	*0.000*	*0.000*	*0.000*	*0.000*	*0.000*	*0.000*	*0.000*
Coast × g				−0.006						
				0.481						
p1992× g					−0.013	−0.013	−0.012	−0.012	−0.015	−0.015
					0.002	*0.001*	*0.003*	*0.003*	*0.000*	*0.000*

(continued)

Table 7.3. Continued

Independent variable	(1)	(2)	(3)	(4)	(5)	(6)	(7)	(8)	(9)	(10)
Liberalization						0.066				0.070
						0.085				*0.097*
Economic structure							0.024			0.048
							0.572			*0.284*
Education								−0.022		−0.021
								0.280		*0.324*
Inflation									−0.066	−0.093
									0.168	*0.054*
Adjusted R^2	0.081	0.680	0.809	0.809	0.803	0.801	0.803	0.802	0.803	0.794
	Globalization indicator: 1st principal component of trade/GDP and FDI/GDP									
Globalization g	0.012	0.013	0.021	0.051	0.045	0.045	0.046	0.046	0.052	0.057
	0.040	*0.020*	*0.004*	*0.036*	*0.000*	*0.000*	*0.000*	*0.001*	*0.000*	*0.000*
Per capita income y	−0.151	−0.372	−0.395	−0.408	−0.425	−0.434	−0.430	−0.434	−0.453	−0.497
	0.000	*0.000*	*0.000*	*0.000*	*0.000*	*0.000*	*0.000*	*0.000*	*0.000*	*0.000*
Coast × g				−0.030						
				0.194						
p1992 × g					−0.015	−0.018	−0.015	−0.015	−0.018	−0.021
					0.015	*0.008*	*0.020*	*0.016*	*0.006*	*0.003*
Liberalization						0.164				0.237
						0.201				*0.083*
Economic structure							0.156			0.282
							0.164			*0.027*
Education								0.004		0.006
								0.878		*0.782*
Inflation									−0.094	−0.112
									0.062	*0.032*
Adjusted R^2	0.084	0.682	0.811	0.810	0.804	0.803	0.804	0.804	0.803	0.796

Notes: See Table 7.2.

Table 7.4. Globalization and the income shares of the poor in China: bottom 5 per cent

Independent variable	(1)	(2)	(3)	(4)	(5)	(6)	(7)	(8)	(9)	(10)
	Globalization indicator: trade/GDP ratio									
Globalization g	0.046	0.013	0.040	0.036	0.036	0.038	0.037	0.031	0.047	0.051
	0.000	*0.372*	*0.032*	*0.119*	*0.055*	*0.042*	*0.050*	*0.093*	*0.022*	*0.017*
Per capita income y	−0.179	−0.393	−0.420	−0.421	−0.450	−0.478	−0.450	−0.401	−0.484	−0.481
	0.000	*0.000*	*0.000*	*0.000*	*0.000*	*0.000*	*0.000*	*0.000*	*0.000*	*0.000*
Coast × g				0.008						
				0.799						
p1992× g					−0.012	−0.016	−0.011	−0.012	−0.016	−0.019
					0.027	*0.009*	*0.064*	*0.029*	*0.008*	*0.005*
Liberalization						0.077				0.091
						0.055				*0.032*
Economic structure							0.048			0.089
							0.346			*0.105*
Education								−0.020		−0.020
								0.373		*0.380*
Inflation									−0.096	−0.133
									0.097	*0.029*
Adjusted R^2	0.068	0.663	0.808	0.809	0.801	0.801	0.802	0.803	0.803	0.784
	Globalization indicator: FDI stock/GDP ratio									
Globalization g	0.009	0.007	0.012	0.012	−0.001	0.006	−0.001	−0.001	−0.002	0.005
	0.373	*0.373*	*0.219*	*0.205*	*0.923*	*0.648*	*0.914*	*0.946*	*0.890*	*0.668*
Per capita income y	−0.143	−0.404	−0.433	−0.426	−0.427	−0.467	−0.427	−0.373	−0.447	−0.443
	0.002	*0.000*	*0.000*	*0.000*	*0.000*	*0.000*	*0.000*	*0.000*	*0.000*	*0.000*
Coast × g				−0.007						
				0.495						
p1992× g					−0.015	−0.015	−0.014	−0.014	−0.017	−0.017
					0.002	*0.001*	*0.002*	*0.003*	*0.000*	*0.000*
Liberalization						0.078				0.082

(continued)

Table 7.4. Continued

Independent variable	(1)	(2)	(3)	(4)	(5)	(6)	(7)	(8)	(9)	(10)
						0.075				*0.089*
Economic structure							0.022			0.049
							0.654			*0.334*
Education								−0.023		−0.023
								0.310		*0.351*
Inflation									−0.076	−0.104
									0.165	*0.059*
Adjusted R^2	0.068	0.662	0.808	0.808	0.799	0.798	0.797	0.798	0.796	0.785
	Globalization indicator: 1st principal component of trade/GDP and FDI/GDP									
Globalization g	0.014	0.015	0.025	0.059	0.053	0.053	0.054	0.055	0.061	0.067
	0.041	*0.021*	*0.003*	*0.035*	*0.000*	*0.000*	*0.000*	*0.001*	*0.000*	*0.000*
Per capita income y	−0.158	−0.409	−0.439	−0.453	−0.473	−0.483	−0.478	−0.491	−0.506	−0.562
	0.000	*0.000*	*0.000*	*0.000*	*0.000*	*0.000*	*0.000*	*0.000*	*0.000*	*0.000*
Coast × g				−0.033						
				0.206						
p1992× g					−0.017	−0.020	−0.017	−0.018	−0.021	−0.024
					0.015	*0.008*	*0.020*	*0.016*	*0.006*	*0.003*
Liberalization						0.184				0.268
						0.208				*0.088*
Economic structure							0.170			0.318
							0.185			*0.031*
Education								0.007		0.010
								0.794		*0.706*
Inflation									−0.110	−0.130
									0.057	*0.032*
Adjusted R^2	0.070	0.663	0.811	0.809	0.799	0.799	0.798	0.799	0.797	0.785

Notes: See Table 7.2.

magnitude of this salutary effect of trade is rather small, about one-tenth of the negative effect of aggregate income growth. Inferring from the estimates in Table 7.2, a doubling of the trade/GDP ratio would only increase the income share of the bottom quintile by about 3 per cent from, say, 12 per cent to 12.4 per cent, assuming other things being equal. The elasticity appears to be slightly higher for the bottom decile and the bottom 5 per cent, but not by a large margin.

When an interaction term of trade openness with either a location dummy for the coastal provinces or a time dummy for the post-1992 years is added to the regression equation,[20] the above results concerning α_1^* and β_1 continue to hold. As indicated by the estimates in column 4, the trade effect is not exclusive to the coastal provinces. While this is reassuring, the results in column 5 would give some cause for concern. It seems that the equalizing effect of trade openness has weakened substantially since the early 1990s, and all the more so for the poorer groups.

All the preceding findings constitute only half of the picture. On moving to the second panel, one can no longer identify any significant effect of globalization on the income shares of the poor. Furthermore, the negative and significant coefficient on the time interaction term (p1992) actually points to an inequality-increasing role of globalization since 1992. The crucial difference between the regressions in the first panel and those in the second panel is, of course, the use of different globalization indicators. It is not our intention here to investigate what accounts for the differing effects of openness to trade and openness to foreign investment, or what mechanism has been at work to have brought about the attenuation of the positive trade effect. Many a model in the literature has demonstrated that the distributional effects of trade and FDI can be sensitive to assumptions about labour mobility, market distortions, production technology and specialization, and a range of initial conditions. Most probably, the results seen above were produced by a confluence of many forces. We will nevertheless venture two conjectures: (1) compared with domestic indigenous export firms, foreign-funded export firms employ more advanced technology and thus require relatively more skilled labour; and (2) China's export growth has been increasingly led by foreign-funded enterprises (FFEs). If the first conjecture holds true, an increase in exports by domestic firms would raise the demand for unskilled labour and thus improve the lot of the poor, whereas an increase in exports by FFEs would raise the demand for more skilled labour, leaving little effect on or even depressing the income of the poor. Since both domestic firms and FFEs engage in trade, we would observe a positive effect of trade on the income shares of the poor and a near zero or no effect on the part of FDI as long as domestic

[20] Deng Xiaoping's tour of South China in 1992 is widely viewed as marking the resumption of China's reform and opening-up process that had stalled after 1989.

firms contribute a growing share to total trade volume. If the growth of trade is led by FFEs, as postulated in conjecture (2), the positive distributional effect of trade will then diminish.[21]

Given the contrasting distributional effects of trade and FDI, what would be the overall evaluation of the influence of globalization? The estimates in the third panel provide a tentative answer. The globalization indicator utilized here is constructed from trade/GDP and FDI/GDP ratios. By construction, it reflects variations in both series. As can be seen, a pattern very similar to that in the first panel emerges. Hence, it might be concluded that on the whole globalization increases the income shares of the poor. It is not the case that the poor in inland provinces have been excluded from the globalization process, as is held in popular belief. If anything, the results suggest that the poor in the coastal provinces have benefited (proportionately) less than their counterparts in the inland. Somewhat disturbingly, the magnitude of the positive impact has decreased since the 1990s.

7.3.2. Sensitivity Tests

Thus far we have restricted the specification of our regression equation down to the minimal. This has the clear virtue of saving on the degrees of freedom. We might also draw some comfort from the fact that the average adjusted *R*-square of the IV-estimated regressions with fixed effects is well over 0.81. However, relying on such a simple specification does risk introducing serious biases into the model that stem from misspecified functional form and/or omission of important explanatory variables. To test the robustness of the findings in section 7.3.1, a range of sensitivity tests have been conducted.

We first consider the possibility that the distributional effect of globalization is non-linear. One type of non-linearity is that the effects of globalization depend on the level of economic development. A second type of non-linearity resembles the shape of the 'Laffer curve'—namely, globalization has an adverse effect on income distribution up to a threshold level beyond which its effect turns positive.[22] We test for the presence of both forms of non-linearity by adding into the regression in column 5 an interaction term between $\bar{y}_{kt}$ and g_{kt} and the quadratic term of g_{kt}. Whether they are entered separately or together, neither of the added terms turns out to be significant while the coefficient estimates on $\bar{y}_{kt}$, g_{kt} and the interaction term between g_{kt} and the 1992

[21] We note two facts supporting these conjectures. First, many of China's indigenous export firms are township and village enterprises engaged in such industries as garment, footwear, and toys that do not require sophisticated machinery and equipment. Second, FDI inflows to China were considerably higher in the 1990s than in the 1980s.

[22] Agénor (2003) examines the 'Laffer curve' effect of globalization on the absolute level of poverty.

dummy remain virtually unchanged. We thus conclude that the possibility of non-linearity can be rather safely excluded.[23]

One might also suspect that the ameliorative effect of globalization identified earlier is spurious on the ground that it is simply a consequence of both globalization and the income shares of the poor being correlated with a third variable/factor in the same direction. We examine four of such factors that are frequently mentioned in studies on poverty and income distribution in China. The first of these is the extent to which market reform has progressed. It is often argued that a more open economy is also a more liberalized economy. By allowing room for private businesses to flourish, a more liberalized economy in turn offers more employment opportunities for the poor. We use the proportion of the labour force employed in the non-state sector as a proxy for the extent of liberalization. Adding this variable to the regression produces the results in column 6 of Tables 7.2–7.4. It can be easily seen that liberalization can indeed exert a positive effect on the income shares of the poor. Equally clear is the result that the positive effect of liberalization does not knock out the positive effect of globalization.[24]

The second factor we consider is the economic structure of the local economy. In an extensive study on poverty in China, Ravallion and Chen (2007) find that agricultural growth has a greater impact on poverty reduction at the national level than does the growth of either the industrial or the service sector. In addition, they do not find evidence for any significant effect of trade openness on poverty. Will these conclusions apply when the subject of investigation is changed to relative poverty in urban areas? In column 7 of Tables 7.2–7.4, the estimation results from including the GDP share of manufacturing industries are reported. Across the nine regressions in this column, globalization retains its significance, whereas the newly added variable proves insignificant. When we substitute this variable alternately with the GDP share of the entire industrial sector and with the GDP share of the service sector, there is still little sign of any significant relationship between the income shares of the poor and the economic structure. Herein lies an important caveat, however. Because no sectoral breakdown of urban GDP is available at the provincial level, the GDP shares used in the regressions are calculated from provincial totals. For individual provinces, these shares may or may not capture the economic structure in their urban areas.

The next factor on the list is the average stock of human capital. The rationale for testing the effects of this factor comes from the observation that the

[23] We have also tried replacing the trade/GDP ratio with exports/GDP and FDI stock/GDP with FDI flow/GDP. The results are expectedly similar, given the high correlations within the two pairs of ratios.

[24] When using the share of non-state enterprises of gross industrial product as the measure of liberalization, we obtained similar results.

distribution of human capital among the Chinese provinces, much like that of physical capital, is weighted in favour of the coastal region. For the lack of a more appropriate measure, the average schooling of the labour force is adopted and the regression results are shown in column 8. The correlation between the income shares of the poor and average schooling is weak, insignificant, and in most cases negative. It should be noted, however, that average schooling is a poor measure of the type of human capital required for the poor to participate better in aggregate growth. The latter is more appropriately anchored to the completion of primary education and basic vocational training, for which we do not have sufficient data. Therefore, while the results in column 8 confirm the robustness of the impact of globalization, they do not serve as the basis for dismissing the effect of augmenting the human capital of the poor.

The last factor we examine is the rate of inflation. For an economy of China's size, it is no surprise that both the absolute level of and the changes in prices can vary widely across regions. The evidence from cross-country studies shows that the poor stand to lose more from inflation than the rest of the population.[25] In Ravallion and Chen (2007), it is noted that changes in inflation rates are poverty increasing. If it so happens that the extent of openness of a province is negatively correlated with its inflation rate, a positive relationship between globalization and the income shares of the poor might show up even if there is no underlying relationship between the two. This proposition does not ring true in our case, however, as the results in column 9 demonstrate. Inflation does have a dampening effect on the income shares of the poor, but the effect of globalization still comes through.

As a final check, we run a regression where all the aforementioned control variables are included in the specification. As can be seen in column 10, the coefficient on g_{kt} remains positive and significant in the first and third panels while the coefficient on the interaction term between g_{kt} and the 1992 dummy remains negative and significant. To summarize the analysis in this section, our findings in section 7.3.1 prove to be robust to additional control variables and non-linearity in functional forms.

7.4. Conclusion

This chapter examines how globalization affects urban poverty in China, with two major objectives in mind: one substantive and one methodological. Our substantive objective is to conduct the analysis at the provincial level. Such a set-up allows us to take into account the rich diversity in levels of development and degrees of openness across the Chinese provinces, an advantage over

[25] See, for example, Easterly and Fischer (2001).

studies at the cross-country or national level. Our methodological objective is to tap into the wealth of statistical methods and econometric models developed for cross-country studies, and to apply some of them at the sub-national level. More specifically, we adopted the kernel density estimation technique of Sala-i-Martin (2002a; 2002b) to recover provincial income distributions from irregularly grouped survey data. The income shares of the three poorest groups (the bottom 20 per cent, 10 per cent, and 5 per cent of the urban residents along the Lorenz curve) are obtained and used in the econometric framework of Dollar and Kraay (2002) to assess the impact of globalization on the poor in urban China.

Our focus on the subnational level resulted in several interesting findings that are either different from those in cross-country or national level studies or are completely overlooked in those studies. First, we found that average income growth has an adverse effect on the income shares of the poor while globalization in general, and trade openness in particular, increases the income shares of the poor. Both findings are in disagreement with related results in Dollar and Kraay (2002). Second, it is seen that openness to trade and openness to FDI have differential, if not diametrically opposed, distributional effects. The inequality-reducing effect of trade was significantly attenuated after 1992, suggesting possible changes in the nature of the growth of trade and in the way trade impacts on the labour market. Finally, the benefit from globalization accrues to the poor in the inland provinces just as much as it does to their counterparts in the coastal region. These findings are robust to alternative specifications where the effect of globalization enters non-linearly or where additional control variables are included.

The above results, however, must be subject to three important caveats. First, the global economic environment during the period examined in this chapter was by and large favourable to export-led growth. In particular, the USA, China's largest export market, saw uninterrupted growth in 1991–2000, the longest expansion in its modern history. China encountered nearly no significant external shocks during these years, and emerged unscathed from the Asian Financial Crisis thanks partly to a closed capital account and partly to the strength of consumer demand in the USA and Europe. However, a decade after the 1997–8 Asian Crisis, worldwide food shortages and oil price hikes in 2007–8 led to sharp increases in food and fuel prices in China in spite that the government still retained strong controls over these prices. And, although China's financial system has remained relatively unaffected by the current financial crisis, the impact has been widely felt in China's coastal region where tens of thousands of factories have been shut down owing to slack demand for exports.[26] For economies as intertwined with the world economy

[26] The *New York Times* (Wong 2008) reported that the slowdown in exports caused more than 6,700 factory closures in the first half of 2008 alone.

as today's China, it is impossible to stay immune to external shocks. The differential impacts of such shocks on different social groups are not invariant, but the poor are often the most vulnerable to their adverse effects. The food and fuel price hikes, for instance, erode the real income of lower income groups disproportionately because non-discretionary expenses on food, transport, lighting, heating, and so on make up a greater share of their living expenditure.[27] Further integration into the world economy, therefore, entails greater income uncertainty and increased vulnerability for the poor. If globalization is to be deployed as a positive force in alleviating urban poverty, then it is necessary to ensure, in addition to the poor sharing the proceeds from general income growth, that a social safety net is in place to cushion the blows from negative shocks.

Second, the income data used in this chapter does not include the 'floating population' of the cities—rural migrant workers without urban household registration. There are no hard figures on the size of the migrant population. The official estimate puts it at around 130 million (Anderlini and Dyer 2009), which would make the migrants more than one-fifth of the 577 million urban residents (NBS 2007). Migrants and laid-off workers of state-owned enterprises are the two largest groups making up the urban 'new poor'. It is estimated that the poverty incidence among migrants is 50 per cent higher than official urban residents (ADB 2004). Hence, if rural migrants are included in the urban population, the income shares of the poor are probably lower than the estimates in this chapter.

Globalization has played an important role in accelerating China's rural–urban migration. The regional pattern of globalization correlates highly with the geographical distribution of rural migrants. Large FDI inflows to the coastal region and the accompanying export boom created millions of jobs offering higher rates of return on labour than does farming. Research shows that the four coastal provinces Guangdong, Zhejiang, Fujian, and Jiangsu, along with Beijing and Shanghai, attracted more than 80 per cent of the rural migrants (Tunñón 2006). Many of these migrants work in factories manufacturing labour-intensive products for the export market. The high geographical and sectoral concentrations of migrant labour imply, however, that migrant workers are susceptible to international business cycles. The current global economic downturn has resulted in more than 20 million migrants, or 15.3 per cent of the total, losing their jobs (Anderlini and Dyer 2009). The plight of the migrants is compounded by their exclusion from the urban social safety net.[28] For

[27] Between the urban and rural poor, the former group are likely to be more severely affected in this case because, as suppliers, farmers benefit from higher prices for farm produce.

[28] Currently there are two welfare programmes targeted at the urban poor: the unemployment insurance scheme and the minimum-living-standard-guarantee scheme. Both are restricted to official urban residents.

migrant workers, therefore, the loss of employment means a return to their rural homes. Such return migration would have an adverse impact on rural poverty reduction as many poor rural households have grown dependent on remittances from migrant workers and, by adding to rural surplus labour, it can cause a deterioration of labour productivity in farming.

Poverty is a multidimensional phenomenon, and income poverty is but one of its many facets. Hence, the third qualification on our results is that they do not reflect the impacts of globalization on the other aspects of urban poverty. In particular, the environmental consequences of globalization and the impact of environmental changes on urban poverty are not considered. There is little dispute that China's rapid economic growth in the past three decades has been achieved at considerable cost to the environment. According to the State Environmental Protection Administration, 60 per cent of the Chinese cities suffer from severe air pollution, and 90 per cent suffer from some form of underground water pollution. The World Bank estimates that air and water pollution now cost China 3.5 per cent to 8 per cent of its GDP per year (World Bank 2007: ix). China is expected to become the world's largest emitter of carbon dioxide in 2009 (IEA 2006). Some of the environmental degradation is clearly linked to globalization. For example, roughly one-third of China's total carbon emissions come from the production of exports. Anecdotal evidence is not in short supply that, whether inadvertently or not, multinational corporations seeking ever-lower production costs encouraged environmentally irresponsible behaviour on the part of their Chinese suppliers. If such environmental externalities are taken into account, the positive effect of globalization on income growth would have to be discounted. The benign distribution effect of globalization on urban poverty as suggested by our results may also be put in a less favourable light. This is so because poor households, especially rural migrants, often live in substandard housing close to polluting factories, waste dumps, or railway tracks, or in areas at high flood risk. Hence, the urban poor suffer disproportionately from the health hazards posed by overcrowding, lack of sanitation facilities, and air and noise pollution. Compared with other urban residents, they are also more vulnerable to floods, storms, and other extreme weather events.

One of the basic lessons learned from economic history is that economies urbanize as they develop. Although China is still a rural society, there is little doubt that urbanization will proceed apace once restrictions on internal migration are removed. Among the many potential 'growing pains' is a resurgence of urban poverty. Increasingly, the battle against poverty will have to be waged in urban as well as in rural areas. Should promoting international trade and foreign investment remain part of the weaponry? On the one hand, the evidence from this study should allay fears that globalization is merely pro-rich or pro-coastal provinces. On the other hand, further research is needed to look into the negative distribution effect of FDI and the impact of globalization on aspects of urban deprivation beyond income poverty.

APPENDIX

Data Sources and Definitions

The data on household income distribution are collected from various provincial statistical yearbooks. The data for all the other variables are from *Comprehensive Statistical Data and Materials for 50 Years of New China* (Beijing: China Statistics Press, 1999) and updated to 2001 using the *Statistical Yearbook of China* 2000, 2001, and 2002 <http://www.stats.gov.cn/english/statisticaldata/yearlydata/>.

The variables involved in the regressions in section 7.3 are defined as follows:

(1) *l*: the logarithms of the income shares of, respectively, the bottom quintile, decile, and 5 per cent of the provincial residents along the Lorenz curve. The method of calculating these income shares are detailed in section 7.2 of the text.

(2) *y*: the logarithm of real per capita income. This is obtained by deflating the nominal average incomes recorded in the survey data by the provincial price levels provided in Brandt and Holz (2004).

(3) *g*: alternatively defined as the ratio of the sum of imports and exports to GDP, the ratio of the stock of FDI to GDP, and the first principal component of the preceding two ratios. The stock of FDI is accumulated from the annual flows of utilized FDI using the perpetual inventory method. The nominal values of FDI flows are converted to real values using the provincial implicit GDP deflators. The depreciation rate is set at 0.09.

(4) *Coast*: dummy variable for coastal provinces, which include Beijing, Fujian, Guangdong, Hainan, Hebei, Jiangsu, Liaoning, Shanghai, Shandong, Tianjin, and Zhejiang.

(5) *Time*: dummy variable for 1992–2001.

(6) *Liberalization*: the logarithm of the proportion of the labour force employed in the non-state sector.

(7) *Economic structure*: the logarithm of the share of manufacturing industries in provincial GDP.

(8) *Education*: average years of schooling obtained from Wan, Lu, and Chen (2004).

(9) *Inflation*: annual inflation rate (as a decimal). The rates are calculated from the price levels in Brandt and Holz 2004.

References

Anderlini, J., and G. Dyer (2009) 'Downturn Causes 20m Job Losses in China', *Financial Times*, 2 Feb. 2009.

Agénor, P.-R. (2003) 'Does Globalization Hurt the Poor?'. Washington, DC: World Bank. mimeo.

Asian Development Bank (ADB) (2004) *Poverty Profile of the People's Republic of China*. Manila: ADB.

Barro, R. J. (1999) 'Inequality, Growth and Investment'. National Bureau for Economic Research Working Paper 7038. Cambridge, Mass.: NBER.

Brandt, L., and C. A. Holz (2004) 'Spatial Price Differences in China: Estimates and Implications'. Hong Kong: Hong Kong University of Science and Technology, Social Science Division. mimeo.

Buckley, P. J., J. Clegg, and C. Wang (2002) 'The Impact of Inward FDI on Performance of Chinese Manufacturing Firms', *Journal of International Business Studies*, 33: 637–55.

Démurger S., and J. C. Berthélemy (2000) 'Foreign Direct Investment and Economic Growth: Theory and Application to China', *Review of Development Economics*, 4: 140–55.

Dollar, D., and A. Kraay (2002) 'Growth is Good for the Poor', *Journal of Economic Growth*, 7: 195–225.

Easterly, W., and S. Fischer (2001) 'Inflation and the Poor', *Journal of Money Credit and Banking*, 33: 160–78.

Hussain, A. (2003) 'Urban Poverty in China: Measurement, Patterns, and Policies'. Geneva: ILO.

International Energy Agency (IEA) (2006) *World Energy Outlook 2006*. Paris: International Energy Agency.

Kanbur, R., and X. Zhang (2005) 'Fifty Years of Regional Inequality in China: A Journey through Central Planning, Reform and Openness', *Review of Development Economics*, 9: 87–106.

Khan, A. (1998) 'Poverty in China in the Period of Globalization: New Evidence on Trend and Pattern'. Issues in Development Discussion Paper 22. Geneva: ILO.

——K. Griffin, and C. Riskin (1999) 'Income Distribution in Urban China during the Period of Economic Reform and Globalization', *American Economic Review*, 89: 296–300.

Khan, J., and M. Landler (2007) 'China Grabs West's Smoke-spewing Factories', *New York Times*, 21 Dec. 2007.

Milanović, B. (2002) 'The Ricardian Vice: Why Sala-i-Martin's Calculations of World Income Inequality are Wrong'. Washington, DC: World Bank. mimeo.

National Bureau of Statistics of China (NBS) (1999) Comprehensive Statistical Data and Materials on 50 Years of New China. Beijing: China Statistics Press.

——(2007) *China Statistical Yearbook 2007*. Beijing: China Statistics Press.

Nissanke, M., and E. Thorbecke (2005) 'Channels and Policy Debate in the Globalization–Inequality–Poverty Nexus', *World Development*, 34: 1338–60.

Ravallion, M. (2001) 'Growth, Inequality and Poverty: Looking Beyond Averages', *World Development*, 29: 1803–15.

——(2003a) 'Measuring Aggregate Economic Welfare in Developing Countries: How Well do National Accounts and Survey Agree?', *Review of Economics and Statistics*, 85: 645–52.

——(2003b) 'Inequality Convergence', *Economics Letters*, 80: 351–6.

——(2004) 'Looking Beyond Averages in the Trade and Poverty Debate'. Policy Research Working Paper 3461. Washington, DC: World Bank.

——and S. Chen (2007) 'China's (Uneven) Progress Against Poverty', *Journal of Development Economics*, 82: 1–42.

Rodriguez, F., and D. Rodrik (2001) 'Trade Policy and Economic Growth: A Skeptic's Guide to the Cross-national Evidence'. In B. Bernanke and K. S. Rogoff (eds), *NBER Macroeconomics Annual 2000*. Cambridge, Mass.: MIT Press for NBER.

Sala-i-Martin, X. (2002a) 'The Disturbing Rise in Global Income Inequality'. National Bureau for Economic Research Working Paper 8904. Cambridge, Mass.: NBER.

——(2002b) 'The World Distribution of Income'. National Bureau for Economic Research Working Paper 8905. Cambridge, Mass.: NBER.

Shorrocks, A., and G. Wan (2004) 'A Simple Method for Generating Income Data from Lorenz Coordinates'. Helsinki: UNU-WIDER. mimeo.

Spilimbergo, A., J. L. Londono, and M. Szekely (1999) 'Income Distribution, Factor Endowments, and Trade Openness', *Journal of Development Economics*, 59: 77–101.

Stiglitz, J. E. (2003) 'Globalization and Growth in Emerging Markets and the New Economy', *Journal of Policy Modeling*, 25: 502–24.

Tunñón, M. (2006) 'Internal Labour Migration in China: Features and Responses'. Beijing: ILO Office. mimeo.

UNU-WIDER. (2008) World Income Inequality Database V2.0c. Helsinki: UNU-WIDER. <http://www.wider.unu.edu/research/Database/en_GB/database/>.

Wan, G., M. Lu, and Z. Chen (2004) 'Globalization and Regional Income Inequality: Evidence From Within China'. Discussion Paper 2004/10. Helsinki: UNU-WIDER.

Wei, S.-J. (1995) 'The Open Door Policy and China's Rapid Growth: Evidence from City Level Data'. In T. Ito and A. O. Krueger (eds), *Growth Theories in Light of the East Asian Experience*. Chicago: University of Chicago Press.

——and Y. Wu (2002) 'Globalization and Inequality without Differences in Data Definition, Legal System and Other Institutions'. Washington, DC: IMF. mimeo.

Wong, E. (2008) 'Factories Shut, China Workers Are Suffering', *New York Times*, 13 Nov. 2008.

World Bank (2007) 'Cost of Pollution in China: Economic Estimates of Physical Damages Report'. Washington, DC: The World Bank.

Zhang, Y., and G. Wan (2006) 'Globalization and the Urban Poor in China'. Research Paper 2006/42. Helsinki: UNU-WIDER.

Part III

Latin America

8

Trade Liberalization, Employment Flows, and Wage Inequality in Brazil

Francisco H. G. Ferreira, Phillippe G. Leite, and Matthew Wai-Poi[1]

8.1. Introduction

The hypothetical link between 'globalization' and inequality (within developed countries, within developing countries, or between them) has been the subject of a vast literature over the last twenty years. Even a cursory review of this literature reveals that 'globalization' has been a 'catch-all term that is used to describe phenomena as diverse as trade liberalization, outsourcing, increased immigration flows, removal of capital controls, cultural globalization, and generally faster transmission of international shocks and trends' (Goldberg and Pavcnik 2004: 1). In this chapter, we focus on evidence pertaining directly to trade liberalization, although in some cases it is difficult to separate the impacts of trade liberalization strictly defined from those of outsourcing, or of increased flows of technical and managerial knowledge.

Most of the literature on trade liberalization in Latin America has focused on Mexico, Chile, and Colombia, and suggests that it has contributed to an *increase* in inequality (or at least in the gap between skilled and unskilled wages). Since there was a presumption that Latin America, like most other developing regions, was abundant in unskilled labour, this empirical finding appears to contradict the predictions of the ('two countries, two goods, two factors' version of the) Stolper–Samuelson theorem in the Heckscher–Ohlin trade theory.

[1] We are grateful to Nina Pavcnik and Norbert Schady for kindly sharing their constructed industry concordance with us, and to Gustavo Gonzaga, Will Martin, Nina Pavcnik, Guido Porto, Martin Ravallion, and Erik Thorbecke for helpful conversations or comments. All errors and omissions are exclusively our responsibility. The views expressed in this chapter are solely those of the authors, and they should not be attributed to the World Bank, or any other organization.

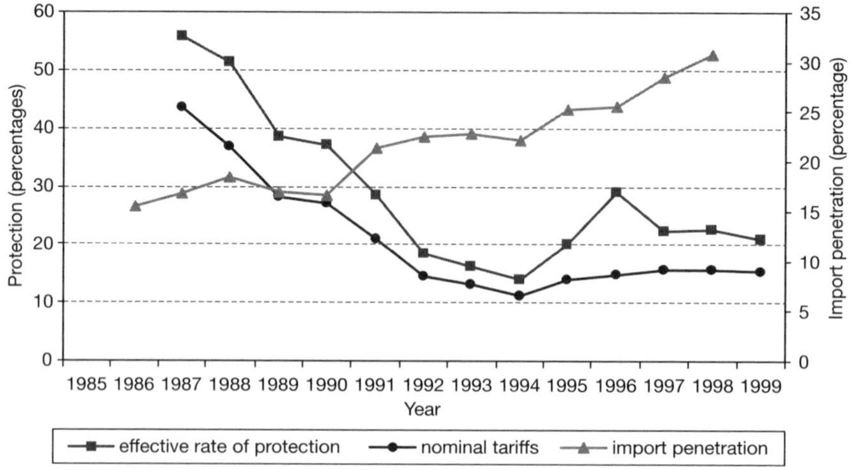

Fig. 8.1. Protection and import penetration in Brazil, 1985–99

Source: Tariffs and rates of protection from Kume, Piani, and de Souza (2000) in de Paiva Abreau (2004); import penetration from Muendler (2003).

Although the next section briefly reviews some of this literature, this chapter focuses on Brazil, a country where trade liberalization appears to have been *inequality reducing*.

Previously one of the most heavily protected economies in the world, Brazil, experienced an episode of marked trade liberalization between 1988 and 1995. Average nominal tariffs (weighted by lagged industry imports) fell from 43.4 per cent in 1987 to 13.9 per cent in 1995. Effective rates of protection fell from 55.8 per cent to 20.0 per cent in the same period. These large changes in protection had a correspondingly large impact on trade flows: import : consumption ratios across all manufacturing sectors rose from 15 per cent in 1986 to 31 per cent in 1998. Figure 8.1 shows the evolution of both tariff rates and trade flows over the 1985–99 period.[2] It has also been argued that this episode of trade liberalization had a substantial impact on labour and total factor productivity growth, with the latter increasing by 6 percentage points in annual rate terms (Ferreira and Rossi 2003).

During this period Brazilian inequality, which had been rising until 1989, started a gradual but persistent decline. Figure 8.2 shows the long-term evolution of two commonly used inequality measures, the Gini and the Theil indices,

[2] The data reported in Table 8.1 weigh tariff rates by lagged industry imports. An alternative weighting scheme (by industry value added) generates an even more pronounced decline: citing data from Kume, Piani, and de Souza (2000), de Paiva Abreu reports a decline in nominal tariffs from 54.9 per cent in 1987 to 10.8 per cent in 1995 (de Paiva Abreu 2004). Effective rates of protection fell from 67.8 per cent to 10.4 per cent in the same period.

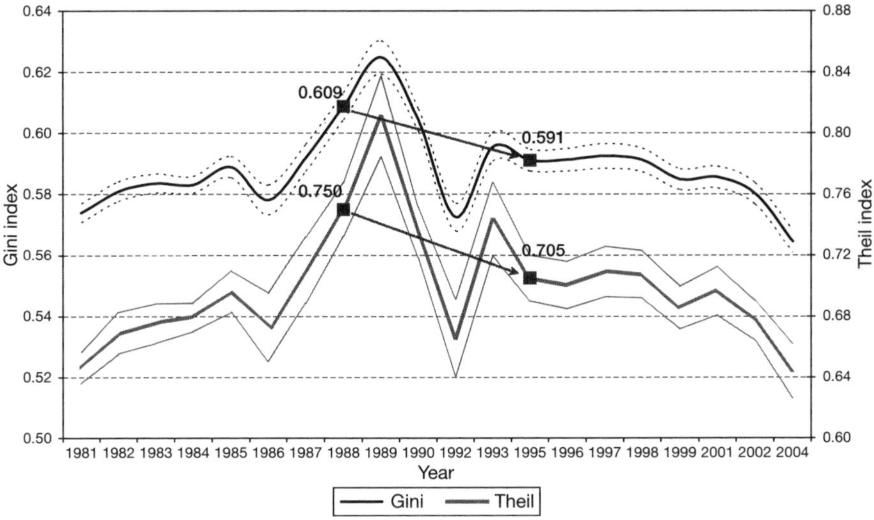

Fig. 8.2. Household per capita income inequality in Brazil, 1981–2004

Source: Ferreira, Leite, and Litchfield (2008).

between 1981 and 2004, for household income per capita. The bands around the point estimates denote the 95 per cent bootstrapped confidence intervals. The figure highlights the trade liberalization period of 1988–95, during which inequality briefly rose (for one year) and then began to fall. The Theil index fell from 0.75 to 0.71 and the Gini fell by almost two points from 0.61 to 0.59 over this seven-year interval. Both declines are statistically significant at the 1 per cent level. As shown in Figure 8.3, inequality also fell in the distribution of hourly wages: the Gini fell by almost three points, from 0.61 to 0.58 and the Theil fell from 0.78 to 0.72. Both declines are significant at the 5 per cent level. The economy-wide skill premium (defined as the ratio of the wages of skilled workers to those of unskilled workers) fell by 14.3 per cent (see Figure 8.4).[3] Looking only at the skill premium in manufacturing, Gonzaga, Menezes-Filho, and Terra (2006) find a similar (15.5 per cent) decline between 1988 and 1995.

Were these two phenomena linked? Did trade liberalization, and other aspects of increased openness which took place alongside it, cause at least part of the contemporaneous decline in Brazilian inequality? The literature is somewhat inconclusive. Focusing on the specific channels of industry wage premiums and industry-specific skill premiums, Pavcnik et al. (2004) find no

[3] We use an education-based definition of skill: skilled workers have eleven or more years of schooling, and unskilled workers are those with ten or fewer. We return to a discussion of this definition and alternatives below.

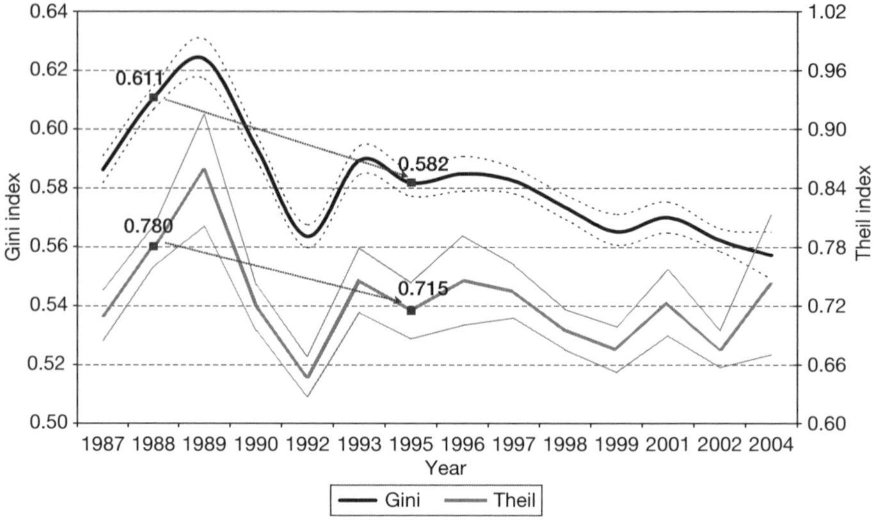

Fig. 8.3. Hourly wage inequality in Brazil, 1987–2004

Source: Authors' calculation from PNADs.

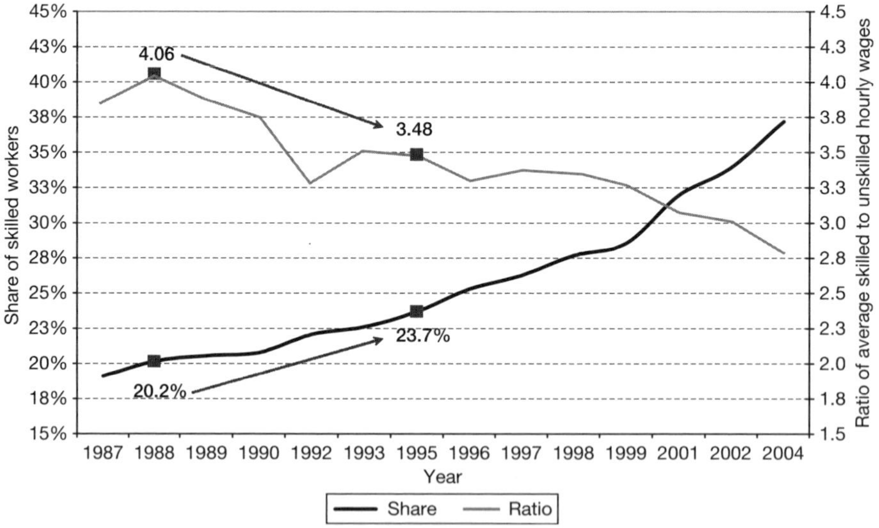

Fig. 8.4. Skill wage premium and share of skilled workers in total employment, 1987–2004

Notes: Unskilled workers have ten or fewer years of schooling; skilled workers have eleven or more years of schooling.

Source: Authors' calculation from PNADs.

evidence of any effect from trade liberalization on the Brazilian wage distribution. More recently, Gonzaga, Menezes-Filho, and Terra (2006) argue persuasively that through the more general channel of changes in the economy-wide skill premium (as opposed to industry-specific premiums), trade liberalization did reduce wage disparities in Brazil. Although these two studies cover the same period, they use different datasets and methodologies, which lead them to focus on different aspects of the same phenomenon.

Despite their differences, both studies focus on workers in manufacturing only. The manufacturing sector accounted for 16 per cent (13 per cent) of total employment in 1988 (1995) and there can be no *a priori* presumption that changes in the skill premium in that sector drive national wage inequality. During this same period, there has also been a convergence between urban and rural incomes in Brazil, which is often attributed to agricultural growth.[4] Although agriculture is eminently tradable, to our knowledge it has not been included in any analysis of liberalization and distribution in Brazil.

This chapter seeks to revisit the evidence on Brazil's trade liberalization in a more comprehensive way. We innovate in four ways. First, we combine the approach used by Pavcnik et al. (2004) to study trade-mandated changes in industry-specific wage and skill premiums, with a consideration of the economy-wide skill premium on which Gonzaga, Menezes-Filho, and Terra (2006) focus, and ask what was the combined effect of the two channels on the wage distribution in Brazil. Second, unlike previous studies, our analysis covers workers in all sectors of the economy, including agriculture and services. Third, we explicitly consider employment responses to the tariff and exchange rate changes that took place over the period, investigating a channel of impact which is generally acknowledged as potentially important in theory, but seldom studied in practice. Fourth, we use our estimated models of wages and employment levels to simulate counterfactual wage distributions which allow us to decompose the changes in distribution actually observed over the seven years of trade liberalization into various components—some directly attributable to trade reforms, some which may or may not reflect trade changes, and some which are most likely independent of trade factors.

Our main findings are, first, that trade liberalization in Brazil did in fact contribute to the observed reduction in wage inequality in the entire Brazilian economy, and not just in manufacturing. As argued by Gonzaga, Menezes-Filho, and Terra (2006)—and unlike in Chile, Mexico, and Colombia—Brazil's pre-liberalization tariffs (adjusted by import penetration) were highest for skill-intensive goods. These tariffs fell by more than those for other goods, leading to a decline in their relative prices. Consistent with the simple Stolper–Samuelson theorem, this decline led to a decline in skilled wages, relative to those of unskilled workers, and to a movement of workers away from previously

[4] See Ferreira, Leite, and Litchfield (2008).

protected industries. As Pavcnik et al. (2004) find, other channels of impact through industry-specific wage and skill premiums were unimportant.

Second, the decomposition results suggest that:

(i) Changes in industry-specific wage premiums and skill premiums were unimportant. Although changes in tariffs have the expected sign, the overall effect on the wage distribution was negligible.

(ii) The bulk of the trade impact on the wage distribution occurs through the employment and occupational reallocation that took place in response to changes in tariffs and relative prices. This effect accounts for a substantial fraction of the observed reduction in inequality between 1988 and 1995.

(iii) Changes in the economy-wide returns to skill, which may be at least partly driven by trade reforms, contributed to a further reduction in inequality (as did changes in other returns).

(iv) Changes in the joint distribution of (observed and unobserved) worker characteristics were inequality increasing, and partly offset some of the trade-driven changes in inequality.

The chapter is organized as follows. The next section provides a very brief overview of the literature, focusing on the conceptual channels through which trade reforms affect the distribution of incomes, and on five or six specific theoretical mechanisms through which openness has been hypothesized to affect wages and employment. Section 8.3 describes our datasets and the methodological approach. Section 8.4 presents the estimation results for a set of wage and employment regressions. Section 8.5 discusses a decomposition of the changes in Brazil's wage distribution between 1988 and 1995, drawing on counterfactual distributions constructed on the basis of the models estimated in Section 8.3. It also discusses the implications of the wage decomposition for poverty and inequality more broadly, measured in the distribution of household per capita incomes. Section 8.6 concludes.

8.2. A Brief Literature Review

The literature on the relationship between 'globalization' and distribution is now so extensive that Goldberg and Pavcnik open their recent survey of the subject by noting that 'the number of literature reviews alone is so large by now, that it seems that a review of literature reviews would be appropriate' (Goldberg and Pavcnik 2004: 1). Given the existence of two excellent recent surveys—Winters, McCulloch, and McKay (2004) and Goldberg and Pavcnik (2004)—we make no attempt at an exhaustive review here. Instead, this section briefly reviews two subthemes which are of particular importance for our analysis in this chapter: the channels through which trade reforms affect the distribution of income (and hence inequality and poverty), and the recent evidence on the distributional effects of trade reform in Latin America in general, and in Brazil in particular.[5]

8.2.1. *Channels of Impact from Trade Liberalization to Household Incomes*

If openness to the international economy brings persistent gains in terms of access to new knowledge and technology, or sustained gains in the growth rate of total factor productivity, then it is possible that trade liberalization leads to faster long-run economic growth. Whether or not this is, in fact, the case has been the subject of a debate, with Sachs and Warner (1995) and Edwards (1998) among the proponents, and Rodriguez and Rodrik (2001) leading the sceptics. The current balance of opinion seems to be that 'despite the econometric and conceptual difficulties of establishing beyond doubt that openness enhances income levels, the weight of experience and evidence seems strongly in that direction' (Winters, McCulloch, and McKay 2004: 78).

If this is indeed the case, the effect of trade on growth, whether it is mediated through a faster rate of technology adoption or through greater dynamic efficiency gains from competitive pressures, is likely to be of first-order importance in any understanding of the relationship between 'globalization' and poverty, and policymakers should bear it very much in mind. Nevertheless, this chapter belongs to the (large) strand of literature that seeks to understand the static or short-term impacts of trade liberalization on the distribution of incomes. When tariffs (or non-tariff barriers) are reduced or eliminated, the domestic prices of the relevant goods change. These price changes can affect household incomes (or consumption) through five main direct channels—namely:

Output and input prices. If household members are self-employed, producing, trading, and consuming different goods, then the first-order approximation to the change in their welfare as a result of changes in the price vector is simply $\Delta W = \sum_i (q_i - c_i)\Delta p_i$.[6] The basic insight is that net producers of those goods whose prices fall as a result of trade reforms lose out, while net consumers gain.

Wages. For household members who are employed, the first effect of price changes is through the knock-on effect on factor prices, and crucially on the individual's wage. The exact transmission mechanisms depend on the degree of competition in both factor and product markets, but the benchmark result under competitive markets is that as protection declines and relative goods prices move against the previously protected good, relative factor prices also move against the factor in which the protected good is intensive. This is the

[5] See also Nissanke and Thorbecke (2006) for a thoughtful discussion of the links between globalization and distribution.

[6] See Deaton (1997) and discussion in Winters, McCulloch, and McKay (2004).

well-known Stolper–Samuelson theorem in the Heckscher–Ohlin trade theory.[7]
Employment. In response to changes in profitability that arise because of the aforementioned changes in product and factor prices, the composition of production typically changes after trade reforms. Industries whose product prices have fallen contract, and those whose relative product prices have risen, expand. In response, there is a reallocation of employment across sectors and, in imperfect labour markets, changes in unemployment and/or the size of the informal sector.
Consumption prices. Self-employed workers are not the only people who consume. Employed workers, who are affected on the income side through changes in their wages and employment sector, are also affected by the changes in the relative prices of the goods they consume. Trade models often pay little heed to this channel because, if preferences are identical across individuals and homothetic, then changes in relative prices will affect all households equi-proportionately. But if preferences are not, in fact, homothetic, or if they differ across households, then the *shares* of different goods in their consumption bundles will vary, and relative price changes will affect different households differently. Under this channel, we also include changes in the *quality* of consumption goods available to consumers, either directly because of differences in quality between imported and domestically produced goods, or because of improvements in domestic production as a result of import competition, or of the availability of imported inputs.
Taxes and public expenditures. As tariffs change, so in general, will tariff revenues. Although there is much evidence that it is possible to reduce protection in a revenue neutral—or even revenue enhancing—manner, if revenues do fall, then there will either be a decline in the level of some public service or transfer, or a rise in some other tax.[8] The incidence of these changes is entirely dependent on which expenditures or taxes are altered, and on their (marginal) incidence.

Ultimately, all trade reforms must affect household welfare—and its distribution—through one of these five primary channels. Much of the discussion in the literature has focused, however, on the nature of the mechanism through which tariff changes affect wages and employment levels. A trade reform that lowers tariffs for a number of goods may affect relative wages and the

[7] The theorem generates less-clear-cut results in a world with more than two countries, goods, or factors of production but, as we shall see, the basic insight from the $2 \times 2 \times 2$ version of the theorem remains remarkably powerful.

[8] The evidence suggests, however, that it has in many cases been possible to liberalize trade without loss in revenues. This may occur because non-tariff barriers generate rents for private agents, rather than government revenue, because some tariffs may initially be above their revenue-maximizing level, or because some trade reforms occur concomitantly with enhancements in the efficiency of customs agencies. See Ebrill, Stotsky, and Gropp (1999) and the discussion in Winters, McCulloch, and McKay (2004).

composition of employment through the standard Stolper–Samuelson channel, as described above, but it may also work in a number of different ways. These have been reviewed in some detail by Goldberg and Pavcnik (2004), and we provide only a sketch below.

There may be changes in the wage premiums to *specific occupations* (as opposed to industries), such as managers and highly skilled professionals (see Cragg and Epelbaum 1996).

- Trade liberalization may be accompanied by adjustments not only in the national composition of production, but in the *international* composition, with some activities being outsourced from developed- to developing-country locations. One hypothesis is that some of these activities are intensive in workers that are unskilled by rich country criteria, but skilled in developing countries. See, for instance, Feenstra and Hanson (1996).
- Technical change that raises firms' relative demand for skill is known as *skill-biased technical change* (SBTC). Whereas in developed countries SBTC is typically seen as a competing explanation (vis-à-vis trade openness) for increases in skill premiums, it has recently been argued that in developing countries SBTC may be spurred on by trade liberalization. See Acemoglu (2003) and Thoenig and Verdier (2003) for different models of how trade liberalization might lead to SBTC in developing countries. If indeed trade liberalization leads to changes in the relative demand for skilled and unskilled workers because of induced changes in technology, then this is a separate effect, additional to Stolper–Samuelson.
- Related to the previous two channels is the possibility that greater openness changes the *quality composition of domestic output*. Most goods (shoes, textiles, cars, or computers) can be produced with very different quality, and there is some evidence that greater participation in world trade shifts production towards higher quality goods in (at least some) domestic firms. This may be in response to greater import competition, or because exchange rate changes shift resources from non-exporters to exporters. If higher-quality varieties are more intensive in skilled workers, this effect too could raise the relative demand for skills in the labour force. See Verhoogen (2006) and Shigeoka, Verhoogen, and Wai-Poi (2006) for evidence from Mexico.
- Finally, wage levels for observably identical workers are not the same across different industries, either because of imperfect competition that gives rise to industry rents, or because of compensating differentials, or industry-specific skills. It is possible that tariff and mandated price changes affect these differentials, in addition to any impact they may have on the economy-wide skill premium. See, for example, Goldberg and Pavcnik (2005) on Colombia.

8.2.2. The Distributive Impact of Trade Liberalization in Latin America

Contrary to what was found in the earlier liberalization episodes of the less-developed countries, notably in East Asia, Latin American trade liberalizations during the 1980s and 1990s have been predominantly contemporaneous with *increases* in the economy-wide wage-skill premium, which is typically defined as the ratio of wages of skilled workers to the wages of unskilled workers.[9] Although this ratio is not a particularly good measure of wage inequality, and certainly a very poor indicator of inequality in household incomes, it has been the focus of most empirical work.[10]

Evidence of a rising skills gap has been comprehensively established for Mexico by Feenstra and Hanson (1996), Cragg and Epelbaum (1996), Feliciano (2001), and Hanson and Harrison (1999), among other works. It has also been documented for Chile by Beyer, Rojas, and Vergara (1999), for Colombia by Attanasio, Goldberg, and Pavcnik (2004), and for Costa Rica by Robbins and Grindling (1999). Given the presumption that developing countries are abundant in unskilled labour, the first reaction to these results was that it seemed to contradict the Stolper–Samuelson theorem, and considerable effort has been expended in proposing alternative explanations, many of which were described in general terms in the preceding subsection.

Wood (1997) argues that the simplest version of Stolper–Samuelson may not apply, because Latin American countries are perhaps abundant in land and natural resources, rather than unskilled labour, or because of the entry into the international trading system of countries even more unskilled-labour abundant, such as China and India. As discussed, Feenstra and Hanson (1996) suggest that part of the increase in the demand for skill in Mexico was due to outsourcing. Cragg and Epelbaum (1996) argue that it was driven by the increases in the returns to specific occupations, such as managers and administrators, who were highly skilled (rather than by returns to all skilled workers in the economy). Others argue that greater openness has spurred a process of technological change that is skill-biased, as also discussed above. Attanasio, Goldberg, and Pavcnik (2004) interpret their finding that increases in demand for skilled workers were largest for sectors with the largest tariff cuts as supporting the thesis of an endogenous skill-biased change in technology that occurs in response to competitive pressures and to the availability of inputs brought about by greater openness.

Each of these alternative stories—occupational rewards, skill-biased technical change, quality upgrading, outsourcing—is plausible, and each is supported by

[9] It matters whether skill levels are measured in practice by education levels as typically done in studies based on household survey data or by production vs. non-production workers as commonly done in studies using firm level data.

[10] Later in this chapter we investigate how changes in skill premium map into changes in more general measures of inequality.

at least some of the available evidence. But it is also true that an examination of the patterns of protection in Chile, Colombia, and Mexico prior to liberalization reveals that tariffs were generally higher for industries intensive in unskilled labour (than for skill-intensive industries). In this case, a fall in the relative prices of these goods, and thus in the price of the factor they are intensive in, is perfectly in line with the Stolper–Samuelson theorem in the first place.[11]

Brazil was an exception, in that effective protection prior to liberalization was higher for skill-intensive industries. The correlation between tariffs and industry skill shares in 1988 was mildly positive and much stronger once tariffs are adjusted by the industry import-penetration rates, which account for differences in the pass-through between tariffs and prices in different sectors.[12] Gonzaga, Menezes-Filho, and Terra (2006) show that, as tariffs were (partly) harmonized between 1988 and 1995, the tariff and effective rates of protection (ERPs) declines for skill-intensive industries were greater than for industries intensive in unskilled workers. In accordance with the Stolper–Samuelson predictions, the relative prices of skill-intensive goods then fell, as did the relative wages of more skilled workers. Using mandated wage equations, these authors estimate that the decline in the manufacturing skill premium over this period was of the order of 25 per cent—larger than the actually observed 15 per cent decline.

In addition, the pattern of labour reallocation was more consistent with a Stolper–Samuelson effect of trade liberalization than with a Rybczynski-style effect of increases in the endowment of skilled labour: the manufacturing employment share of skilled workers rose by 2.67 per cent, which decomposed into a 3.34 per cent within industries effect, and a negative 0.67 per cent between industry effect. This contraction in the employment share of skill-intensive industries would not be expected if the dynamics were driven primarily by expansion in the endowment of skilled workers in Brazil, but is consistent with the expected employment reallocation in response to a trade shock.

The evidence presented by Gonzaga, Menezes-Filho, and Terra (2006) strongly suggests that the Brazilian trade liberalization of 1988–95 played some role in the decline of inequality in Brazil which began during that period. It appears to have done so through the classic channel of changes in the economy-wide skill premium, in line with the prediction of the Heckscher–Ohlin trade theory, leading to a sizable decline in the wage gap between skilled and unskilled workers in manufacturing.[13]

[11] See Goldberg and Pavcnik (2004) for discussion.

[12] See Gonzaga, Menezes-Filho, and Terra (2006) on the importance of this correction.

[13] The literature suggests that alternative channels of impact were less important. Pavcnik and colleagues, for instance, find no evidence that changes in industry-specific wage premiums or in skill premiums specific to certain industries changed in response to trade liberalization (Pavcnik et al. 2004).

But how important was this change in the skill premium for the actual size distribution of hourly wages in Brazil? There are two reasons why its importance is far from guaranteed: one is that skilled and unskilled workers are large and heterogeneous groupings. There is considerable wage variation within each group, and the two group distributions do overlap. The second reason is that Gonzaga, Menezes-Filho, and Terra (2006) consider only manufacturing workers, which accounted for 16 per cent (13 per cent) of total employment in 1988 (1995). Changes in their relative position vis-à-vis workers in agriculture (which were also affected by changes in tariffs) and in services (which were indirectly affected by changes in tariffs, and also by changes in the exchange rate) may have led to overall changes in wage inequality which are quite different from those mandated by the Stolper–Samuelson effects within manufacturing.

In the remainder of this chapter we examine two basic questions. First, we seek to place the changes in wage inequality that can be attributed to trade policy changes in the context of other changes that were concurrently affecting the wage distribution. Second, and more specifically, we also seek to quantify the contribution of the trade-mandated employment reallocation effects to changes in the wage distribution. A third, albeit more tentative, contribution is to investigate the implications of these trade-driven changes in the wage distribution for poverty and inequality in the distribution of household incomes per capita.

8.3. Data and Methodology

8.3.1. The Datasets

The data used in this study come from two different sources. The first of these is the household survey data with information on wages, hours of work, occupations, education levels, age, gender, race, and location of workers. We use eleven waves of the *Pesquisa Nacional por Amostra de Domicílios* (PNAD), fielded by the *Instituto Brasileiro de Geografia e Estatística* annually between 1987 and 1999.[14] The PNAD is a nationally representative household survey, with a stratified and clustered sampling design which ensures coverage of rural and urban areas in every state of the federation, except for the rural areas of Acre, Amapá, Amazonas, Pará, Rondônia, and Roraima.[15] Sample sizes varied somewhat from year to year, but totalled approximately 300,000 individuals per year.

For our wage analysis, we considered all workers aged 15–65 who reported positive earnings during the survey's reference week. Since we are interested in

[14] There are eleven waves because the survey was not carried out in 1991 and 1994.

[15] These rural areas roughly correspond to the Amazon rainforest, which was excluded from PNAD sampling until 2003. Census data suggest that these areas account for 2.3 per cent of the Brazilian population.

quantifying the importance of trade- and openness-related changes in explaining overall changes in the wage distribution, we include all workers in agriculture, industry, and services, regardless of formality or own-account status. Effective sample sizes for this analysis were 107,195 workers in 1988 and 123,455 workers in 1995. This is an important difference between our analysis and those of Gonzaga, Menezes-Filho, and Terra (2006) or Pavcnik et al. (2004), which focus exclusively on workers in manufacturing.[16] The wage definition is hourly wages, calculated as a quarter of the monthly wage, divided by the number of hours worked on the average week. All monetary values are inflated to September 2004 prices, using the *Índice Nacional de Preços ao Consumidor* deflator with the Corseuil and Fogel (2002) adjustment to the 1994 index. See Ferreira, Leite, and Litchfield (2008) for the full deflator in each PNAD reference month.

As in all PNAD-based studies, we use years of schooling as our measure of a worker's skill.[17] In earnings regressions, we group workers into nine schooling groups: zero years, 1–3 years, 4 years, 5–7 years, 8 years (completed primary), 9–10 years (some high school), 11 years (completed high school), 12–14 years (some university), 15+ years (completed university). We also use this variable to construct a dichotomous skill indicator, classifying workers with 0–10 years of schooling as unskilled, and those with 11 or more (completed high school and above) as skilled. Earnings regressions were also estimated with an alternative indicator, which classified only workers with 15 years of schooling or more as skilled, and all results were qualitatively robust. Since workers with completed university accounted for 4.5 per cent of the labour force in 1988, while workers with complete high school and above represented 16.4 per cent, we chose the latter classification as more meaningful for Brazil. See Gonzaga, Menezes-Filho, and Terra (2006) for a similar discussion of this classification.

The second dataset used for this study comprises the trade-related variables for twenty-two industries across the 1987–99 period. Six trade-related variables are used: nominal tariffs and effective rates of protection come from Kume, Piani, and de Souza 2000, as reported in de Paiva Abreu 2004; import penetration and export shares by industry come from Muendler 2003; and import-weighted and export-weighted industry-specific exchange rates were constructed by the authors, based on the methodology suggested by Goldberg

[16] The sample in Pavcnik et al. (2004) is, in addition, based on the Pesquisa Mensal de Emprego and is thus only representative of the country's six main metropolitan areas.

[17] Use of education to define a worker's skill is in fact common to most household or labour-force survey-based studies. Articles relying on firm-level data typically classify production workers as unskilled, and non-production workers as skilled. Although Slaughter (2000) shows that the two definitions do not seem to lead to very different conclusions in the USA, Gonzaga, Menezes-Filho, and Terra (2006) show that the distinction does matter for Brazil. Like the latter authors, we feel that the education classification is more appropriate in the Brazilian case, since trade liberalization and outsourcing of support activities led to considerable changes in the employment levels of non-production workers during the period.

Table 8.1. Trade variables by industry, 1988 and 1995

Industry	Nominal tariffs		ERP		Import penetration		Export share of production		M-REAR		X-REAR	
	1988	1995	1988	1995	1988	1995	1988	1995	1988	1995	1988	1995
Agricultural products	17	7	15	8	na	na	na	na	5,347	7,351	110	193
Mining products	20	3	15	0	8	12	98	77	149	196	135	209
Oil and coal extraction	6	0	−3	−2	130	117	0	1	16	24	441	777
Non-metallic minerals	39	10	46	12	1	3	2	4	105	169	180	297
Steel, non-ferrous, and other metallurgy products	33	11	37	14	3	7	28	28	92	131	6,021	8,158
Machinery and tractors	47	19	50	18	14	31	18	36	105	172	232	324
Electrical equipment, electronic equipment	50	21	59	30	12	18	7	10	56	86	114	182
Auto, trucks, and buses; parts, components, and other vehicles	43	31	45	74	9	16	13	12	91	147	296	414
Wood products and furniture	30	11	29	12	0	1	4	10	311	540	29	45
Cellulose, paper, and printing	32	10	30	10	2	6	6	11	40	55	143	221
Rubber products	49	13	59	15	4	10	6	8	195	299	248	414
Chemical elements and products	66	15	76	16	56	87	33	39	30	46	118	189
Oil refining and petrochemicals	34	4	70	3	12	30	31	7	103	392	96	160
Pharmaceutical and perfumery products	45	8	52	8	6	13	2	3	45	73	208	346
Plastic products	57	15	72	21	2	7	2	3	60	92	311	435
Textile products	57	15	84	22	10	59	27	29	217	334	164	264
Apparel	76	20	94	24	0	3	1	2	162	253	109	185
Footwear	41	18	40	24	3	7	25	36	479	708	18	31
Processing of vegetable products	42	12	86	16	9	15	21	15	112	146	65	111
Meat packing, dairy industry, vegetable, and other food products	63	20	73	21	3	7	50	47	52	83	85	140
Unclassified manufacturing	49	14	64	15	0	0	0	0	101	169	102	265
Simple average	44	17	52	21	19	28	22	22	390	566	456	652
Non-tradable	0	0	0	0	0	0	0	0	67	104	91	147

Source: Nominal tariffs and effective rates of protection from Kumm, Piani, and de Souza 2000, reported in de Paiva Abreu (2004). Import penetration and export share of production from Muendler 2003. Import- and export-weighted real-exchange rates are authors' calculations from World Bank (2006) and UN Comtrade. For more details, see Appendix.

Table 8.2. Industry concordance

Trade industry	PAD code	PAD industry	Final code	Final industry
Agricultural products	11–42	Various crops, horticulture, and forestry	1	Agricultural products
Mining products	50, 53–59	Prospecting and extraction of non-oil/gas/coal minerals	2	Mining products
Oil and coal extraction	51–52	Oil, gas, and coal	3	Oil and coal extraction
Non-metallic minerals	100	Non-metal processing	4	Non-metallic minerals
Steel products	110	Steel products	5	Steel, non-ferrous and other metal products
Non-ferrous metallurgy	110	Non-steel metal products	5	Steel, non-ferrous, and other metal products
Other metallurgical products	110		5	Steel, non-ferrous, and other metal products
Machinery and tractors	120	Manufacture of machines and equipment	6	Machinery and tractors
Electrical equipment	130	Manufacture of electrical and electronic equipment	7	Electrical and electronic equipment
Electronic equipment	130	Manufacture of electrical and electronic equipment	7	Electrical and electronic equipment
Automobiles, trucks, and buses	140	Manufacture of vehicles and parts	8	Automobiles, trucks, and buses; parts, components, and other vehicles
Parts, components, and other vehicles	140	Manufacture of vehicles and parts	8	Automobiles, trucks, and buses; parts, components, and other vehicles
Wood products and furniture	150–1, 160	Manufacture of wood products and furniture	9	Wood products and furniture
Cellulose, paper, and printing	170, 290	Pulp and paper products, printing, and newspapers	10	Cellulose, paper, and printing
Rubber products	180	Rubber products	11	Rubber products
Chemical elements	200	Chemical products	12	Chemical elements and products
Oil refining	201	Oil and petroleum products	13	Oil refining and petrochemicals
Pharmaceutical and perfumery products	210, 220	Pharmaceuticals and toiletries	14	Pharmaceutical and perfumery products

(continued)

Table 8.2. Continued

Trade industry	PAD code	PAD industry	Final code	Final industry
Plastic products	230	Plastics	16	Plastic products
Textile products	240, 241	Textiles	17	Textile products
Apparel	250	Apparel and clothing	18	Apparel
Footwear	251	Footwear	19	Footwear
Coffee industry			21	Meat packing, dairy industry, vegetable, and other food products
Processing of vegetable products	280	Tobacco and other vegetable processing	20	Processing of vegetable products
Meat packing	260	Food preparation	21	Meat packing, dairy industry, vegetable, and other food products
Dairy industry	260	Food preparation	21	Meat packing, dairy industry, vegetable, and other food products
Sugar	17	Sugar cane extraction	21	Meat packing, dairy industry, vegetable, and other food products
Vegetable products	260		21	Meat packing, dairy industry, vegetable, and other food products
Other food products	260–1, 271	Other foods and drinks	21	Meat packing, dairy industry, vegetable, and other food products
Other industries	300	Various scientific instruments	99	Unclassified manufacturing
	340–903	Construction, services, retail, finance, government, etc.	22	Non-tradable
Omitted	190	Leather and skins		
	202	Manufacture of synthetic materials (nylon, etc.)		

(2004), and using data from the World Bank's *World Development Indicators* and the UN's Comtrade.[18] Table 8.1 presents initial (1988) and terminal (1995) values for each of these variables for the twenty-two industries into which we have grouped Brazilian firms.[19] As in Pavcnik et al. (2004), our use of household survey and trade data with different industry definitions necessitated a concordance between the various datasets, mapping the more disaggregated industry classifications in the trade data to the broader PNAD classifications. In addition to the standard *Nível 80* to *Nível 100* concordance,[20] we developed concordances of our own. The main one is based on (but not identical to) Pavcnik et al. (2004), and is presented in Table 8.2.[21] A more detailed description of the steps taken to clean, construct, and match the data is included in the Appendix to this chapter.

8.3.2. Methodology

Since the objective is to understand and quantify the role of trade-induced changes in the wage distribution in relation to the overall observed changes, we combine an extended version of the two-stage estimation framework which has recently been used to investigate the effect of trade reforms on wage premiums in a number of settings, with a more general decomposition of changes in the entire wage distribution. Following Pavcnik et al. (2004), our first stage regresses log-hourly wages (w_{ij}) on a vector of worker *i*'s characteristics (including sex, race, experience, education, residential region, urban/rural status, household headship status, and formality status), a vector of industry *j* indicators (I_{ij}), and a set of interactions between industry indicators and skill category:[22]

$$\ln w_{ij} = X_{ij}\beta + I^{*}_{ij}wp_j + (I^{*}_{ij}S_{ij})sp_j + \varepsilon_{ij} \tag{1}$$

[18] As Goldberg notes, 'At the national level, analyses of exchange rate moves often rely on aggregate trade weighted exchange rates. However, aggregate indexes can be less effective than industry specific indexes in capturing changes in industry competitive conditions induced by moves in specific bilateral exchange rates' (Goldberg 2004: 1).

[19] Although we use data until 1999 in our estimation stage, the key initial and terminal years for our wage decomposition analysis are 1988 at the onset of trade liberalization and 1995 the year in which it was completed.

[20] Available on Marc-Andreas Muendler's excellent website of Brazilian data resources <www.econ.ucsd.edu/muendler/html/brazil.html>. *Nível 80* and *Nível 100* are official Brazilian industry classifications.

[21] We are grateful to Nina Pavcnik and Norbert Schady for graciously making the details of their concordance available to us. A further concordance between *Nível 100* and the trade categories used in Kume, Piani, and de Souza (2000) were also constructed, but are too detailed to present here.

[22] Recall, 'skilled workers' are defined here as having completed high school or eleven or more years of schooling.

Equation 1 is estimated separately for each year in the dataset, from 1987 to 1999. In addition to the wage equation, our first stage also includes a model of employment for each year in the sample, where an individual's occupation is regressed on a similar set (Z_{ij}) of personal characteristics, as well as whether or not he or she has children, and the spouse's occupational status. Given the polychotomous nature of the occupational choice, this relationship is estimated with a multinomial logit model:

$$\Pr\{j = s\} = P^s(Z_i, \lambda) = \frac{e^{Z_i \lambda_s}}{e^{Z_i \lambda_s} + \sum_{j \neq c} e^{Z_i \lambda_j}} \tag{2}$$

In equation (2), there are ten possible occupational choices (j) corresponding to inactivity, unemployment, self-employment, employer status, and formal or informal employment in each of three broad sectors: agriculture, manufacturing, and services. The full specification of models (1) and (2) is presented in the next section, alongside results.

In the second stage, three sets of estimated coefficients from the first stage are pooled over time and regressed on a set of trade-related industry characteristics. The dependent variables in this stage are: (i) the industry premiums coefficients from equation (1), wp_{jt}; (ii) the industry-specific skill premiums coefficients from equation (1), sp_{jt}; and (iii) the constant terms λ_{0jt} for each occupation from equation (2). Each of these variables $v_{jt} = \{wp_{jt}; sp_{jt}; \lambda_{0jt})$ is regressed (in first differences) on a set of trade-related variables (T_{jt}), including industry-specific effective rates of protection, import- and export-weighted exchange rates, import penetration, and export shares:

$$\Delta v_{jt} = \Delta T_{jt} \gamma + \eta_{jt} \tag{3}$$

In addition to estimating a two-stage employment model, which we have not seen in the trade literature, there are other differences between these estimations and those reported in Pavcnik et al. (2004). Our data come from a nationally representative household survey (the PNAD), and include workers in agriculture and non-tradable industries (for which industry-specific exchange rates can be constructed,[23] and affect relative prices). Rather than relying on the manufacturing sector in the six largest metropolitan areas of Brazil, our sample is therefore much more broadly representative of the country. Possibly, as a result, some of our estimation results are different from those in Pavcnik et al. (2004), and we discuss them briefly in the next section.

But the main purpose of estimating equations (1) to (3) is to use them in the decomposition of all changes in the full wage distribution between 1988 and

[23] We use economy-wide import- and export-weighted exchange rates for the non-tradable sector.

1995. Following Juhn, Murphy, and Pierce (1993), one can decompose the difference between the wage distribution prior to the liberalization (say, in 1988) and the wage distribution afterwards (say, in 1995) into three components: one due to changes in observed worker characteristics (X), one due to changes in the returns to those characteristics (measured by regression coefficients β), and a final one due to changes in the distribution of residuals (ϵ). Writing the distribution function of the residuals of equation (1) as $\theta_{it} = F_t(\epsilon_{it})$, a standard Juhn–Murphy–Pierce (JMP) decomposition would proceed as follows:[24]

After estimating earnings regressions (like (1)) in both initial and terminal years:

$$\ln w_{i88} = X_{i88}\beta_{88} + F_{88}^{-1}(\theta_{i88}) \text{ and}$$
$$\ln w_{i95} = X_{i95}\beta_{95} + F_{95}^{-1}(\theta_{i95})$$

one would simulate two counterfactual wage distributions, as follows:

$$\ln w_i^a = X_{i88}\beta_{95} + F_{88}^{-1}(\theta_{i88}) \quad (4)$$
$$\ln w_i^b = X_{i88}\beta_{95} + F_{95}^{-1}(\theta_{i88}) \quad (5)$$

The difference between wage distributions $G(w_{88})$ and $G(w^a)$ would be interpreted as being due to differences in returns between the 1988 and 1995. The difference between $G(w^a)$ and $G(w^b)$ would be due to changes in the distribution of (or returns to) unobservable worker characteristics. Finally, the difference between $G(w_{95})$ and $G(w^b)$ would be due to changes in the joint distribution of observed worker characteristics.[25]

Using our estimates of equations (1) to (3), we construct an expanded set of such counterfactual wage distributions, which also form an exact decomposition of the observed change between 1988 and 1995.[26] We construct six counterfactual wage distributions, chosen to shed light on different channels of effect from the trade liberalization. Not all of the channels discussed in section 8.2 are covered, but the key wage and employment channels are addressed.

Departing from equation (1), our first counterfactual is:

[24] We say 'a standard JMP decomposition' because there are variations on the basic theme. Alternative orderings could be used, or average coefficients instead of final-year coefficients, etc. The specific interpretation varies, but the essence of the insight is the same.

[25] As noted in Juhn, Murphy, and Pierce (1993), and in the closely related works DiNardo, Fortin, and Lemieux (1996) and Bourguignon, Ferreira, and Lustig (2004), this is an accounting decomposition. Changes in the return structure are clearly causally related to changes in the distribution of characteristics in more than one way. The decomposition exercise does not disentangle these causal relations but provides a description of the observed changes.

[26] As in the original JMP decomposition, and indeed in any generalized Oaxaca–Blinder decomposition, the order of the simulations matters: the decomposition is path dependent. See Lemieux (2002) and Bourguignon, Ferreira, and Lustig (2004) for discussions.

$$\ln w_{ij}^{1} = X_{ij}^{88}\beta^{88} + I_{ij}^{88} * wp_{j}^{s} + (I_{ij}^{88} * S_{ij}^{88})sp_{j}^{88} + F_{88}^{-1}(\theta_{i88}) \tag{6}$$

where $wp_{j}^{s} = (T_{j}^{95} - T_{j}^{88})\gamma_{wp}$ and γ_{wp} are the estimated coefficients in the second-stage regression (3) for the industry wage premiums. This first simulation therefore corresponds to changes in the wage distribution due only to those changes in industry wage premiums which are mandated by changes in the exogenous trade variables included in the second stage equation (3) The second counterfactual is:

$$\ln w_{ij}^{2} = X_{ij}^{88}\beta^{88} + I_{ij}^{88} * wp_{j}^{s} + (I_{ij}^{88} * S_{ij}^{88})sp_{j}^{s} + F_{88}^{-1}(\theta_{i88}) \tag{7}$$

where $sp_{j}^{s} = (T_{j}^{95} - T_{j}^{88})\bar{\gamma}_{sp}$ and $\bar{\gamma}_{sp}$ are the estimated coefficients in the second-stage regression (3) for industry-specific skill premiums. The third counterfactual is:

$$\ln w_{ij}^{3} = X_{ij}^{88}\beta^{88} + I_{ij}^{s} * wp_{j}^{s} + (I_{ij}^{s} * S_{ij}^{88})sp_{j}^{s} + F_{88}^{-1}(\theta_{i88}) \tag{8}$$

where I_{ij}^{s} is a counterfactual vector of occupations, constructed by substituting $\gamma_{0j}^{s} = (T_{j}^{95} - T_{j}^{88})\gamma_{\lambda_0}$ into the occupational multinomial logit in equation (2), and then using it to predict the corresponding counterfactual distribution of occupations.[27] This third simulation therefore corresponds to the overall effect of industry premiums, industry-specific skill premiums and employment changes mandated by the second stage trade variables, under the maintained functional form assumptions in equation (3).

The power of the preceding counterfactuals to simulate the changes in the wage distribution that arise from trade reforms depends entirely on the ability of the linear second-stage equations to identify the impact of changes in tariffs and exchange rates on wage premiums and employment probabilities. They also miss, so far, a key theoretical channel through which trade liberalization is likely to impact on wage differences in the economy—namely, changes to the *economy-wide* skill premium. After all, the wp_j and sp_j coefficients capture only changes in industry-specific remuneration rates, controlling for changes in the average returns to education. Our fourth counterfactual is therefore:

$$\ln w_{ij}^{4} = X_{ij}^{88}\beta^{s} + I_{ij}^{s} * wp_{j}^{95} + (I_{ij}^{s} * S_{ij}^{88})sp_{j}^{95} + F_{88}^{-1}(\theta_{i88}) \tag{9}$$

where $\beta^{s} = \{\beta_{ed}^{95}; \beta_{-ed}^{88}\}$. The difference between equation (9) and (8) is twofold: the industry and industry-specific skill-premium coefficients mandated by the

[27] As noted above, the ten occupational categories specified in Equation 2 were more aggregated than the twenty-two industries for which wage and skill premiums are estimated. In constructing $G(w^3)$, workers whose predicted occupations differed from those observed in 1988 owing to changes in λ_{0j} were allocated to specific industries within the broad sector to which they were mapped by the multinomial logit, by random draws with probabilities derived from the 1995 employment distribution across industries.

second stage are replaced with those estimated in 1995, and the economy-wide returns on schooling coefficient is replaced with its 1995 value. This simulation therefore corresponds to a 'more-generous' estimate of the 'price effects' of trade liberalization, in which the full changes in returns to education and to industry membership—rather than only those mandated by the second stage—are included. Although the main channel through which trade reforms might affect β_{ed}^{95} is the Stolper–Samuelson effect of reduced protection in skill-intensive industries, there may be other channels too. If one is prepared to accept that skill-biased technical change in Brazil, or skill-demanding changes in the quality composition of domestic output, are endogenous to trade liberalization, as discussed in section 8.2, then one may come closer to the view that all changes in the returns to schooling between 1988 and 1995 are, in some way or another, related to trade. Be that as it may, we see this particular counterfactual wage distribution as a generous estimate of the joint wage and employment effects of trade on the wage distribution. The true contribution of trade liberalization to changes in Brazilian inequality is likely to lie somewhere between the changes accumulated up to equation (8) and those corresponding to equation (9).

Three remaining steps (and two counterfactual distributions) complete the decomposition—and represent changes that are less likely to have been driven by trade reforms. The first of these (in equation 10) computes the additional changes in the structure of returns to observed characteristics (like experience, location, race, gender, etc.). The second (in equation 11), brings in the distribution of residuals from 1995, in a rank-preserving transformation:

$$\ln w_{ij}^{5} = X_{ij}^{88}\beta^{95} + I_{ij}^{s} * wp_{j}^{95} + (I_{ij}^{s} * S_{ij}^{88})sp_{j}^{95} + F_{88}^{-1}(\theta_{i88}) \tag{10}$$

$$\ln w_{ij}^{6} = X_{ij}^{88}\beta^{95} + I_{ij}^{s} * wp_{j}^{95} + (I_{ij}^{s} * S_{ij}^{88})sp_{j}^{95} + F_{95}^{-1}(\theta_{i88}) \tag{11}$$

Finally, the difference between (11) and the equation estimated for 1995:

$$\ln w_{ij}^{95} = X_{ij}^{95}\beta^{95} + I_{ij}^{95} * wp_{j}^{95} + (I_{ij}^{95} * S_{ij}^{95})sp_{j}^{95} + F_{95}^{-1}(\theta_{i95}) \tag{12}$$

corresponds to differences in the joint distribution of observed characteristics between 1995 and 1988 (except for the changes in occupational structure due to trade, which had been predicted in equation 8). This step also accounts for changes in the correlation between the observed characteristics and the residual terms, including any changes in selection into the labour force.

Only equation (1), for 1988, and equation (12), for 1995 are estimated on observed data. Equations (6)–(11) give rise to simulated wage distributions $G(w^1)$ to $G(w^6)$. In section 8.5, simulation results are presented in two ways. First, a number of inequality indicators are computed for each counterfactual distribution, so that we can decompose the observed changes between 1988 and 1995 into the components corresponding to each counterfactual. Second, we can see a fully disaggregated picture by plotting the observed wage growth

Table 8.3(a). First-stage regression results: wages

	1987	1988	1989	1990	1992	1993	1995	1996	1997	1998	1999
Male	0.321	0.32	0.336	0.297	0.249	0.271	0.222	0.214	0.228	0.214	0.216
	(0.007)***	(0.007)***	(0.007)***	(0.007)***	(0.006)***	(0.006)***	(0.006)***	(0.006)***	(0.006)***	(0.006)***	(0.005)***
Experience	0.048	0.047	0.045	0.044	0.038	0.039	0.036	0.036	0.036	0.034	0.035
	(0.001)***	(0.001)***	(0.001)***	(0.001)***	(0.001)***	(0.001)***	(0.001)***	(0.001)***	(0.001)***	(0.001)***	(0.001)***
Experience squared	−0.001	−0.001	−0.001	−0.001	0	0	0	0	0	0	0
	(0.000)***	(0.000)***	(0.000)***	(0.000)***	(0.000)***	(0.000)***	(0.000)***	(0.000)***	(0.000)***	(0.000)***	(0.000)***
White	0.135	0.143	0.185	0.157	0.139	0.153	0.156	0.165	0.165	0.159	0.161
	(0.005)***	(0.005)***	(0.006)***	(0.005)***	(0.005)***	(0.005)***	(0.005)***	(0.005)***	(0.005)***	(0.005)***	(0.004)***
Yellow	0.294	0.318	0.319	0.303	0.264	0.348	0.346	0.398	0.439	0.351	0.285
	(0.035)***	(0.038)***	(0.044)***	(0.038)***	(0.042)***	(0.040)***	(0.040)***	(0.043)***	(0.046)***	(0.035)***	(0.040)***
1–3 years education	0.213	0.19	0.203	0.195	0.143	0.172	0.145	0.146	0.14	0.144	0.124
	(0.009)***	(0.009)***	(0.009)***	(0.009)***	(0.009)***	(0.009)***	(0.008)***	(0.009)***	(0.009)***	(0.008)***	(0.008)***
4 years education	0.393	0.4	0.398	0.392	0.324	0.356	0.307	0.304	0.288	0.281	0.266
	(0.009)***	(0.010)***	(0.010)***	(0.009)***	(0.009)***	(0.009)***	(0.009)***	(0.009)***	(0.009)***	(0.009)***	(0.009)***
5–7 years education	0.578	0.582	0.573	0.561	0.463	0.496	0.436	0.406	0.41	0.398	0.373
	(0.011)***	(0.011)***	(0.011)***	(0.011)***	(0.010)***	(0.010)***	(0.009)***	(0.010)***	(0.009)***	(0.009)***	(0.009)***
Completed primary school	0.815	0.812	0.806	0.767	0.666	0.709	0.628	0.605	0.602	0.586	0.547
	(0.012)***	(0.013)***	(0.013)***	(0.012)***	(0.011)***	(0.012)***	(0.011)***	(0.011)***	(0.011)***	(0.010)***	(0.010)***
9–10 years education	0.955	0.967	0.981	0.944	0.82	0.848	0.746	0.741	0.726	0.705	0.664
	(0.015)***	(0.015)***	(0.016)***	(0.015)***	(0.014)***	(0.014)***	(0.013)***	(0.013)***	(0.012)***	(0.012)***	(0.012)***
Completed high school	1.23	1.274	1.224	1.096	0.933	1.047	0.968	1.002	1.001	0.938	0.896
	(0.058)***	(0.060)***	(0.061)***	(0.049)***	(0.047)***	(0.049)***	(0.047)***	(0.047)***	(0.047)***	(0.046)***	(0.041)***
12–14 years education	1.623	1.691	1.656	1.511	1.283	1.426	1.39	1.439	1.404	1.35	1.307
	(0.060)***	(0.062)***	(0.063)***	(0.051)***	(0.049)***	(0.052)***	(0.049)***	(0.049)***	(0.049)***	(0.048)***	(0.043)***
Completed university	2.05	2.147	2.05	1.915	1.649	1.82	1.791	1.824	1.81	1.761	1.738
	(0.059)***	(0.061)***	(0.062)***	(0.050)***	(0.049)***	(0.051)***	(0.048)***	(0.049)***	(0.048)***	(0.047)***	(0.042)***
Formal employee	0.22	0.333	0.237	0.17	0.401	0.357	0.184	0.182	0.198	0.207	0.228
	(0.006)***	(0.006)***	(0.006)***	(0.006)***	(0.006)***	(0.006)***	(0.005)***	(0.006)***	(0.005)***	(0.005)***	(0.005)***

Self-employed	0.274	0.295	0.338	0.319	0.302	0.337	0.257	0.268	0.205	0.184	0.197
	(0.008)***	(0.008)***	(0.008)***	(0.008)***	(0.007)***	(0.008)***	(0.007)***	(0.007)***	(0.007)***	(0.007)***	(0.006)***
Employer	0.966	0.974	1.07	0.938	0.925	0.972	0.938	0.903	0.908	0.853	0.876
	(0.018)***	(0.019)***	(0.017)***	(0.015)***	(0.016)***	(0.016)***	(0.014)***	(0.016)***	(0.014)***	(0.014)***	(0.014)***
North-east region	−0.369	−0.353	−0.441	−0.443	−0.291	−0.404	−0.29	−0.276	−0.296	−0.228	−0.244
	(0.009)***	(0.010)***	(0.010)***	(0.010)***	(0.011)***	(0.011)***	(0.010)***	(0.010)***	(0.010)***	(0.010)***	(0.009)***
South-east region	−0.077	−0.025	−0.092	−0.124	0.097	−0.021	0.072	0.105	0.1	0.13	0.112
	(0.009)***	(0.009)***	(0.010)***	(0.009)***	(0.010)***	(0.010)**	(0.010)***	(0.010)***	(0.009)***	(0.009)***	(0.009)***
South region	−0.146	−0.107	−0.16	−0.165	0.063	0.026	−0.003	0.013	0.034	0.055	0.02
	(0.010)***	(0.011)***	(0.011)***	(0.011)***	(0.011)***	(0.011)**	−0.01	−0.011	(0.010)***	(0.010)***	(0.010)**
Central west region	−0.019	−0.005	−0.079	−0.045	0.055	0.068	0.014	0.055	0.047	0.064	0.042
	(0.010)*	−0.01	(0.011)***	(0.010)***	(0.011)***	(0.011)***	−0.01	(0.011)***	(0.010)***	(0.010)***	(0.010)***
Metropolitan residence	0.319	0.331	0.328	0.313	0.302	0.307	0.321	0.326	0.317	0.295	0.252
	(0.009)***	(0.009)***	(0.009)***	(0.009)***	(0.009)***	(0.009)***	(0.008)***	(0.009)***	(0.008)***	(0.008)***	(0.008)***
Urban residence	0.198	0.127	0.146	0.158	0.135	0.145	0.157	0.15	0.122	0.108	0.091
	(0.008)***	(0.009)***	(0.009)***	(0.008)***	(0.009)***	(0.009)***	(0.008)***	(0.008)***	(0.008)***	(0.007)***	(0.007)***
Head of household	0.208	0.203	0.193	0.189	0.159	0.166	0.175	0.17	0.156	0.156	0.149
	(0.007)***	(0.007)***	(0.007)***	(0.007)***	(0.006)***	(0.006)***	(0.006)***	(0.006)***	(0.005)***	(0.005)***	(0.005)***
Industry indicators	Yes	Yes	Yes	Yes	Yes	Yes	Yes	Yes	Yes	Yes	Yes
Industry* skill indicators	Yes	Yes	Yes	Yes	Yes	Yes	Yes	Yes	Yes	Yes	Yes
Observations	112,655	112,730	114,961	116,882	118,075	119,949	128,360	124,017	131,202	129,719	133,310
R-squared	0.59	0.59	0.57	0.58	0.55	0.55	0.56	0.54	0.56	0.56	0.56

Notes: Robust standard errors in parentheses.
*Significant at 10%,
**Significant at 5%,
***Significant at 1%.
Dependent variable is real hourly wage from principal job.
Regions are relative to north region.
White and yellow are relative to black.
Education-attainment indicators are relative to no education.
Informal employee and self-employed coefficients are relative to formal employees.

Table 8.3(b). First-stage regression results: industry wage premiums

	1987	1988	1989	1990	1992	1993	1995	1996	1997	1998	1999
Mining products	0.514	0.578	0.488	0.433	0.238	0.315	0.316	0.213	0.347	0.393	0.349
	(0.001)	(0.001)	(0.001)	(0.001)	(0.001)	(0.001)	(0.001)	(0.001)	(0.001)	(0.002)	(0.001)
Mining products	0.514	0.578	0.488	0.433	0.238	0.315	0.316	0.213	0.347	0.393	0.349
	(0.001)	(0.001)	(0.001)	(0.001)	(0.001)	(0.001)	(0.001)	(0.001)	(0.001)	(0.002)	(0.001)
Oil and coal extraction	0.678	0.666	0.680	0.727	0.835	0.874	0.817	1.043	0.677	0.824	0.994
	(0.009)	(0.011)	(0.010)	(0.011)	(0.013)	(0.018)	(0.012)	(0.018)	(0.019)	(0.013)	(0.018)
Non-metallic minerals	0.202	0.203	0.225	0.242	0.188	0.191	0.274	0.269	0.353	0.353	0.314
	(0.000)	(0.000)	(0.001)	(0.000)	(0.000)	(0.000)	(0.000)	(0.000)	(0.000)	(0.000)	(0.000)
Steel, non-ferrous, and other metallurgy products	0.398	0.398	0.373	0.458	0.381	0.378	0.476	0.484	0.494	0.492	0.432
	(0.000)	(0.000)	(0.000)	(0.000)	(0.000)	(0.000)	(0.000)	(0.000)	(0.000)	(0.000)	(0.000)
Machinery and tractors	0.538	0.539	0.520	0.636	0.406	0.473	0.516	0.508	0.562	0.504	0.495
	(0.001)	(0.001)	(0.001)	(0.001)	(0.001)	(0.001)	(0.001)	(0.001)	(0.001)	(0.001)	(0.001)
Electrical equipment, electronic equipment	0.467	0.493	0.450	0.614	0.507	0.404	0.551	0.503	0.611	0.577	0.458
	(0.001)	(0.001)	(0.001)	(0.001)	(0.001)	(0.001)	(0.001)	(0.001)	(0.001)	(0.001)	(0.001)
Auto, trucks, and buses; parts, components, and other vehicles	0.509	0.608	0.529	0.680	0.646	0.590	0.685	0.692	0.662	0.657	0.628
	(0.001)	(0.001)	(0.001)	(0.001)	(0.001)	(0.001)	(0.001)	(0.001)	(0.001)	(0.001)	(0.001)
Wood products and furniture	0.035	0.020	0.041	0.157	0.091	0.131	0.274	0.299	0.290	0.303	0.298
	(0.000)	(0.001)	(0.000)	(0.000)	(0.000)	(0.000)	(0.000)	(0.000)	(0.000)	(0.000)	(0.000)
Cellulose, paper, and printing	0.325	0.382	0.328	0.437	0.410	0.343	0.484	0.456	0.512	0.490	0.466
	(0.001)	(0.001)	(0.001)	(0.001)	(0.001)	(0.001)	(0.001)	(0.001)	(0.001)	(0.001)	(0.001)
Rubber products	0.480	0.536	0.325	0.515	0.293	0.387	0.553	0.665	0.433	0.394	0.473
	(0.003)	(0.003)	(0.004)	(0.003)	(0.004)	(0.004)	(0.003)	(0.005)	(0.002)	(0.005)	(0.005)

Chemical elements and products	0.410	0.326	0.300	0.394	0.383	0.288	0.421	0.421	0.458	0.403	0.454
	(0.001)	(0.001)	(0.001)	(0.001)	(0.001)	(0.001)	(0.001)	(0.001)	(0.001)	(0.001)	(0.001)
Oil refining and petrochemicals	0.563	0.709	0.600	0.571	0.696	0.677	0.532	0.508	0.566	0.511	0.554
	(0.010)	(0.008)	(0.011)	(0.007)	(0.007)	(0.009)	(0.008)	(0.007)	(0.004)	(0.005)	(0.011)
Pharmaceutical and perfumery products	0.343	0.418	0.294	0.396	0.431	0.445	0.434	0.485	0.565	0.533	0.521
	(0.003)	(0.003)	(0.004)	(0.003)	(0.003)	(0.004)	(0.004)	(0.003)	(0.004)	(0.003)	(0.003)
Plastic products	0.360	0.364	0.382	0.465	0.315	0.317	0.423	0.375	0.425	0.435	0.374
	(0.001)	(0.002)	(0.003)	(0.002)	(0.002)	(0.001)	(0.001)	(0.001)	(0.001)	(0.001)	(0.001)
Textile products	0.153	0.239	0.207	0.253	0.195	0.223	0.321	0.285	0.386	0.338	0.184
	(0.001)	(0.001)	(0.001)	(0.001)	(0.001)	(0.001)	(0.001)	(0.001)	(0.001)	(0.001)	(0.001)
Apparel	0.267	0.310	0.334	0.482	0.267	0.259	0.331	0.317	0.380	0.342	0.310
	(0.000)	(0.001)	(0.001)	(0.001)	(0.000)	(0.000)	(0.000)	(0.000)	(0.000)	(0.000)	(0.000)
Footwear	0.210	0.121	0.278	0.412	0.253	0.176	0.249	0.268	0.271	0.209	0.237
	(0.000)	(0.001)	(0.001)	(0.001)	(0.001)	(0.001)	(0.001)	(0.000)	(0.000)	(0.000)	(0.000)
Processing of vegetable products	0.306	0.360	0.192	0.276	0.522	0.408	0.640	0.477	0.426	0.446	0.174
	(0.013)	(0.008)	(0.014)	(0.008)	(0.008)	(0.011)	(0.007)	(0.010)	(0.005)	(0.014)	(0.006)
Meat packing, dairy industry, vegetable, and other food production	0.151	0.169	0.166	0.270	0.180	0.225	0.298	0.316	0.328	0.331	0.277
	(0.000)	(0.000)	(0.000)	(0.000)	(0.000)	(0.000)	(0.000)	(0.000)	(0.000)	(0.000)	(0.000)
Unclassified manufacturing	0.068	0.065	0.100	0.160	0.080	0.071	0.095	0.196	0.159	0.147	0.103
	(0.001)	(0.001)	(0.001)	(0.001)	(0.001)	(0.001)	(0.001)	(0.001)	(0.001)	(0.001)	(0.000)
Non-tradable	0.164	0.149	0.149	0.300	0.184	0.171	0.306	0.328	0.371	0.367	0.327
	(0.000)	(0.000)	(0.000)	(0.000)	(0.000)	(0.000)	(0.000)	(0.000)	(0.000)	(0.000)	(0.000)

Notes: Standard errors in parentheses.

Table 8.3(c). First-stage regression results: industry skill premiums

	1987	1988	1989	1990	1992	1993	1995	1996	1997	1998	1999
Mining products	0.089	0.108	0.267	0.400	0.462	−0.052	0.163	0.258	0.180	0.326	0.220
	(0.018)	(0.013)	(0.010)	(0.014)	(0.015)	(0.018)	(0.014)	(0.017)	(0.013)	(0.011)	(0.012)
Oil and coal extraction	0.465	0.411	0.537	0.495	0.293	0.202	0.151	0.039	0.380	0.143	0.081
	(0.020)	(0.022)	(0.021)	(0.029)	(0.023)	(0.030)	(0.022)	(0.031)	(0.032)	(0.028)	(0.025)
Non-metallic minerals	0.123	0.184	0.162	0.090	0.144	0.130	0.225	0.184	0.059	0.044	0.107
	(0.008)	(0.011)	(0.013)	(0.009)	(0.009)	(0.008)	(0.006)	(0.007)	(0.007)	(0.005)	(0.005)
Steel, non-ferrous, and other metallurgy products	0.030	−0.071	0.096	0.125	0.148	0.132	0.090	−0.020	0.000	0.037	0.051
	(0.005)	(0.005)	(0.006)	(0.004)	(0.004)	(0.005)	(0.004)	(0.004)	(0.004)	(0.003)	(0.003)
Machinery and tractors	−0.080	−0.119	−0.121	0.020	0.218	0.082	0.050	−0.008	−0.014	0.036	0.001
	(0.006)	(0.008)	(0.008)	(0.006)	(0.005)	(0.007)	(0.006)	(0.005)	(0.004)	(0.004)	(0.004)
Electrical equipment, electronic equipment	0.082	0.073	0.069	0.113	0.039	0.104	0.093	−0.035	−0.052	0.031	0.096
	(0.006)	(0.007)	(0.007)	(0.005)	(0.007)	(0.006)	(0.005)	(0.006)	(0.005)	(0.005)	(0.004)
Auto, trucks, and buses; parts, components, and other vehicles	−0.007	−0.018	−0.072	−0.014	0.113	0.253	0.020	−0.104	−0.010	0.056	0.001
	(0.006)	(0.007)	(0.007)	(0.005)	(0.006)	(0.006)	(0.004)	(0.005)	(0.004)	(0.004)	(0.004)
Wood products and furniture	−0.051	0.036	−0.125	0.121	0.050	0.020	−0.008	−0.179	−0.218	−0.059	−0.143
	(0.010)	(0.009)	(0.009)	(0.007)	(0.006)	(0.007)	(0.007)	(0.006)	(0.006)	(0.005)	(0.003)
Cellulose, paper, and printing	−0.046	−0.131	0.000	0.046	0.006	−0.079	0.032	−0.069	−0.067	0.005	−0.067
	(0.006)	(0.008)	(0.007)	(0.006)	(0.005)	(0.005)	(0.005)	(0.005)	(0.004)	(0.004)	(0.004)
Rubber products	−0.025	−0.273	0.054	−0.136	0.109	0.337	0.158	−0.018	0.179	0.258	−0.197
	(0.032)	(0.029)	(0.022)	(0.026)	(0.025)	(0.015)	(0.017)	(0.021)	(0.024)	(0.015)	(0.021)
Chemical elements and products	0.155	0.175	0.223	0.282	0.254	0.327	0.225	0.173	0.139	0.156	0.073
	(0.007)	(0.008)	(0.007)	(0.006)	(0.006)	(0.007)	(0.005)	(0.007)	(0.006)	(0.008)	(0.005)

Oil refining and petrochemicals	0.456	0.216	0.074	0.374	0.287	0.201	0.294	0.215	0.380	0.308	0.250
	(0.019)	(0.015)	(0.026)	(0.015)	(0.017)	(0.016)	(0.017)	(0.017)	(0.013)	(0.012)	(0.018)
Pharmaceutical and perfumery products	0.088	−0.057	0.184	0.211	0.193	0.078	0.243	0.152	−0.052	0.111	0.066
	(0.011)	(0.012)	(0.015)	(0.012)	(0.011)	(0.012)	(0.011)	(0.010)	(0.011)	(0.008)	(0.007)
Plastic products	0.050	0.110	−0.080	0.170	0.125	−0.084	0.133	0.074	0.055	−0.030	0.043
	(0.018)	(0.014)	(0.022)	(0.010)	(0.010)	(0.011)	(0.011)	(0.010)	(0.010)	(0.008)	(0.006)
Textile products	−0.002	0.153	0.086	0.117	0.235	0.145	0.181	0.143	−0.099	0.002	0.123
	(0.010)	(0.009)	(0.009)	(0.007)	(0.007)	(0.008)	(0.007)	(0.009)	(0.007)	(0.008)	(0.006)
Apparel	−0.185	−0.288	−0.224	−0.116	−0.160	−0.242	−0.230	−0.289	−0.119	−0.194	−0.135
	(0.008)	(0.008)	(0.009)	(0.006)	(0.006)	(0.005)	(0.005)	(0.005)	(0.006)	(0.005)	(0.003)
Footwear	−0.058	−0.062	−0.024	0.061	−0.105	−0.113	−0.155	−0.084	−0.157	−0.054	−0.153
	(0.019)	(0.015)	(0.018)	(0.009)	(0.010)	(0.010)	(0.010)	(0.012)	(0.009)	(0.007)	(0.006)
Processing of vegetable products	0.126	0.024	−0.069	0.329	0.242	0.001	−0.280	0.117	0.229	0.257	0.332
	(0.025)	(0.041)	(0.024)	(0.031)	(0.023)	(0.022)	(0.047)	(0.022)	(0.032)	(0.032)	(0.017)
Meat packing, dairy industry, vegetable, and other food product	0.000	−0.009	0.019	0.010	0.125	−0.003	0.069	−0.064	−0.006	0.016	0.032
	(0.005)	(0.006)	(0.006)	(0.004)	(0.004)	(0.004)	(0.003)	(0.003)	(0.003)	(0.003)	(0.002)
Unclassified manufacturing	0.110	0.056	0.282	0.357	0.233	0.035	0.232	0.081	0.140	0.137	0.167
	(0.008)	(0.012)	(0.010)	(0.008)	(0.006)	(0.006)	(0.006)	(0.006)	(0.006)	(0.006)	(0.004)
Non-tradable	0.194	0.141	0.185	0.265	0.204	0.158	0.130	0.055	0.053	0.095	0.101
	(0.003)	(0.004)	(0.004)	(0.002)	(0.002)	(0.002)	(0.002)	(0.002)	(0.002)	(0.002)	(0.002)

Notes: Standard errors in parentheses.

incidence curve between 1988 and 1995, $g(p) = (w_p^{95} - w_p^{88})/w_p^{88}$, and presenting each intermediate counterfactual growth incidence curve: $g^s(p) = (w_p^s - w_p^{88})/w_p^{88}$, $s = 1, \ldots, 6$.[28]

8.4. Estimation Results

Before we turn to the simulation results in the next section, this section presents the estimation results on which they build. Table 8.3(a) presents the main first-stage results for the wage equation (1), while Tables 8.3(b) and 8.3(c) report the industry-specific wage and skill premiums coefficient estimates, respectively. Each model was estimated for each year in the 1987–99 interval for which data were available. The results in Table 8.3(a) are in line with existing analysis of the Brazilian labour market (see, e.g., Ferreira and Paes de Barros 1999). There are large and significant returns to education, and smaller and concave returns to experience. Measured with respect to zero years of schooling, returns to education fell consistently over the period. This decline was most pronounced for intermediate education categories (4–10 years of schooling). Returns to experience have also fallen. There is a substantial male wage premium, which has also been declining. In contrast, racial premiums of both whites and Asians with respect to Afro-Brazilians have persisted or increased. Controlling for other observed characteristics, employers, the self-employed, and formal employees all earn more than informally employed workers. Metropolitan and urban location premiums vis-à-vis rural workers of identical characteristics have also fallen over the period, though they remain statistically significant. All specifications also include industry and interacted-industry skill indicators, the coefficients on which are reported in Tables 8.3(b) and 8.3(c). These coefficients are then pooled and regressed on a vector of trade variables in the second stage.

Table 8.4(a) reports the first stage results for the employment model in equation (2), as marginal effects of unit changes in each independent variable, with all other variables held at their mean values. These estimates are also mostly in line with expectations. Workers with more experience and education are less likely to be employed in agriculture or informally. In addition, those with higher education are also more likely to be employers, as are whites and Asians, and to work in the formal non-tradable sector, presumably often as professionals. We also see some evidence over time of more females entering the labour force. While men are more likely to be working, the male coefficient falls between 1988 and 1995 across most industries. The industry constants, which are pooled and used in the second stage, are summarized in Table 8.4(b).

[28] The 'wage growth incidence curve' is an application to the distribution of wages of Ravallion and Chen's (2003) concept of the growth incidence curve, which those authors originally defined on the distribution of household incomes or expenditures.

Table 8.4(a). First-stage regression results, 1988 and 1995 (employment multinomial logit: marginal effects)

				Agriculture		Manufacturing		Non-tradable sector		
	Not economically active	Unemployed	Self-employed (all industries)	Informal	Formal	Informal	Formal	Informal	Formal	Employer (all industries)
Column	0	1	2	3	4	5	6	7	8	9
					1988					
Probability (at mean)	0.329	0.026	0.186	0.046	0.013	0.016	0.080	0.108	0.173	0.022
Male		0.009***	0.137***	0.091***	0.025***	0.017***	0.081***	−0.010***	0.087***	0.032***
Experience		0.001***	0.005***	−0.001***	0.000***	−0.001***	0.008***	−0.010***	0.015***	0.005***
Experience squared		0.000***	0.000***	0.000***	0.000***	0.000***	0.000***	0.000***	0.000***	0.000***
White		−0.008***	0.013***	−0.015***	−0.002***	−0.001	0.005***	−0.031***	−0.026***	0.015***
Yellow		−0.030***	0.093*	0.042**	−0.032***	0.003	0.006	−0.098***	−0.076***	0.022***
1–3 years education		0.007***	−0.013	−0.030***	−0.004***	−0.001	0.020***	0.007***	0.032***	0.013***
4 years education		0.005***	−0.010***	−0.056***	−0.008***	−0.002	0.039***	−0.003***	0.065***	0.024***
5–7 years education		0.013***	−0.048***	−0.088***	−0.014***	−0.003	0.048***	0.003***	0.088***	0.029***
Completed primary school		0.012***	−0.044**	−0.120***	−0.018***	−0.006**	0.051***	−0.005	0.130***	0.040***
9–10 years education		0.009***	−0.071***	−0.130***	−0.026***	−0.009***	0.042***	−0.011	0.165***	0.042***
Completed high school		0.018***	−0.074	−0.131***	−0.017***	−0.011**	0.055***	0.033***	0.222***	0.052***
12–14 years education		0.001	−0.122***	−0.188***	−0.033***	−0.013***	0.046***	0.078***	0.229***	0.054***
Completed university		0.009***	−0.039***	−0.132***	−0.017*	−0.012	0.053***	0.117***	0.238***	0.058***
Region 2		0.008***	−0.013	0.027***	0.014***	0.000	−0.014**	−0.003	−0.002	−0.002
Region 3		0.005***	−0.085***	0.036***	0.030***	−0.005	0.064***	−0.002***	0.024***	0.001***
Region 4		0.009***	−0.021***	0.011***	0.023***	−0.007	0.059***	−0.021***	0.054***	−0.001***
Region 5		0.000	−0.052***	0.038***	0.021***	0.001	−0.048***	0.021***	0.044***	0.003***
Metropolitan residence		0.033***	−0.203***	−0.163***	−0.041***	0.006***	0.099***	0.073***	0.191***	−0.013***

(*continued*)

Table 8.4(a). Continued

				Agriculture		Manufacturing		Non-tradable sector		
	Not economically active	Unemployed	Self-employed (all industries)	Informal	Formal	Informal	Formal	Informal	Formal	Employer (all industries)
Column	0	1	2	3	4	5	6	7	8	9
					1988					
Urban residence		0.026***	−0.198***	−0.069***	−0.019***	0.004***	0.066***	0.082***	0.140***	−0.007***
Head of household		0.004***	0.095***	0.014***	0.014***	0.007***	0.082***	0.065***	0.145***	0.030***
Children 0–14 years in household		−0.003***	−0.011***	−0.001***	0.001***	−0.001***	−0.014***	−0.005***	−0.042***	−0.002***
Has a spouse who works		−0.972***	1.870***	0.439***	0.124	0.159***	0.753***	1.033***	1.660***	0.218***
Observations					177,376					
					1995					
Probability (at mean)	0.308	0.046	0.203	0.034***	0.013	0.015	0.061	0.103	0.190	0.027
Male		−0.004***	0.160***	0.073***	0.026***	0.015***	0.061***	−0.040***	0.050***	0.036***
Experience		0.001***	0.008***	0.000***	0.001***	−0.001***	0.007***	−0.005***	0.021***	0.006***
Experience squared		0.000***	0.000***	0.000***	0.000***	0.000***	0.000***	0.000***	0.000***	0.000***
White		−0.008***	0.023	−0.013***	−0.002***	−0.002***	0.003**	−0.022***	−0.028***	0.014***
Yellow		−0.029***	0.114***	0.016	−0.006	−0.008	−0.017**	−0.041***	−0.133***	0.039***
1–3 years education		−0.001***	0.004***	−0.022***	−0.005***	−0.002	0.019***	−0.004***	0.052***	0.010***
4 years education		−0.003***	0.001***	−0.039***	−0.009***	−0.001***	0.034***	−0.017***	0.092***	0.025***
5–7 years education		0.006***	−0.016***	−0.062***	−0.013***	0.000***	0.043***	−0.021	0.115***	0.029***
Completed primary school		0.008***	−0.017***	−0.080***	−0.026***	−0.003	0.047***	−0.049***	0.171***	0.038***
9–10 years education		0.008***	−0.042*	−0.095***	−0.031***	−0.007	0.046***	−0.045***	0.206***	0.049***

Completed high school	0.006***	−0.028***		−0.103***	−0.028***	−0.007	0.054***	−0.053***	0.293***	0.059***
12–14 years education	−0.003***	−0.048***		−0.150***	−0.036***	−0.010	0.048***	−0.045	0.321***	0.068***
Completed university	−0.009***	−0.016***		−0.096***	−0.027***	−0.010	0.059***	−0.049***	0.358***	0.075***
Region 2	−0.011	0.016***		0.008***	0.018***	−0.005***	−0.007	0.006***	0.000**	−0.002
Region 3	−0.012***	−0.081***		0.023***	0.035***	−0.004	0.054***	0.002***	0.042***	−0.001***
Region 4	−0.007***	−0.036***		0.014***	0.031***	−0.004	0.062***	−0.003***	0.043***	0.004***
Region 5	−0.006***	−0.071***		0.029***	0.028***	−0.004***	−0.021***	0.020***	0.029***	0.003*
Metropolitan residence	0.054***	−0.216***		−0.108***	−0.049***	0.003	0.048***	0.074***	0.186***	−0.016***
Urban residence	0.045***	−0.216***		−0.047***	−0.019***	0.002***	0.033***	0.077***	0.139***	−0.011***
Head of household	0.011***	0.013***		0.007***	0.012***	0.003***	0.046***	0.040***	0.104***	0.022***
Children 0–14 years in household	0.005***	−0.024***		0.000***	0.001*	−0.001***	−0.003***	−0.007***	−0.028***	−0.005***
Has a spouse who works	−0.055***	0.156***		0.013***	0.005***	0.005***	0.019***	0.021***	0.077***	0.021***
Observations					208,400					

Notes: Marginal effects reported. 'White' and 'yellow' are race indicators (black is omitted category). 0 years of education is omitted education category. Columns headed 0–9 indicate multinomial logit results for each employment classification.

Table 8.4(b). First-stage regression results, 1988 and 1995 (employment multinomial logit: industry participation constant)

	1987	1988	1989	1990	1992	1993	1995	1996	1997	1998	1999
Unemployed	−4.428	−3.787	−4.476	−4.234	−2.984	−2.783	−2.978	−3.106	−2.802	−2.659	−2.572
	(0.134)***	(0.124)***	(0.142)***	(0.092)***	(1.30)***	(0.092)***	(0.091)***	(0.087)***	(0.080)***	(0.077)***	(0.072)***
Self-employed	−1.157	−1.177	−1.052	−1.168	−1.427	−1.523	−1.75	−2.158	−2.106	−2.135	−2.054
	(0.060)***	(0.060)***	(0.060)***	(0.059)***	(0.057)***	(0.057)***	(0.055)***	(0.055)***	(0.054)***	(0.054)***	(0.053)***
Informal agriculture	−1.374	−1.973	−1.39	−1.483	−2.161	−2.253	−2.648	−3.175	−2.949	−2.631	−2.73
	(0.117)***	(0.128)***	(0.125)***	(0.120)***	(0.128)***	(0.125)***	(0.129)***	(0.135)***	(0.128)***	(0.129)***	(0.129)***
Formal agriculture	−4.487	−5.104	−4.55	−4.358	−5.934	−6.382	−5.984	−6.483	−7.11	−6.019	−6.919
	(0.240)***	(0.267)***	(0.284)***	(0.236)***	(0.311)***	(0.314)***	(0.291)***	(0.310)***	(0.417)*-	(0.294)***	(0.388)***
Informal manufacturing	−3.161	−3.059	−3.054	−2.944	−3.73	−3.433	−3.614	−4.07	−4.038	−4.096	−4.408
	(0.141)***	(0.140)***	(0.133)***	(0.139)***	(0.145)***	(0.135)***	(0.138)***	(0.141)***	(0.133)***	(0.140)***	(0.141)***
Formal manufacturing	−4.395	−4.462	−4.116	−4.136	−5.138	−5.153	−5.394	−5.524	−5.273	−5.474	−5.302
	(0.091)***	(0.092)***	(0.090)***	(0.091)***	(0.101)***	(0.101)***	(0.102)***	(0.101)***	(0.097)***	(0.102)***	(0.103)***
Informal non-tradable	−1.369	−1.578	−1.456	−1.44	−1.324	−1.206	−1.558	−1.753	−1.744	−1.636	−1.791
	(0.064)***	(0.065)***	(0.065)***	(0.063)***	(0.066)***	(0.062)***	(0.062)***	(0.060)***	(0.059)***	(0.058)***	(0.058)***
Formal non-tradable	−3.123	−2.967	−2.841	−2.919	−3.62	−3.575	−3.802	−3.727	−3.797	−3.802	−3.814
	(0.064)***	(0.063)***	(0.063)***	(0.063)***	(0.062)***	(0.062)***	(0.061)***	(0.058)***	(0.058)***	(0.059)***	(0.058)***
Employer	−7.571	−8.099	−6.581	−6.615	−7.724	−8.007	−7.83	−8.185	−8.477	−8.365	−8.205
	(0.149)***	(0.156)***	(0.128)***	(0.122)***	(0.136)***	(0.139)***	(0.145)***	(0.144)***	(0.13)***	(0.138)***	(0.135)***
Observations	177,399	177,376	179,938	184,724	193,931	197,658	208,400	209,264	219,710	221,088	227,369

Notes: Robust standard errors in parentheses;
*Significant at 10%,
**Significant at 5%,
***Significant at 1%.
Non-economically active is an omitted category.

One concern that is typically voiced with respect to multinomial logit models such as in equation (2) is that they assume that the odds ratios of any two possibilities (p_j/p_k) are independent of the number and nature of alternative outcomes. This is known as the independence of irrelevant alternatives (IIA) hypothesis. When alternative polychotomous discrete choice models that do not make this assumption, such as multinomial probits, are unstable or display convergence problems, one can test for the validity of the assumption using, for instance, the Hausman specification test which, in essence, tests for the stability of parameter estimates as alternative outcomes are excluded from the model. This test failed to reject the null hypothesis (that IIA is satisfied) for eight out of our nine outcome categories for 1995. Although results were poorer for 1988, with four rejections of the null, the overall picture is not one of overwhelming rejection of the multinomial logit specification.[29]

Table 8.5 reports the second-stage regression of industry wage premiums on effective rates of protection, import penetration, export shares, and import- and export-weighted real exchange rates. All specifications are in first differences. Import penetration rates and export shares are entered only in lags, so as to reduce possible simultaneity concerns. The basic argument for treating changes in effective rates of protection—the main variable of interest—as exogenous is the same as in Attanasio, Goldberg, and Pavcnik (2004) and Pavcnik et al. (2004): trade reforms in Latin America in the late 1980s and early 1990s arose as a response to becoming GATT/WTO members, or to a central policy decision to comply with previously negotiated rules.

> This reflects the government's objective to reduce tariffs across industries to more uniform rates negotiated with the WTO. Policymakers accordingly cater less to special lobby interests, so that tariff declines in each industry are proportional to the industry's pre-reform tariff levels ... alleviating concerns about endogeneity at least in the economic sense. (Goldberg and Pavcnik 2004: 4)

Eight different specifications are presented in Table 8.5. While ERPs are insignificant when differences are entered contemporaneously, they become robustly statistically significant in first lags (specifications 4–8). The coefficients on lagged ERPs have the expected positive sign and are statistically significant at the usual levels, suggesting that larger declines in protection were associated with larger declines in the industry wage premium over this period in Brazil.[30]

[29] Details from the Hausman specification test are available from the authors on request.

[30] Although Pavcnik et al. (2004) expected these results ('The models predict a positive association between industry tariffs and wages, so that declines in industry tariffs lead to proportional declines in industry wages' (Pavcnik et al. 2004: 321)), they did not find them. This may have been due to their use of the less-representative PME data, or to specifications that did not include lagged ERPs. Lagging ERPs accounts for the fact that the effects of reduced protection on industry premiums may take time to flow through. Our protection results are, however, consistent with those for Colombia (Attanasio, Goldberg, and Pavcnik 2004); and Mexico (Revenga 1997).

Table 8.5. Industry wage premiums and trade exposure

Dependent variable is industry wage premium	(1)	(2)	(3)	(4)	(5)	(6)	(7)	(8)
ERP	0.0005	0.0005	0.0005					
	(0.0005)	(0.0006)	(0.0006)					
ERP* lagged import penetration		−0.0001	−0.0005					
		(0.0019)	(0.0019)					
Lagged ERP				0.0003	0.0003	0.0005	0.0003	0.0005
				(0.0001)*	(0.0001)**	(0.0002)***	(0.0001)**	(0.0002)***
Lagged ERP* lagged import penetration						−0.0015		−0.0015
						(0.0011)		(0.0012)
Lagged import penetration		−0.1531	0.0992		−0.1196	−0.0926	0.1245	0.1508
		(0.1533)	(0.1757)		(0.1452)	(0.1505)	(0.1645)	(0.1746)
Lagged export share		−0.0524	−0.1251		−0.0284	−0.0282	−0.1008	−0.1008
		(0.1313)	(0.1354)		(0.1298)	(0.1306)	(0.1334)	(0.1341)
Lagged import Pen* lagged import weighted RER			−0.001				−0.001	−0.001
			(0.0004)***				(0.0004)***	(0.0004)***
Lagged export shr* lagged export weighted RER			0.0001				0.0001	0.0001
			(0.0000)**				(0.0000)**	(0.0000)**
Observations	210	207	210	207	207	207	207	207
R-squared	0.01	0.01	0.03	0.01	0.02	0.02	0.03	0.04

Notes: Robust standard errors in parentheses.
*Significant at 10%,
**Significant at 5%,
***Significant at 1%.

Nevertheless, the estimated size of the impact is small: using the ERP coefficient from specification 8, the fall in average ERP from 51.4 per cent in 1988 to 20.0 per cent in 1995 (with all other variables held at their mean values) would result in a 1.6 per cent decrease in average industry wage premium.

Although theory suggests that the pass through of tariffs to product prices, and thus to wages, is mediated by the sector's import penetration (see Gonzaga, Menezes-Filho, and Terra 2006), import penetration does not appear to be important in mediating the effect of tariffs on industry-specific wage premiums, as shown by the insignificant coefficients on the interaction terms. The same is not true of (import-weighted) exchange-rate effects, which have the predicted (negative) sign[31] when interacted with lagged import penetration: as the currency appreciates and imports become more competitive for a particular industry, wage premiums in that industry decline. When the real exchange rate (RER) is export-weighted and interacted with lagged export share, the effect is positive and significant.[32]

Table 8.6 presents the second stage results for the regression of industry-specific skill premiums on the same set of trade-related variables. For industry-specific skill premiums, once the economy-wide returns to skill are controlled for in the first stage, there are no particular theoretical predictions, and we find that the coefficients on ERPs are insignificant across all specifications. Interestingly, however, we find a fairly robust pattern of negative and significant coefficients on lagged import penetration, suggesting that skill premiums were falling for those industries where the growth in import penetration was largest. We know that these were largely skill-intensive industries that were most highly protected prior to 1988, as seen in Table 8.1. This movement in industry-specific skill premiums is therefore consistent with the decline in the economy-wide skill premium which was documented in Gonzaga, Menezes-Filho, and Terra 2006, and which we also observe. Controlling for the growth in import penetration, there appears to be some evidence that a stronger currency increases the skill premium.[33]

Table 8.7 reports the second-stage results for the regression of industry participation constants from the employment multinomial logit model on the same set of trade-related variables. These results are somewhat harder to interpret, since the ten occupational categories used in the estimation are much more aggregated than the twenty-two industries used in the previous two tables, and are basically at the agriculture, manufacturing, and services level.[34] Partly as a

[31] An increase in our exchange rates means an appreciation in the currency.

[32] This probably reflects the fact that an increase in an industry's export share would be expected to increase that industry's wage premium.

[33] This may be evidence of quality upgrading in the face of increased import competition.

[34] Both formal and informal agriculture categories are regressed on trade variables for the agricultural industry. Formal and informal manufacturing use manufacturing trade variables averaged over the various manufacturing industries, using lagged imports as weights. Formal and informal non-tradables, employers, and the self-employed categories are assigned zero ERPs, import penetration, and export share, but use economy-wide import- and export-weighted real exchange rates.

Table 8.6. Industry skill premiums and trade exposure

Dependent variable is industry skill premiums	(1)	(2)	(3)	(4)	(5)	(6)	(7)	(8)
ERP	−0.0004	0	0					
	(0.0005)	(0.0007)	(0.0007					
ERP* lagged import penetration		−0.0031	−0.0027					
		(0.0028)	(0.0027)					
Lagged ERP				−0.0003	−0.0004	−0.0004	−0.0003	0.0004
				(0.0003)	(0.0003)	(0.0003)	(0.0003)	(0.003)
Lagged ERP* lagged import penetration						−0.0001		0.0002
						(0.0012)		(0.0014)
Lagged import penetration		−0.2762	−0.486		−0.3476	−0.3453	−0.3578	−0.361
		(0.1652)*	(0.1855)***		(0.1509)**	(0.1551)**	(0.1886)*	(0.1928)*
Lagged export share		−0.0746	−0.1151		−0.0445	0.0446	0.0826	0.0826
		(0.1493)	(0.1577)		(0.1510)	(0.1514)	(0.1591)	(0.1595)
Lagged import pen* lagged import-weighted RER			−0.001				0.0012	0.0012
			(0.0005)*				(0.0005)**	(0.0005)**
Lagged export shr* lagged export-weighted RER			0				0.0001	0.0001
			(0.0001)				(0.0001)	(0.0001)
Observations	204	201	201	208	201	201	204	204
R-squared	0.00	0.01	0.02	0.01	0.02	0.02	0.03	0.04

Notes: See Table 8.5.

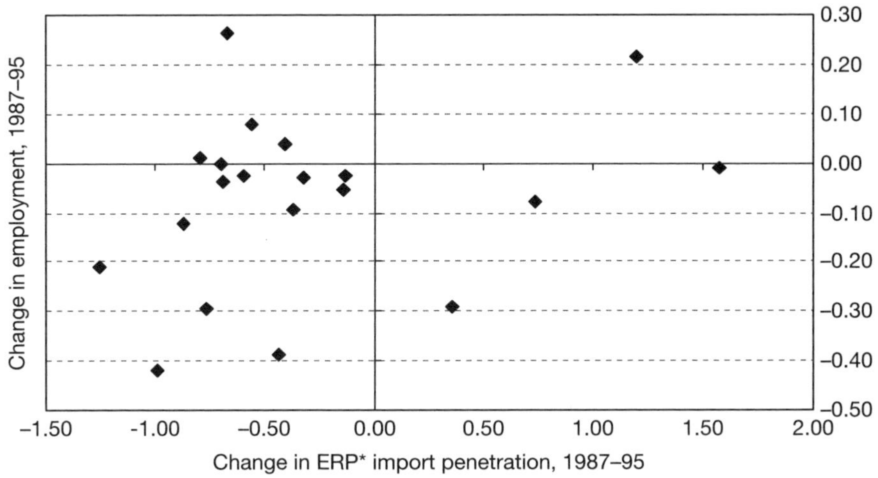

Fig. 8.5. Change in employment versus change in ERP* import penetration by industry, 1987–95

Source: Authors' calculations. Rates of protection from Kume, Piani, and de Souza (2004) in de Paiva Abreau (2004); import penetration from Muendler (2003); employment from PNADs.

result, there is a counter-intuitive negative sign on lagged ERPs, which suggests a (conditional) movement *towards* the industries experiencing the greater declines in protection. This result is explained by a movement towards the tradable sectors (particularly agriculture) of the reference category of workers in the employment model. Once we look at the unconditional pattern of employment changes for all workers at the disaggregated industry level, in Figure 8.5, we observe the expected positive correlation: employment levels seem to have fallen by more in industries experiencing larger declines in protection.

The only other statistically significant result in Table 8.7 is easier to interpret: lagged export shares are positively correlated with conditional increases in employment, suggesting that industries that succeeded in increasing their exports suffered smaller declines in employment than others.

Taken together, these results paint a mixed picture. The signs and significance are broadly—if not wholly—consistent with theoretical expectations from models that feature barriers to labour movement across sectors. Larger falls in protection and an exchange rate that makes imports more competitive domestically imply lower industry wage premiums. More exports in an industry are associated with increased wage premiums and employment. Greater import penetration is associated with falls in wage premiums which are greater for more skilled workers (who work mostly in industries that suffered the largest

Table 8.7. Industry participation and trade exposure

Dependent variable is industry participation	(1)	(2)	(3)	(4)	(5)	(6)	(7)	(8)
ERP	0.0087	−0.0025	−0.0043					
	(0.0076)	(0.0213)	(0.0229)					
ERP* lagged import penetration		0.0849	0.0965					
		(0.1407)	(0.1574)					
Lagged ERP				−0.0148	−0.0139	−0.015	−0.015	−0.0161
				(0.0041)***	(0.0045)***	(0.0047)***	(0.0069)**	(0.0077)**
Lagged ERP* lagged import penetration						0.0437		0.0483
						(0.0326)		(0.0723)
Lagged import penetration		−1.5541	−0.2417		(1.3357)	(1.2278)	0.4760	1.2010
		(3.9782)	(5.7256)		(1.4342)	(1.5567)	(3.8118)	(4.6518)*
Lagged export share		5.9193	4.9226		3.328	4.0074	2.5479	2.9954
		(2.0965)***	(3.4338)		(1.1175)***	(1.0568)***	(2.3503)	(2.3160)
Lagged import pen* lagged import-weighted RER			−0.0091				−0.0049	−0.0024
			(0.0152)*				(0.0105)	(0.0080)
Lagged export shr* lagged export-weighted RER			0.0053				−0.0014	0.005
			(0.0183)				(0.0152)	(0.0223)
Observations	80	72	36	72	72	72	36	36
R-squared	0.02	0.02	0.05	0.05	0.06	0.06	0.11	0.12

Notes: Robust standard errors in parentheses.
*Significant at 10%:
**Significant at 5%;
***Significant at 1%.

increase in penetration). These results are perhaps more in line with theory and with other accounts of trade liberalization in Brazil than previous attempts at estimating these relationships in Brazil, notably by Pavcnik et al. (2004).

Yet, they leave much to be desired. Empirically, the R^2 of each second-stage regression is never higher than 0.12. For the wage equations, they are never higher than 0.04, suggesting that however economically important the joint variation in the trade variables may be it accounts for a small share of the observed variation in wage premiums across industries and over time. Conceptually, these wage regressions focus on only one of the five mechanisms through which trade reforms are thought to influence changes in wages in developing countries (which were reviewed in section 8.2)—namely, changes in industry-specific wage and skill premiums.

However, if workers can move across industries over the medium run, and if market imperfections in labour and product markets are not particularly severe, then it is likely that the main effects of the changes in protection observed in Brazil over this period manifest themselves through (i) worker reallocation across industries and (ii) changes in the economy-wide skill premium. This prediction would accord with the Stolper–Samuelson theorem, but might also be consistent with economy-wide trade-induced SBTC or quality ladder models. In the next section, we turn to the full decomposition of wage changes in Brazil between 1988 and 1995, in an effort to place the changes implied by the second-stage regressions reported in Tables 8.5–8.7 into context—both vis-à-vis other changes that may be associated with trade channels, and vis-à-vis other economic processes that are less likely to be driven by trade reforms.

Table 8.8. Actual and counterfactual hourly wage distributions

	P_{90}/P_{10}	GE(0)	GE(1)	Gini
$w_{ij}^{88} = \exp\left(X_{ij}^{88}\beta^{88} + I_{ij}^{88} * \mathrm{wp}_j^{88} + (I_{ij}^{88} * S_{ij}^{88})\mathrm{sp}_j^{88} + F_{88}^{-1}(\theta_{i88})\right)$	16.9	0.703	0.780	0.611
$w_{ij}^{1} = \exp\left(X_{ij}^{88}\beta^{88} + I_{ij}^{88} * \mathrm{wp}_j^{s} + (I_{ij}^{88} * S_{ij}^{88})\mathrm{sp}_j^{88} + F_{88}^{-1}(\theta_{i88})\right)$	16.9	0.705	0.784	0.611
$w_{ij}^{2} = \exp\left(X_{ij}^{88}\beta^{88} + I_{ij}^{88} * \mathrm{wp}_j^{s} + (I_{ij}^{88} * S_{ij}^{88})\mathrm{sp}_j^{s} + F_{88}^{-1}(\theta_{i88})\right)$	16.7	0.699	0.774	0.609
$w_{ij}^{3} = \exp\left(X_{ij}^{88}\beta^{88} + I_{ij}^{s} * \mathrm{wp}_j^{s} + (I_{ij}^{s} * S_{ij}^{88})\mathrm{sp}_j^{s} + F_{88}^{-1}(\theta_{i88})\right)$	14.6	0.653	0.731	0.593
$w_{ij}^{4} = \exp\left(X_{ij}^{88}\beta^{s} + I_{ij}^{s} * \mathrm{wp}_j^{95} + (I_{ij}^{s} * S_{ij}^{88})\mathrm{sp}_j^{95} + F_{88}^{-1}(\theta_{i88})\right)$	12.9	0.600	0.669	0.572
$w_{ij}^{5} = \exp\left(X_{ij}^{88}\beta^{95} + I_{ij}^{s} * \mathrm{wp}_j^{95} + (I_{ij}^{s} * S_{ij}^{88})\mathrm{sp}_j^{95} + F_{88}^{-1}(\theta_{i88})\right)$	12.3	0.581	0.657	0.566
$w_{ij}^{6} = \exp\left(X_{ij}^{88}\beta^{95} + I_{ij}^{s} * \mathrm{wp}_j^{95} + (I_{ij}^{s} * S_{ij}^{88})\mathrm{sp}_j^{95} + F_{95}^{-1}(\theta_{i88})\right)$	12.0	0.587	0.691	0.571
$w_{ij}^{95} = \exp\left(X_{ij}^{95}\beta^{95} + I_{ij}^{95} * \mathrm{wp}_j^{95} + (I_{ij}^{95} * S_{ij}^{95})\mathrm{sp}_j^{95} + F_{95}^{-1}(\theta_{i95})\right)$	12.4	0.617	0.715	0.582

Source: Authors' calculation from PNADs.

8.5. Decomposition Results

8.5.1. The Distribution of Hourly Wages

Table 8.8 summarizes the results of the decomposition described in section 8.2. It presents four measures of inequality for the 1988 and 1995 hourly wage distributions in Brazil, as well as for the six intermediate counterfactual distributions previously described. The measures are the 90th/10th percentile ratio, the mean log deviation (also known as GE(0), or Theil-L index), the Theil-T index (or GE-1), and the Gini coefficient. Figures 8.6–8.11 plot the observed wage-growth incidence curve (WGIC) between 1988 and 1995, as well as different counterfactual WGICs, each corresponding to one of the counterfactual distributions listed in Table 8.8. The figures provide a full distribution, disaggregated decomposition of wage changes.

The differences between $G(w^1)$ and $G(w^{88})$, which correspond to the impact of the trade-mandated changes in industry wage premiums, are economically insignificant: counterfactual inequality measures hardly move, and the counterfactual WGIC in Figure 8.6 remains very close to the x-axis. Despite statistically significant coefficients on the tariffs in the second-stage estimation described in the previous section, it appears that changes in the wage distribution due to industry wage premiums between 1988 and 1995 were immaterial. The same is true of changes in industry-specific skill premiums, which are incorporated into $G(w^2)$, in Figure 8.7. Thus, although our second-stage regression coefficients are statistically significant (while theirs are not), we reach the same essential conclusion on the economics of these impacts as Pavcnik et al. (2004): trade liberalization did not affect the Brazilian wage distribution *through industry-specific premiums*.

But when relative prices and wages change, firms and industries contract and expand in response. Workers flow across sectors and industries, and their movement is highly selective (on observed and unobserved characteristics). The difference between $G(w^2)$ and $G(w^3)$ is meant to capture those occupational (employment) changes which took place in response to changes in trade-related variables (as predicted by the second-stage regressions). These counterfactual changes are much larger than those associated with industry-specific wage and skill premiums. All four inequality measures for $G(w^3)$ move closer to their 1995 values: the difference in inequality between this simulation and 1988 ranges between 51 per cent of the 1995–88 difference (for p90/p10) and 76 per cent (for the Theil-T). Figure 8.8 reveals that the bulk of the underestimate is due to the bottom of the distribution: whereas $G(w^3)$ generates a remarkably good prediction of changes in the wage distribution from the 20th percentile upwards, it considerably underestimates gains for the bottom quintile.

Allowing for changes in the economy-wide returns to education (and thus in a flexible version of the economy-wide skill premium) contributes to a further reduction in inequality, which now in fact overshoots the 1995 targets (for three of the four measures).[35] Consistent with the decline in returns to higher levels of schooling, this simulation does not affect the bottom of the distribution much, but lowers counterfactual incomes in the middle and at the top (Figure 8.9).

It is harder to attribute these changes to trade reforms, since this counterfactual imports *observed* 1995 coefficients (on education, as well as on industry dummies and industry skill premiums), rather than those mandated by the second stage. The bulk of the difference between $G(w^3)$ and $G(w^4)$ is due to β_{ed}^{95} which, by its very nature as an economy-wide vector of returns, does not vary by industry and cannot be estimated in a second stage. But the fact that it cannot be included in a Pavcnik et al.-style second stage does not mean that it does not reflect trade changes. In fact, as discussed above, if output and labour markets are reasonably well-functioning, a number of theories of trade would predict an important effect of trade liberalization on this coefficient. The Stolper–Samuelson effect would predict a decline in the economy-wide skill premium, and thus an inequality reduction from importing β_{ed}^{95}. Trade-induced SBTC, as well as most versions of the outsourcing or quality ladder stories, would imply an increase in the demand for skilled workers, and thus an increase in inequality from β_{ed}^{95}.

On the other hand, changes in β_{ed}^{95} clearly also reflect other economic and demographic changes, notably changes in the supply of skilled workers. As shown in Figure 8.4, there was indeed some growth in the skills of the Brazilian labour force over this period, with the share of skilled workers rising from 20 per cent to 24 per cent. All in all, this decomposition method does not allow us to separate these changes in inequality into components due to each of the alternative trade hypotheses, and a component due to changes in the supply of skills (or to technology changes unrelated to trade). All that can be said is that the net effect suggests that the Stolper–Samuelson channel and the effects of increased skill supply (which go in the same direction) seem to have outweighed any effects of SBTC or quality compositional changes that might have occurred as a result of trade liberalization.

The two final steps in the decomposition incorporate changes in the remainder of the earnings-regression coefficients (the other elements of β) to generate $G(w^5)$, and a rank-preserving transformation in the distribution of residuals to generate $G(w^6)$. Finally, the differences between $G(w^6)$ and $G(w^{95})$ are residually due to changes in the joint distribution of observed characteristics. Although effects of trade on the returns to experience, or to unobserved skills, cannot be ruled out, these are not channels on which the literature has focused. Accordingly, we interpret these remaining changes as those which are not attributable to trade effects. Changes in non-education returns are mildly equalizing, and

[35] This result is reminiscent of the Gonzaga, Menezes-Filho, and Terra (2006) finding that trade-mandated changes in the economy-wide skill premium were larger than those actually observed.

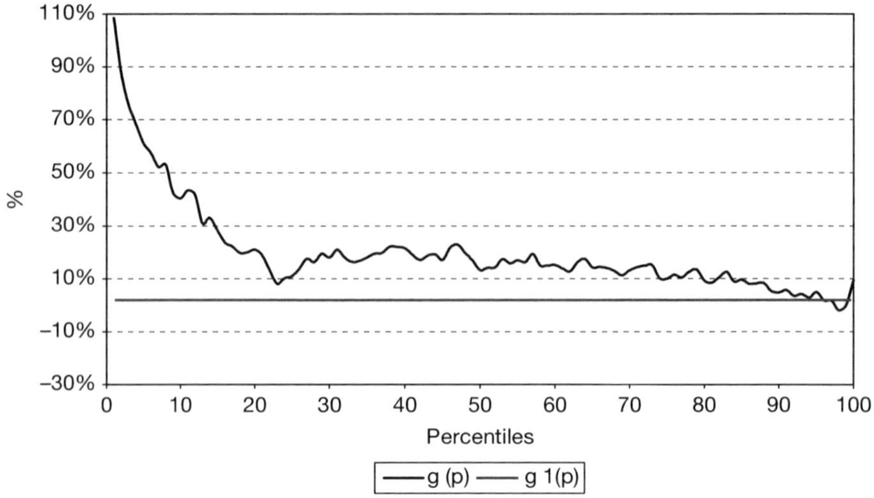

Fig. 8.6. Observed and counterfactual wage growth incidence curves, 1988–95, industry wage premiums

Source: Authors' calculation from PNADs.

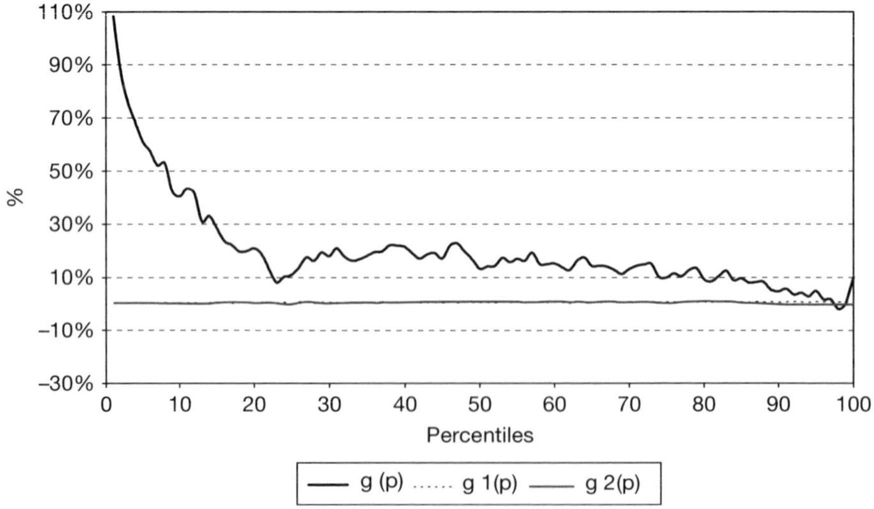

Fig. 8.7. Observed and counterfactual wage growth incidence curves, 1988–95, industry wage and skill premiums

Source: Authors' calculation from PNADs.

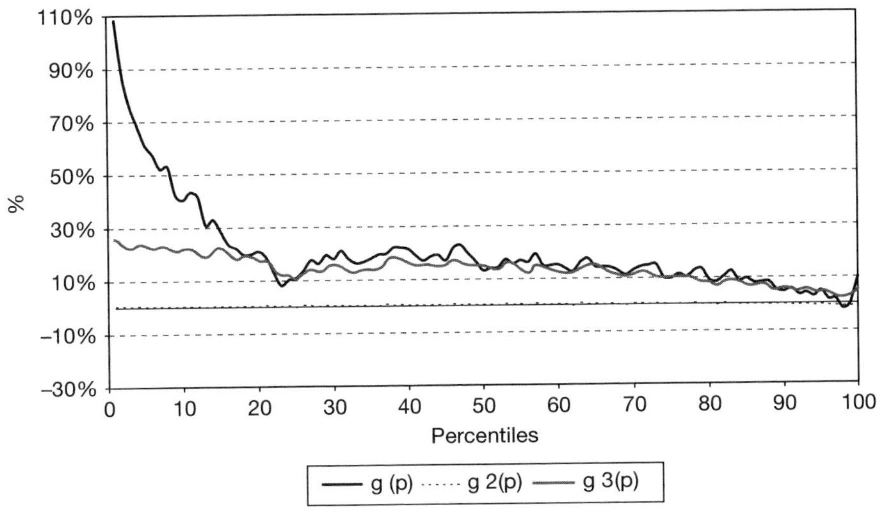

Fig. 8.8. Observed and counterfactual wage growth incidence curves, 1988–95, all trade mandated changes from second stage

Source: Authors' calculation from PNADs.

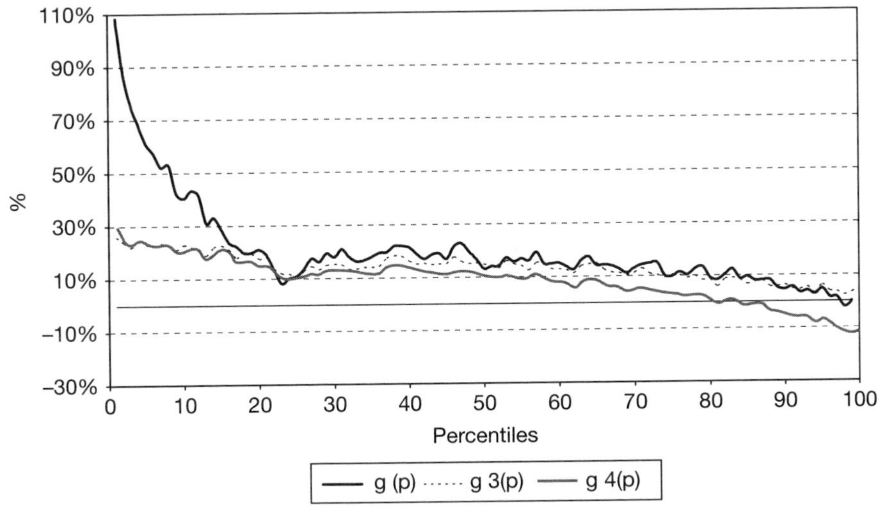

Fig. 8.9. Observed and counterfactual wage growth incidence curves, 1988–95, upper bound on trade effects

Source: Authors' calculation from PNADs.

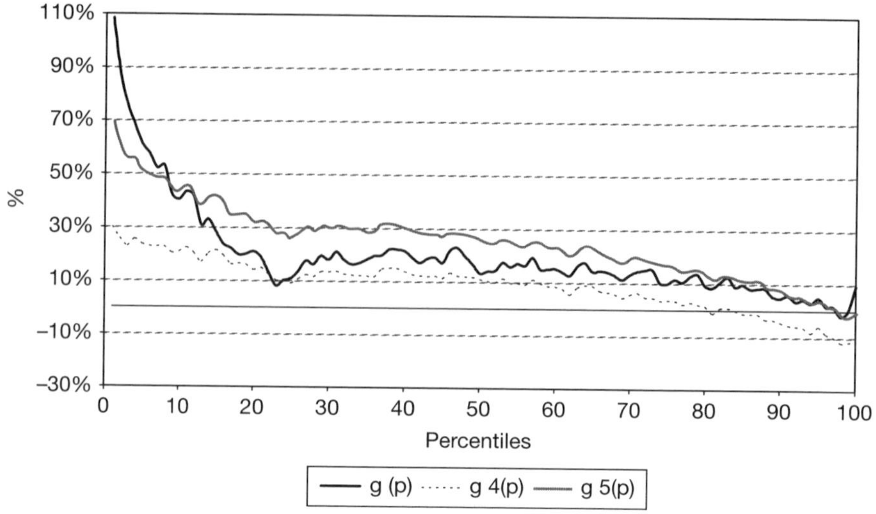

Fig. 8.10. Observed and counterfactual wage growth incidence curves, 1988–95, trade effects and other price changes

Source: Authors' calculation from PNADs.

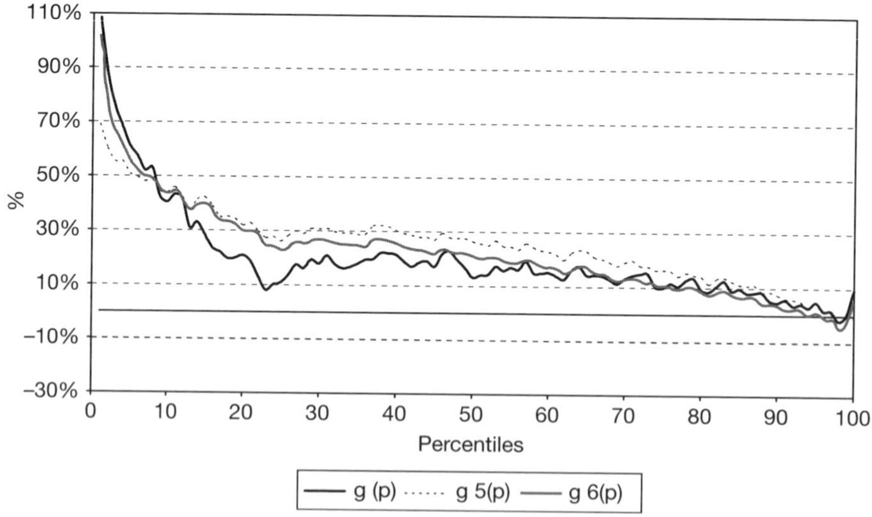

Fig. 8.11. Observed and counterfactual wage growth incidence curves, 1988–95, trade effects, price changes, and changes in residuals

Source: Authors' calculation from PNADs.

Table 8.9. Actual and counterfactual household per capita income distributions

	P_{90}/P_{10}	GE(0)	GE(1)	Gini	Poverty line R$87.55		
					FGT(0)	FGT(1)	FGT(2)
$HPCI_{ij}^{88}$	19.3	0.717	0.750	0.609	27.7	11.5	6.7
$HPCI_{ij}^{1}$	19.9	0.729	0.760	0.613	27.7	12.1	7.1
$HPCI_{ij}^{2}$	19.7	0.724	0.755	0.611	27.8	12.1	7.1
$HPCI_{ij}^{3}$	16.9	0.658	0.692	0.589	21.2	8.7	4.9
$HPCI_{ij}^{4}$	15.3	0.613	0.644	0.571	21.2	8.6	4.9
$HPCI_{ij}^{5}$	15.4	0.616	0.645	0.572	19.0	7.6	4.3
$HPCI_{ij}^{6}$	15.2	0.621	0.663	0.575	19.7	7.8	4.4
$HPCI_{ij}^{95}$	16.9	0.660	0.706	0.592	23.8	10.5	6.3

Notes: This is a relative poverty line, calculated to represent 50 per cent of the median household per capita income in 1988 (expressed in 2004 prices).
Source: Authors' calculations from the PNADs.

poverty reducing. Changes in the distribution of residuals contribute to lower incomes in the middle of the distribution and higher incomes at the very top. The net effect is mildly inequality increasing (except for p90/p10). The effect of changes in the distribution of observed characteristics further lowers incomes in the middle of the distribution and raises them above the 75th percentile.

8.5.2. The Distribution of Household Income per Capita

Once the six counterfactual wage distributions $G(w^1)$ to $G(w^6)$ have been simulated, it is a simple matter to create the corresponding counterfactual distributions of household income per capita. Household identifiers link each worker in our dataset to a particular household, and information is available on all of its other sources of income (subject to the usual misreporting and measurement issues in an income survey like the PNAD). It is therefore possible to simulate the impact of these counterfactual changes in wages on the distribution of household incomes, and on the inequality and poverty levels associated with it. These results are reported on Table 8.9, and in Figures 8.12–8.17, for the same inequality indices used so far and for the three standard Foster–Greer–Thorbecke poverty measures. We adopt a relative poverty line of R$87.55 in 2004 prices, which corresponds to 50 per cent of the 1988 median household per capita income.

Before discussing these results, it is important to recognize that their limitations are even greater than those for the wage distribution decompositions analysed so far. In addition to the same caveat about path dependence, now the absence of general equilibrium effects extends to any indirect impacts of trade (or any other changes) on family composition, or on the occupational decisions of household members other than spouses. There are also important changes in other, unrelated policy parameters, such as the real value of pension payments and other transfers, which are consigned to the residual—which is therefore larger than in the decomposition described in Table 8.8.

As in the hourly wage distribution, trade-mandated changes in industry wage premiums and industry-specific skill premiums have very limited effects (although they are somewhat more inequality increasing, suggesting that the workers hardest hit by wage declines in contracting industries belonged to poorer households (Figures 8.12 and 8.13). The biggest impact, as before, comes in the transition from the second to the third counterfactual (Figure 8.14). The changes in occupations across the distribution which occur in response to changes in the occupation-specific terms in the multinomial logit model are vastly poverty and inequality reducing. They contribute a decline of six points in the headcount index, actually overshooting the observed decline. Inequality measures move very close to the observed 1995 values, and the counterfactual growth incidence curve corresponding to these 'full trade effects' lies quite close to the observed growth incidence curve (GIC) (1988–95).

Allowing for changes in the returns to education β_{ed}^{95} in simulation 4 contributes to a further reduction in inequality, as in the wage distribution, and to an underprediction of all, but particularly the highest, incomes (Figure 8.15). That is partly corrected by allowing the other earnings regression coefficients (including the constant) to take their 1995 values (Figure 8.16). Finally, replacing the earnings regression residuals with a rank preserving transformation of the 1995 residuals leads to column 6 (household per capita income, HPCI) in Table 8.9, and to the counterfactual GIC in Figure 8.17.

The underestimates in poverty and inequality implied in this final counterfactual reflect two main factors. First, there were substantial changes in labour-force participation and informality over this period which were unrelated to trade and are thus not captured by the simulation. Second, there were also important changes in the incidence of non-labour incomes, with a decline in the real value of minimum-wage-linked pensions at the bottom of the distribution, and an increase in the real value of retirement earnings at the top. Both of these trends, which are documented in Ferreira and Paes de Barros (1999), help account for the difference between the counterfactual and the actual GICs in Figure 8.17 (and between the two bottom lines of Table 8.9).

These earnings-based simulations are *not* the most suitable way for understanding differences between full household income distributions. The extended version of this approach, which is described in Bourguignon, Ferreira, and

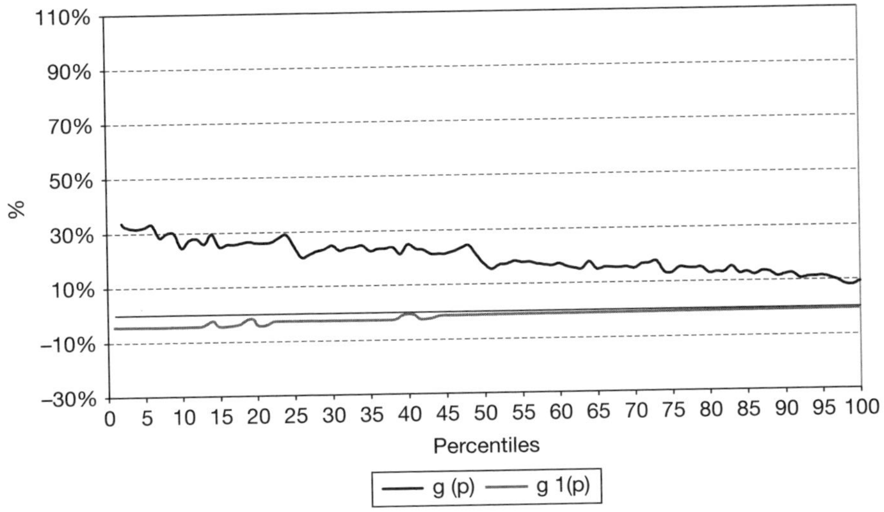

Fig. 8.12. Observed and counterfactual household per capita income growth incidence curves, 1988–95, industry wage premiums

Source: Authors' calculation from PNADs.

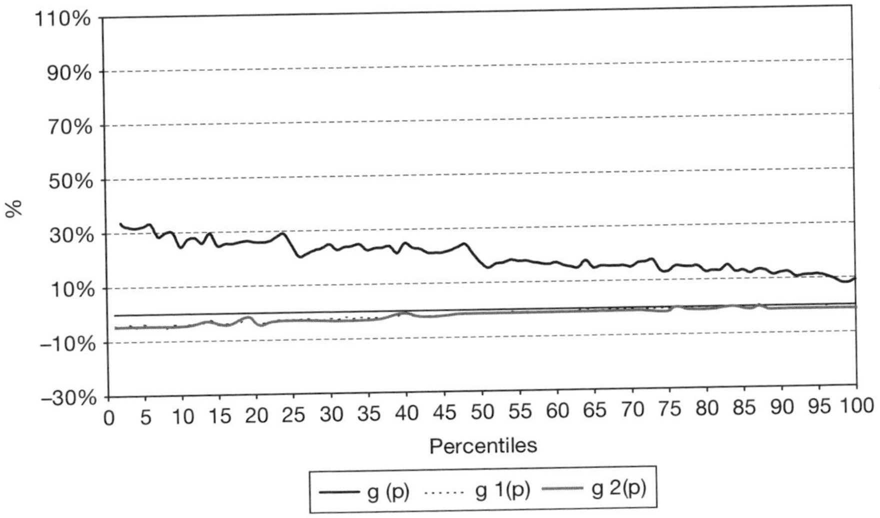

Fig. 8.13. Observed and counterfactual household per capita income growth incidence curves, 1988–95, industry and skill wage premiums

Source: Authors' calculation from PNADs.

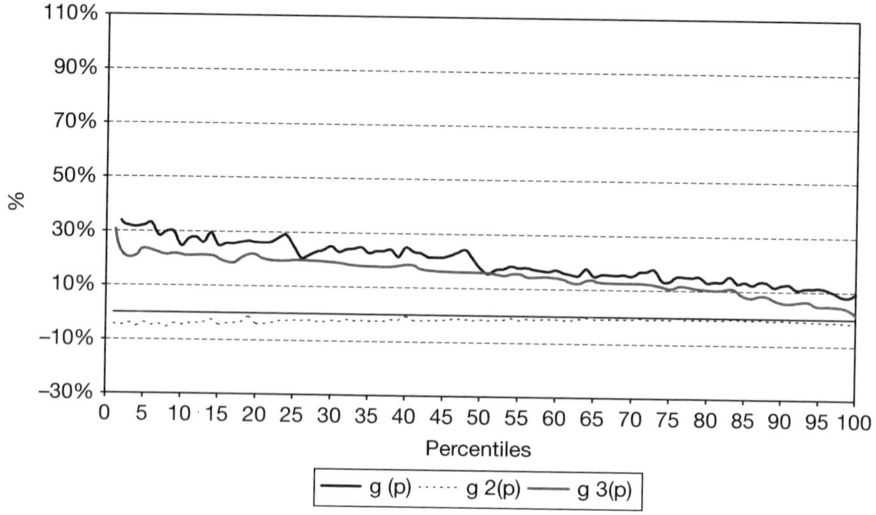

Fig. 8.14. Observed and counterfactual household per capita income growth incidence curves, 1988–95, all trade mandated changes from second stage

Source: Authors' calculation from PNADs.

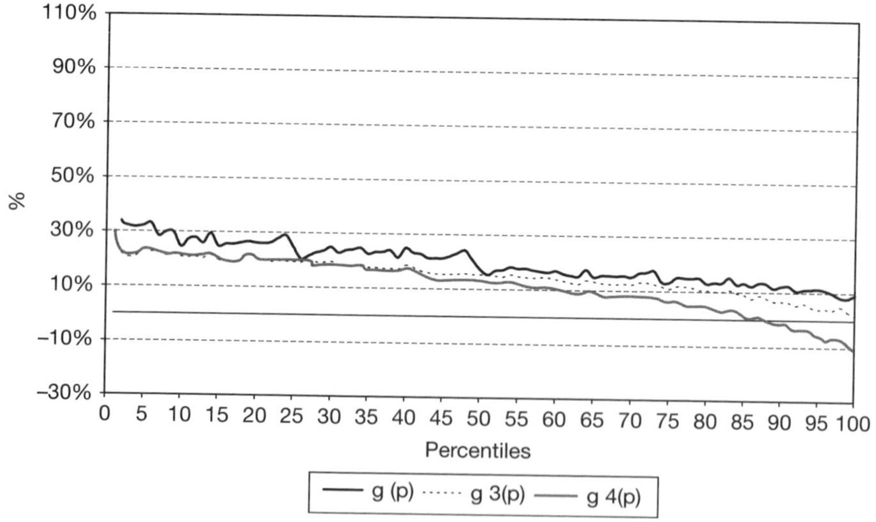

Fig. 8.15. Observed and counterfactual household per capita income growth incidence curves, 1988–95, upper bound on trade effects

Source: Authors' calculation from PNADs.

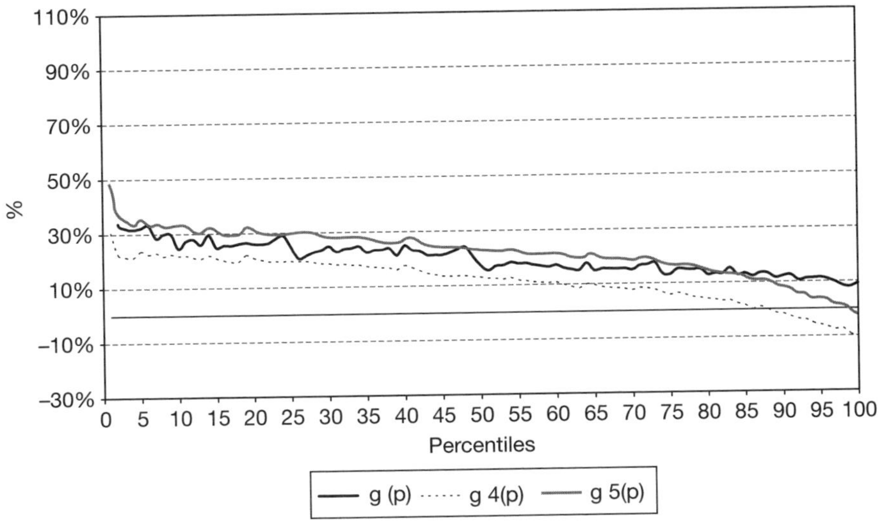

Fig. 8.16. Observed and counterfactual household per capita income growth incidence curves, 1988–95, trade effects and other price changes

Source: Authors' calculation from PNADs.

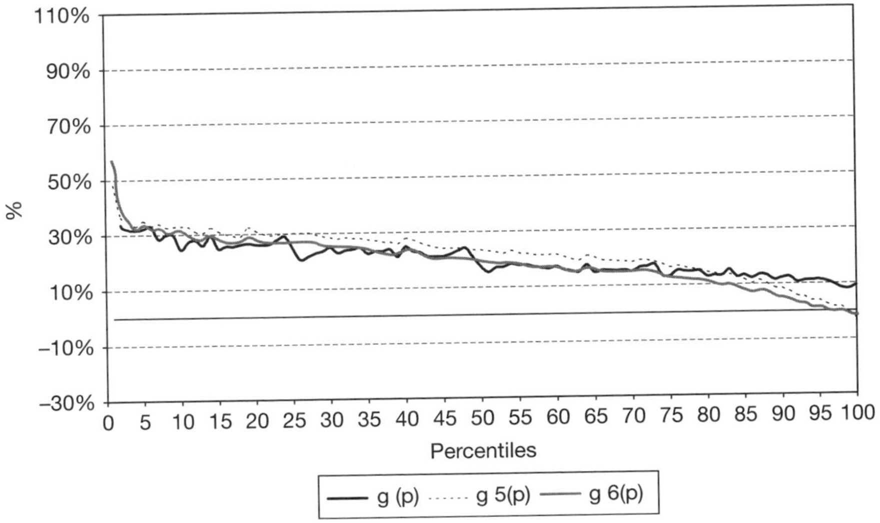

Fig. 8.17. Observed and counterfactual household per capita income growth incidence curves, 1988–95, trade effects, price changes, and changes in residuals

Source: Authors' calculation from PNADs.

Lustig (2004), would be much more appropriate.[36] The aim of this subsection, then, was merely to point out that the links between trade (and, in particular, trade-mandated employment flows across sectors and formality status) and wage inequality do appear to carry through to the changes we have observed in the distribution of HPCI in Brazil over this period, including a substantial part of the observed poverty reduction.

8.6. Conclusions

Using a nationally representative sample of workers in all sectors of the economy, this chapter has sought to quantify the impacts of the 1988–95 trade liberalization episode on the Brazilian wage distribution. Our results confirm previous findings that changes in industry wage premiums and industry-specific skill premiums did not meaningfully contribute to changes in the distribution of hourly wages. Trade reforms *did* contribute to the observed reduction in inequality, but this happened through other channels. Chief among them were trade-induced changes in employment levels across sectors, industries, and formality categories (formal, informal, self-employed, employer). The reallocation of workers that our model predicts to have arisen from changes in levels of protection, exchange rates, import penetration, and export shares between 1988 and 1995 accounts for more than half of the observed changes in three out of four measures of inequality in hourly wages.

The other key channel through which trade reform is likely to have affected the distribution of wages is through changes in the economy-wide skill premium. This is the channel on which Gonzaga, Menezes-Filho, and Terra (2006) focused, and they argue that changes in the skill premium mandated by a Stolper–Samuelson model of trade would account for more than the actual change in skill premium *in manufacturing* during 1988–95. While our approach is unable to identify changes in the economy-wide skill premium which are due to trade variables from those which are not, our findings are consistent with the Gonzaga, Menezes-Filho, and Terra results: returns to education fell over the period, contributing to a decline in inequality which did overshoot the observed decline. If there was any skill-biased technical change, or if other forces for greater demand for skill were at work, they

[36] Yet another alternative approach would be to decompose both the actual and counterfactual changes in inequality between 1988 and 1995 into 'horizontal' and 'vertical' components. The former reflects differences in the income *changes* affecting households at similar initial levels of welfare, while the latter captures differences in conditional mean changes across different levels in the initial welfare distribution. See Ravallion and Lokshin (2004) for a specific decomposition, applied to a counterfactual trade reform in Morocco.

were more than offset by the joint force of the Stolper–Samuelson effect of trade liberalization in an economy that used to protect skill-intensive industries, and of increases in the supply of more educated workers.

Overall, even if one does not attribute the decline in the economy-wide returns to education to the trade reforms (despite evidence from other sources that part of it is attributable to the Stolper–Samuelson effect), our results suggest that trade liberalization did play an important part in the reduction of wage inequality in Brazil during 1988–95. The counterfactual wage growth incidence curve that includes the combined wage and employment effects mandated by changes in trade variables accounted for 59 per cent of the observed change in the Theil-L index, 61 per cent of the change in the Gini coefficient, and 76 per cent of the change in the Theil-T index. Among the combined effects, changes in occupation and employment levels across industries were by far the most important. These reductions in wage inequality did appear to extend to declines in household income inequality, and in the poverty rate.

Some of the implications of these findings are as follows. There is no reason why researchers concerned with the distributional effects of trade liberalization should focus exclusively on the manufacturing sector, or only on industry-specific wage premiums. Indeed, it would seem that employment flows and changes in the occupational structure of the labour force play a central role, and should be considered explicitly. For policymakers, it would seem that in countries where protection was stronger for industries intensive in skilled workers (which was not the case in Mexico, Chile, or Colombia, but was the case in Brazil), there need be no mandatory trade-off between gains in efficiency and productivity on the one hand, and increases in inequality or poverty on the other. Quite the contrary: the same liberalization efforts that lead to productivity gains may also lead to wage gains at the bottom of the distribution, and to reductions in poverty and inequality.

APPENDIX

This Appendix outlines how each trade variable in our second-stage regressions was constructed. The main trade variables are industry-specific real exchange rates, effective rates of protection, import penetration rates, and export shares of production.

Industry-specific Trade-weighted Real Exchange Rates

Adapting Goldberg 2004, we construct both export- and import-weighted real exchange rates for each industry *j*. Goldberg suggests, respectively:

$$xer_t^j = \sum_c w_t^{jc} \times rer_t^c, \text{ where } w_t^{jc} = \frac{X_t^{jc}}{\sum_c X_t^{jc}}, \text{ and}$$

$$mer_t^j = \sum_c w_t^{jc} \times rer_t^c, \text{ where } w_t^{jc} = \frac{M_t^{jc}}{\sum_c M_t^{jc}}$$

where rer_t^c are the bilateral real exchange rates with each Brazilian trading partner *c*.

Rather than derive real exchange rates for every trading partner by industry and year (a large undertaking) we have ranked countries by decreasing size of imports (exports) in each industry, and included those countries which (i) make up the first 95 per cent of imports (exports) and (ii) whose imports (exports) are over 1 per cent of the total within that industry. To reduce spurious volatility in the exchange rate series due to a changing composition of the set of countries in the annual weights, we depart from Goldberg by defining our weighted exchange rates with constant weights across the period:

$$xer_t^j = \sum_c w_{8599}^{jc} \times rer_t^c, \text{ where } w_{8599}^{jc} = \frac{\sum_{t=1985}^{1999} X_t^{jc}}{\sum_c \sum_{t=1985}^{1999} X_t^{jc}}, \text{ and}$$

$$mer_t^j = \sum_c w_{8599}^{jc} \times rer_t^c, \text{ where } w_{8599}^{jc} = \frac{\sum_{t=1985}^{1999} M_t^{jc}}{\sum_c \sum_{t=1985}^{1999} M_t^{jc}}$$

These weights are based on a country's share of trade over the period 1985–99. All trading partners of significance over the period are included, and their real exchange rates are weighted identically in each year, so the variation in the aggregate industry exchange rate comes from changes in trading partners' exchange rates, rather than trade volume or inclusion/exclusion in different years.

We use trade data from UN Comtrade at the SITC 4-digit level. A concordance was constructed to match each SITC2 4-digit industry code to the more aggregated industries of the ERP data from Kume, Piani, and de Souza (2000). Imports (exports) are then summed by country over these ERP industries to give us $M_t^{jc}(X_t^{jc})$. Bilateral real exchange rates were constructed by multiplying each country's nominal exchange rate (in local currency per Real) by the ratio of the Brazilian price index to the partner country price index, where the wholesale price index (WPI) was used where available, and the consumer price index (CPI) otherwise. Countries for which neither a full-time series of WPI or CPI were available were excluded. For the non-tradable sector, we constructed economy-wide real exchange rates, using imports and exports with trading partners across all industries to derive country weights.

EFFECTIVE RATES OF PROTECTION

ERPs from 1985–99 are available from Kume, Piani, and de Souza (2000). We have used them as reported in de Paiva Abreu (2004). However, the industry classifications differ from those available in the PNAD. Adapting the concordance used by Pavcnik et al. (2004), we averaged ERPs across certain ERP industries using lagged industry imports as weights. The summary final concordance is reported in Table 8.2.

IMPORT-PENETRATION RATE AND EXPORT SHARE OF PRODUCTION

Both of these variables were constructed in the same way; the raw data for both are from Muendler (2003) (available at <http://www.econ.ucsd.edu/muendler/html/brazil.html>). These data are given by *Nível 80* (an official Brazilian classification), a different industry classification from that afforded us by the PNAD. So a concordance from *Nível 80* to *Nível* 100 (also available on Muendler's website) was used to move to *Nível 100*, and a second concordance from *Nível 100* to the ERP industry categories was constructed by the authors to standardize industries. As with ERPs, import weights were then used to average certain industry import penetration and export share to arrive at data series for the final industries used in the chapter.

Table A8.1. Industry standardization: steps and concordances

Trade variable	Initial industry classification	Concordance steps	Concordances used
Trade-weighted RER	SITC2	SITC2 to ERP	SITC2-ERP (authors)
		ERP to final (PNAD)	ERP-PNAD (authors)
ERP	Unknown (referred to here as ERP)	ERP to final (PNAD)	ERP-PNAD (authors)
Import Penetration	Nível 80	Nível 80 to Nível 100	Nível 80-Nível 100 (Muendler)
		Nível 100 to ERP	Nível 100-ERP (authors)
		ERP to final (PNAD)	ERP- PNAD (authors)
Export share	Nível 80	Nível 80 to Nível 100	Nível 80-Nível 100 (Muendler)
		Nível 100 to ERP	Nível 100-ERP (authors)
		ERP to final (PNAD)	ERP-PNAD (authors)

CONCORDANCES

There are a number of concordances used to standardize industries across the various trade data. The final industry classifications were driven by those available in the PNAD. The concordances used were:

- ERP industry (i.e., the industry classification used by Kume, Piani, and de Souza 2000, which is similar to *Nível 50*) to our final industry classification (author-constructed).
- ERP to PNAD (author-constructed, based on Pavcnik et al. 2004).
- *Nível 80* to *Nível 100* (available from Muendler).
- *Nível 100* to ERP (author-constructed).
- SITC2 to ERP (author-constructed).

The steps taken to standardize each trade variable's industry classifications are listed in Appendix Table A8.1.

References

Acemoglu, D. (2003) 'Patterns of Skill Premia', *Review of Economic Studies*, 70: 199–230.

Attanasio, O., P. Goldberg, and N. Pavcnik (2004) 'Trade Reforms and Income Inequality in Colombia', *Journal of Development Economics*, 74: 331–6.

Beyer, H., P. Rojas, and R. Vergara (1999) 'Trade Liberalization and Wage Inequality', *Journal of Development Economics*, 59: 103–23.

Bourguignon, F., F. H. G. Ferreira, and N. Lustig (2004) *The Microeconomics of Income Distribution Dynamics in East Asia and Latin America*. Washington, DC: World Bank and Oxford University Press.

Corseuil, C. H. L., and M. N. Fogel (2002) 'Uma Sugestão de Deflatores para Rendas Obtidas a Partir de Algumas Pesquisas Domiciliares do IBGE'. Texto para Discussão 897. Rio de Janeiro: IPEA.

Cragg, M., and M. Epelbaum (1996) 'Why Has Wage Dispersion Grown in Mexico? Is it the Incidence of Reforms or the Growing Demand for Skills?', *Journal of Development Economics*, 51: 99–116.

de Paiva Abreu, M. (2004) 'Trade Liberalization and the Political Economy of Protection in Brazil since 1987'. INTAL-ITD Working Paper SITI-08B. Washington, DC: IDB.

Deaton, A. (1997) *The Analysis of Household Surveys: A Microeconometric Approach to Development Policy*. Baltimore, Md.: Johns Hopkins University Press.

DiNardo, J., N. Fortin, and T. Lemieux (1996) 'Labor Market Institutions and the Distribution of Wages, 1973–1992: A Semiparametric Approach', *Econometrica*, 64: 1001–44.

Ebrill, L., J. Stotsky, and R. Gropp (1999) 'Revenue Implications of Trade Liberalization'. Occasional Paper 180. Washington, DC: IMF.

Edwards, S. (1998) 'Openness, Productivity and Growth: What Do We Really Know?', *Economic Journal*, 108: 383–98.

Feenstra, R. C., and G. Hanson (1996) 'Foreign Investment, Outsourcing and Relative Wages'. In R. C. Feenstra, G. M. Grossman, and D. A. Irwin (eds), *Political Economy of Trade Policy: Essays in Honor of Jagdish Bhagwati*. Cambridge, Mass.: MIT Press.

Feliciano, Z. (2001) 'Workers and Trade Liberalization: The Impact of Trade Reforms in Mexico on Wages and Employment', *Industrial and Labor Relations Review*, 55: 95–115.

Ferreira, F. H. G., and R. Paes de Barros (1999) 'The Slippery Slope: Explaining the Increase in Extreme Poverty in Urban Brazil, 1976–1996', *Brazilian Review of Econometrics*, 19: 211–96.

—— P. G. Leite, and J. A. Litchfield (2008) 'The Rise and Fall of Brazilian Inequality: 1981–2004', *Macroeconomic Dynamics*, 12: 199–230.

Ferreira, P., and J. L. Rossi (2003) 'New Evidence from Brazil on Trade Liberalization and Productivity Growth', *International Economic Review*, 44: 1383–405.

Goldberg, L. S. (2004) 'Industry-specific Exchange Rates for the United States', *Federal Reserve Bank of New York Economic Policy Review*. New York: Federal Reserve Bank.

Goldberg, P., and N. Pavcnik (2004) 'Trade, Inequality, and Poverty: What Do We Know? Evidence from Recent Trade Liberalization Episodes in Developing Countries', *Brookings Trade Forum*, 223–69.

—— (2005) 'Trade Protection and Wages: Evidence from Colombian Trade Reforms', *Journal of International Economics*, 66: 75–105.

Gonzaga, G., N. Menezes-Filho, and C. Terra (2006) 'Trade Liberalization and the Evolution of Skill Earnings Differentials in Brazil', *Journal of International Economics*, 68: 345–67.

Hanson, G., and A. Harrison (1999) 'Who Gains from Trade Reform? Some Remaining Puzzles', *Journal of Development Economics*, 59: 125–54.

Juhn, C., K. Murphy, and B. Pierce (1993) 'Wage Inequality and the Rise in Returns to Skill', *Journal of Political Economy*, 101: 410–42.

Kume, H., G. Piani, and C. F. de Souza (2000) 'A Política Brasileira de Importação no Período 1987–1998: Descrição e Avaliação'. Rio de Janeiro: IPEA. mimeo.

Lemieux, T. (2002) 'Decomposing Changes in Wage Distributions: A Unified Approach', *Canadian Journal of Economics*, 35: 646–88.

Muendler, M.-A. (2003) 'Series of Market Penetration by Foreign Products, Brazil 1986–1998'. San Diego, Calif.: University of California.

Nissanke, M., and E. Thorbecke (2005) 'Channels and Policy Debate in the Globalization–Inequality–Poverty Nexus'. Discussion Paper 2005/08. Helsinki: UNU-WIDER.

Pavcnik, N., A. Blom, P. Goldberg, and N. Schady (2004) 'Trade Policy and Industry Wage Structure: Evidence from Brazil', *World Bank Economic Review*, 18: 319–44.

Ravallion, M., and S. Chen (2003) 'Measuring Pro-poor Growth', *Economics Letters*, 78: 93–9.

—— and M. Lokshin (2004) 'Winners and Losers from Trade Reform in Morocco'. Washington, DC: World Bank, Development Research Group. mimeo.

Revenga, A. (1997) 'Employment and Wage Effects of Trade Liberalization: The Case of Mexican Manufacturing', *Journal of Labor Economics*, 15: S20–S43.

Robbins, D., and T. H. Grindling (1999) 'Trade Liberalization and the Relative Wages for More-skilled Workers in Costa Rica', *Review of Development Economics*, 3: 140–54.

Rodriguez, F., and D. Rodrik (2001) 'Trade Policy and Economic Growth: A Skeptic's Guide to the Cross-national Evidence'. In B. Bernanke and K. S. Rogoff (eds), *NBER Macroeconomics Annual 2000*. Cambridge, Mass.: MIT Press for NBER.

Sachs, J., and A. Warner (1995) 'Economic Reform and the Process of Global Integration', *Brookings Papers on Economic Activity*, 1–118.

Shigeoka, H., E. Verhoogen, and M. Wai-Poi (2006) 'Chinese Competition and the Mexican Manufacturing Sector: Plant-level Evidence and Implications for Policy'. New York: Columbia University. mimeo.

Slaughter, M. (2000) 'What are the Results of Product-prices Studies and What Can We Learn from their Differences?'. In R. Feenstra (ed.), *The Impact of International Trade on Wages*. NBER Conference Report. Chicago: University of Chicago Press, 129–70.

Thoenig, M., and T. Verdier (2003) 'A Theory of Defensive Skill-biased Innovation and Globalization', *American Economic Review*, 93: 709–28.

Verhoogen, E. (2008) 'Trade Quality Upgrading and Wage Inequality in the Mexican Manufacturing Sector', Quarterly Journal of Economics, 123(2): 489–530.

Winters, A., N. McCulloch, and A. McKay (2004) 'Trade Liberalization and Poverty: The Evidence So Far', *Journal of Economic Literature*, 62: 72–115.

Wood, A. (1997) 'Openness and Wage Inequality in Developing Countries: The Latin American Challenge to East Asian Conventional Wisdom', *World Bank Economic Review*, 11: 33–57.

World Bank (2006) *World Development Indicators*. Washington, DC: World Bank.

9

Globalization and the Urban Poor

Janice E. Perlman

9.1. The Heart of the Matter

At the heart of the discourse on globalization is the question of how it affects poverty and inequality among and within regions and nations, and the consequences for marginalized groups and individuals. Hardly a day passes without this issue arising in newspapers, magazines, academic publications, and policy speeches—by defenders and detractors of the 'new world order' as exemplified in the direct quotes below.

> Rising inequality is the dark side to globalization. [But] no one wants a return to outright protectionism. Paul Krugman, *New York Times*, 14 May 2007.

> [In] the modern globalization debate... no [issue] is more important than who benefits and who loses, absolutely and relatively, in both advanced and developing countries. Danny Leipziger and Michael Spence, *Financial Times*, 15 May 2007.

> An impoverished ghetto of one billion people will be increasingly impossible for a comfortable world to tolerate. Paul Collier, *The Bottom Billion: Why the Poorest Countries are Failing and What Can Be Done about It* (Oxford: Oxford University Press, 2007).

> There is mounting evidence that economic growth is less effective in reducing poverty in the face of rising trends in inequalities. United Nations Press Release, Associated Press, 8 Feb. 2007.

> Making globalization work for the masses is the central economic issue of the day.
> Larry Somers, *Financial Times*, 30 Oct. 2006.

> Economic globalization has outpaced political globalization. We need collective action to temper capitalism ... but we have yet to create the political structures to do so. Joseph Stiglitz, *US News and World Report*, 18 Sept. 2006.

These quotations and the articles from which they are excerpted raise fundamental questions regarding the inevitability of globalization, its costs, and whether its perverse consequences for those excluded can be mitigated (or reversed) through international agreements or domestic policies.

The literature on the growth–poverty–inequality nexus which regards inequality as the filter between growth and poverty (Thorbecke and Nissanke 2005; 2006; and 2007) and the literature on what I call the *globalization–urban poverty–public policy nexus* (Maricato 2006) are mutually reinforcing. The logic of globalization supposedly concentrates wealth and deepens inequality in a parallel manner within and among cities, countries, and continents (i.e., developing countries). My starting hypotheses to be tested are as follows:

(i) *The world is not flat* and never was. The process of globalization over the past several decades has exacerbated pre-existing inequalities and divergence. Advanced capitalism has produced 'advanced marginalization' (Wacquant 1996; 1999) whereby those limited to the 'space of place' and excluded from the 'space of flows' (Castells 2000) have been reduced from unimportant to irrelevant.

(ii) *Globalization is not an act of nature.* It is the result of policies which make the market supreme, allowing concentration of capital to trump concern for excluded countries, communities, and citizens. Therefore, different policies, rules and incentives—internationally or nationally—could theoretically mitigate or reverse this trend, given sufficient political will.

(iii) *Globalization is not new.* It is more far reaching now due to technological advances such as those in telecommunications, information, and transportation that facilitate the flows of capital, labour, information, and ideas.[1] The same historical logic of centre/periphery in the world system is reproduced at every level from continents to communities, continually reinforcing the vicious cycle of uneven development (or 'the development of underdevelopment' (Furtado 1964; 1982)).

(iv) *Globalization is not unidimensional.* Each aspect may have different consequences for different constituencies at different times. It can be good, bad, or indifferent depending upon your position in the hierarchy of winners and losers. This varies by context and specific circumstances, often lost in sweeping generalizations about the wonders or evils of a globalized world order.

(v) *Reducing poverty is not sufficient to redress the inequalities* created or exacerbated by globalization. Poverty levels may improve in absolute terms while the gap between the 'haves' and 'have nots' widens. Inclusive growth depends on policy interventions to share the fruits of growth with the bottom third of world population.

[1] Some scholars argue that globalization is *not* linked with advanced capitalism, and is *not* a consequence of policy pressure to follow the Washington consensus, but is the 'manifestation of an age-old drive natural to the human spirit . . . the urge to profit by trading, the drive to spread religious beliefs, the desire to exploit new lands, and the ambition to dominate others by armed might—all had been assembled by 6000 BCE to start the process we now call globalization' (Chanda 2007: 23).

Policymakers seeking ways to put a 'human face' on globalization are discussing taxes on international transactions, stipends for salaries of displaced workers up to previous levels, education/job-training geared to entry into the information economy—and various other income redistribution measures from the mundane to the utopian (see Scheve and Slaughter 2007). It is unclear whether the political will exists to implement any such redistributive measures or whether the self-perpetuating logic of globalization can be moulded by regulatory or contractual arrangements. What is certain is that globalization is not reversible—there is no going back.

9.2. The Urban Question[2]

The focus of this chapter is how the current stage of globalization affects poverty and inequality in urban areas on the periphery of the world hierarchy of cities (Friedmann 1986; 1995). Specifically it addresses the effects on marginalized communities—slums, squatter settlements, and shantytowns—collectively called 'informal settlements'. This is a particularly relevant theme, given that over the next twenty-five to thirty years virtually all of the population growth worldwide will be in the cities of developing countries[3] and will be largely concentrated in such settlements. The UN *State of the World Population* Report (27 June 2007) states:

> The growth of cities will be the single largest influence on development in the twenty-first century . . . Over the next 30 years, the population of African and Asian cities will double, adding 1.7 billion people—more than the current populations of the USA and China combined.

A careful look at globalization and urban poverty reveals complex—often contradictory—relationships. The nature of the linkages depends on how broadly or narrowly you define globalization, how rigorous you are in distinguishing causality from coterminality, how you measure poverty over time, and whose viewpoint you assume.

If the definition of globalization is construed to include all economic, political, social, cultural, and ideological changes that have occurred with the

[2] The title of this section references Manuel Castells' (1977) book, *The Urban Question: A Marxist Approach*.

[3] The term 'developing countries' is contested and bears an ideological valence as does the term 'globalization'. The discussion of such signifiers is itself part of a global debate (Sachs 1992). The evolution of terms for countries on the periphery of the capitalist system (from the pejorative 'underdeveloped' to the comparative 'late-industrializing to the 'geo-political' 'third-world' to the critical 'dependent-capitalist' to 'the global-south' to 'newly industrialized countries' to the 'fourth-world' (irrelevant altogether) and most recently to 'emerging markets') tells an eloquent story of unequal development ending in the transformation of the nation state into a market opportunity for consumption of goods and services (see Fiori 1995).

'restructuring of capitalist production' (Harvey 2003), there is little that remains outside its purview. Deconstructing the various implications of the term could lead to a rather arbitrary exercise of parsing whether each component (such as free trade agreements, technological advances in transportation and communication, or privatization) would have—or could have—occurred without the current form of globalization and how each relates to social justice in the city (Harvey 2003) in the short, medium, and long terms. We would need to unravel which elements of the package are precursors of globalization, inherent in it, or consequences of it. To what extent is the polarization between winners and losers of globalization inherent in capitalism itself with its historic inequalities which are then reinforced by the logic of capital concentrating at the top? Wouldn't the displacement of unskilled labour by mechanization and robotics have occurred under protective import substitution policies as well, perhaps more slowly? My guess is that urban factories would eventually close and footloose capital move to less expensive regions within the same country—causing lay-offs, unemployment, and downward pressure on wages—as long as the market economy had free reign.

The urban question is how the lives of the 40 per cent of urbanites living in the slums and shantytowns of Asian, African, and Latin American cities differ in the absence of the current incarnation of globalization. What would be the impact on poverty, inequality, violence, and voice?

Ultimately these questions can only be addressed by empirical evidence on a case-by-case basis. Case studies on the dynamics of poverty from an earlier period of relative national isolation to the currently pervasive globalization of ideas, icons, and identities may provide some insight. Without a grounded understanding of how globalization affects poverty in specific localities, we cannot hope to refine theory or to transform policy.

9.3. The Case of Rio de Janeiro

This chapter is based on a longitudinal multigenerational study of the urban poor in the *favelas*[4] of Rio de Janeiro[5] that I conducted over the period 1968 to

[4] *Favela* is the Brazilian term for informal settlements or shantytowns. Typically, migrants to the city, lacking the means to rent or buy housing, invade unused land and build their homes there, gradually forming communities as people from their families or hometowns come to join them in the city. These vacant lands, which are generally ignored by their public or private owner, are found in undesirable locations such as hillsides too rocky or steep to build on, marshlands prone to flooding, landfill made from refuse dumping, or narrow parcels alongside roads, water basins, or riverbeds.

[5] Rio de Janeiro is a city municipality with 6 million inhabitants, a metropolitan region of over 12 million, and a state with 14.4 million. Unless specified otherwise, this chapter refers to the municipality.

2008. During that period Brazil experienced major economic political and policy transformations:

(i) from a protected 'import substitution' economy to an increasingly free trade economy actively participating in Mercosul and in NAFTA (ratified in 1993);
(ii) from the economic miracle of the 1960s to triple-digit inflation, stagnation, and eventual stabilization (following the 1994 Plano Real pegging local currency to the dollar);
(iii) from a military dictatorship through a gradual process of opening to full restoration of democracy in 1985; and
(iv) from massive *favela* eradication programmes to on-site upgrading, reaching considerable scale between 1994 and 2004.

In the twenty-two years since the end of dictatorship, Brazil attained 'middle income' status by worldwide standards but its deep socio-economic inequalities have excluded a large part of the population. Brazil has one of the highest levels of inequality of any large country in the world. Not only does this prevent the poor from achieving their full human potential, from being treated with dignity, and from becoming full citizens, but it also sets limits on economic growth, depriving the country of the intellectual capital, productive and consumer potential, and political participation of a third of the urban population.[6]

If globalization had a polarizing effect between rich and poor as would be expected from the five propositions at the beginning of this chapter, income inequality should have become more acute starting in the 1990s. Looking at income distribution data for Brazil and Rio between 1992 and 2003 (Urani; IETS; PNAD) shows a high level of inequality but one that has remained relatively stable over the time period covered by this study.[7] Poverty figures are also fairly consistent over time. Using UNDP definitions of poverty (US$2 a day or less) and extreme poverty (US$1 a day or less), about a third of Brazil's population and about a fifth of Rio's population are in poverty—less than the national average, due in part to not adjusting measures by purchasing power parity.[8] The percentage of poor people in Rio declined slightly from 1992 to

[6] See Blofield (2007) for comparisons with Latin America in general.

[7] In Brazil the bottom 10 per cent earned less than 1 per cent of the national income while the top 10 per cent had close to 50 per cent. The percentage going to the lowest decile ranged in a narrow band from a low of 0.6 per cent (1993, 1996, and 1997) to a high of 0.8 per cent (2002), with all other years staying constant at 0.7. The top 10 per cent of the population likewise had a narrow range and high degree of consistency over the decade, with a high of 48.6 per cent (1993) to a low of 45.8 per cent (1992) and 46 per cent to 47 per cent in all other years.

[8] The highest percentage of Brazilians under the poverty line over this period was 41.7 per cent (1993) and the lowest was 32.7 per cent (1998) with 33 per cent to 34 per cent in all other years, showing no strong globalization effect at the macro level. For Rio, the rates declined slightly between 1992 (26.6 per cent) and 2003 (23.4 per cent) accompanying an increase in the percentage in extreme poverty.

2003, while the percentage of indigent poor increased slightly (Bourguignon, Ferreira, and Menéndez 2007; Ferreira, Leite, and Litchfield 2008; Gacitúa Marió and Woolcock 2005).

I would hesitate to draw conclusions about globalization's consequence or lack thereof from these figures on inequality and poverty over the past decade. Chapter 8 in the current volume by Francisco H. G. Ferreira, Phillippe G. Leite, and Matthew Wai-Poi does an excellent job in this regard. Many intervening variables are in play and it is always possible that strong negative and positive effects cancel each other out. But there is no doubt that the economic decline in the city of Rio (absolutely and in relation to the other metropolitan areas) has had deleterious effects on its inhabitants and particularly the most vulnerable among them.

During the period of the re-study (1999 and 2003), the city of Rio had a lower growth rate (in GDP per capita) and lower rates of upward mobility than the city of São Paulo, the state of Rio, all of the major regions of the country, and Brazil as a whole. Although Rio's GDP per capita is relatively high, the cost of living is even higher—and its level of inequality is worse than that of Brazil (Gini coefficient of 0.616 compared with 0.593). According to the ratings of the human development index, the 'quality of life' ranges from levels comparable to that of Belgium (in Gávea, an upscale neighbourhood in the South Zone, ninth in world ranking) to those comparable to Vietnam (in the Complexo de Alemão, in the North Zone, 108th of 177 countries).[9] As many studies have shown, this extreme inequality in Rio—and in Brazil—presents an obstacle to social mobility (Bourguignon, Ferreira, and Menéndez 2003; Gacitúa Marió and Woolcock 2005).

Other factors contributing to the decline in Rio's economy include loss of the national capital to Brasília, loss of financial, service, intellectual, and cultural headquarters to São Paulo, deindustrialization, the decline of the shipping industry and the port area, and the loss of tourism (and business investment) due to perceived and real violence. The consolidation of the built environment and technological advances in construction meant a drop in construction jobs which had absorbed a large proportion of poor male workers, and the squeeze on the middle class along with labour-saving technology and takeaway (takeout) services meant a drop in demand for domestic service which had absorbed a large portion of poor female workers. The rising bar for entry-level positions has made it difficult for those without an advanced degree to move into better-paying jobs.

9.3.1. Growth of the Favela

One clear indicator of the way this economic decline has played out in the job market along with the continued allure of Rio for cityward migrants is that the

[9] The average per-capita income of Gávea at RBL 2,140/month is more than twelve times that of Complexo de Alemão at RBL177. In 2000, when this was calculated, the exchange rate was 2.7 Reais to the US$.

number and size of Rio's *favelas* have increased steadily. According to the Instituto Pereira Passos (IPP), the city urban planning agency, the rate of growth of the *favelas* exceeded that of the city as a whole in every decade from 1950 to 2000, including in the 1970s, when 100,000 *favela* residents were evicted and their communities demolished. During the 1990s, Rio grew by 7 per cent and the *favelas* by 24 per cent (IPP 2005), and over 2000–5, the *favela* population grew at six times the rate of non-*favela* population (ibid.).

As of 2005, there were 752 *favelas* in Rio, housing for 1.1 million residents, the largest *favela* population of any Brazilian city (IPP 2005). During the original 1969 study, Rio had a total population of three million inhabitants, a third of whom lived informally (without legal title) in *favelas*. By 2000, when the re-study began, Rio had grown to 5.8 million inhabitants of whom 38 per cent were living informally: 19 per cent in the *favelas*, 9 per cent in illegal subdivisions (*loteamentos clandestinos*), 8.6 per cent in public housing complexes (*conjuntos habitionais*), and 1.7 per cent in 'areas of risk' (in environmental danger). This provides an excellent opportunity to look more closely at the dynamics of urban poverty and to explore the relationships between these dynamics and the multiple processes of globalization.

9.4. The Rio Research, 1969–2005

I conducted the original research in 1968–9 in three *favelas* at varying distances from the relatively affluent part of the city (Perlman 1976). In each community[10] a random sample of 200 males and females between 16 and 65 years of age and a purposive sample of fifty leaders were interviewed, totalling 750 people. Informal short-term follow-up studies were undertaken in 1973 and 1980. In 1999, a rigorous re-study was initiated. It took two years to locate as many of the surviving members of the original sample as possible. With a local research team and help from the children of the original study participants, we succeeded in finding 41 per cent of the original sample (308 of 750 people).

In 2001, interviews were conducted with these participants from the original study and with a random sample of their children and grandchildren.[11] This yielded data on both intra- and intergenerational mobility.[12] With basic information already collected on the location, education, and occupation of the parents of the original sample members, we were able to trace the dynamics of poverty and social spatial mobility across four generations spanning the entire

[10] The communities were Catacumba in the upscale South Zone, Nova Brasília in the industrial North Zone, and areas of Caxias in the peripheral Baixada Fluminense.

[11] The average age of the original interviewees was 64 years, of children 40 years, and of grandchildren 24 years remembering that we excluded children and grandchildren under 16 years of age to maintain comparability with our original sample.

[12] For an excellent literature review of intra-generational mobility, see Yaqub (1999).

twentieth century into the twenty-first century. This captures the transition of migrants from countryside to city and the reflection of that in the year-by-year life histories collected from each interviewee along with their responses to the survey questions.

The next phase of the study, conducted in 2003, involved the application of the same survey instrument questionnaire and life-history matrix to new random and leadership samples in the three original study communities. We selected 400 people at random from each community and twenty-five leaders according to their position and reputation. This enabled us to compare snapshots of the same places at two points in time and to go beyond the same circle of families from the 1969 study to cross-check for attrition bias (Perlman 2003; Cano 2005).

Although this small sample in a single city cannot represent all the urban poor in Rio, much less in Brazil, the longitudinal comparisons provide a grassroots view of what has changed in the lives of over 2,000 families in Rio's *favelas*. Subsequent studies have given us no reason to believe that there was anything particularly different in the cases that comprise the study. It is thought provoking to see the changes in this sample and these sample communities as one type of window into the effects of globalization in so far as the original study in 1968–9 pre-dated the current manifestation of globalization in Brazil. It was a time when import substitution still prevailed, the 'economic miracle' was booming, and the military dictatorship was at the height of power. By 2003, when the re-study of the communities was conducted, globalization was all pervasive, free trade was the norm (US and European protectionism notwithstanding), and relative economic stability had been achieved.

The re-study (based on 2,182 new interviews) does not pretend to be representative of the urban poor or of all *favelas* in Rio de Janeiro, much less the city as a whole. The original random sample of 200 residents in each of the three *favelas* in 1968 was selected quite meticulously (Perlman 1976: Appendix) and was representative of the residents in those communities at the time of the study. Likewise, the new random sample of 400 residents, each drawn with painstaking care in the same places in 2003 (Cano 2005), *is* representative of those communities at that time. However, no three *favelas* (regardless of care to select different types) could ever be considered 'typical' of the 752 *favelas* or more now existing in the city of Rio.

The strength of this work lies in its success in finding and following up a large number of original study participants thirty to thirty-five years later, in interviewing their children and grandchildren, and in drawing new samples in the same locations decades later. The depth of the data, its continuity over several decades, and the tracking of life histories over multiple generations is quite unusual. We collected over 6,000 variables for each person and designed the survey instrument to insure that the questions held the same meaning for diverse types of respondents, that probes were included to elicit the specifics of the answers, and that people's words were recorded exactly in the open-ended part of the interviews. This is exactly the opposite of standard economic analysis which relies on a very large sample but is limited in the questions asked and subject to doubt about the precise meaning of the answers.

It is reassuring that our results (Perlman 2006; 2007; and 2008) are corroborated by the much larger studies on inequality in Brazil using census data and household surveys (PNAD) and creating matched cohorts in different years as a proxy for following the same individuals. Recent publications such as the excellent work of Bourguignon, Ferreira, and Menéndez (2003); Gacitúa Marió and Woolcock (2005); and Ferreira, Leite, and Litchfield (2008) support the validity of our findings (and vice versa).

9.5. The Perspective of the Poor

What does globalization look like from the perspective of the poor in Rio de Janeiro? To address this question we asked 'How has globalization affected your life?' This was an open-ended question and the interviewers recorded the answers exactly as spoken. The results reported below are based on the first answers each person gave. The responses did not differ significantly by gender, race, birthplace, current community, or socio-economic status.

The overwhelming finding was that the majority of respondents across all three generations said that globalization had not made any difference. In their words, 'things are the same', 'there wasn't any change', or 'it had no direct effect'.[13] The percentage saying this declined with each generation, from 85 per cent of original interviewees to 59 per cent of the children to 52 per cent of the grandchildren. This coincides with increasing educational levels for each successive generation, but still represented a majority. This result is surprising, given that by the time of the re-study, almost everyone, regardless of generation, reported watching television every day[14] and that so much of the programming and the products adverted were 'made in the USA'.

Among the minority of respondents who reported that globalization did affect their lives, the range of responses covered most of the points in the academic literature. Using the recorded open-ended answers of those who responded positively we found that:

[13] A rising percentage from each generation (from 3 per cent to 22 per cent) said they 'did not know' or refused to answer. All percentages reported are 'valid per cents' after the removal of this group.

[14] As reported, 90 per cent of original interviewees, 98 per cent of their children, and 97 per cent of their grandchildren watched television on a daily basis, as compared with 37 per cent in 1969. This is consistent with the findings in 2003 that 97 per cent of the new random sample in the three study sites having 'watched television daily or almost daily'.

- In every generation the most frequently mentioned impacts of globalization were a tighter labour market, increased unemployment, decline in financial security, lower salaries, and less purchasing power. The percentages giving these responses varied from a low of 6.8 per cent among the original interviewees to a high of 19.7 among their children.
- Among the original interviewees the second most frequent response was 'created economic dependency on other countries' or 'makes us slaves to the global economy'. The percentages were all below 5 per cent of the total sample. Leaders who had experienced the struggles in the 1960s and 1970s and were much more politicized than the random sample and more likely to give such answers.
- Three positive consequences of globalization were mentioned by children and grandchildren: 'improved life in general', 'improved access to information and communication', and 'improved technology, such as cell phones and computers'. Taken together these three answers were given by none of the original study participants, 7 per cent of their children, and 24 per cent of their grandchildren.
- The next most common answer was 'higher requirements for study, knowledge, and certification', which can be seen as positive or negative.
- Only the children and grandchildren mentioned the final factor which was 'facilitated purchase of imported products'.

In follow-up in-depth interviews with the most and least successful individuals from the original sample, we found that those who saw globalization as beneficial often mentioned reduced prices of imported goods, while those who saw it as detrimental made the connection between globalization and cheap imported goods leading to the loss of manufacturing jobs, citing lay-offs, and factory closings. The displaced workers were never told whether their factory was going out of business, relocating to other areas of Brazil, or moving to other countries with cheaper labour and production costs.

When I asked what made work so hard to find these days, one person said, 'the poor don't have a chance' (*o pobre não tem vez*). He added:

> 'Before, there wasn't so much mechanization. Now there are even robots to do the work we used to do and the boss doesn't have to think about anyone. In the Campo Grande garbage dump, which employed lots of people, there is now only one worker, a robot, and a computer. Formerly there were garbage men who threw the trash into the truck. Now there is a machine that scoops it up and dumps it into the truck, so only the driver has a job.'

Others speculated that international competition raised the standards of production and thus the bar on educational and skill requirements for job entry, which helps explain why their educational gains were not sufficient to break into the professional, prestigious, and highest-paid jobs.

Two other considerations that arose in regard to globalization's impact were the consumer culture and the havoc wreaked by the international arms and drugs trades. The ubiquitous television images of the global consumer society created 'new needs'. The youth are especially vulnerable to the constant bombardment of images of status symbols and markers of prestige only attainable (for them) through entering the drug trade.[15] Television advertisements create a pseudo reference group for youngsters who experience relative deprivation in terms of what they see and what they have.[16]

Local non-profit organizations (such as Affro Reggae and Nos do Morro) have tried to reinforce the cultural identity of Afro Brazilians and of *favela* dwellers but, for the most part, the status symbols continue to be international brand-named shirts and trainers along with cars, motorcycles, mobile phones, and pagers. I have seen several young people wearing multiple pagers and mobile phones (that do not work) as prestige signifiers. If the message of the global media is 'you are what you own' then the message of the local setting is that drug lords are the role models.

The extent of violence, and of lethal violence in particular, was the most striking difference in *favela* life in the interim between the two studies. One of every five people we interviewed had lost a family member to homicide. The highest death rates are among male youth (15–24 years old). The violence follows poverty. The death rates in *favelas* are similar to those in the housing projects (conjuntos) and in the peripheral (albeit legal) neighbourhoods where the poor live.

There are constant 'wars' among the three major gangs (the CV—the Red Command; the TC—the Third Command; and the ADA—Friends of Friends) competing over sales territories. Many innocent people are caught in the crossfire in these wars and there is no police presence to bring the killers to justice. On the contrary, the police are considered even more violent than traffickers. They stage periodic raids into the *favelas* to hunt down the dealers, and kill innocent residents and bystanders with impunity, making no distinction between residents and 'bandidos'.

This drug–related violence is inseparable from globalization.

In the mid-1980s, coinciding with the end of the dictatorship and the rise in globalization, Rio de Janeiro became the main South American distributor for cocaine (and, to a lesser extent, marijuana) to European markets via East Africa and to the US markets via Miami and New York.

[15] Young men and women explained to me that they turned down job offers on the basis of calculating how long they would have to work in order to buy 'brand name' clothing or shoes, after deducting their transportation and lunch costs.

[16] Studies have shown that perceived satisfaction is more a function of one's position relative to the reference group than of absolute income or socio-economic status or of one's own upward or downward mobility. The reference group could be created by international images of teenagers on television.

The marijuana trade had been present in Brazil at least since I lived there in the 1960s, but it was a home-grown product and not accompanied by sophisticated weapons and organized networks of gang members. It was the re-routing of the cocaine trade through Rio that created the explosive mixture of cash and crime which has had devastating consequences for life in the *favelas*.[17]

Brazil does not have the proper climate for the cultivation of coca, the raw material used to make cocaine. Coca grows ideally at high altitudes in cool climates. Brazil became involved as a repackaging and distribution hub when the US 'war on drugs' closed down Colombia's borders, creating the need for new routes for distribution. It was a natural option owing to the impossibility of controlling Brazil's vast perimeters and the opportunity of entering the country by land or water. More recently, the jungles of Brazil at the borders with Paraguay, Bolivia, Colombia, and Peru have become the site of processing laboratories for the manufacture of cocaine from the raw coca brought across the borders.

The increased volume of cargo trade due to trade liberalization and globalization makes it even easier to hide material in air or ship freight for import and export. Rio is an ideal port as well as distribution centre. Cargo ships sailing from Rio are checked for drugs and found clean. They then pull out of the harbour and small fishing vessels come out at night and load the precious freight. The same thing happens when boats arrive in Rio. The ships stop and offload the drugs onto islands just beyond the bay—again by fishing boats—and the ships come in for official inspection squeaky clean.

When the shipments enter the city, they come in bulk and require a hiding place for repackaging and distribution. Rio's *favelas* are ideal for this. They have sales points called *bocas de fumo* (mouths of smoke, a name given to them in the time of marijuana) where the rich playboys can come to buy. Their lack of police protection and particular topography discussed above makes them particularly useful. Poor neighbourhoods fulfil particular functions in an extensive and often globalized value chain of production, refinement, manufacturing, warehousing, distribution, and consumption in local, national, and global markets. Around these activities, drug-based gangs exercise near total control of the territories in which they are located, often in collusion with elements in the security forces.

As one of the leaders of a *Favela* explained to me:

> 'The main way that international trade is destroying the lives of Rio's poor is through the vast international market for drugs (particularly cocaine) and the imported supply of sophisticated arms (many from the USA) which the drug traffickers use to intimidate the police and take control of communities and the city.'

[17] For more detail on this, see Dowdney (2003: 25); Leeds (1996: 52–6); Castells (1997); and Naím (2005).

Table 9.1. The reasons for foreign companies to be in Brazil

	1969		2003	
Foreign companies are in Brazil to	Frequency	%	Frequency	%
Help Brazil's progress	188	36.9	253	21.7
Take care of their own interests	191	37.5	522	44.8
Exploit Brazilians	131	25.7	391	33.5
Total	510	100.0	1,166	100.0

His view was that if there were an international embargo on arms sales to Brazil, the violence and death rates would drop dramatically.

9.5.1. The Role of Foreign Investment

Our survey instrument had one other question which sheds light on the changing perception of one aspect of globalization from 1969 to 2003. It asked about perceptions about the role of foreign companies in Brazil. It was an open-ended question on the basis of which we developed three coding categories. The question was: 'Foreign companies are in Brazil in order to (i) help Brazil to progress; (ii) take care of their own interests; or (iii) exploit the Brazilian people.' These options were not read to the interviewees. Their answers were recorded in full and then coded. The valid percentages based on the 85 per cent who answered in 1969 and the 95.5 per cent who responded in 2003 are shown in Table 9.1.

The tendency between 1969 and 2003 was a decline in the percentage of *favela* residents who perceived global investment as positive. This may reflect the increased presence of foreign companies (and difficulties for *favela* residents to get jobs in such companies) but also the overall climate of scepticism about who benefits from international investment. The neutral answer 'take care of their own interests' was given by 45 per cent of the respondents, while over a third saw it as 'exploiting Brazilian labour' (taking advantage of low wages, long hours, and less restrictive health, safety, and environmental regulations). The percentage of those believing that foreign investment creates jobs and attracts capital for economic growth that will eventually help the poor dropped by almost half. Still, one-fifth of the sample saw foreign investment as 'helping Brazil'. Further analysis is needed to explore the income, education, occupation, race, gender, and age of those giving each of these answers.

In short, from the viewpoint of the urban underclass, globalization is mostly seen as irrelevant, and among those who do perceive an impact, only slightly more point out the negative effects than those who see the positive. The expected perception according to the five premises listed above would be that globalization, if not deepening poverty per se, certainly deepened inequality.

Later in the chapter we explore changes in living conditions over the past three decades. This raises a prior question about how any contextual changes—whether at the international, national, or city levels—materially affect the lives of the poor regardless of whether they perceive the effects or not. Are those who fail to see the effects of globalization on their lives reflecting 'false consciousness', naivety, or an accurate assessment of reality?

9.6. Micro Impacts of Macro Changes

One of the major goals of the longitudinal research project was to see if there were reflections in the lives of the poor that coincided with (or appeared after a certain time lag) larger-scale changes in the political economy and public policy. Several approaches were used to explore connections between transformations in the broader context (global, national, and local) and periods of ups and downs in the lives of the urban poor—either as self-reported or measured through indicators in the questionnaire and life-history matrix.

The study traced the chronology of benchmark changes in the economic, political, spatial, and policy contexts for Brazil as a whole and for Rio specifically.[18] To see if these periods coincided with fluctuations in poverty for *favela* residents, we used the year-by-year life-history data to map periods of individual (and collective) upswings and downswings on such variables as unemployment, types of job, educational attainment, number of children, degree of crowding, and location/type of residence.[19]

To triangulate findings we also asked each interviewee to specify the best and worst periods of their lives in terms economic well-being: employment (their own and contributing members of the household) and assets and overall financial security. We then plotted the timing of these periods against the opening of trade, the booms and busts of the Brazilian economy, and major policy changes—and against the poverty variations as indicated by the life-history data. No clear pattern emerged.

The absence of overall correspondence between macro-level changes and micro-level repercussions might be attributable to the interviewees' lack of recall or cognitive disconnect between larger trends and family fates, to

[18] We looked at starting periods and lag periods of place-targeted programmes (such as on-site upgrading focused on the territory of *favelas*, clandestine lots, or public housing), poverty targeted programmes (such as the early conditional cash transfers, based on poverty measures regardless of place of residence), and universal programmes (such as changes in the minimum wage or access to credit that applied to all citizens but would affect the people in our sample directly).

[19] Income was not included as a variable in the life-history matrix, as prior studies have shown lack of recall, reliability, and validity.

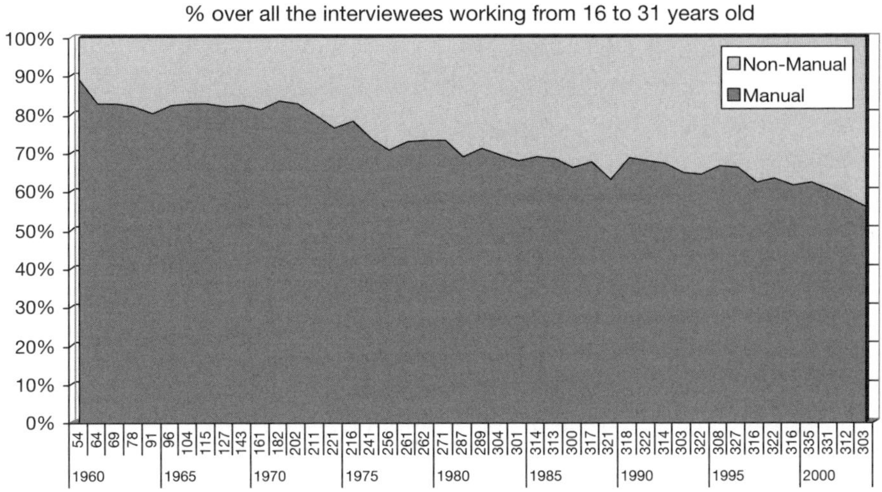

Fig. 9.1. Occupation, non-manual versus manual jobs, 1960–2003

Source: Random Sample 2003 Survey, Phase III.

methodological flaws, and/or to the overwhelming number of intervening variables. We did, however, find two clear reflections of structural or policy changes.

The first was in patterns of insertion in the labour force. Our life-history data on occupational status indicated for each year whether each person was working or not; if not working, whether they were looking for work; if so, were they working formally, self-employed (had a commercial establishment/their own business), or doing odd jobs (*biscates*) on an irregular basis. The division between manual or non-manual labour was the indicator that revealed the most consistent picture over time.

Controlling for age and life-cycle stage by using the same age cohort (16- to 31-year-olds) for each calendar year, we plotted the changes (for those working) between manual and non-manual for each year. The resulting graph is shown in Figure 9.1.[20] The tendency from 1960 to 2003 revealed a progressive transition from manual to non-manual occupations.

The marked decline in the percentage of working-age *favelados* doing manual labour and the concomitant rise in non-manual labour do reflect structural

[20] In each year the sample is composed of different people. As the years progress from 1960 to 2003, new individuals enter the sample when they reach 16 years of age and others leave the sample once they turn 32. When the number of subjects for any year became fewer than fifty we discontinued the sequence. We used the Life History Matrices starting with the current year and tracing each change in occupational status from 2003 back to their first job at or after 16 years of age.

changes in the job market in Rio de Janeiro which, in turn, is affected by national and possibly international labour market trends. These shifts undoubtedly reflect the stage of advanced capitalism and the globalization of labour, capital, information, and technology.

The second clear pattern emerged from the qualitative interviews. As a result of the Real Plan, tying the national currency to the US$ so as to curb inflation and increase global competitiveness, there was a consumption bonanza among the urban poor as their purchasing power rose while incomes stayed the same. While many respondents did not know the name of the Real Plan, or the exact year, many spoke of this one-time opportunity to acquire consumer durables at deflated prices. Family after family in each of the low-income communities proudly showed off heavy wooden furniture, large television and sound systems, washer/driers, and air conditioners saying, 'if we had not bought this, then we would never have been able to afford it again'.

Despite these two suggestive findings it was difficult to detect systematic reflections of macro changes on poverty fluctuations in the *favelas*. The proximate events of personal and family crises such as illness, death, marriage, divorce, births, and job loss, of natural disasters such as floods and fires, or of community-related events, such as community eradication and resettlement in the 1970s, the closing of a nearby factory, school, or clinic, or the drug wars between competing gangs or the gangs and the police, completely obliterated the effects of more distal patterns. The uncertainties of daily life for people on the margins are so huge that they can hardly cope on a moment-to-moment basis and there is no safety net to help them to bounce back from crises.

The question once again is: are the findings reported above on the perceived lack of effect of globalization and the absence of strong co-variation between macro and micro events due to denial, inadequate poverty measures, an over-abundance of intervening variables—or do they convey an accurate portrait of reality? The next section adds to the evidence of this by comparing conditions of life in the same *favela* communities at two points in time.

9.7. Community Level Comparisons over Time

Looking at the community as the unit of analysis permits comparisons of the random samples of the same *favelas* in isolationist 1969 and globally integrated 2003 to explore the nature of change in those thirty-four years and whether the perceptions and chronological disconnects discussed above are borne out by other indicators of advances and setbacks.

The answer to the question 'did life get better or worse for those in these *favela* communities?' depends on what dimensions of life you consider. It is a bit like the proverbial blind men and the elephant. If you look at indicators of individual and collective consumption or educational levels, you would conclude that there have been striking improvements. If you look at unemployment or violence, you would conclude that life is much worse now. What balance sheet can weigh gains in physical comforts and educational attainment against lack of work and constant fear of being caught in the crossfire between drug gangs and police?

Starting with improvements, we found that the level of individual goods, household appliances, and urban services has risen dramatically. The average *favela* household in these older *favelas* studied[21] now enjoys amenities formerly available only to the elite, such as washing machines, microwave ovens, and air conditioners. The mobile phone is ubiquitous and has made an enormous difference in people's ability to get jobs and offer services (as well as run the drug traffic). Urban services, such as running water in the home, closed sewer pipes (separate from open drainage ditches), rubbish collection, paving of access roads and passageways, and metered electricity are almost universal, improving health and liberating women from many time-consuming backbreaking daily tasks. When the electricity company Light was privatized, it included *favela* residents as a profitable new market and lowered their costs as compared with the prior illegal connections controlled by a clique within the community.

Housing also improved noticeably. The incremental upgrading of the dwellings has visually transformed the landscape of the *favela* communities. The precarious shacks of wattle and daub (dried mud packed into a latticework of branches or boards), wood, and other scavenged materials have been replaced by solid multi-storey structures. In 1969, less than half (46 per cent) of the dwellings were made of *alvenaria* (bricks or cinder blocks); by 2003, nearly all (97.7 per cent) were constructed with these durable materials. Aerial views reveal densely packed two- to four-storey homes, many with an open area on the top floor for drying laundry, flying kites, catching a cool breeze, and attaching the satellite dish.

At the individual level, the major gain was a near doubling of the average years of education. In 1969, 42 per cent of the sample had never attended school; in 2003, it had dropped to 4 per cent. Those completing elementary school rose from 14.4 per cent to 83.6 per cent over that same period, and those who had some secondary schooling rose from none to nearly a third. Some 6 per cent had even started university: something unimaginable three decades earlier.

One downside to the story is that these educational gains have not been fully reflected in jobs or income. In fact, the income gap between *favelados* and

[21] This is not necessarily true for the newer *favelas* which are much poorer and more similar to the condition of our study sites in the late 1960s. Many lack the amenities and services enjoyed by the 'consolidated *favelas*', the ones that have existed since the 1960s or before.

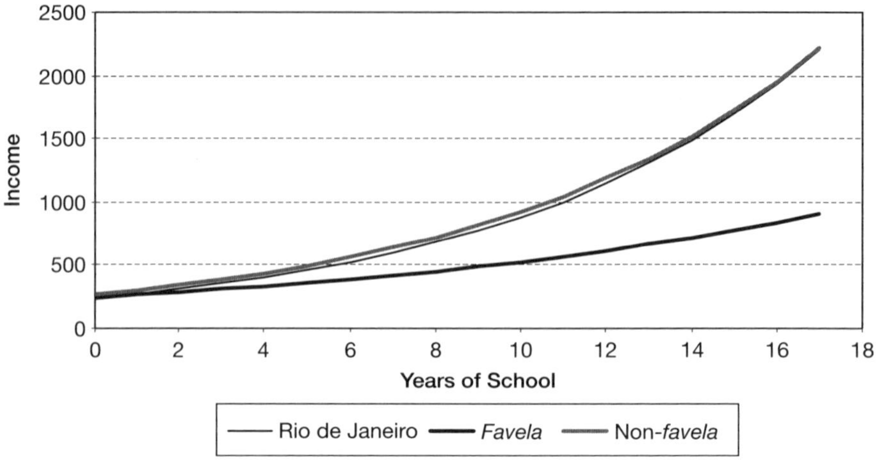

Fig. 9.2. Lower-income returns to education for the *favelados*

Source: Compiled by Valeria Pero from the 2000 Census.

non-*favelados* increased with each additional year of schooling after the first four, as shown in Figure 9.2.

This increasing gap probably reflects differing levels of quality in education, differing social and cultural environments in *favelas* versus neighbourhoods, and discrimination against people from *favelas* in the job market. The lower than expected return to education, even controlling for race and gender (Pero 2003; 2004), explains why many *favelados* became disillusioned with education. This showed up in their responses to the query about 'what is the most important factor for a successful life'. Whereas in the earlier study the vast majority responded that education was most important, in the re-study, the majority across generations said 'a good job' (79 per cent of original interviewees and 96 per cent of their children). Those I spoke to explained that they would be happy with either employment (*emprego*) in the formal sector or independent work (*trabalho*) as long as they had a chance to do decent work with decent pay.

Occupational achievements also lag behind educational advances. Following individual families enabled us to do a case-by-case analysis, comparing each person with his or her own parents. While 75 per cent of the children had more education than their parents, only 66 per cent had better jobs. In part this reflects the fact that educational requirements for the same jobs had also been rising. A higher educational bar to employment also contributes to the higher unemployment rates for each succeeding generation despite greater educational attainment. Between the first study and the re-study, the proportion of our sample that reported being unemployed—or *parado* (literally, stopped)—for more than six consecutive months at any point in their working lives rose from 32 per cent to 51 per cent. The average unemployment rate in the city of Rio was 10 per cent at the time of the re-study.

Indeed, it is harder to find any work now than it was during the Brazilian economic miracle of the late 1960s. The entry requirement for most jobs has risen faster than educational attainment. Changing job markets were linked to external forces, but the particular problems of Rio de Janeiro also combined with the stigma of living in a *favela* to reduce employment opportunities. Many people reported that their job interviews had ended once they gave an address which indicated that they lived in a *favela*. Our sample ranked 'living in a *favela*' a greater obstacle to employment and a greater source of discrimination than race, gender, place of birth, or overall appearance.

9.8. The Inequality Issue

Did the gap between *favelas* and other Rio residents narrow or widen? Looking at the balance sheet of gains and losses for the urban poor does not address the issue of inequality. Meaningful interpretation is contextually dependent on comparisons with the urban population as a whole. In order to narrow the inequality gap, gains for the *favela* population would have to exceed gains of the non-*favela* population. If the trends of globalization are applicable at the city level, the gap is predicted to become even greater.

To test this we compared our data from the 1969 sample with the census data from 1970, and the data from our 2003 sample with census data from 2000. To get an overall measure of convergence or divergence, we constructed an index of socio-economic status (SES) matching the variables used by the census—education, household goods, and density.[22]

The results indicate that the mean SES score of our communities was and still is lower than that of the city, but that the gap was reduced. There was significant upward mobility of *favela* residents in our three study communities relative to the population of Rio as a whole. The *favelas*, although they remain stigmatized spaces, did not reflect the chronic poverty discussed in the literature of the Chronic Poverty Research Group in Manchester (Green and Hulme 2005;

[22] Our SES index is composed of education, consumption, and density (people per room). To compare this with the census, an index of SES for the whole population of the municipality in the 2000 census was created by applying a principal components analysis to: (i) years of schooling; (ii) number of people per room; and (iii) number of domestic items to which they had access (from 0 to 9). The first factor (i.e., the SES score) explained 61.2 per cent of the total variance. We introduced the average of our three communities into the factor equation and obtained a factor score for these communities. The resulting score was −0.437 standard deviations below the mean of the general population of the municipality. Our results remained remarkably close to those obtained through the individual income index.

Moore 2005), nor did they follow the patterns of advanced marginality described by Wacquant for Chicago ghettos and French *banlieues* (Wacquant 1996). Instead, there was a gradual improvement in living conditions in the older *favelas* vis-à-vis the city at large, while more recent migrants, who are settling in newly formed *favelas* (or clandestine subdivisions) in the West Zone, filled in the lower ranks of poverty.

When we compared the 1969 random sample with the 1970 Rio census, using the same composite SES index in both cases, our sample scored between the 10th and 11th percentile from the bottom. When we repeated this comparison using our 2003 random sample and the 2000 Rio census in the same communities, the position of the *favelas* had risen to between the 26th and the 27th percentile. This is not to say they have reached the mean or median—but it does indicate that the gap is closing and that a quarter of Rio's population today lives in deeper poverty than those living in the *favelas* of our original study.[23] Those who live in our communities today are more likely to be Rio-born and the Rio-born tend to have higher SES than migrants.[24] The hope of a better life in the big city seems to have been fulfilled, both then and now: 83 per cent of migrants in the original 1969 study said they were better off than those who stayed behind, and 76 per cent of migrants in the 2003 sample said the same.

Separating out educational level comparisons shows that schooling attained by our study population is still lower than that of Rio's general population, but the gap has diminished since the first study. In 1969, the average schooling for our sample was 2.1 years as compared with 6.1 for Rio's population. In 2003, the average number of years of schooling of our sample rose to 7.3 while Rio's rose to 8.8, narrowing the difference from four years to a year and a half.[25]

Table 9.2 shows the general structural gains in education Rio-wide as well as the shrinking gap over time between our samples and the rest of Rio's population. The highlighted areas are those where the comparisons are most starkly seen. In 1969–70, 42 per cent of the *favela* sample had *no* education at all compared with only 11 per cent in the overall Rio census. In 2000–3, the entire bar has shifted upward, with almost everyone having attended school and very

[23] The growth of new *favelas* has been primarily in the West Zone, which was sparsely settled grazing land in the late 1960s. The new *favelas* followed the expansion of the upscale areas into the Barra de Tijuca, leading to a 108 per cent growth in the population of West Zone *favelas* (1980 and 1992) compared with 21 per cent growth in the South Zone *favelas*, 14 per cent in the North Zone, and 8 per cent in the centre.

[24] In 1969, 43.7 per cent of our sample was born in Rio state, and in 2003 this was 71.5 per cent. In both cases those born in Rio had significantly higher SES than migrants.

[25] One caveat is that while the 2003 data on SES used only the *favela* territories originally designated in 1969, the data on school, domestic goods, and incomes included random samples of the public housing projects where residents of the best located *favela* had been resettled after the forced removal of their community in 1970. This might inflate the numbers somewhat as not all of those in the housings projects were from that single *favela*, but the trend is strong enough that even discounting for this potential bias the gap is clearly closing.

Table 9.2. Ownership of domestic goods (as percentage)

	1969 Sample	1970 Census	2003 Sample	2000 Census
TV	26	70	97	99
Refrigerator	31	73	97	98
Radio	75	84	94	97
Washing machine			60	65
Air conditioner			35	38
Video viewer			57	71
Microwave			23	37
Computer			15	26
Car or truck	1	19	18	42

close to a third of the *favela* sample and census having entered or completed high school (30 per cent of our sample versus 34 per cent of the 2000 census). It gives cause for hope that 6 per cent of our sample had reached university—despite the fact that it was three times as high for urban residents in general.

This same narrowing of the gap between the population of the consolidated *favelas* and the rest of the city shows up in household crowding or density as well. In 1969, the average number of people per room in our sample was 1.96, which was almost double as compared with nearly 1.10 in the city. By 2003, the density in the study communities had dropped to 0.84 per room, while the city density dropped to 0.76—not eliminating, but clearly reducing the gap.

This convergence is especially apparent in the consumption of domestic goods. By 2003, many *favela* households owned appliances only available to the upper classes if at all in earlier times. New 'created needs' converted televisions, refrigerators, washing machines, air conditioners, and video players into 'basic household goods' in *favelas*. The only notable differences in ownership between our 2003 random sample and the city as a whole were microwave ovens, cars, and computers (as shown in Table 9.1). Two factors help explain the high rates of consumption relative to income: more disposable income due to low or no housing costs or property taxes and the quest for status through possessions. Regardless of household income, a *favela* family cannot buy legitimacy or title to their land (even if they have been living there for several generations), so they upgrade their houses and buy household goods and personal consumer items.

This high rate of consumption and convergence towards the norm was not what was expected from the literature on the poverty trap. Even looking at those consumer categories where a relatively large gap exists, it is impressive that 23 per cent of our households have a microwave oven, 18 per cent a motor vehicle, and 15 per cent a computer. The households with computers would probably have entered the global information society through the World Wide

Web. However, I found that only a fraction of those who own computers can connect to the Internet since this requires a landline telephone, uncommon in *favela* communities. A father who proudly told me that he gave a desktop computer to his daughter for her fifteenth birthday specifically said he did not want her on the Internet and did not want her to send or receive emails.

Nonetheless, Internet access is easily available (a direct result of globalization). Most of the residents' associations in *favelas* now have several computers online (sometimes twenty-four hours a day) and usually a group of people waiting to use them. One non-profit organization had arranged for the donations of these computers and their link-ups and for free training for *favela* residents. Other non-profits offer computer access to community residents at their headquarter offices around the city. Online work strikes me as great opportunity for avoiding stigma, as the worker cannot be traced to a geographic location anymore than a call from a mobile phone can be traced to a luxury apartment or a *favela* association.

The inequality reduction reflects the cumulative benefits of urban life for that segment of the population living in the older, more consolidated *favelas* and is confirmed by self-reported life improvements. In both 1969 and 2003, interviewees assessed trends in Brazil more negatively than in their own lives. A small majority of the 1969 interviewees said that life in Brazil had improved over the past five years (probably affected by the 'economic miracle' and the shift from rural to urban life) and a small majority in 2003 said Brazil had got worse (likely owing to drugs, violence, and corruption), but when it came to their own lives, national trends seemed irrelevant: 74 per cent in both time periods judged their lives as better than five years ago. Optimism about their future was even higher: 92 per cent in 2003 and 81 per cent in 1969 said they thought their lives would be better in the next five years.

In the 2001 intergenerational interviews, 61 per cent across all three generations rated their lives as better than in the past (the past thirty years for original interviewees and the past ten years for the children and grandchildren). The original interviewees saw their lives as better than that of their parents (53 per cent), but only 44 per cent thought that their children's lives were (or would be) better than their own. The children's assessments were even more negative: only 35 per cent of children and only 23 per cent of grandchildren believed that their lives would be better than their parents. I would tend to attribute this negative assessment to the rising levels of violence.

9.9. The Fear Factor: Drugs, Arms, and Violence

Without a doubt, the most dramatic and destructive change in life for *favelas* has been the arrival of the drug and arms traffic into the communities. The earlier fear of *favela* eradication has been replaced by fear of dying in crossfire between rival drug gangs or during police raids. The mortality rate is intensified by sophisticated, largely imported arms, which might be termed 'weapons of mass destruction' since the levels of fatal violence now rival those of a city in the midst of a civil war (Cano 2004).[26]

When not one faction is dominant, the wars over contested turf (sales points called *bocas*) are the most prolonged and violent, with gang members from other *favelas* often joining the fight. Millions of dollars are at stake. When the police come into the *favela* in what is locally called a '*blitz*' no one is safe, not even in the privacy of one's own bedroom. The police open fire indiscriminately, not giving much value to the lost life of a 'marginal'. Residents report feeling 'trapped between the dealers and the police'. They say both have harmed them more than helped, negating the idea that the 'traffic' is a 'parallel power' providing services, financing, and protection ordinarily the providence of the state.

According to reconstructed community histories that groups of residents in each *favela* collectively developed during an all-day workshop, the starting-point of drug traffic as a menace to daily life was in the mid-1980s. They recall the unspoken deal between the then governor and the police that as long as security was maintained in the rest of the city, they were not responsible for what happened inside the *favelas*. This coincided with the crackdown by the United States on the Columbian borders and the consequent re-routing of cocaine through Brazil to external markets in Europe and the USA.

In the 2001 interviews we asked each person: 'Have you, or a family member, ever been a victim of violent crime?' One of every five people interviewed had lost a family member to homicide. Those who managed to move out of the *favelas* to modest areas on the far fringes of the city in attempt to escape the violence were followed by the drug traffic operations within a year or two. The public housing projects that house those forcibly evicted from *favelas* in the early 1970s are equally plagued by the gang wars.

The police are complicitous. They confiscate drugs and weapons from one group and sell them to another. The judiciary does not hold police accountable and there is no rule of law that the poor can turn to in the face of injustice. The highly organized gangs, with more sophisticated weapons than the police and ample funds for bribes, have demonstrated their power by shutting down government and commerce in Rio and most of São Paulo, most recently by a drug kingpin from within prison.[27] Governors are reluctant to call in federal troops to control widespread chaos in the streets as they fear it will jeopardize their future aspirations for presidency by appearing weak. The state has lost control of governance.

[26] The homicide rate for young males is higher in Rio than in Colombia (268 per 100,000 in Rio and 213 per 100,000 in Colombia).

[27] Sometimes drug lords prefer to command their operations from prison where they are protected from rival gang members as they conduct their business.

At the start of the re-study in 2000, about half the *favelas* in Rio still had independent residents' associations with popularly elected presidents. One by one the local leaders were driven out or killed, and by 2005 almost all the residents' associations were controlled by drug traffickers, resulting in the loss of collective voice and bargaining power these independent associations had provided.[28] Now the dealers also control entrance and exit from the community, functioning or closing of schools, clinics, commerce, and social programmes, and, most recently, the distribution of the large propane cylinders used for cooking.[29]

The all-pervasive fear in the *favelas* has deprived them of their greatest assets. It has depressed the sale or rental value of homes, forced many local shops and restaurants to close, discouraged new investments in the area, and scared away service providers—teachers, healthcare workers, non-profit organizations—and commercial deliveries. Worse still, it has destroyed the social capital essential for conviviality and coping. Local residents have become afraid to leave their homes after dark, stopped inviting friends and relatives to visit, limited participation in community-based organizations (except evangelical churches), and stopped congregating in public spaces. This showed up in our study as a marked decline of trust in one's neighbours and in the previously strong sense of community unity.[30]

In these ways life is much worse than it was in the earlier years when everyone was free to come and go and to enjoy community activities. People are living under constant stress, unable to sleep through the sound of gunshots, and terrified that their children will be shot while playing on the front step or returning from school. This 'state of siege' atmosphere takes its toll on the mental and physical heath of the residents.

9.10. Implications and Considerations

9.10.1. Summary

The case study of the urban poor in Rio de Janeiro has shown evidence of positive and negative patterns coexisting in the lives of *favela* residents between

[28] The one exception, Rio das Pedras, is drug-free but is controlled by matadores—death squads made up of retired or active police who use their own power to keep drug dealers out. Anyone selling or buying is killed on sight.

[29] As the price of cocaine has recently dropped, the drug dealers are making up the difference by charging fees to residents for permission to deliver cooking gas canisters (propane cylinders).

[30] In 1969, 85 per cent of the original interviewees said their communities were 'united or very united'. By 2001, this had dropped to 51 per cent of the original interviewees, 45 per cent of children, and 42 per cent of grandchildren. The frequency of socializing with friends and neighbours and the degree of trust in neighbours had plunged. In 1969, 51 per cent reported that they could count on 'most or all' of their neighbours, but by 2001 only 31 per cent to 35 per cent said they could—the same was reported among all three generations.

the pre-globalization era and the current globally integrated era. Conditions have improved rather than deteriorated in many areas, but not all. The *favela* communities have become physically more integrated into the urban fabric as the city has expanded around them and transportation improvements have shortened commuting time. Infrastructure, services, domestic goods, and educational levels have improved. Although unemployment rates have risen, for those who are working, they are more likely to be in 'routine non-manual' jobs, considered more respectable than construction work or domestic service, although the pay is often lower and the hours longer.

The gap in living conditions between the study sites and the rest of the city has narrowed not widened on several quality-of-life indicators. This apparent 'catching up' of the informal city with the formal cities appears to contradict the logic of globalization—that the poor become poorer, wealth concentrates upward, and inequality increases. Nonetheless, we cannot infer the opposite causal relationship by imputing the gains of the urban poor to the globalization process. There are many missing links in the chain. The new migrants, who are now the poorest, do not share in the urban amenities accrued over forty years (or more) of urban life and are now living in the same conditions of poverty that was found in the study sites in the late 1960s. It is now widely known that life in a big city offers more economic, political, and social opportunities than in the rural areas. It is also widely known that birth rates drop with urbanization, that education and occupational levels rise, that greater opportunities for 'bridging networks' (diverse contacts) are available, and that the longer the urban exposure the greater the advantages (Granovetter 1973). Thus, with or without globalization, it would be expected that there would be gains in living standards across time and generations.

On the other hand, the negative changes observed over time are equally dramatic. Unemployment rose, income gains did not fully reflect educational advances, and only a handful entered professional jobs or moved into desirable neighbourhoods. The cumulative improvements were not sufficient to make the *favela* residents feel accepted as part of the urban citizenry. The barriers to improved livelihoods/upward mobility included:

(i) *economic obstacles*, such as labour market conditions, extreme inequality, and stigma as an impediment to being hired;

(ii) *political obstacles*, such as less bargaining power, lack of state accountability or protection under the rule of law (symptoms of cronyism and corruption that militate against fair play); and

(iii) *social obstacles*, including deepening exclusion, reduced social capital, and the high toll of living in a state of fear of violence.

This suggests that even as progress is being made at the material and educational levels, the goal of breaking out of poverty to become *gente* (a respectable person) is a moving target that is always out of reach.[31] Even significant educational and economic achievements are not sufficient to erase the lingering marginalization, exclusion, and stigma associated with 'urban informality' (Roy and Al Sayyad 2004).

9.10.2. Effects of Globalization

The majority of *favela* residents who said that globalization did not make a difference in their lives may have made an important point. There are many intervening variables at the national, state, local, and community levels that have a more proximate and direct impact on the lives of the poor than international trade agreements. Local level differences such as proximity to upscale neighbourhoods and job markets, levels of violence and security, access to government or NGO programmes, good schools, health clinics, recreational facilities, computer and arts mentors, and the relationships of the ruling drug faction with the political party in power, all have immediate and long-term effects. Any unexpected crisis affects the marginalized population disproportionately as they have no safety net to fall back on. Anything from a flood or fire to a factory closing, to prolonged illness or death of the principal breadwinner, can consume the savings of a lifetime, and leave an entire family destitute, globalization or not.

Structural improvements in the city over time would be expected. It is a big leap to say that these are the effects of globalization. The challenge I have proposed throughout the chapter is whether it is possible to pinpoint which of the improvements and degradations in the lives of the poor might still have occurred in the relative absence of globalizing influence, if Brazil had continued with import substitution and perhaps invested in human capital and technological innovation instead of servicing a large international debt and focusing on international investment ratings.[32]

The mixed findings in the Rio case do not prove that the premises laid out at the beginning of the chapter are wrong overall. It is thought-provoking that not all the results from this study conform to their underlying assumptions but do not close the question. In fact, the intent and value of the study is to go beyond the facile positions and ideological platitudes often surrounding the globalization debate and raise questions for further research. Similar research conducted in

[31] For more on the elusive attainment of becoming *gente*, see Perlman (2008).

[32] Maricato (2006) observes that in Brazil the finance ministry had become so powerful during the past several administrations that the ministry of cities programmes, already approved and funded by international donors the Inter-American Development Bank, was held up for years because of creditworthiness and political power plays. In the Fernando Henrique Cardoso, as well as the Lula, administrations, many social programmes were not funded or were underfunded in order to service debts and keep the IMF happy.

major world cities, especially those in India, China, and South Africa, would provide much needed points of comparison.

Perhaps we need to distinguish between national, regional, and international inequalities on one hand and local or urban inequalities on the other. At the more global level, issues such as the relegation of Sub-Saharan Africa to inconsequential would be confronted while, at the local level, issues of the divide between Ralph Ellison's *Invisible Man* (1953) and Tom Wolfe's 'master of the universe' (1987) would be faced. Current proposals to tax profits on international trade and redistribution of the surplus to poor regions or nations, or compensation to displaced workers (presumably in developed countries) for salary differentials will not reach the slums of Asia, Africa, or Latin America. They are too distant to trickle down and too many hands will take their piece of the pie before any poor person benefits.

Unless nation states and cities make a new social contract with the poor who service their needs, build their cities and homes, and produce/consume their products, the pattern of stunted development, missed opportunities, wasteful resource use, and mismanaged governance (i.e., non-sustainability) will be self-replication and self-fulfilling. No country or city can afford to neglect/ignore the intellectual capital, creative potential, productive capacity, or purchasing power of 30 per cent to 40 per cent of its population, the average portion of urban population currently living in slums.

There is no level playing field on the pathway towards respect. To create conditions for inclusion or advancement on the basis of merit and effort, the entire social contract condoning extreme inequality will have to be re-examined and confronted. Inequality is the fundamental impediment to upward mobility, economic growth, poverty alleviation, and reduction of violence. What is needed is a direct challenge to the comfortable culture of privilege that perpetuates itself at the expense of the common good.

References

Associated Press (2007) United Nations Press Release, 8 Feb. 2007.

Blofield, M. (2007) 'Proposal for the Observatory on Inequality in Latin America'. Miami: Center for Latin American Studies, University of Miami. mimeo.

Bourguignon, F., F. H. G. Ferreira, and M. Menéndez (2003) 'Inequality of Outcomes and Inequality of Opportunities in Brazil'. Policy Research Working Paper 3174. Washington, DC: World Bank.

——(2007) 'Inequality of Opportunity in Brazil', *Review of Income and Wealth*, 53: 585–618.

Cano, I. (2004) 'O Impacto da Violência em Rio de Janeiro'. Working Paper. Rio de Janeiro: Universidade do Estado do Rio de Janeiro.

——(2005) 'Phase III Report for Rio: Re-Study'. Rio de Janeiro.

Castells, M. (1977) *The Urban Question: A Marxist Approach* (trans. Alan Sheridan). London: Edward Arnold.
——(2000) *The Rise of the Network Society, the Information Age: Economy, Society and Culture*, i, 2nd edn. Oxford: Blackwell.
Chanda, N. (2007) *Bound Together: How Traders, Preachers, Adventurers, and Warriors Shaped Globalization*. New Haven, Conn.: Yale University Press.
Collier, P. (2007) *The Bottom Billion: Why the Poorest Countries are Failing and What Can Be Done about It*. Oxford: Oxford University Press.
Dowdney, L. (2003) *Crianças do Tráfico: Um Estudo de Caso de Crianças em Violência Armada Organizada no Rio de Janeiro*. Rio de Janeiro: 7 Letras.
Ellison, R. (1953) *Invisible Man*. New York: Random House.
Ferreira, F. H. G., C. E. Velez, and R. Paes de Barros (eds) (2004) *Inequality and Economic Development in Brazil*. World Bank Country Study. Washington, DC: World Bank.
——P. G. Leite, and J. A. Litchfield (2008) 'The Rise and Fall of Brazilian Inequality, 1981–2004', *Macroeconomic Dynamics*, 12: 199–230.
Fiori, J. L. (1995) *Em Busca do Dissenso Perdido*. Rio de Janeiro: INsight Editorial.
Friedmann, J. (1986) 'The World City Hypothesis', *Development and Change*, 18: 69–84.
——(1995) 'Where We Stand: A Decade of World City Research'. In P. Knox and P. J. Taylor (eds), *World Cities in a World System*. Cambridge: Cambridge University Press.
Furtado, C. (1964) *Dialética do Desenvolvimento*. Rio de Janeiro: Fundo de Cultura.
——(1982) *A Nova Dependência, Dívida Externa e Monetarismo*. Rio de Janeiro: Paz e Terra.
Gacitúa Marió, E., and M. Woolcock (eds) (2005) *Mobilidade Social no Brasil*. Brasilia: Instituto de Pesquisa Econômica Aplicada (IPEA)/World Bank.
Granovetter, M. (1973) 'The Strength of Weak Ties', *American Journal of Sociology*, 78: 1360–80.
Green, M., and D. Hulme (2005) 'From Correlates and Characteristics to Causes: Thinking about Poverty in a Chronic Poverty Perspective', *World Development*, 33: 867–97.
Harvey, D. (2003) *The New Imperialism*. New York: Oxford University Press.
Instituto Perreira Passos (IPP) [Urban Planning Division of Rio Municipal Government] (2005) '*Favelas* in Rio: Data and Changes'. Presentation by Sergio Besserman. Rio de Janeiro.
Krugman, P. (2007) 'Divided Over Trade'. *New York Times*, 14 May 2007.
Leeds, E. (1996) 'Cocaine and Parallel Polities in the Brazilian Urban Periphery: Constraints on Local-level Democratization', *Latin American Research Review*, 31: 47–83.
Leipziger, D., and M. Spence (2007) 'Globalization's Losers Need Support', *Financial Times*, 15 May 2007.
Maricato, E. (2006) 'Globalization and Urban Policy on the Periphery of Capitalism'. Working Paper: São Paulo: University of São Paulo.
Moore, K. (2005) 'Thinking about Youth Poverty through the Lenses of Chronic Poverty, Life-Course Poverty and Intergenerational Poverty'. Working Paper 57. Manchester: University of Manchester, Chronic Poverty Research Centre.
Naím, M. (2005) *Illicit: How Smugglers, Traffickers and Copycats are Hijacking the Global Economy*. New York: Doubleday.
Nissanke, M., and Thorbecke, E. (2005) 'Channels and Policy Debate in the Globalization–Inequality–Poverty Nexus'. Discussion Paper 2005/08. Helsinki: UNU-WIDER.

———(2006) 'A Quest for Pro-poor Globalization'. Research Paper 2006/46. Helsinki: UNU-WIDER.
———(2007) 'Linking Globalization to Poverty'. Policy Brief 2. Tokyo: United Nations University.
Perlman, J. E. (1976) *The Myth of Marginality: Urban Poverty and Politics in Rio de Janeiro*. Berkeley, Calif.: University of California Press.
——(2003) 'Longitudinal Research Methodologies in Rio de Janeiro's *Favelas*'. In C. Moser (ed.), 'Urban Longitudinal Research Methodology'. Working Paper 124. London: University College, Development Planning Unit.
——(2006) 'The Metamorphosis of Marginality: Four Generations in the *Favelas* of Rio de Janeiro'. *ANNALS of the American Academy of Political and Social Science*, 606: 154–77.
——(2007) 'Elusive Pathways Out of Poverty: Intra- and Intergenerational Mobility in the *Favelas* of Rio de Janeiro'. In D. Narayan and P. Petesch (eds), *Moving out of Poverty: Cross-disciplinary Perspectives on Mobility*. Washington, DC: Palgrave Macmillan and the World Bank.
——(2008) *Favela: The Dynamics of Urban Poverty in Rio de Janeiro, 1968–2005*. New York: Oxford University Press.
Pero, V. (2003) 'Mobilidade Social no Rio de Janeiro'. Rio de Janeiro: Federal University, Instituto de Economia. mimeo.
——(2004) 'Mobility out of the *Favela*: Features and Determining Factors'. Commissioned Report to the Mega-Cities Rio Re-Study Project, Rio de Janeiro.
Roy, A., and N. Al Sayyad (eds) (2004) *Urban Informality in an Era of Liberalization: A Transnational Perspective*. Lanham, Md.: Lexington Books.
Sachs, W. (1992) *The Development Dictionary: A Guide to Knowledge as Power*. London: Zed Books.
Scheve, K., and M. Slaughter (2007) 'A New Deal for Globalization', *Foreign Affairs*, 86: 34–49.
Somers, L. (2006) *Financial Times*, 30 Oct. 2006.
Stiglitz, J. (2006) 'Interview', *US News and World Report*, 18 Sept. 2006.
Wacquant, L. (1996) 'The Rise of Advanced Marginality: Notes on its Nature and Implications', *Acta Sociológica*, 39: 121–39.
——(1999) 'Urban Marginality in the Coming Millennium', *Urban Studies*, 36: 1639–47.
Wolfe, T. (1987) *Bonfire of the Vanities*. New York: Farrar, Straus and Giroux.
Yaqub, S. (1999) 'Born Poor, Stay Poor? A Literature Review'. Technical Report. Brighton: University of Sussex, Institute of Development Studies.

10

Globalization, Crop Choice, and Property Rights in Rural Peru, 1994–2004

Alfred J. Field and Erica Field[1]

10.1. Introduction

Global integration of the world economy in many dimensions has been taking place at a noteworthy pace for the past two decades. The policy changes that have accompanied and facilitated the increased flows of goods, services, and resources have impacted economies at both the micro and macro levels. Investment and technology flows along with changes in relative prices both within and between sectors have resulted in changes in production structures and changes in the relative demand for factor inputs and accompanying factor payments. Any time that changes such as these take place at such rapid rates in a relatively short period of time, there are winners and losers. In terms of the international trade aspect, changes in prices of import goods resulting from a decrease in protection directly benefit the consumers of those goods and indirectly those who consume goods that use imported inputs in their production. At the same time, factors used relatively intensively in import competitive industries tend to suffer with the fall in domestic prices as the trade policy price distortions are removed. On the positive side, trade liberalization which leads to an expansion of exports clearly has a positive effect on the owners of the factors of production used relatively intensively in its production. To the extent that factors lack internal mobility, these effects are clearly enhanced. Thus, while it is often suggested that less restricted world trade should lead to an increase in demand for unskilled labour and hence income and

[1] We are grateful to Lauren Raymer and Jorge de la Roca for dedicated research assistance and to Dennis Appleyard, Patrick Conway, Karen Macours, and the UNU-WIDER project conference participants for helpful comments and suggestions.

perhaps wages in the developing world, there is legitimate concern that poor and unskilled labour is, in fact, being made worse off, both relatively and absolutely.

A significant body of literature already exists on the many links between globalization and poverty. It has been effectively summarized in the recent surveys by Harrison (2005) and Winters, McCulloch, and Mckay (2004). In addition, the recent work by Bardhan (2005; 2006), which provides an overview on the links between globalization and rural poverty, lays out the many direct and indirect ways that reducing barriers to international transactions and domestic market imperfections can influence rural output, productivity, and poverty through various consumption and production effects. It is obvious from these surveys that considerable work has been carried out at the aggregate level both across and within countries. However, better to gauge the effects of key factors such as changes in relative prices, changes in technology, and increased international mobility of capital, it is imperative that more empirical research be carried out at the household level in a variety of settings.

This chapter describes the results of initial work analysing a sample of rural households in Peru over the period from 1994 to 2004 to determine how these households responded to and were affected by globalization and the corresponding change in relative prices of traditional versus export-oriented products. Our principal interest was to identify the impact of opening the economy to international trade on rural household decision-making and to understand better how household responses to globalization influence rural welfare and poverty dynamics. Since a large percentage of Peruvians living in poverty are located in rural areas, learning more about how these households responded to the changing external economic environment should provide insights into factors that affected their ability to improve their economic position, both absolutely and relatively.

In brief, the results of our analysis indicate that changes in relative prices between traditional and export-oriented crops had a significant impact on the adoption of these new products, as did property ownership and access to regional and local markets. It also reaffirms the fact that geographical characteristics such as altitude, rainfall, and growing climate preclude the possibility of many households changing cropping patterns. Finally, by examining changes in household expenditures from the beginning to the end of the period, our analysis suggests that those households who did adopt the new export-oriented crops experienced growth in consumption in proportion to the change in the fraction or amount of land devoted to exportable products, and were much less likely to be classified as impoverished at the end of the period.

10.2. Background: The Peruvian Economy, 1994–2004

Peru is the fourth largest country in Latin America with a current population of 27.2 million and a rural population of approximately 7.3 million. The International Fund for Agricultural Development has classified Peru as a severely indebted, middle-income country, with a per capita GDP of US$2,806 in 2005. The rural areas are found in each of the three major zones of the country: the Pacific coastal area (coast), the Andean highlands (highlands), and the Amazon basin (jungle). The largest segment of the rural poor are found in the highlands, consisting of approximately 5,500 peasant communities and accounting for approximately 4.9 million people. It has been estimated that in 2001 some 73 per cent of the rural highland population were living below the poverty line and 27 per cent were living in extreme poverty (Massler 2004). The 2006 *World Development Report* (World Bank 2006) indicates that in 1997 49.0 per cent of the total Peruvian population lived below the poverty line, including 64.7 per cent of the rural population and some 40.4 per cent of the urban population. In 2000, it was estimated that 18.1 per cent of the total population received below US$1 a day (poverty gap: 9.1 per cent) and 37.7 per cent received less than US$2 a day (poverty gap: 18.5 per cent). Given our focus on the rural areas, it is useful to note that the importance of agriculture has increased over the recent decade, accounting for approximately 9 per cent of GDP in 2000 as opposed to 7 per cent in 1990, a trend which is presumably related in part to structural adjustment measures over the period that included significant reductions in state-owned enterprises.

The period 1990–2004 is particularly interesting and tumultuous inasmuch as Peru undertook a number of policy reforms and also experienced several outside shocks that impacted on the entire economy. A list of the most important events is provided in Table 10.1. One of the most significant changes was the freeing up of capital markets and the enactment of a rather extensive trade reform in 1994, which remained essentially in place over the following ten-year period, through which the Peruvian economy became much more open and subject to changes in the global economy. Prior to the trade liberalization reform in August 1990, Peruvian foreign trade policy was characterized by a system of high tariffs with considerable dispersion (fifty-six different levels from 10 per cent to 84 per cent) between commodities and many quotas. The simple average tariff was 66 per cent and the weighted average 44 per cent, which jointly resulted in both negative and extremely high positive rates of effective protection. For example, the effective rates of protection were 261 per cent for clothing and 189 per cent for daily products (Webb, Camminati, and Thorne 2005). Although significant changes occurred in 1990, reductions in trade barriers continued throughout the 1990s, with important reductions happening in 1997 and 2001. Reflecting Peru's increasingly broad-based open trade regime, total merchandize trade grew at an average annual rate of 7.2 per

Table 10.1. Factors impacting on the Peruvian economy, 1990–2002

Economic reforms

- Price subsidies eliminated
- Farmgate pricing abolished
- New central bank law
- Agrarian Bank abolished, replaced by commercial lenders and NGOs
- Adoption of a unified floating exchange rate
- Major reductions in tariff levels and tariff dispersion
- Import prohibitions, para tariff measures and state import monopolies eliminated
- Capital flows and foreign currencies freed
- Major banking reforms undertaken
- Creation of private pension system
- Privatization promoted with establishment of several commissions and autonomous regulating entities
- National Institute for Competition and Intellectual Property Defence created
- State deregulation involving reduction in number of state workers
- Labour markets deregulated and constitution altered to partially eliminate labour stability
- Payroll taxes eliminated
- Social programmes created and focused on poverty initiated
- Highlands rural poverty reduction strategy initiated in 2002

External factors

- El Niño climate shocks to production, 1997–8
- Asian-led international financial crises, 1997–8
- Growth in world demand and resulting increase in prices of mineral/metal products in late 1990s, which has continued up to present
- US ATPDEA which reduced or eliminated tariffs on more than 6,000 agricultural products from Peru, Bolivia, Columbia, and Ecuador

Source: This table relies heavily on Webb, Camminati, and Thorne (2005); Zorilla (n.d.); and USAID (2001).

cent from 1990 to 2004, and total merchandize exports grew at an annual rate of 7.9 per cent over the same period (World Bank 1996; 2000; and 2006).

Even in the presence of fairly major incidents such as El Niño and tumultuous political events, the data show a continuing growth in exports and a declining trade deficit in recent years. With respect to agriculture, exports grew more rapidly than total imports from 1991 to 1998, but less rapidly in the years following, in part due to the effects of El Niño. The volume response was somewhat different from the value response owing to decreases in world prices of some grains, milk, and meat products, which continued to be the major import groups. Regarding exports, the more traditional export products like coffee, sugar, and cotton were accompanied by a rapid growth in non-traditional exports such as tomatoes and asparagus. Not surprisingly, given the differences in the geographical characteristics, the nature of the rural production response differed between the coastal, highlands, and jungle areas.

Recent country indicators for Peru by the Inter-American Development Bank (IDB) (see Appendix I to this chapter) provide a useful overview of the performance of the economy from 1995 to 2005. Key measures of Peru's economic and social development during this period show that while growth was erratic due in part to the effects of El Niño, the economy grew considerably. The inflation rate fell substantially over the period, from well over 20 per cent in the early 1990s to 2 per cent in 2003. The sizeable trade deficit of the early 1990s first increased (especially during the El Niño period) and then decreased. By 2004, the trade balance had become positive. Much of this turnaround can be traced to the increase in mineral and metals prices. Using the traditional measure of openness, the economy became more open over the ten-year period from 1994 to 2004 as exports plus imports as a share of GDP rose from 23 per cent to nearly 39 per cent. As a result of the improving trade balance, the external debt fell from 1996 to 2002. However, net foreign investment proved somewhat erratic, falling through the late 1990s and then recovering slightly between 2000 and 2004.

Because of the influence of many different domestic and external factors during this period, it is virtually impossible to isolate the unique effect of globalization on overall poverty in the rural sectors of Peru during the past decade. Thus, this research focuses on the nature of the rural household production response to the change in relative prices between exportable and traditional crops in the presence of other direct and indirect effects of globalization. We look specifically at the roles of property rights and market access in influencing household crop choice, and examine these and other barriers to production responses to price incentives. Furthermore, to the extent possible, we test the assumption that those who take advantage of the relative price regime shifts are more likely to increase their income by estimating the returns of switching to export-oriented production among households that were more able to do so as a result of quasi exogenous factors. This allows us to draw some inferences about the influence of globalization on poverty among our household sample over the period.

The ability to take advantage of changes in relative prices depends on the degree to which factors are appropriately mobile and/or production structures are flexible. This is indicated to some degree by observing which producers did in fact alter their production in response to the increased openness of the Peruvian economy over this period. More specifically, we focus on the household response to these relative price effects by examining the degree to which household production shifted towards greater relative production of export versus domestic crops driven by both the 1997 and 2001 reductions in tariff rates that reduced the relative price of commodities such as grains, and the preferential tax treatment for nearly all agricultural exports to the USA granted under the Andean Trade Preference and Drug Eradication Act (ATPDEA). The

Table 10.2. Tariff rates on Peruvian imports

	1994	1997–2001	2001–4	Change, 1994–2004
Wheat	25	20	17	−8
Potato	25	20	20	−5
Barley	18	12	12	−6
Rice	25	20	20	−5
Yucca	18	12	12	−6
Corn	18	12	12	−6
Maize	18	12	12	−6
Beans	25	20	20	−5
Fruit/vegetables	25	20	20	−5

Source: Tariffs in the first three columns provided by SUNAT and the Ministry of Agriculture (General Direction of Agrarian Information).

former led to an increase in grain imports and the latter led to increases in US demand for Peruvian exports of fruit and vegetables.

Table 10.2 gives the average changes in tariffs over the period of study for the primary crop categories in our sample. Although tariff reductions were nearly universal, differences in the elasticity of export demand to reductions in trade barriers generate important variation in the post-reform increases in returns to the cultivation of specific crops. Specifically, even though tariffs on nearly all fruit and (non-grain) vegetables fell from 25 per cent to 20 per cent between 1994 and 2004, increased export demand for specific fruit and vegetable products such as citrus rose (in great part due to the increase in US imports) and more than offset the price effects of reduced protection. Meanwhile, grain products, which were highly protected prior to the reforms, experienced a fall in domestic price and consequently there was a dramatic rise in wheat imports. On account of these changes, by 2003, Peru was a net grain importer, and grains (specifically wheat, corn, dry peas, lentils, and rice) composed nearly half of US agricultural exports to Peru. US exports of grain accounted for US$114 million in 2003, up 24 per cent from the previous year; wheat accounted for 88 per cent of the total.

At the same time, the price of export-oriented produce was rising over this period in response to increasing demand from abroad. Import penetration in the US fruit and vegetable market—Peru's most important export destination—has increased significantly in recent years, most of which is sourced from western hemisphere suppliers. Indeed, tropical fruit consumption rose significantly at the same time as domestic production was falling, such that Mexico and Peru now supply almost all of the mangos, papayas, and limes consumed in the USA. Over the period 1994–2003, US imports of horticultural products increased by 121 per cent (from US$9.9 billion to US$21.9 billion). Excluding

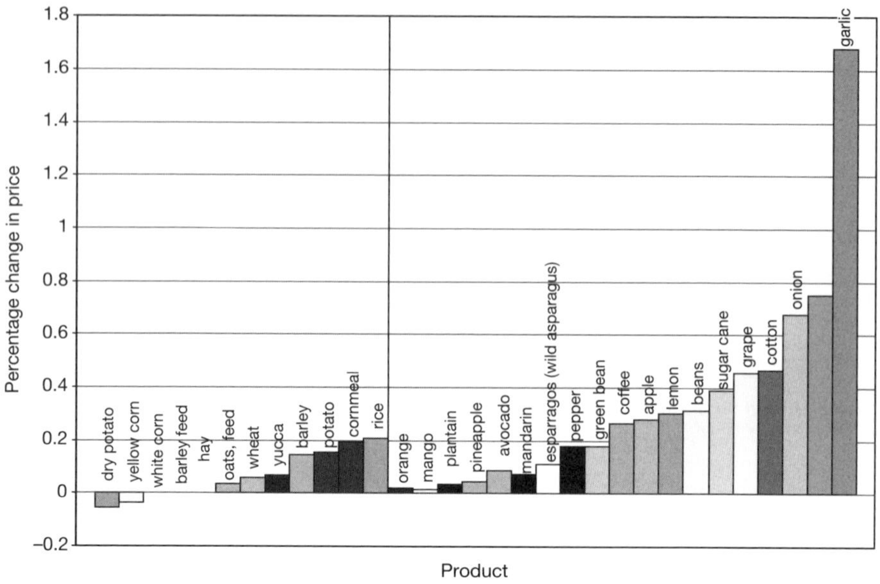

Fig. 10.1. Price changes, grains versus fruit/vegetables/industrial crops

Source: Crop prices from the Peruvian Ministry of Agriculture monthly crop specific price series from January 1996 to December 2004 (based on data from Regional Agricultural Directions).

bananas and melons, imports of fresh fruit rose from 11.6 per cent to 19 per cent of fresh domestic consumption during the same period, while imports of fresh vegetables rose from 7.5 per cent to 13.5 per cent between 1990 and 2002.

As can be seen in Figure 10.1, these market changes are reflected in the changing price of export-oriented agricultural products relative to import competitive products in Peru during the period. This shows the difference in the average domestic price of the most common agricultural products, collected by the Ministry of Agriculture on a monthly basis beginning in 1996. The data show the difference in average annual prices before and after the first wave of tariff reductions in 1997. As can be seen by observing price changes to the right and left of the vertical line separating grains and traditional crops from fruit, vegetables, and industrial crops, the former experienced very little price change over this period relative to the latter.

10.3. Determinants of Crop Adoption

Our empirical study tests specific hypotheses regarding factors influencing the adoption of export-oriented crops in place of grains. Household decisions to adopt new export products are dependent on household information regarding the product and its relative price, feasibility of growing the export crop in the household's geographical environment, adoption costs such as the availability and cost of inputs, and accessibility to product markets. All of these are functions of various characteristics of the household and its local environment.

With respect to price incentives, while little work has been done on rural household decisions to adopt export crops in the presence of trade opening, there has been considerable work examining the decision of rural households to switch from household or locally consumed traditional crops to commercial crops. Of notable interest is a study by Cadot, Dutoit, and Olarreaga (2006) focusing on the cost of moving out of subsistence crops, and that of Vakis, Sadoulet, and de Janvry (2003) focusing on transactions costs of shifting from traditional to commercial crops in Peru. While the adoption of export crops in response to globalization effects may involve a movement away from subsistence crops, it also is likely to involve the shifting from production of domestic commercial crops to export crops. Thus, household decision-making regarding the adoption of export crops is assumed to involve the same critical elements as decisions regarding switching from traditional to commercial crops. For instance, household production is influenced by land size and the percentage of land cropped. In addition, geographical factors such as climate, altitude, and length of growing season determine the production possibilities in the area. Furthermore, willingness to adopt a new export product is more likely if the household has previous experience producing commercial crops in addition to the traditional crops of the region. Hence, the likelihood of adoption will be increasing in the fraction of initial total output that is commercial production.

Traditional household characteristics such as size of household, age and gender of the household head, education of the household head, and farm experience are also assumed to play a role in household decisions to alter the mix of products. In addition, other institutional variables such as local producer organizations, labour opportunities for household members outside the household, and the availability and cost of hired labour can enter into the final decision. Consideration of risk also suggests that the closer the household is to the poverty level, the less willing they will be to risk undertaking a new production endeavour. Finally, the ability to carry out this change may also depend on access to credit needed to acquire inputs.

Lastly, production of exportable crops is influenced by market access, a function of household characteristics such as distance or time to hard surface roads and walking distance to local commercial markets and major centres of agricultural trade. Since products can be either marketed locally, at the farm gate to buyers who travel from farm to farm, or sold in distant, more major markets, the decision to produce new crops depends on the availability and prices of these marketing choices. Since, by definition, export crops are destined for shipments abroad, the accessibility to export marketing centres is more likely to be critical in the adoption decision. Thus, quality of road and distance to the markets should play a significant role in the decision process. Vakis, Sadoulet, and de Janvry (2003) provide a comprehensive analysis of the role of information, search costs and bargaining in the selection of markets and quantities in Peru with regard to the commercial sales of potatoes by rural households. Switching products also depends on the household knowledge of product alternatives, and expected prices and costs of necessary inputs, which are likely to increase with proximity to centres of trade. This information may also depend upon the technical assistance available or the past experience of other members of the community in adopting commercial crops.

Finally, land rights may be an important predictor of household price responses for a number of reasons. First, switching costs may require sufficient credit from institutions such as agricultural banks. Without property titles, households may lack the resources needed to pay for the fixed costs of adoption or to take on the risk involved in doing so. Second, household tenure insecurity may reduce the incentive to invest in agricultural products with longer investment time horizons, such as fruit trees which have a three- to five-year gestation period. Third, because property rights increase gains from trade in land, titled households may have greater opportunity to respond to relative prices of agricultural products by buying or selling land.

10.4. Changes in Rural Ownership Rights, 1994–2004[2]

Interestingly, the period of 1994 to 2004 was one in which rural households in Peru experienced dramatic changes in ownership rights through a large nationwide land-titling programme. The map in Appendix II shows the distribution of households participating in the Programa especial de titulación de la tierra [Special land-titling and registration project] (PETT). Each point on the map corresponds to a rural community, and the small, black dots indicate whether the titling programme operated in the community, while the bigger, grey dots show the rate of export crop adoption at the community level aggregated from the household survey data.

Prior to the reforms, possession of formal property titles in rural areas was limited, largely on account of lengthy and expensive registration procedures. In response to this concern, in 1991 the government implemented PETT through Legislative Decree 25902. PETT's field operations started in 1993 in the coastal region of the country. The programme was initially aimed at issuing property titles and developing a cadastre for beneficiaries of the agrarian reform, owners of uncultivated land, and native communities. In 1996, the government of Peru

[2] This section borrows heavily from Field and Torero (2005).

signed an agreement with the IDB to speed the titling process and increase its coverage to all rural estates. The agreement included financing a four-year project aimed at surveying 1.1 million parcels for rural cadastre and registering 1.1 million property titles in the coast and highlands. By 2000, the project had surveyed 1.9 million parcels for rural cadastre, registered 900,000 new property titles, and moved into the jungle region.

Based on 1996–8 information from a sample of farms in the northern coastal provinces of Piura and Ica, the 1994 Agricultural Census, and the National Superintendency of Registry Offices, an IDB evaluation of PETT's performance found effects of the titling programme on agricultural practices and credit markets. Production on titled and registered parcels in Ica was 67 per cent higher than those that were titled but unregistered and 179 per cent higher than those with no title at all. This fact may be related to farmers switching production from potatoes, beans, and corn to grapevines and asparagus. In the case of credit markets, the study found that rural areas that were titled through PETT experienced increases in the number of mortgages and sales of land. A decline in livestock herds—substituted with other means of saving and borrowing—was also documented in Ica. Antle et al. (2003) analyses the impact of titling on investment in terraces in the province of Cajamarca (northern Peru). It finds that the probability of investments in terraces increased by 6.6 per cent with registration. Likewise, Aldana and Fort (2001) documents that registry and titling have a significant impact on access to formal credit and a positive, albeit smaller, effect on informal credit. Nevertheless, they find that these effects tend to fall rapidly with land size, so that no significant effect is predicted for producers with less than one hectare. In this sense, titling does not necessarily imply a substantial increase in access to credit among farmers in our sample, 25 per cent of whom have less than one hectare of land in 1994. Furthermore, results from the last two studies should be interpreted with caution since in both cases possession of a title is not limited to cases reached by the government programme, so endogeneity concerns are likely to be significant.

Because the sudden shift in ownership status brought about through PETT coincided with the opening of the economy to international trade, it is a prime opportunity to examine whether lack of ownership rights presents a significant barrier to the adoption of commercial crops or modern farming practices. To the extent that participation was quasi exogenous to other household features influencing production choices, the titling programme serves as a natural experiment in tenure status that enables us to compare the influence of price incentives across untitled and newly titled households.

Table 10.3. Panel decomposition (number of households)

Initial panel		682
Non-agricultural households	31	
Only in agricultural activities in 1994 wave	55	
Only in agricultural activities in 2004 wave	23	
Households involved in agricultural activities		573
No information on crops in both waves	13	
Did not harvest crops in 1994 wave	6	
Did not harvest crops in 2004 wave	36	
Final panel		581

Source: Calculated by authors from bridge file linking the 1994 Peruvian LSMS and the 2004 PETT.

10.5. Data

To examine household responses to changes in relative agricultural prices, we use data from a nationwide panel of rural households linked across two large surveys: the 1994 Peruvian Living Standard Measurement Survey (LSMS) and the 2004 PETT. PETT was a nationally representative rural household survey conducted between April and July 2004, which drew its sample from the collection of rural households that participated in the 1994, 1997, and 2000 LSMS surveys. The sample was stratified by three regions in the country in order to maintain representative samples from each region. The survey collected detailed individual and household information including members' characteristics (age, sex, education, health, labour, etc.), assets, income and expenses, ownership rights, including title status of the dwelling and participation in PETT, access to credit, and agricultural production, where survey questions were designed to match the LSMS survey instrument for comparison across years.[3] Additional geographic information was gathered through land coordinates identifying the exact location of each household, from which we constructed a village-level measure of altitude, average rainfall, and walking distance to the district capital.

The spatial distribution of households in our sample is shown on the map in Appendix II. As detailed in Table 10.3, the initial panel consisted of 682 households—51 per cent of the 1994 rural LSMS sample—of which 651 were at one or both periods involved in agriculture. Among these, 10 per cent either entered or abandoned farming over the ten-year period. An additional fifty-five households did not harvest any crops in one or both waves during the preceding twelve months, which reduced the panel to 518. Six others had missing crop data. An important limitation of the data is the fact that the subsample of households in the 1994–2004 panel is subject to selection driven by all forms

[3] Details on the construction of the total expenditure variable are provided in the Appendix to this chapter.

of sample attrition over the period. While this is potentially relevant to the interpretation of results, it implies no obvious selection bias. Furthermore, expanding the analysis to include the eighty-one households that stopped producing during the ten-year period has little effect on the results.

10.6. Patterns of Agricultural Production, 1994–2004

Table 10.4 provides basic summary statistics on crop choice and demographic characteristics of households in our sample. As discussed previously, trade opening influenced the price of export-oriented crops (fruit, coffee, and cacao) relative to import crops (grains) and therefore presumably altered household incentives to produce fruit and vegetables versus grains. Indeed, a cursory look at the data in Table 10.4 indicates that agricultural households have switched away from wheat and other grains towards export-oriented fruit, industrial crops, and legumes. According to the summary statistics, the most significant changes in agriculture over this panel appear to happen in jungle and highlands regions. In highland villages, the total decrease in agricultural production outweighs substitution across categories of products. In the jungle, we observe a significant reduction in the fraction of households cultivating cereals and a significant increase in the fraction cultivating fruit and legumes. In fact, over the period of study, fruit and industrial crops (bananas, coffee, mango, avocado, orange, cocoa) have become the main type of crops in the jungle, and legumes (kidney beans and peas) have significantly increased their incidence in the highlands and jungle. Figure 10.2 reveals that this change in farm activity is occurring primarily among wealthier households in the coast and highlands, while change in land devoted to export crops is independent of 1994 income in the jungle. This probably reflects higher fixed costs of switching to irrigated crops as well as the stronger relationship between climate and income in dryer regions.

Table 10.5 provides additional information regarding the specific nature of crop adoption over the period. Unfortunately, the structure of the questionnaire in 1994 allows the respondent to specify a maximum of eleven crops while the 2004 survey only allows a maximum of six crops, which precludes us from recognizing as adopters those that produce only a minimal amount of the new export crop. As a result, we considered two possible definitions for an 'adopter'. The first scenario involves ranking all harvested crops according to the fraction of land size devoted to each one and then considering only changes in the top six crops.[4] The result was 347 adopter households (68 per cent of the sample), 134 of which are adopters of export-oriented crops. The second

[4] Maize has been simplified as a uniform crop category when possible, to avoid greater variation in results.

Table 10.4 Summary statistics from the living standard measurement survey (LSMS)/programa especial de titulación de la tierra (PETT) survey panel

	1994			2004		
	Coast	Highlands	Jungle	Coast	Highlands	Jungle
	Land					
Median size (m^2)	30,000	12,500	50,000	25,000	7,568	60,000
Median size with crops (m^2)	25,000	10,000	27,500	20,000	6,666	50,000
Mean size (m^2)	39,386	19,914	95,204	42,065	16,690	93,925
Mean size with crops (m^2)	33,269	14,739	30,271	39,599	13,971	87,847
Proportion of land with crops	0.89	0.85	0.63	0.95	0.90	0.94
	Crops					
Number of crops	2.53	4.04	3.77	1.59	2.75	3.14
Fruit	0.15	0.01	0.36	0.14	0.06	0.66
Industrials	0.10	0.01	0.26	0.05	0.02	0.41
Cereals	0.75	0.89	0.72	0.78	0.85	0.67
Vegetables	0.22	0.05	0.06	0.11	0.04	0.03
Legumes	0.25	0.25	0.06	0.18	0.31	0.09
Tubers	0.08	0.61	0.43	0.07	0.60	0.46
Forages	0.04	0.11	0.01	0.04	0.03	0.02
Pastures	0.08	0.06	0.00	0.04	0.03	0.01
Adopted any crop				0.44	0.54	0.67
Adopted any export crop				0.21	0.12	0.50
Adopted any long term crop				0.14	0.07	0.48
	Land title and infrastructure					
PETT	0.45	0.33	0.37	0.12	0.22	0.19
Other title				0.41	0.33	0.36
No property title	0.55	0.67	0.63	0.47	0.44	0.45

Time to: nearest paved highway (min.)				28.00	79.00	87.00
Nearest market (min.)				30.00	50.00	48.00
Access to: formal loans	0.01	0.00	0.01	0.27	0.05	0.06
informal loans	0.18	0.17	0.19	0.16	0.07	0.08
	Demographics					
Household size	5.60	5.60	6.00	4.30	4.60	4.80
Same household head in 2004	1.00	1.00	1.00	0.95	0.91	0.82
Age of household head	50.10	46.40	45.20	59.30	56.00	54.00
Sex of household head	0.92	0.91	0.92	0.93	0.90	0.84
Schooling years of household head	4.50	4.70	4.60	4.50	5.10	4.50
	Employment outside of household					
Total weekly hours per: all members	44.7	33.2	33.8	27.0	36.1	37.6
males	30.8	22.4	21.3	16.2	25.4	27.2
females	13.9	10.8	12.5	10.8	10.7	10.5
Weekly hours per: worker	37.1	30.9	34.4	38.2	38.3	37.4
male worker	42.2	33.1	32.7	37.0	39.7	38.2
female worker	30.2	27.7	37.5	42.9	37.0	38.9
	Production					
Agricultural production: quantity	19,366	4,266	9,565	21,479	3,328	12,421
value	12,451	2,748	5,050	14,397	1,791	14,863
percentage sold	0.85	0.37	0.59	0.87	0.36	0.77
percentage consumed	0.05	0.42	0.26	0.09	0.44	0.17
Agricultural subproducts: quantity		387	2,604	275	556	2,013
value		166	2,586	170	348	1,047
percentage sold		0.44	0.84	0.40	0.08	0.51
percentage consumed		0.55	0.12	0.60	0.82	0.49

(continued)

Table 10.4 Continued

	1994			2004		
	Coast	Highlands	Jungle	Coast	Highlands	Jungle
Pecuarian production: quantity	−11.7	−7.5	−20.8	−9.0	−10.5	−55.4
value	958	651	574	929	1,099	1,017
percentage sold	0.41	0.47	0.38	0.61	0.66	0.41
percentage consumed	0.57	0.47	0.57	0.39	0.33	0.57
	Expenditure and poverty					
Monthly per capita expenditure *(S/.)*	125	74	77	174	79	97
Real per capita expenditure *(S/.)*				104	47	58
Negative shock in last 2 years				0.10	0.24	0.19
Change in expenditures (%)				64.9	40.9	68.8
Change in expenditures (% -medians)				23.2	9.9	24.6
N	73	315	124	73	315	124

Note: Data from subsample of all households that can be linked to across the 1994 Peruvian LSMS and the 2004 PETT. Mean values reported in cells.

Table 10.5. Crop choice, 1994 and 2004

Living standard measurement survey 1994				Programa especial de titulación de la tierra 2004			
Rank	Crop	No. of Households	(%)	Rank	Crop	No. of Households	(%)
1	Wheat	81	23.3	1	Yellow corn	105	30.3
2	Yellow corn	67	19.3	2	Potato	50	14.4
3	Potato	59	17.0	3	Lima beans	36	10.4
4	Barley	52	14.9	3	Wheat	36	10.4
5	Corn (chala)	33	9.5	5	Plantains	35	10.1
6	Green beans	28	8.0	6	Yuca	30	8.6
7	Rice	25	7.2	7	Beans	28	8.1
8	Yuca	24	6.9	8	Peas	22	6.3
9	Lima beans	20	5.7	9	Barley	20	5.8
10	Peas	18	5.2	10	Avocado	16	4.6
11	Alfalfa	15	4.3	11	Rice	13	3.7
11	Quinua	15	4.3	12	Cocoa	10	2.9
13	Oca	13	3.7	12	Coffee	10	2.9
14	Dry potato	10	2.9	12	Coca	10	2.9
15	Onion	7	2.0	12	Mango	10	2.9
15	Coca	7	2.0	12	Orange	10	2.9
18	Corn (choclo)	7	2.0	17	Corn (chala)	8	2.3
19	Cotton	6	1.7	17	Quinua	8	2.3
19	Peanut	5	1.4	19	Corn (choclo)	6	1.7
19	Tomato	5	1.4	19	Squash	6	1.7
19	Carrot	5	1.4				
N	348 observations			N	347 observations		

Notes: There are slight differences in categories across years since different crop classifications are used in the two surveys. PETT uses Encuesta Nacional de Hogares (ENAHO) classification and LSMS as a broader set of categories.

Source: Data from subsample of all households that can be linked to across the 1994 Peruvian LSMS and the 2004 PETT.

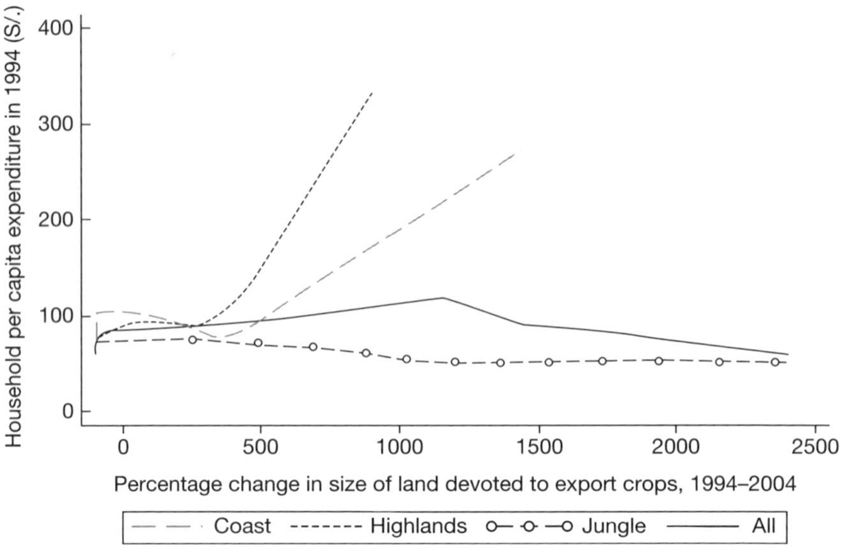

Fig. 10.2. Change in size of land devoted to export crops, 1994–2004

Notes: Lowess regressions with bandwidth of 0.8. Analysis considered, as a maximum, a 2,500 per cent change in land devoted to exports, eliminating nine observations with extreme right values. In addition, twelve households that produce export crops in 2004 but not 1994 are excluded since we cannot estimate a percentage change.

Source: Data from subsample of all households that can be linked across the 1994 Peruvian LSMS and the 2004 PETT. Authors' calculations.

scenario considers all crops harvested in both years, such that any new crop introduced in the 2004 survey turns a household into an adopter, which yields 306 households (60 per cent).

Among these, 65 per cent (115 households) are adopters of export-oriented crops. The remainder of the analysis focuses on the second definition of adopter since it makes use of all possible information and is therefore more likely to pick up genuine crop adoption.

Based on this definition, there is a clear movement from traditional crops to both long-term and short-term export crops such as fruit and vegetables. For instance, the fraction of households producing wheat fell from 23 per cent to 10 per cent, and the fraction producing barley fell from 16 per cent to 6 per cent. Among traditional crops, only yellow corn increased significantly in production, moving from 19 per cent to 30 per cent of households.

Table 10.6 provides a glimpse of the differences between household characteristics and crop choices of those who adopted new crops or export crops in 1994 and 2004. Both the mean and median land sizes of export adopters were larger than those of all adopters, and all adopters were larger than non-adopters. The proportion of land cropped increased for all categories over the period. In

Table 10.6. Summary statistics in 1994 and 2004, adopters versus non-adopters

	1994				2004			
	All adopters	Others	New exporters	Others	All adopters	Others	New exporters	Others
		Land size						
Median size (m^2)	20,000	19,000	30,000	15,000	15,000	10,000	30,000	10,000
Median size with crops (m^2)	15,000	15,000	21,000	12,500	12,450	10,000	25,000	10,000
Mean size (m^2)	45,590	31,901	64,516	33,389	46,063	24,348	66,609	30,166
Mean size with crops (m^2)	21,305	20,745	28,766	18,624	41,529	23,162	60,840	27,375
Proportion of land with crops	0.78	0.85	0.74	0.82	0.91	0.92	0.91	0.92
	Crops							
Number of crops	3.86	3.54	3.99	3.68	3.02	1.95	3.33	2.46
Fruit	0.12	0.10	0.17	0.09	0.29	0.06	0.68	0.06
Industrials	0.12	0.01	0.22	0.04	0.17	0.01	0.46	0.01
Cereals	0.76	0.96	0.68	0.88	0.76	0.87	0.54	0.88
Vegetables	0.09	0.04	0.16	0.05	0.07	0.01	0.18	0.01
Legumes	0.16	0.30	0.10	0.24	0.29	0.14	0.11	0.28
Tubers	0.47	0.53	0.44	0.51	0.52	0.42	0.40	0.52
Forages	0.10	0.03	0.02	0.10	0.04	0.00	0.02	0.03
Pastures	0.06	0.02	0.07	0.04	0.03	0.01	0.04	0.02
	Land title							
PETT	0.38	0.31	0.46	0.33	0.21	0.18	0.20	0.20
Other title					0.36	0.33	0.44	0.32
No property title	0.62	0.69	0.54	0.67	0.43	0.48	0.36	0.48
Time to nearest paved road					77	67	69	75
Time to nearest market (minimum)					47	46	36	50

(*continued*)

Table 10.6. Continued

	1994				2004			
	All adopters	Others	New exporters	Others	All adopters	Others	New exporters	Others
	Demographics							
Household size	5.75	5.63	5.80	5.68	4.60	4.63	4.43	4.67
Different household head in 2004					0.13	0.06	0.18	0.08
Age of household head	47.20	45.40	47.80	46.20	56.30	55.30	57.30	55.5
Sex of household head	0.91	0.92	0.90	0.91	0.88	0.93	0.83	0.91
Schooling years of household head	4.60	4.70	4.70	4.60	5.00	4.70	4.80	4.90
Monthly per capita expenditure (S/.)	79	88	100	76	87	86	107	80
Real per capita expenditure (S/.)					52	51	64	48
Negative shock in last 2 years					0.23	0.16	0.25	0.19
N	347	165	126	386	347	165	126	386

Source: Data from subsample of all households that can be linked to across the 1994 Peruvian LSMS and the 2004 PETT. Authors' calculations.

addition, the average number of crops produced fell for all categories, indicating a move towards greater specialization. A higher percentage of new exporters had title to property (64 per cent) in 2004, compared with 52 per cent for those not classified as new exporters. On the positive side, monthly per capita expenditures were substantially higher for new exporters in both 1994 and 2004 than for others, while all adopters' expenditures increased at the same time that expenditures of others declined slightly such that there was little difference between expenditures for 'all adopters' and 'others' in 2004. Finally, adopters of new crops experienced more negative shocks in 2003–4 than did non-adopters, suggesting that there is a higher risk associated with undertaking a change in crop production structure.

The second element of interest relates more directly to changes in poverty that took place during this period. We are interested in whether those households that experienced changes in product prices and were both able to—and chose to—respond experienced an increase in real income. For some this could mean a movement out of absolute poverty, while for others it implies moving further above the poverty line. Using monthly per capita expenditures as an indicator of household income, the summary statistics in Table 10.4 and Appendix III suggest that conditions improved for coastal households, and changed little for households in the highlands, the most impoverished region. The relationships are also illustrated in Figure 10.3. The situation in the jungle is less clear. While the variance as well as the mean of household income increased in both the coast and the jungle, in the poorer of the two regions—the jungle—this rise in inequality resulted in a significant increase in the fraction of households below the poverty line, reflecting the general vulnerability of households in this part of the country. In the highlands, there is almost no noticeable change in poverty, either in terms of the poverty gap or fraction of households below the poverty line. The highlands result is not surprising inasmuch as this region is substantially more insulated from national markets, its altitude and climate preclude the adoption of the new export type crops, and the low level of income and assets prevent residents from being able to change.

The fact that in the jungle region where export crop adoption was highest, average expenditures increased at the same time as the fraction of households below the poverty line suggests one of two possibilities: either high variance in the returns to crop adoption, or high returns to crop adoption along with a decline in the returns to traditional crops. The latter story implies that the degree of traditional crop subsidization was particularly high in the jungle region, which could arise from higher average marketing costs given the remoteness of households in this region. In particular, price distortions were likely to be higher in the jungle relative to the highlands and the coast on account of the government's traditional policy of farm gate pricing, or guaranteeing a price per unit independent of location, which was abolished in the 1990s (Table 10.1). Our empirical analysis of the returns to crop adoption will help distinguish between these two scenarios.

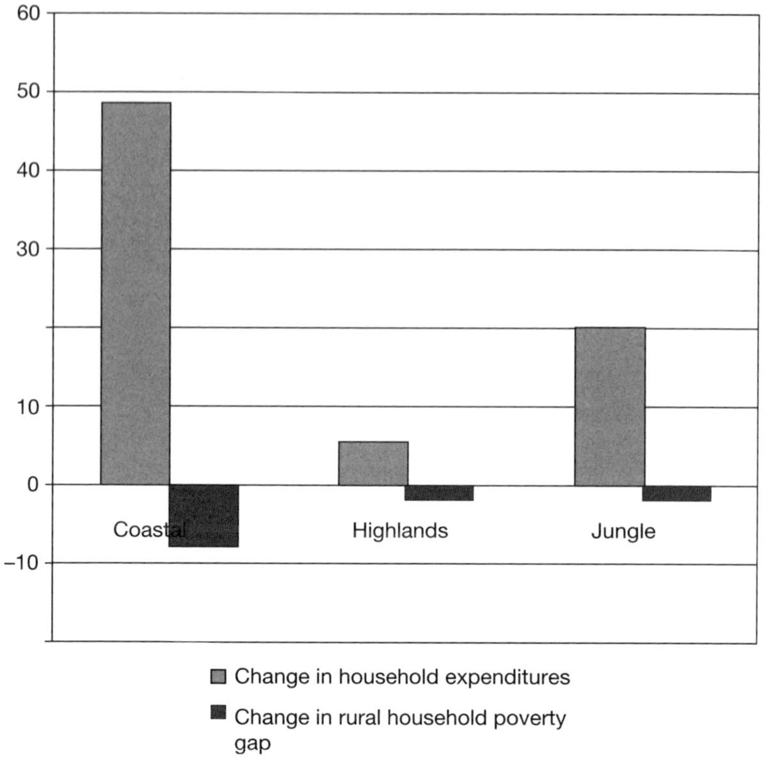

Fig. 10.3. Changes in household expenditure and poverty gap by region, 1994–2004

Source: Data from subsample of all households that can be linked to across the 1994 Peruvian LSMS and the 2004 PETT. Authors' calculations.

10.7. Empirical Analysis of Crop Adoption

To test hypotheses regarding determinants of crop adoption, we examine the interaction between specific household characteristics and price incentives to reorient production to export industries. The first specific hypothesis we explored is whether changes in household crop cultivation were influenced by the presence of legal ownership rights of the household. To do so, we used variation in household ownership rights stemming from regional variation in programme activity of the Peruvian rural land titling programme, PETT. Between 1994 and 1998, PETT distributed property titles to over 1.1 million rural households, one of the largest formalization programme targeted to rural areas in the developing world. As shown in Table 10.4 and Appendix IV, approximately 20 per cent of households in our sample received a land title through the PETT programme in the late 1990s, the majority of which resided in the highlands where the bulk of programme activity took place. By 2004, 35 per cent had acquired a title independently of the programme and approximately 45 per cent of households in our sample still had no legal ownership rights to their land. As indicated by the rate of non-PETT titles in 1994, virtually all new titles obtained between 1994 and 2004 resulted from the PETT programme.

We examine more formally determinants of changes in the amount of land devoted to crops destined for export markets by running the following fixed effects regression that controls for differences in production choices within each of eight climate zones (*c*) based on temperature and altitude:

$$\begin{aligned} crop\_adoption_{ic} &= \alpha + \beta_0(\mathrm{Pr_{pc}}) + \beta_1(\mathrm{T_{ic}}) + \beta_2(\mathrm{C_{ic}}) + \beta_3(\mathrm{M_{ic}}) + \beta_4(\mathrm{P_{ic}}) \\ &\quad + \beta_5(\mathrm{X_{ic}}) + \mu_c + \mu_{ic} \end{aligned}$$

The regression analysis considers four measures of change in crop choices for household *i* in climate zone *c* between 1994 and 2004 as outcome variables in the above equation: change in hectares of land devoted to export-oriented crops, change in fraction of land devoted to export crops, change in fraction of cultivated land devoted to export crops and whether the household introduced any export-oriented crop by the 2004 survey.[5] The right-hand side variables of interest are agricultural product prices, property rights, access to product markets, climate, and household demographic characteristics. Hence, *Pr* is a vector of agricultural product prices in 1996 and 2004. We consider the role of changes in prices that occurred during the period as a result of general increased openness and tariff reductions using the 1996 and 2004 prices of the most widely grown traditional crop (destined primarily for domestic markets) in the province in 1994, which encompasses nine separate products. Crop status as import competing or export-oriented was determined following criteria of volume and FOB amounts according to data provided by the National Superintendence of Tax Administration (SUNAT) and the Ministry of Agriculture (General Direction of Agrarian Information) for the period December 2004–5. Import-competing (import) crops were defined as all crops that were not exported abroad at all or represented an insignificant amount of exports. The most common crop by province was determined by aggregating frequencies for each household crop at the province level from the 1994 LSMS. In the case of a tie, the crop to which more land was devoted in the province was selected. Monthly crop prices were obtained from the Ministry of Agriculture based on price series between January 1996 and December 2004 constructed

[5] Considering only the fraction of cultivated land yields virtually identical results.

from data from regional agricultural directions.[6] In total, real prices of the most common products fell over the period for about half of the sample and rose for the other half. *Pr* also contains the interaction of 2004 prices with acquisition of a PETT property title and distance to nearest paved road.

In addition, *T* is a vector of binary indicators of whether the household possessed formal title to its land in 1994 and whether it received a title through the government titling programme between 1994 and 2004, *C* includes altitude and mean rain fall (mapped to climate data from GPS data collected by survey takers), *M* includes distance to nearest paved road, distance to province capital, and urbanicity, and *X* includes number of household members in 1994 and 2004, age and education level of household head in 1994, and household expenditures per person in 1994. Finally, we control for the following characteristics of household production (*P*): land holdings in 1994 and 2004, fraction of farm produce sold in 1994, land devoted to export crop production in 1994, financial losses due to drought or weather conditions during the past year, whether the household belonged to a local producers' association, and binary indicators of the top two crops categories produced.[7] Although land and household size are both potentially endogenous, we include them to increase the precision of the estimates and run robustness checks excluding these variables.

The regressions include fixed effects for each of eight climatic zones. The results are presented in Table 10.7. In the first column, for the binary outcome of whether any export-oriented crop was adopted, a probit model was run with the same set of controls. The estimates in column 1 suggest that household production of export crops increased in response to falling prices of grains in the domestic market. A 10 per cent reduction in the price of a province-level traditional crop is associated with a 12 per cent increase in the likelihood that a producer begins growing fruit or vegetables. With respect to ownership status, we observe that possession of a property title is also a strong predictor of changes in production. Households that acquired a property title between 1994 and 2004 are an estimated 68 per cent more likely to begin producing an export-oriented crop. Furthermore, households that received property titles through the government titling programme appear to be more responsive to changes in price incentives. In particular, the coefficient on the interaction term between province-level import prices and participation in the titling programme is positive and statistically significant. Finally, market access in terms of hours of travelling time to the district capital is a strong predictor of crop adoption: with each additional ten hours of travel time, households are 16 per cent less likely to switch from a traditional to an export-oriented crop.

[6] For a few crops, prices are only available since 1997. Hence, the earliest price available in most cases (Jan. 1996) was used as a proxy for the 1996 price. Prices in 2004 are taken from May since this was the month of the PETT survey. All estimates are robust to using annual averages in place of monthly data.

[7] Categories are: vegetables, legumes, fruit, cereals, grasses, tubers, and industrial crops.

Table 10.7. Determinants of export crop adoption, 1994–2004

	Adopter of any export crop, 2004	Change in fraction of land to export crops, 1994–2004	Change in fraction of cultivated land to export crops1994–2004	Change in hectares of land to export crops1994–2004
PETT title, 2004	0.676 [0.172]***	0.117 [0.094]	0.122 [0.084]	2.402 [1.189]**
Price of most common import crop by province (1994)	0.212 [0.139]	−0.015 [0.095]	−0.176 [0.086]**	−2.788 [1.214]**
Price of most common import cropby province (2004)	−0.197 [0.099]**	−0.148 [0.066]**	−0.099 [0.059]*	1.208 [0.840]
(Price of most common import crop by province (2004))*(PETT title in 2004)	−0.675 [0.188]***	−0.080 [0.117]	−0.078 [0.105]	−2.139 [1.483]
(Price of most common import crop by province (2004))*(Distance to capital)	0.000 [0.001]	0.000 [0.000]	0.000 [0.000]	−0.007 [0.006]
Mean altitude of CCPP	0.000 [0.000]***	0.000 [0.000]***	0.000 [0.000]***	0.000 [0.000]
Mean precipitation level of CCPP	0.060 [0.014]***	0.022 [0.008]***	0.027 [0.007]***	0.293 [0.103]***
Belongs to a producers' group	−0.017 [0.063]	0.091 [0.047]*	0.065 [0.043]	1.249 [0.604]**
Time (minimum) to nearest paved highway	−0.001 [0.000]	0.000 [0.000]	0.000 [0.000]	0.007 [0.004]*
Time to capital of CCPP (hours)	0.016 [0.006]**	0.003 [0.005]	0.003 [0.004]	0.022 [0.061]
Household head age, 1994	−0.002 [0.002]	0.000 [0.001]	0.000 [0.001]	0.009 [0.013]
Household size, 1994	−0.001 [0.009]	0.007 [0.006]	−0.005 [0.005]	−0.038 [0.074]
Household size, 2004	0.000 [0.010]	−0.001 [0.006]	−0.006 [0.006]	−0.105 [0.083]
Level of education attained by household head, 1994	0.012 [0.021]	0.006 [0.015]	0.017 [0.013]	−0.110 [0.188]
Log of per capita expenditure, 1994	0.023 [0.037]	0.060 [0.024]**	0.005 [0.021]	−0.016 [0.300]
HH head is another person, 2004	0.029 [0.053]	0.042 [0.036]	0.071 [0.032]**	1.134 [0.452]**

(continued)

Table 10.7. Continued

	Adopter of any export crop, 2004	Change in fraction of land to export crops, 1994–2004	Change in fraction of cultivated land to export crops1994–2004	Change in hectares of land to export crops1994–2004
Size of land in 1994 (m^2)	0.000 [0.000]*	0.000 [0.000]	0.000 [0.000]*	0.000 [0.000]*
Size of land devoted to export crops, 1994	0.000 [0.000]	0.000 [0.000]***	0.000 [0.000]***	0.000 [0.000]
Per cent of agricultural value sold, 1994	−0.119 [0.074]	−0.088 [0.048]*	−0.128 [0.043]***	−1.046 [0.606]*
Property title in 1994	0.066 [0.046]	0.001 [0.028]	0.011 [0.025]	0.447 [0.360]
One of top 2 crops in 1994 is: industrial	0.038 [0.101]	−0.269 [0.066]***	−0.324 [0.059]***	−2.991 [0.837]***
cereal	−0.080 [0.061]	0.134 [0.037]***	0.066 [0.033]**	0.497 [0.467]
vegetables	0.236 [0.108]**	−0.081 [0.052]	−0.053 [0.046]	−0.268 [0.657]
legume	−0.016 [0.054]	0.023 [0.034]	0.018 [0.030]	−0.225 [0.429]
tuber	0.039 [0.043]	0.032 [0.028]	0.003 [0.026]	0.404 [0.362]
grass	0.111 [0.120]	0.058 [0.062]	−0.006 [0.055]	−0.560 [0.786]
Drought losses in household in last 2 yrs	0.208 [0.113]	0.076 [0.047]	0.071 [0.042]*	−0.418 [0.596]
Constant		−0.317 [0.178]*	0.173 [0.160]	1.093 [2.266]
Observations	502	512	512	512
R-squared		0.29	0.34	0.23

Notes: Robust standard errors in brackets:
*. significant at 10%,
**. significant at 5%,
***. significant at 1%. Coefficient estimates from ordinary least squares regressions.
CCPP = geographic centre of village (GPS measurements taken at time of PETT survey).

Source: Data from subsample of all households that can be linked to across the 1994 Peruvian LSMS and the 2004 PETT.

With the continuous measure of intensity of adoption, the relationships are not as strong. For all four outcome measures, crop adoption falls with the price of the most common traditional crop produced in the province, as measured in either 2004 or 1996. However, the effect of a property title on the amount of land devoted to export crops only shows up as significant when the outcome is measured in absolute terms rather than percentage terms. Not surprisingly, climate characteristics including average rainfall and altitude are strong predictors of changes in production. Households that live in high altitudes and those with little rainfall are significantly less likely to begin producing fruit or vegetables or expand production of these crops. This relationship is clearly shown in Figure 10.4. Similarly, production choices in 1994 are strong predictors of production choices in 2004, reflecting both switching costs as well as unobservable determinants of relative returns to specific products.

More surprisingly, agricultural losses due to drought significantly *increase* the likelihood that a household adopts a new crop. Although the loss in income from a shock to production presumably works against the household's ability to alter or expand production, response to risk and loss of long-term investments appear to encourage new crop choices so that the net effect is positive.

While likely to matter, the influence of demographic characteristics such as education are swamped by the more fundamental influences of climate and prices such that their effect on crop adoption cannot be detected in the regression estimates. Meanwhile, membership in a local producers' association is also a significant determinant of increases in export-oriented production, which could reflect an important role of spillovers in technology adoption.

Because production choices are endogenous to many household characteristics, we instrumented for changes in the amount of land devoted to export crop production by making use of household participation in the PETT titling programme and province-specific changes in the price of imported agricultural products. We estimated the following instrumental variables (IV) model, where A_{ic} is predicted crop adoption of household *i* based on the first-stage regression estimate detailed in the first equation:

$$\begin{aligned} \textit{crop\_adoption}_{ic} = {} & \alpha + \beta_0(\mathrm{Z}_{ic}) + \beta_1(\mathrm{T}_{ic}) + \beta_2(\mathrm{C}_{ic}) + \beta_3(\mathrm{M}_{ic}) + \beta_4(\mathrm{P}_{ic}) + \beta_5(\mathrm{X}_{ic}) \\ & + \mu_c + \mu_{ic} \end{aligned}$$

$$\begin{aligned} \textit{pc\_consumption}_{ic} = {} & \gamma + \lambda_1(A_{ic}) + \lambda_2(\mathrm{T}_{ic}) + \lambda_3(\mathrm{C}_{ic}) + \lambda_4(\mathrm{M}_{ic}) + \lambda_5(\mathrm{P}_{ic}) \\ & + \lambda_6(\mathrm{X}_{ic}) + \epsilon_c + \mathrm{V}_{ic} \end{aligned}$$

The following instruments are contained in Z: province-level agricultural product prices in 1996 and 2004, whether the household received a property title through the government titling programme between 1994 and 2004, and 2004 prices interacted with receipt of a property title and distance to nearest paved road. The level effect of distance to nearest paved road and other indicators of market access, along with ownership rights prior to the government

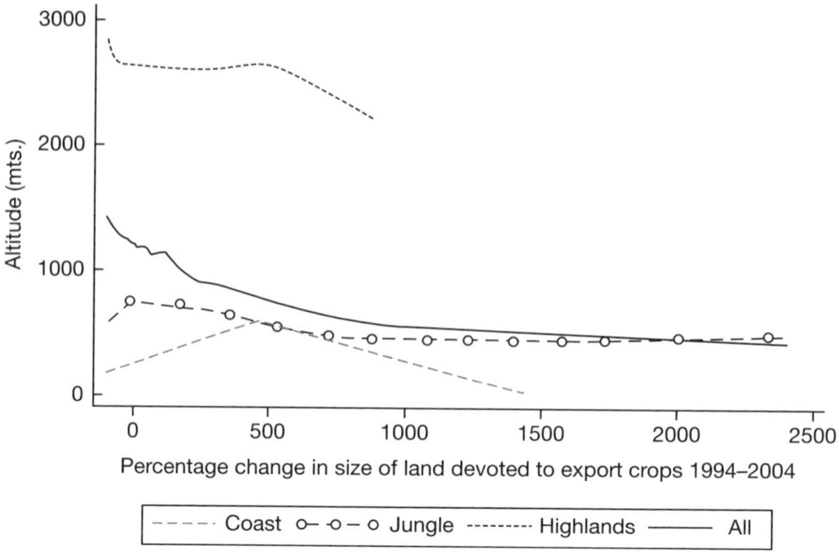

Fig. 10.4. Percentage change in size of land devoted to export crops, 1994–2004, by altitude

Notes: Lowess regressions with bandwidth of 0.8. Analysis considered, as a maximum, a 2500 per cent change in land devoted to exports, eliminating nine observations with extreme right values. In addition, 12 households that produce export crops in 2004 but not 1994 are excluded since we cannot estimate a percentage change.

Source: Data from subsample of all households that can be linked to across the 1994 Peruvian LSMS and the 2004 PETT.

programme, are included in both regressions in the set of control variables. Hence, our identification strategy makes use of participation in the titling programme and variation in product prices, which we argue are exogenous to other determinants of crop choice conditional on baseline property rights in 1994, and the differential impact of this variation on households based on distance to market and ownership of land.

One concern is that participation in the property titling programme was not exogenous to household determinants of land use. As an area-wide titling scheme, the programme was intended to target all households residing within large areas of land, regardless of household characteristics. Consistent with this, a comparison of baseline characteristics across PETT and non-PETT households show no clear pattern of difference in socio-economic level between participating and non-participating households (Field and Torero 2005). Furthermore, even if households inside and outside of PETT centres of activity are systematically different, our estimates, which study changes in household behaviour before and after the PETT programme, are valid as long as PETT households are not subject to distinct time trends. While there is no obvious reason to anticipate this, based on programme objectives, it is impossible to verify with existing data. It is therefore acknowledged this is a possible limitation of the instrument.

The regression results in Table 10.7 reveal that the instruments have statistical power in predicting variation in crop adoption, the first requirement for instruments to be valid. However, since the first-stage F-statistic falls between 5.79 and 7.12, there is potential concern over 'weak instruments' bias. In addition, identification of the causal effect of changes in agricultural production in the above set of regressions requires that the instruments (Z_{ic}) are uncorrelated with the household expenditures conditional on the observables contained in *T, C, M, P,* and *X*. If differences in the likelihood of receiving a property title are positively related to other factors that encourage changes in production conditional on *T, C, M, P,* and *X*, then the estimates will overstate the true effect of crop adoption on income and poverty. With respect to prices, this is unlikely to present a problem since product prices are measured at the national level and reflect changes in prices driven by global markets which are unaffected by local supply decisions. Variation across provinces in the modal crop is therefore likely to reflect region-specific comparative advantage in the production of certain plant types and possibly institutional infrastructure that favours specific products.

10.8. Effect of Crop Adoption on Income and Poverty

In the second stage of the analysis, we study the returns to crop adoption by estimating the effect of changes in production on household income and poverty status. Our first outcome of interest is the natural log of per capita household expenditure in 2004 conditional on log expenditures in 1994.[8] Expenditure data collected in the 1994 and 2004 surveys were designed to include consumption from own production and income in kind. We also consider the effect of crop adoption on poverty status by classifying households as impoverished if per capita income falls below 100 soles per month, which corresponds to the international standard for 'absolute poverty line' of US$1 a day.

As far as the titling programme is concerned, we treat receipt of a property title between 1994 and 2004 as exogenous to household production choices conditional on 1994 household income, tenure status in 1994, and geographic and production characteristics of the household. This assumption is supported by previous analyses of programme expansion and participation criteria, detailed in Field and Torero 2005. Although possession of a land title in 1994 is likely to be correlated with household wealth, assets, and use of technology, and conditional on climate zone and 1994 expenditures, participation in the PETT programme appears to be independent of household production or other observables.

The instrumental variables (IV) regression results are presented in Table 10.8. Not surprisingly, household size, head's education level, and household

[8] Data were converted to 2004 prices using the consumer price index estimated by the Peruvian National Statistical Institute on a monthly basis.

Table 10.8. Crop adoption and changes in household consumption, 1994–2004

	Log of per capita expenditure, 2004	Whether extremely poor, 2004	Log of per capita expenditure, 2004	Log of per capita expenditure, 2004
Change in fraction of all land devoted to export crops, 1994–2004	1.441 [0.752]*	−1.652 [0.819]**		
Change in fraction of cultivated land devoted to export crops, 1994–2004			1.694 [0.778]**	
Change in hectares of land devoted to export crops, 1994–2004				0.106 [0.059]*
Mean altitude of CCPP	0.000 [0.000]	0.000 [0.000]**	0.000 [0.000]	0.000 [0.000]
Mean precipitation level of populated centres (CCPP)	−0.016 [0.023]	0.046 [0.025]*	0.028 [0.026]	−0.018 [0.024]
Belongs to a producers' group	−0.001 [0.140]	0.013 [0.151]	0.026 [0.134]	0.018 [0.139]
Time to capital of populated centres (CCPP) (hours)	0.021 [0.012]*	0.039 [0.019]**	−0.019 [0.012]	−0.013 [0.012]
Time (minimum) to nearest paved highway	0.000 [0.000)	0.000 [0.000]	0.000 [0.000]	0.000 [0.000]
Household head age, 1994	−0.003 [0.003]	−0.002 [0.003]	0.002 [0.003]	0.001 [0.003]
Household size, 1994	−0.017 [0.015]	−0.008 [0.016]	0.035 [0.016]**	0.027 [0.014]*
Household size, 2004	−0.154 [0.016]***	0.111 [0.019]***	−0.144 [0.018]***	−0.142 [0.018]***
Level of education attained by household head, 1994	0.088 [0.036]**	−0.052 [0.039]	0.063 [0.041]	0.102 [0.037]***
Log of per capita expenditure, 1994	0.188 [0.072]***	−0.050 [0.081]	0.264 [0.061]***	0.268 [0.059]***
Household head is another person, 2004	−0.139 [0.097]	0.081 [0.093]	−0.209 [0.115]*	−0.192 [0.116]*
Size of land in 1994 (m^2)	0.000 [0.000]	0.000 [0.000]	0.000 [0.000]	0.000 [0.000]
Size of land devoted to export crops, 1994	0.000 [0.000]**	0.000 [0.000]*	0.000 [0.000]**	0.000 [0.000]
Percentage of agricultural value sold, 1994	−0.236 [0.128]*	−0.171 [0.138]	−0.312 [0.148]**	0.213 [0.126]*
Property title in 1994	0.076 [0.070]	0.025 [0.076]	0.057 [0.074]	0.036 [0.076]
One of top 2 crops in 1994 is industrial	−0.148 [0.252]	−0.220 [0.303]	−0.012 [0.288]	−0.222 [0.233]

One of top 2 crops in 1994 is cereal	−0.369 [0.122]***	0.442 [0.131]***	−0.268 [0.096]***	−0.232 [0.090]**
One of top 2 crops in 1994 is vegetables	−0.003 [0.139]	−0.046 [0.142]	−0.019 [0.140]	−0.080 [0.130]
One of top 2 crops in 1994 is legume	−0.221 [0.084]***	0.195 [0.071]***	−0.223 [0.088]**	−0.174 [0.085]**
One of top 2 crops in 1994 is tuber	−0.053 [0.076]	0.075 [0.084]	−0.020 [0.073]	0.049 [0.077]
One of top 2 crops in 1994 is grass	0.273 [0.170]	−0.230 [0.206]	−0.326 [0.155]**	−0.456 [0.135]***
Drought losses in household in last 2 years	0.289 [0.127]**	0.291 [0.055]***	−0.301 [0.132]**	−0.142 [0.120]
Constant	4.558 [0.497]***		4.019 [0.388]***	3.956 [0.375]***
Observations	511	508	511	511
R-squared	0.35		0.28	0.32

Notes: Robust standard errors in brackets:
* significant at 10%,
** significant at 5%,
*** significant at 1%.

Source: Coefficient estimates from ordinary least squares regressions. Data from subsample of all households that can be linked to across the 1994 Peruvian LSMS and the 2004 PETT.

expenditures in 1994 are the strongest predictors of expenditures and poverty status in 2004. Furthermore, households whose principal product in 1994 is a grain do significantly worse in terms of expenditures and poverty status, even conditional on climate zone and changes in production over the period. Negative shocks over the past ten years, particularly agricultural losses from weather shocks, are also likely to drive a household into poverty. These characteristics, along with climate zone fixed effects, soak up most of the variation in per capita expenditures and poverty classification in 2004.

However, results from the IV regressions also indicate high returns to expansion of production and adoption of new export-oriented crops. Based on all three continuous measures of expansion in production, our estimates indicate that switching towards export-oriented crops is a significant determinant of growth in expenditures over the period. According to the estimate in column 1, a 10 per cent expansion in the fraction of land devoted to export crops corresponds to a 14 percentage point increase in expenditures per capita. The same change is associated with an estimated 16 per cent reduction in the likelihood of being classified as extremely poor in 2004 (column 2). These estimates are independent of whether changes in production are measured in terms of cultivated or total land holdings (column 3). Similarly, column 4 suggests that each additional hectare of land devoted to export-oriented production is associated with an 11 percentage point increase in household consumption. These changes are illustrated graphically in Figure 10.5, which shows a steady improvement in estimated income with the amount of land dedicated to export-oriented production marked by the straight line. The plotted lines also indicate a higher rate of return in coast and jungle areas, although the confidence bands are too large for interpretation in the regional graphs, particularly for changes in production greater than 500 m^2, of which there are very few.

It is important to note in all of these IV regression results, the possible role of bias due to weak instruments in light of the fact that the first-stage F-statistic does not surpass the critical value believed to indicate sufficiently strong instruments (Staiger and Stock 1994). Hence, the results on poverty and household expenditures should be taken as suggestive rather than solid evidence of the high returns to crop adoption in rural Peru over this period.

10.9. Conclusions

This chapter examined rural household decision-making in Peru over the period of 1994–2004. It focused on how these households responded to the changes in economic environment accompanying economic reforms of the period which reduced domestic market distortions, opened up the economy, and changed relative prices between traditional agricultural crops and those produced primarily for export. The econometric results confirmed that changes in

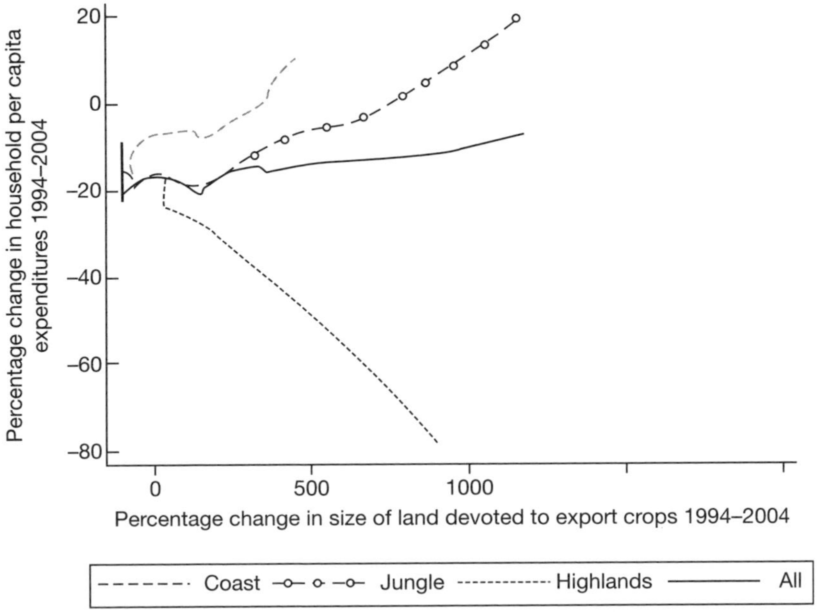

Fig. 10.5. Percentage change in size of land devoted to export crops, 1994–2004

Notes: Lowess regressions with bandwidth of 0.8. Analysis considered, as a maximum, a 2500 per cent change in land devoted to exports and a 300 per cent change of expenditures, eliminating 18 observations with extreme right values. In addition, 12 households that produce export crops in 2004 but not 1994 are excluded since we cannot estimate a percentage change.

Source: Data from subsample of all households that can be linked to across the 1994 Peruvian LSMS and the 2004 PETT. Mean values reported in cells.

these relative prices increased the likelihood that households would shift production towards these new export products. These tendencies appear to be strengthened if the household obtained title to their property over the period, which indicates that weak property institutions may inhibit the degree to which households can reap the benefits of a globalized market place. Additional work is needed to disentangle the possible channels through which ownership security could matter for crop adoption, which has relevance for the steps necessary to counter the negative influence of weak institutions on growth. Adoption of these crops was also found to be dependent upon geographical characteristics such as altitude and rainfall, initial cropping pattern, and membership in a technical assistance group. Interestingly, these factors appeared to dominate the effects of head of household characteristics.

We then examined how changes in cropping pattern related to the changes in household expenditures and poverty. Our results indicated high returns to adoption of export products and that households which began producing an export-oriented crop over the period under review were much less likely to be classified as impoverished in 2004. The obvious implication is that those who were unable to alter production due to reasons such as geographical location, access to credit, or lacking title to their property continued to produce traditional crops and were not able to escape poverty. This finding reaffirms the idea that liberalizing markets must be accompanied by appropriate social programmes or institutional reforms directed to the unique situational problems of different subgroups in poverty if the broader poverty issue is to be improved.

Based on the results of our analysis, it is difficult to predict the impact of the current global recession and the accompanying crisis in worldwide financial institutions on the rural poor on Peru. When the economic slide in the USA began in the summer of 2007, the rest of the world initially showed little signs of stress. Indeed, this was the case for Peru where growth jumped to well over 7 per cent in 2007 in the presence of higher world prices for minerals and metals, continued growth in exports of non-traditional agricultural commodities, and investment optimism reflecting the governments continued openness to trade and investment. Since turning positive in 2006, the current account balance has remained positive and the exchange rate has remained remarkably stable up through December 2008. The economic downturn has now surfaced worldwide and will certainly affect the Peruvian economy as world demand declines, lower minerals and metals prices persist, and investors remain risk averse. The impact of these changes on the Peruvian economy and poverty in general will certainly depend in part on the degree to which exports of minerals, metals, textiles, and agricultural goods slow down. World Bank endorsed figures indicate that the overall poverty level in Peru fell from 44 per cent in 2006 to 39 per cent in 2007, primarily due to improved economic conditions in the urban sector.[9] In agriculture, consistent with the results of our analysis, the coastal agricultural areas have clearly benefited from the recent export boom, while the highlands have continued to show little improvement poverty wise and average incomes remain below the US$1 a day poverty level in many areas. To the extent poverty has declined in the highland areas it has largely been the result of the mining expansion and the redistribution of the mining tax income. Thus, rural poverty may well get worse if the global recession and financial crisis reduces overall demand for these exports resulting in reduced mining income and reduced exports of the non-traditional agricultural goods. On the brighter side, it is clearly possible that some of the negative global factors will be mitigated in part by the implementation of the new free trade agreement between Peru and the USA which will go into effect in January 2009. There is no doubt that increased globalization increases the exposure of developing countries to outside economic forces. However, it is not yet clear whether the rippling effects of, for example, the US economic recession on developing countries such as Peru may show up more gradually, be mitigated by positive aspects of

[9] See <http://www.fco.gov.uk/en/about/the/fco/country/profiles/south/america/peru>.

globalization such as increased economic integration, or ultimately be longer in duration as a greater number of countries find themselves having to adjust to the financial and economic shocks emanating from the major industrialized countries.

APPENDIX I

Construction of Total Household Expenditures

The 1994 annual expenditure measure was built by 'Instituto CUANTO', the institution in charge of developing the Peruvian LSMS. The final expenditure variable assesses the total annual expenditures of all members in the household. It is divided among nine categories according to recurrence or periodicity of expenditures and their incidence in the basket of goods. Monthly per capita expenditure is calculated by the simple division of annual household expenditure by twelve divided by household size. The nine categories considered are the following:

- *Food, beverages, and tobacco.* Includes all expenditures made in these categories during the last fifteen days. Any self-produced or self-supplied item, and any payment in kind is included in the estimation. Results are multiplied by twenty-six to obtain annual figures.
- *Clothing and footwear.* Includes all clothing and footwear bought, self-produced, or self-supplied during the last three months. Payments in kind are also considered. Results are multiplied by four to obtain annual figures.
- *Rents, fuel, and electricity.* Includes nominal monthly payments for rent in case the dwelling is rented. For other property options (owned, by invasion, etc.) a hypothetical monthly rent is provided. Monthly payments for home taxes and utilities such as fuel, electricity, or water are considered. Payments in kind are also included. Results are multiplied by twelve to obtain annual figures.
- *Pieces of furniture, belongings, and maintenance of dwelling.* Includes all personal care and cleaning products bought during the last fifteen days. Also, accounts for home furniture and kitchen products and appliances bought in the last three months. Payments in kind and self-supplied items are also considered. Finally, this category includes payments for house-cleaning services. Results are multiplied by twenty-six and three accordingly, in order to obtain annual figures.
- *Health and medicines.* Includes all expenditures related to health services and medicines during the last three months. Results are multiplied by four to obtain annual figures.

- *Transport and communication*. Includes all expenditures made in public transport, communication, and gas during the last fifteen days. Expenditures incurred during the last three months in car maintenance or repair, national or international trips, and purchase of motorized vehicles are also considered. Finally, monthly telephone bills (landlines or mobile phones) are also included. Results are multiplied by twenty-six, three, and twelve accordingly, in order to obtain annual figures.
- *Leisure, cultural, and educational services*. Includes all expenditures incurred in recreational activities during the last three months. Also, expenditures in books, newspapers, magazines, subscriptions to journals, or purchases of electronic items (cameras, radio, TV, etc.) are considered. 'Educational services' comprise tuition payments made to universities, schools, or kindergartens, and any additional expenditure incurred in those institutions (transport, snacks, school supplies, etc.). Results are multiplied by four and nine (length of academic year) in order to obtain annual figures.
- *Other goods and services*. Includes all additional purchases or consumptions incurred in the last fifteen days, quarter, or year. Some examples are food consumed in restaurants, purchase of a particular electronic item, insurance premiums, etc. Results are multiplied accordingly to obtain annual figures.
- *Transfers*. Includes any monetary transfer incurred in the last year such as alimony, contributions to social security, donations, consignments, etc. Figures are already expressed in annual terms.

The 2004 expenditure measure was built following the same criteria used to construct the 1994 expenditure variable. However, the 'expenditure module' in the 2004 survey was shorter than the one in 1994. For this reason, a typical expenditure category in 1994 includes a greater set of items compared with a category in 2004. Although there is no change in the wording between the two surveys, the data in 1994 presents more detailed information.

The expenditure module in 2004 is divided according to periodicity or recurrence of expenditures:

- Last fifteen days. Includes aggregates for 'food and non-alcoholic beverages consumed in the household', 'cigarettes and alcoholic beverages', 'personal care and cleaning products', and 'transport'. Results are multiplied by two to obtain monthly figures.
- Last month. Includes monthly bills or expenditures paid for telephone (landline), public telephone, mobile phone, electricity, water, and Internet. Information is already provided in monthly terms.
- Last three months. Includes aggregates for 'clothing and footwear' and 'other goods and services' (such as newspapers, magazines, car repair, recreation, etc.). Result is divided by three to obtain monthly figures.
- Last twelve months. Includes aggregates for 'educational services' (tuitions, school supplies, registration fees, etc.) and 'transfers' (alimony, child support, donations, any big electronic or furniture purchase, etc.). Result is divided by twelve in order to obtain monthly figures.

- Health expenditures during the last twelve months. Includes aggregates for 'adults' health expenditures' (medicines, consultations, medical equipment, etc.), and 'children's health expenditures' (medicines, vaccines, consultations, etc.) Result is divided by twelve to obtain monthly figures.

Finally, a monthly hypothetical rent is included in the final estimation. Respondents are asked for a market rent value of their homes in case the dwelling is owned, partially owned, owned by invasion, etc. This value is upper-bounded in case the amount provided exceeds thirty per cent of total expenditure.

APPENDIX II

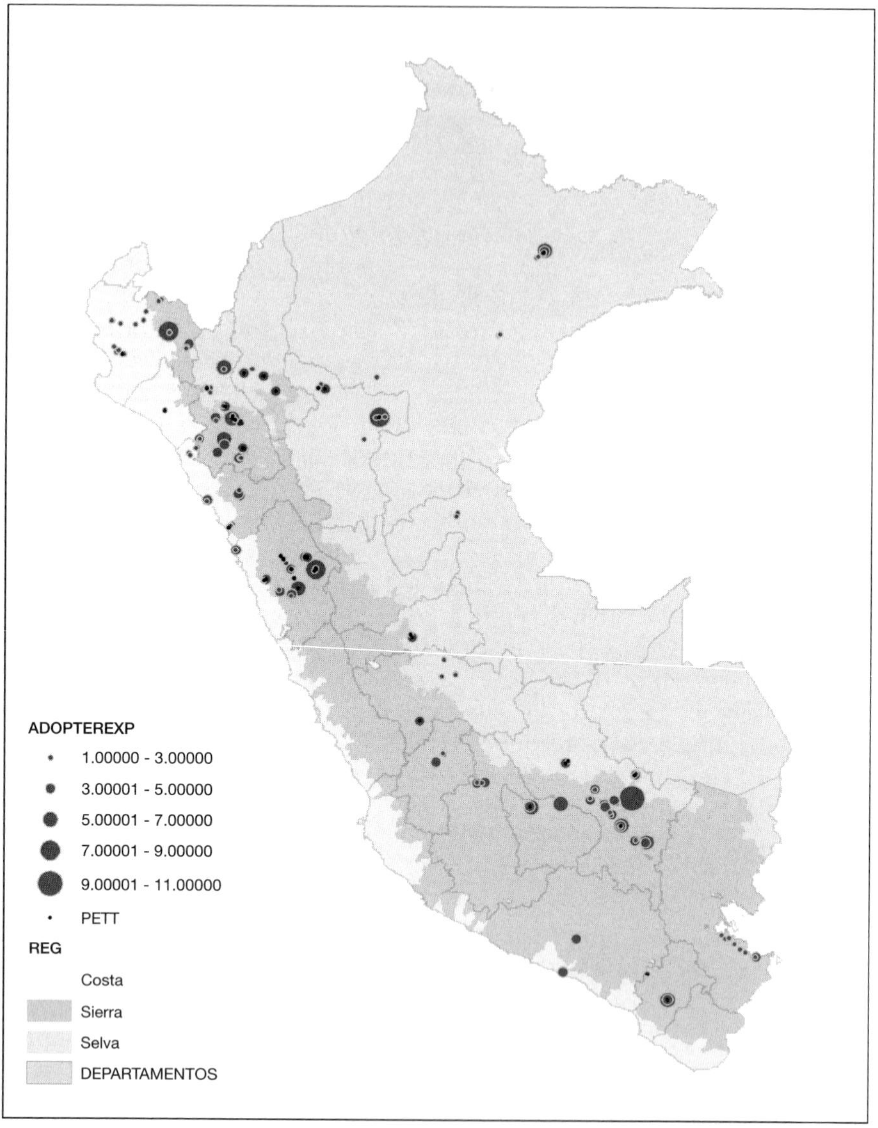

Distribution of sample, property titles, and change in crop adoption

Source: GIS coordinates and crop adoption data from the 1994 Peruvian LSMS and the 2004 PETT. Authors' calculations.

APPENDIX III

Region	1994		2004	
	Sol	Percentage	Sol	Percentage
Coast (n = 73)				
Per capita mean household expenditures	125.2		173.7	
Expenditure range	21.7		30.7	
	to		to	
	1,000.0		1,170.0	
	60			
Standard deviation	134.2		195.1	
Household below poverty line[2]		56.2		45.2
Mean poverty gap[3]	40.1		32.1	
Highlands (n = 314)				
Per capita mean household expenditures	73.8		78.9	
Expenditure range	102.0		8.7	
	to		to	
	850.3		476.7	
Standard deviation	79.3		67.3	
Household below poverty line		80.3		83.4
Mean poverty gap	49.5		47.6	
Jungle (n =1124)				
Per capita mean household expenditures	76.8		96.7	
Expenditure range	9.9		12.1	
	to		to	
	448.8		343.5	
Standard deviation	55.1		67.8	
Household below poverty line		65.3		80.6
Mean poverty gap	43.3		41.1	

Regional household monthly per capita expenditures and poverty[1]

Notes: 1 Poverty line is estimated to be 100 sol. per capita per month, based on the UN poverty line of 1US$ a day.
2 Households in poverty/regional sample size, n.
3 S/100 minus mean per capita HH expenditures among households with income below S/100.

APPENDIX IV

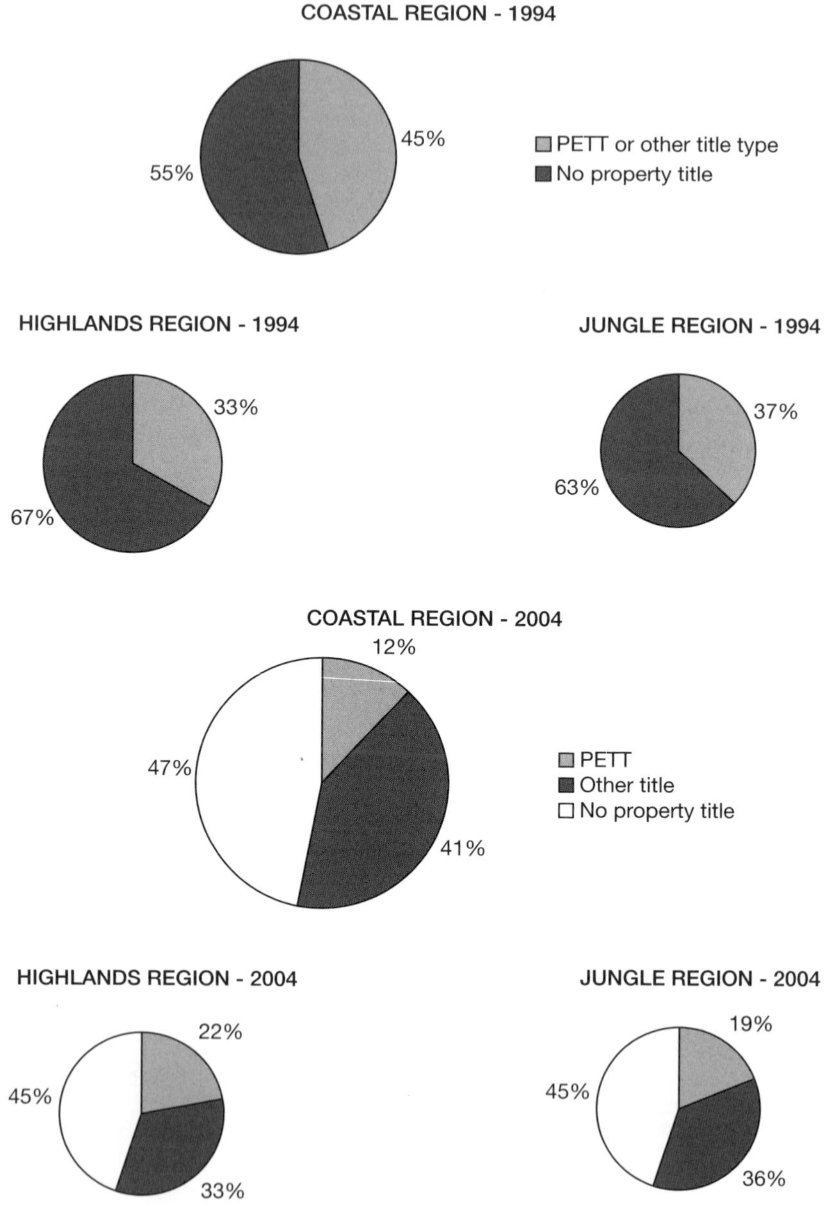

Land ownership, 1994 and 2004

Source: Land ownership data from the 2005 PETT. Authors' calculations.

References

Aldana, U., and R. Fort (2001) 'Efectos de la titulación y registro de tierras sobre el grado de capitalización en la agricultura peruana: una estimación basada en el III Censo Agropecuario'. Lima: Grupo de análisis para el desarrollo. mimeo.

Antle, J. M., D. Yanggen, R. Valdivia, and C. C. Crissman (2003) 'Endogeneity of Land Titling and Farm Investments: Evidence from the Peruvian Andes'. Working Paper Series (08–2004). Bozeman, Mont.: Montana State University Department of Agricultural Economics and Economics.

Bardhan, P. (2005) 'Globalization and Rural Poverty'. Research Paper 2005/30. Helsinki: UNU-WIDER.

——(2006) 'Globalization, Inequality and Poverty'. Research Paper. Washington, DC: Inter-American Development Bank Integration and Regional Programmes.

Cadot, O., L. Dutoit, and M. Olarreaga (2006) 'How Costly is it for Poor Farmers to Lift Themselves Out of Subsistence?'. Policy Research Working Paper 3881. Washington, DC: World Bank.

Field, E., and M. Torero (2005) 'Impact of Land Titles over Rural Households'. Working Paper OVE/WP-07. Washington, DC: Inter-American Development Bank Office of Evaluation and Oversight.

Harrison, A. (2005) 'Globalization and Poverty'. Cambridge, Mass.: NBER. mimeo.

IDB (Inter-American Development Bank) (n.d.) 'Country Indicators Peru'. <http://www.iadb.org/countries/indicators.cfm?language=English&id_country=PE&pLanguage=ENGLISH&pCountry=PE&parid=8>.

Massler, B. (2004) 'Innovative Strategies for Reducing Poverty in the Southern Highlands of Peru'. Working Paper. Washington, DC: World Bank.

Staiger, D., and J. H. Stock (1994) 'Instrumental Variables Regression with Weak Instruments'. National Bureau for Economic Research Technical Working Paper 0151. Cambridge, Mass.: NBER. <http://www.nber.org/papers/t0151.pdf>.

USAID.(2001) 'Country Strategic Plan for Peru: FY 2002–FY 2006'. 30 June 2001. <http://www.bvcooperacion.pe:8080/biblioteca/bitstream/123456789/2020/1/BVCI0001966.pdf>.

USAID Program Profiles (2006) USAID website. <http://www.usaid.gov/locations/latin_america_caribbean/country/program_profiles/peruprofile.html>.

Vakis, R., E. Sadoulet, and A. de Janvry (2003) 'Measuring Transactions Costs from Observed Behavior: Market Choices in Peru'. CUDARE Working Papers. Berkeley, Calif.: University of California at Berkeley.

Webb, R., J. Camminati, and R. L. Thorne (2005) 'Antidumping Mechanisms and Safeguards in Peru'. Policy Research Working Paper 3658. Washington, DC: World Bank.

Winters, L. A., N. McCulloch, and A. Mckay (2004) 'Trade Liberalization and Poverty: The Evidence So Far', *Journal of Economic Literature*, 47: 72–115.

World Bank (1996) *World Development Report 1996*. Washington, DC: World Bank.

——(2000) *World Development Report 2000*. Washington, DC: World Bank.

——(2006) *World Development Report 2006*. Washington, DC: World Bank.

Zorilla, J. T. (n.d.) 'Peru–WTO Agreement on Agriculture: The Implementation Experience. Developing-country Case Studies'. Rome: FAO Corporate Document Repository. <http://www.fao.org/DOCREP/005/Y4632E/y4632e0o.htm#bm24.1>.

Part IV

Africa

11

Globalization, Growth, Inequality, and Poverty in Africa: A Macroeconomic Perspective

Jeffery I. Round[1]

11.1. Introduction

The last decade or so has witnessed the process of globalization, a process characterized by an increasing degree of market openness and more integration—between countries and within the global economy more generally (Nissanke and Thorbecke 2005). Market openness is reflected in increasing cross-border movement in goods, people, capital, and the transfer of technology and information. While the globalizing forces in respect of commodities and, to some extent, of factors, stem from the increasingly liberalized international policy regime of the 1980s and 1990s (Dollar 2005), evidence on the degree or the extent of globalization in its various manifestations is not easy to assemble at the individual country level, and still less so at a regional or world level. In particular, while there are some assertions, there is much less by way of hard evidence on the extent of globalization in Sub-Saharan Africa (SSA) relative to other regions, and on what impact increasing global interdependence is having on poverty in countries in Africa.[2] There is also relatively little knowledge about the channels of the impact of globalization on poverty in African countries.

This chapter has one single overarching objective. It is to outline the macro-evidence on the extent to which globalization is taking place and poverty is

[1] I am grateful to Machiko Nissanke and Erik Thorbecke, and participants of the WIDER project meeting in Johannesburg, for many useful comments and suggestions on an earlier draft. I also thank Matthew Odedokun for his very helpful and incisive comments. However, I remain responsible for the views expressed and any errors or omissions.

[2] Throughout this chapter 'Africa' is used synonymously with 'Sub-Saharan Africa' unless otherwise stated.

reducing in Africa, and to consider this in relation to both characteristics of the Africa region (i.e., within the region) and relative to other global regions. This draws on some of the most recent evidence about the globalizing processes in various forms in order to try to determine the speed and extent of globalization in Africa. This is potentially important in helping to put into proper perspective the likely impact of globalization on poverty and inequality. It is therefore essentially a partial and descriptive approach, at best indicative of associations, and is therefore not analytically rigorous enough to identify the channels of influence and possible causal relationships discussed by Nissanke and Thorbecke (2005) and Bourguignon (2004).

Some important previous studies take a similarly broad perspective and examine the evidence on globalization, inequality, and the poverty nexus in Africa. In particular, in a broad-ranging paper, Geda and Shimeless (2005) examine many patterns of association between social and economic variables, including poverty, inequality and openness, in an attempt to establish whether there is a causal link between greater global interdependence and poverty. Likewise, Kayizzi-Mugerwa (2001) addresses the same issue, but with reliance on evidence from selected African countries, though with less reference to poverty and inequality indicators. Various reports, in particular by the United Nations Economic Commission for Africa (UNECA) (1999; 2004; and 2005) and the United Nations Conference on Trade and Development (UNCTAD) (2002; 2003; 2004a; and 2005) provide very useful and extensive statistical and economic analyses around these broad issues. Several other papers empirically examine aspects of globalization, growth, and/or poverty and inequality more formally in an African context. These include Christiaensen, Demery, and Paternostro (2003), which examines some macro- and micro-perspectives on growth and poverty, Collier and Gunning (1999), which reviews the empirical evidence on Africa's relatively poor growth performance, and many country-specific econometric and simulation studies. The present chapter does not attempt to replicate any of this previous work, but instead the attempt is to look afresh at some of the most recent empirical evidence.

11.2. The Sub-Saharan Africa Region in a Global Context

11.2.1. Identifying Trends in Globalization, Growth, Poverty, and Inequality

To make any significant headway in identifying the channels of impact of globalization on poverty in Africa, it is helpful to find ways of tracking the broad globalizing features of African countries, both over time and relative to other countries and regions. For analytical purposes there are clear advantages in seeking quantifiable evidence, as there are obvious difficulties in relying on qualitative evidence, even though some facets of globalization are extremely hard to quantify.

GLOBALIZATION VIA TRADE

Many writers suggest that globalization is a process that has several interpretations (Bigsten and Durevall 2003), though it is universally recognized to reflect increasing global integration, not just from the liberalization of commodity and factor markets, but also of cross-border movements of labour and capital, transfers of incomes and technology, and an increase in communication and the flow of information between countries. It is probably true that most research has focused on economic globalization, and most often on trade liberalization. There are two good reasons for this. Clearly, one is to do with tractability and, in particular, measurability. Estimates of exports of goods and non-factor services are routinely assembled as part of countries' national accounts and balance-of-payments statistics, and, moreover, they are internationally comparable. International movements of capital, human migration, and international transfers of technology are more difficult to track. But, besides the data issue, there is a second good reason. Trade liberalization is a policy-determined influence and it is relatively more tractable to analysis than might be the case with many other kinds of globalizing influences, especially those involving social and political variables. Empirically, trade liberalization is usually measured via outcome variables such as trade openness (Sachs and Warner 1995) or via policy input measures such as average tariff rates or quota restrictions.

In order to examine some features of globalization trends in Africa relative to other global regions, in Table 11.1 we show some summary data on performance in SSA in respect of trade openness, alongside evidence on economic growth, over the period 1980 to 2004. Estimates are shown for five-year periods for each of the regions (low- and middle-income countries) where comparable data are available. Clearly, such selectivity over periods of time can be problematic because we may miss events and macro-features of individual years. However, this span covers the period when many African countries embarked on economic reform programmes, and it includes the decade or so of their aftermath.

Turning first to the evidence on trade openness, following Sachs and Warner 1995 we use a measure of trade intensity, that is, imports plus exports relative to GDP (measured in current US$). Three important issues about measuring trade intensity should be noted. First, *ceteris paribus*, one would expect the ratio to decline with income, so if a ratio for a region is based on country ratios weighted by GDP, then this is likely to be lower than an equivalent ratio using (equal) country weights. Second, if trade and GDP are valued at PPP units, then the ratios are also likely to be lower (as GDP in PPP prices for low income countries are higher than in current dollars, while trade values would remain the same). Table 11.1 is therefore based on average trade intensity

Table 11.1. Global comparisons of trade openness and growth

	1980–4	1985–9	1990–4	1995–9	2000–4
	Trade openness[1]: (X+M)/GDP				
Sub-Saharan Africa	55.4	53.0	54.8	60.1	65.3
Latin America and Caribbean	27.3	29.2	32.0	39.3	43.4
South Asia	19.2	17.8	22.4	27.5	32.6
East Asia	29.2	36.6	50.7	59.8	73.9
Eastern Europe and Central Asia	n/a	n/a	59.1	67.3	73.9
Middle East and North Africa	57.6	41.5	59.7	54.0	56.9
World total	37.9	36.6	38.8	43.9	48.5
Sub-Saharan Africa (with country weights)[2]	69.3	65.3	68.6	70.4	75.7
	Growth of GDP per capita (average annual)[3]				
Sub-Saharan Africa	−1.2	−0.2	−2.0	0.8	1.5
Latin America and Caribbean	−0.8	0.3	1.7	0.9	0.8
South Asia	3.2	3.6	2.8	4.0	3.7
East Asia	5.7	6.2	7.7	5.4	6.5
Eastern Europe and Central Asia	n/a	n/a	−5.4	1.6	5.3
Middle East and North Africa	0.7	−1.2	1.8	1.7	2.5
World total	0.5	2.0	0.8	1.7	1.6

Notes: n/a = not available.

Source:

1 World Bank 2005 (calculated from current US$ estimates).

2 Own calculations based on World Bank 2005.

3 Average annual percentage (World Bank 2005).

measured in current US$. Third, the ratio is likely to be affected by country- or region-specific effects, which has led some researchers to control for these factors before making comparisons across regions.

The first panel of Table 11.1 shows the expected general trend towards greater openness over the two decades across all global regions between 1980 and 2004, based on GDP weights. The trend is not uniform, either across regions or over time, and this is an important feature. At first sight, openness in SSA is higher than in other regions in almost all years shown, but this is potentially misleading because of region-specific factors (IMF 2005). Low levels of per-capita income, geographical location, and the composition of trade (predominantly exports of primary goods and imports of manufactured and capital goods) make African countries relatively more dependent on trade (relative to their income) (UNCTAD 2004b). Average trade intensity has increased in Africa in line with the overall global increase, but not as rapidly as almost all other low and middle income regions. East Asia increased from 29 per cent in 1980–4 to 74 per cent in 2000–4, and Latin America and South Asia also increased by more than Africa. Table 11.1 also shows the trade-intensity ratios for Africa calculated with equal country weights. They confirm expectations that the ratios are considerably higher than those with GDP weights although the trend between each five-year period is broadly comparable.[3]

In spite of the increase in trade intensity, Africa's share of total world trade has fallen over these two decades.[4] UNCTAD (2003) attributes the reasons for this downturn to the region's primary commodity dependence and the structure of international trade, and to market access and the agricultural policies of industrialized countries. Similarly, Bigsten and Durevall 2003 suggests two conflicting inferences: either that Africa has not globalized, at least to the same extent as other regions, or, that it has done as well as it could, given its underlying geography and characteristics. But the reduction in the share of total world trade and the increase in the trade intensity ratio are consistent with the relatively poor performance of Africa in terms of economic growth. There are also endemic obstacles to intra-African trade through high transaction costs (non-tariff barriers, and poor infrastructure) (UNCTAD 2004b).

Relying solely on trade intensity as an indicator of trade liberalization is problematic, and still more so as a measure of globalization, because there are many factors that may influence the ratio besides liberalization policies. Some researchers prefer to use a policy input measure, such as average tariff rates (weighted or unweighted) but this does not necessarily take into account the full consequential effect of tariffs and non-tariff restrictions. And, finding the tariff equivalents of non-tariff restrictions is difficult. Pritchett (1996) and others consider a 'structure-adjusted trade intensity' measure along with other alternative measures of outward orientation. He corrects trade intensity for structural characteristics (size, GDP per capita, and resource endowment characteristics) similar to the Chenery–Syrquin adjustments in measuring country typologies. This is also similar to controlling for region-fixed effects. Table 11.1 therefore needs to be interpreted with some caution.

GROWTH

Relative growth performance of Africa compared with other regions is shown in the lower panel of Table 11.1. The table confirms the now well-established fact that Africa's growth performance (GDP per capita) has been worse, period by

[3] Averages are based on those countries for which trade intensity ratios have been recorded. So the estimates are subject to errors due to composition.

[4] UNCTAD (2003: table 1) reports Africa's share of world exports falling from about 6 per cent to 1.5 per cent, and imports from 5 per cent to 1.5 per cent merchandize trade over the period from 1980 to 2002.

period, than any other region since 1980, with the possible exception of Eastern Europe prior to economic reform. In fact, more detailed estimates show this to be so throughout the decade of the 1990s, with growth rates also being predominantly negative. However, a reversal occurred in 2000 and 2001, and the most recent estimates suggest that per-capita growth is continuing to rise sharply, with rates of 2.1 and 2.8 per cent being recorded in 2003 and 2004 (ADB 2005). Many authors offer explanations for the relatively poor performance, such as economic policy failures, low levels of education and skills of the labour force, poor infrastructure, conflict and political instability, rent-seeking behaviour (Bigsten and Durevall 2003), poor institutions (Acemoglu, Johnson, and Robinson 2001). What the table does not adequately show is the relatively strong growth performance in the Africa region since 2002, relative, that is, to performance before 2002, although growth is still low compared with other regions.

The link between trade and growth has been examined by many authors, most prominently recently in Frankel and Romer (1999); Dollar and Kraay (2004); Rodriguez and Rodrik (1999); Greenaway, Morgan, and Wright (1998); and with the literature usefully reviewed in an Africa context by Hammouda (2004). Whether there is a causal link, or a correlation that is controlled by other factors, is still a matter of some controversy. However, the estimates in Table 11.1 suggest that global regions which showed the greatest increase in openness also experienced the fastest growth, and that Africa recorded relatively little increase in openness and slow growth in this period.

GLOBALIZATION VIA FOREIGN DIRECT INVESTMENT

Since the early 1990s, many developing countries have enhanced their efforts to attract foreign direct investment (FDI), and the most successful have been those engaged in exporting fuels and mining products and fast-growing exporters of manufactures (UNCTAD 2005). Within Africa, as in any of the global regions, there is considerable variance across countries in this regard. However, the relative increase in growth of FDI has sometimes been used as another indicator of globalization (Geda and Shimeless 2005), partly to indicate the degree of integration into world capital markets. Table 11.2 shows estimates of FDI flows (inflows and outflows combined) expressed relative to GDP and (net inflows) as shares of the total net FDI received by developing countries, in both cases shown at the regional level.[5] Because FDI is a relatively volatile measure, Table 11.2 again shows estimates smoothed as five-year averages. The top panel does confirm the marked increase in FDI relative to GDP over the twenty-five-year period, and especially in the last decade. Africa does better than most

[5] Clearly, shares of the total can only be calculated for net figures. Inflows of FDI greatly exceed outflows for Africa. But the opposite may be true in the case of private capital flows other than FDI.

Table 11.2. Global comparisons of FDI

	1980–4	1985–99	1990–4	1995–9	2000–4
	FDI: FDI(I+O)/GDP (%)[1,a]				
Sub-Saharan Africa	0.30	0.50	0.72	2.04	2.74
Latin America and Caribbean	0.83	0.75	1.17	3.26	3.16
South Asia	0.07	0.10	0.23	0.68	0.67
East Asia	0.57	0.90	2.99	3.98	3.13
Eastern Europe and Central Asia	0.06	0.07	0.47	2.22	2.81
Middle East and North Africa	0.46	0.47	0.91	0.76	1.08
World total	0.54	0.77	0.84	2.00	2.64
Sub-Saharan Africa (with country weights)[2]	0.84	0.94	1.31	4.53	4.56
	FDI: FDI[1,2,b] (regional shares of total)[c]				
Sub-Saharan Africa	0.06	0.09	0.04	0.04	0.06
Latin America and Caribbean	0.47	0.42	0.31	0.40	0.34
South Asia	0.01	0.02	0.02	0.02	0.03
East Asia	0.31	0.35	0.51	0.37	0.33
Eastern Europe and Central Asia	0.01	0.02	0.10	0.15	0.21
Middle East and North Africa	0.13	0.10	0.04	0.02	0.03
Developing countries as a share of world total	0.21	0.12	0.26	0.26	0.18

Notes: [a] I (inflows) and O (outflows).
[b] Net inflows only: net inflows dominate net outflows in these regions.
[c] Regional shares of total net inflows across the six regions. (These may include flows between regions.)

Source:
[1] World Bank 2005 (average annual ratios).
[2] Own calculations based on World Bank (2005).

other regions, increasing from 0.30 per cent in the first period to 2.74 per cent in the final five-year period. The same ratio based on (equal) country weights suggests an even greater increase, reflecting the high ratios in some very low-income countries (e.g., Chad). In terms of the regional shares of FDI, the estimates are far less favourable to Africa. The second panel shows that around 6 per cent of total net FDI inflows to developing countries have accrued to Africa throughout this period. The increase in the share of world FDI that was received by developing countries in the 1990s (a globalizing feature?) did not significantly impact on Africa—Africa's share fell to 4 per cent of the total during this period.

POVERTY

There are significant and well-known conceptual problems in making poverty comparisons. Ideally a combination of monetary- (income or consumption) and non-monetary-based measures should be used. In the case of the former, alternative poverty lines and appropriate aggregate poverty measures can help to track outcomes for the chronic and hard core poor.

Table 11.3 shows estimates of income poverty (based on the US$1 a day international poverty line) taken from the latest published estimates in Chen and Ravallion 2007. For Africa, the estimates are significant. They indicate little progress in poverty reduction over the two decades, and arguably a worsening outcome. Based on this measure, the number of poor increased in this region, almost doubling from about 168 million to 298 million. Over the same period, the world total fell, largely due to a dramatic reduction in the number of poor in China.[6] Table 11.3 also shows that the proportion of the world's poor who are in Africa rose from about 11 per cent in 1981 to approximately 31 per cent in 2004. In terms of headcount indices, which normalize these poverty estimates to levels of population, the results look somewhat different. For Africa the incidence of poverty is fairly constant for most of the two decades, rising from 42 per cent in 1981 to 47 per cent during the 1990s, though falling back

Table 11.3. Global comparisons of poverty trends

	1981	1987	1993	1999	2004
	Income poverty (headcount ratios)				
Sub-Saharan Africa	42.3	47.2	45.5	45.7	41.1
Latin America and Caribbean	10.8	12.1	8.4	9.7	8.6
South Asia	49.6	45.1	36.9	34.9	30.8
East Asia and Pacific	57.7	28.0	25.2	15.5	9.1
Eastern Europe and Central Asia	0.7	0.4	3.6	3.8	0.9
Middle East and North Africa	5.1	3.1	1.9	2.1	1.5
World total	40.1	28.7	25.6	22.1	18.1
Ratio: SSA/World	1.05	1.64	1.78	2.07	2.27
	Income poverty (numbers million)				
Sub-Saharan Africa	167.5	222.8	252.3	296.1	298.3
Latin America and Caribbean	39.4	50.0	38.3	49.0	47.0
South Asia	455.2	471.1	436.7	463.4	446.2
East Asia and Pacific	796.4	428.8	420.2	276.5	169.1
Eastern Europe and Central Asia	3.0	1.6	16.9	17.9	4.4
Middle East and North Africa	8.8	6.4	4.5	5.7	4.4
World total	1470.3	1180.7	1170.2	1108.6	969.5
Ratio: SSA/World	0.11	0.19	0.22	0.27	0.31

Source: Chen and Ravallion (2007): table 1 based on international poverty line of US$1.08, 1993 PPP.

[6] Note that these results are sensitive to the choice of the poverty line. With a US$2 a day measure, while the number in poverty in SSA still rises dramatically, and very nearly doubles, the world total now rises, but less sharply. This is due to quite different outcomes for China and India: over this period the fall is less dramatic for China while there is an increase for India.

to 41 per cent by 2004 (Chen and Ravallion 2007: table 1). Using the world headcount ratio as a benchmark, we see that the outcome for the Africa region is far worse than the rest of the world. The relative size of the poverty incidence in Africa increased sharply, the ratios rising from just over 1.1 in 1981, to 1.8 in 1993, and well over 2.2 by 2004.

INEQUALITY

There are very few comparative estimates of levels and changes in inequality on a global or regional basis. As in the case of poverty, we focus only on income (or expenditure) inequality. Milanović (2005) and Ravallion (2004) identify several significant issues in measuring inequality. These issues are due not only to the scarcity of data but also to alternative conceptual bases for measurement. In particular, Milanović[7] distinguishes between inter-country inequality (concept 1, country weights), international inequality (concept 2, population weights), and global inequality (concept 3, this includes intra-country inequality). Thus, with access to individual-level data from household surveys, the true spread of incomes (concept 3) is a combination of inequality within countries and between countries.[8] Milanović (2002) estimates regional inequality (using Gini coefficients) for broad regional groups, corresponding closely to the years 1988 and 1993. His global (concept 3) estimates are reproduced in Table 11.4(a).

The results show a general world increase in inequality during this period, together with a corresponding increase in Africa. Inequality changes in other regions vary considerably, with slight reductions in Western Europe, North America, Oceania (WENAO), and in Latin America, a sharp increase in Eastern Europe, and a comparable increase in Asia to that of Africa.

Detailed analysis and decomposition for Africa suggest that this overall increase for Africa arises from a slight decline in intra-country inequality, a sharp increase in between-country inequality, and (in consequence) a reduction in the 'overlapping' component. Nevertheless, the between-country inequality in Africa is a good deal lower than the between-country inequality in Asia.

From the point of view of assessing the impacts of globalization at the country level (within the Africa region, or within other regions), estimates of inter-country inequality (based on country Ginis, using country weights) might be more appropriate. Table 11.4(b) shows estimates taken from Milanović 2003 for countries in Africa compared with the rest of the world, for the decades of the 1970s, 1980s, and 1990s. The evidence is fragmentary, with few African countries having comparable individual-based household survey data in these decades. Nevertheless, the results do confirm that intra-country inequality in

[7] Milanović (2005) refers to these as 'concept 1', 'concept 2', and 'concept 3' inequality, respectively.

[8] Of course, not all inequality measures are exactly decomposable. For the Gini coefficient, which is not decomposable, Milanović (2002; 2005) includes an 'overlapping' component.

Table 11.4(a). Regional Gini coefficients in 1988 and 1993

	1988	1993
Africa	42.7	48.7
Asia	55.9	61.8
Latin America and Caribbean	57.1	55.6
Eastern Europe	25.6	46.4
WENAO	37.1	36.6
World	62.8	66.0

Notes: 'Africa' includes North Africa: only eight of the twelve countries included in the dataset (common sample) were from SSA. The results are based on household survey data.
Source: Milanović 2002: tables 10 and 16.

Table 11.4(b). Regional Gini coefficients over time

	Africa	Rest of world
1970s	47.0	34.2
1980s	41.0	36.9
1990s	45.9	37.8

Source: Milanović 2003: table 2 (calculated from the World Income Inequality Database dataset, and based on the relatively few countries for which Gini coefficients have been estimated for all periods).

Africa does appear to be higher than in the rest of the world (ibid.). This is further confirmed by a finer rest-of-the-world regional breakdown reported by Geda and Shimeless (2005) based on UNECA (1999).[9] What is even more noteworthy from Tables 11.4(a) and 11.4(b) is that the degree of income inequality in Africa has increased sharply between the 1980s and the 1990s.

11.2.2. Measuring Globalization: A Composite Index

The issue of whether outcome measures or input measures are most appropriate cuts across whether globalization is, or should be, viewed as a phenomenon under the control of domestic policymakers (e.g., domestic trade policy), or whether it is a global phenomenon which is outside a country's control (communications, technology, trade policy of other countries) and is therefore exogenously determined. Studies have generally considered facets of globalization such as trade, FDI, and capital flows, and the changing role of institutions and democratic processes as separate phenomena. There have been a few

[9] Survey comparability might be an issue here. Milanović (2003) includes only individual-based household surveys, whereas the latter include household-based household survey evidence.

attempts to construct globalization indices which embrace more than just measures of trade and take into account some additional non-economic as well as economic factors.

Responding to an initial attempt by Kearney (2001), Lockwood (2004) and subsequently Lockwood and Redoano (2005) have recently constructed an all-embracing CSGR[10] index applied at country, region, and world levels annually for the period 1982–2004. The overall index is a composite (an unweighted average) of three indices: an economic globalization index (EGI), a social globalization index (SGI), and a political globalization index (PGI). The EGI is based on four variables, all measuring international flows, standardized with respect to GDP: these include trade (the standard openness measure), FDI, portfolio investment, and factor-income remittances. The SGI is constructed from nine variables, four are included in a 'people' sub-index and five are in an 'ideas' sub-index. The 'people' sub-index includes stocks and flows of foreign population, and tourists, expressed as proportions of total population, and worker remittances as a proportion of GDP. The 'ideas' sub-index includes phone calls, Internet users, the sum of books and newspapers imported and exported, and mail, all expressed per capita. The PGI is derived from three variables: the numbers of embassies in a country, and UN missions and international organizations in which the country participates. Each variable is normalized (actually, 'panel normalized', so as to enable comparisons to be made across countries and over time), weighted, and aggregated to form EGI, SGI, and PGI indices for each country. The unweighted average of these indices yields an overall globalization index for each country. The regional indices are a weighted average of country indices, where the weights are equal to individual country GDP (at PPP values). The regional indices are, therefore, susceptible to composition effects as more countries enter the sample over time.

Clearly, whatever virtues the index may have in indicating changes in globalization processes over time or in making comparisons of globalizing influences across countries or regions, there are many problems and deficiencies of the CSGR index, too. The choice of variables is obviously crucial. A major influence in the choice is the availability of data, and the sixteen variables listed above represent a first attempt based on a reasonable coverage of data. However, Lockwood and Redoano (2005) have attempted to choose variables that measure outcomes, rather than policy inputs directly. Also, for the trade openness measure especially, geographic and economic characteristics (such as population size, land area, and isolation) will influence the outcome measure. So, what they do is to control for country characteristics in the measures of all their economic variables.

Table 11.5 shows the CSGR index results at a regional level, concentrating only on the EGI and the overall index. The movement of the EGI for SSA shows

[10] University of Warwick, Centre for the Study of Globalization and Regionalization <http://www2.warwick.ac.uk/fac/soc/csgr/>.

Table 11.5. Centre for the Study of Globalization and Regionalization (CSGR) globalization index

Region	1983	1987	1990	1993	1997	2000	2004
	(a) Economic globalization index						
Sub-Saharan Africa	0.034	0.058	0.064	0.080	0.126	0.128	0.123
Latin America and Caribbean	0.094	0.096	0.102	0.103	0.112	0.120	0.123
South Asia	0.009	0.021	0.023	0.133	0.139	0.144	0.146
East Asia and Pacific	0.113	0.107	0.114	0.112	0.122	0.135	0.138
Eastern Europe and Central Asia	0.025	0.013	0.002	0.010	0.122	0.133	0.130
Middle East and North Africa	0.046	0.049	0.057	0.076	0.079	0.097	0.105
North America	0.115	0.118	0.121	0.123	0.132	0.136	0.133
Western Europe	0.139	0.134	0.140	0.142	0.152	0.174	0.160
World	0.111	0.113	0.115	0.119	0.132	0.143	0.140
	(b) Overall globalization index						
Sub-Saharan Africa	0.020	0.054	0.075	0.126	0.206	0.237	0.270
Latin America and Caribbean	0.080	0.135	0.179	0.251	0.268	0.238	0.286
South Asia	0.008	0.023	0.030	0.353	0.408	0.359	0.394
East Asia and Pacific	0.171	0.198	0.235	0.281	0.316	0.413	0.524
Eastern Europe and Central Asia	0.024	0.014	0.002	0.021	0.332	0.323	0.376
Middle East and North Africa	0.055	0.069	0.097	0.169	0.182	0.228	0.313
North America	0.363	0.371	0.489	0.664	0.764	0.786	0.872
Western Europe	0.254	0.277	0.343	0.537	0.555	0.670	0.754
World	0.242	0.264	0.320	0.455	0.513	0.583	0.675

Notes: Sources of data are set out at <http://www2.warwick.ac.uk/fac/soc/csgr/index/guide/sources/>.
Source: Lockwood and Redoano (2005).

an increase from a value of 0.034 in 1983 to a value of 0.123 in 2004. By way of comparison, the 2004 does not reach the value achieved in Western Europe at the beginning of the period in 1983 of 0.139; although the index for this region only rose to 0.160 in 2001. Better comparators might be the South Asia region or the Latin American and Caribbean regions. The former started at an even lower value of 0.009 in 1983 and rose to 0.146 in 2004: evidence of a much stronger globalizing outcome. The latter started higher at 0.094 and rose less strongly to 0.123 in 2001. In SSA a big shift occurred in the early 1990s, the index rose from 0.080 in 1993 to 0.126 in 1997, with little change since then. The SGI and PGI indices (not shown) reflect similar sluggish movement, both over time and in comparison with other regions. For SSA the overall index of globalization shows a slightly stronger gradient in outcomes than we observe from the EGI alone, as in all regions and hence at the world level. But in 2004 it still falls well behind South Asia, although it seems to be on a par with Latin America and the Caribbean.

Other empirical evidence on relative levels and changes in globalization between regions and over time does exist but is similarly fragmentary. Heshmati (2005) computes several composite indices of globalization—for example, one is based on the Kearney *Foreign Policy* index which combines a similar vector of components (but with equal weights) and a second which extracts the principal components of this vector (and hence has unequal weights). Amongst several methodological differences to the CSGR index, Heshmati relies on a balanced panel of data and hence the total number of countries included is only sixty-two worldwide. Of this total, only five countries from SSA are included in his dataset.[11] Nevertheless, SSA emerges near the bottom of the rank order of world regions on the basis of all indices of globalization.

The evidence is flimsy and we have to be cautious by not putting too much weight on the precise numerical scores, but the evidence is nevertheless quite compelling. Sub-Saharan Africa has not 'globalized' at the same pace, or to the same extent, as that of any other world region. It lags way behind what have been the outcomes in other regions where poor countries are also predominantly found. It may also be the case that the ways in which African countries are linked to the rest of the world are different, so that a scaling up of linkages might not be sufficient to reduce inequality and poverty in the region. This evidence on the slow rate of integration might also help to put into context some measures of other outcomes, including performance in terms of growth, poverty, and inequality discussed earlier.

11.3. Assessing the Evidence across Countries in Sub-Saharan Africa

Against this background of the average broad trends and performance of SSA relative to other global regions, there is much variation across and within the countries of the region. This variation and, in particular, the relatively poor performance of particular countries obviously explain the aggregate performance. There has been a recent and quite dramatic upturn in the growth performance in SSA as a whole. But there is, as yet, only very limited evidence in terms of how this translates into poverty reduction. However, it is useful to examine some features of this macroeconomic performance more deeply and to set this against particular country characteristics.

[11] The countries are Nigeria, Botswana, South Africa, Senegal, Kenya, and Uganda.

11.3.1. A Typology Approach to the Analysis of Globalization and Growth Performance

Table 11.6 shows some comparisons of globalization and growth performance in subgroups of countries, chosen according to different criteria. Note that the analysis is based on averages across countries with country weights. Clearly, this has the disadvantage that small countries are given the same weight as large countries, but is consistent with the use of country weights in standard regression analysis. Also, there has been no attempt to exclude outliers, although all the subgroups are sufficiently large that outliers do not affect the average values unduly. The analysis is restricted to two periods within the past decade, roughly the second half of the 1990s and the first half of the 2000s, primarily to identify any broad changes over time but in the most recent period. Comparisons are made in terms of real GDP growth, real GDP growth (in non-oil sectors), real GDP per capita-growth, trade intensity (trade to GDP ratios), FDI to GDP ratios, and the terms of trade (TOT). All of the reported measures are annualized averages, in real terms, and hence are smoothed and broadly comparable.[12] The distinction between GDP and non-oil GDP is based on a treatment suggested by IMF (2005). We assume for the latter that they simply exclude the oil (extraction and refining) sectors but it is, of course, difficult to account for the indirect effects on other sectors.

One long-standing basic hypothesis suggests that countries' growth performance may be inextricably linked with their natural resource endowments, especially minerals and oil. Some evidence on recent growth performance across oil and non-oil producing countries is reproduced as the first typology in Table 11.5. A comparison of growth performance in terms of real GDP and real GDP per capita[13] confirms that oil-producing countries have experienced higher growth rates on average than non-oil-producing countries in both periods. Even when the oil sectors are excluded, the disparity remains. Interestingly, the trade intensity ratio is much higher (in both periods) in oil-producing countries, although the ratio increased slightly, on average, in non-oil-producing countries between the first and second periods. Confirming expectations, the FDI:GDP ratios are considerably higher on average in oil-producing countries: oil attracts FDI inflows. The estimates show a slight increase, on average, in oil countries between the two periods and a slight fall in non-oil countries. Also, the TOT index indicates a rising trend for oil countries, and a falling trend for non-oil countries. A cursory analysis of these results suggests that oil-producing

[12] The analysis may also be subject to exclusion bias, as small numbers of countries are excluded from parts of the analysis, owing to absence of data. Missing observations have simply been treated as 'missing'.

[13] Note that as these averages are based on country weights, and exclude some countries for which data are not available, the estimates are not consistent with the aggregate SSA estimates shown in Table 11.1.

Table 11.6. A typology of growth and globalization trends in Sub-Saharan African (SSA) countries, 1995–2005

	Real GDP growth		Real GDP growth (non-oil)		Real GDP per-capita growth		Trade intensity		FDI/GDP		Totals (Index: 2000=100)	
Subgroups	1997–01	2002–5	1997–2001	2002–5	1995–9	2000–4	1995–9	2000–3	1995–9	2000–3	1997–2001	2002–5
Oil-producing countries[1]	4.3	6.2	5.0	5.8	4.3	2.6	97.3	94.3	10.7	11.0	85.3	108.3
Non-oil-producing countries	2.8	3.8	2.8	3.8	2.2	1.3	63.7	71.6	3.2	2.8	104.3	99.2
Resource intensive[2]	7.3	7.0	4.5	6.1	2.9	3.1	85.4	81.1	6.8	8.9	89.1	95.7
Coastal, resource poor	4.0	3.4	4.0	3.2	1.8	1.1	69.6	80.9	2.7	3.1	104.2	105.0
Landlocked, resource poor	2.9	3.7	2.9	2.7	1.5	1.0	58.6	64.7	3.2	4.2	105.7	95.5
Fast growers in 1990–4[a]	7.1	3.9	4.7	3.6	1.5	4.1	85.6	87.9	8.1	5.0	98.0	93.1
Slow growers in 1990–4	2.9	5.0	3.2	4.0	−3.2	0.6	60.1	67.5	2.3	4.1	102.0	103.3

Notes:
a 'Fast growers' are those countries whose average annual rate of growth of GDP per capita in the period 1990–4 was positive, the average for SSA in this period was −0.2 (see Table 11.10).

Source:
1 The categories are based on classifications in IMF (2005).
2 The categories are based on classifications in IMF (2005) which are in turn based on Collier and O'Connell (2004).

countries may have had a tendency towards experiencing faster growth (and not necessarily confined to the oil sectors) and to have become more globalized than has been the case in the non-oil-producing countries.

A second analysis is shown in Table 11.6 with respect to resource-intensity levels and geographical aspects, as suggested by Sachs and Warner 1997 and Collier and Gunning (1999).[14] Again, the results reveal expected outcomes. Resource-intensive countries[15] have consistently grown faster on average than resource-poor countries, and have generally had higher trade-intensity ratios, higher FDI:GDP ratios (high prices of key commodities attracting new exploration projects from overseas), and rising TOT indices (although lower on average than the benchmark year 2000). The average difference in performance between the coastal and landlocked categories of resource-poor countries is also discernable in both periods, though the differences are not dramatic. Coastal countries on average grew slightly faster (in terms of real GDP growth, real non-oil GDP growth, real GDP per-capita growth) and the average trade intensity was higher. However, the FDI:GDP ratios were lower, though not by a margin that would suggest an appreciable difference. The TOT indices for the coastal resource-poor countries are approximately the same in both periods and are falling for landlocked resource-poor countries, suggesting a pattern (a divergence) consistent with the other indicators. Clearly, the sustainability of the high growth performance of resource-rich economies will depend heavily on the primary commodity markets and commodity prices, and, whether the windfalls from commodity booms are used 'purposely' for economic transformation (Nissanke and Thorbecke 2008).

The third typology tackles a division between relatively fast- and relatively slow-growing countries. In the five-year period 1990–4, many African countries recorded low, even negative average annual rates of growth, the overall average growth rate (country weights) was −0.2 per cent. Faced with the choice of subdividing countries into those above and below this average and those with positive and negative average growth rates, it was decided to go along with the latter. On this basis, twenty-five countries were deemed to be relatively fast-growing and seventeen relatively slow-growing. Either way, there are some anomalies: Zimbabwe is categorized as fast-growing and, on the chosen split, South Africa is deemed to be slow-growing. Nevertheless, in spite of the arbitrariness of the division, the results are noteworthy. The fast-growing countries (in 1990–4) continue to have an average growth rate (of real GDP or GDP per capita) that exceeds that of previously slow-growing countries, but oil appears to explain most of this, because the comparison of average real non-oil GDP

[14] The classifications are based on Collier and O'Connell (2004).

[15] These include all the oil-producing countries, with the exception of Chad and the Côte d'Ivoire, which were not included because their oil reserves were discovered only relatively recently, plus Botswana, Guinea, Namibia, Sierra Leone, and Zambia.

growth in the two subsequent periods shows very little difference and even a suggestion of a reversal in the second period. The globalization indicators, trade intensity and FDI:GDP ratios, confirm expectations: with relatively high average ratios for the previous fast growers.

The typologies considered here can be extended further. The work of Dollar and Kraay (2004) has been key to distinguishing the performance (in growth and poverty reduction) between 'globalizers' and 'non-globalizers' (defined according to trade-intensity ratios) while Birdsall and Hamoudi (2002) suggest that these categories are closely aligned to 'least' and 'most' commodity-dependent countries (UNCTAD 2003; 2004). These are not pursued here but there is a point to be made that the alternative classifications are not necessarily orthogonal, and may indeed be highly correlated, as is already apparent in the three typologies selected above.

The overall picture of globalization and growth performance in Africa in the last decade gained from this typology analysis is quite pronounced. There seems to be a considerable variation across countries, and some clear differences between subgroups defined according to their natural resource endowments (especially oil), to geographical features (landlocked versus coastal), and according to growth experience in the immediate previous five-year period. The analysis is cursory, relying on averages, and with averaging over two periods of approximately five years so that some important variations may have been smoothed out. Nevertheless the differences between all subgroups are large and systematic, indicating that the following conclusions may be robust. There seems to be some association between growth and globalizing features (as measured by trade intensity and FDI:GDP ratios), and between natural resource endowments (including oil) and globalization. Clearly, this is simply a cursory analysis based only on averages. It does not take into account within subgroup variation, nor does it control for other factors that might affect the association, so causality cannot be inferred.

11.3.2. Globalization, Growth, and Governance

Many authors now attribute at least part of Africa's poor growth performance to poor governance, weak or inappropriate institutions, and continuing conflict (Sachs and Warner 1997; Bigsten and Durevall 2003),[16] the combination of which creates impediments to the accumulation of capital and the necessary structural change. Continuing the theme of exploring patterns and associations between key variables measured at the country level, the first relationship considered is between the change in a country's governance and growth in

[16] Plus several classic papers on institutions and growth referred to and providing the background to the report by the Commission for Africa (2005), which places a heavy emphasis on the improvement of governance as a key to growth and poverty reduction in Africa.

GDP per capita. Governance is measured using the Kaufmann governance indicator (Kaufmann, Kraay, and Mastruzzi 2003), which is a composite indicator based on six indicators of governance.[17] Figure 11.1 shows the plot between the change in the aggregate governance indicator (1998–2004) and the average annual growth in real GDP per capita (2000–4), the underlying assumption being that if there is a relationship it should be observed between growth and a change in governance over a longer horizon. From the plot, there is a discernible positive association between these variables, confirmed by a sample correlation coefficient of 0.459 (p-value: 0.0014), which suggests the linear association is highly significant.

In Figure 11.2, a second association is explored between governance (as defined above) and the change in the trade intensity. Again, to smooth out as much volatility in the annual openness ratios as possible, the change in trade intensity is measured as the proportional change in the averages of the trade openness ratios in the periods 1995–9 and 2000–4. Again, the plot is indicative of some positive association (an improvement in governance being associated with more openness), confirmed by a correlation coefficient of 0.277, although this is not statistically significant (p-value: 0.069).

The Kaufmann governance indicators are based on a wide range of responses about the quality of governance at the country level, derived from expert groups, institutes, NGOs, and international organizations. They are predominantly subjective but are widely regarded as reputable indicators. The plots in

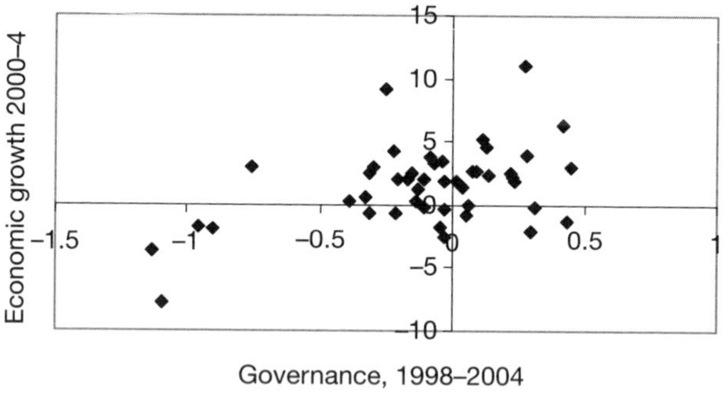

Fig. 11.1. Growth versus governance

Notes: Own calculations based on observations for forty-six African countries.
Source: World Bank (2005), Kaufmann, Kraay, and Mastruzzi (2003).

[17] The six components are: (i) voice and accountability; (ii) political stability; (iii) government effectiveness; (iv) regulatory quality; (v) rule of law; and (vi) control of corruption. Each component in each country is assessed on a scale from −2.5 to 2.5. Our calculations are based on an unweighted average of these six component indicators.

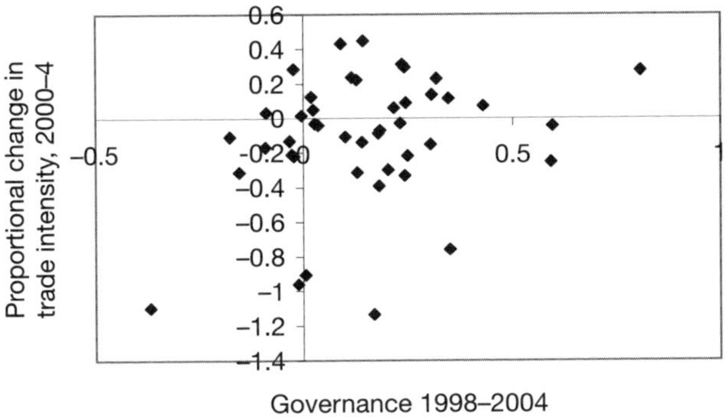

Fig. 11.2. Change in trade intensity versus governance

Notes: Own calculations based on observations for forty-six African countries.

Source: World Bank (2005), Kaufmann, Kraay, and Mastruzzi (2003).

both Figures 11.1 and 11.2 are only intended to be indicative of relationships and, at best, do just that. Formal (often panel data-based econometric) analyses of governance and economic performance in Africa are already underway (e.g., Amin, Bussari, and Ntilivamunda 2005). There is also a view that governance may be endogenous. Hence it might be important to heed caution in putting too much reliance on bivariate associations and to recognize there may be a multiplicity of causal factors in the governance–growth–globalization nexus. Sachs (2003) is prominent in cautioning not to place all the weight on a single factor explanation of growth and development and, while Acemoglu, Johnson, and Robinson (2001) and others show that institutions and governance are important contributory factors, but so are geography, health, and human capital, etc. (Sachs 2003). The focus in the present chapter is on the growth, globalization (and poverty) nexus, hence it is sufficient to indicate that governance may be a related factor, alongside resource endowments and geography, and more credence ought not to be inferred from it than this.

11.3.3. Evidence on Globalization at the Country Level in Africa

For completeness, Table 11.7 shows some results from calculations of the EGI for countries in Africa (Lockwood and Redoano 2005). The table includes only those countries for which sufficient data were available to compute the index between 1983 and 2004. Some countries enter the series during this period. This is a problem and is due entirely to the lack of data. There are also significant country omissions, such as Ghana, Tanzania, Uganda, Madagascar, Burundi, and Ethiopia, some of which figure prominently in empirical and analytical

Table 11.7. Economic globalization index for countries in Africa

	1983	1987	1990	1993	1997	2000	2004
Angola							0.219
Benin			0.079	0.100	0.101	0.097	0.084
Burkina Faso	0.094	0.098	0.094	0.102	0.099	0.099	0.089
Botswana	0.183	0.201	0.159	0.136	0.163	0.154	0.135
Côte d'Ivoire	0.134	0.128	0.128	0.124	0.146	0.145	0.154
Cameroon		0.081	0.085	0.083	0.102	0.115	0.114
Congo, Republic of					0.202	0.194	0.195
Comoros	0.047	0.039	0.029	0.038	0.048	0.030	0.033
Cape Verde						0.085	0.097
Gabon					0.129	0.136	0.134
Guinea						0.093	0.102
Guinea-Bissau							0.096
Kenya	0.116	0.115	0.129	0.168	0.137	0.136	0.127
Liberia	0.146	0.126	0.128	0.132	0.137	0.107	0.091
Mali							0.131
Mozambique							0.151
Mauritania				0.138	0.113	0.110	0.119
Mauritius			0.168	0.131	0.128	0.132	0.127
Malawi	0.105	0.109	0.109	0.100	0.137	0.150	0.128
Namibia							0.144
Niger	0.089	0.098	0.097	0.099	0.088	0.093	0.180
Nigeria		0.157	0.181	0.210	0.193	0.202	0.101
Rwanda	0.060	0.058	0.050	0.058	0.067	0.064	0.069
Sudan							0.097
Senegal	0.135	0.095	0.100	0.093	0.111	0.120	0.124
Sierra Leone	0.054	0.082	0.104	0.084	0.055	0.084	0.090
São Tomé and Príncipe	0.017	0.002	0.000	0.025	0.057	0.082	0.125
Swaziland	0.195	0.213	0.210	0.219	0.204	0.201	0.223
Seychelles			0.090	0.078	0.100	0.129	0.129
Togo	0.137	0.129	0.131	0.102	0.121	0.127	0.131
South Africa					0.119	0.126	0.135
Zambia					0.135	0.136	0.121
Zimbabwe	0.091	0.104	0.106	0.127	0.151	0.123	0.072

Notes: Some countries are excluded owing to the lack of data necessary to compile the index to date. These include Burundi, Central African Republic, Eritrea, Ethiopia, Ghana, the Gambia, Equatorial Guinea, Lesotho, Madagascar, Mayotte, Somalia, Chad, Tanzania, Uganda, and Congo Democratic Republic.

Source: Lockwood and Redoano (2005).

work on globalization and poverty in Africa.[18] Viewing and comparing the outcomes for 2004, the results suggest that Swaziland is the most globalized African country, closely followed by Angola, and that Comoros is the least globalized. According to Lockwood and Redoano's calculations, a half of the twenty-five countries for which estimates exist are less globalized in 2004 than they were in 2000. Overall, the mixed picture across countries is a significant feature of the table. Some countries appear to show signs of steady globalization (South Africa, Cameroon), some show a downward trend (Liberia), some show U-shaped tendencies (Côte d'Ivoire), and others are inverse U-shaped (Zimbabwe, Nigeria). So the average trends for Africa reported earlier (Table 11.5) subsumes considerable variation across countries. Clearly, these results are questionable, and may say as much about the inadequacies of the data and methodology than about the level or trends in globalization. On the other hand, the fact that there is so much variation, with few countries showing striking changes, may confirm the view that Africa is not showing significant signs of globalization.

11.3.4. Evidence on Change in Poverty Levels at the Country Level in Sub-Saharan Africa

Evidence on the level and change in (income) poverty in SSA, either at the all-Africa level or country level across Africa, is relatively scarce (Ali and Thorbecke 2000). There has been a sequence of important studies by Ravallion and Chen (most recently, for example, Chen and Ravallion 2007) in attempting to make international poverty comparisons at the global and regional levels. This project has helped significantly in assembling a database of household surveys, although there are well-known issues of data quality and comparability, both between surveys for individual countries (i.e., over time) and across countries, that make comparisons difficult. In their study making international poverty comparisons Chen and Ravallion (2004; 2007) rely on a small number of countries, and benchmark their poverty comparisons to international poverty lines, including the US$1 per day (US$30.42 per month) line.

Ali and Thorbecke (2000) assesses the level and change in poverty in Africa based on secondary information for sixteen SSA countries (representing about 47 per cent of the total population of SSA). As in the present study, their objective is mainly descriptive and uses countries as the units of observation. However, instead of using absolute poverty lines (e.g., international poverty lines), they estimate relative poverty lines, but build in a non-proportional

[18] The introduction of countries or complete omission into the EGI for SSA is also problematic for interpreting the regional index. Countries are weighted by GDP PPP to form the aggregate index, so the EGI index is affected as and when countries are included, and the weights are adjusted.

variation of the poverty lines with income, thereby avoiding the usual assumption that 'poverty changes over time are not affected by the growth in mean income' (Ali and Thorbecke 2000: 13). Their study focuses on an analysis of rural versus urban poverty, the relationship between the change in poverty and the change in mean income, and the change in distribution (inequality). Their results show that change in inequality matters, especially as regards the results for urban poverty. Importantly, the research is based on secondary data generated by PovcalNet, a programme for calculating poverty measures from grouped data developed in Chen and Ravallion (2004).

In this section we also use PovcalNet, but advance one stage further into the realm of secondary data by generating some observations on poverty (headcount ratios) and inequality (Gini coefficients) for selected African countries from PovcalNet. PovcalNet generates these summary statistics based on grouped data drawn from a databank of household surveys for selected countries, and chosen poverty lines. The default poverty line is the PPP-based US$1 a day international line, although this can be varied. In view of the availability of this database and software, PovcalNet was applied to all the datasets available for African countries, selecting those countries for which there are at least two household surveys. This gave rise to results for nineteen countries, spanning the period 1985 to 2000. Chen and Ravallion (2004) and earlier papers discuss in detail the problems of the comparability and consistency of household surveys, and there are many.[19] So in those cases where more than two household surveys are available, two surveys were selected to achieve what seemed to be the best degree of comparability. The surveys chosen were not always the earliest and latest surveys available for each country, and the intervals between surveys are quite variable, ranging from two years (Zambia) to ten years (Uganda), with an average gap of 5.6 years. PovcalNet generates estimates of the headcount, poverty gap (PG) and squared PG ratios, and the Gini coefficient. However, for our purposes, we confine our attention to the headcount ratio and Gini coefficient, and simply observe the directions of change that are indicated by these respective estimates in each country and disregard the magnitude of change.[20] Table 11.8 sets out the results.

Overall, the results in Table 11.8 show a preponderance of countries where it appears poverty (headcount ratio) has been falling between survey years. In twelve countries the headcount ratio fell, in six countries it rose, and in

[19] Detailed notes accompanying PovcalNet indicate that surveys for individual countries may not be comparable: Priority Surveys alongside LSMS surveys, Integrated Household Surveys, income and expenditure surveys, welfare monitoring surveys, etc.

[20] For those countries in which there are more than two surveys, the direction of change is not always uniform, and this is a further complication of this cursory analysis. It might, of course, be possible to use other information (maybe country poverty assessments) to ascertain whether poverty has been generally falling, rising, or changing direction during the past fifteen to twenty years.

Table 11.8. Poverty and inequality change at the country level in Africa: some evidence based on PovcalNet

Country	Survey years	Headcount (%)	Change (+/−)	Gini coefficients	Change (+/−)
Botswana	1985–93	33.3–32.1	−	54.2–66.7	+
Burkina Faso	1994–8	51.4–44.9	−	50.7–46.9	−
Burundi	1992–8	45.2–54.6	+	33.3–42.3	+
Cameroon	1996–2001	32.5–17.1	−	46.8–44.6	−
Côte d'Ivoire	1993–8	9.9–15.5	+	36.9–43.8	+
Ethiopia	1995–2000	31.3–23.0	−	40.0–30.0	−
The Gambia	1992–8	53.7–27.1	−	47.8–50.2	+
Ghana	1988–98	45.5–40.5	−	36.0–40.8	+
Kenya	1994–7	26.5–20.1	−	44.5–42.5	−
Lesotho	1986–95	30.3–36.4	+	56.0–63.1	+
Madagascar	1993–9	46.3–66.0	+	46.1–39.1	−
Malawi	1997–2004	41.7–21.3	−	50.3–39.0	−
Mali	1994–2001	72.3–36.4	−	50.5–40.0	−
Mauritania	1995–2000	28.6–25.9	−	37.3–39.0	+
Niger	1992–4	41.7–54.8	+	36.1–41.5	+
Nigeria	1992–6	59.2–77.9	+	45.0–52.0	+
Rwanda	1984–99	35.7–51.8	+	28.9–45.4	+
Senegal	1994–2001	24.0–17.0	−	41.4–41.3	=
South Africa	1993–2000	10.0–10.7	=	59.3–57.8	−
Uganda	1989–99	39.2–26.4	−	44.4–43.1	−
Zambia	1996–8	72.6–65.7	−	49.8–52.4	+
Zimbabwe	1990–5	54.4–56.1	+	56.2–50.1	−

Notes: PovcalNet is software written by Chen and Ravallion which computes headcount (and poverty gap and squared poverty gap) indices based on a chosen poverty line and household survey data, usually in grouped data format. In this table the poverty line is the US$1-a-day international poverty line, converted into local currency (within PovcalNet), using PPP estimates.

Source: PovcalNet <http://iresearch.worldbank.org/PovcalNet/jsp/index.jsp> and Chen and Ravallion (2004).

one country (South Africa) it was virtually unchanged. This pattern is broadly consistent with the overall estimates produced by Chen and Ravallion (2007) and reproduced earlier in Table 11.3. As regards inequality (Gini coefficient), PovcalNet generated results showing six countries where inequality fell, eleven in which it increased, and two countries (Kenya[21] and Uganda) in which it was virtually unchanged. It suggests a tendency for inequality to have increased

[21] The results for Kenya are perhaps surprising and questionable on the grounds that this change was based on a short time-interval (1994–7) and that it excludes results from the 1998–9 Integrated Household Survey, which indicated a marked increase in inequality.

overall. Of potentially greater interest is the outcome in terms of both poverty and inequality in each country. In those countries where poverty increased, the predominant outcome was that inequality also increased, whereas in those countries where poverty decreased, there was no clear direction of change in inequality. Obviously, it is difficult to draw firm conclusions without introducing information on growth rates and other controlling variables at the country level, so as ascertain whether it is the growth in incomes (or the lack of it) and/or changes in inequality that best describe the outcome on the change in poverty. Nevertheless, the pattern of results at the country level does not appear to be clear-cut. Also, as noted earlier, we need to be cautious about the comparability of surveys and of placing too much reliance on just two data points for each country.

The evidence above on the level and change in poverty and inequality on the one hand and the relative indices of economic globalization on the other permit us to carry out some tentative associations between variables. Tables 11.7 and 11.8 show there are twelve countries[22] for which estimates exist on the levels and change in poverty and inequality, between various years, and globalization indices for 2004. As the poverty and inequality estimates for countries span varying time-periods, to standardize the changes, the estimates shown in Table 11.7 are divided by the span of years. Figures 11.3, 11.4, and 11.5 show simple plots of the 2004 economic globalization index versus the level of poverty, and versus the change in poverty, and versus the change in inequality.

The simple linear correlation coefficients between the globalization index and (i) the level of poverty is −0.30; (ii) the change in poverty is 0.32; and (iii) the change in inequality is 0.71. Only in (iii) is the coefficient significantly different from zero. These results suggest that globalization may be associated with an increase in inequality, with an increase in poverty, though with a lower *level* of poverty. Thus, countries which are more 'globalized' tend to have a lower level of poverty although poverty is increasing in these countries and so is inequality. This suggests that globalization may be associated with increasing inequality and (hence) with an increase in poverty. However, the evidence is not strong and is at best indicative.

11.3.5. Other Country-level Dimensions of Change in Poverty in Africa

This study has focused exclusively on income poverty. Other socio-economic dimensions of well-being have not been considered and it is a moot point whether, and to what extent, health, education, environmental sustainability, gender imbalance, etc., have been affected by (and in turn may influence) globalization and growth. But this would broaden the scope of the chapter

[22] The countries included are Botswana, Burkina Faso, Cameroon, Côte d'Ivoire, Kenya, Mauritania, Niger, Nigeria, Senegal, South Africa, Zambia, and Zimbabwe.

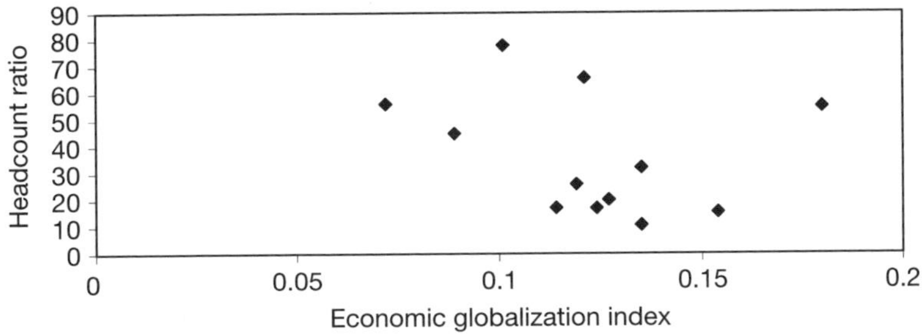

Fig. 11.3. Poverty versus globalization

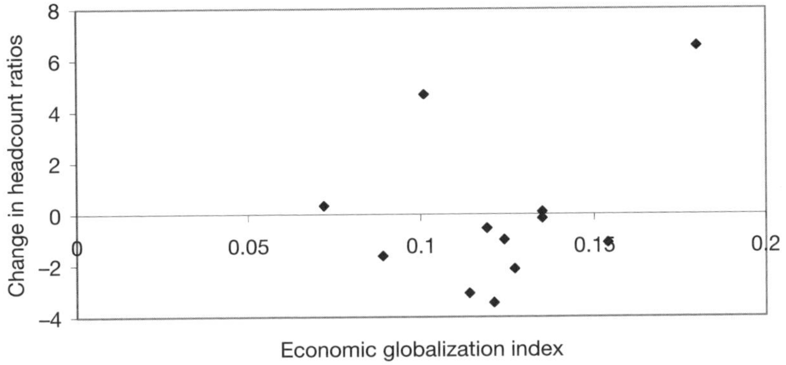

Fig. 11.4. Change in poverty versus globalization

beyond feasible limits. Useful sources of evidence for Africa are summarized in Geda and Shimeless (2005); UNECA (2005); and Commission for Africa (2005).

What perhaps is more useful as a prelude to analytical work is the evidence on structural profiles in African countries. Structural features are now considered to be central to understanding the channels through which globalization impacts on growth, poverty, and inequality (Nissanke and Thorbecke 2005; Culpeper 2005) and also underpin the possible policy initiatives underlying 'pro-poor growth'. Structural features are wide-ranging, going beyond product or sectoral disaggregations, and include rural–urban dimensions, gender, labour markets (by skill, formal–informal employment), and the ownership of enterprises (private–public, foreign and domestic ownership). Many of these profiles are discussed, and some evidence presented, in the reports for the Economic Commission for Africa (UNECA 2005) and in a study by Fielding (2001).

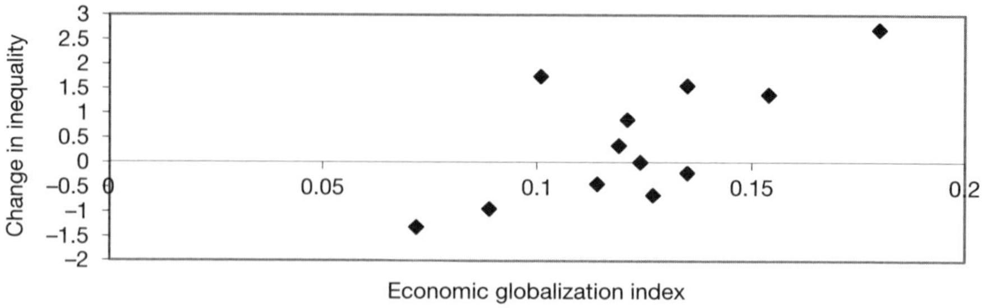

Fig. 11.5. Change in inequality versus globalization

Source: For Figs. 11.3, 11.4, and 11.5, the plots are based on Tables 11.7 and 11.8.

According to the standard HOS (Heckscher–Ohlin–Samuleson) trade model, trade liberalization in Africa should lead (or have led) to an expansion of use of its most abundant factor resource, low-skilled labour. Because of the anti-agricultural bias of trade protection (UNECA 2005) this should be expected to boost, *ceteris paribus*, an expansion of small-scale agriculture, and a relative reduction of rural poverty. In their summary of the extent of poverty in Africa, Ali and Thorbecke 2000 notes that at the beginning of the 1990s, rural poverty was very widespread and substantially higher than urban poverty.[23] So what we have produced in Table 11.9 is the available evidence on rural and poverty headcount ratios at the country level in Africa, based on published household survey data post-1990 in *World Development Indicators 2005* (World Bank 2005). We assume that the survey results for urban and rural households are more likely to be comparable than between countries or over time. Out of thirty-two surveys reported in Table 11.9, in thirty cases there was a positive differential between rural and urban poverty, and in many cases this is recorded as a double-digit difference.[24] So rural poverty in Africa remains persistent and is substantially higher than in urban areas (Wood 1998). In only ten countries is there reported evidence from more than one survey and (as mentioned earlier) it is questionable whether the surveys for each country are directly comparable. Nevertheless, in half of the countries, the rural–urban differential in headcount ratios fell and in half they rose: at best, this is an inconclusive result.

[23] Note that the urban and rural poverty lines were not the same, because their estimates were based on relative and country-specific poverty lines. But still, the rural and urban poverty ratios headcount, poverty gap, and squared PG were substantially different.

[24] These results are based on national not international poverty lines and we must assume that in most cases if not all there are no separate rural and urban poverty lines. This may exaggerate the rural–urban differential, but they are still considered large.

Table 11.9. Rural–urban differentials of poverty ratios (headcount ratios)

Country	Survey year	Rural-urban poverty differential (% headcount ratio)
Benin	1995	−3.3
	1999	9.7
Burkina Faso	1994	40.6
	1998	34.6
Burundi	1990	−7.0
Cameroon	1996	18.2
	2001	27.8
Chad	1996	4.0
Ethiopia	1996	13.7
	2000	8.0
The Gambia	1998	13.0
Ghana	1999	31.9
Kenya	1994	18.0
	1997	4.0
Madagascar	1997	12.8
	1999	24.6
Malawi	1998	11.6
Mali	1998	45.8
Namibia	1996	35.4
	2000	35.8
Mozambique	1997	9.3
Nigeria	1993	6.0
Niger	1993	14.0
Rwanda	2000	51.4
Senegal	1992	16.8
Sierra Leone	2004	22.4
Tanzania	1991	9.6
	2001	9.2
Zambia	1996	36.8
	1998	27.1
Zimbabwe	1992	32.4
	1996	40.1

Source: Based on UNECA (2005: fig. 11.3). Own calculations from data derived from World Bank (2005).

Table 11.10. Subgroups of Sub-Saharan African countries used in Table 11.6

Oil-producing countries	Resource intensive	Coastal, resource poor	Landlocked, resource poor	Fast growers (g > 0: 1990–4)	Slow growers (g < 0: 1990–4)
Angola	Angola	Benin	Burkina Faso	Equatorial Guinea	Angola
Cameroon	Botswana	Cape Verde	Burundi	Nigeria	Cameroon
Congo, Republic of	Cameroon	Comoros	Central African Republic	Botswana	Congo, Republic of
Equatorial Guinea	Congo, Republic of	Côte d'Ivoire	Chad	Namibia	Sierra Leone
São Tomé and Príncipe	Equatorial Guinea	The Gambia	Congo, Democratic Republic	Benin	Zambia
Côte d'Ivoire	Gabon	Ghana	Ethiopia	Cape Verde	Côte d'Ivoire
Chad	Guinea	Guinea-Bissau	Lesotho	Ghana	Madagascar
Gabon	Namibia	Kenya	Malawi	Guinea-Bissau	Togo
Nigeria	São Tomé and Príncipe	Madagascar	Mali	Mauritius	Burundi
	Sierra Leone	Mauritius	Niger	Mozambique	Central African Republic
	Zambia	Mozambique	Rwanda	Seychelles	Congo, Democratic Republic
		Senegal	Swaziland	Burkina Faso	Niger
		Seychelles	Uganda	Lesotho	Rwanda
		South Africa	Zimbabwe	Swaziland	Guinea
		Tanzania		Uganda	São Tomé and Príncipe
		Togo		Mali	Comoros
				Chad	Zimbabwe
				Gambia, The	Kenya
				Gabon	Senegal
					South Africa
					Tanzania
					Ethiopia
					Malawi

Source: IMF (2005: tables A2, A3).

11.4. Analytical Approaches and Empirical Evidence for Africa

11.4.1. Deeper Analytical Approaches

A more rigorous empirical investigation of the channels of influence and possible causal relationships within the globalization–growth–inequality–poverty nexus, set out and discussed in Nissanke and Thorbecke (2005), invites several alternative approaches of analysis.[25] Each analytical approach has both advantages and disadvantages: there is no universally acceptable way in which one can assess the impacts of a globalization shock, or indeed of any impulse, conclusively. Theory alone is not sufficient and it is necessary to pursue an evidence-based (empirical) approach to assess the linkages and impacts further. At the risk of some oversimplification, existing studies may be dichotomized into econometric and simulation approaches. We first briefly set out some of the pros and cons of these approaches because this is relevant to a review of the studies we consider subsequently.

11.4.2. Econometric Analysis

Apart from their reliance on consistent data, whether cross-section, time series, or even panel data, econometric models are usually estimated as reduced-form relationships, and therefore the approach is quite problematic in ascertaining channels of effect linking policy variables with outcomes (Devarajan and Robinson 2005). These links ideally need to be identified via structural relationships (Fielding 2001). The econometric approach has therefore most often been used in the context of estimating channel 'segments', such as trade-growth, growth-inequality, trade-wages, export-performance-productivity relationships. Tied up with the difficulty of estimating structural relationships, there is the problem of choosing the relevant control variables so as to identify the channels of effect. For example, the magnitude of many responses (say, the income effects of price shocks) will depend crucially on sociopolitical factors as well as economic factors, of a country-specific or time-specific nature such as the institutional capability, local conflicts, geography, etc. (Bigsten and Fosu 2004). These are not easy to quantify and therefore not easy to account for in regressions. Nevertheless, the econometric approach has proved popular and useful in statistical (as opposed to structural) analyses of growth and inequality, determining regularities over time and across countries.

[25] Hertel and Reimer (2005) have recently surveyed alternative models of the effects of trade policy on the poor.

11.4.3. Simulation Modelling

Simulation models (such as computable general equilibrium, CGE, or linked micro-simulation-CGE models) are an alternative empirical approach to ascertaining magnitude and directions of effect explicitly via channels of impact, and are more suited to counterfactual rather than predictive analysis (Devarajan and Robinson 2005). There are several examples of their application in an African context, some of which are reviewed in the next section. Amongst the main advantages of CGE models is their ability to trace the effects of an exogenous 'shock' (in this case, for example, a globalizing shock such as the removal of tariffs, or inflows of capital) through the system as it impacts on markets and on real incomes of households. They are representative of the classic counterfactual experimentation, and the literature is vast. Many scholars would caution about the drawbacks and even dangers of CGE modelling. For example, econometricians are sceptical of the use of single datapoint 'estimates' or even 'guesstimates' of parameters. Macroeconomists are wary of the primitive or even ad hoc macroeconomic features that many models employ along with large dimensional equilibrium representations of product and factor markets (Robinson and Lofgren 2005). For sure, it has been shown many times over that the macro 'closure' rules drive the results to a very significant degree. Most of the applications of CGE models are large-scale comparative static models showing impacts on representative household groups. To analyse poverty effects with these models, a further link has to be included, either within the model or bolted on to the model outcomes (Decaluwé et al. 1999). Recently, more technical advances have generated CGE models with dynamic features and several incorporating 'real' households (as opposed to models with 'representative household groups' usually referred to as RHG models) using micro-simulation methods. It is not yet possible to provide an assessment, let alone a blanket assurance, that these more complex models are better able to capture poverty impacts than their first-generation RHG counterparts.

11.4.4. Evidence for Africa

The specific links identified by Nissanke and Thorbecke (2005) are: globalization and growth, globalization and inequality, growth and inequality (bi-directional), and growth inequality on poverty. Within these broad links there may be several channels of effect. At first sight, there appear to be few studies that have specifically tackled the globalization–poverty relationship in the African context. But it is not difficult to uncover many studies that qualify on the grounds that either they deal with specific links (e.g., openness–growth) or they consider policy shocks (e.g., structural adjustment programmes and economic reform) that have related liberalizing features.

LINK 1: GLOBALIZATION AND GROWTH

There is a good deal of mainly cross-section econometric evidence on the linkage between trade openness and growth. The most highly regarded studies are those that include a SSA dummy (possibly including interaction effects with other explanatory variables) in a more globally based dataset. This is more likely to increase the explanatory power with more degrees of freedom. Interestingly, after controlling for geography and income, Frankel and Romer (1999) find no additional distinguishing factors for SSA. Greenaway, Morgan, and Wright (1998) provides a panel analysis of trade reforms and growth, based on data for seventy-three countries, worldwide. Again, they find strong evidence of trade-reform-induced effect on growth. They point out, however, that this is not necessarily a strong, or even a positive, effect for every country. But, importantly, they do not include separate regional effects, so one cannot generalize about Africa from their study. Harrison (1996) has also performed an earlier panel analysis of openness and growth, and she too finds a positive relationship. Alongside this positive evidence there is no counter evidence as such—that is, to demonstrate that openness is 'bad' for growth. The closest the dissenting voices (e.g., Ocampo and Taylor 1998) get to it are challenges to the assumptions made about the underlying microeconomic conditions and the potential regressive effects of globalization.

The specific evidence for Africa obtained from the global growth regressions is discussed by Collier and Gunning (1999). They report on four well-known studies that include Africa dummies. The studies are Barro and Lee (1994); Easterly and Levine (1997); Sachs and Warner (1997); and Collier and Gunning (1999). The periods covered are closely comparable, predominantly covering the 1960s to the 1980s. All studies include an openness variable along with many other similar explanatory variables, with different interaction terms, but all have an African (shift) dummy. In two of the studies (Barro–Lee and Easterly–Levine), the Africa dummy is significant while in the others (Sachs–Warner and Collier–Gunning), the inclusion of an openness variable renders the dummy insignificant. While these studies are searching for broader explanations for relatively poor growth performance in Africa, they do provide us with evidence that openness does have a growth-enhancing effect in the region. It is the strength of this effect that is more questionable.

While the cross-country growth regressions dominate, other studies provide significant and specific insights into the globalization–growth relationship, either at an individual country or sectoral level. A relatively early econometric study, Van Frausum and Sahn (1993), examines the possible macroeconomic effects of four exogenous shocks, including currency devaluation, in Malawi. There are many examples of similar models for other African economies. What they have in common is an attempt to track the consequences on other variables besides output. And this highlights channels of effect on households other than via growth. There are also early examples of fairly aggregative country-specific CGE models, which make no attempt at tracing the effects of shocks through to individual household groups, but nevertheless examine the short-run consequences of trade liberalization on the economy. Classic examples are Rattsø and Torvik 1998, both in an SSA and Zimbabwe context (they examine import rationing and trade liberalization but recognize the sensitivity of the results to alternative macro closure rules), and Davies, Rattsø, and Torvik (1998), who consider the macroeconomic effects of trade liberalization in Zimbabwe. Bigsten and Fosu (2004) uses an econometric approach using data for Cameroon, Ghana, Kenya, and Zimbabwe to demonstrate that under trade liberalization increases in exports of manufacturing firms lead to efficiency gains.

LINK 2: GLOBALIZATION AND INEQUALITY

The second primary macro-meso channel links globalization with income inequality. There are many possible channels of effect. According to trade theory, the impact of globalization on economies well-endowed with unskilled labour should see the demand for this labour increase and income inequality should fall (Nissanke and Thorbecke 2008). However, the extent to which globalization impacts on factor markets, goods markets, and on government income and expenditure, etc., is much more complex. Kanbur (1999) sets out the attendant problems of four facets of globalization on income distribution (principally the factoral distribution) in an African context. He provides no empirical evidence as such, but he urges caution against using theory to assume that the opportunities of globalization are a 'win-win' situation. Kanbur argues that inequality may well worsen, and is more concerned that this will induce policymakers into a retreat from globalization rather than managing the risk that inequality may increase. The direction and magnitude of the overall effect of globalization on inequality is not easy to assess analytically; it is largely an empirical issue.

In their econometric study of the long-term changes in the ratio of manufacturing wages and agricultural wages (a proxy for skilled–unskilled wage inequality) in Kenya, Bigsten and Durevall (2006) finds that greater openness was linked directly to a reduction in wage inequality. On the other hand, there is evidence in several African economies that there has been an increased urban–rural inequality, and that this is a source of the overall increase in inequality. Nicita and Razzaz (2003) looks at the impact of an increase in textile exports on labour income in Madagascar and finds significant differences by gender. Textiles are a highly labour-intensive good, and tracing the effects through labour markets is an excellent way to see how the benefits impact on households: who benefits and how?

Fagernäs (2004) constructs a CGE model for Zimbabwe (based on the well-known, standard IFPRI model) to simulate the effects of adjustment and stabilization policies (devaluation and expenditure reduction). She considers the distributional implications for household groups (defined according to socio-economic group) and finds that while agricultural households gain, many other household lose under combinations of policies. It is of interest to note that she tries to compare her results with those of Davies, Rattsø, and Torvik (1998). Although the scenarios are different, her enquiry leads her to question the plausibility of her own results and to question the plausibility/validity of the macroeconomic closure rules of both models. This is a virtue of good-practice simulation work. Finally, Devarajan and van Mensbrugghe (2000) has also conducted a standard (RHG) CGE model analysis of the impact of trade reform on the income inequality between household defined according to their ethnic background and by income level. They show that trade reform could benefit black South Africans at the expense of white South Africans, although inequality would worsen within the black population and improve within the white population.

LINK 3: GROWTH AND INEQUALITY

Based on empirical evidence at a global level, Ferreira and Ravallion (2007) formulated a series of stylized facts about growth, poverty, and inequality[26] one of which is that 'economic growth tends to be distribution neutral on average in developing countries, in that [income] inequality tends to increase about as often as it decreases in growing economies' (Ferreira and Ravallion 2007: 17). They also offer some explanations for this outcome. While growth might be expected to generally reduce earnings inequality (through greater labour-force participation, higher returns to education, etc.) this might not apply universally across the population and earnings inequality might increase. Furthermore, they suggest that while greater (lower) earnings inequality might be expected to translate into greater (lower) household income inequality, this is not always the case.[27]

Evidence on the growth–inequality relationship in an African context is sparse. The global evidence on the correlates of income inequality, including economic growth and the level of development, has not been replicated for Africa, mainly due to the paucity of data. But, some evidence is now emerging. Two studies in particular arise. First, Odedokun and Round (2004) studied the bi-directional relationship between income inequality and growth in Africa using essentially cross-section evidence. The results suggest two things: first, that based on African data, the postulated causality from economic growth to inequality does not seem to be evident. Structural and geographical features were stronger explanations of inequality than growth per se. Second, the results suggest that inequality did appear to hinder growth in the countries sampled and, moreover, that inequality is associated with channels that adversely affect growth such as sociopolitical

[26] Based on 290 observations from 80 countries.

[27] In Taiwan, the entry of relatively skilled women into the labour force reduced earnings' inequality, but, as these women were married to skilled men, household income inequality increased (Ferreira and Ravallion 2008: 17).

instability, high fertility, and low school enrolment rates. In related work, Fielding and Torres (2006) attempt to investigate further the reasons for the negative African dummy in growth regressions. They conclude that the reasons can be partly attributed to 'ethno-linguistic fractionalization', geography and sociopolitical factors, underlining the earlier suggestion that channels of effect from inequality to growth may be multifarious and complex.

LINK 4: GROWTH AND INEQUALITY ON POVERTY

The question of the links from growth and inequality to determining the impacts on households groups and individuals has been addressed mainly (though not exclusively) via simulation models. Sahn, Dorosh, and Younger (1996) carry out a study of ten African countries to examine the effects of adjustment policies and agricultural reforms on the poor, but they use an eclectic mix of analytical tools to do so, ranging from econometric models, through partial equilibrium models and CGE models. Apart from the significance of their main conclusions—that the adjustment programmes were marginally beneficial to the poor, in that they precipitated a redistribution of benefits, though without positive growth effects—the study was instrumental in provoking a useful debate about the appropriateness of the methodology used. There are many other good examples of the use of CGE models in this context for African countries, including Chitiga (2000); Chitiga, Kandeiro, and Mabugu (2005) for Zimbabwe; and, most recently, Emini, Cockburn, and Decaluwé (2006) for Cameroon and Abdelkhalek (2006) for Morocco. Some of the most recent examples are highly innovative in having fully linked microsimulation and recursive dynamic features, thereby potentially embracing a fuller range of macro- and meso-level effects on households. The results from these models are not at all clear-cut and easy to summarize. There is a good deal of country-specificity: some evidence of inequalizing effects of trade policy shocks, and of poverty consequences that do not show dramatic improvement. There are some other studies that do not fit comfortably within this framework of analysis, but nevertheless provide valuable insights into what the data tell us. For example, Bigsten et al. (2003) uses panel data from household surveys in Ethiopia between 1994 and 1997 (the post-economic reform era) to examine the extent to which changes in poverty can be attributed to growth and distribution effects. The study is insightful. The authors conclude that increasing inequality offsets the potential poverty reduction from growth.

CASE-STUDY APPROACH

The studies reviewed above suggest that whatever methodological approach is pursued, a country case study may offer the best prospect of identifying the links, the channels of effect and their importance within the globalization–poverty nexus. There is clearly considerable country-specificity, and whether this generalizes across countries, or across groupings of countries according to typology, is a more open question.

A good example is South Africa, which is notable for its high degree of income inequality that has persisted in the post-apartheid era and throughout the recent era of globalization and liberalization. The indications are that there has been a decline in the dispersion of racial incomes and an increase in within-group income inequality. Several studies (e.g., Jenkins and Thomas 2004) indicate that there are several reasons for this, including, for example: (i) labour market imperfections and segmentation (wage differentials and unequal access to unemployment); and (ii) marked inequalities in asset-distribution, education, social spending, and land. Naudé and Coetzee (2004) and others suggest that globalization may have induced higher inequality through technological change, higher unemployment, and less wage income towards poorer/unskilled households.

11.4.5. Lessons from Asia?

In Chapter 4 in the present volume, Terutomo Ozawa analyses the widespread growth and poverty reduction across countries in Asia that has occurred, especially in the past three decades. Ozawa notes that the so-called 'flying geese' model of economic development characterizes the events in Asia well; whereby growth in the region as a whole can be characterized as a sequence of catch-up events in constituent economies. In that case, an early high-ranking 'follower-goose' (that is, to the 'lead-goose' the United States) was Japan, thereby creating a growth cluster, and hence a succession of middle-ranking 'follower-geese'. As Ozawa notes, many conditions and circumstances (including pro-growth and pro-poor policies) contributed to Asia's success in reducing poverty through significant growth, but the analysis also raises important questions as to what might be missing in the context of Africa. There are no straightforward answers to be reported here although two observations might be pertinent. First, it is not so obvious what 'lead-geese' are on the horizon for Africa. It is not clear who the 'lead-geese' are that would create the demand stimulus. The United States, China, and other industrializing countries in Asia are not obviously in the frame and, in any case, the emerging global recession and falling primary commodity prices will inevitably hamper any such stimulus. Second, and in a similar vein, Nayyar (2008) considered the potential for South Africa to become an engine for growth, in the same way that China, India, and Brazil stimulated growth in their regions. His analysis suggested that South Africa does not yet exhibit such potential.

11.5. Conclusions

The results here confirm that globalization has generally been a gradual and, indeed, a slow process in Africa relative to other global regions, whether globalization is perceived fairly narrowly as a process of greater trade openness or as a combination of several kinds of globalizing processes. The mechanisms through which globalization in its various manifestations impact on growth, inequality, and poverty are still a matter of intense debate. Some authors claim that globalization is good for poverty reduction by promoting growth, although the outcome may be affected (even mitigated or offset) by the effects on inequality. The net effects for Africa suggest that poverty incidence has remained persistently high alongside a relatively slow globalizing process and generally sluggish growth performance.

What the present study has shown is that there is considerable variation within these broad regional outcomes. For a start, income inequality within Africa (notwithstanding the difficulty as to how best to measure this) seems high relative to other regions and is persistently so. A priori expectations of the impact of globalization on distribution are not clear-cut (Kanbur 1999; Nissanke and Thorbecke 2005) and this is borne out by the evidence. Indeed, there are good reasons to expect that trade liberalization will not necessarily be inequality-reducing, as would be the naive expectation under the standard Heckscher–Ohlin–Samuelson model. Segmented factor markets (including rural and urban dichotomies) and entrenched social and culturally based gender and ethnic dimensions mean there is considerable country-specificity and no easy 'all-Africa' prediction. But, as regards globalization and growth outcomes since the early 1980s, the typology analysis has revealed marked variation across subgroups. In particular, and predictably, oil-producing and resource-intensive countries have grown faster, are significantly more open to trade, and attract a higher proportion of FDI relative to GDP than resource- poor countries. Geography also seems to matter in that amongst the resource-poor countries there appears to be some difference in the average performance of landlocked and coastal countries, although the differences are less clear-cut and maybe less significant.

The evidence on changes in poverty and inequality across African countries is more fragmentary, and therefore difficult to assess. There are several issues and difficulties here. First, there are relatively few African countries that are able to report household survey evidence on changes in income (or expenditure) on a comparable basis during the past twenty-five years. The partial evidence that does exist has been assessed for the Africa region as a whole by Chen and Ravallion (2004; 2007) and this underpins the outcome that suggests poverty incidence remains high. But, it is quite difficult to investigate changes in poverty incidence at a country level—for example, in line with typologies. Second, many works (amongst others, Ali and Thorbecke 2000) argue strongly for the use of country-specific (and locally based) poverty lines for country-level poverty monitoring and analysis. However, cross-country analysis can only be satisfactorily undertaken with international poverty lines. In this case, and based on Chen and Ravallion's PovcalNet software, we observe the broadly comparable changes in poverty incidence and income inequality across nineteen countries, and note that slightly more of the countries show a decline in poverty incidence, while roughly the same number of countries show an increase in inequality as show a decrease. There is still insufficient evidence to pursue cross-country empirical analysis suggested by Sahn and Younger (2004) or undertaken for selected countries by Christiaensen, Demery, and Paternostro (2003). In any case, there is so much country-specificity and so many problems with cross-country analysis, that it is likely that the only way to trace the various channels and mechanisms of globalization is through country studies.

References

Abdelkhalek, T. (2006) 'Trade Liberalization and Poverty in Morocco: A General Equilibrium Micro-simulation Analysis'. MPIA Working Paper 2006–12. <http://ssrn.com/abstract/906588>.

Acemoglu, D., S. Johnson, and J. A. Robinson (2001) 'The Colonial Origins of Comparative Development: An Empirical Investigation', *American Economic Review*, 91: 1369–401.

African Development Bank (ADB) (2005) *African Development Report 2005*. Oxford: Oxford University Press.

Ali, A., and E. Thorbecke (2000) 'The State and Path of Poverty in Sub-Saharan Africa: Some Preliminary Results', *Journal of African Economies*, 9 (Suppl.): 9–40.

Amin, A. A., D. Bussari, and T. Ntilivamunda (2005) 'Reforms, Governance and Africa's Growth Performance'. Paper presented at the international conference, 'NEPAD and the Future of Economic Policy in Africa', 9–12 Nov., Sénégal: IDEP (African Institute for Economic Development and Planning).

Barro, R., and J.-W. Lee (1994) 'Losers and Winners in Economic Growth', *Proceedings of the 1993 Annual World Bank Conference of Development Economics*, 267–97. Washington, DC: World Bank.

Bigsten, A., P. Collier, S. Dercon, et al. (2003) 'Risk Sharing in Labor Markets', *World Bank Economic Review*, 17: 349–66.

——and D. Durevall (2003) 'Globalization and Policy Effects in Africa', *World Economy*, 26: 1119–36.

————(2006) 'Openness and Wage Inequality in Kenya, 1964–2000', *World Development*, 34: 465–80.

——and A. Fosu (2004) 'Growth and Poverty in Africa: an Overview', *Journal of African Economies*, AERC Supplement 1: 1–15.

——A. Shimeles, B. Kebede, and M. Taddesse (2003) 'Growth and Poverty Reduction in Ethiopia: Evidence from Household Panel Surveys', *World Development*, 31: 87–106.

Birdsall, N., and A. Hamoudi (2002) 'Commodity Dependence, Trade, and Growth: When "Openness" is not Enough'. Working Paper 7. Washington, DC: Center for Global Development.

Bourguignon, F. (2004) 'The Poverty–Growth–Inequality Triangle'. Working Paper 125. New Delhi: Indian Council for Research on International Economic Relations.

Chen, S., and M. Ravallion (2004) 'How Have the World's Poorest Fared Since the Early 1980s?', *World Bank Research Observer*, 19: 141–70.

——(2007) 'Absolute Poverty Measures for the Developing World, 1981–2004'. Policy Research Working Paper 4211. Washington, DC: World Bank.

Chitiga, M. (2000) 'Distribution Policy under Trade Liberalization in Zimbabwe: A CGE Analysis', *Journal of African Economies*, 9: 101–31.

——T. Kandeiro, and R. Mabugu (2005) 'Computable General Equilibrium Micro-simulation Analysis of the Impact of Trade Policies on Poverty in Zimbabwe'. Cahiers de Recherche PEP-MPIA 2005-1. Montreal: PEP.

Christiaensen, L., L. Demery, and S. Paternostro (2003) 'Macro and Micro Perspectives of Growth and Poverty in Africa', *World Bank Economic Review*, 17: 317–47.

Collier, P., and J. W. Gunning (1999) 'Explaining African Economic Performance', *Journal of Economic Literature*, 37: 64–111.

——and S. O'Connell (2004) 'Growth in Africa: Opportunities, Syndromes and Episodes'. Paper presented at the African Policy Institutes Forum, 15–16 Nov., Harare.

Commission for Africa (2005) *Our Common Interest*. Report of the Commission for Africa. London: Commission for Africa.

Culpeper, R. (2005) 'Approaches to Globalization and Inequality with the International System'. Overarching Concerns Programme Paper 6. Geneva: UNRISD.

Davies, R., J. Rattsø, and R. Torvik (1998) 'Short-run Consequences of Trade Liberalization: A Computable General Equilibrium Model of Zimbabwe', *Journal of Policy Modeling*, 20: 305–33.

Decaluwé, B., A. Patry, L. Savard, and E. Thorbecke (1999) 'Poverty Analysis in a General Equilibrium Framework'. Cahiers de recherche PEP-MPIA 9909. Montreal: Université Laval, Département d'économique.

Devarajan, S., and D. van Mensbrugghe (2000) 'Trade Reform in South Africa: Impact on Households'. Paper presented at the conference, 'Poverty and the International Economy', 20–1 Oct., Stockholm.

——and S. Robinson (2005) 'The Influence of Computable General Equilibrium Models on Policy'. In T. Kehoe, T. N. Srinivasan, and J. Whalley (eds), *Frontiers in Applied General Equilibrium Modelling*. Cambridge: Cambridge University Press.

Dollar, D. (2005) 'Globalization, Poverty and Inequality since 1980', *World Bank Research Observer*, 20: 145–75.

——and A. Kraay (2004) Trade, Growth and Poverty', *Economic Journal*, 114: F22–F49.

Easterly, W., and R. Levine (1997) 'Africa's Growth Tragedy: Policies and Ethnic Divisions', *Quarterly Journal of Economics*, 112: 1203–50.

Emini, C. A., J. Cockburn, and B. Decaluwé (2006) 'The Poverty Impacts of the Doha Round in Cameroon: The Role of Tax Policy'. In T. Hertel and L. A. Winters (eds), *Poverty and the WTO: Impacts of the Doha Development Agenda*. Washington, DC: World Bank.

Fagernäs, S. (2004) 'Analysing the Distributional Impacts of Stabilization Policy with a CGE Model: Illustrations and Critique for Zimbabwe'. ESAU Working Paper 4. London: Overseas Development Institute.

Ferreira, F. H. G., and M. Ravallion (2008) 'Global Poverty and Inequality: A Review of the Evidence'. Policy Research Working Paper 4623. Washington, DC: World Bank.

Fielding, D. (2001), 'Why Is Africa So Poor? A Structural Model of Economic Development and Income Inequality'. Working Paper 143. Oxford: Centre for the Study of African Economies. <http://www.bepress.com/csae/paper143>.

——and S. Torres (2006) 'A Simultaneous Equation Model of Economic Development and Inequality', *Journal of Economic Inequality*, 4: 253–77.

Frankel, J., and D. Romer (1999) 'Does Trade Cause Growth?', *American Economic Review*, 89: 379–99.

Geda, A., and A. Shimeless (2005) 'Openness, Inequality and Poverty in Africa'. Addis Ababa: University of Ethiopia Department of Economics. mimeo.

Greenaway, D., W. Morgan, and P. Wright (1998) 'Trade Reform, Adjustment and Growth: What Does the Evidence Tell Us?', *Economic Journal*, 108: 1547–61.

Hammouda, H. B. (2004) 'Trade Liberalization and Development: Lessons for Africa'. Work in Progress Paper. Addis Ababa: Economic Commission for Africa, African Trade Policy Centre.

Harrison, A. E. (1996) 'Openness and Growth: A Time Series, Cross-country Analysis for Developing Countries', *Journal of Development Economics*, 48: 419–47.

Hertel, T., and J. Reimer (2005) 'Predicting the Poverty Impacts of Trade Reform', *Journal of International Trade and Economic Development*, 14: 377–405.

Heshmati, A. (2005) 'The Relationship between Income Inequality, Poverty, and Globalization'. Research Paper 2005/37. Helsinki: UNU-WIDER.

International Monetary Fund (IMF) (2005) *Regional Economic Outlook: Sub-Saharan Africa*. World Economic and Financial Surveys. Washington, DC: IMF.

Jenkins, C., and L. Thomas (2004) 'The Changing Nature of Inequality in South Africa'. In G. A. Cornia (ed.), *Inequality, Growth, and Poverty in an Era of Globalization*. Oxford: Oxford University Press for UNU-WIDER.

Kanbur, R. (1999) 'Income Distribution Implications of Globalization and Liberalization in Africa'. Ithaca, NY: Cornell University. mimeo.

Kaufmann, D., A. Kraay, and M. Mastruzzi (2003) 'Governance Matters III: Governance Indicators for 1996–2002', *World Bank Economic Review*, 12 (updated dataset 2005).

Kayizzi-Mugerwa, S. (2001) 'Globalization, Growth and Income Inequality: The African Experience'. Working Paper 86. Paris: OECD Development Centre.

Kearney, A. T. (2001) 'Measuring Globalization', *Foreign Policy*, 122: 56–65.

Lockwood, B. (2004) 'How Robust is the Kearney/Foreign Policy Globalization Index?', *World Economy*, 28: 507–23.

——and M. Redoano (2005) 'The CSGR Globalization Index: An Introductory Guide'. Working Paper 155/04. Warwick: Centre for the Study of Globalization and Regionalization. <http://www2.warwick.ac.uk/fac/soc/csgr/index/download/>.

Milanović, B. (2002) 'True World Distribution, 1988 and 1993: First Calculation Based on Household Surveys Alone', *Economic Journal*, 112: 51–92.

——(2003) 'Is Inequality in Africa Really Different?'. Washington, DC: World Bank, Development Research Group. mimeo.

——(2005) *Worlds Apart*. Princeton, NJ: Princeton University Press.

Naudé, W., and R. Coetzee (2004) 'Globalization and Inequality in South Africa: Modelling the Labour Market Transmission', *Journal of Policy Modeling*, 26: 911–25.

Nayyar, D. (2008) 'China, India, Brazil, and South Africa in the World Economy: Engines of Growth?'. Discussion Paper 2008/05. Helsinki: UNU-WIDER.

Nicita A., and S. Razzaz (2003) 'Who Benefits and How Much?: How Gender Affects Welfare Impacts of a Booming Textile Industry'. Policy Research Working Paper 3029. Washington, DC: World Bank.

Nissanke, M., and E. Thorbecke (2005) 'Channels and Policy Debate in the Globalization–Inequality–Poverty Nexus'. Discussion Paper 2005/08. Helsinki: UNU-WIDER.

————(2008) 'Introduction: Globalization–Poverty Channels and Case Studies from Sub-Saharan Africa', *African Development Review*, 20: 1–19.

Ocampo, J. A., and L. Taylor (1998) 'Trade Liberalization in Developing Countries: Modest Benefits but Problems with Productivity Growth, Macro Prices, and Income Distribution', *Economic Journal*, 108: 1523–46.

Odedokun, M., and J. I. Round (2004) 'Determinants of Income Inequality and its Effects on Economic Growth: Evidence from African Countries', *African Development Review*, 16: 287–327.

Pritchett, L. (1996) 'Measuring Outward Orientation in LDCs: Can It Be Done?', *Journal of Development Economics*, 49: 307–35.

Rattsø, J., and R. Torvik (1998) 'Economic Openness, Trade Restrictions and External Shocks: Modelling Short-run Effects in Sub-Saharan Africa', *Economic Modelling*, 15: 257–86.

Ravallion, M. (2004) 'Competing Concepts of Inequality in the Globalization Debate'. Policy Research Working Paper 3243. Washington, DC: World Bank.

Robinson, S., and H. Lofgren (2005) 'Macro Models and Poverty Analysis: Theoretical Tensions and Empirical Practice', *Development Policy Review*, 23: 385–403.

Rodriguez, F., and D. Rodrik (1999) 'Trade Policy and Economic Growth: A Skeptic's Guide to the Cross-national Evidence'. Working Paper 7081. Cambridge, Mass.: NBER.

Sachs, J. D. (2003) 'Institutions Matter, but Not for Everything', *Finance and Development*, June: 38–41.

——and A. M. Warner (1995) 'Economic Reform and the Process of Global Integration', *Brookings Papers on Economic Activity*, 1: 1–118.

————(1997) 'Sources of Slow Growth in African Economies', *Journal of African Economies*, 6: 335–76.

Sahn, D. E., and S. D. Younger (2004) 'Growth and Poverty Reduction in Sub-Saharan Africa: Macroeconomic Adjustment and Beyond', *Journal of African Economies*, 13 (AERC Suppl. 1): i66–i95.

——P. Dorosh, and S. D. Younger (1996) 'Exchange Rate, Fiscal and Agricultural Policies in Africa: Does Adjustment Hurt the Poor?', *World Development*, 24: 719–47.

UNCTAD (United Nations Conference on Trade and Development) (2002) *The Least Developed Countries Report 2002: Escaping the Poverty Trap*. New York and Geneva: United Nations.

——(2003) *Economic Development in Africa: Trade Performance and Commodity Dependence*. New York and Geneva: United Nations.

——(2004a) *The Least Developed Countries Report 2004: Linking International Trade with Poverty Reduction*. New York and Geneva: United Nations.

——(2004b) *Economic Development in Africa: Trade Performance and Commodity Dependence*. New York and Geneva: United Nations.

——(2005) *Trade and Development Report 2005*. New York and Geneva: United Nations.

UNECA (United Nations Economic Commission for Africa) (1999) *Economic Report on Africa 1999: The Challenge of Poverty Reduction and Sustainability*. Addis Ababa: Economic Commission for Africa.

——(2004) *Economic Report on Africa 2004: Unlocking Africa's Trade Potential*. Addis Ababa: Economic Commission for Africa.

——(2005) *Economic Report on Africa 2005: Meeting the Challenges of Unemployment and Poverty*. Addis Ababa: Economic Commission for Africa.

Van Frausum, Y., and D. E. Sahn (1993) 'An Econometric Model of Malawi: Measuring the Effects of External Shock and Policies', *Journal of Policy Modeling*, 15: 313–27.

Wood, A. (1998) 'Globalization and the Rise of Labour Market Inequalities', *Economic Journal*, 108: 1463–81.

World Bank (2005) *World Development Indicators 2005*. Washington, DC: World Bank.

12

Globalization and Marginalization in Africa: Poverty, Risk, and Vulnerability in Rural Ethiopia

Stefan Dercon[1]

12.1. Introduction

The impact of globalization on the poor is one of the most emotive debates in the development policy community. Non-governmental organizations (NGOs) have been arguing that it is a process with disproportionate benefits for rich countries and multinationals, leaving poor countries and people behind (e.g., Oxfam 2000). The World Bank argued in its influential report on globalization (World Bank 2002) that it is not true that globalization makes rich people richer and poor people poorer since poverty is falling rapidly in those poor countries that are integrating into the global economy. In this chapter, we will revisit some of the arguments used in this debate, but with a focus on one particular context, Ethiopia, one of the poorest countries in the world. We examine the impact of globalization on the poor in this country, using evidence from rural panel data, and focusing not just on the level of poverty and its change but also on the risks in the livelihoods of the poor that may follow from globalization. The key finding is that not all will benefit in the same way, and any growth benefits are likely to be dependent on having access to good local infrastructure and communications. Households living further away from good roads and other forms of infrastructure risk further marginalization. Furthermore, liberalization and globalization are likely to shift the nature of the risks faced by households towards market-related risks, such as prices and demand shocks,

[1] I am grateful for useful comments obtained from the project directors of the UNU-WIDER project on 'The Impact of Globalization on the World's Poor' and the participants to the workshop in Johannesburg in Dec. 2005. Excellent research assistance by Sonya Krutikova is also gratefully acknowledged. All errors are mine.

requiring mechanisms to cope with risk other than those commonly used in rural economies.

One point should be clear from the outset. Given the nature of the question—the impact of globalization—empirical analysis using actual observed microdata is highly problematic and close to impossible. We can point to two methodological reasons for this. First, in the general debate, globalization is used as an evocative term describing the closer integration of societies and economies around the world. Integration is linked to lower trade barriers, reduced costs of transport, faster communication, including of ideas, and rising capital flows. It is a composite concept and, by its nature, vague in terms of what it actually describes. It is also a gradual process rather than a well-defined change at one particular moment in time.

Second, there is no doubt that something like 'globalization' is taking place across the world and Ethiopia is to some extent affected. But, even if one is able to define a general process as describing 'globalization', inference on its impact is highly problematic by the common lack of a well-defined counterfactual in the data available. Most studies appear to attribute observed changes over time in living standards and risk to globalization or specific elements of it. However, many aspects change over time, and many of them are represented by common factors in the data. Typically, therefore, they cannot be separately identified in the data. For example, simply observing an increase in the exports of a crop such as coffee (Ethiopia's most important export crop) may be due to opportunities offered by globalization, but it could also be due to improved extension services increasing productivity, or just a terms of trade (TOT) change related to domestic returns to alternative crops. In short, analysing 'globalization' as a 'natural experiment' is hardly possible, and more structural modelling is required to understand its impact.

There is no perfect solution. In this chapter, we simply try to bring persuasive evidence on one particular aspect of globalization: the likely impact of further trade liberalization on households, in terms of returns to their activities, their growth rate, and the risks they face. It will be done by assessing the impact of one specific period of liberalization in terms of its short-run impact on household living standards and its subsequent impact on risks faced. The period is well defined (the liberalization from a strict control regime between 1989 and 1991) and even though other factors may have caused some of the observed evolution of living standards, the evidence is sufficiently compelling to offer a persuasive narrative of how that episode of liberalization worked. In particular, in line with the theory of the impact of trade liberalization and the empirical evidence surrounding it (Winters, McCulloch, and McKay 2004), there seem to be relative winners and losers. Furthermore, since the evidence comes from panel data, one can look at some more long-run impact of the relative price change, thereby approximating the 'growth' effect of liberalization. Finally, since some continuing data collection took place to monitor the impact of risk and shocks, one can at least offer some suggestive evidence on how this period may have changed the risk environment faced by Ethiopian rural households. Taken together, a sense of the impact on poverty, poverty changes, and the vulnerability to poverty related to this liberalization episode can be constructed.

However, in order to put this micro-level evidence into better perspective, we offer first a more general view of how we think that globalization is currently affecting a country such as Ethiopia, given its defining and problematic features in the African context. This discussion is first introduced in the next section, which covers relatively well-trodden terrain and where it is argued that despite some apparent advantages of integration into the world economy, large parts of Africa may well have missed the boat. In section 12.3, this discussion is made more specific to an economy such as Ethiopia. Section 12.4 then introduces the liberalization phase studied, and examines the micro-level evidence between 1989 and 1999. Section 12.5 then offers some insights on the changing risk environment that may have affected the risk-related vulnerability faced by the studied households. As most of the evidence in this chapter is from the 1990s, we briefly comment in the conclusion on the situation since 2005, with high food and fuel prices, and its implications for the globalization process as seen from Ethiopia.

12.2. The Globalization Debate and Africa: Theory and Macro-evidence

In this section, we introduce some elements of the debate on globalization and the poor in Africa. In covering rather familiar arguments, we are preparing the ground for testing the plausibility of these in the context of a country like Ethiopia. In identifying the relevant 'theory' of beneficial globalization, we focus specifically on the impact of trade liberalization on Africa's poor. Simply speaking, globalization theory, as applied to trade, is the combination of standard arguments for free trade and markets, combined with an appeal to a *growth* effect from the trade regime. This is different from standard trade theory, which simply predicts 'gains from trade' from exploiting comparative advantage—effectively a once-and-for-all increase in output and income. The 'globalization' argument appeals to ever-increasing output or growth induced by openness. In the parlance of the endogenous growth literature, it suggests that trade orientation is a specific 'initial condition', offering a source of 'increasing returns', affecting long-run steady state output and growth. The mechanism by which openness affects growth could be manifold, ranging from incentives to increase efficiency following more competition to the development of better market-oriented institutions from the confrontation with the rest of the world.

As is well known, the effect on the poor is typically not well identified in theory—if only because most growth models are representative agent models. However, this effect can be identified as an extension of the standard distributional impact of trade liberalization in standard theory based on the Heckscher–Ohlin model, or related insights from the Stolper–Samuelson set-up. In particular, labour is the most abundant factor in most poor developing countries, so that trade liberalization will encourage specialization in labour-intensive production, increasing labour demand. Since labour is usually the only asset of the poor, trade liberalization will result in poverty reduction. The growth effects from openness further contribute to poverty reduction, via increased labour demand.

There is empirical evidence of the expansion of labour-intensive production in developing countries, consistent with their comparative advantage. Davis and Weinstein (2003) find that developing country exports as a whole are now indeed labour intensive. Countries such as China, India, Bangladesh, Sri Lanka, and Indonesia—the populations of which constitute the majority of that of the developing world—all have a share of manufacturing in total exports above or close to the world average. There is also evidence of substantial poverty reduction in a number of developing countries over recent decades, most notably in China, where between and 1999 the number of poor declined by more than 200 million. Other more recent success stories include Vietnam, where poverty was cut by half in the 1990s, as well as India and Uganda. These trends are possibly directly linked with the growth of labour-intensive exports.

A hotly debated issue is the role of trade liberalization and openness as causes of growth and poverty reduction. With some minimally imaginative presentation of the available data, the success in poverty reduction is typically larger in countries that have been able to increase their share of trade to GDP substantially since the 1980s. World Bank (2002) defines the 'globalizers' as the top third of developing countries in terms of the extent to which they have been able to increase their trade share in this period. In total there are about 3 billion people in these countries, dominated by China and India in terms of population.[2]

It is indeed the case that on average these 'globalizers' have been more successful both in terms of growth and poverty reduction than the other developing countries. Because of the magnitude of their population share, the presence of China and India in this group is largely responsible for a global decline in absolute poverty levels in the 1990s. This needs to be qualified by the fact that inequality has nevertheless increased in the largest 'globalizer', China, although not necessarily in other countries in this group.

But, the use of the term 'globalizers' may be misleading:[3] the fact that trade increased is not necessarily caused by a conscious policy of trade, exchange rate,

[2] The group also includes Argentina, Bangladesh, Brazil, Malaysia, Mexico, the Philippines, and Thailand, and some other smaller countries.

[3] The World Bank is aware of this possible misleading use of the term 'globalizers' noting that the rise in trade may not have been the consequence of pro-trade policies but 'may have been due to other policies or even to pure chance' (World Bank 2002).

and financial liberalization. While the association between openness, growth, and poverty reduction is evident, the causal link between these is harder to prove, and remains a hotly debated issue. For example, Dollar (1992); Sachs and Warner (1995); and Dollar and Kraay (2001) claim that liberal trade policies cause growth. Rodriguez and Rodrik (1999) argues that these studies are methodologically flawed and that they mainly show that good economic institutions rather than trade orientation matter for growth. In Rodriguez and Rodrik's view, liberalization may not be all that important; in their view, activist policies could well bring about more substantial trade and growth increases. Further, there is a line of literature assessing the impact of growth on poverty through its effect on inequality. Dollar and Kraay (2001) shows that there is a one-to-one relationship in mean income growth and income growth of the poorest 20 per cent. This result indicated that, proportionately, the gap between the poor and the mean individual remains constant so that inequality remains unaffected, leading the authors to the insight that 'growth is good for the poor'. They further argue that trade does not change this relationship. Ravallion (2003) finds compelling evidence that while on average openness does not affect inequality, in low-income countries it is associated with greater inequality. He also finds that even though on average growth is inequality neutral, beyond this average there is a diversity of experiences across the world, with some growth episodes coinciding with increases in inequality and others with decreases in inequality.

The notion that openness may not deliver growth and poverty reduction should be qualified. There is no evidence of any countries succeeding in bringing down poverty substantially without increasing growth (Ravallion 2003). There is also not much evidence of countries delivering substantial growth via persistent protection, or of countries that have been able to increase their growth rates by increasing protection. Openness may well be a characteristic of successful economies, possibly a necessary condition, but its importance and sufficiency are still debatable.

While some developing countries have been able to increase growth and their trade share, and reduce poverty, many others have failed in all these respects. Most of Africa and quite a few Asian and Latin American countries are in this situation, comprising roughly one billion people. If anything, many of these countries appear to become increasingly marginalized in the world economy, with negative per-capita growth rates in the recent decade and small but significant increases in poverty levels; there is even evidence of 'club convergence' towards permanently lower levels of income per capita. A key issue is then to understand the reasons for this trend. A simple explanation may be that such countries have had bad policies, not least in TOT orientation. But this cannot be the full story—quite a few of these African, Asian, and Latin American countries did introduce some trade liberalization in the last two decades, but with little impact in terms of sustained growth. A related explanation is that even with trade liberalization, growth is being stifled by poor infrastructure, low education, and corruption. Again, this would suggest that policymakers bear a substantial part of the responsibility for low growth and the persistence of poverty.

However, there are alternative possible explanations. An intuitively appealing one is that some countries suffer from the fundamental disadvantages of location: landlocked, disease-prone, tropical countries with harsh natural environments face a fundamental cost disadvantage (Sachs and Warner 1995). There is indeed evidence for Africa that marketing and transport costs are substantially higher, and these are not just caused by 'geography'. But are they largely influenced by poor investment in the quality of infrastructure or its management? For example, Collier and Gunning (1999) report that port charges in Abidjan in Côte d'Ivoire are far higher than in Antwerp: a container costs US$200 in the former compared with US$120 in the latter. Further, air transport in Africa is four times as expensive as in Asia, while rail freight charges are about double. In short, the differential growth experience between some of the largest Asian economies compared with Africa cannot easily be explained by simple geographical disadvantage: past investment patterns, linked to policy decisions, or at least lacking investment, are to blame as well.

Whatever the explanation for the past failure of some developing countries to increase their growth rates and trade shares, there is reason to be concerned that they may 'have missed the boat' (World Bank 2002). For instance, increasing returns in manufacturing activities and general agglomeration effects—that is, positive externalities to locating in the same geographical areas, mean that firms tend to locate in clusters. Once firms have set up in selected labour-abundant economies, latecomers have little to offer even if initially clusters could have been formed within these countries. Furthermore, the mere fact that some developing countries that have *not* missed the boat had similar initial characteristics to those that have, may induce further negative externalities from globalization. Since increased capital market liberalization in the globalizing economies will make capital inflows easier, not only will firms not locate in the latecomers, capital will be encouraged to flow away from these marginal economies into the globalizing ones. This could happen, via illegal capital flight, even if the marginal economies do not liberalize capital markets. For example, by 1990, 40 per cent of private African wealth was held outside Africa, even though capital is scarcer in Africa than anywhere else in the world (Collier, Hoeffler, and Pattillo 2001). Another self-perpetuating mechanism of marginalization includes the apparent higher risk of civil war in economies more heavily dependent on primary commodities; this increases the cost of failure to engage in the world economy (ibid.).

All this paints rather a bleak future for these marginal economies, not least in Africa. They may be stuck in a growth and poverty trap—an equilibrium outcome with permanently low growth and high poverty. While plausible, there is no reason for uniform pessimism, although naive optimism would be misplaced as well. In the recent few decades, a number of countries, often written off by experts, have been able to transform themselves. For example, the World Bank (2002) quotes how Nobel winner Gunnar Myrdal wrote off Indonesia in the 1960s only for it to emerge in the 1980s as a fast-growing economy substantially reducing poverty, aided by labour-intensive manufacturing exports. Even after the serious crisis of the late 1990s, poverty is far lower than in the early 1980s. Similarly, after descending into chaos and civil war in the first part of the 1980s, Uganda has emerged as a fast-growing economy, delivering large poverty reduction in both rural and urban areas.

However, the change required in many developing countries is substantial. If the current outcomes are an equilibrium growth and poverty trap, then mere small changes would be ineffective. If there are indeed multiple equilibria at play, then only a substantial 'shock' may bring these countries onto a higher growth path. Few would argue that mere trade orientation would do the trick. A drastic transformation of the investment climate, with better institutions and infrastructure, would be required, as well as much improved public service delivery of education and health services. These would in turn serve to increase the human capital likely to be required in order fully to capture the benefits from new investment. Globalization may have moved the production processes of many goods across the world, making multinational companies the scourge of anti-globalization campaigners. But many multinationals do not appear to be even considering investment in the marginal economies, not least in Africa.

12.3. Globalization, Marginalization, and Ethiopia

Suppose, as is plausible, that many African economies are best characterized as having 'missed the boat' in world economic growth and are characterized by a lower steady state growth rate than some of the Asian emerging economies. Furthermore, suppose that, as is again plausible, the international process of allocating capital has few if any incentives at present to move capital to Africa. This can be seen as caused by a combination of poor 'initial characteristics' such as a poor political and physical infrastructure and a related high-risk investment climate. Furthermore, as was argued before, a growth 'trap' may have developed with little or no incentives currently to move any manufacturing activities at any scale to Africa due to increasing returns in manufacturing activities and general agglomeration effects. This will create further constraints to Africa's rise to the challenge and induce a virtuous cycle of export-led growth (with its plausible self-reinforcing productivity enhancing process to sustain growth) or indeed any other growth process.

Before discussing the implications for understanding the impact of globalization on Ethiopia specifically, it is worth qualifying the above to account for some of the clear heterogeneity in Africa.[4]

Broadly speaking, one could consider three Africas: one consists of the resource-rich economies such as Nigeria, Congo, or Botswana. A second group is coastal Africa, with potential access to relatively low-cost transport of commodities to the rest of the world, with parts of countries such as Ghana, Côte d'Ivoire, or Kenya and Tanzania, and the third group is landlocked Africa, without harbours and with limited natural resources—Ethiopia clearly springs to mind, but also Uganda or Burkina Faso. The main constraints on these countries effectively engaging in world economic growth and, indeed, just attaining growth and poverty reduction at home, are quite different.

Take the resource-rich economies. Here the problem is not so much a problem of scarcity, but to some extent a problem of apparent affluence. The main issue for growth and poverty reduction would appear to be macroeconomic policy and general governance issues: how to ensure that the economy is not fundamentally undermined by the pressures caused by Dutch disease effects of natural resource windfall (including the incentives to move away from productive and tradable activities), and how to ensure that the richness earned by the government and by the country in general can be handled in a transparent, incorrupt way to enhance living standards and to invest in the future, such as in health, education, and infrastructure. The globalization process presents further opportunities and pressures but is possibly not the essential tool for the growth and poverty reduction in these economies.

The second set of countries, those with relatively good connections to world markets due to their location in coastal Africa, definitely have more to gain or lose from globalization. For these countries, trying to be competitive in attracting investment for manufacturing production (or indeed keeping African capital in their own continent for productive purposes) is the real challenge. The continuing rise of an export-oriented manufacturing industry across Asia, including China and, more recently, India, consistent with the presence of agglomeration effects, make the emergence or indeed survival of domestic industrial production difficult. Key policies here have to include the promotion of domestic competitiveness (including issues related to trade or labour market regulation), further infrastructural development, as well as basic macroeconomic management, including financial market development. WTO rules are bound to limit the range of instruments allowed to promote the emergence or sustaining of the export manufacturers in these latecomers in the globalizing economy. Liberalizing reforms, combined with substantial investment in human capital (health, education, and skills) appear necessary but are bound not to

[4] The classification in this chapter is closely related to the framework used by Ndulu et al. (2008).

be sufficient. The hurdles they have to overcome are tremendous, and a dependence on some preferential treatment vis-à-vis Asian manufacturing industries in terms of access to European and US markets may well be necessary and desirable.

But there is a third group for whom the luxury of natural resources and the opportunities of relatively good location and infrastructure are missing: landlocked economies with few resources, largely dependent on agriculture and an urban-based service sector with only a small manufacturing base without much export orientation. While their dependence on agriculture means that export earnings will continue to have to come from this sector, an increasingly integrated world economy means that graduating from an export-oriented agricultural sector to a more diversified export-oriented non-agricultural sector will be a slow and difficult process. Agricultural productivity growth may be a partial solution—but the poor location of these countries may make the move of some of their population to more coastal or, at least, better-connected areas a more effective strategy. Of course, this should not be attained by coercion but, rather, if immigration policies allow it, by the voluntary move in response to increased incentives from these areas. A landlocked economy fitting this bill is Burkina Faso, with much of its productive population already active in countries such as Côte d'Ivoire for many decades, even though the recent conflict and tension in the host economies have made this strategy a less plausible one for the Burkinabes.

So where does this leave a country like Ethiopia? Arguably, it starts with some of the worst endowments possible for an active part in the globalization game. It is (since 1996) landlocked, on poor terms with at least two of its neighbours, Eritrea and Somalia, and dependent on Djibouti for any exports. Its economic base is still largely agricultural, with coffee as the main export earner. In principle, it has embraced the necessity to liberalize the economy in order to engage in the world economy. In practice, however, while over the last decade it has initiated economic reform geared towards a more market-oriented economy, it is hard to find evidence of a real transformation. Some quarters of Addis Ababa appear to experience booms, but these tend to result from aid-fuelled, real-estate-led expansion of the non-tradable sector. Some urban centres and their surrounding countryside appear to have experienced strong growth in recent years, but their scale is too small to suggest the establishment of serious growth poles. Ethiopia remains on the fringes of the world economy, with only its coffee ever appearing in shopping baskets in Europe or the USA. Poverty levels have declined a little, but population growth has meant that the number of poor has probably increased in the last ten years.

Furthermore, Ethiopia has only recently emerged from another war, this time with Eritrea, which it granted independence only ten years ago. Even if observers and most international donors do not pin much blame on the Ethiopian government for the conflict, it again underlined the regional political instability, with civil war also raging in neighbouring Sudan and continuing anarchy in parts of former Somalia. It has just brought an end to another military adventure in Somalia, with little prospect of improved border conditions. Its own political institutions remain characterized by a reluctance to grant much voice to opposition groups, after a brief recent relaxation of some of the restrictions on freedom of expression in the national media around the 2005 elections. Ethnic tensions remain substantial. While infrastructure has improved in recent years, the road and communications networks remain very limited. There is evidence of some improvement in education as well, but skill and health levels remain generally poor. As one would expect in this type of risky environment, only limited Ethiopian capital is productively used within Ethiopia. Most strikingly this applies to human capital, with many skilled Ethiopians living abroad, if possible, in the USA or Canada, occupying low-skilled professions such as taxi driving in Washington, DC.

But, Ethiopia should be given some credit. It has a relatively competent and, broadly speaking, not corrupt civil service. While using antiquated and opaque procedures, its governance tends to be relatively efficient. Its macroeconomic policy management has made the birr a remarkably stable currency, even during the years of civil war and famine.[5] In 2008, the world food price fuelled macroeconomic instability after the 2005 elections, leading to strong inflationary and exchange rate pressure. On past performance, stabilization will be high on the agenda and likely to result in relatively effective measures to restore macroeconomic stability.

It also appears committed to reform, even though the process of opening up appears to be slow, not least after the recent war with Eritrea and the political tensions related to the 2005 elections. Recurrent drought and the recent high food prices put a lot of pressure on efforts to transform agriculture, even if there is also evidence of improved ability to manage these drought-induced crises in the short run using food aid and other transfer mechanisms. Ethiopia's policy-makers recognize the importance of agricultural growth, and there is some evidence of growth in agricultural productivity but only for a limited number of crops (such as maize). Even for these crops, however, growth remains well below the expectations raised by the agricultural extension and input programmes that started in the mid-1990s.

Poverty and growth traps may ask for bold measures, in the form of risk taking in economic policy to enforce a regime change, even though recent economic history across the world suggests that success cannot be guaranteed. The political economy in Ethiopia is characterized by serious suspicions

[5] In 1970, the Kenyan shilling, the Tanzanian shilling, the Ugandan shilling, and the Ethiopian birr were all trading at 2 to the US$. The exchange rates are now about 80 Kenyan shillings per US$, 1,375 Tanzanian shillings per US$ and 1,985 Ugandan shillings per US$, while the Ethiopian birr is trading at 10.6 birr per US$.

towards the government among the nascent middle classes. As a result, although possibly insufficient, only gradual reform may be possible. An improved investment climate requires not only a commitment to change, but one that is credible to local and foreign investors. At present, the policy environment is not sufficiently credible for donors to be willing to commit to the provision of large-scale foreign aid necessary to support the transformation of institutions, public services, and infrastructure.

But, even if economic and political regime change may come about, the nature of Ethiopia's landlocked, agricultural economy means that expectations cannot be too high. Liberalization of the economy, and increased export orientation are likely to constitute a sensible strategy, contributing to some further investment in different sectors.[6] At best, however, this approach will (in terms of sustained long-term growth) only be able to contribute to a modest growth. Export agriculture can provide a steady source of growth, but evidence from other countries suggests that it is hardly likely to generate much high productivity job creation, necessary for large-scale poverty reduction.

Still, in Ethiopia, this type of growth is essential to avoid falling further behind. The main first round impact from any process towards globalization will have to come from trade liberalization and its impact on the rural sector. Consequently the focus of the remainder of this chapter is on the short and long term impacts of increased liberalization on the rural sector and its poor, based on assessing its impact in a rural panel data sample.

12.4. Evidence from a Trade Liberalization Episode on Living Standards and Poverty in Ethiopia, 1989–95

Identifying the impact of trade liberalization on living conditions and poverty is complicated since most episodes occur both gradually and in the context of numerous other reforms. However, as is argued further, the biggest change in TOT liberalization in Ethiopia occurred around 1991. The data available for this period allow one to assess the impact of the episode on rural Ethiopia, providing a unique opportunity to determine the differential effect of such change on households in terms of subsequent living-standard levels and growth, as well as on risk.[7]

[6] For example, one has seen in recent years some horticultural investment (including for rose production) focused on the export market by air. Again, while important and innovative, the scale remains relatively small.

[7] In Chap. 6 of this volume, Hayami offers a discussion of the changes in the levels and structure of rural incomes and employment in a village in the Philippines during a period of 'globalization' between 1966 and 1996. Relative price changes were only indirectly a factor in that context as the main changes were rapid technology-driven changes in yields and rising urban and international demand for labour-intensive products.

Our method is to try first to identify the impact of the liberalization in the shortrun, via its impact on relative prices, as well as its subsequent impact on consumption and poverty outcomes in a number of villages in rural Ethiopia by 1994. We then extend the analysis to the medium term, by assessing whether the particular episode has a clear impact on the subsequent growth between 1994 and 1999 in these villages. This is important, since one of the main arguments in favour of these liberalization episodes is related to subsequent growth effects, not just 'first round' short-run effects of relative price change. Finally, we put the results into a somewhat broader context by using a larger sample briefly to comment on some of the factors that appear to matter substantially for growth. In the next section, we will briefly extend the analysis to 'risk' related to this and other liberalization episodes.

As part of its moves to a more market-based economy from a centrally controlled 'socialist' economy, the Ethiopian government liberalized its domestic agricultural markets between 1989 and 1992. Combined with the end of the civil war in 1991 and the liberalization of the movement of goods across regions around the same time, this change can be seen as overall trade liberalization between regions, from a situation of regionally closed economies. Before 1989, most trade between regions was either banned or very heavily taxed (Dercon 2002), so that internally the Ethiopian economy resembled a set of closed economies with high tariff barriers limiting the free flow of goods and services. The liberalization within Ethiopia from 1989 was then, in the first instance, a move to greater openness *between* regions *within* a country, not unlike the changes advocated by international institutions *between* countries. The growth and distributional impact of these changes can be studied using the Ethiopian Rural Household Survey (ERHS), a panel data survey covering households in different communities from 1989 until 2004. Lessons from studying welfare changes in this period are likely to be relevant to understanding the implications of trade and investment policy liberalization on the poor. Dercon and Krishnan (2002) and Dercon (2002) give more details on the data and the findings. The results related to the first phase of trade liberalization, between 1989 and 1995, are briefly summarized below. They are based on only a small sample of 354 households in six different communities across the country. No other data covering this period exist in Ethiopia. Dercon (2006) gives much more detail. Our focus is on the relative price changes resulting from liberalization, and the impact of these on households. The first issue is then to identify the price change induced by liberalization.

The policy measures meant that, compared with the years before 1989, agricultural crops could move freely across regional borders within the country without trade restrictions and heavy tariffs. Cereals such as teff, wheat, and maize were most strongly affected. This resulted in downward pressure on staple food-crop prices in food-deficit areas and upward pressure in surplus areas. Further measures allowing free entry into many trade and other business activities meant that food and other markets became spatially more integrated, resulting in lower marketing margins between the prices in surplus and deficit areas (Dercon 1995). These measures had less impact on previously smuggled crops, such as coffee and chat; once these began to be legally traded, prices settled at levels close to those seen in black markets before the liberalization. A subsequent decline in world coffee prices, however, resulted in actual declines in prices for coffee farmers. Finally, crops that were typically not traded across regional borders, bulky permanent crops like enset and yams, for instance, became relatively less interesting to grow, since they tended to be grown in cereal deficit areas, where consumers now could benefit from decreases in staple food prices. The overall result was that TOT moved very favourably for farmers in food surplus areas, especially in cereal areas, but farmers specializing in export crops such as coffee and chat, as well as in less-traded crops such as enset, experienced a relative decline. The evidence from the six survey villages broadly confirms these patterns. Table 12.1 gives the finding on the real producer price changes (i.e., relative to a food price deflator) between 1989 and 1995. Note that these changes in indexes are based on average changes per village: the underlying index is household-specific, with weights related to the share of income from each crop at the household level. As a result there is household-specific heterogeneity in this index, which is useful for further analysis.

On average, the villages saw their TOT[8] improve by about a quarter. The highest positive change in tradable crop prices occurred in villages situated in

Table 12.1. Real producer prices (percentage increases relative to 1989)[1]

	Dinki	Debre Berhan	Adele Keke	Koro Degaga	Gara Godo	Domaa	Average
All crops	+28	+21	+12	+65	−37	+35	+26
Tradables[2]	+28	+23	+15	+65	−12	+49	+31
Non-tradables[3]	....	....	−38	....	−77	−23	....
Food	+31	+21	+25	+65	−37	+35	+28
Coffee	....	....	....	....	+49	....	....
Chat	....	....	−9	....	....	....	....

Notes:
[1] Percentage changes in TOT, based on the movement of producer prices relative to food price inflation. The producer prices for different crops are weighted using the contribution to total crop income in 1994 of each crop (including production for home consumption), with different weights for each household. The reported figures are based on the producer price indexes, averaged across households in each community and across the sample. Producer prices for all indexes were taken from publications on rural producer prices at the subregional level, collected by the Central Statistical Authority. To achieve maximum comparability, only consumer prices collected by the Central Statistical Authority were used as well. Data were compiled for the same months so that differences do not reflect seasonality.
[2] Tradables: regularly traded food and cash crops in Ethiopia, i.e., most cereals and cash crops.
[3] Non-tradables: crops such as enset and sweet potatoes.

Source: Ethiopian Rural Household Survey and Central Statistical Authority.

[8] Terms of trade (TOT) are here defined as a Laspeyres output-weighted producer price deflated by a local consumer price index, using 1989 as a base.

broad surplus areas (Korodegaga, for example, is near Arsi, one of the main cereal producing areas in the country), while non-tradables generally saw declines in their prices. Tradable prices went up, but not in deficit areas—such as in Gara Godo, the only coffee village in the sample, despite the boom in coffee prices.

These trends confirm a standard result of the impact of liberalization: good for producers, net sellers of tradables and net buyers of non-tradables, not so good for net buyers of tradables and for producers of non-tradables. In a rural economy, all possible combinations of these types of households coexist, although typically in different areas. It leads to an important point for further analysis: the impact of the relative price change in terms of incentives to produce will depend on whether the household is net seller of what it produces.

Next, we build on Dercon (2006) to provide a simple regression analysis of the impact of the improved price incentives for tradables after liberalization, by regressing consumption growth between 1989 and 1995 on changes in the TOT, allowing for differential responses between food surplus farmers and deficit farmers.[9] In order to analyse the impact of the relative price change, one needs to ensure that any inference is not spurious. Therefore, we need to try to control for any other underlying factors that may explain changes in food consumption (note that no non-food consumption data are available for 1989). This is clearly important, given the substantive size of the consumption changes observed in these villages, as shown in Table 12.2.

Overall, poverty, based on absolute poverty line, declined substantially in the sample over this period: the number of poor households declined by about a third in our sample, even though more than 40 per cent of households remained poor. There appears to be a correlation between the TOT changes and the extent of the poverty decline per village. In fact, in the two villages where TOT declined, poverty did not decline at all; in one of them it increased substantially. However, this is not the full story. First, TOT changes do not affect every household in a village in the same way. Second, other measures undertaken as part of the liberalization may also provide opportunities or impose costs on households.

In order to control for both this heterogeneity in the impact across households and the possibility of spurious correlation, we run a regress growth in food consumption on a variety of controls for initial assets and characteristics, including land, household size (measured in terms of adult equivalent units), education, geography (distance to nearest town), and road infrastructure (whether any all-weather roads exist or not), 'exogenous' changes in these characteristics (in land and household size), and rainfall and serious illness shocks in this period. Note that the price changes are defined at the household level. Table 12.3 gives the results. One factor that is hard to control for is the

[9] Note that, by definition, all farmers are net sellers of non-food crops, such as coffee and chat. Even though some coffee and chat tend to be consumed as well this seems a safe assumption.

Table 12.2. Changes in food consumption per adult equivalent between 1989 and 1994–5[1]

	Dinki	Debre Berhan	Adele Keke	Koro Degaga	Gara Godo	Domaa	All
Mean food consumption 1989	50.0	53.0	64.0	37.0	27.0	25.0	42.0
Mean food consumption 1994	62.0	96.0	108.0	40.0	20.0	80.0	64.0
Headcount 1989	0.42	0.34	0.42	0.73	0.80	0.86	0.61
Poverty gap 1989	0.14	0.12	0.10	0.39	0.46	0.45	0.29
Squared poverty gap 1989	0.07	0.05	0.05	0.25	0.30	0.27	0.17
Headcount 1994–5	0.57	0.26	0.16	0.62	0.95	0.39	0.51
Poverty gap 1994–5	0.19	0.06	0.04	0.22	0.53	0.23	0.22
Squared poverty gap 1994–5	0.09	0.02	0.02	0.10	0.34	0.16	0.12

Notes:
[1] In birr, 1994 prices (n=354) (6 birr≈1 US$).

Source: Own calculations from Ethiopian Rural Household Survey. Food consumption is deflated by a food price deflator, using regional prices collected by the Central Statistical Authority. Consumption is expressed in 1994 prices. The nutritional equivalence scales used, and more details on the data are described in Dercon (2002).

impact of the end of the civil war. However, there is little reason to expect a relative price change from this. In addition, it is likely to be a common experience across all these villages as they were all far from the frontline. At least for our purposes, this impact is likely to be more of a 'fixed' effect for the entire sample which does not need to be controlled for explicitly as it is captured by the constant term.

The results suggest that many of the controls matter; important effects from road infrastructure and distance to town ('good' geography and roads meant much higher consumption growth), rainfall shocks ('better' rain has a strong impact), some role for initial characteristics (initial land), as well as exogenous changes in land.[10] However, a strong impact from the direct effect of the reform programme is also found: general improvement in the rural TOT, with much larger impact for surplus farmers. In sum, the changes in the rural TOT, quite clearly attributable to the reform programme, contributed to growth in food consumption in this period. But let us not forget that this effect will be negative for those who faced with declining TOT (including on average one village) during this reform period. Overall, there are clearly winners and losers from relative price changes induced by this process of trade liberalization.

Of particular interest is the impact on the poor. As was seen in Table 12.2, there was a considerable poverty decrease in this period, not dissimilar to the increase in consumption. It is possible to provide a decomposition of the change in consumption based on this linear regression using standard Blinder–Oaxaca decompositions. It is less known that one can also do a decomposition of the Watts poverty index using a linear regression-based decomposition. The Appendix to this chapter shows the method. The result is that one can identify the contributing factors to the total change in both the average change in food consumption and the poverty change.

Table 12.4 presents these results. First, it brings together the factors contributing to actual growth and poverty changes. Then, the table reports on an additional counterfactual: the case in which there were no reforms, so that none of the increases in returns and prices actually took place. The growth effect is derived simply by excluding the factors noted, based on the first column results, to contribute to actual growth and poverty changes from the findings. Since the poverty decompositions in contributing factors are counterfactual dependent (i.e., they are only correct to describe the contributing factors to a particular overall change), they cannot be derived directly from the second column (for details, see Dercon 2006). They are obtained by constructing a specific counterfactual distribution and then apply the decomposition as before.

[10] Note that these land changes are 'exogenous' to the household in that land is state owned and land is allocated, even though statistically one cannot exclude some placement effects and therefore problems with inference. Since this is not a variable of particular interest at this stage, we ignore this problem below.

Table 12.3. Change in log food consumption between 1989 and 1994

	Model 1		
	Coeff	t-value	Sample mean
Constant	0.185	(1.43)	1.000
ln (land in ha. +0.1)	0.211	(2.07)	0.160
Δln (land in ha. + 0.1)	0.239	(3.24)	0.327
ln (adults in 89)	−0.090	(−1.23)	1.549
Δln (adults)	0.287	(1.18)	0.091
ln (years adult education +1)	0.016	(0.07)	0.202
ln (number of adults serious ill +1)	−0.205	(−0.92)	0.188
Δ (% real terms of trade)	0.371	(3.67)	0.263
Δ (% real terms of trade) squared	0.642	(3.28)	0.187
Surplus farmer *Δ (% real terms of trade)^2	0.664	(3.50)	0.015
Δln (rain last season)	0.826	(4.12)	−0.179
ln (distance to town)[1]	−0.223	(−2.18)	0.000
Road infrastructure[1]	0.205	(2.36)	0.706
Adjusted R^2		0.09	

Notes: Linear regression: explaining changes in consumption; dependent variable: change in log food consumption between 1989 and 1994 (mean 0.3733; N=354); ordinary least squares regression with robust standard errors corrected for village cluster effects.

[1] Road infrastructure is a dummy whether the road linking the village to the nearest town is an all-weather road or not. The distance variable is the distance in km to the nearest town scaled relative to the mean distance in the sample.

Total per adult growth (defined by the change in the logs of per adult equivalent food consumption) was 32 per cent, while the poverty gap declined by 29 per cent. The table gives the contribution in percentage points to this change. Since the percentage change in both is very close in absolute terms (suggesting a scaled Watts poverty elasticity of −0.90), the percentages are directly comparable.

From Table 12.4, it can be concluded that growth in these villages was largely fuelled by relative price changes induced by reforms (and probably helped by peace); better TOT prices and better returns to location explain most of the growth. Poverty reduction is determined by similar factors, but scant rains for some hindered the decline. Crop price increases, a factor most directly linked to the reforms, contributed more to the decline in poverty than in growth. The poor benefited somewhat more than proportionately from better returns to roads, even though they include a significant remote group with poor infrastructure. Poor households grew in size in this sample by more than average, contributing to lower per-adult growth and higher poverty. Land increases for some of the poor meant that this contributed more to poverty reduction than to growth. Given the current (relatively equal) land distribution within

Table 12.4. Decomposition of growth *per adult* and poverty gap (percentage point contribution to total growth)

	Actual		Counterfactual, no reforms	
	growth	poverty	growth	poverty
Increase in land	7	−11	1	−1
Changes in returns to land	0	−0		
Terms of trade change	15	−30		
Rainfall shock	−8	25	−8	29
Returns to road infrastructure/location	19	−17		
Constant	5	−6	5	−7
Residual	0	3	0	6
Change in adult equiv. units	−5	7	−5	7
Percentage growth (sum of above)	32	−29	−7	34

Notes: Based on restricted version of model 1 in Table 12.3, re-estimated after imposing (and testing) linear restriction that insignificant variables are zero.

communities and the history of land reform in Ethiopia, however, this is not easily repeatable, nor desirable as a strategy. Since the poor typically have low potential or little land, they could not benefit from the increased returns to land, relative to the average household. Finally, the poor suffered disproportionately from sparse rains, limiting the poverty decline.

Nevertheless, inspecting these results further, it is found that the largest part of this poverty decline is driven by one group. More than 80 per cent of the actual poverty decline is accounted for by those leaving poverty between 1989 and 1994. Analysis in Dercon (2006) shows that this group had relatively good endowments, had experienced the most substantial crop price increases and were lucky with good rains. Those remaining in poverty experienced limited growth: their poverty gap only declined by an insignificant 4 per cent. With poor endowments and poorly accessible locations, increased returns via better prices were limited and virtually wiped out by poor rains. This is not dissimilar to the findings reported by Winters, McCulloch, and McKay (2004) from other studies: the ability to respond to the opportunities offered by liberalization seems to be determined by the endowments of the households involved.

The counterfactual result is to speculate, using the econometric model, what the consequences for local growth and poverty reduction would have been if policies had not changed. Recall, however, that the impact on prices appears to have been largely from liberalizing measures. In this simulation, none of the increased returns are assumed to have taken place, also implying a correction for the return on the changes in land (and optimistically assuming that they could have taken place). The relatively poor local rainfall in a few villages and population growth are then predicted to have resulted in a 7 per-cent decline in per adult consumption and a 34 per-cent increase in poverty. Looking further into this, most of this increase in poverty is for those who were poor in 1989 and remained poor in the actual data; those who actually moved out of poverty would have experienced zero poverty growth in this counterfactual scenario. This confirms that even if reforms did not benefit all poor households in the same way, *no* reforms clearly would have made the plight of this persistently poor group even worse.

In short, growth and the reforms appear to have been relatively pro-poor. The growth and poverty reduction in the surveyed villages appear to have been fuelled by these reforms. Nevertheless, the reforms were not pro-all-poor: the poor with good land, good location, and high producer price increases—about a quarter of the sample—benefited more than any other group. At the same time, however, a third of the sample, the poorly endowed poor in terms of land and location, experienced the lowest price increases and limited benefits from the reforms. Still, without the reforms the counterfactual analysis suggests that growth would have been negative and poverty would have increased.

However, one can hardly speak of 'growth' when considering the changes in the levels of consumption between two periods that are relatively close to each other with the last observation only a few years after the liberalization. In order to examine growth further, we investigated whether we could find any correlation between growth in the subsequent five years (1994–9) and the relative price shock linked to the liberalization episode. The analysis is hindered by the high likelihood of incidences of other developments during this period that may convolute the impact of the relative price shock. Nevertheless, a positive correlation would constitute strongly suggestive evidence of a *growth* effect of liberalization, beyond an initial level effect (a 'once-and-for-all' effect, in line with standard trade theory). To focus on the actual relative price incentive changes for household farmers, we controlled for all other 'village-specific changes' between 1989 and 1994 and subsequently[11] by doing a village fixed-effect regression. Recall again that the price changes are defined at the household level, and therefore are now identified using within village variation. It should also be emphasized that all alternative specifications of our test yielded the same results. Table 12.5 gives the econometric findings. The first model is effectively the same as before but without the community variables and including village fixed effects. The second model is the same specification on the right-hand side, but now using growth in the subsequent five years, 1994–9, as the left-hand-side variable.

[11] The motivation was to ensure that other community-wide changes, for which the model does not control, do not affect changes in the 1994–9 period. However, many other specifications were tried but the general result was the same: the impact of the relative price change of 1989–94 on growth in 1994–9 is insignificantly different from zero.

Table 12.5. Change in log food consumption between 1989–94 and 1994–9

	Model 1: 1989–94		Model 2: 1994–9	
	Coefficient	t-value	Coefficient	t-value
Δ (% real TOT)	0.219	1.70	0.285	0.55
Δ (% real TOT) squared	0.674	7.08	−0.070	0.34
Surplus farmer *Δ (% real terms of trade)	0.643	3.27	−0.161	0.16
Adjusted R^2		0.13		0.06

Notes: Linear regression: explaining changes in consumption; dependent variable: change in log food consumption between 1989–94 and 1994–9 (n=354); ordinary least squares regression with village fixed effects and robust standard errors corrected for village cluster effects.

The results from model 1 are (unsurprisingly) close to those from the previous regression, showing significant effects from increases in TOT, especially for surplus farmers. But, the results from model 2 are striking: there is no sign of a further 'growth' effect from the improved TOT. Note that there is no evidence of reversal of the earlier gains (which would be reflected in a negative and significant coefficient of similar value). In other words, in line with the simple standard trade theory, the relative price change stimulated by liberalization induced 'once-and-for-all' improvement in incomes for those experiencing better TOT, but without the expected 'growth' effect in a theory of globalization.

There are, of course, limitations to the analysis above. For example, it could be argued (as in Winters McCulloch, and McKay 2004) that 'spillover' effects from initial growth spurts related to liberalization could play a role, creating growth externalities for households or areas initially not positively affected by the liberalization measures. This could possibly explain the findings above: while initially only those within the village that directly experienced favourable relative price changes experienced growth after liberalization, subsequently everybody benefits similarly due to externalities. Similarly, there is evidence that can identify further some of the general sources of growth in this period. For example, Dercon (2004) shows that growth in the same six villages between 1989 and 1997 was strongly determined by the nature of the road infrastructure connecting the village to other areas: the growth externalities of living in a village with a good road result in almost 4 per cent higher growth in consumption per year. Again, it is plausible that there is a complementarity between road infrastructure and liberalization, so that these villages with better infrastructure are able to benefit from the liberalization more, creating externalities for all in the communities. Still, this narrative is only consistent with the evidence and is not directly tested.

In another paper (Dercon, Hoddinott, and Woldehanna 2005), the link between road infrastructure and growth is further tested in the full sample, using data between 1994 and 1999 (based on three rounds of the ERHS). It is noted that yearly growth rates are strongly affected by road infrastructure and its quality. The regression analysis in that paper links growth in consumption to *changes* in road infrastructure and quality in a fixed-effects regression framework, providing strong and econometrically well-identified effects. The effects on road quality are based on detailed investigation of the quality of roads: improvement in roads leading to local towns, say, from a road poorly accessible to buses and trucks to one reasonably accessible for these vehicles in the rainy season results in 3.5 per-cent higher growth. Improvements in accessibility due to better transport have a further impact, resulting in a 6.1 per-cent higher growth rate in this period. Furthermore, there is a persistent and divergent effect linked to the road quality: the better *level* of past road quality increases *growth*. Such a result is again consistent with externalities from road infrastructure. This also means that those with poor road infrastructure experience systematically lower growth, at the risk of being totally left behind. Again, if liberalization is one of the factors necessary to offer growth opportunities for rural Ethiopia, this growth tends to benefit largely those with good geographical and infrastructural endowments. Of course, the parallel with the marginalization argument at play at the international trade level is clear: geographical externalities (possibly induced by local spillovers) mean that trade benefits certain areas, not just increasing levels of income, but also stimulating growth, while other areas are marginalized—they may not gain much or even lose in the first round effects, and subsequently have lower growth, staying behind permanently.

Overall, this leads to the following conclusions. Further liberalization, and engagement with the world economy in the age of globalization, may offer new opportunities for some rural areas. But, the impact is likely to be largely confined to those areas with good infrastructure and communications. Currently, growth in such areas appears to be outpacing growth in other areas. It is unlikely to get better without concerted efforts in terms of infrastructure development.

12.5. Risk and Vulnerability in a Period of Liberalization

In this final section, we will briefly comment on another apparent impact of liberalization: the risk related to markets. It is useful to look at this, since liberalization not only results in changes in levels of income and the standard of living, but also potentially introduces new risks, related to further integration into world markets and the world economy. Risk-related vulnerability to poverty is a concept that does not just look at the observed 'ex-post' realizations of poverty but includes the threat of poverty linked to downside risk (i.e., the 'bad' part of the risk distribution) (Calvo and Dercon 2005). It could help to show whether a more comprehensive 'poverty' concept in the face of trade liberalization is fruitful, not just in terms of emphasizing the change in the mean of income or consumption after liberalization but also the changes in downside risk related to liberalization.

Assessing this 'vulnerability to poverty' is, however, very data intensive, and requires the calibration of outcomes in different states of the world. It typically requires the equivalent of a forecasting model of consumption or another dimension of well-being, not just of the household mean of consumption but also its distribution. Assessing the changes in the distribution of risk after liberalization in Ethiopia is not fully possible, not least since so many other factors have changed in recent years (including regionalization, a war with Eritrea, and vast market-distorting aid flows). Consequently, the calibration of a counterfactual risk-due-to-liberalization distribution was not feasible. Instead, we only present some suggestive evidence on the risks faced by households, and the implications of these. In particular, in 1995, the 1,477 households in ERHS were asked to name the shocks that seriously affected their standard of living or asset position in the last twenty years, based on a long list of possible shocks. Subsequently, in 2004, the survey asked the same households to nominate the experiences related to the same set of potential shocks, but this time referring to the last five years. The question was similar, although the order of questions and the categories used were different, possibly affecting the answers. The findings were, nevertheless, very suggestive.

As Table 12.6 showed, besides natural and life-cycle risks (health, death), and diseases or deaths of livestock, high-frequency problems are those that relate to the economic and political regime during the period 1974 until 1991. Among problems in this category, forced labour, the ban of migration, high rural taxes, as well as problems concerning the land tenure and redistribution system feature highly. Problems related to the functioning of markets were rarely if ever mentioned. The explanation is simple: markets were effectively repressed and an economic control regime was instead in operation, at times resulting in serious and identifiable shocks to the living standards of the households. This type of problem is mentioned much less by 2004 with reference to the preceding five years. Of course, the length of the recall period is relevant here, but, in order of importance, economic and political regime is definitely not as high on the list of problems anymore. Instead, issues related to output and input markets appear to feature much more importantly now. This is the main conclusion from this analysis: liberalization introduces new risks to households, even though others may disappear.

Whether overall risk has increased or decreased cannot be assessed from these data, and this possibly is not the most important issue. Households use strategies to manage and cope with risks. One should not overstate the role of these strategies because, despite them, most evidence points out that shocks are only partially handled and consumption and other welfare outcomes are not fully smoothed. Nevertheless, the introduction of new risks will challenge existing mechanisms.

Table 12.6. Shocks faced by rural households in Ethiopia, 1974–94

Type of shocks households reported to be affected by, leading to serious loss of assets, income, or consumption, of those affected by a shock	Percentage of households reporting hardship episode in last twenty years
Drought or other source of harvest failure	78
Policy shock (taxation, forced labour, ban on migration)	42
Illness or death of household members	40
Diseases or death of oxen or other livestock	39
Land problems ('villagization', land reform)	17
Asset losses (fire, loss)	16
War	7
Crime/banditry (theft, violence)	3

Source: Own calculations based on ERHS (1994–7).

Evidence from Dercon, Hoddinott, and Woldehanna (2005) suggests that these new risks are significant in affecting consumption outcomes. Table 12.8 demonstrates this, using the outcomes of regressing the log of consumption per capita in 2004 on a number of characteristics in 1999, and shock variables based on the same questions as in Table 12.7. Besides the more 'standard' shocks, such as those related to the drought in 2002, and illness shocks, the other two shocks that show up significantly relate to the inability to sell output or a collapse of output prices, and a failing demand for non-agricultural products in a particular period. These shocks appear to have reduced consumption in 2004 by 15 per cent to 20 per cent—clearly

Table 12.7. Shocks faced by rural households in Ethiopia, 1999–2004

Type of shocks households reported to be affected by, leading to serious loss of assets, income, or consumption, of those affected by a shock	Percentage of households reporting hardship episode in last five years
Drought	47
Death or serious illness of head, spouse, or other person	43
Inability to sell outputs or decreases in output prices	15
Pests or diseases that affected crops	14
Crime/banditry (theft, violence)	13
Difficulty in obtaining inputs or increases in input prices	11
Policy/political shocks (land redistribution, state confiscation of assets, resettlement, forced contributions, or arbitrary taxation)	7
Pests or diseases that affected livestock	7

Source: Own calculations based on Ethiopian Rural Panel Data Survey (2004).

a large impact.[12] In sum, this is suggestive evidence that shifting risks towards market-related risks may not have suitable responses, thereby suggesting a possible further effect from liberalization policies, at least in the medium run.

12.6. Conclusion

There is a close correlation between the role of trade in GDP, overall growth, and poverty reduction in developing countries. Growth and poverty reduction have accelerated in those economies that have successfully increased their trade share in income. However, whether there is a direct causal link between trade policy, growth, and poverty reduction is still disputed. Still, the substantial poverty reductions in some developing countries, such as China and, more recently, parts of India are beyond doubt.

However, for many other developing countries, globalization is still far removed. In fact, there are concerns that these countries may well become further marginalized. The reasons include poor policy environment but also poor geographical endowments. It will be a difficult task to stop this process of marginalization, not least since there are risks that these economies may get trapped in permanently low growth and high poverty owing to the externalities related to globalization and marginalization. Concerted efforts within these countries with substantial outside support are likely to be needed to improve the investment climate in these economies.

There is some evidence that particular groups and areas may also risk becoming marginalized within the globalizing economies. High growth may provide the means to prevent this process from becoming self-perpetuating, but in any case action would be needed. The factors correlated with this marginalization are typically poor local endowments in terms of geography and infrastructure, as well as poor household endowments in terms of labour and assets. In many ways, the factors causing marginalization on the global scale are similar to the factors causing within country marginalization.

These insights were illustrated using Ethiopia as a case study. Ethiopia has started a process of market and international trade liberalization, but definitely still belongs to the group of 'marginalized' economies in the world. Growth remains limited, and poverty is highly persistent. The welfare impact of the domestic market liberalization in the first part of the 1990s also illustrates the risks related to further marginalization of some of the poor in Ethiopia. While one substantial group of the poor has been able to take advantage of the recent

[12] Of course, this regression may suffer from missing variable bias, such as those reporting these shocks may have other unobservable characteristics. Since this regression could not be estimated with household-fixed effects, there is no obvious way to control for these characteristics besides entering observable characteristics, as we did.

Table 12.8. Impact of shocks on (log) consumption per capita, 2004

	Estimated coefficient	t-statistic (absolute value)
Drought, 2002–4	−0.163	2.46**
Drought, 1999–2001	−0.137	2.72**
Pests or diseases that affected crops, 2002–4	−0.006	0.07
Pests or diseases that affected crops, 1999–2001	−0.052	1.05
Pests or diseases that affected livestock, 2002–4	−0.002	0.18
Pests or diseases that affected livestock, 1999–2001	0.022	0.24
Difficulty in obtaining inputs or increases in input prices, 2002–4	0.055	0.63
Difficulty in obtaining inputs or increases in input prices, 1999–2001	0.001	0.02
Inability to sell outputs or decreases in output prices, 2002–4	−0.187	2.23**
Inability to sell outputs or decreases in output prices, 1999–2001	−0.026	0.36
Lack of demand for non-agricultural products, 2002–4	−0.037	0.19
Lack of demand for non-agricultural products, 1999–2001	−0.195	2.28**
Crime shocks, 2002–4	−0.018	0.36
Crime shocks, 1999–2001	0.083	0.99
Death of head, spouse or another person, 2002–4	0.043	0.69
Death of head, spouse or another person, 1999–2001	−0.001	0.02
Illness of head, spouse or another person, 2002–4	−0.019	0.32
Illness of head, spouse or another person, 1999–2001	−0.151	2.33**
R^2	0.34	
Sample size	1,290	

Notes: Specification includes controls for female headship, age head, schooling, household size, dependency ratio, land holdings (quintiles), livestock, ethnic minority, religious minority, holding official position in Peasant Association or important place in social life, all in 1999. PA dummies, month of interview dummies and perceptions of rainfall in previous harvest year are also included but not reported.
Standard errors are robust to locality cluster effects.
*Significant at 10%,
**Significant at 5%.

Source: ERHS (1999–2004) and Dercon, Holdinott, and Woldehanna (2005).

improved economic environment, another group seems to have become increasingly marginalized. Investment in infrastructure provides one useful strategy to overcome some of the inherent marginal endowments in terms of infrastructure and other assets. The evidence from the 1990s from Ethiopia reported in this chapter suggests that improving infrastructure had very substantial growth effects. In any case, geographic diversity in these infrastructural investments seems to be correlated with differential growth experience, suggesting that more marginal areas within Ethiopia are at risk of becoming even more marginalized during the age of globalization.

One should also realize that liberalization and more market orientation will bring other risks, which households have to find ways of coping with. Evidence from self-reported shocks suggests that market-related risks (in the form of failing demand or price shocks) are more common now than they were before liberalization. This does not have to be a fundamental problem, since other risks (such as locally covariate risks) may be better spread across geographical areas. Nevertheless, it points to the need for other instruments, including those available to households, to cope with these emerging risks.

Recent events in the international economy, such as the international food price rises, high fuel prices, and the global credit crunch and recession offer a case in point. By far the largest impact on Ethiopia was the food and fuel price rise. Domestic food prices rose more than international prices, as, beyond high world prices, domestic food prices increases were also linked to rising transport costs, as well as both fuelled by and contributing to a derailment of the macro-economy. The net result was an increase in food prices between 2007 and 2008 by more than 50 per cent, creating huge relative price changes in the economy, providing an example of a market-related risk affecting households across the country. The burden on urban areas was likely to be high, but our analysis also suggests important distributional differences in impacts in rural areas, not least since some areas were also affected by the failure of the short rains in 2007, while others have no doubt benefited from the high prices. A further study comparing the experience in relative price changes in rural Ethiopia in the last few years to the evidence presented in this chapter is bound to give interesting evidence on whether and how the Ethiopian economy is changing.

APPENDIX

A Regression-based Poverty Decomposition

Suppose one is specifically interested in investigating the contribution to poverty changes of some variables crucial in explaining growth. We use an additive separable poverty index that is for each person linear in log consumption. The normalized poverty gap, defined over the log of consumption as the underlying welfare measure, satisfies this property.

Following Dercon 2006, formally, denote z as the log of the poverty line, y_{ht} the log of consumption of household h at t, and q_t as the number of people falling below the poverty line at time t and n as the total number of individuals, which are observed over time. If one orders all individuals from poor to rich in each period, then this measure can be defined as:

$$P_t = \frac{1}{n}\sum_{h=1}^{q_t}\frac{z - y_{ht}}{z} \tag{1}$$

Let us consider two periods of time, 0 and 1, and introduce a specific counterfactual, in which the change of consumption over time is equal to X_h. For example, this could be the change in consumption stemming from the actual change in one of the endowments (as used in the regression analysis in the main text). It is then possible to calculate the counterfactual consumption for person h, $y_{h1}{}^*$, as:

$$y^*_{h1} = y_{h0} + X_h \tag{2}$$

Given this change, the number of poor will change. Let us call the actual and counterfactual number of poor in period 0 and 1, respectively, q_0 and $q_1{}^*$. One can then define the change in poverty between period 1 and 0 as:

$$P^*_1 - P_0 = \frac{1}{n}\sum_{h=1}^{q^*_1}\frac{z - y_{h1}}{z} - \frac{1}{n}\sum_{h=1}^{q_0}\frac{z - y_{h0}}{z} \tag{3}$$

Let us now order the individuals, so that the poor in both periods are from h=1,... $q^*{}_{11}$; those moving into poverty h=$q^*{}_{11}$+1, ... $q^*{}_{01}$ (i.e., non-poor in period 0 and poor in period 1); those moving out of poverty ranked h=$q^*{}_{01}$+1, ...$q^*{}_{10}$; and, finally, those non-poor in each period as h=$q^*{}_{10}$+1,..., n. Then (3) can be written as:

$$P^*_1 - P_0 = \frac{1}{n}\sum_{h=1}^{q^*_{11}}\left(\frac{z - y^*_{h1}}{z} - \frac{z - y_{h0}}{z}\right) + \frac{1}{n}\sum_{h=q^*_{11}+1}^{q^*_{01}}\frac{z - y^*_{h1}}{z} - \frac{1}{n}\sum_{i=q^*_{01}+1}^{q^*_{01}}\frac{z - y_{h0}}{z} \tag{4}$$

That is, the change in the gap consists of the change of the gap of those poor in both periods, plus the gap of those poor in the second, but not in the first period, minus the gap in the first period of those leaving poverty.[13] Dividing the left- and right-hand side of (4) by ($P_1{}^*$ – P_0) yields a decomposition in terms of the contribution to the total poverty

[13] As suggested earlier, and using the notation as before, the Watts poverty measure is defined as:

$$W_t = \frac{1}{n}\sum_{h=1}^{q_t} z - y_{ht}$$

so that the decomposition is effectively a decomposition of the Watts poverty measure. Just like the squared poverty gap it is convex in levels of consumption implying that consumption levels far below the poverty line have a higher weight than levels closer to the poverty line: unlike the poverty gap, which is linear in levels of consumption.

change of those staying poor, those becoming poor, and those leaving poverty. Note that this is an additive decomposition. This can be rewritten in terms of changes in consumption. The part in brackets in the first term of (4) is directly defined in terms of $y_{h1}* - y_{h0} = X_h$. Pre-multiplying the terms within the summation sign for each of the two subsequent terms by $(y_{h0} - y_{h1}*)/(y_{h0} - y_{h1}*)$. Slightly rewritten, (4) becomes:

$$P_1^* - P_0 = \frac{1}{n}\sum_{i=1}^{q_{11}^*}(\frac{-X_i}{z}) + \frac{1}{n}\sum_{i=q_{11}^*+1}^{q_{10}^*}(\frac{-X_i}{z})(\frac{z - y_{i1}^*}{y_{io} - y_{i1}^*}) - \frac{1}{n}\sum_{i=q_{01}^*+1}^{q_{10}^*}(\frac{z - y_{i0}}{y_{io} - y_{i1}^*})(\frac{-X_i}{z}) \qquad (5)$$

This expression suggests (rather self-evidently) that when calculating the total counterfactual poverty change, for households who leave or enter into poverty, only the consumption change up to or counting from the poverty line will be taken into account, while for those staying poor, their entire consumption change is relevant. This allows us to define the share of the consumption change that has to be taken into account as:

$$s_h^* = 1 \quad \text{for} \quad q_h \in \{1, \ldots \theta_{11}^*\} \qquad (6a)$$

$$s_h^* = \frac{z - y_{h1}^*}{y_{h0} - y_{h1}^*} \quad \text{for} \quad q_h \in \{\theta_{11} + 1, \ldots, \theta_{01}^*\}, \text{and} \qquad (6b)$$

$$s_h^* = \frac{z - y_{h0}}{y_{h1}^* - y_{h0}} \quad \text{for} \quad q_h \in \{\theta_{01}^* + 1, \ldots, \theta_{10}\} \qquad (6c)$$

Note that these shares s_h* are dependent on the specific counterfactual studied, and between 0 and 1.

Using (6a), (6b), and (6c), (5) can be rewritten as:

$$P_1^* - P_0 = \frac{1}{n}\sum_{h=1}^{q_{10}^*} s_h^* \left(\frac{-X_h}{z}\right) \qquad (7)$$

Equation (7) may seem only of limited interest: if only one factor is considered in the counterfactual, the equation only describes what in practice is calculated via simulations. Calculating the weights s_h* is probably more time-consuming than calculating the change in poverty directly from the derived and the actual distribution. Furthermore, (7) is restricted to very specific poverty measures, while micro-simulations can handle any measure. Nevertheless, (7) becomes more interesting when X is itself determined by different variables.

First, let us consider a case in which the counterfactual consists of two parts (V and W), and assume that for each h, $X_h = V_h + W_h$. Now, (7) can be used to study the contribution of each factor V_h and W_h in the total counterfactual change. For a given total change in consumption, the shares s_h* will be constant, so that (7) can be written as:

$$P_1^* - P_0 = \frac{1}{n}\sum_{h=1}^{q_{10}^*} s_h^*\left(\frac{-V_h}{z}\right) + \frac{1}{n}\sum_{h=1}^{q_{10}^*} s_h^*\left(\frac{-W_h}{z}\right) \tag{8}$$

This implies that, for a given total change, the contribution of different factors to the change in poverty can be directly derived from (8). Note that these contributions sum to 1, but also that they are always defined relative to a particular total counterfactual change. For example, let us define $P_1^V (P_1^W)$ as poverty in period 1 when V (W) has been added to y_{h0}. Even though $(y_{h0} + X_h) = (y_{h0} + V_h + W_h)$, it can be easily seen that:

$$P_1^* - P_0 \neq (P_1^V - P_0) + (P_1^W - P_0)$$

In other words, the total poverty change due to adding both V and W to consumption is not simply equal to the poverty change induced by adding V and W separately. This means that the decomposition has to be carefully interpreted. Equation (8) can be easily generalized to more factors; it will be used below to interpret the contribution to poverty changes of different factors linked to economic reform.

One counterfactual is of particular interest for the current research: assessing the contribution of different factors to the *actual observed* total change in poverty $(P_1 - P_0)$. With an appropriate residual term (ϵ_h), equation (1) provides a prediction model for changes in consumption for each person, based on different factors. Or, more in general, suppose $X_h = V_h + W_h + \epsilon_h$. Equation (8) can then be rewritten as (dropping asterisks, since the counterfactual considered is the actual change in poverty):

$$P_1 - P_0 = \frac{1}{n}\sum_{h=1}^{q_{10}} s_h\left(\frac{-V_h}{z}\right) + \frac{1}{n}\sum_{h=1}^{q_{10}} s_h\left(\frac{-W_h}{z}\right) + \frac{1}{n}\sum_{h=1}^{q_{10}} s_h\left(\frac{-\epsilon_h}{z}\right) \tag{9}$$

Equation (9) provides, then, simple ways of describing the contribution of these different factors (and the error term) to the observed poverty changes, using shares s_h based on the *actual* observed poverty transitions. It shows a direct link between changes in individual consumption over time and the poverty outcome. The overall result is a decomposition of the poverty gap into the effects of changes in fixed endowments, changes in input and output prices, and random events, for a given total change in poverty. The decomposition will now be applied to data related to 1989 and 1994/5, before and after a major set of reform measures were implemented. The decomposition of consumption changes is exact when using an estimation method which imposes that the sum of the residuals is 0, such as ordinary least squares (OLS) decompositions based on (9) are additive in terms of the contributing factors but not exact and the contribution of the error term will have to be added.

References

Calvo, C., and S. Dercon (2005) 'Measuring Individual Vulnerability'. Economics Series Working Paper 229. Oxford: University of Oxford Department of Economics.

Collier, P., and J. W. Gunning (1999) 'Explaining African Economic Performance', *Journal of Economic Literature*, 37: 64–111.

——A. Hoeffler, and C. Pattillo (2001) 'Flight Capital as a Portfolio Choice', *World Bank Economic Review*, 15: 55–80.

Davis, D. R., and D. E. Weinstein (2003) 'Market Access, Economic Geography and Comparative Advantage: An Empirical Test', *Journal of International Economics*, 59: 1–23.

Dercon, S. (1995) 'On Market Integration and Liberalization: Method and Application to Ethiopia', *Journal of Development Studies*, 32: 112–43.

——(2002) 'The Impact of Economic Reform on Households in Rural Ethiopia, 1989–1995'. Washington, DC: World Bank.

——(2004) 'Growth and Risk: Evidence from Rural Ethiopia', *Journal of Development Economics*, 74: 309–29.

——(2006) 'Economic Reform, Growth and the Poor in Rural Ethiopia', *Journal of Development Economics*, 81: 1–24.

——J. Hoddinott, and T. Woldehanna (2005) 'Shocks and Consumption in 15 Villages in Rural Ethiopia', *Journal of African Economies*, 14: 559–85.

——and P. Krishnan (2002) 'Changes in Poverty in Villages in Rural Ethiopia, 1989–1995'. In A. Booth and P. Mosley (eds), *The New Poverty Strategies: What Have They Achieved? What Have We Learned?* Basingstoke: Macmillan.

Dollar, D. (1992) 'Outward Oriented Developing Countries Really Do Grow More Rapidly: Evidence from 95 LDCs, 1976–1985', *Economic Development and Cultural Change*, 40: 523–44.

——and A. Kraay (2001) 'Growth is Good for the Poor'. Policy Research Working Paper 2587. Washington, DC: World Bank.

Ndulu, B. J., S. A. O'Connell, R. H. Bates, P. Collier, and C. C. Soludo (2008) (eds), *The Political Economy of Economic Growth in Africa, 1960–2000*. Cambridge: Cambridge University Press.

Oxfam (2000) 'Globalisation, Submission to the Government's White Paper on Globalisation'. Oxfam Policy Papers 5/00. Ivanhoe: Fitzroy Oxfam.

Ravallion, M. (2003) 'The Debate on Globalization, Poverty and Inequality: Why Measurement Matters'. Policy Research Working Paper 3058. Washington, DC: World Bank.

Rodriguez, F., and D. Rodrik (1999) 'Trade Policy and Economic Growth: A Skeptic's Guide to the Cross-national Evidence'. Working Paper 7081. Cambridge, Mass.: NBER.

Sachs, J. D., and A. Warner (1995) 'Economic Reform and the Process of Global Integration', *Brookings Papers on Economic Activity*, 1: 1–118.

Winters, A., N. McCulloch, and A. McKay (2004) 'Trade Liberalization and Poverty: The Evidence So Far', *Journal of Economic Literature*, 42: 72–115.

World Bank (2002) *Globalization, Growth, and Poverty: Building an Inclusive World Economy*. Washington, DC: World Bank.

13

Inequality and Poverty in Africa in an Era of Globalization: Looking Beyond Income to Health and Education

David E. Sahn and Stephen D. Younger[1]

13.1. Introduction

How globalization affects poverty and inequality in developing countries is the subject of considerable debate, a debate that is complicated by the fact that globalization means different things to different people. For applied work, the question of how to define globalization in a conceptually meaningful and empirically feasible way is quite demanding, with little clear agreement in the literature as to the best way forward. More specifically, it is possible to identify four major aspects of economic globalization: increased trade, more capital flows, greater movement of people, and greater diffusion of knowledge and technology. Taking each of these aspects of globalization, it is possible to tell a complex story, both positive and negative, about the potential impact of greater global economic integration on living standards. And, of course, the intensity of globalization defined along the four dimensions differs from one context to the next, further complicating the process of drawing generalizable conclusions, especially given that there are important temporal dimensions under which the outcomes of globalization need to be considered.

In practice, there are undoubtedly winners and losers from globalization, whose characteristics differ from one country and region to the next, depending on the economic structure and related opportunities that prevail in a given context. And, despite the conflicting views and perspectives on the impact of globalization, there is little doubt that there are risks and opportunities for the

[1] This research is supported by SAGA, a cooperative agreement between USAID and Cornell and Clark Atlanta Universities. See <http://www.saga.cornell.edu>.

poor associated with increased interdependence along a range of dimensions, including economic, social, cultural, and political.

But, if the literature to date has been less than decided about the proper definition of globalization and its link to poverty and inequality, it has been quite consistent in as far as both poverty and inequality are almost always measured in terms of income (or proxies for it), especially in the empirical literature (Deaton 2004 is an important exception). Our goal in this chapter is to challenge that consistency by examining poverty and inequality in non-income dimensions of well-being. In doing so, we take seriously Sen's argument that well-being is multidimensional and includes capabilities such as good health and education (Sen 1979; 1985; and 1987; Drèze and Sen 1989). More traditional money-metrics of poverty, particularly as measured by income (or consumption expenditure) are *instrumentally* important to these capabilities, but it is the capabilities themselves that are *intrinsically* important, and merit recognition and measurement in their own right (Sen 1985; 1987).

Even though Sen's argument is widely accepted in theory, in practice it is usually ignored. Most empirical poverty research still focuses on measuring material living standards. Indeed, one important exception is the human development index which, inspired by Sen's work, includes an income indicator (GDP per capita), a health indicator (life expectancy at birth), and an education indicator (adult literacy). We focus on the latter two pillars, and compare progress in these dimensions both in terms of levels of deprivation—measured in terms of the share of the population that are malnourished and have not completed primary schooling—as well as the changes in the distribution of these outcomes among the population. Our reliance on readily available and useful empirical measures of the non-income dimensions of well-being is not to say that income poverty and inequality are unimportant, but, rather, that income is not the only dimension of well-being that matters, in theory and in applied work.

To further motivate our work, it is important to recognize that there is a low correlation between incomes and many other measures of living standards, particularly health. This is the case both when the correlations are done for households within a country, as well as when cross-country correlations are examined (Haddad et al. 2003; Appleton and Song 1999). Most importantly for the present analysis, in a prior paper using similar methods, we find that in Latin America, where progress on income poverty has been modest and where income inequality may well be worsening, health and education poverty and inequality have both decreased significantly over the past fifteen to twenty years in virtually every country for which we have data. This chapter examines whether the same is true in Africa.

Yet another argument for focusing on health and education is that public policy has an important role in providing for the basic needs of the population. Indeed, it is often far easier to mobilize public support and resources for targeted programmes to improve health and education than more general income-transfer schemes. This is consistent with a welfarist view of the role of the state, international donors, and non-governmental organizations (NGOs). A focus on health and educational objectives is also further motivated by the reasonable expectation that there are substantial public goods, aspects of improving health and education, as well as externalities of raising living standards of the poor in these dimensions, including externalities that benefit the non-poor.

Finally, there are a number of practical considerations that motivate our focusing on health and education outcomes in this chapter. First, such indicators are measured at the individual rather than household level, as are income and expenditures. Thus, we need not make arbitrary assumptions about how resources are allocated among household members, or similar unidentifiable assumptions about economies of scale and equivalence units (Deaton and Muellbauer 1980). Such problems do not arise when measuring individual outcomes. There is also comparable and widely available data for many countries and at several points in time during the past fifteen to twenty years[2] on health and education outcomes that do not suffer from the types of measurement errors associated with money-metric indicators. Thus, we can examine a large number of spells of change in these indicators with a minimum of concern over data quality and comparability.

While we are greatly concerned with broadening the definition of poverty and inequality in empirical work, we are modest in terms of our objectives and aspirations. While we will examine some correlations between our poverty and inequality measures and a standard measure of openness (trade divided by GDP), for the most part we assume that globalization is occurring in Africa (as elsewhere) and that there is more of it now than there was fifteen to twenty years ago. Given that assumption, observed changes in non-income poverty and inequality can be correlated with globalization, though inferring causation would be a heroic leap.

Our methods are largely descriptive. We first examine how health and education poverty and inequality change over time in a given country. We then decompose the observed changes in poverty into a component due to the change in the mean and another due to the change in the dispersion of the distribution. That is, we examine to what extent the change in health and education poverty across spells can be attributed to a change in the mean of the distribution, holding the dispersion constant, versus the change in the dispersion while keeping the mean constant. Doing so allows us to relate and compare the relative importance of changes in inequality to the overall process of improvement or deterioration in living standards. Based on our empirical results, we highlight the limited progress observed in Africa in improving health

[2] Specifically, we rely upon the demographic and health survey DHS data described next.

and education outcomes, and contrast that with other regions of the world where globalization has been accompanied by more favourable outcomes.

13.2. Data and Methods

With large sample sizes and questionnaires that are consistent throughout various countries as well as over time, the demographic and health surveys (DHSs) are nationally representative surveys that provide data that are well suited for our analysis. We use data from sixty-four DHSs from twenty-three African countries. We have selected countries that have data from at least two DHSs. These data provide us with forty spells—usually around five years in length—of change in health and education outcomes that we use here. A standard stratified and clustered design is used in most surveys to select households. The subject of the interview in each household is one woman aged 15–49, selected randomly. Additionally, children, 60 months or younger (but sometimes 36 months or younger), of the female interview subject are weighed, and their heights recorded. For our analysis, we use the data that reference these women and children.

Since we are interested in *distributions* of well-being, we, therefore, must use continuous variables. Discrete variables such as mortality or literacy rates are not appropriate for our study. Similarly, predicted variables, such as mortality probabilities, pose problems, because the distribution is compressed when such predicted variables are derived.

The particular measures that we use are children's heights, women's body mass, and women's educational attainment. The first two are good measures of health, the third of education.

To amplify, we use standardized height of pre-school-aged children as a health indicator because it is particularly predictive and captures general health far better than the alternative measures of health. Specifically, many other researchers find that a child's growth provides an excellent objective indicator of his or her general health status. See, for example, Cole and Parkin (1977); Mata (1978); Tanner (1981); Mosley and Chen (1984); WHO (1995); Martorell et al. (1975); Beaton et al. (1990); Strauss and Thomas (1995); and Behrman and Deolalikar (1988). As Beaton et al. put it, growth failure is 'the best general proxy for constraints to human welfare of the poorest, including dietary inadequacy, infectious diseases and other environmental health risks' (Beaton et al. 1990: 2). Furthermore, they note the utility of stature as an indicator is due to the fact that it embodies the multiple dimensions of health and development, as determined by an individual's socio-economic and environmental circumstances.

Most analyses of children's heights (or weights) measure them in z-scores: the distance the child's height is from the median of a reference population of healthy children, measured in standard deviations and standardized by age and gender (WHO 1983). This age and gender standardized measure basically reflects the standard deviations and can be negative (and usually are negative among the poor). Most standard *distributional* statistics, however, necessitate positive value for the welfare measure. Therefore, we choose to work with 'standardized heights', calculating this variable as the height that this child would have if she or he were a twenty-four-month-old girl. We basically assign a child the height corresponding to the same z-score in the twenty-four-month-old girls' distribution. We thereafter assign a poverty line for this variable defined as the standardized height two standard deviations below the median of the distribution of the reference population of healthy children.

Second, we employ the body mass index (BMI) for women aged 15–49, as another health indicator. The BMI is calculated as weight (in kilograms) divided by height (in metres squared). For the BMI variable we choose a conventional cut-off point of 18.5 as a poverty line, as determined by the WHO. An important consideration with the use of BMI is that welfare (unlike for height, education, or income) does not necessarily increase monotonically with BMI. Although 'more is better' is a standard axiom of most distributional measures, the share of overweight or obese women in Africa is small enough to allow us to interpret our results for this variable as if this axiom applied.

Third, to assess changes in level of education and education inequality, we analyse years of schooling for women. We seek to eliminate from consideration any women who have not yet reached the age to complete their post-secondary school;[3] thus, we limit our analysis to women at least 22 years of age. The upper limit of our indicator, 30 years of age, ensures that we focus our attention on women who have completed their education relatively recently. We note the limitation in the use of years of schooling as an indicator of well-being since it does not take into account differences in school quality that may affect the value of the education received. The variability in school quality, however, is implicitly assumed to be negligible for our study since we are making our comparisons within countries and over relatively short time-periods (usually five years). We arbitrarily define the education poverty line as having completed six years of schooling. We also varied the education poverty line three years above and below the defined six-year line to test the sensitivity of our measure and find that such choices did not significantly affect our results.

13.2.1. Measuring Poverty Inequality

Given the poverty lines defined above, we use the headcount as our poverty measure—that is, the share of the sample that falls below the poverty line. For

[3] Because few of the women in the survey actually attend post-secondary school, we could have chosen a lower limit of 18 rather than 22. We find that the results we report later in this paper would be almost the same had we chosen eighteen as our lower boundary for our indicator.

inequality, we follow the standard approach used in the income literature where we examine the variation or dispersion of a health or educational outcome per se.[4] This 'univariate' approach to measuring non-income dimensions of inequality contrasts with the more common approach to examining health (and education) inequality which examines differences in health (or other social indicators) across a variety of social and economic strata such as race, ethnicity, location, gender and, most commonly, income. Making comparisons of health or education across populations with different social and economic characteristics is often referred to in the literature as the 'gradient' or 'socio-economic' approach to health inequality.[5]

We would argue that the univariate approach is the correct one, at least in the context of our efforts to promote the notion that well-being should be measured in multiple dimensions. The gradient approach implicitly gives primacy to inequality in the income dimension. Inequality in the dimension of health or education is only relevant insofar as it is correlated with income inequality. By implication, a given distribution of health or educational outcomes is only undesirable if it is correlated with the income distribution, but acceptable if it is not, an implication of the gradient approach which makes it undesirable for our purposes. Given our univariate approach, we use the Gini coefficient to measure inequality.

13.2.2. Decomposition

To decompose changes in poverty, we note that any distribution can be characterized by its mean and its Lorenz curve. Datt and Ravallion (1992) demonstrate that it is possible to decompose the change in the share of the population that falls below the poverty line into two components. The first is changes in the mean of the distribution, and the second is changes in its dispersion. Following Datt and Ravallion, then, we express the share of a population that are poor as a function of its mean, μ, its Lorenz curve, L, and the poverty line, z. The change in poverty between two periods can then be decomposed, first, into a growth component representing the change in poverty resulting from a

[4] We follow previous work using the univariate approach, including Thomas, Wang, and Fan (2000) and Lopez, Thomas, and Wang (1998), which develop the concept of an education Gini index based on school attainment data for working-age adults, and Pradhan, Sahn, and Younger (2003); Le Grand (1987); and Murray, Gakidou, and Frenk (1999), which apply the univariate approach to health.

[5] See, for example, van Doorslaer et al. (1997); Wagstaff, Paci, and van Doorslaer (1991); Wagstaff and van Doorslaer (2004) in the case of health; and Filmer and Pritchett (2001) in the case of education. The gradient approach is useful for examining the correlation of a health or educational outcome with a given characteristic. Interest in this correlation arises from various types of discrimination, prejudice, and other legal, social, and economic norms that may contribute to stratification and fragmentation, and subsequent inequality in access to material resources and various correlated welfare outcomes.

change in the mean of the distribution, while holding the Lorenz curve constant at that of the reference sample, and second, a redistribution component reflecting the change in the Lorenz curve, while holding the distribution's mean constant with that of the reference sample (Datt and Ravallion 1992).

We avoid the problem that the Datt and Ravallion decomposition is not robust to the choice of reference sample, by relying on Kakwani's (1997) approach, and averaging the Datt and Ravallion decompositions calculated with each sample as the reference. We and others have previously employed this method (Sahn and Younger 2005; McCulloch, Cherel-Robson, and Baulch 2000; Dhongde 2002; Shorrocks and Kolenikov 2001). This practice is both consistent with the axiomatic properties discussed by Kakwani, and also eliminates the residual in the decomposition methodology.

13.3. Results

We first consider the headcounts and Gini coefficients for each of our indicators of well-being in each country and survey (Tables 13.1, 13.2, and 13.3). To summarize our findings for children's heights: among the thirty-nine spells, the headcount worsened in thirteen cases, improved in thirteen, and remained unchanged for thirteen. Important differences, both between countries and within a single country, for which we have more than one spell, are necessarily obscured by such a summary. A closer look reveals, for instance, that between 1992 and 2000, there was a marked decline in the share of children who are stunted in Namibia, whereas in Niger, for the same period, just the opposite was observed. We also observe that for those countries with more than one spell, quite often the changes over time occur in different directions. This is illustrated by the case of Zimbabwe, which experienced a marked decline in the headcount between 1988 and 1994, only to witness a substantial worsening between 1994 and 1999. In Nigeria, the health of children that deteriorated between 1986 and 1990, and, again between 1990 and 1999, similarly, showed improvement in 2003 when a substantial decline in the headcount was observed. Thus, looking at these specific cases between and within countries, it is evident that no steady improvement in children's heights can be clearly observed.

For inequality of children's heights, we also find more cases of worsening than improvement. Specifically, there are twenty-three cases where height inequality increased, eight where it declined, and eight where it remained constant over time. Mozambique between 1997 and 2003 stands out among those countries that showed the greatest improvement (i.e., decline) in inequality, while Burkina Faso, Mali, and Zimbabwe stand out by witnessing a worsening degree of inequality across the multiple spells in each country.

While the inequality figures have some interest in their own right, our major concern is the extent to which changes in inequality are contributing to, or

Table 13.1. Poverty headcounts and Gini coefficients for children's heights

			Tests for equality				Tests for equality		
	Survey	Headcount	vs 1st	vs 2nd	vs 3rd	Gini	vs 1st	vs 2nd	vs 3rd
Burkina Faso	1992	0.353				0.0386			
	1999	0.383	1.96			0.0399	1.54		
	2003	0.406	4.09	1.76		0.0444	8.33	5.83	
Benin	1996	0.294				0.0346			
	2001	0.320	1.82			0.0362	2.05		
Côte d'Ivoire	1994	0.289				0.0342			
	1998	0.245	−2.61			0.0346	0.50		
Cameroon	1991	0.272				0.0342			
	1998	0.355	4.65			0.0378	3.64		
	2004	0.348	4.42	−0.42		0.0390	5.01	1.34	
Chad	1997	0.431				0.0440			
	2004	0.437	0.41			0.0490	5.83		
Ethiopia	2000	0.511				0.0388			
	2005	0.475	−2.62			0.0438	6.19		
Ghana	1988	0.320				0.0336			
	1993	0.307	−0.78			0.0353	1.80		
	1998	0.236	−5.20	−4.33		0.0339	0.31	−1.55	
	2003	0.304	−1.00	−0.20	4.24	0.0361	2.77	0.96	2.55
Guinea	1999	0.284				0.0389			
	2005	0.371	5.00			0.0423	3.22		
Kenya	1993	0.355				0.0368			
	1998	0.355	0.00			0.0397	3.43		
	2003	0.347	−0.60	−0.59		0.0370	0.20	−3.41	

(*continued*)

Table 13.1. Continued

			Tests for equality				Tests for equality		
	Survey	Headcount	vs 1st	vs 2nd	vs 3rd	Gini	vs 1st	vs 2nd	vs 3rd
Madagascar	1992	0.567				0.0330			
	1997	0.564	−0.25			0.0360	4.23		
	2003	0.502	−4.32	−4.17		0.0437	12.71	9.11	
Mali	1987	0.272				0.0347			
	1995	0.368	5.45			0.0405	5.91		
	2001	0.408	7.87	3.75		0.0429	8.25	3.85	
Malawi	1992	0.496				0.0360			
	2000	0.506	0.71			0.0418	8.11		
Mozambique	1997	0.440				0.0401			
	2003	0.425	−1.09			0.0365	−4.93		
Nigeria	1986	0.302				0.0335			
	1990	0.425	8.11			0.0422	9.66		
	1999	0.504	10.80	4.65		0.0519	14.86	8.42	
	2003	0.422	7.57	−0.19	−4.63	0.0453	12.25	3.61	−5.54
Niger	1992	0.439				0.0394			
	1998	0.497	4.18			0.0387	−1.00		
Namibia	1992	0.330				0.0343			
	2000	0.238	−5.60			0.0322	−2.34		
Rwanda	1992	0.489				0.0345			
	2000	0.427	−4.47			0.0402	7.37		
	2005	0.479	−0.66	3.62		0.0377	3.92	−3.07	
Senegal	1986	0.230				0.0311			
	1992	0.262	1.66			0.0346	3.04		

	2005	0.164	−3.38	−7.16		0.0329	1.44	−2.06	
Togo	1988	0.341				0.0342			
	1998	0.262	−4.86			0.0337	−0.52		
Tanzania	1992	0.451				0.0343			
	1996	0.466	1.19			0.0364	2.97		
	1999	0.442	−0.58	−1.47		0.0334	−1.25	−3.71	
	2004	0.385	−5.75	−6.67	−3.62	0.0313	−5.21	−7.97	−2.85
Uganda	1988	0.472				0.0368			
	1995	0.412	−4.25			0.0354	−1.75		
	2000	0.407	−4.53	−0.38		0.0349	−2.38	−0.70	
Zambia	1992	0.428				0.0335			
	1996	0.448	1.58			0.0361	3.93		
	2001	0.512	6.40	4.95		0.0393	8.10	4.49	
Zimbabwe	1988	0.321				0.0305			
	1994	0.254	−4.04			0.0319	1.59		
	1999	0.312	−0.52	3.51		0.0402	9.40	8.75	

Source: The results in columns 2–5 are from Sahn and Younger (2008).

Table 13.2. Poverty headcounts and Gini coefficients for women's BMI

	Survey	Headcount	Tests for equality			Gini	Tests for equality		
			vs 1st	vs 2nd	vs 3rd		vs 1st	vs 2nd	vs 3rd
Burkina Faso	1992	0.137				0.0682			
	1999	0.125	−1.50			0.0633	−3.30		
	2003	0.197	9.12	11.07		0.0816	9.85	14.29	
Benin	1996	0.140				0.0770			
	2001	0.101	−5.02			0.0936	8.92		
Côte d'Ivoire	1994	0.079				0.0769			
	1998	0.082	0.53			0.0886	6.09		
Cameroon	1998	0.070				0.0834			
	2004	0.064	−0.89			0.0963	6.37		
Chad	1997	0.194				0.0710			
	2004	0.202	0.93			0.0772	4.13		
Ethiopia	2000	0.281				0.0686			
	2005	0.246	−5.38			0.0717	3.01		
Ghana	1993	0.113				0.0823			
	1998	0.107	−0.68			0.0897	2.68		
	2003	0.091	−2.77	−2.15		0.1011	7.88	4.95	
Guinea	1999	0.113				0.0789			
	2005	0.121	1.09			0.0820	1.75		
Kenya	1993	0.094				0.0784			
	1998	0.109	2.19			0.0832	2.60		
	2003	0.118	4.05	1.43		0.0985	13.40	9.19	
Madagascar	1997	0.190				0.0635			
	2003	0.184	−0.74			0.0732	8.51		
Mali	1995	0.146				0.0728			
	2001	0.114	−5.43			0.0844	9.63		

Malawi	1992	0.086				0.0692		
	2000	0.080	−0.97			0.0728	2.68	
Mozambique	1997	0.109				0.0696		
	2003	0.081	−4.45			0.0796	6.93	
Nigeria	1999	0.156				0.1182		
	2003	0.141	−1.75			0.1003	−6.55	
Niger	1992	0.177				0.0744		
	1998	0.190	1.49			0.0723	−1.35	
Namibia	1992	0.128				0.1007		
Rwanda	2000	0.082				0.0713		
	2005	0.092	2.07			0.0710	−0.30	
Senegal	1992	0.137				0.0875		
	2005	0.174	4.48			0.1084	10.56	
Togo	1998	0.105				0.0779		
Tanzania	1992	0.089				0.0729		
	1996	0.088	−0.16			0.0773	2.93	
	2004	0.095	1.25	1.35		0.0871	11.79	6.80
Uganda	1995	0.089				0.0685		
	2000	0.094		0.78		0.0785	6.73	
Zambia	1992	0.097				0.0784		
	1996	0.083	−2.25			0.0757	−1.82	
	2001	0.141	7.08	10.14		0.0838	3.80	6.02
Zimbabwe	1994	0.047				0.0849		
	1999	0.054	1.45			0.0922	3.76	

Source: The results in columns 2–5 are from Sahn and Younger (2008).

Table 13.3. Poverty headcounts and Gini coefficients for women's years of schooling

			Tests for equality				Tests for equality		
	Survey	Headcount	vs 1st	vs 2nd	vs 3rd	Gini	vs 1st	vs 2nd	vs 3rd
Burkina Faso	1992	0.940				0.8779			
	1999	0.947	0.95			0.8975	4.13		
	2003	0.905	−4.64	−5.71		0.8552	−5.14	−10.10	
Benin	1996	0.893				0.8100			
	2001	0.898	0.54			0.7564	−8.71		
Côte d'Ivoire	1994	0.862				0.7101			
	1998	0.835	−1.80			0.6723	−4.58		
Cameroon	1991	0.718				0.5462			
	1998	0.543	−9.37			0.4643	−10.08		
	2004	0.523	−11.83	−1.29		0.4061	−19.21	−9.54	
Chad	1997	0.966				0.8718			
	2004	0.947	−2.88			0.8390	−6.69		
Ethiopia	2000	0.878				0.8493			
	2005	0.870	−1.17			0.7870	−17.56		
Ghana	1988	0.507				0.5119			
	1993	0.530	1.23			0.4792	−3.67		
	1998	0.492	−0.83	−2.04		0.4486	−7.39	−3.63	
	2003	0.494	−0.73	−1.98	0.12	0.4330	−9.57	−5.71	−2.02
Guinea	1999	0.927				0.8671			
	2005	0.931	0.52			0.8385	−5.78		
Kenya	1988	0.482				0.4056			
	1993	0.386	−6.41			0.3498	−9.49		
	1998	0.276	−14.38	−7.75		0.2974	−19.67	−10.26	
	2003	0.261	−15.76	−9.01	−1.14	0.3037	−18.33	−8.91	1.33

Madagascar	1992	0.726				0.4891			
	1997	0.748	1.51			0.4982	1.59		
	2003	0.741	1.01	−0.56		0.4760	−2.34	−4.13	
Mali	1987	0.943				0.8962			
	1995	0.933	−1.12			0.8657	−5.55		
	2001	0.929	−1.64	−0.65		0.8603	−6.79	−1.36	
Malawi	1992	0.809				0.6402			
	2000	0.739	−5.52			0.4978	−22.87		
Mozambique	1997	0.924				0.6549			
	2003	0.893	−3.93			0.6190	−6.72		
Nigeria	1986	0.661				0.4990			
	1990	0.809	8.87			0.6706	22.91		
	1999	0.625	−2.04	−15.34		0.5329	4.63	−24.03	
	2003	0.599	−3.41	−16.49	−1.84	0.5484	6.40	−19.62	2.57
Niger	1992	0.972				0.9230			
	1998	0.947	−4.08			0.8845	−8.78		
Namibia	1992	0.408				0.3551			
	2000	0.228	−11.13			0.2594	−17.46		
Rwanda	1992	0.762				0.5701			
	2000	0.640	−8.81			0.4895	−13.47		
	2005	0.804	3.39	13.72		0.4665	−18.04	−4.64	
Senegal	1986	0.910				0.8433			
	1992	0.903	−0.68			0.7956	−7.49		
	1997	0.871	−3.70	−3.16		0.7509	−15.16	−7.52	
	2005	0.848	−6.32	−5.92	−2.54	0.7196	−22.52	−14.27	−6.26

(continued)

Table 13.3. Continued

	Survey	Headcount	Tests for equality			Gini	Tests for equality		
			vs 1st	vs 2nd	vs 3rd		vs 1st	vs 2nd	vs 3rd
Togo	1988	0.836				0.6979			
	1998	0.881	3.38			0.6304	−8.72		
Tanzania	1992	0.433				0.4319			
	1996	0.320	−8.29			0.3884	−6.61		
	1999	0.328	−6.36	0.44		0.3824	−6.15	−0.74	
	2004	0.346	−6.68	1.98	1.14	0.3672	−10.50	−3.40	−1.96
Uganda	1988	0.795				0.5494			
	1995	0.758	−2.59			0.5088	−5.70		
	2000	0.699	−6.62	−4.41		0.4580	−13.17	−8.45	
Zambia	1992	0.453				0.3480			
	1996	0.465	0.79			0.3527	0.85		
	2001	0.476	1.44	0.67		0.3407	−1.32	−2.36	
Zimbabwe	1988	0.532				0.3301			
	1994	0.286	−13.15			0.2953	−5.63		
	1999	0.157	−21.61	−8.89		0.2397	−15.37	−10.75	

impairing, progress in terms of the overall reduction in poverty. Tables 13.4, 13.5, and 13.6 present the Datt–Ravallion and Kakwani decompositions of the change in the headcounts for children's heights, women's BMI, and women's educational attainment, respectively. For heights, in thirty out of forty-one spells, the absolute value of the mean component of the decomposition is larger than the dispersion share. This is particularly true when the changes are large. A good example of this is found in the three spells from Ghana: in each case the share of the overall change contributed to by the mean shift is at least twice the magnitude of the change in the dispersion. The predominance of the changes in the mean in driving changes in poverty, however, is not to say that the dispersion component is trivial or important. For example, over half of the increase in stunting over the spell in Cameroon, from 27 per cent to 35 per cent, was accounted for by the declining inequality in children's health. We finally note that averaging the impact of both the mean and dispersion affects across all spells, the former equals −0.01 and the latter 0.01. Thus, overall, the average effects of both components of our decomposition are basically zero.

We would expect to see improvements in children's heights concentrated in the leftmost part of the distribution, since there is an upper bound to heights that individuals can attain. If that were the case, then we would tend to observe a correlation between increases in the mean and reductions in the dispersion of the distribution.[6] But that is not the case here. The mean and dispersion components for children's heights move together in about half of the cases and against each other in half.

Because women's anthropometry was not a standard consideration of the health module of the earlier DHS, we have less data, with fewer spells of information for the case of the share of underweight women. Unlike the results seen upon examining the information on child health, there was no change in the majority of cases in the share of women who are severely underweight (Table 13.2). An increase was observed for the share of underweight women in only five of twenty-six spells, while a decline was seen in six cases. Our examination of Ginis for BMI indicates increasing inequality: in twenty out of twenty-six spells, the BMI distribution became less equal. This rise in inequality is largely due to increased skewing in the right-hand tail of the distribution—reflecting in part the increase in BMI of women who were already at the high end of the distribution, even where the share of underweight women in the population remained largely unchanged.

When we examine the BMI decompositions, we find that there are more cases, thirteen out of twenty-six, where the mean shift is of a greater magnitude than the dispersion effect. In fact, when taking the average of the mean and dispersion effects across all spells, we find the average of the former is −2 per

[6] We do, in fact, find this consistently in Latin America (Sahn and Younger 2006).

Table 13.4. Datt–Ravallion and Kakwani decompositions for children's heights

Country	Period	First	Second	Difference	t-value	Mean	Dispersion
Burkina Faso	1992–9	0.351	0.380	0.030	−1.940	0.053	−0.023
	1999–2003	0.380	0.402	0.021	−1.584	0.003	0.018
Benin	1996–2001	0.290	0.318	0.028	−1.920	0.024	0.004
Côte d'Ivoire	1994–8	0.286	0.240	−0.046	2.697	−0.052	0.006
Cameroon	1991–8	0.271	0.349	0.078	−4.405	0.035	0.043
	1998–2004	0.349	0.346	−0.003	0.154	−0.011	0.008
Chad	1997–2004	0.426	0.434	0.009	−0.604	0.011	−0.002
Ethiopia	2000–5	0.509	0.471	−0.037	2.705	−0.071	0.034
Ghana	1988–93	0.320	0.303	−0.016	0.984	−0.026	0.009
	1993–8	0.303	0.232	−0.071	4.333	−0.057	−0.014
	1998–2003	0.232	0.301	0.068	−4.268	0.050	0.018
Guinea	1999–2005	0.282	0.368	0.086	−4.952	0.063	0.023
Kenya	1993–8	0.352	0.352	0.000	0.003	−0.031	0.031
	1998–2003	0.345	−0.007	0.004	0.000	−0.011	0.000
Madagascar	1992–7	0.567	0.562	−0.005	0.339	−0.011	0.006
	1997–2003	0.562	0.502	−0.060	4.089	−0.084	0.024
Mali	1987–95	0.271	0.366	0.095	−5.412	0.069	0.025
	1995–2001	0.366	0.406	0.040	−3.771	0.025	0.015
Malawi	1992–2000	0.491	0.505	0.014	−0.963	−0.009	0.022
Mozambique	1997–2003	0.438	0.423	−0.015	1.128	0.017	−0.032
Nigeria	1986–90	0.301	0.421	0.119	−7.902	0.073	0.046
	1990–9	0.421	0.502	0.081	−4.783	0.035	0.047
	1999–2003	0.502	0.420	−0.082	4.639	−0.045	−0.037

Niger	1992–8	0.437	0.495	0.058	−4.177	0.068	−0.010
Namibia	1992–2000	0.329	0.235	−0.094	5.686	−0.080	−0.014
Rwanda	1992–2000	0.486	0.424	−0.062	4.487	−0.093	0.030
	2000–5	0.424	0.474	0.050	−3.512	0.066	−0.016
Senegal	1986–92	0.230	0.258	0.028	−1.434	0.000	0.028
	1992–2005	0.258	0.162	−0.095	6.980	−0.078	−0.017
Togo	1988–-98	0.340	0.259	−0.082	4.969	−0.083	0.001
Tanzania	1992–6	0.448	0.463	0.015	−1.178	0.006	0.009
	1996–9	0.463	0.441	−0.022	1.357	0.001	−0.024
	1999–2004	0.441	0.382	−0.059	3.730	−0.059	0.001
Uganda	1988–95	0.470	0.408	−0.062	4.376	−0.052	−0.010
	1988–2000	0.470	0.404	−0.066	4.619	−0.051	−0.015
	1995–2000	0.408	0.404	−0.004	0.341	−0.002	−0.003
Zambia	1992–6	0.426	0.446	0.020	−1.539	0.018	0.002
	1996–2001	0.446	0.508	0.062	−4.790	0.054	0.008
Zimbabwe	1988–94	0.319	0.252	−0.066	4.033	−0.082	0.016
	1994–9	0.252	0.306	0.054	−3.311	0.004	0.050

Source: Sahn and Younger (2008).

Table 13.5. Datt–Ravallion and Kakwani decompositions for women's BMI

Country	Period	First	Second	Difference	t-value	Mean	Dispersion
Burkina Faso	1992–9	0.137	0.125	−0.011	1.501	0.011	−0.022
	1999–2003	0.125	0.197	0.071	−11.069	0.006	0.065
Benin	1996–2001	0.140	0.101	−0.039	5.016	−0.090	0.051
Côte d'Ivoire	1994–8	0.079	0.082	0.004	−0.534	−0.023	0.027
Cameroon	1998–2004	0.070	0.064	−0.006	0.888	−0.038	0.032
Chad	1997–2004	0.194	0.202	0.008	−0.931	−0.023	0.031
Ethiopia	2000–5	0.281	0.246	−0.035	5.379	−0.045	0.011
Ghana	1993–8	0.113	0.107	−0.007	0.677	−0.029	0.022
	1998–2003	0.107	0.091	−0.016	2.155	−0.066	0.050
Guinea	1999–2005	0.113	0.121	0.008	−1.092	−0.004	0.012
Kenya	1993–8	0.094	0.109	0.015	−2.188	0.001	0.014
	1998–2003	0.109	0.118	0.009	−1.429	−0.044	0.053
Madagascar	1997–2003	0.190	0.184	−0.006	0.736	−0.047	0.041
Mali	1995–2001	0.146	0.114	−0.031	5.429	−0.066	0.035
Malawi	1992–2000	0.086	0.080	−0.006	0.972	−0.016	0.011
Mozambique	1997–2003	0.109	0.081	−0.027	4.445	−0.056	0.028
Nigeria	1999–2003	0.156	0.141	−0.015	1.747	0.030	−0.044
Niger	1992–8	0.177	0.190	0.013	−1.487	0.011	0.002
Rwanda	2000–5	0.082	0.092	0.010	−2.074	0.009	0.000
Senegal	1992–2005	0.137	0.174	0.036	−4.483	−0.036	0.072
Tanzania	1992–6	0.089	0.088	−0.001	0.163	−0.012	0.011
	1996–2004	0.088	0.095	0.007	−1.355	−0.018	0.025
Uganda	1995–2000	0.089	0.094	0.005	−0.776	−0.030	0.034
Zambia	1992–6	0.097	0.083	−0.014	2.253	−0.010	−0.004
	1996–2001	0.083	0.141	0.058	−10.144	0.035	0.023
Zimbabwe	1994–9	0.047	0.054	0.008	−1.446	−0.014	0.022

Source: Sahn and Younger (2008).

Table 13.6. Datt–Ravallion and Kakwani decompositions for women's years of schooling

Country	Period	First	Second	Difference	t-value	Mean	Dispersion
Burkina Faso	1992–9	0.940	0.947	0.007	−0.950	0.016	−0.009
	1999–2003	0.947	0.905	−0.043	5.710	−0.052	0.009
Benin	1996–2001	0.893	0.898	0.006	−0.536	−0.012	0.018
Côte d'Ivoire	1994–8	0.862	0.835	−0.026	1.802	−0.095	0.068
Cameroon	1991–8	0.718	0.543	−0.175	9.367	−0.189	0.014
	1998–2004	0.543	0.523	−0.020	1.288	−0.038	0.018
Chad	1997–2004	0.966	0.947	−0.019	2.880	−0.021	0.002
Ethiopia	2000–5	0.878	0.870	−0.008	1.175	−0.011	0.002
Ghana	1988–93	0.507	0.530	0.023	−1.227	−0.026	0.049
	1993–8	0.530	0.492	−0.039	2.044	−0.029	−0.009
	1998–2003	0.492	0.494	0.002	−0.121	0.032	−0.030
Guinea	1999–2005	0.927	0.931	0.004	−0.520	0.006	−0.001
Kenya	1988–93	0.482	0.386	−0.095	6.411	−0.039	−0.057
	1993–8	0.386	0.276	−0.110	7.753	−0.122	0.012
	1998–2003	0.276	0.261	−0.015	1.138	0.036	−0.051
Madagascar	1992–7	0.726	0.748	0.022	−1.508	0.017	0.005
	1992–2003	0.726	0.741	0.014	−1.014	−0.017	0.031
	1997–2003	0.748	0.741	−0.008	0.559	−0.017	0.010
Mali	1987–95	0.943	0.933	−0.010	1.117	−0.014	0.004
	1995–2001	0.933	0.929	−0.004	0.647	−0.010	0.006
Malawi	1992–2000	0.809	0.739	−0.070	5.518	−0.136	0.066
Mozambique	1997–2003	0.924	0.893	−0.030	3.930	−0.022	−0.008
Nigeria	1986–90	0.661	0.809	0.148	−8.869	0.136	0.011
	1990–9	0.809	0.625	−0.184	15.337	−0.147	−0.038
	1999–2003	0.625	0.599	−0.026	1.837	−0.092	0.066

(continued)

Table 13.6. Continued

Country	Period	First	Second	Difference	t-value	Mean	Dispersion
Niger	1992–8	0.972	0.947	−0.025	4.076	−0.049	0.024
Namibia	1992–2000	0.408	0.228	−0.180	11.126	−0.127	−0.054
Rwanda	1992–2000	0.762	0.640	−0.121	8.811	−0.126	0.005
	2000–5	0.640	0.804	0.163	−13.722	0.078	0.085
Senegal	1986–92	0.910	0.903	−0.007	0.676	0.044	−0.052
	1992–7	0.903	0.871	−0.032	3.163	−0.059	0.028
	1997–2005	0.871	0.848	−0.023	2.537	−0.072	0.049
Togo	1988–98	0.836	0.881	0.045	−3.378	0.026	0.019
Tanzania	1992–6	0.433	0.320	−0.113	8.290	−0.014	−0.099
	1996–9	0.320	0.328	0.007	−0.441	−0.007	0.014
	1999–2004	0.328	0.346	0.018	−1.144	−0.014	0.033
Uganda	1988–95	0.795	0.758	−0.036	2.589	−0.036	0.000
	1995–2000	0.758	0.699	−0.059	4.409	−0.145	0.086
Zambia	1992–6	0.453	0.465	0.012	−0.794	−0.042	0.055
	1996–2001	0.465	0.476	0.010	−0.671	−0.039	0.049
Zimbabwe	1988–94	0.532	0.286	−0.246	13.151	−0.199	−0.046
	1994–9	0.286	0.157	−0.129	8.890	−0.027	−0.102

Source: Sahn and Younger (2008).

cent and the average of the latter is +2 per cent. So, while the mean effect is contributing to declining average undernourishment among women across the survey, and the dispersion effect just the opposite, the overall magnitudes cancel each other out. The importance of the dispersion effects at the country level can be illustrated by the most recent spell in Burkina Faso. Between 1999 and 2003, there was a 7 per cent increase in the share of wasted women. This was almost entirely due to increases in inequality, despite that the mean remained nearly constant. Another interesting case of the mean shift and dispersion effects nearly cancelling each other out is the final spell in Kenya, between 1998 and 2003. There was only a one percentage point increase in the share of underweight women. However, if the dispersion remained the same, and the observed mean shift occurred, the share of wasted women would have declined over six percentage points.

We also find that the mean and dispersion effects tend to move in opposite directions in the case of BMI. Thus, we find many instances, for example, where the dispersion is increasing, mostly driven by increases in the right-hand tail of the distribution, which also contributes to overall increases in the mean.

For our final measure of well-being—the years of schooling for women aged 22 to 30—we find a greater proportion of positive spells than with the other indicators. Using a cut-off point of six years of schooling for our headcount measure, we find a statistically significant decline in school poverty in twenty-one out of forty-one spells, a worsening in two cases (Nigeria between 1986 and 1990 and Rwanda between 2000 and 2005), and no change in the remainder of the cases. Most notable improvements were seen in Kenya and Zimbabwe across multiple spells. To the contrary, there are several countries, largely in Francophone West Africa, with very high shares of women lacking schooling of six or more years, little improvement is noted over one or more spells in these countries. Within this region, Cameroon is the only country, based on the 1991 to 1998 spell, but not the 1998 to 2004 spell, where a substantial improvement is seen in the share of women who have competed six years of schooling.

When we look at the change in univariate inequality of schooling, and its overall contribution for changes based on the mean dispersion decompositions, we find first that in thirty-three of the thirty-four spells the overall level of education inequality had declined. Like both health indicators, the mean shift is of a greater magnitude than the impact of the changes in dispersion in terms of explaining overall differences in the headcount. This is the case in thirty-four out of forty-one spells. Overall, the average dispersion effect across all spells is 1 per cent, while the average mean shift effect is −4 per cent, indicating it is the latter which is driving improvements in the education poverty headcount. Nevertheless, the dispersion effects often prove to be quite important in explaining the overall level of improvement, or lack thereof. For example, in Uganda between 1995 and 2000, the education headcount declined from 76 per cent to 70 per cent. The improvement in the share of women with six or more years of schooling would have been much greater, with the headcount declining from 76 per cent to 61 per cent, were it not for the increased inequality of education during this period in Uganda. The increase in the percentage of women that completed six years of schooling in Nigeria between 1999 and 2003, similarly, would have been 10 percentage points, rather than merely three, had inequality of education not negatively affected the decomposition.

As with the BMIs, the mean and dispersion effects for the years of schooling indicator tend to move in opposite directions, again, reflecting that most of the improvement in these indicators, unlike the case of child health, is in the right side of the distribution.

A final point we take up is the question of whether the spells of changes have any association with changes in several indicators of globalization. First, we look at the relationship between our welfare indicators and various indexes of globalization. These include a simple measure of trade openness defined as imports plus exports/GDP and four indices of globalization constructed by researchers at Warwick University.[7] The first is an index of economic globalization, composed of measures of trade openness as defined above, inflows plus outflows of FDI as a proportion of GDP, and employee compensation. The second is an index of social globalization which includes foreign population as proportion of total, inflows of foreign population as proportion of total population, worker remittances as a proportion of GDP, number of tourists as proportion of total population, international outgoing telephone traffic in minutes per capita, Internet users as a percentage of population, number of films, books, and newspapers imported and exported per capita, and pieces of international mail. The third index is of political globalization, which includes the number of foreign embassies in the country, the number of UN peacekeeping operations in which a country participates, and the number of memberships of international organizations. Finally, there is an aggregate globalization index that combines these three components. These annual indexes are constructed to be consistent over time and across countries.

Despite the difficulties of attributing causation, we none the less look at simple correlations to get some insight into the relationship of our welfare indictors, both in terms of headcount ratios and Gini coefficients, and these indicators of globalization. In Table 13.7, we first report the results of the simple correlations for the various globalization indexes and the headcount. We present correlation results first when the headcounts and the indexes are for the same years, and also when the indexes are lagged three years for the height-for-age of children less than 36 months of age, and where the indexes are lagged ten years for the schooling correlations.[8] While the lags are somewhat arbitrary, the

[7] For more details, see <http://www2.warwick.ac.uk/fac/soc/csgr/index/>.

[8] The results in general are not sensitive to the choice of lags. For example, if we lag education by ten years, all the significant results are the same sign and magnitude.

Table 13.7. Correlations between globalization and non-income measures of well-being

		Height-for-age z-score (HAZ)		Body mass index (BMI)		Years of schooling	
		Headcount	Gini	Headcount	Gini	Headcount	Gini
Trade openness	coefficient p-value	−0.2849[1]	−0.0315[2]	−0.3327[a]	0.4928	−0.3620	−0.3090
		0.0406	0.8246	0.0385	0.0014	0.0071	0.0230
Economic globalization	coefficient p-value	0.1037	0.4081	−0.2873	0.5013	−0.3554	−0.3413
		0.6143	0.0385	0.2194	0.0243	0.0634	0.0755
Economic globalization lagged	coefficient p-value	0.1363	0.4349	−0.0486	0.6898	−0.1756	−0.1442
		0.4807	0.0184	0.8256	0.0003	0.4230	0.5117
Social globalization	coefficient p-value	−0.4665	−0.0769	−0.4791	0.1309	−0.2823	−0.1281
		0.0216	0.7209	0.0326	0.5823	0.1623	0.5327
Social globalization lagged	coefficient p-value	−0.4786	−0.1333	−0.5598	0.1140	−0.2097	−0.0529
		0.0155	0.5253	0.0083	0.6227	0.5130	0.8702
Political globalization	coefficient p-value	−0.2213	0.2373	−0.0432	0.5982	−0.3890	−0.2728
		0.1394	0.1123	0.8112	0.0002	0.0063	0.0607
Political globalization lagged	coefficient p-value	−0.1183	0.2904	−0.0429	0.6852	−0.4361	−0.3344
		0.4035	0.0368	0.7954	0.0000	0.0035	0.0284
Aggregate globalization	coefficient p-value	0.0681	0.5612	0.3919	0.7016	−0.2889	−0.1307
		0.8095	0.0295	0.1854	0.0075	0.2607	0.6170

Notes: [1] Positive coefficient means that an increase in openness over time is associated with an increase in the share of stunted individuals—e.g., higher headcount.
[2] Positive coefficient implies that an increase in openness is associated with an increase in the Gini—e.g., greater inequality.

logic of the use of lags for the correlation with children's growth is that height-for-age captures the accumulation of effects of economic, social, and health conditions over the past few years which may be better captured by the lagged indexes. And, given that the children in the sample are 0 to 36 months of age, we consider a three-year lag to be a reasonable one to employ. In contrast for education where our headcounts are for young women aged 22 to 30,[9] we report the results with a ten-year lag, which generally corresponds to a period of time in terms of the indexes when most of the women would have been in their teens, an age when they would have been in secondary school if they had not dropped out early.

In the case of the height-for-age headcount, we find that there is a negative and significant correlation with our trade openness indicator and the social globalization index, both with and without lags. For the BMI headcount, we find the same result for the openness and social globalization indexes. When it comes to years of schooling, we again observe several negative and significant correlations for trade openness, economic globalization, political globalization, and political globalization with lags.

In the case of the correlations with the Gini coefficients, we find that the higher the globalization indexes, the greater the health inequality in terms of both the child health and BMI indicators. More specifically, for the height-for-age headcount, the correlation is positive and significant in the cases of economic and political globalization, as well as the aggregate index. And in the case of BMI, this applies to the trade openness indicator, economic globalization, political globalization, and aggregate globalization indexes.

Just the opposite finding is noted in the case in term of years of schooling where greater openness is accompanied by less inequality. This applies to the trade openness, economic globalization, and political globalization indexes. Perhaps the difference with the health outcomes captures the fact that there has never been much gender discrimination in either health for kids or access to food for adults, but there has been for schooling. This, however, seems to be improving (Glick, Saha, and Younger 2004), mostly at the primary level, as secondary school remains rare for girls in Africa. Thus one could envisage a situation where there is both a significant reduction in education poverty (measured at primary graduation) and reduced inequality as the gender gap is closed.

Table 13.8 reports correlations of the changes in both globalization indexes and our non-income outcomes. The difference correlations control for country-specific characteristics that do not vary over time, including those that are

[9] As noted earlier, we choose not to use the entire sample of women aged 15–49 because at the younger end we want to avoid censoring for women who have not yet reached the age at which they should have completed post-secondary school and at the older end we want to limit our attention to those who have finished their schooling in the not-too-distant past.

Table 13.8. Correlations between changes in globalization and changes in non-income measures of well-being

		Height-for-age z-score (HAZ)		Body mass index (BMI)		Years of schooling	
		Headcount	Gini	Headcount	Gini	Headcount	Gini
Differences in trade openness	coefficient p-value	−0.3265	0.3542	−0.2513	0.4519	−0.0409	0.1872
		0.0682	0.0467	0.2993	0.0521	0.8183	0.2890
Differences economic globalization	coefficient p-value	−0.0691	0.2429	−0.0661	−0.1214	−0.3677	−0.1838
		0.8225	0.4240	0.8881	0.7954	0.1776	0.5120
Differences economic globalization lagged	coefficient p-value	0.3939	0.4215	−0.1393	−0.2203	0.2465	0.4729
		0.1312	0.1039	0.7010	0.5409	0.4649	0.1418
Differences social globalization	coefficient p-value	−0.2880	−0.0458	0.0160	−0.0752	−0.4031	−0.0274
		0.3641	0.8877	0.9700	0.8595	0.1529	0.9259
Differences social globalization lagged	coefficient p-value	−0.1098	−0.0321	−0.1141	0.0563	−0.9668	0.7897
		0.7086	0.9133	0.7536	0.8772	0.1645	0.4205
Differences political globalization	coefficient p-value	−0.0349	0.1851	−0.3216	−0.2838	−0.1451	−0.2205
		0.8656	0.3654	0.2839	0.3473	0.4613	0.2595
Differences political globalization lagged	coefficient p-value	0.0102	0.0188	0.0582	0.2162	0.0256	0.2904
		0.9557	0.9186	0.8131	0.3741	0.9076	0.1788
Differences aggregate globalization	coefficient p-value	0.2450	0.3617	−0.2912	−0.7866	−0.5156	−0.3779
		0.6399	0.4812	0.7088	0.2134	0.1909	0.3561
Differences aggregate globalization lagged	coefficient p-value	0.5486	0.5537	0.4977	−0.0268	na	na
		0.2023	0.1973	0.3955	0.9658	na	na

Notes: See Table 13.7.

difficult or impossible to measure and thus control for. If the relationship between openness and the outcomes is linear, this correlation of differences provides more reliable estimates of that relationship.

As can be seen in Table 13.8, there are only three significant correlations: a positive correlation between changes in the headcount index and changes in the trade–openness indicator, and two positive correlations—for the height-for-age and BMI Ginis. While these three correlations can be interpreted to suggest that an increase in globalization is accompanied by more poverty and inequality, overall, the lack of significance indicates that we do not find any relationship between changes in globalization and changes in non-income poverty headcounts or inequality.

13.4. Discussion

Our aim in this chapter is to describe changes in non-income measures of well-being in Africa over the past fifteen to twenty years, a period during which we assume that Africa has been 'globalizing'. We adopted this focus because, while there is much discussion in the literature on *income* poverty and inequality, there is very little on other dimensions of well-being that we feel deserve equal consideration when evaluating a country's economic and social progress. We were also encouraged by evidence from Latin America that indicates that measures of education and health have improved significantly, and that their inequality has decreased in the past two decades, even as traditional income poverty has declined only a little and income inequality may well have increased (Sahn and Younger 2006).

Our hope was to find similar results for Africa where, like Latin America, income poverty and inequality are not improving. This is not an unreasonable aspiration. The underlying factors that determine income inequality are different from those that contribute to health and education inequality. For example, the nature of labour market is an important determinant of income inequality, as are the distribution of productive assets, the differential returns to human capital, and the role of non-earned incomes, including remittances from overseas workers. In contrast, education and health inequality are strongly influenced by public provision of basic services and social infrastructure. The availability and access to these institutions may have little relationship to the underlying distribution of incomes.

Progress in the provision of public services (including access to and adoption of basic health technologies such as oral rehydration) and the focus of public spending in the social sector, such as building primary schools, is expected to contribute to declining poverty and inequality in health and education, even in an environment of stagnant or worsening levels of income poverty. Investments in health and education as a share of GDP in Africa have been commensurate, and in many cases greater than in other regions of the world (Table 13.9). Even in terms of per capita expenditures in real dollars, Africa does better than South Asia in terms of health, and East Asia and the Pacific, and South Asia in terms of education. Furthermore, there has been a push in Africa over the past decade to focus on the delivery of primary services in the social sectors. We thus expected that such policies would have reduced inequalities and lifted up those at the bottom of the distribution of well-being measured in terms of health and education outcomes, even in the absence of substantial improvements in incomes and income equality.

Unfortunately, our priors were wrong. In the area of health, changes in children's heights suggest that little progress is being made in terms of reducing stunting, a clear manifestation of poor overall health. Indeed, only one-third of the spells indicated improvement along these dimensions, and there were more spells indicating a worsening in the headcount ratio of stunted children. Likewise, our health inequality measure showed that while there were a few instances of reduced inequality along this dimension, there was, on balance, little evidence of success in improving equality of outcomes, despite efforts to focus expenditures and interventions on those in the bottom end of the distribution.

Our examination of underweight women as an indicator of general current health status of adults indicated that in only six of twenty-six spells did the share of underweight women decline. And, even more disheartening, inequality in women's standardized weights actually worsened in most cases, an artefact of standardized weights increasing far more among women in the upper ranges of the BMI distribution than those in the bottom of the distribution.

With regards to education, the story is somewhat more positive: schooling poverty declined in twenty-one or forty-one spells for which we have data, and, likewise, for inequality in the vast majority of cases. But, even here, we had somewhat higher expectations, given all the investments and attention paid to raising primary school enrolments.

In this chapter, we also attempted to relate directly changes in non-income indicators of poverty and inequality to various indexes of globalization. A general story emerges that countries that are more globalized tend to show a lower rate of stunting among young children, underweight among women, and low levels of school enrolments. It is also the case that in the same countries greater globalization is associated with more inequality in terms of health, but not education. Despite that there were several strong correlations between globalization measures and health and education poverty and inequality, we would admonish against drawing the conclusion that these are causal relationships. In fact, when we control for fixed effects looking at the correlation of differences over time, almost all of the correlations become statistically insignificant. This applies to whether we look at contemporaneous changes or lag globalization indexes relative to the various outcomes analysed. There is just nothing here to suggest that globalization is correlated (positively or

Table 13.9. Indicators of health and education spending by region

Region	Years	Openness	Percentage openness change (1995–2001)	Health (percentage GDP)	Health/cap (current US$)	Education (percentage GNI)	Education/cap (current US$)
East Asia and Pacific							
	1995	59.923					
	1996	55.541					
	1997	58.889					
	1998	62.506		4.411	35.653	2.284	17.042
	1999	62.378		4.553	40.466	2.265	18.205
	2000	71.598		4.914	47.824	2.313	20.064
	2001	70.102	16.987	5.068	51.757	2.309	20.821
South Asia							
	1995	27.148					
	1996	26.769					
	1997	27.185					
	1998	27.801		4.779	19.961	3.195	13.265
	1999	28.653		5.208	22.871	3.208	13.953
	2000	31.632		5.606	25.055	3.477	15.397
	2001	31.282	15.224	5.472	24.805	3.498	15.703
Latin America and Caribbean							
	1995	37.911					
	1996	39.152					
	1997	39.570					
	1998	39.701		6.931	280.352	4.04	159.513
	1999	40.378		7.119	252.071	4.074	140.345
	2000	42.066		6.906	265.859	3.977	149.966
	2001	41.460	9.360	7.046	259.49	4.096	146.982

Sub-Saharan Africa						
1995	59.760					
1996	59.712					
1997	60.145					
1998	60.336		6.49	33.847	4.944	24.58
1999	60.540		6.593	33.581	4.893	23.616
2000	64.828		6.279	32.228	4.85	23.14
2001	64.912	8.621	6.326	31.467	4.605	21.27
Middle East and North Africa						
1995	57.019					
1996	55.028					
1997	53.119					
1998	52.253		5.325	69.073	5.189	84.561
1999	52.621		5.222	68.7	5.254	84.32
2000	55.697		5.073	71.959	5.29	90.279
2001	54.419	−4.561	5.329	73.832	5.322	59.65

negatively) with health and education outcomes. While these results may be viewed as somewhat disappointing, they probably reflect the complexity and context-specific nature of the dynamic processes that both contribute to changes in the globalization indexes employed, and how they transmit through very different economic and social structures to affect non-income poverty.

Finally, we acknowledge that we are not capturing all non-income dimensions of well-being, broadly speaking, nor even all dimensions of health and education poverty and inequality. For those dimensions other than child stunting, mother's BMI, and years of schooling, the story of limited progress in eliminating health and education poverty and inequality may not hold, although, we suspect it does. None the less, we need to be cognizant of this possibility and appropriately cautious in generalizing from the limited dimensions over which we conduct our analysis. This implies a need to consider further other indicators of well-being. But, more important is to gain a fuller understanding of the processes that contribute to differences in income versus other indicators of inequity and poverty, as well as explaining the relatively discouraging outcomes presented in this chapter. This is best done through intensive country studies, rather than painting with a broad brush as we have done in this chapter. However, the bottom line seems clear: the evolution of income inequality and poverty in Africa during the 1990s and first part of the new millennium gives little cause for complacency or optimism.

References

Appleton, S., and L. Song (1999) 'Income and Human Development at the Household Level: Evidence from Six Countries'. Oxford: Oxford University Centre for the Study of African Economies. mimeo.

Beaton, G. H., A. Kelly, J. Kevany, R. Martorell, and J. Mason (1990) 'Appropriate Uses of Anthropometric Indices in Children: A Report Based on an ACC/SCN Workshop'. UN Administrative Committee on Coordination/Subcommittee on Nutrition. ACC/SCN State-of-the-Art Series, Nutrition Policy Discussion Paper 7. New York: United Nations.

Behrman, J. R., and A. B. Deolalikar (1988) 'Health and Nutrition'. In H. Chenery and T. N. Srinivasan (eds), *Handbook of Development Economics*, i. Amsterdam: North-Holland Elsevier.

Cole, T. J., and J. M. Parkin (1977) 'Infection and its Effect on Growth of Young Children: A Comparison of the Gambia and Uganda', *Transactions of the Royal Society of Tropical Medicine and Hygiene*, 71: 196–8.

Datt, G., and M. Ravallion (1992) 'Growth and Redistribution Components of Changes in Poverty Measures: A Decomposition with Applications to Brazil and India in the 1980s', *Journal of Development Economics*, 38: 275–95.

Deaton, A. (2004) 'Health in an Age of Globalization'. Working Paper 10669. Cambridge, Mass.: NBER.

—— and J. Muellbauer (1980) *Economics and Consumer Behavior.* Cambridge: Cambridge University Press.

Dhongde, S. (2002) 'Measuring the Impact of Growth and Income Distribution on Poverty in India'. Riverside, Calif.: University of California, Department of Economics. mimeo.

Drèze, J., and A. Sen (1989) *Hunger and Public Action.* Oxford: Oxford University Press for UNU-WIDER.

Filmer, D., and L. Pritchett (2001) 'Estimating Wealth Effects without Expenditure Data or Tears: An Application of Educational Enrolment in States of India', *Demography,* 38: 115–32.

Glick, P., R. Saha, and S. D. Younger (2004) 'Integrating Gender into Benefit Incidence and Demand Analysis'. Cornell Food and Nutrition Policy Program Working Paper 167. Ithaca, NY: Cornell University. http://www.cfnpp.cornell.edu/info/workpap.html.

Haddad, L., H. Alderman, A. Appleton, et al. (2003) 'Reducing Child Malnutrition: How Far Does Income Growth Take Us?', *World Bank Economic Review,* 17: 107–31.

Kakwani, N. (1997) 'On Measuring Growth and Inequality Components of Changes in Poverty with Application to Thailand'. Sydney: University of New South Wales School of Economics. mimeo.

Le Grand, J. (1987) 'Inequalities in Health: Some International Comparisons', *European Economic Review,* 31: 182–91.

Lopez, R., V. Thomas, and Y. Wang (1998) 'Addressing the Education Puzzle: The Distribution of Education and Economic Reforms'. Working Paper 2031. Washington, DC: World Bank.

McCulloch, N., M. Cherel-Robson, and B. Baulch (2000) 'Growth, Inequality and Poverty in Mauritania 1987–1996'. Brighton: University of Sussex, Institute of Development Studies. mimeo.

Martorell, R., J.-P. Habicht, C. Yarbrough, et al. (1975) 'Acute Morbidity and Physical Growth in Rural Guatemalan Children', *American Journal of Diseases in Childhood,* 129: 1296–301.

Mata, L. (1978) *The Children of Santa Maria Cauque: A Prospective Field Study of Health and Growth.* Cambridge, Mass.: MIT Press.

Mosley, W. H., and L. C. Chen (1984) 'An Analytical Framework for the Study of Child Survival in Developing Countries', *Population and Development Review,* 10: 25–45.

Murray, C. J. L., E. E. Gakidou, and J. Frenk (1999) 'Health Inequalities and Social Group Differences: What Should We Measure?', *Bulletin of the World Health Organization,* 77: 537–43.

Pradhan, M., D. E. Sahn, and S. D. Younger (2003) 'Decomposing World Health Inequality', *Journal of Health Economics,* 22: 271–93.

Sahn, D. E., and S. D. Younger (2005) 'Improvements in Children's Health: Does Inequality Matter?', *Journal of Economic Inequality,* 3: 125–43.

—— —— (2006) 'Changes in Inequality and Poverty in Latin America: Looking Beyond Income', *Journal of Applied Economics,* 9: 215–34.

—— —— (2008) 'Living Standards in Africa'. In S. Anand, P. Segal, and J. E. Stiglitz (eds), *Debates in the Measurement of Global Inequality.* New York: Oxford University Press.

Sen, A. (1979) 'Personal Utilities and Public Judgment: Or What's Wrong with Welfare Economics?', *Economic Journal,* 89 (355): 537–58.

Sen, A. (1985) *Commodities and Capabilities*. Amsterdam: North-Holland Elsevier.

—— (1987) 'The Standard of Living, Lecture II: "Lives and Capabilities" '. In G. Hawthorn (ed.), *The Standard of Living*. Cambridge: Cambridge University Press.

Shorrocks, A., and S. Kolenikov (2001) 'Poverty Trends in Russia during the Transition'. Helsinki: UNU-WIDER. mimeo.

Strauss, J., and D. Thomas (1995) 'Empirical Modelling of Household and Family Decisions'. In J. Behrman and T. N. Srinivasan (eds), *Handbook of Development Economics*, iiiA. Amsterdamml: North-Holland Elsevier.

Tanner, J. M. (1981) *A History of the Study of Human Growth*. New York: Cambridge University Press.

Thomas, V., Y. Wang, and X. Fan (2000) 'Measuring Education Inequality: Gini Coefficients of Education'. Education Policy Research Working Paper 2525. Washington, DC: World Bank.

van Doorslaer, E., A. Wagstaff, H. Bleichrodt, et al. (1997) 'Income-related Inequalities in Health: Some International Comparisons', *Journal of Health Economics*, 16: 93–112.

Wagstaff, A., P. Paci, and E. van Doorslaer (1991) 'On the Measurement of Inequalities in Health', *Social Science and Medicine*, 33: 545–57.

—— and E. van Doorslaer (2004) 'Overall versus Socioeconomic Health Inequality: A Measurement Framework and Two Empirical Illustrations', *Health Economics*, 13: 297–301.

World Health Organization (WHO) (1983) 'Measuring Change in Nutritional Status: Guidelines for Assessing the Nutritional Impact of Supplementary Feeding Programmes for Vulnerable Groups'. Geneva: WHO.

—— (1995) 'Physical Status: The Use and Interpretation of Anthropometry: Report of WHO Expert Committee'. Geneva: WHO.

14

Post-apartheid South Africa: Poverty and Distribution Trends in an Era of Globalization

Servaas van der Berg, Ronelle Burger, and Megan Louw[1]

14.1. Introduction

South Africa's political transition culminated in 1994 with the holding of the country's first democratic elections. This date can also be regarded as the turning-point in South Africa's reintegration into the world economy. Under apartheid, protectionism was first an activist industrial policy instrument and later a defence against growing international isolation. The political realities of the time constrained policy choice and prevented progress in the first hesitant moves to open up the South African economy. Whatever liberalization impetus existed was strongly countered by the effect of threatened sanctions against the apartheid state—later de facto financial sanctions—and the debt standstill of 1985. Within this constellation of political events, policymakers could do no more than accept the reality of a relatively closed economy and continue with the industrial policy stance of import substitution.

Economic liberalization and South Africa's full acceptance into the international fold brought new possibilities for economic policymaking. In the main, reintegration brought sustained, if unspectacular, growth that reversed the long decline in per capita incomes. The economic upswing that continued until the world financial crisis of 2008 was the longest sustained one in South Africa's economic history. But, economic performance has not been spectacular and the adjustment required by liberalization has left its scars in job shedding in much of the industry—in order to become internationally competitive—and in mining, given rising mine wages and more recently a strengthening currency.

[1] The authors wish to thank Derek Yu for his technical assistance.

This is in line with international evidence that the positive employment effects of trade liberalization take some time to be realized—although Rama (2003) contends that the initial loss of 'privileged' employment in monopolistic and state-owned industries is eventually counteracted by new export jobs. Disappointing employment growth in the face of an expanding labour force have fed a trend of rising unemployment rates in an economy with only a small informal sector and no safety net of subsistence farming. This implies that formal sector unemployment has become a major cause of poverty.

The apparently adverse implications of such market-driven trends for the South African income distribution have been revealed in several recent studies. Using household survey data, Leibbrandt, Levinsohn, and McCrary (2005) observe that the returns to human capital have collapsed in the post-transition period, while Hoogeveen and Özler (2004) find that poverty has worsened substantially. However, both of these studies are based on the income and expenditure surveys (IES) of 1995 and 2000: surveys that are known to suffer from serious deficiencies in terms of reliability and comparability. Indeed, the massive income decline implied by a comparison of these surveys—about 40 per cent in per capita terms in the first five years of the post-transition period—contradicts the trend observed in the national accounts and is also greatly at odds with other data. For instance, government revenues from VAT, income tax, and company tax increased in real terms by 19 per cent, 26 per cent, and 33 per cent, respectively, over the measurement period. Few observers of the South African scene regard such large income declines as credible, thus raising the need for alternative data sources to be able to assess whether money-metric poverty and polarization have indeed increased.

Given the known shortcomings of recently collected official datasets and the desire to evaluate poverty trends since the turn of the century, this study draws on an alternative source of data: the all media and products survey (AMPS). Evidence of a marked reduction in poverty during the second half of the first decade of democracy is presented, and largely attributed to the recent large-scale expansion of the social grants system. Poverty dominance testing is used to show that the main conclusions reached are not sensitive to the selection of poverty line or poverty measure. However, a caveat applies when drawing inference regarding the link between globalization and poverty. No matter how well poverty is measured or how robust the findings are to the specification of a poverty line, empirical analysis does not allow one to draw strong conclusions on the role of globalization in determining the course of poverty. The reason for this is that it is extremely difficult to establish a causal relationship between globalization and changes in the income distribution.

Survey data are also used to construct a polarization measure developed by Duclos, Esteban, and Ray (2004) and a bi-polarization index developed by Wolfson (1994). This analysis investigates claims that income has become an increasingly important polarizing force in South African society, and is—to the best of our knowledge—the first of its kind in the South African context. Polarization measures are distinct from standard inequality indicators because they consider not only the spread of the income distribution, but also what Duclos and Échevin refer to as the 'clustering of income around local poles' (Duclos and Échevin 2003). Polarization is usually interpreted as a measure of political and social stability, an issue of particular importance in a newly democratized society. The intuition behind this interpretation is that the existence of individual incomes far from the mean will not fuel social and political action on its own. Some degree of association between groups of observations located far above and far below the mean is required to prompt collective behaviour.

This chapter continues in section 14.2 with a brief review of developments in trade and financial liberalization over the transition and post-transition period, proceeding to a discussion of the labour market implications of such changes. Section 14.3 turns to evaluating trends in poverty and inequality over the past decade, and speculates on how these could have been influenced by globalization. Section 14.4 concludes.

14.2. A Brief History of South Africa's Trade and Financial Liberalization, 1994–2005

14.2.1. Trade Liberalization

Efforts to liberalize South Africa's trade regime were first undertaken during the 1970s, following the release of the Reynders Commission Report. It was already recognized at that time that a more outwardly oriented strategy was superior to the import substituting industrialization strategy that had been in place since as early as 1925 (Ball 2001). However, the increasing political and economic isolation of the country prevented much progress with the envisioned shift towards greater openness until the early 1990s. The move towards liberalization gained steam with the negotiations conducted by the transition government through the mechanism of the National Economic Forum, as the prospect of reintegration into the global economy grew more real.

When the new government took over in April 1994, South Africa was emerging from the poorest decade of economic performance it had experienced during the post-war period (Du Plessis and Smit 2007). Decades of isolation and protectionist policy had left the country with a legacy of production inefficiency and a skewed economic structure that was also associated with South Africa's notoriously severe racial inequality. Embarking on a programme of trade liberalization was therefore viewed as not only symbolic of South Africa's political transition but also as one of the key components of government's strategy to kick-start economic growth. The enthusiasm of the new government with respect to making further progress in trade liberalization was evident when South Africa became a signatory to the Marrakech Agreement of the General Agreement on Tariffs and Trade in 1994. The government thus took its first major step towards reforming the trade regime, committing to an initial five-year phased programme for reducing and rationalizing the country's complex and highly discretionary tariff structure. In terms of the agreement 10,000 tariff lines were to be decreased to 6,000, while tariff rates were to be standardized from more than 100 to only six, varying up to 30 per cent (Ball 2001). Impressively, the largest tariff cuts were made in sectors that had previously enjoyed the most extensive protection, and South Africa's tariff-reduction programme was more ambitious than required by the WTO. This policy stance is in line with the government's 1996 growth, employment, and redistribution (GEAR) framework, which set out an export-led growth strategy.

Initially, substantial progress was made in simplifying the tariff structure. The number of tariff lines was cut by a third from the very high level of 12,500 between 1990 and 1996, while the number of tariff rates was reduced from 200 to 49. The average tariff fell from 28 per cent to 10 per cent during the same period, and the maximum tariff rate was cut to 61 per cent (Lewis 2001). Since 1996, however, progress with liberalization has slowed: there have been small declines in the number of tariff bands and the level of the maximum tariff.[2] Furthermore, there has been less progress since 1990 in reducing *effective* protection than has been the case with nominal protection, given South Africa's tiered protection structure (i.e., high protection on consumer goods, moderate protection on intermediate goods, and low protection on capital goods). In fact, research by Fedderke and Vaze (2001) shows that half of South Africa's output is produced in sectors where effective protection actually rose over the period 1994–8; by contrast, only 15 per cent of the output is produced in sectors where effective protection had fallen by 1998 relative to pre-transition levels. Continuing high levels of effective protection imply that South Africa's anti-export bias has not yet been eliminated.

To evaluate the impact of trade liberalization on the South African economy—and in particular its impact on employment and distribution—at least three issues need to be examined: (i) changes in the volume of trade flows; (ii) changes in the composition of trade; and (iii) the impact of trade on growth. Trade flows have undoubtedly increased. Total trade (measured as the ratio of exports plus imports to GDP) has risen throughout the post-transition period; by 2004, it stood at 54 per cent. This increase should be attributed not only to trade policy reform, but also to favourable world demand conditions and exchange rate depreciation—both factors that strongly influence South Africa's export performance (Tsikata 1999). Manufacturing exports rose rapidly after

[2] Bhorat, Lundall, and Rospabe suggest that this was because the dramatic initial cuts in trade protection were followed with 'more careful and nuanced adjustments that needed to be made in more sensitive industry and product lines' (Bhorat, Lundall, and Rospabe 2002: 3).

1994, with the chemical, metal, and machinery sectors showing the best performance within the sector (Lewis 2001). Liberalization also caused the price of imports to fall as a result of continuing tariff reductions and the removal of sanctions, leading to greater import penetration.[3] Consequently, both imports and exports increased after 1994. On balance, the growth impact of this increased trade was positive: net trade contributed 10 per cent of the rise in gross output between 1993 and 1997 (Edwards 2001a). However, in line with what appears to be a typical trade liberalization experience for developing countries, the bulk of the increase in South Africa's gross output during this period was due to rising domestic final demand—particularly demand for manufactured goods (Lewis 2001).

Turning to the composition of South Africa's trade, it is interesting to note that the country's manufacturing exports are dominated by physical and human capital-intensive goods, contrary to what one might expect given South Africa's abundance of unskilled labour. The share of skill-intensive manufactures in total exports has grown since the early 1990s, from 49.5 per cent in 1992 to 58.5 per cent in 1999 (Lewis 2001). However, this share stagnated from 1996 onwards, at least partly due to a shortage of skilled managerial and technical labour (Lewis 2000). By contrast, manufacturing exports intensive in unskilled labour and natural resources have fallen in importance over the same period; in 1999, the former amounted to only 6.8 per cent of total exports while the latter contributed 19.6 per cent (Lewis 2000). Against the predictions of Heckscher–Ohlin trade models, trade liberalization has thus intensified the structural shift towards capital and skill intensive production in the South African economy. Labour market implications of the structural shift are discussed towards the end of this section.

Next, the impact of trade liberalization on economic growth is considered. Early international empirical studies arguing that trade is unambiguously good for growth have recently come under fire by authors including Rodriguez and Rodrik, for reasons including measurement difficulties (see Rodriguez and Rodrik 1999). Another issue relevant to the interpretation of empirical work on the relationship between trade and growth is drawing the distinction between trade openness and trade reform. Greenaway, Morgan, and Wright (2001) note that there is more solid empirical evidence of trade openness being beneficial for growth than there is for trade reform. Investigating the issue further, these authors report the existence of a robust J-curve relationship: trade reform is growth enhancing, but its benefits are not reaped immediately.

[3] Accounting for 40 per cent of total imports in 2000, the largest import category remains metal products and machinery (Ball 2001). This reflects South Africa's continued reliance on imported intermediate inputs into capital-intensive production techniques.

14.2.2. Financial Liberalization

The South African government initiated financial liberalization following the release of the De Kock Commission reports (1978; 1985) that recommended a more market-oriented monetary policy. However, liberalization efforts were dealt a temporary but severe blow in 1985 with the international debt standstill resulting in a sharp cut in net capital inflows. The scope for pro-liberalization policymaking only broadened again almost a decade later with the election of the ANC-led government in 1994. During this year the trend in private capital flows was reversed as investors responded euphorically to the peaceful transition to democracy, and the South African government was able to re-enter global financial markets with a bond issue of US$750 million (Cross 2003: 104). These substantial capital inflows allowed the government to increase both the Reserve Bank's holdings of gold and foreign exchange—which had been run down to critical levels during the pre-election period—and to sustain a modest current account deficit. Such inflows created substantial leeway for making further progress in liberalizing the financial sector. In addition, a macroeconomic burden of high and variable inflation and substantial public debt provided the government with an urgent financial liberalization imperative.

During the years following 1985, the government had issued a large number of foreign currency guarantees as a result of its lack of access to international capital markets: by March 1995 the net open forward position[4] stood at US$28 billion (Cross 2003). These high levels of public debt made the country vulnerable to currency attacks and thus increased exchange rate risk. In March 1995, the financial Rand system was abolished, ending the operation of a dual exchange rate mechanism. Foreign exchange flows linked to international transactions concerning assets in South Africa thus became available for reducing the Reserve Bank's forward book. During the late 1990s, following harsh criticism by the IMF of the government's intervention in the market through the forward book, the Reserve Bank decided to reduce the net open forward position to zero. Finally, in February 2004, the oversold forward book was closed out. Relaxation of exchange controls also brought benefits to the private sector. Capital controls on non-residents were effectively eliminated when the dual exchange rate system ended, and resident individuals and firms have been allowed to make increasingly large offshore investments since the mid-1990s. In addition, it was decided in 1995 that South African insurers, pension funds, unit trusts, and fund managers could hold a limited proportion of their

[4] During the time of sanctions following 1985, South Africa's access to international credit was cut off. The only way in which the government could raise credit was through providing forward cover to the private sector to protect its access to trade credits; hence the establishment of the forward book. The net open forward position equals the oversold forward book less the Reserve Bank's net gold and foreign exchange reserves.

investments offshore. Collectively, these measures represent a large stride in the direction of capital account openness.

The maintenance of net inflows on the capital account after 1994 allowed South Africa to maintain a modest current account deficit once again. They also allowed the Reserve Bank to replenish its store of foreign exchange reserves. Previously the absence of foreign capital had imposed a balance-of-payments constraint in terms of which the country was forced to run a current account surplus. Together with the high interest rates maintained during the last decade of apartheid, this had placed a limit on South Africa's economic growth prospects. Aside from easing the balance-of-payments constraint, the government was also able to promote growth through reducing interest rates. During the second half of the 1980s, the Reserve Bank had introduced money supply targets in an attempt to directly control spiralling inflation. However, the use of this nominal anchor was unsuccessful in containing inflationary pressure: inflation figures remained double digits during the early 1990s. In 1998, the Reserve Bank replaced money supply targeting with an informal inflation targeting system. This system was formalized two years later, with national treasury setting an initial target band of 3 per cent to 6 per cent. While the inflation rate has not always been kept strictly below the upper limit of the target range, it had been reduced significantly and had been maintained at stable and low levels for a number of years, until a sharply rising world oil price and sharp depreciation of the currency in 2007–8 brought an equally sharp rise in the inflation rate. This reduced the leeway of the Reserve Bank to respond to the world financial slowdown by relaxing its interest rate policy.

The gradualist approach adopted by the government in its financial liberalization programme appears to have paid off. Despite some exchange-rate volatility, financial liberalization has progressed relatively smoothly and has not been accompanied by capital flight, although South Africa was also affected like other emerging markets by capital outflows when the world financial crisis started in 2008. The ANC government's high prioritization of macroeconomic stability—most strongly reflected in the GEAR policy framework—is arguably at least partly the reason for South Africa's successful post-transition financial liberalization experience.[5] It has become conventional wisdom that financial liberalization improves economic growth prospects only if reforms are sequenced correctly—that is, that macroeconomic stability is achieved before the financial sector is liberalized—and if complementary financial sector policies are in place (see, for instance, Eichengreen 2001; Nyawata and Bird 2003). The question of whether financial liberalization has indeed enhanced

[5] Du Plessis and Smit conclude that 'macroeconomic policy prudence' has been a major positive feature of South African policy since the political transition that has encouraged investment (du Plessis and Smit 2007).

growth in South Africa, empirically speaking, is not easily answered. In the international literature, little conclusive support has been found for the robust growth-enhancing impact of financial liberalization (Eichengreen 2001). Given the weakness of international conclusions on a growth-enhancing role for financial liberalization, additional, less-formal evidence on the impact of financial reform on South Africa's growth prospects is presented.

Analysing countries of the Southern African Development Community (SADC), Nyawata and Bird (2003) argue that the available data do not support the hypothesis of a link between financial liberalization and growth. Their study indicates little change in saving or investment rates in South Africa during the second half of the 1990s; substantial post-transition investment inflows were largely offset by investment outflows of a similar size. Constituting 17.1 per cent of GDP, South Africa's investment spending still remains low by world standards (Du Plessis and Smit 2007). Indeed, it is true that many aspects of South Africa's financial liberalization experience support Nyawata and Bird's position. While one might expect the liberalization of the capital account to promote investor confidence in the long term, FDI levels thus far have remained disappointingly low. Portfolio flows have been large and positive at times, although highly volatile, resulting in large fluctuations in the exchange rate, the key price of an open economy. Indeed, a slew of recent international financial crises demonstrated just how risky globalization can be for a government's efforts to maintain macroeconomic stability. On the other hand, it seems intuitive that recently lower interest rates, a stable low inflation rate, and improved availability of foreign capital have contributed positively to growth. In addition, Nyawata and Bird (2003) show that some financial deepening has occurred over the past decade in South Africa. This has positive implications for long-term growth (Levine 1992, cited in Reinhart and Tokatlidis 2003).

While empirical support for the growth-enhancing effects of financial liberalization remains tenuous, there is stronger evidence of a link between financial liberalization and two key macroeconomic aggregates in South Africa. Aron and Muelbauer (2000) find that financial liberalization in South Africa has been associated with large increases in the ratios of both private consumption and household debt to income. The literature often argues that financial liberalization reduces credit constraints when consumption-smoothing households expect higher rates of future economic growth. However, Aron and Muelbauer point out that financial liberalization also increases household consumption and debt through its impact on mortgage markets. It does so by improving the availability of collateral-backed credit and by reducing the deposits required of first-time homeowners. These factors result in young consumers spending more as a result of being required to save for fewer years to accumulate a housing deposit, and consumers who own houses spending more as a result of being able to borrow more in a liberalized market.

14.2.3. The Impact of Globalization on Employment

The picture outlined above is one where both trade and financial liberalization appear to have positively—albeit modestly—influenced economic growth in South Africa. Averaging 3.1 per cent per year in the decade following 1994 (Du Plessis and Smit 2007: 673, table 2), GDP growth has improved, implying that globalization has created some space for reducing unemployment. However, unemployment has not declined: by late 2004, the unemployed accounted for 26.4 per cent of the labour force according to the narrow definition of unemployment, and 41.3 per cent by the expanded definition.[6] These figures are substantially higher than the comparable ones for the mid-1990s. Attempting to determine the extent to which job growth has proven inadequate requires careful consideration of the issues surrounding different sources of employment data, since trends in employment figures differ widely depending on which source is used.

The Statistics South Africa and South African Reserve Bank series of employment in non-agricultural sectors provide the most pessimistic trends, with the Reserve Bank suggesting that non-agricultural employment declined by 13 per cent over the period 1994 to 2003 (South African Reserve Bank 2002, cited at van der Berg 2004: 218). However, the series from which this estimate is derived has major deficiencies, including a major discontinuity in the middle of 2002. The downward trend in employment seems doubtful, particularly given the strengthening in economic performance preceding the world economic slowdown in 2008.

A second source of employment data comes from comparing employment figures in the October household surveys (OHSs) and labour-force surveys (LFSs) over the period 1995–2004. However, there is also a discontinuity between these two series, with the LFS capturing more informal sector participants. Using these two series would overestimate the growth in employment over the period: employment growth of 26 per cent is recorded over the period, as against real GDP growth of 31 per cent. This may be viewed as surprisingly positive employment performance in light of the modest economic growth rates observed during the second half of the 1990s. (For a more-complete discussion of the choice between these alternative employment series, see, *inter alia*, Bhorat 2003; 2004.)

A third option is to accept the surveys as correct, but to take the position that the OHS and LFS are not comparable—that is, to accept that part of the increase between the two series results from differences in methodology. To make them more comparable, the two series are spliced where they meet. The results of this exercise are displayed in Figure 14.1. Estimated employment growth is slower than in the previous case, at 23 per cent over 1995–2004, implying an average

[6] Calculations based on the labour-force survey of Sept. 2004.

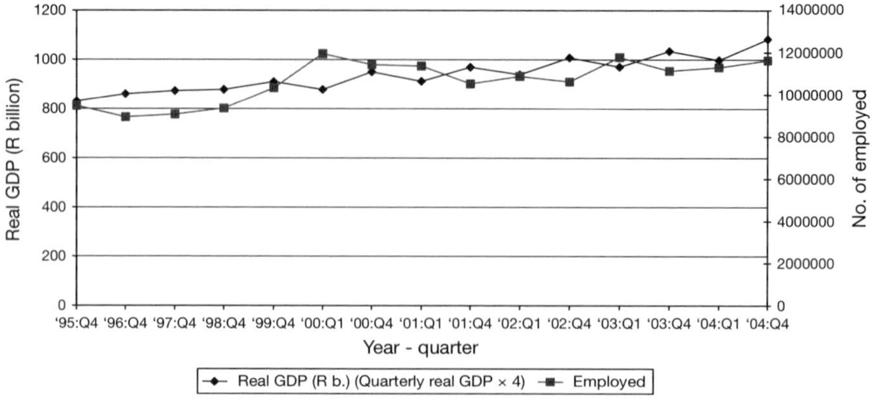

Fig. 14.1. Estimates of total employment, 1990–2004

Source: South African Reserve Bank, OHS/LFS data for various years.

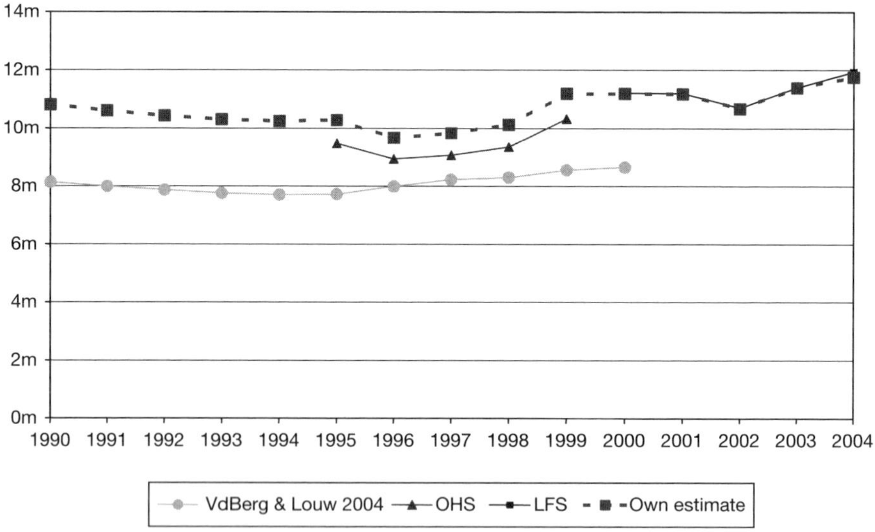

Fig. 14.2. Real GDP and employment, 1995–2004

Source: van der Berg and Louw (2004) and own calculations based on OHS/LFS data for various years.

annual increase of 2.3 per cent per year. On the basis of the spliced employment series (which may be the most accurate set of estimates available), regression analysis yields a relatively high employment elasticity of economic growth of 0.83 over the same period. This is illustrated in Figure 14.1: observe how closely the spliced employment series tracks real GDP over the past decade.

While it would seem that the ability of the economy to generate jobs is surprisingly positive and robust (at least before the economic slowdown), no related discussion would be complete without considering the skills content of employment opportunities recently created and lost. It was pointed out earlier that there has been a skill bias in the structural change of the economy over the past ten years. As a result, jobs have been shed at the lower end of the skill spectrum, reflected in the decline of the share of employment of unskilled labour in the total from 31 per cent in 1995 to 27 per cent in 2002. By contrast, the demand for skilled and semi-skilled labour has risen, with the share of employment of each type of labour increasing by two percentage points over the same period[7] (Bhorat 2004). Thus, the jobs that have been created are largely located towards the upper end of the skill spectrum. Furthermore, the pace of job creation has not managed to keep up with the very rapid growth in the labour force, as Figure 14.2 indicates. Five million individuals entered the labour market between 1995 and 2002,[8] while only 1.6 million found employment. Modest employment growth of 16.75 per cent over the period is implied, contrasted with a much larger 52.38 per cent increase in the size of the labour force (Bhorat 2004). This has compounded an unemployment problem that was already large at the time of political transition. Clearly, employment growth has proven insufficient to absorb more of the unemployed into the formal labour market, and to shift them from traditional (low-wage) to modern (high-wage) sectors—analogous to Arthur Lewis' model of economic development with unlimited supplies of labour. Consequently, the labour surplus has been rising rather than declining during most of the post-transition period. But the problem appears to be not so much the shift away from labour-intensive production as it is an economic growth rate lower than that required to accelerate labour absorption.

Recent developments in the labour market have not affected all groups in society equally. Black workers experienced the second-largest percentage increase in employment over the period 1995–2002,[9] while white workers experienced the smallest increase. This trend can be partly attributed to the introduction of affirmative action policy. However, Bhorat points out that the employment absorption rate was substantially higher for whites (55 per cent) than for blacks (28 per cent) (Bhorat 2004). This suggests that blacks joined the ranks of the unemployed in disproportionately large numbers. The cause of this perpetuation of racial inequality in the labour market can be traced to the interaction between the skills-biased nature of recent economic growth in South Africa and racial human capital stock: firms increasingly demand employees with high levels of education. Between 1995 and 2002, 64 per cent of

[7] Skilled labour accounted for 11 per cent of employment in 2002, while semi-skilled labour accounted for 61 per cent in the same year (Bhorat 2003).

[8] This calculation is made using the expanded definition of unemployment.

[9] Asians experienced the largest increase in employment (Bhorat 2003).

individuals with tertiary education found work, contrasted with only 35 per cent of individuals with matric (high school) and a mere 14 per cent of individuals with incomplete secondary schooling (Bhorat 2004). White workers remain best positioned in the competition for scarce employment in the South African economy, given their historically superior access to education. In 2004, white labour force participants had an average of 12.4 years of schooling, compared with a much lower average of 8.6 years for black labour force participants.[10] Simkins (1998) describes this ongoing disparity as one of the most enduring 'footprints' of apartheid.

Amongst the (predominantly black) individuals who have borne the losses from the structural change associated with recent globalization, those who live in rural areas have been particularly hard hit. Instead of surviving on a purely agricultural basis, rural households in South Africa typically rely on a combination of remittances from urban areas and own access to land-based natural resources (including grazing rights, water, and wood). Indeed, only 5 per cent of household income in the former homelands is generated by subsistence production (van der Berg 2004). Members of impoverished rural households are at a particular disadvantage regarding access to education given the small number and often poor quality of schools in these areas. As a result of this lack of education and skill, they have been severely hit by the drop in unskilled employment in urban areas. On the other hand, the rural poor in South Africa are affected less by agricultural price shocks and changes in production associated with international competition than are the rural poor in other African countries, owing to the relatively low reliance of the former on agriculture for survival (van der Berg 2004). Indeed, simulations performed by Dieden et al. (2005) confirm that the adverse impact of trade liberalization on the poor has been relatively small, with the bulk of modelled job losses affecting workers in the middle of the income distribution.

The discussion above paints a picture in terms of which South Africans in the upper range of the income distribution appear to have reaped most of the gains to globalization—at least in so far as conditions in the labour market have evolved. However, research by Edwards (2001b) suggests that the most significant factors driving recent changes in the labour market are not directly linked to trade. This author employed an input–output decomposition to identify the determinants of changing employment over the early liberalizing years, 1993–7. Edwards finds that increasing domestic final demand expanded employment by 10 per cent during the period, while technological change caused a contraction in employment of 15 per cent (Edwards 2001b). Net trade had a positive but very modest impact on employment, boosting it by only 1 per cent over the five-year period. Interestingly, the strongest driver of the observed change in the skills composition in the workforce over this period appeared to

[10] These calculations are based on the LFS Sept. 2004.

be technological change, rather than trade. Of course, it may be convincingly argued that changes in technology represent a response by domestic suppliers to the challenges associated with liberalization in domestic product markets. In this way, trade liberalization has indirectly benefited affluent, highly skilled workers at the expense of poor, low-skilled workers.

14.3. Trends in Poverty, Inequality, and Polarization

The discussion has focused predominantly on the impact of recent liberalization on labour up to this point, given that wages constitute approximately two-thirds of household income in South Africa (Leibbrandt, Woolard, and Bhorat 2001). It has been argued that globalization-related developments in the labour market have tended to favour better-skilled workers, and would thus have exacerbated inequality, *ceteris paribus*. However, globalization may also have impacted on the South African income distribution through other mechanisms. In particular, the rising share of property income in household income is likely to be driving increased inequality. At the same time, rising economic growth rates (particularly in more recent years) have allowed for a concerted response from the government to the problem of ongoing widespread poverty. As will be shown, the poverty alleviation that has occurred has largely been achieved through expanding the social grant system, which has acted to reduce poverty and counter increases in inequality associated with recent structural trends.

To investigate these issues further, we draw on the results of empirical analysis. First, conventional measures of poverty and inequality are presented, along with stochastic dominance curves that test the robustness of poverty findings. In this subsection, attention is focused mostly on discerning reliable trends in poverty over the past decade, given the controversial findings of several recent studies on the topic. An assessment of poverty trends during an era of reintegration into the global economy is also of particular interest in the context of the globalization focus, even if accepting that the causal relationship cannot be clearly established empirically. Following this exercise, a closer look is taken at South Africa's unequal income distribution through the lens of polarization analysis. It is then asked whether reintegration has been accompanied by any change in the degree of polarization in an already highly economically polarized society.

14.3.1. Distributional Analysis

Given the problems associated with comparing income data from the post-transition sets of censuses or income and expenditure surveys,[11] as well as a

[11] See van der Berg, Louw, and Yu (2008) for a discussion of the hazards involved in a comparison of post-1994 income distributions constructed from either of these datasets.

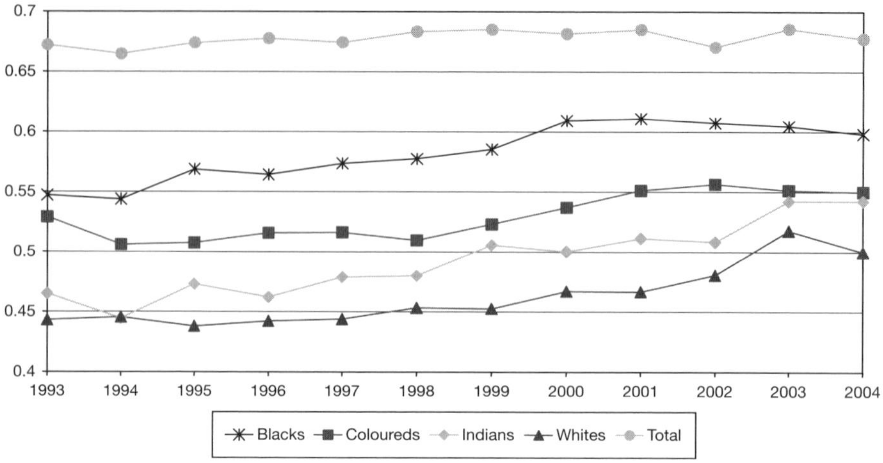

Fig. 14.3. Estimated Gini coefficients, 1993–2004

Source: Own estimates based on AMPS data for various years.

desire to extend the analysis beyond 2001, it was decided instead to draw data from the AMPS.[12] This survey is conducted once or twice a year under the auspices of the South African Advertising Research Foundation. For the purposes of this research, unit data records for the variables of interest were obtained for the period 1993 to 2004. Each dataset contains approximately 25,000 observations, each relating to one individual who provided data for every household sampled. This includes income data. Respondents indicate in which of thirty-two income intervals household income lies. This allows much more disaggregation than some of the expenditure data from official surveys, where far fewer intervals are provided. Before utilizing the AMPS datasets for distributional analysis, these were tested extensively for stability. Encouragingly, per capita incomes calculated from the data for the race groups deviated only once in forty-eight cases (four race groups times twelve years in which growth rates could be calculated) by more than 10 per cent from that in the previous year, indicating that data differences were not driven by large fluctuations caused by sampling and fieldwork questions in different years. Gini coefficients calculated for each race group were even more stable.

Before turning to the analysis of poverty trends, a brief overview of intra-racial inequality is provided. The trends in racial Gini coefficients in Figure 14.3 show increasing inequality of incomes over the period as a whole for each of the

[12] A study by van der Berg and Louw used the IES data to obtain the intra-group distribution and then adjusted these to be consistent with mean income data by race derived from other sources (van der Berg and Louw 2004).

four race groups, consistent with most findings of rising within group inequality in the literature. However, all race groups show individual deviations from this broad pattern, with the most surprising deviation being the declining Gini coefficient of the black population since 2000. This decline, together with the later decline of the Gini for the 'coloured' population, is consistent with a scenario in which the expansion of grants and widening employment opportunities have benefited the poor more than proportionately. Since almost all of the poor belong to the black or 'coloured' groups, these groups would have experienced the greatest inequality reducing benefits of additional transfer income during recent years. The Gini coefficient measuring overall inequality (the net effect of both intra-group inequality and inequality between the race groups) is large but has remained quite stable over the period, implying that the effect of rising intra-racial inequality has been offset to a large degree by the impact of a decline in inter-racial inequality. This is a continuation of a longer-term trend in the South African income distribution that started in the 1970s.

The focus now shifts to determining whether poverty has improved or worsened since political transition. Here, following van der Berg and Louw 2004, the poverty line is set at R250 household income per month or R3,000 per year in 2000 Rand (approximately US$4 per capita per day in 2002 PPP dollars), somewhat above the US$2 a day often used by the World Bank. The poverty line is a conservative measure in the sense that it will identify those living in relatively deep poverty, although it is judged to be high enough to act as a relatively realistic identifier of poverty. Stochastic dominance testing is used to determine the robustness of our conclusions to the specification of poverty line, given that the choice of poverty line is fairly arbitrary by construction. For purposes of measuring poverty, the Foster–Greer–Thorbecke measures are employed: the poverty headcount (P_0) reflects the extent of poverty, the poverty gap index (P_1) reflects the depth of poverty, and the squared poverty gap index (P_2) reflects the severity of poverty.

Table 14.1. Selected indicators of poverty

	1993	2000	2004
P_0 (Headcount ratio)	0.50	0.51	0.47
P_1 (Poverty gap ratio)	0.24	0.25	0.22
P_2 (Squared poverty gap/Poverty severity ratio)	0.15	0.15	0.13
Number of poor (million)	20.0	22.7	21.8
Number of non-poor (million)	20.0	22.0	24.7

Notes: Poverty line set at R3,000 per capita per year in 2000 Rand values.

Source: Computed by authors.

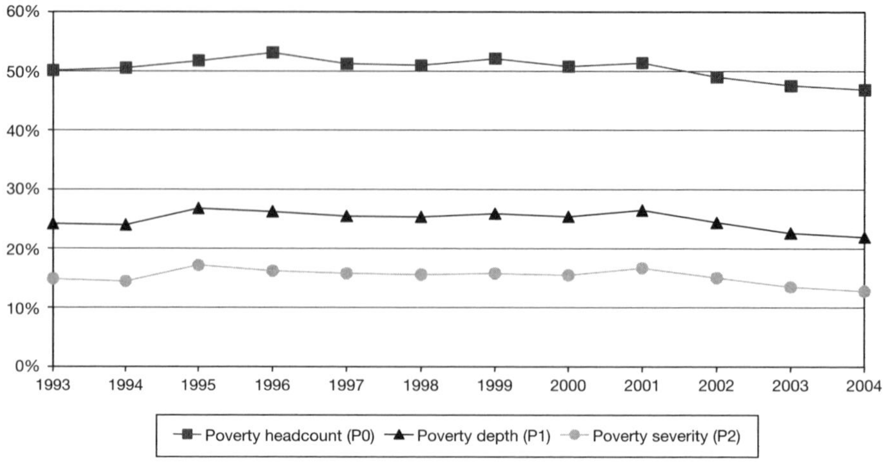

Fig. 14.4. Trends in poverty, 1993–2004

Source: Own estimates based on AMPS data for various years.

Table 14.1 reveals that the headcount poverty rate and poverty-gap index increased slightly over the first part of the period covered, and declined to below their starting levels towards the end of the period covered. The poverty severity ratio remained stable between 1993 and 2000, also dropping after the turn of the century. The proportion of people living in poverty increased over 1993–2000, probably as a result of sluggish economic growth and poor labour market prospects. However, in more recent years the proportion of poor people appears to have declined substantially, possibly due to a combination of faster growth, better labour market prospects, and large-scale expansion of the social grant system. A similar trend applies in terms of the poverty headcount (i.e., the absolute number of people living in poverty), although the number of people living in poverty in 2004 was larger than in 1993 as a result of population growth. The trends in poverty drawn from the analysis on AMPS data are illustrated in Figure 14.4.

The speed at which poverty appears to have declined since 2002 is striking, and may be challenged as being the result of quirks in the AMPS data. To answer such claims, the issue is investigated further.

- The recent expansion of social grants had a major impact on the poor. Real transfers from the government increased by some R22 billion in the last two years (in 2000 Rand), an amount well in excess of R1,000 per poor person. Bear in mind that poverty is defined as income of less than R3,000 per capita per year in this chapter. The grants are targeted through the means test, thus the additional R22 billion flows mainly into poor households. In 1997, the bottom two quintiles of households received three-quarters of grant spending (van der Berg 2006: 209 Table 5.2). Considering that the income of the poor was only R27 billion in 2000, an increase of such magnitude in social grants makes a great difference to the poor and may lift many of them out of poverty, if it is as well targeted as the South African grants.

- Recent analysis of official data (the annual general household surveys) supports the view that poverty has declined. The proportion of households with children reporting that a child went hungry during the previous year declined from 31 per cent in 2002 to 16 per cent in 2006 (van der Berg, Louw, and Yu 2008: 73–4).
- The national accounts show that real remuneration rose by R53 billion between 2002 and 2004, representing an exceptionally large increase by South African standards of 11.7 per cent over this period. This must have had a strongly positive influence on the incomes of many of the poor, either through higher wages or through increased employment.
- Income distribution, particularly in the black population, is relatively clustered around the poverty line. This means that small shifts in the distribution could have large impacts on poverty. The poverty consequences of distributional shifts are particularly severe if black incomes change, given the size of this group and the observed clustering of black incomes near the poverty line. Thus, the impact of grants on poverty is strongest if grants contribute predominantly to black incomes.

The finding that poverty has fallen during the post-transition period stands in direct contrast with the arguments made in several earlier studies, including Hoogeveen and Özler (2004) and Leibbrandt, Woolard, and Bhorat (2005). These papers argued that the extent of poverty had risen strongly during the post-transition period. However, there is reason to believe that the datasets on which these analyses are based (and particularly the IESs) are not directly comparable. The interested reader is referred to van der Berg, Louw, and Yu (2008) for a discussion of the issues affecting the validity of inference drawn from a comparison of these household datasets. Moreover, the period covered by these studies ends before the major decline in poverty observed in this study, and before the full expansion of social grant spending that largely brought this poverty reduction about.

Finally, the sensitivity of findings to the specification of a poverty line is tested using cumulative density functions (CDFs). In each of the CDF graphs, a vertical line is plotted at the level at which the poverty line is drawn—that is, R3,000 per person per year. The CDFs are plotted with alternately income and the log of income on the horizontal axis—the latter allows one to get a better overview of the whole distribution. Figures 14.5(a) and 14.5(b) show that there is poverty dominance in 2004 relative to either of the other years shown—that is, that poverty was lower in terms of extent, depth, and severity in 2004 than in

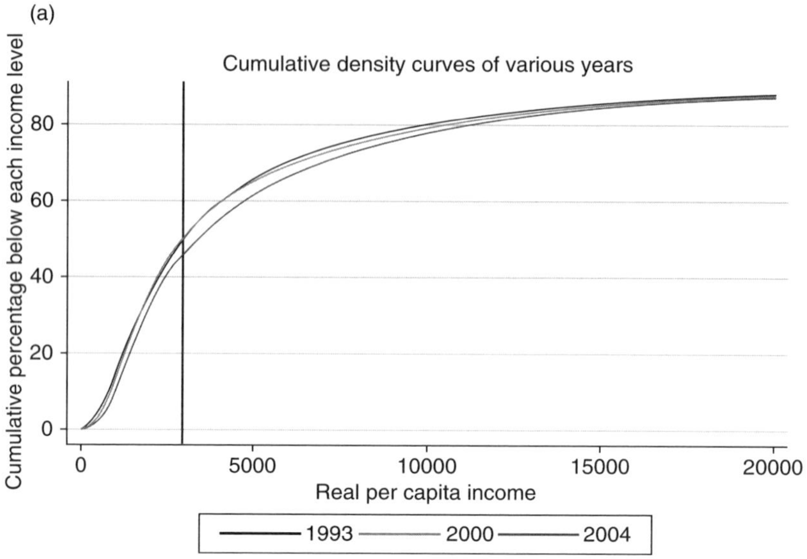

Fig. 14.5(a). Poverty dominance testing, real per capita income

Source: Computed by authors.

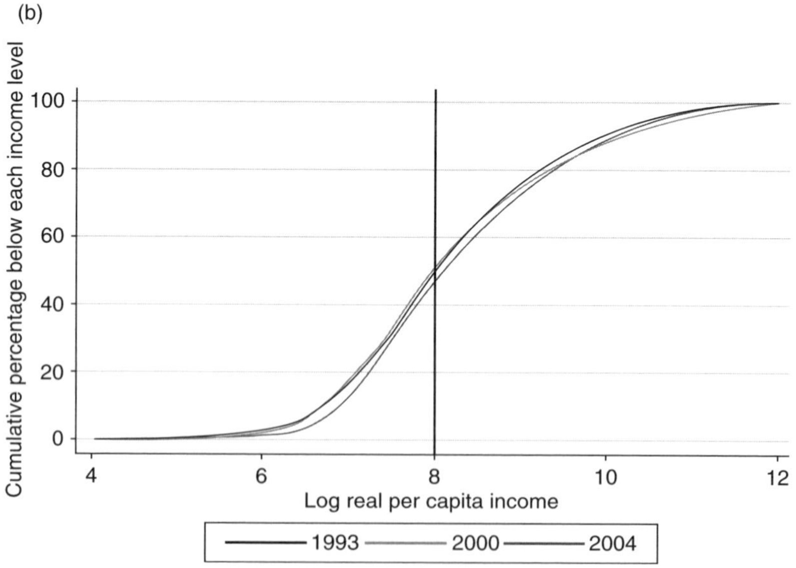

Fig. 14.5(b). Poverty dominance testing, log real per capita income

either of the preceding years. This finding is independent of the choice of poverty line or of the scale chosen (that is, income or the log thereof).

In summary, a robust trend of declining poverty has emerged from the empirical analysis. It appears that government action to address poverty through social grants has been the most important contributor to poverty alleviation, although the improved employment trend may indicate that employment growth is now on course towards a greater sustainable reduction in poverty. This represents an improvement on the initially weak job creating performance of the economy during the first few years after re-entering the world economy.

The flipside of declining poverty is a rise in the number of non-poor, as reflected in Table 14.1. In particular, a swelling black middle class has emerged as one of the most interesting distributional phenomena in recent years. Growth in black per capita incomes during the last two years has been very rapid, due, *inter alia*, to:

- Acceleration in aggregate black remuneration as a result of the improved performance of the economy in creating jobs. For the long-term sustainability of poverty reduction, further trends of this nature are essential. It is too early to determine whether the increased job creation indicates that the job-shedding reaction of many firms in adjusting to international competition has completed its course.
- The rapid growth of transfer income from the government driven by the expansion of the CSG, increased uptake of other grants (particularly disability grants), and higher benefits.

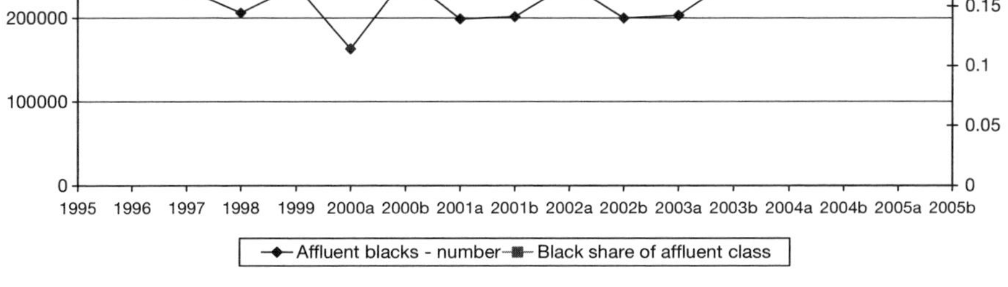

Fig. 14.6. Black middle and upper income earners

Source: Own estimates based on OHS/LFS data for various years.

- An increasing share of transfer income for the blacks, with the initially slow uptake of the CSG in rural areas having yielded to very rapid expansion.
- Slowdown in population growth amongst blacks, which has also meant that the gains from a growing overall income share of blacks have been spread amongst a smaller population, raising per capita incomes as a result.

In Figure 14.6, estimates of black workers likely to form part of the middle and upper classes is presented, both in terms of numbers of people and the black proportion of the total constituting this socio-economic grouping. OHS and LFS data are used for this exercise, and middle and upper earners are identified as those workers earning at least R6,000 per month (2000 Rand values) from their main job. As can be seen, the number of black workers who are well established in the labour market has increased substantially since 2003. Indeed, approximately 150,000 black workers joined these ranks between 1995 and 2005. In addition, the proportion of the total well-earning subpopulation accounted for by the blacks has also risen recently.

14.3.2. Polarization Analysis

The chapter examines trends in polarization as a supplement to the poverty and inequality analysis. As Duclos, Esteban, and Ray (2004) and Wolfson (1997) demonstrate, polarization is a concept that is both theoretically and empirically distinct from inequality.[13] Wolfson (1997) and Seshanna and Decornez (2003) argue that polarization indicators are best suited for describing the distributional trends about which the public and media appear to be most concerned. As Seshanna and Decornez suggest, polarization captures the 'sharpening of the divide' between income classes (Seshanna and Decornez 2003). According to Esteban and Ray, a shortcoming of many of the conventional inequality indicators is that they do not reflect increases in the 'tightness' of clustering around local means (Esteban and Ray 1994).

These polarization measures are interesting in their own right. They reflect social integration more precisely and are thus better predictors of social stability than inequality measures. They can identify changes in social organization such as increased fracturing and marginalization, which often would not be reflected in inequality indicators. Given the evidence that these measures generally produce rankings and trend lines that are distinct and even at odds with those produced using inequality indicators, the authors consider it vital to supplement the inequality and poverty analysis with an investigation of shifts in polarization in South Africa over the last ten years.

[13] Duclos, Esteban, and Ray show, for instance, that for a sample of twenty-one countries, the polarization measure yields country rankings that are vastly different from the rankings based on the size of the Gini coefficient (Duclos, Esteban, and Ray 2004).

Polarization analysis is applied here to two series of datasets. To measure polarization trends for household income, we use the IES datasets for 1995 and 2000. The AMPS data are not ideal for this purpose since this survey captures household income data in intervals. The study also examines polarization trends in wage income for individuals, using the OHS and LFS household surveys available from 1995 to 2005. Note that the OHS for 1996 is excluded from the analysis since incomes are reported in intervals, rendering this data unsuitable for calculation of polarization indices.

In the economics literature, two polarization measures are frequently used: the Wolfson index (1994) and the Duclos, Esteban, and Ray (2004) polarization measure (hereafter referred to as the DER measure). The DER polarization indicator was designed to capture changes in clustering around a number of local means. It measures both the tightness of these identified groups and their distance from other data points, assuming that there are two vital factors underlying polarization: alienation and identification. The authors argue that a sense of detachment is not all that matters, the sense of togetherness and belonging within the isolated groups is a crucial factor to consider since this is expected to be correlated with the likelihood of social mobilization and action. Consequently, Duclos, Esteban, and Ray describe the polarization index as the sum of all 'effective antagonism' in a society (Duclos, Esteban, and Ray 2004).

The alienation between two points is measured by the distance between the points, while the identification metric is captured by the density of observations at the point of interest. In this study, both the alienation of and identification among individuals are measured in terms of income. The algorithm suggested by Duclos, Esteban, and Ray is:

$$P_\alpha(f) \equiv \int\int f(x)^{1+\alpha} f(y)|y - x|dydx$$
$$\text{where } \alpha \in [0.25, 1]$$

In the work reported below, the polarization sensitivity parameter, α, is set to 1. This parameter determines the power of the identification effect. When $\alpha = 0$, the index reduces to double the Gini coefficient. Changes in polarization can be attributed to changes in alienation (distance between incomes) and identification (densities at populated points), as well as to co-movements between these two dimensions (for instance, whether density increases have been at points that are far removed or near to other incomes). Duclos, Esteban, and Ray explain that more variation and 'spikiness' are associated with higher polarization.

The Wolfson index is a bi-polarization index that can be used to detect trends in the divergence of incomes or the so-called 'vanishing middle class'. This index studies clustering around two extreme poles and is thus distinct from the

Table 14.2. Polarization trends for household income per capita, 1995–2000 (DER index)

Survey		IES 1995	IES 2000
All		*n=29 586*	*n=26 142*
		0.1912	0.2049
Race	Black	0.1398	0.1923
	'Coloured'	0.1088	0.1180
	Indian	0.0998	0.0933
	White	0.0952	0.0914
Area	Urban	0.1447	0.1693
	Rural	0.1535	0.1309

Source: Computed by authors.

DER index that investigates the 'tightness' of observations around a number of prominent 'lumps' in the income distribution.

$$W = 2[2[0.5 - L(0.5)] - I_2]\frac{\mu}{Q(0.5)}$$

where Q is the quantile function, I_2 is the Gini index, and L is the Lorenz curve.

In Table 14.2, the calculated values of the DER polarization index for household income per capita between 1995 and 2000 are reported, with α set to 1. The most striking aspect of Table 14.2 is undoubtedly the high level of polarization suggested by the index values. For α set to 1, household per capita polarization is 0.19 and 0.20 in 1995 and 2000, respectively. If South Africa had to be inserted into the DER polarization ranking based on either of these two polarizations estimates, it would achieve the second highest position out of 22, placed after Russia and before Mexico.[14] The DER ranking is based on the fourth wave of the Luxembourg Income Study.

With respect to trends, the calculations in Table 14.2 show that there was a modest increase in overall income polarization between 1995 and 2000. The DER index was also calculated separately for each of the population groups. The within-race polarization calculations reveal that the trend on the aggregate level may be fuelled by the strong increase in income polarization among blacks. As might be expected, given the high income inequality within this group, the level of polarization is highest among blacks. Due to a strong

[14] To make our calculated index values more comparable with the estimates of Duclos, Esteban, and Ray (2004) we follow them by dividing the estimates by two. Note that the resulting index values are still not entirely comparable because Duclos, Esteban, and Ray use post-tax income normalized by an adult equivalence scale.

Table 14.3. Trends in Wolfson bi-polarization index, 1995 to 2000

		Household income per capita	
Survey		IES 1995	IES 2000
All		0.8548	0.6906
Race	Black	0.5839	0.5451
	'Coloured'	0.4697	0.5159
	Indian	0.3959	0.4820
	White	0.3585	0.3841
Area	Urban	0.7353	0.7241
	Rural	0.5274	0.4526

Source: Computed by authors.

increase in income polarization within this group, the substantial racial gap in levels of polarization widened further between 1995 and 2000.

Over this period, income polarization increased in urban areas, but decreased in rural areas. In 1995, income polarization was more or less the same in urban and rural areas. Following the strong increase in polarization in urban areas, observe that polarization was higher in urban than in rural areas by 2000.

Figure 14.7 indicates that between 1995 and 2000, the polarization of individual wage income declined, while household income polarization has increased. Comparable trends are observed for the separate race groups. After 2000, wage polarization rose beyond 1995 levels. As argued before, it is

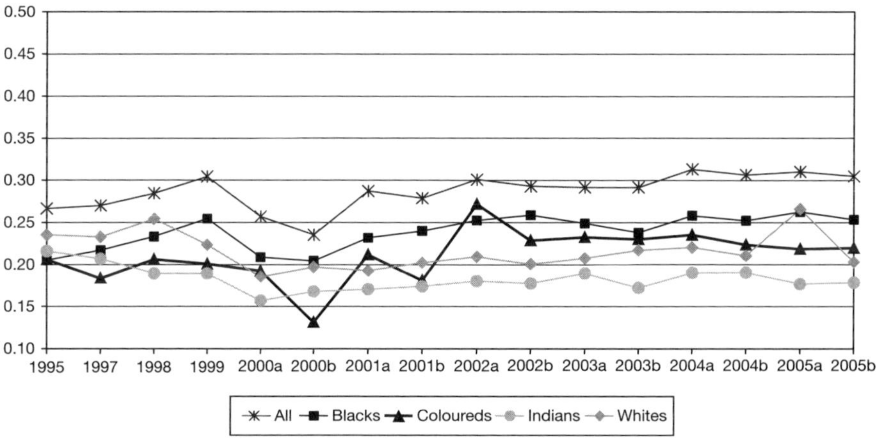

Fig. 14.7. Trends in wage income polarization, 1995–2005 (DER index)

Source: Own estimates based on OHS/LFS data for various years.

impossible to attribute these trends to any one specific event, although the results are consistent with strong unions and increased labour market regulation. Given the household income polarization results, it is not surprising that wage polarization is shown to be the highest among blacks.

It is clear that the DER and Wolfson indices measure different types of polarization. Using the same data, the Wolfson polarization index suggests a considerable decline in household income polarization between 1995 and 2000. This trend is reflected in Table 14.3, contrasting starkly with the noted moderate increase in the DER index over the same period. As mentioned before, the Wolfson index captures bi-polarization, while the DER index detects alienation and clustering around several local means.

The observed decline in income bi-polarization is indicative of an expanding middle class. If there is a bi-polarizing force at work due to the greater openness of economy, it appears that other factors, such as the impact of the expansion of social grants and the increased mobility of black workers in post-apartheid South Africa have countered it. This conjecture of two opposing forces is further supported by the strong rising trend of wage bi-polarization, following the large tariff reductions that occurred between 1990 and 1996. In Figure 14.8, it is shown that this trend was reversed in 2000, with wage polarization starting to taper off again. Post-2000 wage polarization for blacks has declined sharply and started to approach levels observed within other race groups.

The fall in bi-polarization in black and rural incomes between 1995 and 2000 suggests that transfers may have played a role in softening the starkness of

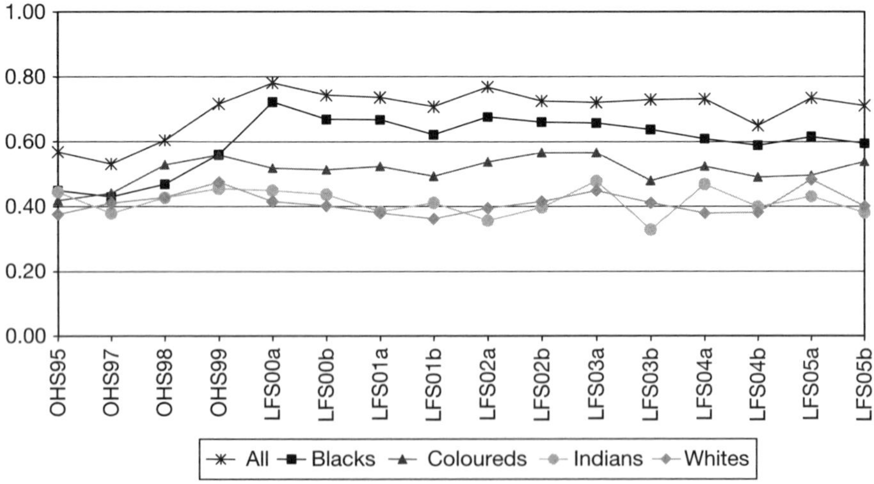

Fig. 14.8. Trends in wage income polarization, 1995–2005 (Wolfson bi-polarization index)

Source: Own estimates based on OHS/LFS data for various years.

disparities in the overall income distribution. Between 1995 and 2000, rural wage polarization grew from 0.60 to 0.81, while rural income polarization dropped from 0.53 to 0.45. However, some of the sharper changes observed here might be due to a deficiency in the comparability of the surveys.

14.4. Conclusion

This chapter has analysed possible links between South Africa's post-1994 globalization experience and the country's income distribution by treating globalization as a triad of political change, financial liberalization, and trade liberalization. It has thus evaluated the likely impacts on the income distribution of a modest improvement in the country's economic growth prospects post-1994 and the implementation of the ANC-led government's poverty alleviation policy. While the process of opening up to international markets has not resulted in a structural switch towards jobless growth, it has been accompanied by rising unemployment and a skills bias in employment creation favouring better-educated workers. Thus, in spite of yielding an estimated employment elasticity of economic growth of approximately 0.8 over the period 1993–2004, it is improbable that the labour market has been responsible for any substantial increase in the incomes of those near the lower end of the income distribution. By contrast, a boost of R22 billion (in 2000 Rand) to social grant expenditures between 2002 and 2004 is highly likely to have improved the material position of the poor, who as a group received only R27 billion in the year 2000. The good targeting of grants (three-quarters going to the poor) contributes greatly to their efficacy in reducing poverty.

A formal analysis of distributional trends shows a small increase in poverty between 1993 and 2000, followed by a marked reduction in poverty. While the recent expansion of the social grant system is the main source of this improvement, at over 3 per cent of GDP it is currently nearing its poverty alleviation ceiling. With respect to inequality, ongoing substitution of inter-racial for intra-racial inequality is observed, continuing an earlier trend. Amongst groups, blacks continue to experience the highest level of inequality, although a small reduction has been observed since the turn of the century. Estimation of two polarization indices complements the inequality analysis by highlighting the extent to which unequal income distribution may be undermining social and political stability. Although one measure—the DER index—provides evidence of increasing 'effective antagonism' within South African society, another—the Wolfson index—suggests that the improvements in living conditions associated with expanding grants and the emergence of a black middle class have dampened to some degree the social tensions associated with material inequality. Importantly, given the caveats required in any discussion of recent achievements in reducing poverty and inequality in South Africa, addressing widespread poverty associated with unemployment and the possible consequences of ongoing high levels of inequality remain critical policy focus areas in this country. This conclusion is strengthened by the present world economic slowdown.

References

Aron, J., and J. Muelbauer (2000) 'Financial Liberalization, Consumption and Debt in South Africa'. CSAE Working Paper 132. Oxford: Oxford University Centre for the Study of African Economies.

Ball, G. (2001) 'The Context: South Africa in the Global Economy since the Political Transition'. Paper 2 in Country Background Report on Poverty and the Role of Rural Institutions in a Globalizing South African Economy. Tokyo: FASID (Foundation for Advanced Studies on International Development).

Bhorat, H. (2003) 'The Post-apartheid Challenge: Labour Demand Trends in the South African Labour Market, 1995–1999'. DPRU Working Paper 03/82. Cape Town: University of Cape Town Development Policy Research Unit.

—— (2004) 'Labour Market Challenges in the Post-apartheid South Africa', *South African Journal of Economics*, 72: 940–77.

—— P. Lundall, and S. Rospabe (2002) 'The South African Labour Market in a Globalizing World: Economic and Legislative Considerations'. Employment Paper 2002/32. Geneva: ILO.

Cross, J. H. (2003) 'Global Integration and Capital Account Liberalization in South Africa'. Bank for International Settlements Paper 15, *China's Capital Account Liberalization: International Perspectives*. <http://www.bis.org/publ/bispap15.htm>.

Dieden, S., L. Edwards, M. Leibbrandt, and K. Pauw (2005) *'Trade and Poverty in South Africa: Traded Sector Employment and Vulnerability'*. Paper presented at the TIPS/DPRU Forum 2005: 'Trade and Uneven Development:Opportunities and Challenges', 30 Nov.–1 Dec. 2005, Johannesburg.

du Plessis, S., and B. Smit (2007) 'South Africa's Growth Revival After 1994', *Journal of African Economies*, 16: 668–704.

Duclos, J.-Y., and D. Échevin (2003) 'Bi-polarization Comparisons'. CIRPÉE Working Paper 03–41. Montreal: Université Laval.

—— J.-M. Esteban, and D. Ray (2004) 'Polarization: Concepts, Measurement, Estimation', *Econometrica*, 72: 1737–72.

Edwards, L. (2001a) 'Trade and the Structure of South African Production, 1984–1997', *Development Southern Africa*, 18: 471–91.

—— (2001b) 'Globalization and the Skills Bias of Occupational Employment in South Africa', *South African Journal of Economics*, 69: 40–72.

Eichengreen, B. (2001) 'Capital Account Liberalization: What Do Cross-country Studies Tell Us?', *World Bank Economic Review*, 15: 341–65.

Esteban, J.-M., and D. Ray (1994) 'On the Measurement of Polarization', *Econometrica*, 62: 819–52.

Fedderke, J., and P. Vaze (2001) 'The Nature of South Africa's Trade Patterns by Economic Sector, and the Extent of Trade Liberalization during the Course of the 1990s', *South African Journal of Economics*, 69: 436–73.

Foster, J. E., J. Greer, and E. Thorbecke (1984) 'A Class of Decomposable Poverty Measures', *Econometrica*, 52: 761–6.

Greenaway, D., W. Morgan, and P. Wright (2001) 'Trade Liberalization and Growth in Developing Countries', *Journal of Development Economics*, 67: 229–44.

Hoogeveen, J. G., and B. Özler (2004) 'Not Separate, Not Equal: Poverty and Inequality in Post-apartheid South Africa'. Washington, DC: World Bank. mimeo.

Leibbrandt, M., I. Woolard, and H. Bhorat (2001) 'Understanding Contemporary Household Inequality in South Africa'. In H. Bhorat, M. Leibbrandt, M. Maziya, et al. (eds), *Fighting Poverty: Labour Markets and Inequality in South Africa*. Cape Town: UCT Press.

——J. Levinsohn, and J. McCrary (2005) 'Incomes in South Africa since the Fall of Apartheid'. Working Paper 11384. Cambridge, Mass.: NBER.

Lewis, J. (2001) 'Reform and Opportunity: The Changing Role and Patterns of Trade in South Africa and SADC'. Africa Region Working Paper Series 14. Washington, DC: World Bank.

Nyawata, O., and G. Bird (2003) 'Financial Liberalization in Southern Africa: An Assessment'. Guildford: University of Surrey Centre for International Economic Studies. mimeo.

Rama, M. (2003) 'Globalization and Workers in Developing Countries'. Policy Research Paper 2958. Washington, DC: World Bank.

Reinhart, C. M., and I. Tokatlidis (2003) 'Financial Liberalization: The African Experience', *Journal of African Economies*, 12 (AERC Suppl. 2): ii53–ii88.

Rodriguez, F., and D. Rodrik (1999) 'Trade Policy and Economic Growth: A Skeptic's Guide to the Cross-national Evidence'. Working Paper 7081. Cambridge, Mass.: NBER.

Seshanna, S., and S. Decornez (2003) 'Income Polarization and Inequality across Countries: An Empirical Study', *Journal of Policy Modeling*, 25: 335–58.

Simkins, C. (1998) 'On the Durability of South African Inequality'. Macarthur Foundation Working Paper. Princeton, NJ: Macarthur Network on Inequality and Poverty.

Tsikata, Y. (1999) 'Liberalization and Trade Performance in South Africa'. Informal Working Papers on Aspects of the South African Economy 13. Washington, DC: World Bank.

van der Berg, S. (2004) 'Poverty and the Role of Rural Institutions in a Globalizing South African Economy'. In Foundation of Advanced Studies on International Development, *Poverty in a Globalizing Economy: The Role of Rural Institutions*. Tokyo: FASID.

——(2006) 'Public Spending and the Poor since the Transition to Democracy'. In H. Bhorat and R. Kanbur (eds), *Poverty and Policy in Post-apartheid South Africa*. Pretoria: HSRC Press, 201–31.

——and M. Louw (2004) 'Changing Patterns of South African Income Distribution: Towards Time Series Estimates of Distribution and Poverty', *South African Journal of Economics*, 72: 546–72.

————and D. Yu (2008) 'Trends in Poverty and Inequality since the Political Transition', *South African Journal of Economics*, 76: 58–76.

Wolfson, M. C. (1994) 'The Inequalities Diverge', Papers and Proceeding of the Hundred and Sixth Annual Meeting of the American Economic Society, May 1994, *American Economic Review*, 84: 353–8.

——(1997) 'Divergent Inequalities: Theory and Empirical Results', *Review of Income and Wealth*, 43: 401–21.

Index